The Interpretation and Application of Law: Assignment Casebook

2011-2012 Edition

Olga A. Posse Esq.

ISBN: 1-4636-9637-X
ISBN-13: 9781463696375

Dedication

In Loving Memory of Cookie, Sam and Max

Contents In Brief

Introduction

After developing four successful undergraduate courses for SUNY Buffalo / Millard Fillmore College over these past fifteen years, I decided to write my own casebook to enhance and supplement the web version of those classes.

A casebook is different from a textbook or a workbook. A casebook is defined as a book containing source materials in a specific area, used as a reference and in teaching. A casebook is a collection of judicial decisions that illustrate the application of specific principles of law that is used in legal education to teach students under the case method system of study. This casebook is a compilation of primary law together with comments, exercises and study aids designed to serve as a source book and departure point for memorandums of law and law related research papers.

I use the case study method extensively to effectively teach legal analysis and critical writing skills in my traditional seated classes (non web classes). In the past I have assigned term paper writing projects in my web classes. But paralegals, law students and lawyers do not write term papers. They write case briefs, appeals, motions and memorandums of law. All of those documents require case study.

So upon writing my casebook I replaced the term paper assignment in each of my web classes with a more *skills relevant* series of case briefing assignments, memorandums of law and law topic related research. Each chapter in my casebook begins with a set of learning objectives and ends with skill building assignments.

I also wrote my casebook because no other casebook on the market was specific enough with regard to the courses I wrote. I did not want to assign a book for a class that would only be used a few times during the semester. I was also shocked at how expensive law related dictionaries, casebooks and textbooks are.

Instead of writing a separate casebook for each of my classes, I wrote one comprehensive casebook. Thus, if you take just one of my classes, or all four, you will only need <u>one</u> book for all of my web classes per academic year. Since this is a casebook, I can adapt my assignments to make them applicable to each web class.

I welcome you to my courses and wish you every success.

Skill Set Goals and Learning Objectives

When used in conjunction with my web course materials, quizzes, and written assignments students will be able to achieve the following goals and objectives:

<u>Goal 1</u>: Students will demonstrate an understanding of the law and its impact on social responsibility. Accordingly, students will be able to:

<u>Objective 1.1</u>: describe how the American legal system operates.

<u>Objective 1.2</u>: describe how lawyers and judges engage in legal reasoning so as to be able to evaluate a judge's argument.

<u>Objective 1.3</u>: explain how the law responds to complex social issues.

<u>Objective 1.4</u>: explain principles of private law (e.g., tort law) and public law (e.g., education law).

<u>Objective 1.5</u>: explain how ethical norms underlie judicial decisions.

<u>Goal 2</u>: Critical and Analytical Skills in Law; Students will apply higher-order thinking skills when analyzing to legal problems (fact patterns). Accordingly, students will be able to:

<u>Objective 2.1</u>: identify components of a legal argument, including the author's issue, conclusion, and reasons in support of the conclusion.

<u>Objective 2.2</u>: evaluate a legal argument, searching for ambiguous words, reasoning fallacies, faulty evidence, and relevant information that was omitted.

<u>Objective 2.3</u>: identify the ethical norms that underlie a legal argument.

<u>Objective 2.4</u>: use integration skills to identify and explain relationships among legal issues and concepts.

<u>Goal 3</u>: Students will demonstrate the ability to apply an informed understanding of the law to individual and social issues. Accordingly, students will be able to:

<u>Objective 3.1</u>: identify and apply legal principles to legal problems.

Objective 3.2: articulate how legal and social responsibility principles can be used to evaluate social issues and to inform public policy.

Objective 3.3: explain how legal decision makers create and maintain an ethical and socially responsible legal system.

Goal 4: Communication Skills in Law; Students will be able to effectively communicate understanding and application of legal and ethical concepts in a different formats, including quizzes, assignments and a written memorandum of law. Accordingly, students will be able to:

Objective 4.1: demonstrate effective writing skills in a range of appropriate formats, including essays, case briefs, case studies, research papers, memoranda and similar forms of composition.

Objective 4.2: recognize the use of different writing techniques and formats for different purposes, and to demonstrate effective written communication for varied purposes of research, information, explanation, persuasion, defense of a position, and similar objectives.

Objective 4.3: demonstrate familiarity with the use and meaning of the language of the law.

Goal 5: Core Values in Law; Students will be able to weigh evidence, tolerate ambiguity, and decide legal issues logically and ethically. Accordingly, students will be able to:

Objective 5.1: recognize the necessity for ethical behavior in using legal means to achieve objectives.

Objective 5.2: tolerate ambiguity and realize that legal explanations will often be complex and tentative.

Objective 5.3: recognize that legal explanations may vary across populations and contexts.

Objective 5.5: appreciate the student-citizens role in influencing the continuing evolution of the law.

Goal 6: Creative Thinking Skills; Students will develop skills that enable them to use knowledge to bring about something new. Accordingly, students will be able to:

Objective 6.1: describe how legal writers, such as attorneys, work creatively.

Objective 6.2: create new ideas, including problem reformulation.

Objective 6.3: recognize the evolutionary nature of law, appreciate the need for continuous self-education in the area, and learn skills to perpetuate and broaden their knowledge of changing legal standards.

Chapter 1
Case Analysis and Critical Thinking

<u>Chapter Learning Objectives</u>:

Upon completing this chapter and the related assignments students will be able to:

- Achieve improvement in their legal research and analytical writing skills through writing assignments that focus on the interpretation of case law and related social issues.

- Understand how issues of race, ethnicity, language, culture and socioeconomic factors are interwoven with academic achievement in urban schools and how positive legal reforms can address the needs of needy urban students.

- Demonstrate critical analysis skills by showing various perspectives on controversial legal issues relating to urban education and the historical lack of access to academic resources—in light of knowledge gained in through case law analysis of relevant court decisions.

<u>What Is Case Law?</u>

Case law is defined as the decisions and interpretations made by judges while deciding on the legal issues before them which are considered as an aid for interpretation of a law in subsequent cases with similar conditions. Case laws are used by advocates to support their views to favor their clients and also it to influence the decision of the judges. Case law is also known as judge—made law.

Unlike statutes, which are legislative acts that proscribe societal conduct by demanding or prohibiting something, case law is a constantly changing and evolving body of law. Each case opinion contains a section that sets out the relevant facts of the case along with the court's holding and an explanation (reasoning) of how the judge reached his conclusion. In addition, a case might contain the concurring or dissenting opinions of other judges.

Case opinions are *legal precedent* created by judges rather than legislatures. In writing case law, judges interpret statutory law, constitutions, or apply the common law to analyze a set of facts and to reach a decision (holding) regarding a central question (legal issue).

Thus, case opinions—judgments given by higher (appellate) courts in interpreting statutes applicable in cases argued before them are called precedent. They are binding on all courts within the same jurisdiction to be followed as the law in similar cases. Over time, these precedent case opinions are affirmed (or possibly overruled) and enforced by subsequent court decisions, thus continually expanding and refining the common law. In comparison, statutes, laws enacted by legislature, and do not recognize any precedent.

In this chapter we will analyze case law opinions that were written by New York trial and appellate court judges. All of the opinions set forth in this chapter are part of just <u>one</u> litigation—*Campaign for Fiscal Equity v. New York State*. It is a New York State case that took 13 years to resolve.

Sometimes legal research involves finding many different case law opinions that are "on point" to a particular set of facts and legal issues. But sometimes legal research involves tracking a single long and complicated litigated matter over a time span of many years. That is what we will do in this chapter. We will track *Campaign for Fiscal Equity v. New York State* from 1993 to 2011.

<u>What Is CFE?</u>

What is the "Campaign for Fiscal Equity (CFE)? It is a coalition of concerned parents and education advocates who sued New York State over underfunding of New York City public schools. It is a non-profit organization, founded in 1993 by a group of parents and education advocates who wanted to fix New York State's school finance system to ensure resources and a sound basic education for all city students. In 1993CFE filed a constitutional challenge to New York State's school finance system, arguing that it underfunded New York City public schools and deprived students of their constitutional right to a sound basic education.

In 2006, after <u>13 years</u> in the New York courts, the state's highest court, the New York Court of Appeals, ruled in CFE's favor by holding that the state must provide public school students with a sound basic education, defined as the "opportunity for a meaningful high school education, one which prepares them to function productively as civic participants." CFE then turned the litigation's outcome and the court rulings into legislation benefitting poor public schools.

The outcome of CFE's 13 year fiscal adequacy lawsuit led to a new era in school finance reform with the enactment of the New York State Education Budget and Reform Act of 2007-2008. With over $7 billion in extra aid scheduled for New York's public schools from FY 2008—FY 2011, the stage was set for change that would result in real progress for students.

The case began in 1993 when the Campaign of Fiscal Equity filed a constitutional challenge to the state school funding system. They argued that the New York State's public school finance system does not provide sufficient funds to New York City public schools and thus deprives its students of their constitutional right to a sound basic education as per the New York constitution.

The Education Article of the New York Constitution states that "the legislature shall provide for the maintenance and support of a system of free common schools, wherein all the children of this state may be educated." The decision in this case defined the meaning of this Education Article and determined that the New York City public school system was in violation. As this case moved up and back through the New York State trial and appeals court system, there were various theories about what the state needed to do to comply with the constitutional requirement. The Appellate Division, an intermediate appellate court, decided that the State Constitution only requires schools to provide an 8th grade education.

The New York State Court of Appeals rejected the 8th grade standard and held that a sound basic education consisted of "the basic literacy, calculating, and verbal skills necessary to enable children to eventually function productively as civic participants capable of voting and serving on a jury." All students in New York public schools therefore have the right to an "opportunity for a meaningful high school education, one which prepares them to function productively as civic participants."

The Court of Appeals held that the New York City public schools violated this right to education provided by the New York State Constitution. It noted the evidence presented at trial of what the school children in our modern society need in order to function productively as civic participants; "inputs" in the education system in New York City such as teacher quality; school facilities and classrooms with respect to environment and class size; and instrumentalities of learning such as textbooks, classroom supplies, and computers, and "outputs" in the system such as school completion rates and test scores of its students.

Sad to say, in every area examined New York City schools were far below average compared with the rest of the state. But in order for the plaintiff CFE to successfully prove its case, it had to prove that the failure to provide a sound basic education was actually *related* to the present funding system.

The Court of Appeals held that CFE <u>did</u> prove a causal link between the present funding system and the failure to provide a sound basic education. New York City schools were shown to have the most student need and the highest local cost, yet the lowest per-student funding from the state and the worst results.

By analyzing the "inputs" into the schools, such as teachers, facilities, and books, and the "outputs" of the students' academic performance afterwards, the Court found a correlation between the state funding scheme and the failure of the New York City schools to provide a sound basic education to its students. It held that state aid to the New York City schools must be increased where the need is high and the local ability to pay is low.

The Sad News

The Campaign for Fiscal Equity legal advocacy organization, whose 13 year long lawsuit brought increased public school funding to the New York City, shut down in 2011 because it ran out of funding. This happened because of a shift in the way philanthropists think about the importance of education advocacy.

In recent years CFE not only went to court, but they also went to Albany to lobby for more funding for public schools. Now that CFE is closing its doors, another strong litigation group dedicated to school finance issues, the Education Law Center, may take over where CFE left off. The Education Law Center's most recent victory came in 2011 when courts ordered New Jersey Governor Christie to spend an extra $500 million on poor public school districts in New Jersey next year. The Education Law Center is an organization with a thirty year history of successful lawsuits related to public school funding.

The Bad News

Governor Cuomo's Budget Takes Back 100% of Remaining CFE Funds Statewide

In February 2011, testimony was heard before a hearing of the New York State Assembly and Senate regarding Governor Cuomo's proposed education budget by the Campaign for Fiscal Equity and the Alliance for Quality Education. Those non- profit organizations presented graphs detailing how the Governor's budget would take back the remaining dollars delivered under the historic 2007 settlement of the Campaign for Fiscal Equity.

In 2007 the legislature and the governor agreed to increase foundation aid (basic classroom operating aid) by $5.5 billion over four years. Over 70% of this foundation aid goes to high need schools and districts in order to ensure every student has access to educational opportunity.

In 2007-08 a foundation aid increase of $1.1 billion was enacted and in 2008-09 the enacted foundation aid increase totaled $1.2 billion.

In 2009-10 state school aid was frozen, and in 2010-11 Governor Paterson enacted a $1.4 billion cut in state aid. Seventy nine percent (79%) of the cut, known as the Gap Elimination

Adjustment, was in foundation aid ($1.1 billion) last year. In this year's budget Governor Cuomo has proposed a record setting $1.5 billion cut in school aid with 79% being attributable to foundation aid. Governor Cuomo's proposed foundation aid cut this year is $1.2 billion bringing schools to pre-CFE funding levels for foundation aid.

In 2007, the State settled the Campaign for Fiscal Equity case in favor of New York's poorest public school students. Students in high needs districts were prioritized. With the CFE reforms and funding in place, students in high need schools began to make progress. The academic achievement gap slowly began to close.

In 2010-2011 $1.4 billion was cut from school aid in the attempt to close the budget deficit. The $1.4 billion cut had terrible consequences. For example, New York City increased class sizes and overcrowding. Even worse, over 10,000 teacher positions were cut. As a result, students were deprived of personnel, programs and services that are critical for academic achievement. The most important consequence of these cuts is the inequity they perpetuate.

CFE was a promise to New York's schoolchildren that the right to a good basic education will be protected. The financial aid formula created in response to the court order was based on student need. The 2011 executive budget proposes the highest dollar cut to schools in New York history at $1.5 billion. This is on top of last year's of $1.4 billion. The proposed cuts will gut CFE, break the promise and move the state away from the path of adequacy and academic excellence.

Historical Overview for Campaign for Fiscal Equity v. State of New York

In 1978, a group of property-poor school districts, joined by the five large urban New York districts, filed a lawsuit _Levittown v. Nyquist_, to challenge the state's public education finance system. In 1982 the Court of Appeals—New York State 's highest court—held that while substantial inequities in funding did exist, the state constitution does not require equal funding for education. The court also held that the state constitution does guarantee students the right to the opportunity for a "sound basic education."

This right was at the center of the _CFE v. State of New York_ complaint filed in 1993 which asserted that New York State was failing in its constitutional duty to provide a sound basic education to hundreds of thousands of school children. In 1995 the Court of Appeals distinguished its _Levittown_ ruling and remanded the case back down to the trial court for trial.

After a seven-month trial, Justice Leland DeGrasse rendered his decision on January 10, 2001 in favor of plaintiffs and ordered the State to ensure that all public schools provide a sound basic education to their students. This decision also ordered a costing-out study as to aid in developing a new school funding system.

In June 2002, the intermediate appeals court overturned the trial court ruling and claimed that an eighth grade education was all the New York State Constitution required. The plaintiffs appealed, and the Court of Appeals issued its decision in favor of plaintiffs on June 26, 2003. The court gave the State until July 30, 2004 to:

- determine the cost of providing a sound basic education

- fund those costs in each school, and

- set up an "accountability" system to ensure that the reforms actually provide the opportunity for a sound basic education.

However, the July 30, 2004 deadline passed without state action. The case went back to Justice DeGrasse who appointed a panel of three "special masters" to hold hearings on the matter and to make recommendations to the court.

On November 30, 2004, the panel issued its Report and Recommendations and urged the court to order the state to enact legislation within 90 days that would:

- provide an additional $5.63 billion for annual operating aid, phased in over a four year period;

- undertake a new cost study every four years to determine the cost of a sound basic education;

- provide an additional $9.2 billion, phased in over a five year period, for building, renovating, and leasing facilities, in accordance with plaintiffs' plan.

In March 2005, the trial court confirmed the special masters' report and its recommendations and ordered the state to comply within 90 days. The state appealed.

In March 2006, the intermediate appeals court ordered the state to increase New York City schools' annual operating funds by at least $4.7 billion per year, to be phased in over four years, and provide an infusion of at least $9.2 billion in facilities funding, to be accomplished within five years. The court set an April 1 deadline, and on April 1 the legislature enacted funding that met the court's requirement. The state did not comply with the operational funding order.

In November 2006, the Court of Appeals reaffirmed its 2003 decision but held that $1.93 billion was the "constitutional floor" for additional operating funds, although the legislature could provide the full amount recommended by the Special Masters and the lower courts.

In January 2007, newly elected Governor Spitzer recommended an increase in funding for New York City public schools of $5.4 billion (of which the City would be responsible for $2.2 billion). He also proposed a range of education finance and accountability reforms. The legislature accepted the Governor's proposals.

The new accountability requirements directed public school districts receiving increases of $15 million in state aid to develop "Contracts for Excellence" that detail plans for using the additional funding. Under this new legislation, the new funding must be devoted to programs that are directly related to:

- class size reduction,

- programs that increase student time on task,

- teacher and principal quality initiatives,

- middle school and high school restructuring,

- and full-day kindergarten or prekindergarten.

Districts were also required to direct the new funding and these programs to students with the greatest educational needs. New York City is also required to develop a five-year plan for reducing class sizes.

Before the Court of Appeals issued its June 2003 order requiring a costing out study, CFE and the New York State School Boards Association announced *"Costing Out: A New York Adequacy Study"*, to be performed by leading national research experts. The research team used professional judgment, successful schools methodologies and economic analyses.

I n early September 2003 the governor announced the formation of the *"Commission on Education Reform,"* which hired Standard and Poors to conduct a separate cost study. Both of these studies were released in the spring of 2004. In early 2004, the New York State Board of Regents also released a cost study as part of its annual school funding proposal.

The three cost studies recommended increases in annual funding between $2.5 billion and $9.0 billion in pre-K–12 education spending–as much as a 26.5 percent increase.

All three developed similar recommendations for changes in the policies and practices of the state's school funding system and urged the state to:

- match school resources to student needs;

- provide state aid based on enrollment instead of attendance;

- apply regional cost adjustments;

- direct most of the increased funding to the New York City School District and most of the remainder to other districts educating high need students;

- simplify the funding system by combining many of the almost 50 separate state aid formulas into one "operating aid" formula.

In its first Contract for Excellence, New York City chose to spend $152 million on class size reduction, $48 million on programs to increase students' time on task, $39 million on teacher and principal quality initiatives, $16 million on middle and high school restructuring, and $182,000 on full-day kindergarten and prekindergarten programs. The City was one of 55 districts around the state to develop Contracts for Excellence relating to the expenditure of a total of $428 million in new funding.

<u>Chronological Outline of CFE and CFE Related Case Opinions</u>

1. Board of Education, Levittown Union Free School District v. Nyquist, 57 N.Y.2d 27, 1982
2. Campaign for Fiscal Equity v. New York State, 162 Misc.2d 493, 1994
3. Campaign for Fiscal Equity v. New York State, 86 N.Y.2d 307, 1995
4. Campaign for Fiscal Equity v. New York State, 187 Misc.2d 1, 2001
5. Campaign for Fiscal Equity v. New York State, 295 AD2d 1, 2002
6. Campaign for Fiscal Equity v. New York State, 100 N.Y.2d 893, 2003
7. Campaign for Fiscal Equity v. New York State, 8 N.Y.3d 14, 2006
8. Campaign for Fiscal Equity v. New York State, 29 A.D.3d 175, 2006

<u>Case Analysis Assignments</u>

1. The dissenting opinion by Judge Read (in case # 6 above) disputed that the plaintiffs had shown a causal connection between the level of state aid and the deficiencies in the New York City Public schools. He wrote that "educational deficiencies are not always attributable to the lack of money or necessarily cured by the infusion of more

funds. A wide variety of non-financial factors may contribute to academic failure." What are some of these non-financial factors? Do you agree or disagree with Judge Read?

2.   Read the statement below and answer the following question: What factors cause the perpetuation of economic disadvantage over multiple generations, and what policy changes might correct and improve upward social mobility within disadvantaged groups? You will need to do some web-based research before attempting to answer this question. The web site listed below is a good place to start.

Race, Racial Concentration, and the Dynamics of Educational Inequity Across Urban and Suburban Schools—by Christy Lleras (2008)

http://hcd.illinois.edu/people/faculty/lleras_christy/publications/Race,%20Racial%20Concentration%20and%20Educ%20Ineq.pdf

"Neglect for the educational needs of children in urban schools threatens the economic welfare of our entire nation. Unless inequalities in education between suburban and urban schools are corrected, schools and their students will remain victims of the divisions between race and class. Deprived students in decaying urban schools say the Pledge of Allegiance to the flag each morning in their classrooms saying "…one nation indivisible, with liberty and justice for all." Children do understand the irony of these words they recite each morning at school."

OPINION #1

Court of Appeals of New York

57 N.Y.2d 27

BOARD OF EDUCATION, LEVITTOWN UNION FREE SCHOOL DISTRICT et al., Respondents-Appellants

and

Board of Education, City School District, Rochester et al., Intervenors-Respondents-Appellants

v

Ewald B. NYQUIST, as Commissioner of Education, et al., Appellants-Respondents

June 23, 1982

School district boards of education and public school students brought declaratory judgment action challenging New York provisions for financing public schools. Boards of education, officials, resident taxpayers and students of four large cities intervened, together with federation of parents and parent-teacher associations. The Supreme Court, Nassau County, L. Kingsley Smith, J., 94 Misc.2d 466, 408 N.Y.S.2d 606, declared that state's public school financing system violated both equal protection clause and constitutional education article, and appeal was taken. The Supreme Court, Appellate Division, 83 A.D.2d 217, 443 N.Y.S.2d 843, modified trial court's judgment and affirmed, and cross appeals were taken. The Court of Appeals, Jones, J., held that:

(1) existing provisions for state aid to finance public education do not violate the equal protection clause of Federal or State Constitution, and

(2) education article's requirement that legislature provide for maintenance and support of system of free common schools in which all children of state may be educated is being met in New York, in which average pupil expenditure exceeds that in all other states but two, and thus present school financing system does not violate the education article.

Order of Appellate Division modified with direction.

Fuchsberg, J., filed a dissenting opinion.

OPINION OF THE COURT

JONES, Judge.

The present amalgam of statutory prescriptions for State aid to local school districts for the maintenance and support of public elementary and secondary education does not violate the equal protection clause of either the Federal or the State Constitution nor is it unconstitutional under the education article of our State Constitution.

This declaratory judgment action challenging the State's provisions for financing our public schools is prosecuted by two groups, representing different constituencies and mounting attacks based on different predicates. The original plaintiffs by which the action was instituted in 1974 are the boards of education of 27 school districts located at various sites in the State and 12 students of public schools located in some of those districts. The intervenors, whose participation in the action was agreed to by the original parties, are the boards of education, officials, resident taxpayers, and students of the Cities of New York, Buffalo, Rochester and Syracuse, together with a federation of parent and parent-teacher associations in the City of New York. Defendants are the Commissioner of Education, the University of the State of New York, the State Comptroller and the Commissioner of Taxation and Finance of the State of New York.

It is the contention of the original plaintiffs (who are "property-poor" school districts) that the system for financing public schools presently in effect in this State (as principally set forth in Education Law, § 2022 [provision for local district financing]; and § 3602 [apportionment of State aid]) by which funds raised by locally imposed taxes are augmented by allocations of State moneys in accordance with a variety of formulas and grants, violates the equal protection clauses of both the State and the Federal Constitutions and the education article of our State Constitution because that system results in grossly disparate financial support (and thus grossly disparate educational opportunities) in the school districts of the State. The intervenors, representing interests in school districts located in four of the largest cities in the State, also assert violations of the same State and Federal constitutional provisions as the result of circumstances said to be peculiar to cities which they contend place them in a position comparable to that of property-poor districts.

Included in these circumstances, they assert, are special financial burdens borne by cities in four categories: (1) demands on municipal budgets (from which local funds for education are secured) for non education needs peculiar to cities ("municipal overburden"), (2) diminished purchasing power of the municipal education dollar, (3) significantly greater student absenteeism (with a resulting adverse effect both because of added operational costs and because State aid is largely allocated on the basis of average daily attendance), and (4) larger concentrations in cities of pupils with special educational needs, all four of which may be comprehended within the term "metropolitan overburden". These factors are said to result in greatly disparate educational opportunities available to children in the cities' public schools when compared to the offerings of some of the school districts not located within cities.

Succinctly stated, it is the gravamen of the complaint of the original plaintiffs (and the findings of the courts below provide factual support for their argument) that property-rich districts have an ability to raise greater local tax revenue enabling them to provide enriched educational programs beyond the fiscal ability of the property-poor districts. The intervenors argue that although they are not disadvantaged in their ability to raise gross revenue from local sources, in consequence of the economic factors of metropolitan overburden the net effective economic ability of the city districts falls well below that of non city districts (and the factual determinations made below support their argument). Both then assert that State aid as presently granted serves to perpetuate, and even to exacerbate, these disparities.

Both courts through which this litigation has progressed have granted declarations favorable to the original plaintiffs and to the intervenors, although not on all the claims asserted. Each court made careful and detailed factual determinations with respect to the financing of the State's educational system, the operation of the various State aid statutory provisions, and their practical impact on various school districts, individually and comparatively. In the case of the Appellate Division there was consideration not only of the public school finance system as it existed at the time the action was commenced in 1974 but also of the effect of alterations accomplished by legislation up to and through chapters 53 and 148 of the Laws of 1981. In reaching our disposition we proceed on these factual determinations made by both courts below as to the details of the various school district programs and operations and their comparison with one another, as well as the impact on them of the present State aid programs.

After an extended nonjury trial which produced 23,000 pages of transcript and 400 exhibits, the Justice presiding issued a judgment declaring that the State's public school finance system violates both the equal protection clause (art. I, § 11) and the education article (art. XI, § 1) of the State Constitution and, as to the cities whose interests are represented by the intervenors, the equal protection clause (14th Amdt., § 1) of the Federal Constitution as well, 94 Misc.2d 466, 408 N.Y.S.2d 606.

The Appellate Division, by a divided court, modified the judgment of the trial court; while concurring in the determination that the provisions of the State Constitution had been violated, the appellate court rejected the conclusion that the intervenors had also established a violation of the Federal Constitution. Justice Hopkins, concurring in part and dissenting in part, rejected all claims of denial of equal protection, but concluded that the present "maze of convoluted intricacies and provisos" of State aid fails to constitute a "basic State-wide fiscal *system* for education" as required in his view by the education article of the State Constitution 83 A.D.2d 217, 267-268, 443 N.Y.S.2d 843).

We now modify the order of the Appellate Division and direct that judgment be entered declaring that the present admixture of statutory provisions for State aid to local school districts, considered in connection with the existing system for local financing, is constitutional under the equal protection clause of the Federal Constitution and under both the equal protection clause and the education article of the State Constitution.

At the outset it is appropriate to comment briefly on the context in which the legal issues before us arise. Although New York State has long been acknowledged to be a leader in its provision of public elementary and secondary educational facilities and services, and notwithstanding that its per pupil expenditures for such purposes each year are very nearly the highest in the Nation, it must be recognized that there are nonetheless significant inequalities in the availability of financial support for local school districts, ranging from minor discrepancies to major differences, resulting in significant unevenness in the educational opportunities offered. These disparities may properly be ascribed in some respects to the wide variances between the property assessments bases on which local district taxes are imposed.

Similarly, it may be accepted that the four major cities represented by the intervenors, by reason of the factors encompassed in metropolitan overburden, are forced to provide instructional services and facilities of a lesser quantity, variety, and quality than those provided in some other school districts. No claim is advanced in this case, however, by either the original plaintiffs or the intervenors that the educational facilities or services provided in the school districts that they represent fall below the State-wide minimum standard of educational quality and quantity fixed by the Board of Regents; their attack is directed at the existing disparities in financial resources which lead to educational unevenness above that minimum standard.

The determination of the amounts, sources, and objectives of expenditures of public moneys for educational purposes, especially at the State level, presents issues of enormous practical and political complexity, and resolution appropriately is largely left to the interplay of the interests and forces directly involved and indirectly affected, in the arenas of legislative and executive activity. This is of the very essence of our governmental and political polity.

It would normally be inappropriate, therefore, for the courts to intrude upon such decision-making (see *Matter of Board of Educ. v. City of New York*, 41 N.Y.2d 535, 538, 394 N.Y.S.2d 148, 362 N.E.2d 948; *Matter of Anderson v. Krupsak*, 40 N.Y.2d 397, 402-403, 386 N.Y.S.2d 859, 353 N.E.2d 822; *New York Public Interest Research Group v. Steingut*, 40 N.Y.2d 250, 257, 386 N.Y.S.2d 646, 353 N.E.2d 558; cf. *James v. Board of Educ.*, 42 N.Y.2d 357, 397 N.Y.S.2d 934, 366 N.E.2d 1291).

With full recognition and respect, however, for the distribution of powers in educational matters among the legislative, executive and judicial branches, it is nevertheless the responsibility of the courts to adjudicate contentions that actions taken by the Legislature and the executive fail to conform to the mandates of the Constitutions which constrain the activities of all three branches.

That because of limited capabilities and competences the courts might encounter great difficulty in fashioning and then enforcing particularized remedies appropriate to repair unconstitutional action on the part of the Legislature or the executive is neither to be ignored on the one hand nor on the other to dictate judicial abstention in every case. In the discharge of our judicial responsibility in this case, recognizing the existence of the very real disparities of financial support as found by the lower courts, we nonetheless conclude that such disparities do not establish that there has been a violation of either Federal or State Constitution.

Considering first the claim that the existing provisions for State aid to finance public education in this State violate the equal protection clause contained in the Fourteenth Amendment of the United States Constitution, we agree with the Appellate Division that this claim must fail. The equal protection argument as developed by the original plaintiffs is that, because what are termed property-rich districts (those districts having a greater amount of assessable real property per pupil) are able to generate, through local taxation approved by taxpayers in those districts, a larger amount of money per pupil for education than is generated through the same process of local tax approval by property-poor districts (resulting in a lower per pupil expenditure in the latter districts), the financial resources (and thus education programs and facilities) of the two groups are significantly unequal.

The intervenors assert that, in the case of large cities, although the property wealth per pupil is not low, inequality is nevertheless occasioned by metropolitan overburden which likewise operates to diminish the available financial resources (and thus per pupil expenditures) in those localities. The inequalities existing in property-poor and large city school districts, both argue, are perpetuated and magnified rather than remedied by the existing distribution of State funds allocated to education-apportioned as such funds are in accordance with a formula and variations thereof which supplement local school tax revenue only to the extent of assuring a minimum, uniform per pupil expenditure throughout the State, together with an additional flat grant for each pupil and "save harmless" or special aid provisions which are designed to compensate for inflationary increases in real property values and to ease the effect of decreasing pupil population.

The essence of the original plaintiffs' argument-that disparities in per pupil expenditures, resulting largely from differences in the value of assessable property per pupil among school districts, coupled with a failure by the State to offset such disparities by provision of compensating aid funds, constitute an impermissible discrimination against pupils in the less property-wealthy districts in violation of the Fourteenth Amendment-was considered and rejected by the Supreme Court of the United States in _San Antonio School Dist. v. Rodriguez_, 411 U.S. 1, 93 S.Ct. 1278, 36 L.Ed.2d 16.

Noting that the subject of public school finance involves decisions both with respect to the raising and disposition of public revenues and of persistent, complex, and difficult questions of educational policy areas appropriately within legislative determination-the court held that rational basis, rather than strict scrutiny, was the proper standard against which to examine the Texas public school financing system there under review (which was described by the court as "comparable to the systems employed in virtually every other State".

Applying this standard, the court found in the Texas system a rational relationship to a legitimate State purpose-the permission and encouragement of participation in and control of public schools at the local district level (at p. 49, 93 S.Ct. at p. 1305). As both courts below acknowledged, the conclusions reached in that case dictate a similar result in the present litigation insofar as the original plaintiffs' claim of a Federal Constitution violation is concerned.

With respect to the intervenors' position in this litigation, not _in haec verba_ put before or considered by the Supreme Court in _San Antonio_, that metropolitan overburden is an unequalizing force which must be remedied by compensating increases in State aid to city school districts, a response is found in the opinion by Justice Hopkins at the Appellate Division, which observes that the cited inequalities existing in cities are the product of demographic, economic, and political factors intrinsic to the cities themselves, and cannot be attributed to legislative action or inaction.

While unquestionably education faces competition in the contest for municipal dollars from other forms of public service for which non municipal school districts bear no responsibility, municipal dollars flow into the cities' treasuries from sources other than simply real property taxes-sources similarly not available to non municipal school districts. The disbursement of the funds received from real estate taxes and such other sources and the decisions as to how they shall be allocated are decisions to be made by municipal governmental bodies.

In the words of Justice Hopkins: "It is beyond the power of this court in this litigation to determine whether the appropriations of the intervenor-plaintiffs have been wisely directed or reasonably applied, or whether their budgets are fairly divided in terms of priority of need between the competing services, such as police, fire, health, housing and transportation, and it is, equally, beyond the power of the court to determine whether the resources of the intervenor-plaintiffs can otherwise be employed so that their educational needs can be met." (83 A.D.2d 217, 262, 443 N.Y.S.2d 843.) Accordingly, we conclude that, applying the rational basis test, the intervenors have failed to demonstrate denial of equal protection under the Federal Constitution.

We turn then to the claims of both original plaintiffs and intervenors that, whatever may be determined with respect to the equal protection clause of the Federal Constitution, a violation of the comparable provision of our State Constitution (art. I, § 11) has been demonstrated-the conclusion reached by both courts below. Our attention must first be directed to identification of the standard appropriate to the subject now before us (financial support for public education) for examination as to whether there has been a violation of our constitutional mandate of equal protection (*Montgomery v. Daniels*, 38 N.Y.2d 41, 59, 378 N.Y.S.2d 1, 340 N.E.2d 444).

The Appellate Division, declining to apply the measurement of strict scrutiny that had been employed by the trial court and under which the trial court had found the education finance system invalid, concluded that the intermediate or more careful scrutiny test described in *Alevy v. Downstate Med. Center of State of N. Y.*, 39 N.Y.2d 326, 384 N.Y.S.2d 82, 348 N.E.2d 537 was properly to be employed-justifying this decision by its conclusion that the right to education in this State "represents an important constitutional interest". (83 A.D.2d, at p. 241, 443 N.Y.S.2d 843.)

The choice of that intermediate standard, under which the appellate court also found the system invalid, cannot be sustained however, both for the previously recited reasons articulated in the *San Antonio* case and in face of our decision in <u>*Matter of Levy*, 38 N.Y.2d 653, 382 N.Y.S.2d 13, 345 N.E.2d 556,</u> app. dsmd. *sub. nom.* <u>*Levy v. City of New York*, 429 U.S. 805, 97 S.Ct. 39, 50 L.Ed.2d 66,</u> reh. den. <u>429 U.S. 966, 97 S.Ct. 397,</u> 60 L.Ed.2d 335.

In *Levy* we expressly held that rational basis was the proper standard for review when the challenged State action implicated the right to free, public education. Nothing in the present litigation impels a departure from that decision, made as it was with full recognition of the existence in our State Constitution of the education article (art. XI).

The circumstance that public education is unquestionably high on the list of priorities of governmental concern and responsibility, involving the expenditures of enormous sums of State and local revenue, enlisting the most active attention of our citizenry and of our Legislature, and manifested by express articulation in our State Constitution, does not automatically entitle it to classification as a "fundamental constitutional right" triggering a higher standard of judicial review for purposes of equal protection analysis.

Thus, in <u>*Matter of Bernstein v. Toia*, 43 N.Y.2d 437, 402 N.Y.S.2d 342, 373 N.E.2d 238,</u> where the concern was public assistance to the needy-clearly a matter of significant interest, provision for which is similarly included in our <u>State Constitution</u> (art. XVII, § 1)-we employed the rational basis test as the proper standard for review.

The more careful scrutiny standard has been applied when the challenged State action has resulted in intentional discrimination against a class of persons grouped together by reason of personal characteristics, the use of which called into question the propriety of the particular classifications (<u>*People v. Whidden*, 51 N.Y.2d 457, 434 N.Y.S.2d 937, 415 N.E.2d 927</u> [gender]; <u>*Matter of Fay*, 44 N.Y.2d 137, 404 N.Y.S.2d 554, 375 N.E.2d 735,</u> app. dsmd. *sub. nom.* <u>*Buck v. Hunter*, 439 U.S. 1059, 99 S.Ct. 820, 59 L.Ed.2d 25</u> [illegitimacy]; <u>*Matter of Lalli*, 43 N.Y.2d 65, 400 N.Y.S.2d 761, 371 N.E.2d 481,</u> affd. <u>*sub nom. Lalli v. Lalli*, 439 U.S. 259, 99 S.Ct. 518, 58 L.Ed.2d 503</u> [illegitimacy]). The *Alevy* case itself was one in which race was the factor which pervaded the reverse discrimination alleged by the petitioner.

Our inquiry is therefore only whether there has been demonstrated the absence of a rational basis for the present school financing system, premised as it is on local taxation within individual school districts with supplemental State aid allocated in accordance with legislatively approved formulas and plans. Addressing the submissions of the original plaintiffs, our conclusion is that there has not been such a showing, and that the justification offered by the State-the preservation and promotion of local control of education-is both a legitimate State interest and one to which the present financing system is reasonably related.

Under the existing system the State is divided into more than 700 local school districts, each of which varies from the others and, from time to time, varies within itself, in greater or lesser degree, as to number of pupils and value of assessable real property, as well as with respect to numerous other characteristics, including personal wealth of its taxpayers. Outside the cities in the State (in which school funding is a part of the total municipal fiscal process), funds for the support of the education program offered in the schools of a district are raised through the imposition of local taxes following voter authorization based on approval of a budget prepared and submitted by an elected board of education, reflecting the instructional program (within standards fixed by the State) perceived by the local board of education to be responsive to the needs and desires of the community.

By way of assuring that a basic education will be provided and that a uniform, minimum expenditure per pupil will occur in each district, the Legislature has long provided for payment of supplementing State aid such that presently $1,885 per pupil (and, by a weighting computation, larger amounts for particular types of pupils) is available for education in each district.

Throughout the State, voters, by their action on school budgets, exercise a substantial control over the educational opportunities made available in their districts; to the extent that an authorized budget requires expenditures in excess of State aid, which will be funded by local taxes, there is a direct correlation between the system of local school financing and implementation of the desires of the taxpayer.

It is the willingness of the taxpayers of many districts to pay for and to provide enriched educational services and facilities beyond what the basic per pupil expenditure figures will permit that creates differentials in services and facilities. Justification for a system which allows for such willingness was recognized by the Supreme Court of the United States in _San Antonio School Dist. v. Rodriguez_, 411 U.S. 1, 48, n. 102, 93 S.Ct. 1278, 1304 n. 102, 36 L.Ed.2d 16, _supra_ quoting with approval a statement which accompanied the State of Hawaii's 1968 amendment of its educational finance statute to permit counties to collect funds locally and spend them on their schools over and above the wholly State-funded program: "Under existing law, counties are precluded from doing anything in this area, even to spend their own funds if they desire.

This corrective legislation is urgently needed in order to allow counties to go above and beyond the State's standards and provide educational facilities as good as the people of the counties want and are willing to pay for. Allowing local communities to go above and beyond established minimums to provide for their people encourages the best features of democratic government." (Hawaii Sess. Laws, 1968, act. 38, § 1.)

Any legislative attempt to make uniform and undeviating the educational opportunities offered by the several hundred local school districts-whether by providing that revenue for local education shall come exclusively from State sources to be distributed on a uniform per pupil basis, by prohibiting expenditure by local districts of any sums in excess of a legislatively fixed per pupil expenditure, or by requiring every district to match the per pupil expenditure of the highest spending district by means of local taxation or by means of State aid (surely an economically unrealistic hypothesis)-would inevitably work the demise of the local control of education available to students in individual districts. The *amicus* brief filed on behalf of the 85 school districts puts it well: "For all of the nearly two centuries that New York has had public schools, it has utilized a statutory system whereby citizens at the local level, acting as part of school district units containing people with a community of interest and a tradition of acting together to govern themselves, have made the basic decisions on funding and operating their own schools.

Through the years, the people of this State have remained true to the concept that the maximum support of the public schools and the most informed, intelligent and responsive decision-making as to the financing and operation of those schools is generated by giving citizens direct and meaningful control over the schools that their children attend."

The State-wide $360-per-pupil flat grant provided by State aid legislation is immune from attack under the equal protection clause, for on its face there is no inequality in this per pupil distribution of State aid which is allocated to all school districts without differentiation. Nor does the fact that the "save harmless" or special aid grants accrue to the benefit of only those districts which stand to suffer identified harm by reason of changing property values or of diminishing pupil registration serve to invalidate the school financing system.

In addition to the fact that only a minimal amount of State aid is distributed under this category, we cannot say that there is no rational basis for the Legislature's selection of districts subject to these impacts as those for whom alleviating relief is appropriate and for its provision for such relief so long as the relief is uniformly available to school districts falling within the classifications.

As to the intervenors, their contentions that they are denied equal protection under the State Constitution must be rejected for the same reasons that their comparable claims under the Federal Constitution are rejected (*supra*, at pp. 41-42, 93 S.Ct. at p. 1301).

Finally, we consider the claim, upheld by all the Judges below, that the present school financing system violates the education article (art. XI, § 1) of our State Constitution. It is there required that "[t]he legislature shall provide for the maintenance and support of a system of free common schools, wherein all the children of this state may be educated."

It is significant that this constitutional language-adopted in 1894 at a time when there were more than 11,000 local school districts in the State, with varying amounts of property wealth offering disparate educational opportunities-makes no reference to any requirement that the education to be made available be equal or substantially equivalent in every district.

Nor is there any provision either that districts choosing to provide opportunities beyond those that other districts might elect or be able to offer be foreclosed from doing so, or that local control of education, to the extent that a more extensive program were locally desired and provided, be abolished.

What appears to have been contemplated when the education article was adopted at the 1894 Constitutional Convention was a State-wide system assuring minimal acceptable facilities and services in contrast to the un-systematized delivery of instruction then in existence within the State. Nothing in the contemporaneous documentary evidence compels the conclusion that what was intended was a system assuring that all educational facilities and services would be equal throughout the State.

The enactment mandated only that the Legislature provide for maintenance and support of a system of free schools in order that an education might be available to all the State's children. There is, of course, a system of free schools in the State of New York. The Legislature has made prescriptions (or in some instances provided means by which prescriptions may be made) with reference to the minimum number of days of school attendance, required courses, textbooks, qualification of teachers and of certain nonteaching personnel, pupil transportation, and other matters. If what is made available by this system (which is what is to be maintained and supported) may properly be said to constitute an education, the constitutional mandate is satisfied.

Interpreting the term education, as we do, to connote a sound basic education, we have no difficulty in determining that the constitutional requirement is being met in this State, in which it is said without contradiction that the average per pupil expenditure exceeds that in all other States but two. There can be no dispute that New York has long been regarded as a leader in free public education.

Because decisions as to how public funds will be allocated among the several services for which by constitutional imperative the Legislature is required to make provision are matters peculiarly appropriate for formulation by the legislative body (reflective of and responsive as it is to the public will), we would be reluctant to override those decisions by mandating an even higher priority for education in the absence, possibly, of gross and glaring inadequacy-something not shown to exist in consequence of the present school financing system.

For the reasons stated, the order of the Appellate Division should be modified, without costs, to direct that the judgment of Supreme Court be modified by substituting for the declarations that the State's school financing system violates the equal protection clause and the education article of the State Constitution a declaration that the present statutory provisions for allocation of State aid to local school districts for the maintenance and support of elementary and secondary public education are not violative of either Federal or State Constitution.

As we wrote in _Montgomery v. Daniels_, 38 N.Y.2d 41, 53, 378 N.Y.S.2d 1, 340 N.E.2d 444, _supra_ : "It is not our office to rejoice or to lament. A fair regard for the basic polity of separation of powers dictates judicial respect for the proper role of the legislative branch, and pride in the uniquely and essentially neutral role of the judicial branch. That judicial role is both a privilege and a limitation." It would neither serve the purposes of orderly government nor honor the role of the judiciary to lay aside standards of judicial review recently held appropriate (in decisions in which the dissenter joined) because in this instance corrective measures may, in the view of many, be much needed with respect to the provision of financial support for our educational system.

FUCHSBERG, Judge (dissenting).

I believe the sad record of this case demonstrates that in material manner the public school system of New York State, to which falls responsibility for the education of well over three million children, does not rise to the level dictated by a realistic reading of the State constitutional mandate for the " _maintenance_ and _support_ of a system of free common schools, wherein all the children of this state may be educated" (N.Y.Const., art. XI, § 1).

Justice L. Kingsley Smith of the State Supreme Court, after presiding over the 122-day trial at which this matter was exhaustively explored, found that it failed to do so (94 Misc.2d 466, 408 N.Y.S.2d 606). Justice Leon D. Lazer, writing on this point in a painstaking and penetrating opinion for the Appellate Division, came to the same conclusion (83 A.D.2d 217, 219, 443 N.Y.S.2d 843).

Concurring in this view, Justices James D. Hopkins and Moses M. Weinstein each emphasized his position by writing separately to this effect. Nor did the recent Report and Recommendations of the distinguished official New York State Special Task Force on Equity and Excellence in Education, whose independent inquiry was precipitated by the findings in this case, arrive at a different appraisal. And Governor Hugh L. Carey's Elementary and Secondary School Message, delivered to the current session of the Legislature on February 17, 1982, was in the same vein.

In this connection, it is worthy of special note, in a world where life and law must not live in separate compartments, that the Governor, responding to the decrees of the afore-mentioned courts, and quoting the Task Force's statement that "in the education of children, the demands of morality are as compelling as the commands of legality", recommended a five-year program to "make equal education opportunity a reality".

But the majority of this court, though compelled to accept the now affirmed "careful and detailed factual determinations made by both courts below", insists that "the constitutional requirement is being met in this State". Doing so, it also rejects the lower courts' conclusion that the disparities and discriminations produced by our property-oriented educational finance system offends the equal protection guaranteed by our <u>State Constitution (art. I, § 11)</u>. For the reasons which follow, my disagreement is on all counts.

At the very outset of my analysis, I put at issue the majority's assertion that the inclusion of the education article in our State Constitution, far from carrying the weight of a like insertion in the Federal Constitution, where it has no counterpart, may have little more significance than would a mere "statutory articulation". I would think that a far more likely theory, consistent with our Federal form of Government, is that primary concern for education was to be that of the States rather than of the Union and that the article's placement in the State Constitution was all the more crucial in the context of the pluralistic political process of which the Tenth Amendment speaks (<u>U.S.Const., 10th</u> Amdt.).

In any meaningful ordering of priorities, it is in the impact education makes on the minds, characters and capabilities of our young citizens that we must find the answer to many seemingly insoluble societal problems. In the long run, nothing may be more important-and therefore more fundamental-to the future of our country. Can it be gainsaid that, without education there is no exit from the ghetto, no solution to unemployment, no cutting down on crime, no dissipation of intergroup tension, no mastery of the age of the computer? Horace Mann put it pragmatically that education is not only "the great equalizer of men", but, by alleviating poverty and its societal costs, more than pays for itself. So, too, only this past week, the Supreme Court of the United States reminded us that it had recognized the public school "as the primary vehicle for transmitting the values on which our society rests" (<u>Plyler v. Doe, 457 U.S. 202, 102 S.Ct. 2382, 72 L.Ed.2d 786 [1982]</u>).

Even more pointed is how the sponsors of the education article perceived it. The spokesman for the unanimous Education Committee of the Constitutional Convention which immediately preceded the one at which the article was adopted, reported it in these words: "If there is anything that should be constitutionalized because of its great importance, it is the all-important, overriding interest of education. Sir, I regard it as being paramount to every other interest in this State. I regard this article as being more important to the people of the State, to every man, woman and child in the State, than any other article that has been under consideration in this Convention" (1867-1868 N.Y. Constitutional Convention, 4 Proceedings & Debates, p. 2856).

Though an unrelated political controversy foreclosed *any* amendment of the State constitution that year, when it next was amended, in 1894, the article as we know it today was adopted on a report which apparently had not retreated a bit from the position that "[t]here seems to be no principle upon which the people of this commonwealth are so united and agreed as this, that the first great duty of the State is to protect and foster its educational interests" (1894 N.Y. Constitutional Convention, Doc.No. 62, p. 3).

The report went on to note (at p. 4), "that within the last half century of constitutional revision no other State of the Union has considered it superfluous or unwise to make such an affirmation in its fundamental law" and that the article "requires not simply schools, but a system; not merely that they shall be common, but free, and not only that they shall be numerous, but that they shall be sufficient in number, so that all the children of the State may, unless otherwise provided for, receive in them their education. No desire to confine the new Constitution to the narrowest possible limits of space should prevent the adoption of an enactment declaring in the strongest possible terms the interest of the State in its common schools".

It is in juxtaposition to this contemporary commentary by the fathers of our education article, which, revealingly, came to be known as "the children's Bill of Rights" (2 Lincoln, Constitutional History of New York, p. 206), that a sampling of the facts regarding the actual impact of the system as it now exists should be examined. For this purpose, we may well quote from the Appellate Division's excellent synopses, first, as to the four intervenor cities (Syracuse, Rochester, Buffalo and New York City) and, second, as to the many individual districts who initiated this suit.

The plight of the cities, found to be attributable to the inexorable drain of a municipal overburden left un-remedied by a State aid formula tied to realty resources, is at once seen in the findings that they:

"spent 28% of their tax revenues on education while jurisdictions outside the cities spent 45% [and that the] huge concentration of poverty stricken gave New York City 47% of the State's pupils with special educational needs, although it had only 31% of the total public school population and received only 26% of the State's education operating aid. By 1980-1981 New York City's percentage of the State's special needs pupils had risen to 51% as against 33% of the public school enrollment and 29% of education operating aid.

Furthermore, "the State's reliance on attendance rather than enrollment figures results in a double financial penalty to the cities because of their high rates of absenteeism. Because the high absentee rate is a direct consequence of poverty and underlying social conditions, its effects are inexorable and its financial effects cannot be alleviated by employment of additional attendance officers.

"The significantly higher proportion of physically, mentally and emotionally handicapped and learning impaired pupils resident in the cities and the extra personnel required to administer necessary programs compel the expenditure of greater sums to educate them. While the State aid formula provides additional weightings for handicapped students, the computation is flawed by a failure to account for municipal overburden, reduced purchasing power of city educational dollars, and high absentee rates.

"Reduced aid to the cities also impairs their abilities to instruct students who speak little or no English, although such programs are required under Federal mandate. [Also] the cities have the highest concentration of occupational education students. Because of their large numbers and the greater expense of the programs offered, city school districts are unable to accommodate all students requesting occupational education.

[Indicative of both inferiority and inequality], "results of national, State and local achievement tests demonstrate that unconscionable numbers of children fail to acquire basic educational skills. In Rochester, standardized tests given in 1975 revealed that 45% of the secondary school students were 'educationally disadvantaged'- that is, not performing at grade level and at least two years or more below level in reading-as were 58% of those students in mathematics; 16% of Rochester's twelfth grade students read fifth grade level or below. In a 1976 New York City test, 12% of the ninth grade students were found to read at fourth grade level or below.

These percentages translate into many thousands of high school children, some of whom are totally illiterate while others can read the words without accompanying comprehension and still others cannot apply the meager information they can obtain to problems." (83 A.D.2d, at pp. 229-232, 443 N.Y.S.2d 843).

The Trial Judge's summary is apt: "When the cities concentrate resources on pupils with special needs, other pupils, including those who are in fact disadvantaged but not reached by special programs, are subjected to educational deprivation. Many pupils attend classes in buildings which were shown to be in need of repairs and lacking in facilities for counseling, study or recreation.

Pupils attending schools in the large cities were shown to be provided with less physical security in their schools; less transportation; restricted sports and extracurricular activity; inadequate library and health services and diminished offerings in art and music. In summary, the failure to provide State aid on an equitable basis deprived the children in the large city districts of an equal education opportunity" (94 Misc.2d, at pp. 518-519, 408 N.Y.S.2d 606).

Now, as to the non-intervening plaintiffs, while their problems may not be compounded by municipal overburden, they suffer from a qualitatively, if not, quantitatively related malaise produced by a daunting and difficult finance system so onerous in its effect on districts poor in realty wealth (see 83 A.D.2d 217, 443 N.Y.S.2d 843, esp. at pp. 223-226, 443 N.Y.S.2d 843) and so complex in its application that Justice James D. Hopkins, concurring in the majority's finding that the State is violating the State Constitution's education article, felt called upon to complain that "the design of a uniform and harmonious system conceived by its nineteenth century authors had been frustrated and distorted" into "a veritable jungle of labyrinthine incongruity", "an Ossa of confusion piled on a Pelion of disorder". (83 A.D.2d, at p. 269, 443

N.Y.S.2d 843.) In everyday terms, the net result is illuminated again by the Appellate Division's recitation, this time that:

"The disparities in operating expenditures per pupil in 1974-1975 ranged from $4,215 for the richest district to $936 for the poorest, a ratio of 4.5 to 1. Three districts in Suffolk spent more than $6,300 and four spent less than $2,300 while the ratios between some districts in Nassau and Albany Counties reached 2 to 1. The direct connection between wealth and operating expenses and total expenses is revealed by further statistics, a few of which bear mention here.

"The consequences of [such] disparities are dramatic. To achieve expenditure levels to provide better educational output, low-wealth districts must tax themselves at relatively high rates, as a result of which they encounter difficulties in obtaining school budget approvals, imposition of austerity budgets which limit transportation, supplies, library and textbook purchases, and, ultimately, rises in rates of mortgage foreclosure and community instability. [See, e.g., *Matter of Onteora Cent. School Dist. (Onteora Non-Teaching Employees Assn.)*, 56 N.Y.2d 769, 452 N.Y.S.2d 22, 437 N.E.2d 281.]

"Low-wealth districts are unable to reduce class size and their children lose the resulting individual attention which is particularly important for both the disadvantaged and the gifted. Such districts are compelled to hire fewer nonteaching personnel as guidance counselors, psychologists and therapists and they cannot adequately provide the special attention requisite for students with severe speech and hearing impediments.

Poor districts must ration their speech therapists and other ancillary services to such a degree that long waiting lists exist for these services. Also constrained by insufficient realty wealth are the offer of the number and variety of advanced placement programs (which encourage children to continue in school and provide better preparation for college). Finally, the low-wealth districts experience chronic shortages of equipment and supplies.

"Fund shortages also affect district ability to engage necessary teaching and administrative personnel. At the time of trial, 9 of Brentwood's 12 elementary schools were without assistant principals and the district was unable to follow the Education Department's recommendation for reducing class size in certain courses because it could not afford to hire the requisite additional staff. In Roosevelt, there were no funds for substitute teachers and 23 professional staff members had to be terminated in 1975-1976 to eliminate a budget deficit." (83 A.D.2d, at pp. 227-229, 443 N.Y.S.2d 843.)

Surely, if it were meet to substitute the minimized reading the majority would give the education article for the hope and promise with which the constitutional delegates wrote it, it could not be said as a matter of law that the picture painted by this proof of disparities and discriminations complied with even the undefined "minimal acceptable facilities and services" or the broadly stated "sound basic education" to which it would be thus reduced. The fact is, of course, that in this past century, as high school and college statistics show, the acceptable level of education in our country has risen, not fallen.

Responsively, the constitutional demands of our State's education article, must be deemed to have kept pace. For, while, as a practical matter, the Federal Constitution may be said to fix a floor for the rights of our people, the ceiling may be set by each State's own constitutional charter (see, generally, my dissent in Matter of Esler v. Walters, 56 N.Y.2d 306, 315, 452 N.Y.S.2d 333, 437 N.E.2d 1090).[FN5] And, as great expounders of constitutional law, from Marshall to Holmes, have always made clear, such a document's permanence rests on its adaptability to changing events.

This brings me to the unequal protection phase of this case for, as I see it, whether taken separately or in their combined effect, the guarantees of the two converging constitutional provisions here at stake preclude the unequal and inadequate public schooling which children in property poor or fiscally overburdened areas of this State must endure.

On this score, suffice it to say that I am in agreement with the Appellate Division's determination that, for reasons included among those on which I have already touched, the standard of scrutiny to be brought to bear on this case was the intermediate one heretofore recognized in this State (see *Matter of Fay*, 44 N.Y.2d 137, 404 N.Y.S.2d 554, 375 N.E.2d 735, app. dsmd. *sub nom. Buck v. Hunter*, 439 U.S. 1059, 99 S.Ct. 820, 59 L.Ed.2d 25; *Matter of Lalli*, 43 N.Y.2d 65, 400 N.Y.S.2d 761, 371 N.E.2d 481, affd. *sub nom. Lalli v. Lalli*, 439 U.S. 259, 99 S.Ct. 518, 58 L.Ed.2d 503; *Alevy v. Downstate Med. Center of State of N. Y.*, 39 N.Y.2d 326, 384 N.Y.S.2d 82, 348 N.E.2d 537; Gunther, Supreme Court 1971 Term-Forward: In Search of Evolving Doctrine on a Changing Court: A Model for a Newer Equal Protection, 86 Harv.L.Rev. 1, 28, 35, 44-47).

It then proceeded along an analytical path which included recognition (1) that equality of educational opportunity is an important State constitutional interest in New York (see, also, *Plyler v. Doe*, 457 U.S. 202, 102 S.Ct. 2382, 72 L.Ed.2d 786, *supra*; *Brown v. Board of Educ.*, 347 U.S. 483, 489, 74 S.Ct. 686, 688, 98 L.Ed. 873), (2) that the extensive invidious disparities in the availability of this opportunity are born of the classifications based on property or fiscal wealth of the districts in which the affected children reside, (3) that preservation of local controls, the consideration the State (and now the majority here) offers for imposing the statutory plan, is so confined by what a limited local tax base will permit that its vaunted furtherance of local independence is illusory rather than real, and (4) that by no means had the State shown that the local input it could achieve could not be created by less intrusive means. On these bases, it was decided, correctly I say, that the intermediate standard was an effective bar to the statutory scheme.

Finally, two related equal protection questions may be worthy of comment.

The first of these is that it is not to be assumed that the equal protection clause of the Federal Constitution was not also impinged. Although the Appellate Division, as an intermediate tribunal, thought it best to avoid the question, _San Antonio School Dist. v. Rodriguez_, 411 U.S. 1, 93 S.Ct. 1278, 36 L.Ed.2d 16 may leave more leeway than some believe. In _Rodriguez_, there was no claim that the statute mal-apportioned State school aid by mismeasuring the funding capacities and needs of city districts. Rather, the Supreme Court there expressly stated its concern lest the problems of the "overburdened core-city school districts" in that case be exacerbated rather than eased by recognition of the theory pressed by their plaintiffs.

The second bears on the analysis provisionally suggested in Justice Weinstein's concurring opinion-that strict scrutiny may have been an appropriate test. This formulation was premised largely on the undisputed fact that the existing education aid formulae have an adverse effect, not only on pupils from impoverished families, but also on a large percentage of the nearly 750,000 "minority" students (black, Hispanic, American Indian, Asian and others). About 110,000 are unable to participate in school effectively in English and many are illiterate in their native tongues as well.

Raised, therefore, was the specter of an issue of discrimination involving the approximately 83% of the "minority" people who reside in the intervenor cities. Its occasion would be the inability of these cities, left bereft of the means to do so, to cope with the social and educational breakdown affecting a large group identifiable by race, or country of origin. This issue, of course, is made far less tenuous, if that it ever was, by last week's Federal equal protection decision in _Plyler v. Doe (supra)_. Be that as it may, however, since Justice Weinstein decided to adopt the alternative of joining in the majority's rationale, which in this case would have achieved the same result, suffice it unto the day that the question needs no answer now.

In fine, poor children, no less than rich, and the Nation of which both are a part, are entitled to an education that prepares today's students to face the world of today and tomorrow. Those who took and tolled the testimony tell us that, by any standard that counts, for the multitudinous many no such educational opportunity truly exists. Understandably, then, as the Governor put it to the Legislature just the other month, "Financial inequalities in education are more pronounced than at any time in the State's history" and "There can be no disagreement that New York's school finance program must be reformed".

Because, nevertheless, as the record reveals, our present method of financing education grossly distorts our ability to do so, and because I agree with the Appellate Division that it is constitutionally defective, my vote is to uphold the order of that court.

COOKE, C. J., and JASEN, GABRIELLI, WACHTLER and MEYER, JJ., concur with JONES, J.

FUCHSBERG, J., dissents and votes to affirm in a separate opinion.

Order modified, without costs, in accordance with the opinion herein and, as so modified, affirmed.

N.Y.1982. Board of Educ., Levittown Union Free School Dist. v. Nyquist

57 N.Y.2d 27, 439 N.E.2d 359, 453 N.Y.S.2d 643, 6 Ed. Law Rep. 147

END OF DOCUMENT

OPINION #2

Supreme Court, New York County, New York

162 Misc.2d 493

CAMPAIGN FOR FISCAL EQUITY, INC.; Community School Boards Districts 1, 2, 3, 5, 6, 10, 11, 13, 15, 17, 19, 25, 28, 31, Aminisha Black, Kuzaliawa Black; Innocencia Berges-Taveras, Bienvennido Taveras, Tania Taveras; Joanne Dejesus, Erycka Dejesus; Robert Jackson, Sumaya Jackson, Asmahan Jackson; Heather Lewis, Alina Lewis, Shayna Lewis, Joshua Lewis; Lillian Paige, Sherron Paige, Courtney Paige; Vernice Stevens, Richard Washington; Maria Vega, Jimmy Vega; and Dorothy Young, Blake Young, Plaintiffs

v

STATE of New York; Mario M. Cuomo, as Governor of the State of New York; Thomas Sobol, as President of the University of the State of New York and Commissioner of Education of the State of New York; Donald Dunn, as Acting Comptroller of the State of New York; James W. Wetzler, as Commissioner of Taxation and Finance of the State of New York; Ralph J. Marino, as Majority Leader and Temporary President of the Senate of the State of New York; Manfred Ohrenstein, as Minority Leader of the Senate of the State of New York; Saul Weprin, as Speaker of the Assembly of the State of New York; and Clarence D. Rappleyea, Jr., as Minority Leader of the Assembly of the State of New York, Defendants

CITY OF NEW YORK and The Board of Education of the City of New York, Plaintiffs

v

STATE of New York; Mario M. Cuomo, as Governor of the State of New York; Thomas Sobol, as President of the University of the State of New York and Commissioner of Education of the State of New York; Edward V. Regan, as Comptroller of the State of New York; James W. Wetzler, as Commissioner of Taxation and Finance of the State of New York; Ralph J. Marino, as Majority Leader and Temporary President of the Senate of the State of New York; Manfred Ohrenstein, as Minority Leader of the Senate of the State of New York; Saul Weprin, as Speaker of the Assembly of the State of New York; and Clarence D. Rappleyea, Jr., as Minority Leader of the Assembly of the State of New York

Defendants

June 21, 1994

City, city board of education, city community school board districts, fiscal equity organization, and parents of city public school students brought actions against state challenging constitutionality of state school financing formula. On state's challenge to legal sufficiency of pleadings, the Supreme Court, New York County, DeGrasse, J., held that:

(1) municipality and community school boards lacked standing to bring actions;

(2) complaints challenging constitutionality of state school financing formula sufficiently alleged violations of state constitutional mandate that legislature maintain and support free common schools wherein all children may be educated;

(3) financing system did not violate federal equal protection clause;

(4) complaints sufficiently alleged Title 6 civil rights claim; and

(5) complaints sufficiently stated claims for violation of state constitutional antidiscrimination clause prohibiting discrimination as to civil rights.

Motions granted in part and denied in part.

LELAND DeGRASSE, Justice.

The struggle continues. Lawsuits all around the country are now challenging the inherent inequities in the funding of school districts with local property taxes-creating huge disparities in the resources available to children in city and suburban districts (*Forty Years and Still Struggling*, N.Y. Times, May 18, 1994) at A 22)

The motions before this court challenge the legal sufficiency of pleadings filed in two such lawsuits. The City of New York and the Board of Education of the City of New York have filed a complaint (hereinafter "the municipal complaint") for, *inter alia*, a judgment declaring unconstitutional and granting injunctive relief with respect to the method for distributing funds to local school districts under New York State's education aid scheme. Similar relief is sought in the companion action brought by the Campaign for Fiscal Equity, Inc. (CFE), various New York City community school board districts and parents of New York City public school pupils.

The first causes of action of both complaints are based upon alleged violations of <u>N.Y. Constitution, article XI, § 1</u>, the Education Article. The second causes of action are based upon alleged violations of the Equal Protection Clauses of U.S. Constitution, 14th Amendment, § 1 and <u>N.Y. Constitution, article I, § 11</u>. The third cause of action of the municipal complaint and the fourth cause of action of the CFE complaint are based upon alleged violations of the Civil Rights Act of 1964 (<u>42 USC § 2000d *et seq.*</u>) and regulations promulgated there-under. The third cause of action of the CFE complaint is based upon alleged discrimination on account of race and color which is also proscribed by <u>N.Y. Constitution article I, § 11</u>.

Defendants assert that the City of New York, the Board of Education and the community school boards lack the capacity to bring this action. In general, municipalities and school boards lack the substantive right to challenge the constitutionality of acts of the State Legislature (<u>*Matter of Jeter v. Ellenville Cent. School Dist.*, 41 N.Y.2d 283, 287, 392 N.Y.S.2d 403, 360 N.E.2d 1086</u>). The doctrine is based upon the principle that local governments, as political subdivisions created by the sovereign State, exercise their power subject to the State's direction and control.

As such, impairment of those powers raises no constitutional issue (<u>*Town of Black Brook v. State of New York*, 41 N.Y.2d 486, 488, 393 N.Y.S.2d 946, 362 N.E.2d 579</u>). The rule, however, has its exceptions. For example, a State act may be challenged by a municipality where it would require the municipality to violate a constitutional proscription (*see*, <u>*Matter of Jeter, supra*, 41 N.Y.2d at 287, 392 N.Y.S.2d 403, 360 N.E.2d 1086</u>).

A municipality also has the capacity to sue where the act in question concerns propriety rights conferred upon it by N.Y. Constitution, Article IX, the Home Rule Article (*see*, <u>*Town of Black Brook v. State of New York, supra*, 41 N.Y.2d at 488-489, 393 N.Y.S.2d 946, 362 N.E.2d 579</u>). The instant claims for additional state school funding do not create such proprietary rights (*see*, <u>*Matter of Town of Moreau v. County of Saratoga*, 142 A.D.2d 864, 531 N.Y.S.2d 61</u>). The City and the plaintiff school boards also lack the capacity to assert the Constitutional and Statutory claims on behalf of the school children who reside within the City. Generally, parties to lawsuits may assert claims on behalf of themselves but not others (*MFY Legal Servs. v. Dudley*, 67 N.Y.2d 706, 708, 499 N.Y.S.2d 930, 490 N.E.2d 849). *National Organization of Women v. Terry*, 886 F.2d 1339, cited by plaintiffs is distinguishable because there it was held that the City of New York as a municipality had standing to sue for the purpose of restraining a public nuisance caused by anti-abortion demonstrations (*Id.*, 886 F.2d at 1361). No analogous municipal interests are alleged to exist in the instant actions. Plaintiffs' reliance upon *Caulfield v. Bd. of Educ. of the City of New York*, 486 F.Supp. 862, *aff'd* 632 F.2d 999, *cert. denied* 450 U.S. 1030, 101 S.Ct. 1739, 68 L.Ed.2d 225, is misplaced.

In *Caulfield* the District Court found that local school board officials who had suffered some threatened or actual injury from putatively illegal action had standing to maintain a Title VI action (486 F.Supp. at 878). The standing issue was not reached by the Circuit Court of Appeals which affirmed the dismissal of the complaint on other grounds. The instant complaints do not allege the requisite injury to the municipal plaintiffs.

In 1982, the Court of Appeals held that the amalgam of statutory prescriptions for State aid to local school districts for the maintenance and support of public elementary and secondary education was constitutional under the Education Article of the State Constitution. (*Bd. of Educ. Levittown Union Free School Dist. v. Nyquist*, 57 N.Y.2d 27, 35, 453 N.Y.S.2d 643, 439 N.E.2d 359).

In reaching the conclusion the court recognized the existence of significant inequalities in available financial support for local school districts resulting in significant unevenness of educational opportunities (*Bd. of Educ. Levittown Union Free School Dist. v. Nyquist, supra*, at 38, 453 N.Y.S.2d 643, 439 N.E.2d 359). The *Levittown* court further acknowledged that these factors forced major cities such as New York, Buffalo, Rochester and Syracuse to provide instructional services and facilities of a lesser quantity, variety and quality than those provided in some other school districts (*Bd. of Educ. Levittown Union Free School Dist. v. Nyquist, supra*, at 38, 453 N.Y.S.2d 643, 439 N.E.2d 359). The court was able to harmonize the aforementioned inequalities with the mandates of the Education Article (N.Y. Const., art XI, § 1) of the State Constitution by concluding that the latter was intended to assure only a sound basic education as opposed to a statewide equality of all public educational facilities and services (*Bd. of Educ. Levittown Union Free School Dist. v. Nyquist, supra*, at 47-48, 453 N.Y.S.2d 643, 439 N.E.2d 359).

The Court of Appeals noted that the *Levittown* plaintiffs and municipal intervenors advanced no claim that the educational facilities or services provided in their school districts fell below the Statewide minimum standard of educational quality and quantity fixed by the Board of Regents. (*Bd. of Educ. Levittown Union Free School Dist. v. Nyquist, supra*, at 38, 453 N.Y.S.2d 643, 439 N.E.2d 359). The observation was not gratuitous and it provides the best available insight into the court's definition of "a sound basic education."

Subject to the Legislature's control, the Board of Regents is constitutionally empowered to exercise legislative and policymaking functions with respect to the State's educational system (N.Y. Const. art XI, § 2; Education Law §§ 207). Statewide regulations are promulgated by the Commissioner of Education and approved by the Board of Regents (Education Law § 207). The said regulations set forth minimum educational standards for elementary and secondary schools in areas such as teacher certification (8 NYCRR 80.1 *et seq.*), availability of required Regents courses (8 NYCRR 100.2 [e] and 100.5), guidance programs and suitable building facilities (8 NYCRR 155.1 *et seq.*).

The CFE complaint contains allegations of a widespread failure of New York City public schools to meet minimum standards of Regents and the Commissioner in the foregoing specific areas and others. These specific allegations sufficiently buttress the CFE plaintiffs' assertion that "defendants have not adopted a systematic method for financing education to assure the provision of a sound basic education for all students throughout the State." The municipal plaintiffs' complaint, although primarily focused upon alleged inequalities of educational opportunities, does refer to the New York City Schools' failure to meet State wide minimum standards in building and library facilities.

The Appellate Division, Second Department has recently affirmed an order dismissing a complaint which similarly challenged the constitutionality of the State's public school financing scheme (*Reform Educational Financing Inequities Today [R.E.F.I.T.] v. Cuomo*, 199 A.D.2d 488, 606 N.Y.S.2d 44. As noted by the Court, the *R.E.F.I.T* plaintiffs did not allege any failure on part of the State to provide students with a sound basic education (606 N.Y.S.2d at 46). The *R.E.F.I.T.* IAS Court similarly noted the absence of an allegation that education had become inadequate or below minimum standard (*Reform Education Financing Inequities Today [R.E.F.I.T.] v. Cuomo*, 152 Misc.2d 714, 718, 578 N.Y.S.2d 969).

Unlike the *R.E.F.I.T.* complaint, the pleadings before this court contain allegations of a "gross and glaring inadequacy" which would possibly warrant judicial intervention in the school financing system (*see*, *Bd. of Educ. v Levittown Union Free School Dist. v. Nyquist, supra*, 57 N.Y.2d 27 at 48-49, 453 N.Y.S.2d 643, 439 N.E.2d 359). *R.E.F.I.T.* is, therefore, readily distinguishable with respect to the claimed violations of the Education Article (N.Y. Const., art. XI, § 1).

Based upon the foregoing, this court equates the provision of a sound basic education within the contemplation of *Levittown* with adherence to minimum educational standards approved by the Board of Regents. Accordingly, both complaints sufficiently allege violations of the Education Article (N.Y. Const., art. XI, § 1).

The *Levittown* court also found the statutory prescriptions for State and local school districts to be compatible with the Equal Protection Clauses of the Federal and State Constitutions (*Bd. of Educ. Levittown Union Free School Dist. v. Nyquist, supra*, at 35, 453 N.Y.S.2d 643, 439

N.E.2d 359). Following the holding of _San Antonio School Dist. v. Rodriguez_, 411 U.S. 1, 93 S.Ct. 1278, 36 L.Ed.2d 16, the court rejected the _Levittown_ plaintiffs' equal protection claims based upon a lack of State aid to compensate for disparities in per pupil expenditures caused by differences in the value of assessable property among school districts.

The claims were rejected pursuant to the court's determination that use of the rational basis standard was proper for examination of the State's public school financing system (_Bd. of Educ. Levittown Union Free School Dist. v. Nyquist, supra_, 57 N.Y.2d at 41, 453 N.Y.S.2d 643, 439 N.E.2d 359). The complaints before this court mandate a similar disposition of plaintiffs' equal protection claims. Notwithstanding allegations of a wide rift between affluent and poor school districts, the financing system challenged today appears to be identical to the one passed upon by the _Levittown_ court.

The standard of more careful scrutiny urged by plaintiffs is applicable when challenged State action has resulted in intentional discrimination against a class of persons (_Bd. of Educ. Levittown Union Free School Dist. v. Nyquist, supra_, at 43-44, 453 N.Y.S.2d 643, 439 N.E.2d 359). In both complaints it is alleged that the system of State aid for school funding with its inherent inequalities results in reduced educational resources for minority children who comprised 81% of the City's 1990-91 public school enrollment. Neither complaint, however, sets forth a requisite claim of intentional discrimination which would trigger a heightened scrutiny analysis.

Defendants correctly cite _Alexander v. Choate_, 469 U.S. 287, 105 S.Ct. 712, 83 L.Ed.2d 661, for the proposition that plaintiffs' claims based upon Title VI of the Civil Rights Act of 1964 (42 U.S.C. § 2000d et seq.) are also dependent upon a showing of deliberate discrimination. However, violations of the regulations promulgated there under can be established by a mere showing of discriminatory effect (_Guardians Assn. v. Civ. Serv. Commn. of the City of New York_, 463 U.S. 582, 103 S.Ct. 3221, 77 L.Ed.2d 866).

Both complaints allege violations of 34 C.F.R. § 100.3 which also prohibits discrimination based upon race, color or national origin. In both complaints it is alleged that the current school financing formula creates and perpetuates a dual system which adversely affects the quality of education available to New York City's predominantly minority student body. Liability under the regulation has been sufficiently pleaded based upon the allegation that a substantial number of students are being deprived of meaningful education on the ground of race, color or national origin (_see_, _Serna v. Portales Mun. Schools_, 499 F.2d 1147).

The third cause of action of the CFE complaint is based upon a violation of N.Y. Constitution, article I § 11 which provides that "No person shall, because of race, color, creed or religion, be subjected to any discrimination in his civil rights by any other person or any firm, corporation or institution, or by the state or any agency or subdivision of the state." Citing _People v. Kern_, 75 N.Y.2d 638, 555 N.Y.S.2d 647, 554 N.E.2d 1235, _cert. denied_ 498 U.S. 824, 111 S.Ct. 77, 112 L.Ed.2d 50, defendants contend that the claim is not viable because the foregoing antidiscrimination clause prohibits discrimination only as to civil rights which are elsewhere declared by Constitution, statute or common law.

The argument is refuted by Executive Law § 291(2) which provides that "[t]he opportunity to obtain education without discrimination because of age, race, creed, color, national origin, sex or marital status, as specified in section two hundred ninety-six of this article, is hereby recognized as and declared to be a civil right." A system which is discriminatory in effect albeit not in intent may violate civil rights recognized by the statute (*State Div. of Human Rights v. Kilian Mfg. Corp.*, 35 N.Y.2d 201, 208, 360 N.Y.S.2d 603, 318 N.E.2d 770; *New York Inst. of Technology v. State Div. of Human Rights*, 48 A.D.2d 132, 368 N.Y.S.2d 207, *rev'd on other grounds* 40 N.Y.2d 316, 386 N.Y.S.2d 685, 353 N.E.2d 598). Accordingly the instant claim of discrimination in violation of N.Y. Constitution, article I, § 11 is viable without an allegation of discriminatory intent.

For the foregoing reasons, the motions are granted only to the extent that entire municipal complaint and all claims asserted on behalf of the plaintiff community school board districts in the CFE action are dismissed on the ground plaintiffs lack the legal capacity to sue. The second cause of action of the municipal complaint and the second cause of action of the CFE complaint are dismissed on the ground that they fail to state a cause of action. The third cause of action of the municipal complaint and the fourth cause of action of the CFE complaint are also dismissed for failure to state a cause of action.

Defendants Marino and Rappleyea are granted leave to withdraw the branches of the motions by which they seek dismissal of the complaints on the ground of absolute immunity. The motion by the United Federation of Teachers, the American Civil Liberties Union Foundation, the New York Civil Liberties Union Foundation, the Community Service Society of New York, District Council 37 of the American Federation of State, County and Municipal Employees, AFL-CIO (DC-37) and Local 372 of DC-37 for leave to appear as *amici curiae* is granted without opposition.

END OF DOCUMENT

OPINION #3

Court of Appeals of New York.

86 N.Y.2d 307

CAMPAIGN FOR FISCAL EQUITY, INC., et al., Appellants

v

STATE of New York et al., Respondents

June 15, 1995

Action was brought challenging funding for New York City schools. The Supreme Court, New York County, DeGrasse, 162 Misc.2d 493, 616 N.Y.S.2d 851, dismissed claims under the equal protection clauses and Title VI but denied motion to dismiss claims under the education article and Title VI regulations. The Supreme Court, Appellate Division, 205 A.D.2d 272, 619 N.Y.S.2d 699, granted motion to dismiss remaining claims. The Court of Appeals Ciparick, J., held that:

(1) education article is not merely hortatory and establishes a constitutional floor with respect to education adequacy;

(2) complaint stated cause of action for violation of the education article;

(3) heightened scrutiny under equal protection clause was not applicable to claims;

(4) proof of discriminatory effect suffices to establish liability under Title VI regulations; and

(5) complaint stated cause of action under those regulations.

Affirmed as modified.

Levine, J., filed a concurring opinion.

Simons, J., dissented in part and filed an opinion.

Smith, J., dissented in part and filed an opinion in which Ciparick, J., concurred in part.

OPINION OF THE COURT

CIPARICK, Judge.

Thirteen years after we decided *Board of Educ., Levittown Union Free School Dist. v. Nyquist,* 57 N.Y.2d 27, 453 N.Y.S.2d 643, 439 N.E.2d 359 (hereinafter *Levittown*), we are again faced with a challenge to the constitutionality of New York State's public school financing system. We are called upon to decide whether plaintiffs' (Campaign for Fiscal Equity *et al.*) complaint pleads viable causes of action under the Education Article of the State Constitution, the Equal Protection Clauses of the State and Federal Constitutions, and title VI of the Civil Rights Act of 1964 and its implementing regulations.

Judges Titone, Bellacosa, Smith and I conclude that the nonschool board plaintiffs plead a sustainable claim under the Education Article. Judge Levine concurs in a separate opinion. The Court is unanimous that, as to the nonschool board plaintiffs, that a valid cause of action has been pleaded under title VI's implementing regulations. The remainder of this complaint should be dismissed.

Plaintiffs in this case are (1) Campaign for Fiscal Equity, Inc. (CFE), a not-for-profit corporation whose membership consists of community school boards, individual citizens, and a number of parent advocacy organizations; (2) 14 of New York City's 32 school districts; and (3) individual students who attend New York City public schools and their parents. The defendants are New York State, the Governor, the Commissioner of Education, the Commissioner of Taxation and Finance, and the Majority and Minority Leaders of the Senate and Assembly.

Plaintiffs commenced this action seeking a declaratory judgment against the State defendants, claiming that the State's public school financing system is unconstitutional under the Education Article of the State Constitution (art. XI, § 1), the Equal Protection Clauses of the State (art. I, § 11) and Federal Constitutions (U.S. Const. 14th Amend.), the Antidiscrimination Clause of the State Constitution (art. I, § 11), and is unlawful under title VI of the Civil Rights Act of 1964 (42 U.S.C. § 2000d *et seq.*) and the United States Department of Education's regulations implementing title VI (34 C.F.R. § 100.3[b][2]).

Three defendants-the State of New York, the Senate Majority Leader, and the Assembly Minority Leader-brought the instant motion to dismiss under CPLR 3211(a)(3) and (7), contending "that certain plaintiffs lack the right to bring this action and that the complaint fails to state a cause of action."

Supreme Court granted defendants' motion to the extent of dismissing all claims asserted on behalf of the plaintiff school districts on the ground that they lacked the legal capacity to sue. As to the remaining plaintiffs-CFE and the individual students and parents-the court dismissed their equal protection and title VI claims for failure to state a cause of action, but ruled that the complaint stated valid claims under the Education Article, the Antidiscrimination Clause of the State Constitution, and title VI's implementing regulations.

The Appellate Division modified the order of Supreme Court by fully granting defendants' motion to dismiss and dismissing the claims made under the Education Article, the Antidiscrimination Clause, and the title VI regulations for failure to state causes of action.

The Appellate Division concluded that plaintiffs' allegations that reduced resources have resulted in the failure to provide New York City school children with an opportunity to receive a minimally adequate education were conclusory in nature, and, in any event, embodied a theory "virtually identical to that advanced, fully tried and ultimately rejected on appeal in *Levittown.*" (205 A.D.2d 272, 276, 619 N.Y.S.2d 699.)

The Court also concluded that the prohibition in title VI's regulations against methods of administration which have an unlawful impact on racial and ethnic minorities was not violated by the State's role in allocating a lump sum of education aid to the New York City school system.

Education Article

The first cause of action in plaintiffs' complaint essentially alleges that the State's educational financing scheme fails to provide public school students in the City of New York, including the individual plaintiffs herein, an opportunity to obtain a sound basic education as required by the State Constitution.

Discussion of the constitutional issues raised in this case necessarily takes place against the backdrop of our decision in *Levittown,* 57 N.Y.2d 27, 453 N.Y.S.2d 643, 439 N.E.2d 359, *supra.* The *Levittown* plaintiffs consisted of 27 property-poor school districts, boards of education of 4 of the State's 5 largest cities (including New York City), and a number of school children and their parents residing in the property-poor school districts.

After a 122-day trial, Supreme Court issued a judgment declaring that the 1974 school financing system violated the Equal Protection Clauses of the Federal and State Constitutions and the Education Article of the State Constitution. The Appellate Division agreed, except as to the Federal equal protection claim. This Court modified, by substituting a declaration "that the present statutory provisions for allocation of State aid to local school districts for the maintenance and support of elementary and secondary public education are not violative of either Federal or State Constitution.

We rejected the *Levittown* plaintiffs' Federal equal protection challenge based on the decision of the Supreme Court of the United States in *San Antonio School Dist. v. Rodriguez*, 411 U.S. 1, 93 S.Ct. 1278, 36 L.Ed.2d 16 (*id.*, at 41, 453 N.Y.S.2d 643, 439 N.E.2d 359). The State equal protection challenge was rejected after we applied the rational basis test (*id.*, at 43-46, 453 N.Y.S.2d 643, 439 N.E.2d 359). Finally, the Education Article challenge was found lacking, as the plaintiffs advanced no claim of a deprivation of "minimal acceptable facilities and services" or "a sound basic education".

Article XI, § 1 of the State Constitution, the Education Article, mandates that "[t]he legislature shall provide for the maintenance and support of a system of free common schools, wherein all the children of this state may be educated." In *Levittown,* this Court examined the Education Article's language and history and rejected the plaintiffs' contention that the provision was intended to ensure equality of educational offerings throughout the State (57 N.Y.2d 27, 47, 453 N.Y.S.2d 643, 439 N.E.2d 359, *supra*). Rather, we stated, "[w]hat appears to have been contemplated when the Education Article was adopted at the 1894 Constitutional Convention was a State-wide system assuring *minimal acceptable facilities and services* in contrast to the unsystematized delivery of instruction then in existence within the State." In order to satisfy the Education Article's mandate, the system in place must at least make available an "education", a term we interpreted to connote "a sound basic education".

The Court in *Levittown* acknowledged the existence of "significant inequalities in the availability of financial support for local school districts, ranging from minor discrepancies to major differences, resulting in significant unevenness in the educational opportunities offered." (*Id.*, at 38, 453 N.Y.S.2d 643, 439 N.E.2d 359.) Nonetheless, such unevenness of educational opportunity did not render the school financing system constitutionally infirm, unless it could be shown that the system's funding inequities resulted in the deprivation of a sound basic education (*id.*, at 47-48, 453 N.Y.S.2d 643, 439 N.E.2d 359).

The gravamen of the plaintiffs' complaint in *Levittown* was that "property-rich districts have an ability to raise greater local tax revenue enabling them to provide enriched educational programs beyond the fiscal ability of the property-poor districts." (57 N.Y.2d, at 36, 453 N.Y.S.2d 643, 439 N.E.2d 359). Indeed, we specifically noted:

"No claim is advanced in this case, however, by plaintiffs that the educational facilities or services provided in the school districts that they represent fall below the State-wide minimum standard of educational quality and quantity fixed by the Board of Regents; their attack is directed at the existing disparities in financial resources which lead to educational unevenness above that minimum standard." (*Id.*, at 38, 453 N.Y.S.2d 643, 439 N.E.2d 359.)

We recognized in _Levittown_ that the Education Article imposes a duty on the Legislature to ensure the availability of a sound basic education to all the children of the State. Contrary to the dissenting expression of Judge Simons, we are unable to adopt the view that the constitutional language at issue is, in effect, hortatory. Indeed, we should not do so in the face of _Levittown's_ unambiguous acknowledgment of a constitutional floor with respect to educational adequacy. We conclude that a duty exists and that we are responsible for adjudicating the nature of that duty.

In this case, the principal premise underlying the Appellate Division's dismissal of plaintiffs' Education Article cause of action-that it is "virtually identical" to the theory tried and rejected in _Levittown_-is flawed and fails. Plaintiffs advance the very claim we specifically stated was not before us in _Levittown,_ i.e., that minimally acceptable educational services and facilities are not being provided in plaintiffs' school districts. _Levittown_ does not foreclose plaintiffs' Education Article claim. Rather, a fair, contextual reading of that case compels the contrary conclusion. The Court there manifestly left room for a conclusion that a system which failed to provide for a sound basic education would violate the Education Article (_id.,_ at 48, 453 N.Y.S.2d 643, 439 N.E.2d 359).

Having concluded that _Levittown_ is not an obstacle to plaintiffs' Education Article claim, we turn next to the crucial question: whether plaintiffs have properly stated a cause of action under the Education Article.

That Article requires the State to offer all children the opportunity of a sound basic education Such an education should consist of the basic literacy, calculating, and verbal skills necessary to enable children to eventually function productively as civic participants capable of voting and serving on a jury. If the physical facilities and pedagogical services and resources made available under the present system are adequate to provide children with the opportunity to obtain these essential skills, the State will have satisfied its constitutional obligation. As we stated in _Levittown,_

"The Legislature has made prescriptions (or in some instances provided means by which prescriptions may be made) with reference to the minimum number of days of school attendance, required courses, textbooks, qualifications of teachers and of certain nonteaching personnel, pupil transportation, and other matters. If what is made available by this system (which is what is to be maintained and supported) may properly be said to constitute an education, the constitutional mandate is satisfied." (57 N.Y.2d, at 48, 453 N.Y.S.2d 643, 439 N.E.2d 359.)

The State must assure that some essentials are provided. Children are entitled to minimally adequate physical facilities and classrooms which provide enough light, space, heat, and air to permit children to learn. Children should have access to minimally adequate instrumentalities of learning such as desks, chairs, pencils, and reasonably current textbooks. Children are also entitled to minimally adequate teaching of reasonably up-to-date basic curricula such as reading, writing, mathematics, science, and social studies, by sufficient personnel adequately trained to teach those subject areas.

We note that plaintiffs, throughout their complaint, rely on the minimum State-wide educational standards established by the Board of Regents and the Commissioner of Education, a reliance directly traceable to certain language in *Levittown* (*see*, <u>57 N.Y.2d, at 38, 453 N.Y.S.2d 643, 439 N.E.2d 359</u>).

Contrary to Judge Simons, we see no reason to penalize plaintiffs for referencing those standards in this manner. Construing the allegations liberally and in whole, as we must (*see*, <u>*Leon v. Martinez*, 84 N.Y.2d 83, 87-88, 614 N.Y.S.2d 972, 638 N.E.2d 511</u>), there can be no question that the pertinent pivotal claim made here is that the present financing system is not providing City school children with an opportunity to obtain a sound basic education.

However, because many of the Regents' and Commissioner's standards exceed notions of a minimally adequate or sound basic education-some are also aspirational-prudence should govern utilization of the Regents' standards as benchmarks of educational adequacy. Proof of noncompliance with one or more of the Regents' or Commissioner's standards may not, standing alone, establish a violation of the Education Article.

Plaintiffs also rely on standardized competency examinations established by the Regents and the Commissioner to measure minimum educational skills (*see*, <u>8 NYCRR 100.3</u>[b][2]; 100.5[a][4]). Performance levels on such examinations are helpful but should also be used cautiously as there are a myriad of factors which have a causal bearing on test results.

We do not attempt to definitively specify what the constitutional concept and mandate of a sound basic education entails. Given the procedural posture of this case, an exhaustive discussion and consideration of the meaning of a "sound basic education" is premature. Only after discovery and the development of a factual record can this issue be fully evaluated and resolved.

Rather, we articulate a template reflecting our judgment of what the trier of fact must consider in determining whether defendants have met their constitutional obligation. The trial court will have to evaluate whether the children in plaintiffs' districts are in fact being provided the opportunity to acquire the basic literacy, calculating and verbal skills necessary to enable them to function as civic participants capable of voting and serving as jurors.

A relevant issue at this point is whether plaintiffs can establish a correlation between funding and educational opportunity. In order to succeed in the specific context of this case, plaintiffs will have to establish a causal link between the present funding system and any proven failure to provide a sound basic education to New York City school children. However, we believe that Judge Simons' extended causation discussion (*see*, dissenting in part opn., at 339-340, at 583-584 of 631 N.Y.S.2d, at 679-680 of 655 N.E.2d) is premature given the procedural context of this case.

We turn next more specifically to the complaint. In considering the sufficiency of a pleading subject to a motion to dismiss for failure to state a cause of action under CPLR 3211(a)(7), our well-settled task is to determine whether, "accepting as true the factual averments of the complaint, plaintiff can succeed upon any reasonable view of the facts stated" (*People v. New York City Tr. Auth.*, 59 N.Y.2d 343, 348, 465 N.Y.S.2d 502, 452 N.E.2d 316; *see*, *Jiggetts v. Grinker*, 75 N.Y.2d 411, 414-415, 554 N.Y.S.2d 92, 553 N.E.2d 570; *219 Broadway Corp. v. Alexander's, Inc.*, 46 N.Y.2d 506, 509, 414 N.Y.S.2d 889, 387 N.E.2d 1205).

We are required to accord plaintiffs the benefit of all favorable inferences which may be drawn from their pleading, without expressing our opinion as to whether they can ultimately establish the truth of their allegations before the trier of fact (*see*, *219 Broadway, supra*, at 509, 414 N.Y.S.2d 889, 387 N.E.2d 1205; *Underpinning & Found. Constructors v. Chase Manhattan Bank*, 46 N.Y.2d 459, 414 N.Y.S.2d 298, 386 N.E.2d 1319; *Morone v. Morone*, 50 N.Y.2d 481, 429 N.Y.S.2d 592, 413 N.E.2d 1154). Only recently we recognized the right of plaintiffs "to seek redress, and not have the courthouse doors closed at the very inception of an action, where the pleading meets a minimal standard necessary to resist dismissal of a complaint." (*Armstrong v. Simon & Schuster*, 85 N.Y.2d 373, 379, 625 N.Y.S.2d 477, 649 N.E.2d 825; *see also*, *Leon v. Martinez*, 84 N.Y.2d 83, 87-88, 614 N.Y.S.2d 972, 638 N.E.2d 511, *supra* [court is to "determine only whether the facts as alleged fit within any cognizable legal theory"].)

f we determine that plaintiffs are entitled to relief on any reasonable view of the facts stated, our inquiry is complete and we must declare the complaint legally sufficient.

According to plaintiffs, New York City students are not receiving the opportunity to obtain an education that enables them to speak, listen, read, and write clearly and effectively in English, perform basic mathematical calculations, be knowledgeable about political, economic and social institutions and procedures in this country and abroad, or to acquire the skills, knowledge, understanding and attitudes necessary to participate in democratic self-government (plaintiffs' amended complaint, record on appeal, at 64-65).

Plaintiffs support these allegations with fact-based claims of inadequacies in physical facilities, curricula, numbers of qualified teachers, availability of textbooks, library books, etc. On the basis of these factual allegations, and the inferences to be drawn there-from, we discern a properly stated cause of action sufficient to survive a motion to dismiss and to permit this portion of the action to go forward.

Taking as true the allegations in the complaint, as we must, plaintiffs allege and specify gross educational inadequacies that, if proven, could support a conclusion that the State's public school financing system effectively fails to provide for a minimally adequate educational opportunity. We think it beyond cavil that the failure to provide the opportunity to obtain such fundamental skills as literacy and the ability to add, subtract and divide numbers would constitute a violation of the Education Article. In our view, plaintiffs have alleged facts which fit within a cognizable legal theory (*see*, _Leon v. Martinez, 84 N.Y.2d 83, 87-88, 614 N.Y.S.2d 972, 638 N.E.2d 511, supra_). Accordingly, plaintiffs' cause of action under the Education Article should be reinstated.

Equal Protection

Judges Simons, Titone, Bellacosa and Levine conclude that the second cause of action alleging that the State's school financing scheme violates the Equal Protection Clauses of the Federal and State Constitutions (U.S. Const. 14th Amend; N.Y. Const., art. I, § 11) must be dismissed in light of our decision in _Levittown._

In _Levittown,_ we followed _San Antonio School Dist. v. Rodriguez, 411 U.S. 1, 93 S.Ct. 1278, 36 L.Ed.2d 16, reh. denied 411 U.S. 959, 93 S.Ct. 1919, 36 L.Ed.2d 418, supra_ in holding that education was not a fundamental right under the United States Constitution, and concluded as well that it was not a fundamental right under the State Constitution (57 N.Y.2d, at 41-43, 453 N.Y.S.2d 643, 439 N.E.2d 359). Therefore, we held, the rational basis test was the appropriate standard for equal protection analysis under both Constitutions (*id.*). We concluded in _Levittown_ that any disparities in educational funding among school districts in the State arising from the State's financing scheme were rationally based upon and reasonably related to a legitimate State interest, "the preservation and promotion of local control of education" (*id.*, at 44, 453 N.Y.S.2d 643, 439 N.E.2d 359).

Plaintiffs attempt to distinguish _Levittown_ in two ways. First, plaintiffs contend that absent from the pleadings and proof in the _Levittown_ case was the claim they make here, that the State's funding methodology deprives New York City school children of a "minimum adequate education." Relying on _Plyler v. Doe, 457 U.S. 202, 102 S.Ct. 2382, 72 L.Ed.2d 786, reh. denied 458 U.S. 1131, 103 S.Ct. 14, 73 L.Ed.2d 1401,_ they urge that an intermediate level of scrutiny applies to such a deprivation, thereby shifting the burden to the State to show a substantial relationship of its educational funding scheme to a substantial State interest (*see, id.*, at 224, 102 S.Ct. at 2398 [Brennan, J.]; *see also, id.*, at 239, 102 S.Ct. at 2406-07 [Powell, J., concurring]). This Court today finds this argument unpersuasive for the following reasons.

First, _Plyler v. Doe_ does not stand for the broad proposition that heightened scrutiny applies in all State financing challenges, merely when, as here, the gravamen of the plaintiffs' factual allegations charges violations of the " *state-wide* minimum standard of educational quality and quantity." *Plyler* explicitly disclaimed elevating public education to a " 'right' granted to individuals by the Constitution" (*id.,* at 221, 102 S.Ct. at 2396; *see also, id.,* at 223, 102 S.Ct. at 2397-98).

The Court discerns important differences between the instant case and *Plyler,* i.e., the educational deprivation was absolute in *Plyler* and was intentionally discriminatory toward a defined subclass, the blameless children of undocumented alien adults. Moreover, the reach of *Plyler's* holding was specifically clarified in *Kadrmas v. Dickinson Pub. Schools,* 487 U.S. 450, 108 S.Ct. 2481, 101 L.Ed.2d 399, where the Supreme Court explained:

"We have not extended [*Plyler's* application of a heightened level of equal protection scrutiny] beyond the 'unique circumstances', [*Plyler v. Doe,* 457 U.S., at 239, 102 S.Ct. at 2406] (Powell, J., concurring), that provoked its 'unique confluence of theories and rationales' " (487 U.S., at 459, 108 S.Ct. at 2488).

Thus, as to the claimed violation of the Equal Protection Clause of the Federal Constitution, the Court determines that neither *Plyler* nor any Supreme Court case decided after *Levittown* requires reexamination of our holding in that case rejecting heightened scrutiny and finding a rational basis in the State's educational funding scheme.

Alternatively, plaintiffs' claim that heightened scrutiny is required under the Equal Protection Clause of the State Constitution because, unlike the *Levittown* plaintiffs, in this case they have alleged that the State's educational funding methodology has a disparate impact upon African-American and other minority students.

The Court rejects this contention, noting plaintiffs' concession that no discriminatory intent has been charged in this case. The Court relies on the case law from our Court and the Supreme Court holding that an equal protection cause of action based upon a disproportionate impact upon a suspect class requires establishment of intentional discrimination (*see, Arlington Hgts. v. Metropolitan Hous. Corp.,* 429 U.S. 252, 264-265, 97 S.Ct. 555, 562-563, 50 L.Ed.2d 450; *Washington v. Davis,* 426 U.S. 229, 240, 96 S.Ct. 2040, 2047-48, 48 L.Ed.2d 597; *People v. New York City Tr. Auth.,* 59 N.Y.2d 343, 350, 465 N.Y.S.2d 502, 452 N.E.2d 316, *supra; Board of Educ. v. Nyquist,* 57 N.Y.2d, at 43-44, 453 N.Y.S.2d 643, 439 N.E.2d 359, *supra*).

Title VI

Plaintiffs also complain that the State public education financing system violates title VI and title VI's implementing regulations. Title VI provides:

"No person in the United States shall, on the ground of race, color, or national origin, be excluded from participation in, be denied the benefits of, or be subjected to discrimination under any program or activity receiving Federal financial assistance" (42 U.S.C. § 2000d).

Title VI prohibits discrimination on the basis of race or national origin in programs receiving Federal financial assistance (*see*, <u>42 U.S.C. §§ 2000d</u>-<u>2000d-6</u>). The Supreme Court has ruled that there must be a showing of intentional discrimination to succeed on a title VI claim (*see*, <u>*Guardians Assn. v. Civil Serv. Commn.*, 463 U.S. 582, 103 S.Ct. 3221, 77 L.Ed.2d 866</u>). *Guardians* involved a challenge to the hiring and firing practices of New York City's police department. The principal issue was whether compensation could be awarded for a violation of title VI in the absence of proof of discriminatory intent. Although the Court was divided and no majority opinion issued, seven Justices concluded that proof of discriminatory intent is required in order to make out a violation of title VI (*see*, <u>*Alexander v. Choate*, 469 U.S. 287, 293, 105 S.Ct. 712, 716, 83 L.Ed.2d 661</u>). The instant complaint contains no showing of intentional discrimination.

Plaintiffs also allege a violation of title VI's implementing regulations (*see*, <u>34 C.F.R. § 100.3</u>[b][2]), which provide that recipients of Federal funding may not:

"utilize *criteria or methods of administration* which *have the effect* of subjecting individuals to discrimination because of their race, color, or national origin, or *have the effect* of defeating or substantially impairing accomplishment of the objectives of the program as respect individuals of a particular race, color, or national origin." (Emphasis supplied.)

The regulations incorporate a disparate impact standard.

Under title VI's implementing regulations, proof of discriminatory intent is not a prerequisite to a private cause of action against governmental recipients of Federal funds (*see*, <u>*Choate*, *supra*, at 293-294, 105 S.Ct. at 716</u>). Proof of discriminatory *effect* suffices to establish liability under the regulations promulgated pursuant to title VI: "actions having an unjustifiable disparate impact on minorities [can] be redressed through agency regulations designed to implement the purposes of Title VI" (<u>*id.*, at 293, 105 S.Ct. at 716</u>).

Federal courts have consistently held that the evidentiary standards developed under title VII govern title VI cases as well (*see*, *e.g.*, <u>*Georgia State Conference of Branches of NAACP v. State of Georgia*, 775 F.2d 1403, 1417</u>; <u>*Groves v. Alabama State Bd. of Educ.*, 776 F.Supp. 1518, 1523</u>). Consequently, in order to make out a prima facie case of disparate impact:

"The plaintiff first must show by a preponderance of the evidence that a facially neutral practice has a racially disproportionate effect, whereupon the burden shifts to the defendant to prove a substantial legitimate justification for its practice. The plaintiff then may ultimately prevail by proffering an equally effective alternative practice which results in less racial disproportionality or proof that the legitimate practices are a pretext for discrimination."

A validly stated cause of action under the title VI regulations thus has two components: "whether a challenged practice has a sufficiently adverse racial impact-in other words, whether it falls significantly more harshly on a minority racial group than on the majority-and, if so, whether the practice is nevertheless adequately justified." (*Groves, supra,* at 1523; *see, Georgia State Conference, supra,* at 1417; *Quarles v. Oxford Mun. Separate School Dist.,* 868 F.2d 750, 754, n. 3.) Statistics comparing benefit distribution or access patterns among members of the protected class and the over-all population play a key role in demonstrating an adverse racial impact (*see, Georgia State Conference,* 775 F.2d at 1417 [plaintiffs made prima facie case through statistics showing that the racial composition differed from what would be expected from a random distribution]; *Huntington Branch, NAACP v. Town of Huntington,* 844 F.2d 926, 938; *Sharif v. New York State Educ. Dept.,* 709 F.Supp. 345, 362).

Once a prima facie case is established, the burden of persuasion shifts to the defendant to affirmatively defend the challenged practice by way of a legitimate nondiscriminatory reason (*see, Larry P. v. Riles,* 793 F.2d 969, 982-983). If the defendant meets its burden and demonstrates that the challenged practice is justified or necessary, the plaintiff can still prevail by showing that "less discriminatory alternatives" were available to further the purportedly legitimate interest (*see, Abermarle Paper Co. v. Moody,* 422 U.S. 405, 425, 95 S.Ct. 2362, 2375, 45 L.Ed.2d 280).

Applying the foregoing standards to this case, we conclude that plaintiffs have stated a cause of action under title VI's regulations. The Appellate Division dismissed plaintiffs' claim on the ground that the State's role in allocating a lump sum to the New York City school system is not the "function which results in the disparate impact on minority racial or ethnic groups; rather, it is the method by which plaintiff Chancellor of the City School District divides and sub allocates those funds that may arguably result in the disparate impact complained of here." (205 A.D.2d, at 277, 619 N.Y.S.2d 699.) The Appellate Division misconstrued the nature of plaintiffs' claim.

Plaintiffs complain that it is the *State's* decisions concerning allocation of education aid which constitute the "criteria or methods of administration which have the effect of subjecting individuals to discrimination because of their race". The complaint challenges the manner in which the *State* allocates education aid, alleging that the present methodology has a disparate impact on the State's racial and ethnic minorities, the vast majority of whom attend New York City public schools.

The Appellate Division's reasoning fails to account for the fact that the City can only sub-allocate what the State allocates to it. If, as alleged, the State allocates only 34% of all State education aid to a school district containing 37% of the State's students (81% of whom are minorities comprising 74% of the State's minority student population), then those minority students will receive less aid as a group and per pupil than their nonminority peers who attend public schools elsewhere in the State, irrespective of how the City sub-allocates the education aid it receives.

Initially, it is undisputed that New York State is the recipient of Federal funds for education. Moreover, plaintiffs complain of a benefit distribution practice which allegedly has the *effect* of subjecting minority students to discrimination on the basis of their race, color, or national origin.

Plaintiffs support their allegations statistically, pointing to the disparity between the total and per capita education aid distributed to the City's predominantly minority student population as opposed to the amount distributed to the State's nonminority students. Since defendants have not yet advanced a substantial justification for the challenged practice at this procedural point, plaintiffs' cause of action under the title VI regulations should be reinstated.

The order of the Appellate Division should be modified, without costs, in accordance with the opinion herein and, as so modified, affirmed.

LEVINE, Judge (concurring).

I join with the majority of this Court in holding that plaintiffs have failed to allege legally sufficient causes of action under the Equal Protection Clauses of the Federal and State Constitutions or under title VI of the Civil Rights Act of 1964, but have pleaded a valid cause of action under the United States Department of Education's regulations implementing title VI.

I am also of the view that, under our prevailing liberal pleading standards, the complaint states a cause of action based upon a violation of the Education Article of the State Constitution (N.Y. Const., art. XI, § 1). The complaint invokes the definition of the State's educational duty under the Constitution set forth in *Board of Educ., Levittown Union Free School Dist. v. Nyquist*, 57 N.Y.2d 27, 453 N.Y.S.2d 643, 439 N.E.2d 359 (hereinafter *Levittown*) and alleges that the State's public school financing scheme denies them a "sound basic education" with "minimal acceptable facilities and services" (*id.*, at 47-48, 453 N.Y.S.2d 643, 439 N.E.2d 359).

The complaint also refers to various specific educational deficiencies and alleges that the State's funding scheme denies New York City public school students the opportunity to achieve even basic literacy. These allegations, in my view, are sufficient to withstand the motion to dismiss, despite the inclusion and heavy reliance upon various other factors which I consider essentially irrelevant to a determination of whether the current State school aid formula violates the Education Article of the State Constitution.

I write separately regarding plaintiff's Education Article claim because the constitutional standard for a sound basic education articulated by the majority may be read to extend the State's funding obligation well beyond that envisaged by the *Levittown* Court or justified by the language or history of the adoption of the Education Article.

Before addressing the errors and deficiencies I perceive in the majority's opinion upholding the sufficiency of plaintiffs' Education Article cause of action, I wish to explain why I am unable to agree with Judge Simons' dissent in this case, although I find much merit in its discussion of the extent of the State's constitutional responsibility for funding the State's public education system and of the inherent limitations of courts in making constitutional decisions on educational quality and quantity. That dissent concludes that it "is for other branches of government, not the courts, to define what constitutes a sound basic education" (Simons, J., dissenting in part 631 N.Y.S.2d, at 676 of 655 N.E.2d).

It also finds plaintiffs' Education Article cause of action deficient because their "claim [of a denial of a sound basic education] does not attempt to establish deprivation State-wide; it advances only claims involving some New York City schools." (Simons, J., dissenting in part of 631 N.Y.S.2d, at 679 of 655 N.E.2d.) The dissent apparently concludes that the State's mandate to support the system of education is only breached upon proof of a State-wide failure of the system of public education, but not a failure (attributable to inadequate State funding) in any individual school district. I believe this position is inconsistent with the _Levittown_ decision.

In _Levittown_ we explicitly stated that the Education Article (N.Y. Const., art. XI, § 1) of the Constitution does require the Legislature to put in place and support "a State-wide system _assuring_ minimal acceptable facilities and services", although _not_ necessarily "a system assuring that all educational facilities and services would be equal throughout the State." (57 N.Y.2d, at 47, 453 N.Y.S.2d 643, 439 N.E.2d 359, _supra_ [emphasis supplied].) We further defined the "constitutional mandate" as that of providing a "sound basic education" (_id._, at 48, 453 N.Y.S.2d 643, 439 N.E.2d 359).

This Court in _Levittown_ viewed from an historical perspective the funding role and responsibility of the State in the constitutional scheme contemplated when article XI, § 1 was adopted. We expressly relied upon the historical description, contained in the _amicus_ brief of 85 local school districts, that there has been in this State a nearly 200-year tradition of a dual system of financing public education, already well in place when the Education Article was adopted in 1894, giving local school districts broad autonomy in making policy decisions on the quality and quantity of education and the funding thereof for their respective schools (_see, id._, at 46, 453 N.Y.S.2d 643, 439 N.E.2d 359).

We described the State's funding responsibility under the 1894 constitutional scheme as one of " _assuring_ that a _basic_ education will be provided [through State financial aid to local school districts]" (_id._, at 45, 453 N.Y.S.2d 643, 439 N.E.2d 359 [emphasis supplied]).

These observations were historically accurate and are reflected in the history of the adoption of the Education Article. As early as 1795, the Legislature enacted a common school law providing for State aid to counties and cities to support their local schools, contingent upon matching funds raised by local taxation but not otherwise limiting local school educational expenditures; similar legislation was passed in 1812 (*see*, 3 Lincoln, The Constitutional History of New York, at 526-527).

As we have discussed more extensively in <u>*Reform Educ. Fin. Inequities Today v. Cuomo*, 86 N.Y.2d 279, 631 N.Y.S.2d 551, 655 N.E.2d 647</u> [decided today], the primary purpose of <u>article XI, § 1</u> was to "constitutionalize the established system of common schools rather than to alter its substance" <u>(86 N.Y.2d, at 284, 631 N.Y.S.2d at 552, 655 N.E.2d at 648)</u>.

Moreover, the constitutional history of the Education Article shows that the objective was to "make it *imperative* on the State to provide *adequate* free common schools for the education of *all* of the children of the State" and that the new provision would have an impact upon "places in the State of New York where the common schools are not adequate" (3 Revised Record of Constitutional Convention of 1894, at 695).

In my view, the dissent's conclusions that the determination of what constitutes a sound basic education for constitutional purposes is not a judicial responsibility on this constitutional challenge, and that, in any event, only a State-wide failure to provide funding for a sound basic education will give rise to a constitutional violation, are inconsistent with *Levittown's* description of the State's funding responsibility and with the constitutional history I have cited. The *Levittown* record definitely established, and the courts at all levels recognized that the State's educational aid formula produced significant variations in aggregate per pupil State aid among the various school districts (*see, e.g.*, <u>*Board of Ed., Levittown Union Free School Dist. v. Nyquist*, 94 Misc.2d 466, 502, 408 N.Y.S.2d 606)</u>.

Also established in <u>*Levittown*</u> and found by the trial court was that the cost of the same educational services, resources or facilities varied substantially throughout the State (*see, <u>id., at 503-510, 408 N.Y.S.2d 606)</u>.* If, because of such factors or others, the State aid to an individual school district proved to be insufficient to "assure minimal adequate facilities and services" <u>(57 N.Y.2d, at 47, 453 N.Y.S.2d 643, 439 N.E.2d 359, *supra*)</u> or "to assure[e] that a basic education will be provided" (<u>*id.*, at 45, 453 N.Y.S.2d 643, 439 N.E.2d 359)</u>.

Our <u>*Levittown*</u> decision certainly would lead to the conclusion that the State's constitutional educational funding responsibility, couched in those very terms, would have been violated in that school district. Moreover, the notion that only a State-wide failure to provide sufficient State funds for a basic sound education is sufficient to establish a right to relief under the Education Article is inconsistent with the constitutional debate I have previously quoted, in which it was specifically anticipated that its adoption would have an ameliorative effect upon "places where the common schools are not adequate".

Thus, I conclude that we cannot avoid addressing the meaning and content of the constitutional mandate identified in _Levittown,_ that the Legislature must support a public school system providing an opportunity for students to receive a _sound basic education._

I now turn to a discussion of the serious errors I find in the majority's opinion addressing the meaning and content of that constitutional mandate, to provide school children an opportunity for a sound basic education. Analysis may profitably begin by identifying what the _Levittown_ Court most clearly rejected as the constitutional mandate under the Education Article.

Contrary to the conclusion of the majority here, the Court in _Levittown_ not only had before it the contention that disparities in overall funding and quality of education among local school districts violated the Education Article. The Court also indisputably had before it the claim, supported by findings of fact and conclusions of law by the lower courts, that, irrespective of the existence of disparities, the school children in the plaintiff and intervenor school districts in that case were not receiving the educational opportunities guaranteed by the Education Article. Thus, without reference to disparity, the trial court adopted as the constitutional mandate in New York the construction of a comparable constitutional provision on public education by the New Jersey Supreme Court in _Robinson v. Cahill_ (62 N.J. 473, 515, 303 A.2d 273) (_Levittown,_ 94 Misc.2d, at 533, 408 N.Y.S.2d 606, _supra_):

" 'The Constitution's guarantee must be understood to embrace that educational opportunity which is needed in the contemporary setting to equip a child for his role as a citizen and as a competitor in the labor market'."

The trial court paraphrased that concept of the constitutional obligation as requiring the State to afford all school children the opportunity to acquire those skills "necessary to function as a citizen in a democratic society" _(id.),_ and found that the constitutional responsibility of the State was breached by the State's inadequate funding aid to the large city school districts in the State (_id.,_ at 534, 408 N.Y.S.2d 606).

When the _Levittown_ case reached the Appellate Division, the majority in that Court adopted the same approach in defining the basic education guaranteed by article XI, § 1. It quoted (83 A.D.2d 217, 249, 443 N.Y.S.2d 843) from _Seattle School Dist. No. 1 v. Washington,_ 90 Wash.2d 476, 517, 585 P.2d 71 that the educational opportunities which are constitutionally required to be furnished are those " 'in the contemporary setting to equip our children for their role as citizens and as potential competitors in today's market as well as in the marketplace of ideas' ".

The Appellate Division concluded that "we believe section 1 of article XI of the New York Constitution requires no less" (83 A.D.2d, at 249, 443 N.Y.S.2d 843, _supra_). The Appellate Division majority found that the then-current State funding scheme violated the Education Article in failing to provide children in the school districts represented there with the skills required thus "to function in society" (83 A.D.2d, at 251, 443 N.Y.S.2d 843, *supra*).

The majority of this Court in *Levittown* was also directly confronted with the position of the sole dissenter, Judge Fuchsberg, that under the State Constitution, all children "are entitled to an education that prepares today's students to face the world of today and tomorrow." (57 N.Y.2d, at 60, 453 N.Y.S.2d 643, 439 N.E.2d 359, *supra*.) The dissent also reminded the majority that both lower courts found as a fact that the State's funding scheme denied such educational opportunities for the children in the districts involved in the *Levittown* suit. "Those who took and tolled the testimony tell us that, by any standard that counts, for the multitudinous many no such educational opportunity truly exists."

Despite those findings by the lower courts in *Levittown,* that the children in the subject school districts in that suit were denied the opportunity "to acquire the skills necessary to function as a citizen in a democratic society" (94 Misc.2d, at 533, 408 N.Y.S.2d 606, *supra*) or the skills "to function effectively in society" or prepare them for " 'their role as citizens and as potential competitors in today's market place' " (83 A.D.2d, at 248-249, 443 N.Y.S.2d 843, *supra*), this Court held, as a matter of law, that the plaintiffs and intervenors in *Levittown* had not established (indeed, not even claimed) that the State's public education funding scheme failed to provide the educational opportunity mandated by article XI, § 1, i.e., minimal facilities and services needed for a sound basic education.

The conclusion seems to me inescapable that, if we are to faithfully follow the *Levittown* precedent, the concept of a sound basic education as a constitutional mandate is much more circumscribed than the aspirational, largely subjective standards expressed by the lower courts and the dissent in *Levittown,* representing what typically one would desire as the outcome of an entire public education process-to produce useful, functioning citizens in a modern society or, as Judge Fuchsberg put it, preparation of students "to face the world of today and tomorrow".

Thus, in my view, the majority unmistakably and unwisely departs from *Levittown* in the majority's principal holding here that the sound basic education which is the State's funding responsibility under the Education Article includes imparting these skills "necessary to enable children to *eventually function productively as civic participants* " (majority at 316, at 570 of 631 N.Y.S.2d, at 666 of 655 N.E.2d [emphasis supplied]).

In substance and meaning, this objectively unverifiable standard is indistinguishable from the criteria for the constitutional norm expressed by the trial court and Appellate Division in *Levittown.* The majority's error is further compounded and reinforced by the majority's reference to plaintiffs' allegations, which the majority apparently considers relevant on plaintiffs' cause of action under the Education Article, that New York City students are being deprived of the opportunity, among other things, to "be knowledgeable about political, economic and social institutions and procedures in this country and abroad" (majority opn., at 319, at 571 of 631 N.Y.S.2d, at 667 of 655 N.E.2d.)

Having demonstrably rejected similar standards, the manifest teaching of _Levittown_ is that the State's constitutional educational funding responsibility does not nearly extend to guaranteeing students the opportunity to acquire those skills to "function productively as civic participants", as the majority would have it. The narrower State role, as the _Levittown_ decision explains, flows necessarily from New York's historical tradition of dividing responsibility over public education between the State and local school governments, under which the quality of public education necessary to enable students to "function in society" is largely a matter of local decision and control subject to standards and assistance from the appropriate State executive, legislative and administrative bodies (see, _Levittown_, 57 N.Y.2d, at 45-46, 453 N.Y.S.2d 643, 439 N.E.2d 359, _supra_). As previously pointed out, that division of responsibility was constitutionalized in the adoption of article XI, § 1.

That this Court in _Levittown_ construed the Constitution as imposing only a drastically limited State funding responsibility for guaranteeing the quality of public school education also stems from the _Levittown_ majority's awareness of the inherent and proper limitations of the courts in enforcing the constitutional obligation. The _Levittown_ decision cogently pointed to the "enormous practical and political complexity" (57 N.Y.2d, at 38, 453 N.Y.S.2d 643, 439 N.E.2d 359, _supra_) of deciding upon educational objectives and providing funding for them which, under our form of government, are legislative and executive prerogatives upon which courts should be especially hesitant to intrude (_id.,_ at 39; _see also, id.,_ at 49, n. 9, 453 N.Y.S.2d 643, 439 N.E.2d 359).

Again, the majority here disregards the prudent and jurisprudential advice of _Levittown_ and appears ready to fully enter this arena in delineating a series of "essentials" to which "children are entitled" under the Constitution, including such things as "minimally adequate teaching of reasonably up-to-date curricula" on a wide variety of subjects, "reasonably current textbooks" and "minimally adequate" educational physical plant and equipment. Presumably the determination of the adequacy of all such educational resources will be made by the Trial Judge in this case.

The true, far more limited nature of the State's constitutional responsibility to fund a sound basic education can be gleaned, again, from the language of the Education Article itself and the _Levittown_ opinion. As is well explained in Judge Simons' dissent, article XI, § 1 does not explicitly designate a State responsibility regarding any minimum quality of education. It expressly imposes only the duty upon the Legislature to "provide for the maintenance and support of a _system_ of free public education (N.Y. Const., art. XI, § 1 [emphasis supplied]).

The _Levittown_ Court emphasized that the constitutional mandate is solely to maintain a _system_ of education (57 N.Y.2d, at 48, n. 7, 453 N.Y.S.2d 643, 439 N.E.2d 359). The Court observed that, concededly, a system of public schools did exist in the State through legislation and regulation and appropriations for maintenance of various State-wide minimum educational standards, etc. (*id., at 48, 453 N.Y.S.2d 643, 439 N.E.2d 359)*. The Court then identified the only remaining element of the State's constitutional responsibility under article XI, § 1:

"If what is made available by this *system may properly be said to constitute an education,* the constitutional mandate is satisfied."

Thus, the sound basic education envisaged by the *Levittown* Court as a constitutional mandate subsume those minimal categories of instruction without which whatever the system provides *cannot* "be said to constitute an education". Historically and traditionally, the essential, universally recognized as indispensable elements, the *sine qua non*, of what legitimately might be called an education are the basic literacy (reading and writing) and computational skills and, in a public educational system, citizenship awareness. A public educational system failing to provide the opportunity to acquire those basic skills would not be worthy of that appellation.

Of course, almost all of us would hope for, expect and support as voters and taxpayers funding of a system of public education in this State which offers more than those basics in all school districts, including the furnishing of many of those resources and subjects of instruction plaintiffs claim to be constitutionally mandated and those which, regrettably, may be implied as required from the majority's interpretation of the Education Article.

But *Levittown* held that decisions regarding such concededly worthwhile educational supplements, including the selection thereof and the level of such funding, is to be determined in other forums than by judicial fiat in interpreting the State Constitution. *Levittown* cannot fairly be interpreted as mandating more than the provision of a system in which all children in the State are given an opportunity to acquire basic literacy, computational skills and knowledge of citizenship as the elements of a sound basic education. Deficiencies beyond those basics were certainly established in the *Levittown* record, and were found to exist by both lower courts in that case. Yet this Court in *Levittown* not only found no deprivation of a sound basic education had been proven, *it found none had been claimed.*

The majority's significantly less precise or exacting standard for the sound basic education constitutionally required to be provided invites and inevitably will entail the subjective, unverifiable educational policy making by Judges, unreviewable on any principled basis, which was anathema to the *Levittown* Court.

As I have previously discussed, however, the complaint can be read as alleging that the State's funding scheme denies New York City school pupils the opportunity to acquire the basic literacy and mathematical skills. I, therefore, vote with the majority that plaintiffs' cause of action under the Education Article of the State Constitution is legally sufficient.

SIMONS, Judge (dissenting in part).

There can be no argument about the importance of educating our children or that there are serious shortcomings in the New York City school system. But it is possible to recognize those serious social concerns and still conclude, as I do, that plaintiffs have not successfully pleaded a cause of action charging defendants with violating the Education Article of the State Constitution.

Plaintiffs allege in their first cause of action that defendants have violated <u>article XI, § 1 of the New York State Constitution</u> because children in New York City have been deprived of a sound basic education. They support that conclusion by a number of allegations identifying shortcomings in instruction, facilities and student performance in the City's schools.

The majority and Judge Levine in his concurrence conclude this states a cause of action because they interpret the Education Article as containing a qualitative component. In their view, the Constitution guarantees that all school-age children shall receive a sound basic education. They hold that the definition of a sound basic education, and the standard against which the City's schools are to be measured, is to be judicially determined.

If the instruction, facilities and student performance in New York City schools fail to meet that standard, the State has violated the Constitution and must respond to correct the deficiencies in the City's school system. The majority and Judge Levine differ only on the particulars of the education which the Court should decree necessary.

My review of the history of the Education Article and our *Levittown* decision interpreting it (*Board of Educ., Levittown Union Free School Dist. v. Nyquist,* 57 N.Y.2d 27, 453 N.Y.S.2d 643, 439 N.E.2d 359) (hereinafter *Levittown*) leads me to a different conclusion. I believe that the constitutional duty is satisfied if the State creates the structure for a State-wide system of schools in which children are given the opportunity to acquire an education and supports it.

It is for other branches of government, not the courts, to define what constitutes a sound basic education and, assuming the State has not defaulted on its duty to establish a State-wide system and provide financial support, to ensure that the opportunity to be educated is available to all. In my view, plaintiffs have not successfully pleaded that the State has violated that duty.

I therefore dissent from so much of the majority's decision as sustains plaintiffs' first cause of action alleging a violation of <u>article XI, § 1 of the New York State Constitution</u>.

At the outset, it is helpful to remember that the responsibility for primary and secondary education in New York has been historically, and is by law, a joint undertaking of the State and local school districts. The State, acting through the Legislature and the constitutionally created Board of Regents, establishes standards for curricula, faculty and facilities and annually provides financial aid to the local districts. In 1994-1995 the State distributed almost $10 billion in State funds to school districts in New York State.

The New York City School District received over one third of that sum (*see*, Report of Education Unit, New York State Div. of Budget, Oct. 31, 1994, at 16-17, 26-27). Although individual districts no longer enjoy the power to establish the criteria for instruction and facilities they once had, they remain charged with administering the schools in their districts and possess broad powers for that purpose. They also supply a major part of the funding necessary to support and maintain their schools. They do so by determining annual expenses and, after crediting that sum with State and Federal aid, raising the balance by local taxation.

In the past, the financial needs of the New York City School District were supported by a greater proportion of local funds than State funds. Since 1983, however, the amount of money contributed by the City has steadily declined while the amount contributed by the State has increased. The State now contributes more to the funding of City schools than does the City. This increase in State aid has not, however, resulted in increased or improved services, only in a reduction in City appropriations for education (*see*, Chancellor's Budget Estimate, 1995-1996, Board of Education of City of NY, at 14). The question before the Court on this appeal, broadly stated, is whether the Constitution requires the State to provide an even greater share of the funds than it now does to defray the cost of operating the New York City schools.

Analysis begins with the language of the Constitution. The Education Article provides: "The legislature shall provide for the maintenance and support of a system of free common schools, wherein all the children of this state may be educated."

The words, with utter simplicity, impose a duty on the State to create a "system" for free public education available to all children and to support it. Conspicuously absent are descriptive words, establishing a qualitative or quantitative standard for the education the State must provide. Thus, if the drafters intended to impose on the State a substantive requirement for instruction and facilities, or provide that the State is ultimately responsible for any shortage of funds in individual school districts, it must be found in the history of the Article, not its words.

The section was adopted in 1894 at a time when there were more than 11,000 independent school districts in the State offering vastly different educational opportunities (*see*, 3 Lincoln, Constitutional History of New York, at 550-551). The Convention record reveals that the section was proposed to "express the principle of universal education, and direct the Legislature to use the power of the State to foster that principle" (3 Revised Record of Constitutional Convention of 1894, at 691). Its "evident purpose [was] to impose on that body the absolute duty to provide a general system of common schools" (3 Lincoln, Constitutional History, *op. cit.*, at 554).

Thus, it was said the Legislature must provide "not simply schools, but a system; not merely that they shall be common, but free, and not only that they shall be numerous, but that they shall be sufficient in number, so that all the children of the State may receive in them their education" (*id.*, at 555). The delegates' concern was focused on establishing a State-wide system of free education. The quality of that education was mentioned only in passing, a delegate stating that it should be "adequate" (3 Revised Record on Constitutional Convention, *op. cit.*, at 695). I find no indication that the drafters intended to go beyond this and impose a qualitative component within the Education Article, or to hold the State liable to make up a shortage of funds in particular school districts.

Reviewing this history in *Levittown* (57 N.Y.2d 27, 453 N.Y.S.2d 643, 439 N.E.2d 359), we concluded that the section was intended to require "a State-wide system assuring minimal acceptable facilities and services in contrast to the unsystematic delivery of instruction" which existed when the Constitution was adopted (*Levittown, supra,* at 47, 453 N.Y.S.2d 643, 439 N.E.2d 359).

Levittown, of course, involved a different claim than is asserted here: it dealt with the inequality or disparity of the education offered in various districts of the State whereas plaintiffs here assert that the students of New York City's schools have been deprived of an education meeting constitutional standards. Nevertheless, the *Levittown* Court interpreted the Education Article and the majority, Judge Levine and I all rely on that interpretation to support our differing views. The majority and the concurrence conclude that the *Levittown* decision does not foreclose the courts from defining the ingredients of a sound basic education and ordering the State to assume responsibility for providing it.

They find in *Levittown* an "unambiguous acknowledgement of a constitutional floor with respect to educational adequacy," and from that, assume the power of the courts to override the legislative and executive determinations of what and how much the system must provide (majority at 315, at 569 of 631 N.Y.S.2d, at 665 of 655 N.E.2d). The majority believes that the *Levittown* Court analyzed the article only so far as was necessary to address inequality and maintains that it is acting consistently with that precedent and only resolving issues the *Levittown* Court left unanswered. I conclude that the *Levittown* Court fully considered and determined the scope of the constitutional duty. Our differing interpretation of the same opinion requires a detailed consideration of it.

The decision is best understood by first reviewing the analysis made by the Appellate Division and then this Court's disposition of the matter. The Appellate Division unanimously agreed in *Levittown,* though for different reasons, that the Education Article had been violated (83 A.D.2d 217, 443 N.Y.S.2d 843). Three Justices, speaking through Justice Lazer, stated that the State's educational finance system was unconstitutional because it created inter-district variances in educational quality which disadvantaged urban children (*id.,* at 247-251, 443

N.Y.S.2d 843). Acknowledging that <u>article XI, § 1</u> was "devoid of semantic adornments", the Court nevertheless amplified its wording to attribute to the section concepts of a "thorough and efficient" school system and an "ample" education, importing qualifying words found in the Constitutions of the States of New Jersey and Washington but not found in the Constitution of New York (<u>id., at 248, 443 N.Y.S.2d 843).</u>

Though acknowledging that our Constitution did not explicitly mention a quantitative and qualitative standard, the Appellate Division nevertheless added one, requiring the State to insure that all children are equipped with "certain basic educational skills necessary to function effectively in society" (<u>id., at 248, 443 N.Y.S.2d 843).</u> The Appellate Division looked to statutes (e.g., <u>Education Law § 3204</u>) and to the Regulations of the Commissioner of Education (8 NYCRR part 100) defining the approved curricula to determine the scope of a constitutional guarantee.

The mere existence of these standards did not satisfy the Constitution they said; student performance must meet the Commissioner's standards <u>(83 A.D.2d, at 249-250, 443 N.Y.S.2d 843).</u> In sum, the Court made a qualitative analysis of the State educational system based upon the degree to which the Commissioner's standards were fulfilled and, finding performance levels below those standards in some districts, concluded the cause was insufficient State funding. Accordingly, the Appellate Division held the State had failed to "support and maintain" a State-wide system of schools.

Justice Hopkins agreed that the Education Article had been violated but he analyzed the constitutional mandate differently <u>(83 A.D.2d, at 266-269, 443 N.Y.S.2d 843).</u> He found three key ideas conveyed in the language of <u>article XI</u>: first, a duty was imposed on the Legislature; two, the duty included maintenance and support of a system of common schools; and third, the system had to be available to all children of the State. He found the Legislature had failed to "support and maintain a system of free common schools" because the statutes distributing State aid had become irrational, a "patchwork mounted on patchwork", a "maze of convoluted intricacies." He concluded the financing was unconstitutional because it was unsystematic

When the matter reached this Court, we modified the determination of the Appellate Division, construing the Education Article more narrowly and concluding that the Legislature had not violated it. The Appellate Division read a qualitative component into the Education Article because, it said, absent such a component the clause would be "without parameters" <u>(83 A.D.2d, at 248, 443 N.Y.S.2d 843).</u> We had no difficulty identifying the substance of the provision, however, concluding that it mandated only that the State support and maintain a system of free schools available to all children. We held that the guarantees of the Article had been satisfied because, in the words of the Court, "[t]he Legislature has made prescriptions with reference to the minimum number of days of school attendance, required courses, textbooks, qualifications of teachers and certain nonteaching personnel, pupil transportation, and other matters. If what is available by this system may properly be said to constitute an education, the constitutional mandate is satisfied." (57 N.Y.2d, at 48, 453 N.Y.S.2d 643, 439 N.E.2d 359.)

In other words, the _Levittown_ Court concluded that the system of which the Constitution speaks is a framework of educational programming and, implicitly, regulatory oversight of compliance with that framework. We concluded further that the State manifestly had "supported and maintained" the system because State appropriations for the New York public school system, judged by the fiscal contributions of other States, far exceeded those of all but two others. Based upon those determinations, we held that "a sound basic education" was available for all children in the State and thus the constitutional mandate was satisfied.

We rejected the extensive qualitative analysis of the lower courts, holding that the courts were not free to review the adequacy of the appropriations, except, "possibly", in the case "of gross and glaring inadequacy" of State funding (57 N.Y.2d, at 48-49, 453 N.Y.S.2d 643, 439 N.E.2d 359). In sum, we fully interpreted the Education Article, concluding that the State had met its constitutional obligation because it had created a system-it had defined a sound basic education and the facilities necessary to provide it-and appropriated substantial financial aid to local school districts to support and maintain that system.

The plaintiffs in this action do not contend that the State has defaulted in defining the ingredients of the State-wide system, nor do they allege that the State funding to maintain and support it is grossly inadequate. The position of plaintiffs, the majority and the concurrence is that the State must do more. It must not only set up the structures of a State-wide system, define the ingredients and provide aid to local districts, it must step in with additional financing to ensure that an "education", as defined by the courts, is fully developed and successful in each of the local school districts.

The _Levittown_ Court had before it the same analysis adopted by the majority here, in Judge Fuchsberg's dissent and in the opinion of the Appellate Division majority, and rejected it (see, 57 N.Y.2d, at 49, n. 9, 453 N.Y.S.2d 643, 439 N.E.2d 359).

Plaintiffs have not and cannot successfully plead that the present statutory provisions for allocation of State aid to local school districts for the maintenance and support of elementary and secondary education violate the State Constitution as we interpreted them in _Levittown._

First, plaintiffs' claim does not attempt to establish deprivation State-wide; it advances only claims involving some New York City schools. They contend, and the majority and concurrence agree, that the State's duty is to be measured district by district and requires the State to provide additional funding to rehabilitate ailing districts even though the constitutional obligation is met State-wide.

The concurrence supports that position by relying on language from the constitutional debates to the effect that the new duty would ameliorate conditions in places where the common schools are not adequate" (concurring at 327, at 576 of 631 N.Y.S.2d, at 672 of 655 N.E.2d [quoting from 3 Revised Record of Constitutional Convention of 1894, at 695]).

But the constitutional mandate to support the system of common schools is general in its terms and there is nothing in the debates to suggest that the quoted language meant more than that the Legislature should prescribe standards for a State-wide curricula and facilities to upgrade common schools with inferior standards. Certainly, nothing in the historical materials suggests that the State must step in when a district fails to meet statewide standards and increase State funding to that locality until a satisfactory performance level is achieved.

Confining their argument to New York City's schools, plaintiffs claim deprivation because selected community school districts in the City have inadequate facilities, low student performance ratios and high dropout rates. They have stated those claims by comparing their circumstances to the rest of the State and by comparing the condition of their schools and the performance of City students to the Regents' standards for school registration. Their complaint sounds remarkably similar to the complaint of the _Levittown_ plaintiffs and, as a unanimous Appellate Division held, states no more than a claim based on inter-district disparity.

Significantly, many figures relied upon by plaintiffs to prove their point that an adequate education had not been provided are less substantial than figures relied upon by the Appellate Division and Judge Fuchsberg in _Levittown_ (_see_, 83 A.D.2d 217, 250, 443 N.Y.S.2d 843, 57 N.Y.2d 27, 50, 453 N.Y.S.2d 643, 439 N.E.2d 359, _supra)_.

Plaintiffs further support their claims by assertions that students in New York City make less than "normal progress" than students in other parts of the State, that they perform poorly on achievement tests, and that City children earn fewer Regents' diplomas than students elsewhere in the State. The failure to make "normal progress" does not constitute deprivation and, as plaintiffs' own statistics prove, _most_ students, even in New York City, perform at acceptable levels. Manifestly, then, the State is providing children with the opportunity for a sound basic education.

Having determined that there is a qualitative component in the Education Article, and that the allegations of subpar performance and facilities in New York City alone state a cause of action, the majority approved judicial review of the State funding scheme. But this Court in _Levittown_ clearly stated that judicial review of the State funding scheme would only be warranted if it appeared there had been a "gross and glaring inadequacy" in State funding (_Levittown,_ 57 N.Y.2d, at 48, 453 N.Y.S.2d 643, 439 N.E.2d 359, _supra_). In holding that plaintiffs here have stated a cause of action, the majority simply ignores this limitation on our powers.

Thus, even if I were to accept the majority's analysis that the Constitution guarantees a certain level of instruction and performance and assume that plaintiffs have sufficiently alleged that it has not been satisfied, I still believe plaintiffs have failed to state a cause of action because they have failed to sufficiently plead that State aid to education is grossly inadequate. Unless they can sustain that element, we have no power to declare that defendants must accept responsibility for and cure the shortcomings of the New York City School District.

Plaintiffs allege only in the most conclusory form, and the majority assume without discussion, that the State funding is grossly inadequate and that there is a causal connection between it and the instruction and facilities provided New York City school children and their performance. But the State appropriates almost $10 billion for school aid State-wide-approximately one sixth of the money appropriated for all State purposes-and the New York City School District receives more than a third of it. Even if the State's obligation were imposed district by district, current State appropriations to New York City do not approach a "gross inadequacy" in State funding.

Plaintiffs also complain that they enroll 37% of the State's public school population but receive slightly less than 35% of the total State aid distributed. There is no constitutional requirement, however, that the State maintain exact parity in the financial aid distributed to the several thousand school districts. Insofar as plaintiffs attack the formula by which State aid is calculated, or allege that it is inequitable, their claim is similar to the claim Justice Hopkins accepted in _Levittown_ (83 A.D.2d, at 266, 443 N.Y.S.2d 843). It was rejected by this Court (see, 57 N.Y.2d, at 48, n. 7, 453 N.Y.S.2d 643, 439 N.E.2d 359).

Moreover, there is serious doubt that plaintiffs can establish that any claimed deficiency in the State funding scheme has caused a deprivation of educational opportunity to City students. These claims against the State are presented at a time when New York City is reducing its funding to the City School District when measured both in terms of the dollars appropriated and the percentage of its municipal budget allocated to education (see, Chancellor's Budget Estimate, 1995-1996, _op. cit._, at 14).

And these reductions have occurred even though the City is among municipalities having the lowest residential property tax rate for school purposes in the State and devotes the lowest percentage of its tax revenue to education. The Chancellor of the City School District has stated that the City contributes approximately 20% of its revenues to education, whereas the percentage contributed to education by other localities in the State is almost twice as much.

Based upon this evidence, a court could justifiably conclude as a matter of law that the shortcomings in the City schools are caused by the City's failure to adequately fund City schools, not from any default by the State of its constitutional duty.

Of course, the majority may interpret the State Constitution, or our _Levittown_ decision, as mandating a level of student performance and authorizing judicial determination of the curriculum and facilities and State funding necessary to achieve that level if it chooses, but I believe it unwise to do so for several reasons.

The first was stated by the _Levittown_ Court. In an opinion fully sensitive to the political process by which we are governed and the separation of powers concerns which restrain courts from interfering with responsibilities resting elsewhere, _Levittown_ defined the standard for measuring the constitutional requirement and properly avoided a judicial determination of the highly subjective and policy-laden questions of how much (or little) students must be taught or how well (or poorly) they must perform before a court should intervene. The courts, we held, were not to interfere in constitutional responsibilities assigned to other branches of government unless the executive and legislative branches had, in effect, defaulted on their duty to establish a State-wide system of education and fund it. I find that reasoning persuasive.

The State Legislature, in which New York City is amply represented, annually investigates and reviews the educational needs of the various school districts, and may conduct hearings to solicit further views if it deems them necessary. Based upon the information available to it, the Legislature distributes billions of dollars of educational aid throughout the State.

Surely the legislators are aware that the quality of the educational opportunity in some districts in New York City is inferior to the opportunity in other districts in the City and State. If they conclude that resources of the State call for a certain level of funding notwithstanding those problems and if that funding is not "grossly inadequate", it is not for us to force the State to do more. The Legislature is far more able than the courts to balance and determine State-wide needs and equities and, I need hardly mention, such determinations are well within _its_ constitutional domain.

The majority apparently view the constitutional provision as establishing an entitlement to receive an adequate education. It assumes that there is a point at which the education available is so palpably inadequate that the courts must intervene, determine the extent of the inadequacy and order the problem solved at State expense. And the courts may impose this duty on the State, the majority holds, even though the State has established a structure for the school system and provided adequate funding for it as measured by the State's resources.

If we were dealing with a constitutional right personal to each child in New York, then the Court's power to override the majority's will to protect those rights might be justified. But the

Education Article states a general duty. The Constitution is satisfied if the majority has worked its will through its elected officials and their action represents a reasonable response to the duty imposed. The courts have the power to see that the legislative and executive branches of government address their responsibility to provide the structure for a State-wide school system and support it but we have no authority, except in the most egregious circumstances, to tell them that they have not done enough.

Finally, it is not clear whether increased State aid to New York City is to be provided by increasing appropriations for education generally, or reallocating the current State-wide appropriations so that New York City schools receive a greater share of the aid appropriated. If State aid to education is to be generally increased, the increase will necessarily be achieved at the expense of other equally meritorious programs deprived of some portion of the State resources previously used to fund their activities. If there is to be a reallocation of State aid to provide greater funding for New York City-or a reconstruction of the State aid formula for that purpose-the reallocation will be achieved at the expense of other school districts in the State.

They will then be forced to increase local taxes to fund education for their districts and to do so at a time when New York City is reducing its municipal appropriations for education. Judicially compelling either course encroaches on the Legislature's power to order State priorities and allocate the State's limited resources.

This assumption of power in the field of education sets a precedent for other areas that will be hard for the courts to resist in the future. The State Constitution is a voluminous document covering not only the distribution and scope of power, but also addressing dozens of other matters as diverse as public housing, nursing homes, canals, ski trails and highways. The State, to a greater or lesser degree, is directed to maintain and protect all those services and facilities. It cannot be that each of them are matters calling for quantitative and qualitative judicial oversight in their funding and operation.

To explore just one example, the New York State Constitution provides, in language similar to that contained in article XI, § 1, that the State "shall" provide "aid, care and support of the needy" (N.Y. Const., art. XVII, § 1). There is, and probably always will be, a profound public debate over who should be eligible for public assistance and whether the levels of assistance are too high or too low.

We have assiduously avoided making quantitative and qualitative determinations in this area in the past, concluding that those are questions for the legislative and executive branches to decide (see, *Hope v. Perales,* 83 N.Y.2d 563, 578, 611 N.Y.S.2d 811, 634 N.E.2d 183; *Matter of Barie v. Lavine,* 40 N.Y.2d 565, 388 N.Y.S.2d 878, 357 N.E.2d 349; *Matter of Bernstein v. Toia,* 43 N.Y.2d

437, 402 N.Y.S.2d 342, 373 N.E.2d 238). If the Court is to assume the responsibility of determining what level of educational services and student performance must be achieved under the Constitution, I know of no legal answer for those who will contend that we must resolve similar questions challenging compliance with the Social Welfare Article or other sections of the Constitution.

The temptation to address these school problems judicially is understandable. But the Constitution provides for particularized areas of responsibility and it is not for the courts to mandate that the State must spend more of its finite resources for education and less, say, for housing the poor or healing the sick. Nor is it for us to say that the current resources devoted to education are to be transferred to one part of the State to the loss of others. Those are choices delegated to the people's elected representatives, not Judges, and in the absence of their manifest failure to address the problem, the judiciary should refrain from interfering.

Accordingly, I would dismiss plaintiffs' first cause of action asserting defendants have violated article XI of the State Constitution.

SMITH, Judge (dissenting in part).

I agree with and join the majority opinion in upholding the causes of action based on the Education Article of the New York State Constitution and on a violation of title VI's regulations. I conclude, in addition, that the complaint states a valid equal protection claim under both the Federal and State Constitutions. I would, therefore, reverse this aspect of the Appellate Division decision and deny the motion to dismiss the equal protection claims.

Judge Ciparick agrees only that plaintiffs have made a valid State equal protection claim. the federal equal protection claim

Introduction

The present case should be viewed in its historical context. At least since the latter part of the nineteenth century, African-Americans in New York State have sought equality of education. Like many other parts of the Nation, New York segregated its schools on the basis of race. The end of segregation by law did not end efforts to exclude African-Americans from equal educational opportunities. Much of the twentieth century has been spent by African-American parents and students fighting for equality of education.

Plaintiffs have a right to demonstrate that they are receiving less than a minimal basic education. The Equal Protection Clauses of both the Federal and State Constitutions stand for the proposition that State action, through selective and biased funding, cannot be used to condemn African-American, Latino or other children to an education which is inherently inferior.

While the thrust of the decision in *Brown v. Board of Educ.*, 347 U.S. 483, 74 S.Ct. 686, 98 L.Ed. 873 was that separate facilities, no matter how similar in terms of resources, were inherently unequal, one underlying fact in those cases was that the resources of the separate schools were unequal. And that fact led to the argument of a denial of equal protection.

The Historical Setting

New York State, like many other States, had a history of segregated schools required by law. In 1864, New York State enacted the "Common School Act" (L.1864, 555, tit. 10, § 1), which authorized school authorities in cities and incorporated villages to establish separate schools for the education of the "colored" race. This Act empowered school authorities to establish schools for the exclusive use of colored children and authorized such authorities to exclude colored children from schools provided for white children. In 1873, the State enacted the Civil Rights Act (L.1873, 186) providing that persons of color shall have full and equal enjoyment of any accommodation, advantage, facility or privilege furnished by teachers and other officers of common schools and public institutions of learning.

Chapter 556 of the Laws of 1894 (art. 11, tit. 15, §§ 28-30), again provided for the organization and creation of separate schools for colored children in cities, villages, union districts and school districts organized under a special act. The language of section 31 of that same article provided that colored schools in the City of New York "shall be open for the education of pupils for whom admission is sought, without regard to race or color."

Chapter 492 (§ 1) of the Laws of 1900 expressly provided that "no person shall be refused admission into or be excluded from any public school in the state of New York on account of race or color." Further, section 2 of that chapter repealed section 28 (art. 11, tit. 15) of chapter 556 of the Laws of 1894 regarding the establishment of separate schools with equal facilities for colored children in any city or incorporated village.

Under chapter 140 of the Laws of 1910, section 920 of the Education Law provided that "no person shall be refused admission into or be excluded from any public school in the state of New York on account of race or color." However, section 921 of that same chapter again expressly provided for separate schools for colored children should the inhabitants of any district determine. This apparent inconsistency in the law, of generally prohibiting exclusion from public schools on account of race, but expressly making available the option to establish separate schools, permitted the continuance of segregated schools by law. The gravamen of such disparity resulted in the disparate impact upon the education of children, detrimentally and adversely affecting children of color.

Such dissimilar treatment in education of children was supported by decisions of this Court. _People ex rel. King v. Gallagher_ (93 N.Y. 438 [1883]) involved the denial of admission of a 12-year-old black girl to a local public school in Brooklyn because of her race. The majority affirmed the lower court's denial of admission to the school because the school was open only to white children. The Court determined that the principal of the school, as administrator, was within his discretion to deny the child admission because she was black.

Citing the Common School Act of 1864, which authorized the establishment of separate schools for the education of the colored race within the State, the Court held that such separate schools were not an abrogation of the Privileges and Immunities Clause of the Fourteenth Amendment of the United States Constitution. No impairment was found by the City of Brooklyn requiring separate but equal educational facilities.

The Court further determined that notwithstanding the Civil Rights Act of 1873 (L.1873, ch. 186), repealing and annulling any statute which discriminated against persons of color (93 N.Y. at 456), the establishment of separate schools for black and white children was not discriminatory. Judge Danforth dissented, finding the requirement that black children attend schools designated only for black children was unequal and in violation of the laws protecting equal rights.

Further, in _People ex rel. Cisco v. School Bd.,_ 161 N.Y. 598, 56 N.E. 81 [1900], this Court similarly held that the School Board of Queens was authorized to maintain separate schools for the education of "colored" children and to exclude such children from schools designated for "white" children only. Citing its earlier holding in _Gallagher (supra)_ the Court reasoned that the Civil Rights Act of 1873 required that equal school facilities and accommodations be furnished, not equal social opportunities.

With the passage of legislation prohibiting the exclusion of blacks from schools on the basis of race, the official policy of the State became one of nondiscrimination against black children. Nevertheless, as several cases have shown, the efforts of some governmental officials have continued the previous State policy of racial exclusion. Thus, over the years, a number of lawsuits have been brought to eliminate the exclusion of blacks from white schools (see, _for example, Taylor v. Board of Educ.,_ 191 F.Supp. 181, 195 F.Supp. 231, _affd._ 294 F.2d 36, _cert. denied_ 368 U.S. 940, 82 S.Ct. 382, 7 L.Ed.2d 339 _decree mod._ 221 F.Supp. 275; _United States v. Yonkers Bd. of Educ.,_ 837 F.2d 1181; _Hart v. Community School Bd. of Educ.,_ 512 F.2d 37).

While the major thrust of efforts to fight unequal treatment of black students has been desegregation, at the same time black parents and pupils have insisted that the facilities and opportunities available to black students have been grossly inferior to those available to white students and have challenged that state of affairs on equal protection grounds.

Thus, _Brown v. Board of Educ._ (347 U.S. 483, 74 S.Ct. 686, 98 L.Ed. 873) was clearly decided on the assumption that facilities and other tangible factors of segregated schools were equal even though it was clear that in many instances, the segregated schools were unequal. The Court stated:

"We come then to the question presented: Does segregation of children in public schools solely on the basis of race, even though the physical facilities and other 'tangible' factors may be equal, deprive the children of the minority group of equal educational opportunities? We believe that it does."

Despite this assumption by the Supreme Court in _Brown_, at least two of the complaints in the five cases decided there attacked the inequality in black schools when compared to white schools. The allegations of inadequate education made against the State here are similar to claims of inadequacy made in _Brown._ To the extent that such claims are alleged to be based upon the deliberate action of the State, plaintiffs should be given the opportunity to prove their assertions.

In their complaint in _Brown_, plaintiffs questioned "whether the denial to infant plaintiffs, solely because of race, of educational opportunities equal to those afforded white children was in contravention of the Fourteenth Amendment of the United States Constitution as being a denial of the equal protection of the laws." In _Briggs v. Elliott_, another case reversed in _Brown_, the plaintiffs similarly alleged in their complaint that the "public schools of Clarendon County, South Carolina set apart for white students and from which all Negro students are excluded were superior in plant, equipment, curricula, and in all other material respects to the schools set apart for Negro students."

Plaintiffs argued further that "the defendants by enforcing the provision of the Constitution and laws of South Carolina excluded all Negro students from the 'white' public schools and thereby deprived plaintiffs and others on whose behalf the action is brought solely because of race and color, of the opportunity of attending the only public schools in Clarendon County where they can obtain an education equal to that offered all qualified students who are not of Negro descent" (see also, _Davis v. County School Bd._, 103 F.Supp. 337, 340-341).

In _Belton v. Gebhart_, 32 Del.Ch. 343, 87 A.2d 862, another case decided in _Brown_, the plaintiffs, elementary and high school Negro children, brought an action in the Delaware Court of

Chancery seeking to enjoin enforcement of provisions of that State's constitutional and statutory code requiring segregation in the public schools. The court found for the plaintiffs and ordered the immediate admission of the Negro children into schools that were formerly for white children only.

The court determined that the separate educational facilities were inherently unequal, finding the white schools superior to the Negro schools with respect to pupil-teacher ratio, physical plants, teacher training, aesthetic considerations, extracurricular activities, and time and distance involved in the student's travel to and from school.

he court concluded that the State, through its agencies, had violated the plaintiffs' rights under the Equal Protection Clause of the Fourteenth Amendment, by pursuing a policy of segregation in education which resulted in Negro children, as a class, receiving educational opportunities substantially inferior to those available to white children otherwise similarly situated.

The plaintiffs in the New Rochelle school case also alleged a disparity in the quality of education available to black and white students. The court found it unnecessary to consider those claims in the light of _Brown._

The Present Allegations and Federal Law

One of the major issues here is what level of scrutiny the courts must give to the plaintiffs' equal protection claims-minimal or rational basis, intermediate or strict. The minimal level of scrutiny tests whether a classification or statute "bears some fair relationship to a legitimate public purpose" (_Plyler v. Doe_, 457 U.S. 202, 216, 102 S.Ct. 2382, 2394, 72 L.Ed.2d 786 [1982]; _see also, Alevy v. Downstate Med. Ctr._, 39 N.Y.2d 326, 332, 384 N.Y.S.2d 82, 348 N.E.2d 537). This standard has often been applied in cases dealing with economics and social welfare (_id._). Strict scrutiny applies where a law operates to the disadvantage of a suspect class, or a fundamental constitutional interest is alleged to have been violated (_Plyler v. Doe, supra,_ at 216-217, 102 S.Ct. at 2394-95; _San Antonio School Dist. v. Rodriguez,_ 411 U.S. 1, 18-44, 93 S.Ct. 1278, 1288-1303, 36 L.Ed.2d 16; _Alevy v. Downstate Med. Ctr., supra,_ at 332, 384 N.Y.S.2d 82, 348 N.E.2d 537).

An intermediate level of scrutiny has been applied to legislative classifications which are not "facially invidious" which, nevertheless, "give rise to recurring constitutional difficulties" and require "the assurance that the classification reflects a reasoned judgment consistent with the ideal of equal protection by inquiring whether it may fairly be viewed as furthering a substantial interest of the State (_Alevy v. Downstate Med. Ctr., supra._) Plaintiffs assert that intermediate scrutiny should be the standard used here. I conclude that the facts alleged require at least a standard of intermediate scrutiny.

Defendants rely essentially on three cases in concluding that the Equal Protection Clause of the Fourteenth Amendment is not violated-(1) *San Antonio School Dist. v. Rodriguez (supra),* (2) *Plyler v. Doe (supra)* and (3) *Board of Educ., Levittown Union Free School Dist. v. Nyquist,* 57 N.Y.2d 27, 453 N.Y.S.2d 643, 439 N.E.2d 359 [1982] (hereinafter *Levittown*).

Plaintiffs' basic contention, distinguishing this case from *Rodriguez* and *Levittown,* is the assertion that the pupils in question are not receiving a minimal basic education sufficient to prepare them for contemporary society including, but not limited to, basic literacy, calculating and verbal skills. If such allegations can be proved and it can further be shown that (1) the property tax funding of schools and or (2) the State allocation of its resources is discriminatory, plaintiffs may be entitled to a decision in their favor, in my view, on Federal equal protection grounds as well as on the Education Article ground which a majority of the Court upholds.

In the complaint here, plaintiffs allege that they are not receiving a minimal basic education as the result of the funding system in the State and further buttress that claim with specific allegations. In addition, the complaint addresses the disparate impact of the funding system on minorities.

It is clear that the Supreme Court has not decided the issue raised here, that a minimal basic education is fundamental and should receive heightened scrutiny. The Court noted such in *Papasan v. Allain,* 478 U.S. 265, 106 S.Ct. 2932, 92 L.Ed.2d 209, where it stated:

"The complaint in this case asserted not simply that the petitioners had been denied their right to a minimally adequate education but also that such a right was fundamental and that because that right had been infringed the State's action here should be reviewed under strict scrutiny. App. 20. As *Rodriguez* and *Plyler* indicate, *this Court has not yet definitively settled the questions whether a minimally adequate education is a fundamental right and whether a statute alleged to discriminatorily infringe that right should be accorded heightened equal protection review."* (478 U.S. at 285, 106 S.Ct. at 2944 [emphasis supplied].)

The *Rodriguez* case also does not preclude the claims made here. In *Rodriguez,* the Supreme Court held that the Texas system of funding education did not violate the Equal Protection Clause of the Fourteenth Amendment. There, Mexican-American parents brought a class action attacking the funding of the Texas educational system. One main difference between that case and this is that *Rodriguez* involved no allegation that the education of the children was inadequate.

At another point in *Rodriguez,* the Court stated: "Even if it were conceded that some identifiable quantum of education is a constitutionally protected prerequisite to the meaningful exercise of either right, we have no indication that the present levels of educational expenditures in Texas provide an education that falls short. Whatever merit appellees argument might have if a State's financing system occasioned an absolute denial of educational opportunities to any of its children, that argument provides no basis for finding an interference with fundamental rights where only relative differences in spending levels are involved and where-as is true in the present case-no charge fairly could be made that the system fails to provide each child with an opportunity to acquire *the basic minimal skills necessary for the enjoyment of the rights of speech and of full participation in the political process.*" (411 U.S., at 36-37, 93 S.Ct. at 1298-1299 [emphasis supplied].)

A second point in *Rodriguez* was that there was no showing that the Texas system of financing schools operated to the disadvantage of a suspect class. If it did, the Court noted, the financing scheme would come under strict scrutiny. Instead, the Court concluded that rational basis was the appropriate test. The Court stated:

"This, then, establishes the framework for our analysis. *We must decide, first, whether the Texas system of financing public education operates to the disadvantage of some suspect class or impinges upon a fundamental right explicitly or implicitly protected by the Constitution, thereby requiring strict judicial scrutiny. If so, the judgment of the District Court should be affirmed. If not, the Texas scheme must still be examined to determine whether it rationally furthers some legitimate, articulated state purpose and therefore does not constitute an invidious discrimination in violation of the Equal Protection Clause of the Fourteenth Amendment.* " (411 U.S. at 17, 93 S.Ct. at 1288 .)

In *Plyler,* the Supreme Court held that the Equal Protection Clause of the Fourteenth Amendment was violated by denying children of illegal aliens a basic education. While the Court found in *Plyler* that there was no fundamental right to an education, it applied an intermediate level of scrutiny and held that where a discrete group (children of illegal aliens) was being denied the right to an education, the State had to show a compelling State interest. The Court stated:

"If the State is to deny a discrete group of innocent children the free public education that it offers to other children residing within its borders, that denial must be justified by a showing that it furthers some substantial state interest. No such showing was made here." (457 U.S., at 230, 102 S.Ct. at 2401-02.)

To prove a violation of the Equal Protection Clause of the Fourteenth Amendment, the plaintiffs must prove intentional discrimination. This intent does not have to be overt and express. It is clear that the complaint alleges that the educational funding by the State has a disparate impact on minority students. The complaint also sufficiently alleges intentional discrimination. After addressing the disparities and inequalities of education for minority students, the complaint states the following:

"Over the past ten years, despite knowledge of the facts set forth in the preceding paragraphs, and despite recommendations for major reforms in official reports issued by commissions created by the defendants themselves, the defendants have re-enacted the inequitable state aid scheme without substantial modification to address the blatant inequities and their disproportionate impact on minority students, or to ensure that all students throughout the state of New York have available to them the resources necessary to obtain an education meeting or exceeding the Regents' minimum statewide standards. Defendants have refused to act, even though the detrimental impact of their failure to provide equitable levels of funding on minority students was well-recognized and reasonably foreseeable."

It is also important to note that intent need not be shown on the face of legislation and that disparate impact is only one of the factors by which intent is shown. This is clear in quotations from both _Washington v. Davis, 426 U.S. 229, 96 S.Ct. 2040, 48 L.Ed.2d 597 [1976]_ and _Arlington Hgts. v. Metropolitan Hous. Dev. Corp., 429 U.S. 252, 97 S.Ct. 555, 50 L.Ed.2d 450 [1977]_. In _Washington v. Davis_ the Supreme Court stated:

"The central purpose of the Equal Protection Clause of the Fourteenth Amendment is the prevention of official conduct discriminating on the basis of race. It is also true that the Due Process Clause of the Fifth Amendment contains an equal protection component prohibiting the United States from invidiously discriminating between individuals or groups. _Bolling v. Sharpe, 347 U.S. 497, 74 S.Ct. 693, 98 L.Ed. 884 (1954)_. But our cases have not embraced the proposition that a law or other official act, without regard to whether it reflects a racially discriminatory purpose, is unconstitutional _solely_ because it has a racially disproportionate impact.

"This is not to say that the necessary discriminatory racial purpose must be express or appear on the face of the statute, or that a law's disproportionate impact is irrelevant in cases involving Constitution-based claims of racial discrimination. A statute, otherwise neutral on its face, must not be applied so as invidiously to discriminate on the basis of race.

"Necessarily, an invidious discriminatory purpose may often be inferred from the totality of the relevant facts, including the fact, if it is true, that the law bears more heavily on one race than another. It is also not infrequently true that the discriminatory impact-in the jury cases for example, the total or seriously disproportionate exclusion of Negroes from jury venires-may for all practical purposes demonstrate unconstitutionality because in various circumstances the discrimination is very difficult to explain on nonracial grounds.

Nevertheless, we have not held that a law, neutral on its face and serving ends otherwise within the power of government to pursue, is invalid under the Equal Protection Clause simply because it may affect a greater proportion of one race than of another. Disproportionate impact is not irrelevant, but it is not the sole touchstone of an invidious racial discrimination forbidden by the Constitution. Standing alone, it does not trigger the rule, _McLaughlin v. Florida,_ 379 U.S. 184, 85 S.Ct. 283, 13 L.Ed.2d 222 (1964), that racial classifications are to be subjected to the strictest scrutiny and are justifiable only by the weightiest of considerations." (426 U.S. at 239, 241-242, 96 S.Ct. at 2047, 2048-2049.)

In _Arlington Hgts.,_ 429 U.S., at 264-268, 97 S.Ct. at 562-565, the Court stressed factors which indicate circumstantial and direct evidence of intent, including, whether the action bears more heavily on one race than another, a clear pattern, historical background, a sequence of events, statements of members of the decision-making body, minutes, and testimony of officials. Where the ultimate proof shows intentional discrimination through historical background, a pattern, disparate impact or other factors, plaintiffs would be entitled to relief.

The Levittown Decision

In _Levittown,_ this Court relied on the _Rodriguez_ decision in applying a minimal or rational basis standard of review and in rejecting the claims of the plaintiffs that the Equal Protection Clause of the Fourteenth Amendment had been violated. Moreover, in _Levittown,_ this Court noted the absence of any allegation that educational facilities or services fell below the minimum standard set by the Board of Regents. This Court stated:

"No claim is advanced in this case, however, by either the original plaintiffs or the intervenors that the educational facilities or services provided in the school districts that they represent fall below the State-wide minimum standard of educational quality and quantity fixed by the Board of Regents; their attack is directed at the existing disparities in financial resources which lead to educational unevenness above that minimum standard." (57 N.Y.2d, at 38, 453 N.Y.S.2d 643, 439 N.E.2d 359.)

The difference between this case and _Levittown_ is clear. In _Levittown,_ there was no allegation that African-American, Latino or other students were receiving an education which was below the minimum standard. Here, the allegation of the lack of a minimal basic education is at the heart of the action as to all City public school students and that is why a majority upholds the Education Article cause of action.

In sum, I conclude that the plaintiffs have adequately stated a claim under the Equal Protection Clause of the Fourteenth Amendment. I also conclude that this Court is free to adopt a heightened scrutiny standard in dealing with the allegations of denial of a basic minimal education.

THE STATE EQUAL PROTECTION CLAIM

Judge Ciparick and I conclude that the plaintiffs have stated a valid State equal protection claim. New York's historical and constitutional commitment to public education establishes education as an integral and substantial right of every citizen in our State, and a heightened level of scrutiny should be applied to review the current system of financing public education.

In the procedural posture of this case, the allegations of the amended complaint are sufficient to allege that plaintiffs' equal protection rights, guaranteed by <u>article I, § 11 of the New York State Constitution</u>, have been violated by the State's funding methodology which denies New York City public school students a minimum adequate education. Therefore, for the current educational aid scheme to withstand intermediate review, defendants must demonstrate that the State's method of funding public education is substantially related to the important educational needs of its public school students.

While Judge Ciparick and I recognize that the distribution of educational aid is traditionally the bastion of the Legislature, we cannot overlook the allegations of the deleterious consequences of years of inequitable funding which have led to inadequate and substandard educational services.

The allegation is that a substantial number of New York City public school students do not receive the type of basic education necessary to equip them to exercise all of their established rights under the Federal and State Constitutions and to adequately function in society. In the 13 years since this Court's decision in <u>Levittown,</u> the gross disparities presaged by the <u>Levittown</u> majority are, allegedly, now a reality, and, plaintiffs argue, it is painfully apparent that the Legislature refuses to address what has evolved into an epic constitutional problem, rendering the application of heightened scrutiny particularly appropriate in this case (*see, <u>San Antonio School Dist. v. Rodriguez,</u> 411 U.S., at 99, 108, 93 S.Ct. at 1330-1331, 1335* [Marshall, J., dissenting], *supra;* <u>Dandridge v. Williams,</u> 397 U.S. 471, 519-521, 90 S.Ct. 1153, 1178-1180, 25 L.Ed.2d 491 [Marshall, J., dissenting], *reh. denied* <u>398 U.S. 914, 90 S.Ct. 1684,26 L.Ed.2d 80</u>; <u>Bismarck Pub. School Dist. No. 1 v. State of North Dakota,</u> 511 N.W.2d 247, 259; Hubsch, <u>The Emerging Right to Education Under State Constitutional Law,</u> 65 Temp.L.Rev. 1325 [1992]; *accord,* <u>Levittown, 57 N.Y.2d, at 39, 453 N.Y.S.2d 643, 439 N.E.2d 359, *supra; but see,* <u>Levittown,</u> 57 N.Y.2d, at 50, n. 9, 453 N.Y.S.2d 643, 439 N.E.2d 359).</u>

Assuming the truth of plaintiffs' allegations that New York City public school students are receiving an education below minimum standards because of an educational aid scheme that disparately impacts minority students through an inequitable distribution of public moneys, the focus of the inquiry of our dissent in this aspect of the case is whether New York's funding scheme which includes direct State funding and property-based funding furthers a substantial or important State interest to justify the discriminatory effects.

It is alleged that the disparities in educational opportunities for urban public school children are a reality because the State's method of distributing aid bears no relationship, substantial or rational, to the educational needs of students or the costs of educating students in a particular district.

Since the State is constitutionally charged with providing an educational system that offers "a sound basic education" (_Levittown,_ 57 N.Y.2d, at 48, 453 N.Y.S.2d 643, 439 N.E.2d 359, _supra;_ N.Y. Const., art. XI, § 1), the failure to adequately fund New York City schools allegedly denies New York City public school students equal protection of the laws of this State in contravention of article I, § 11 of the New York State Constitution, by depriving them of equal access to educational opportunities.

Under the current financing methodology, the quantum of taxable property in a school district bears an immediate and direct correlation to the student's access to education. Yet, according to plaintiffs, it is not the existence of disparities among districts that produces the unconstitutional inequity, but the fact that the financing scheme employed by the State to fund the system of free common schools perpetuates profound inequality of educational opportunity. Equal protection "is not addressed to the minimal sufficiency but rather to the unjustifiable inequalities of state action." (_San Antonio School Dist. v. Rodriguez,_ 411 U.S., at 89, 93 S.Ct. at 1325, [Marshall, J., dissenting] _supra._)

Pointing to _Levittown,_ respondents contend that the disparities in funding among districts is the justifiable consequence of local control, long recognized as the legitimate State interest underlying the complex school aid allocation formula. However, these disparities, it is alleged, directly translate into a constitutionally unacceptable result-disparate and diminished educational opportunities for school children who, to their misfortune, reside in districts penalized under the current school aid allocation formula.

It is this result-lesser educational opportunity which denies a sound, basic education, based on wealth discrimination-that allegedly transgresses the Equal Protection Clause of the State Constitution, and would require respondents to demonstrate at trial that the current school funding scheme bears an important and substantial relationship to the State's interest in preserving the current funding scheme and its rationale, which interest cannot be achieved through a less intrusive alternative (_see, e.g., Montgomery v. Daniels,_ 38 N.Y.2d 41, 61, 378 N.Y.S.2d 1, 340 N.E.2d 444; _Matter of Lalli,_ 43 N.Y.2d 65, 400 N.Y.S.2d 761, 371 N.E.2d 481, _affd. sub. nom. Lalli v. Lalli,_ 439 U.S. 259, 99 S.Ct. 518, 58 L.Ed.2d 503; _People v. Whidden,_ 51 N.Y.2d 457, 460, 434 N.Y.S.2d 936, 415 N.E.2d 927; _Califano v. Webster,_ 430 U.S. 313, 316-317, 97 S.Ct. 1192, 1194-1195, 51 L.Ed.2d 360; _Craig v. Boren,_ 429 U.S. 190, 197, 97 S.Ct. 451, 456-457, 50 L.Ed.2d 397, _reh. denied_ 429 U.S. 1124, 97 S.Ct. 1161, 51 L.Ed.2d 574; _Alevy v. Downstate Med. Ctr.,_ 39 N.Y.2d 326, 336, 384 N.Y.S.2d 82, 348 N.E.2d 537, _supra_).

This would be no easy task for respondents, complicated by strongly conflicted viewpoints and policies among the very agents who administer educational policy in New York. The Commissioner of Education and the Board of Regents have characterized the school funding scheme as inequitable, charging that it undermines New York's educational policies. The Commissioner and Board of Regents have assailed the current financing formula for its arbitrariness, asserting that the current methods for allocating State education aid are ineffective and preclude attainment of proposed educational goals.

Accordingly, I reinstate the second cause of action alleging a violation of the Equal Protection Clause of the Fourteenth Amendment of the Federal Constitution. Judge Ciparick and I would reinstate the second cause of action insofar as it asserts a violation of the Equal Protection Clause of the State Constitution.

Majority opinion by Judge CIPARICK, J., and SIMONS, TITONE, BELLACOSA, SMITH and LEVINE, JJ., concur.

LEVINE, J., concurring in result as to the first cause of action based upon a violation of New York Constitution, article XI, 1, the Education Article, in a separate opinion.

SIMONS, J., dissenting in part and voting not to reinstate the first cause of action in a separate opinion.

SMITH, J., dissenting in part and voting to reinstate causes of action on behalf of the municipal plaintiffs as well as the non-municipal plaintiffs and to reinstate the second cause of action in its entirety, alleging violations of the Equal Protection Clauses of the Federal and State Constitutions in a separate opinion.

CIPARICK, J., dissenting in part and voting to reinstate causes of action on behalf of the municipal plaintiffs as well as the non-municipal plaintiffs and to reinstate the second cause of action insofar as it asserts a violation of the Equal Protection Clause of the State Constitution, for reasons stated in Judge SMITH'S dissenting-in-part opinion.

Order modified, without costs, in accordance with the opinion herein and, as so modified, affirmed.

END OF DOCUMENT

OPINION #4

Supreme Court, New York County, New York

187 Misc.2d 1

CAMPAIGN FOR FISCAL EQUITY et al., Plaintiffs

v.

STATE of New York et al., Defendants

Jan. 9, 2001

Students, parents, and organizations concerned with education issues brought action challenging state's funding of New York City's public schools. After remand, <u>271 A.D.2d 379, 707 N.Y.S.2d 94,</u> the Supreme Court, New York County, <u>Leland DeGrasse</u>, J., held that:

(1) state failed to assure that city's public schools received adequate funding to afford their students the "sound basic education" guaranteed by the Education Article of the New York State Constitution;

(2) state's funding mechanisms had an adverse and disparate impact upon city's minority public school students in violation of specific implementing regulations of Title VI of the Civil Rights Act; and

(3) legislature, rather than court, would be given the first opportunity to reform public school financing system.

Judgment for plaintiffs.

<u>LELAND DeGRASSE</u>, J.

Education is perhaps the most important function of state and local governments. Compulsory school attendance laws and the great expenditures for education both demonstrate our recognition of the importance of education to our democratic society. It is required in the performance of our most basic public responsibilities, even service in the armed forces.

It is the very foundation of good citizenship. Today it is a principal instrument in awakening the child to cultural values, in preparing him for later professional training, and in helping him to adjust normally to his environment. In these days, it is doubtful that any child may reasonably be expected to succeed in life if he is denied the opportunity of an education. (*Brown v. Board of Education of Topeka*, 347 U.S. 483, 493, 74 S.Ct. 686, 98 L.Ed. 873 [1954].)

In the years since the *Brown* decision was handed down, state and local governments have struggled with fulfilling the "most important function" of providing universal free primary and secondary education. This case raises an issue that has proved particularly vexing to educators, policy makers, and the general public: how to devise a method of funding public schools that assures students at least a minimally adequate education.

Plaintiffs, comprised of students, parents and organizations concerned with education issues, challenge New York State's funding of New York City's public schools. After pre-trial motion practice, appeals, and discovery, two claims were tried before this court from October 12, 1999 to May 15, 2000. Extensive post-trial briefing followed.

In the first of these two claims, plaintiffs assert that the State has failed to assure that New York City's public schools receive adequate funding to afford their students the "sound basic education" guaranteed by the Education Article of the New York State Constitution (N.Y. Const. article 11, § 1; *Board of Educ., Levittown Union Free School Dist. v. Nyquist*, 57 N.Y.2d 27, 453 N.Y.S.2d 643, 439 N.E.2d 359 [1982]).

In their second claim, plaintiffs assert that the State's funding mechanisms have an adverse and disparate impact upon the City's minority public school students-who comprise 73% of the State's minority students and approximately 84% of the City's public school enrollment-in violation of specific implementing regulations of Title VI of the Civil Rights Act of 1964 (42 U.S.C. § 2000d; 34 C.F.R. § 100.3[b][1], [2]).

The defendants who remained in the case by the time of trial, New York State, Governor George Pataki, and State Tax Commissioner Michael Urbach, vigorously dispute these claims. They argue that New York State spends more per student on education than all but three other states, that New York City spends more per student than any other large school district in the nation, and that this provision of funds is more than is necessary to provide a sound basic education to New York City's public school students.

In the alternative, defendants argue that any failure to provide a constitutionally adequate education is the fault of New York City, for failing to contribute its fair share of school funding, and of the City's Board of Education, for failing to adequately manage the funding it receives from federal, State, and City sources. Defendants also assert that State education aid is allocated on a non-discriminatory basis.

The court holds that the education provided New York City students is so deficient that it falls below the constitutional floor set by the Education Article of the New York State Constitution. The court also finds that the State's actions are a substantial cause of this constitutional violation.

With respect to plaintiffs' claim under Title VI's implementing regulations, the court finds that the State school funding system has an adverse and disparate impact on minority public school children and that this disparate impact is not adequately justified by any reason related to education. Accordingly, plaintiffs have proven their federal law claim as well.

The findings of fact that form the foundation for these legal conclusions are set forth in sections III-VI, below. However, before embarking on an examination of the massive factual record presented by the parties, it will be necessary first to provide a brief procedural history of the case, and a brief description of the arc of school funding litigation nationwide that began in California with _Serrano v. Priest_, 5 Cal.3d 584, 96 Cal.Rptr. 601, 487 P.2d 1241 (1971). This background will help place into context both the parties' arguments and the Court of Appeals' pronouncements concerning the content of the "sound basic education" standard.

I. THE PROCEDURAL HISTORY OF THIS CASE

Plaintiffs filed this action in May 1993 against the current defendants, an array of other elected officials, and the Commissioner of the State Education Department ("SED"). At the same time the City of New York and the New York City Board of Education brought an action against the State and other defendants alleging virtually identical claims. Both actions came before this court.

Defendants moved to dismiss both complaints. This court partially granted defendants' motions as discussed in the following paragraphs.

This court dismissed the City's action on the ground that as a subdivision of the State subject to the State's direction and control the City could not challenge the constitutionality of the acts of its governmental parent. Several New York community school boards, governmental units which are part of the City's Board of Education, were dismissed as plaintiffs from the instant lawsuit on the same grounds (see _Campaign for Fiscal Equity, Inc. v. State of New York_, 162 Misc.2d 493, 496-7, 616 N.Y.S.2d 851 [1994]).

This court also dismissed plaintiffs' federal and State equal protection claims as barred by decisions of the Supreme Court and the New York Court of Appeals, respectively. In _San Antonio Indep. School District v. Rodriguez_, 411 U.S. 1, 93 S.Ct. 1278, 36 L.Ed.2d 16 [1973] the Supreme Court held that Texas' system of financing its school system largely through property taxes, which resulted in large school funding disparities between rich and poor areas of the state, did not violate the "rational basis" test of the equal protection clause of the Fourteenth Amendment to the United States Constitution. In _Board of Education, Levittown Union Free School District_, 57 N.Y.2d 27, 453 N.Y.S.2d 643, 439 N.E.2d 359 [1982] the Court of Appeals reached a similar conclusion with respect to the New York State Constitution's equal protection clause.

The _Levittown_ Court thus rejected an attack on New York State's school funding based on an _equality_ principle, a principle that posits that all school districts must be funded equally. However, it left open the door to an argument based on an _adequacy_ principle, an argument based on the premise that the State must ensure an education to public school students that satisfies some basic minimum requirements (_see Levittown, supra_, 57 N.Y.2d at 38, 453 N.Y.S.2d 643, 439 N.E.2d 359).

Following the distinction between claims based on equality and adequacy set forth in _Levittown_, this court let stand plaintiffs' claim that the State's funding mechanisms cause New York City public school students to receive something less than the sound basic education required by the Education Article of the New York State Constitution.

This court dismissed plaintiffs' claims based on Title VI, which bars discrimination by schools that receive federal funding. The complaint included no allegations of discriminatory intent, a necessary element of a Title VI claim.

By contrast intent is not an element of plaintiffs' claims under various implementing regulations promulgated by the federal Department of Education under Title VI. These regulations incorporate a disparate impact theory of liability. Accordingly this court let stand plaintiffs' claims under Title VI's implementing regulations (_Campaign for Fiscal Equity, supra_, 162 Misc.2d at 499-500, 616 N.Y.S.2d 851).

The result reached by this court was left intact by the Court of Appeals (_see Campaign for Fiscal Equity v. State of New York_, 86 N.Y.2d 307, 631 N.Y.S.2d 565, 655 N.E.2d 661 [1995] [referred to herein as "the 1995 decision"]). While the Court of Appeals affirmed this court's dismissal of certain parties and claims, it disagreed with aspects of this court's analysis of plaintiffs' constitutional claim. The Court of Appeals set forth a "template" to guide this court's determination as to whether defendants are providing New York City public school students with a sound basic education. The Court of Appeals decision is discussed at greater length in section III below.

The parties delivered their opening statements on October 12, 1999. Testimony was taken during 111 court days over a seven-month period. The last of 72 witnesses left the stand on May 15, 2000. Over 4300 documents were admitted into evidence. Extensive post-trial briefs and proposed findings of fact were submitted by the parties, and the court heard closing arguments on July 29, 2000.

II. A BRIEF HISTORY OF SCHOOL FUNDING LITIGATION

School funding litigation in this State, from <u>Levittown</u> to the instant action, has followed a pattern seen in similar litigation around the nation. It is common among commentators to divide school funding litigation into three "waves" defined by the dominant legal theory asserted by plaintiffs (*see* Heise, <u>*State Constitutions, School Finance Litigation, and the "Third Wave": From Equity to Adequacy,*</u> 68 Temp. L. Rev. 1151, 1152 n. 9; Thro, <u>*Judicial Analysis During the Third Wave of School Finance Litigation: The Massachusetts Decision as a Model,*</u> 35 B.C. L. Rev. 597). In fact there is much overlap between the legal theories asserted in these three "waves" (*see* Patt, *School Finance Battles: Survey Says It's All Just a Change in Attitudes,* 34 Harvard C.R.-C.L. L. Rev. 547 [1999]). However, the organization of the relevant cases into waves provides a reasonably accurate means for discussing trends in school funding litigation.

As is well known, most states rely in large measure upon local property taxes for education funding. Because of property value differences certain localities benefit from high tax revenues and others suffer from low tax revenues resulting in uneven funding among school districts.

In the first wave of cases, which ran from the late 1960s to the Supreme Court's <u>San Antonio</u> decision in 1973, plaintiffs argued that these variations in funding amounted to violations of the Equal Protection Clause of the federal Constitution. As noted above, this line of attack was foreclosed by the <u>San Antonio</u> decision, in which the Supreme Court declined to find that education was a "fundamental right" under the federal Constitution or that the plaintiffs in property-poor districts were a protected class.

Accordingly, the <u>San Antonio</u> Court held that disparities in school funding would be judged by the "rational basis" test. The Supreme Court had no difficulty finding that it is permissible for states to jointly fund public schools with localities, and that the inequality in funding caused by differences in property wealth among school districts was a by-product of a state's rational decision to give localities a voice in funding and governing their local schools. (<u>San Antonio, supra,</u> 411 U.S. at 54-5, 93 S.Ct. 1278.)

The second wave of cases, beginning with the landmark New Jersey case of <u>Robinson v. Cahill,</u> 62 N.J. 473, 303 A.2d 273, *cert. denied* <u>414 U.S. 976, 94 S.Ct. 292, 38 L.Ed.2d 219 (1973),</u> concerned arguments based on provisions of state constitutions-usually, but not always, the equal protection and education clauses of state constitutions. With the possible exception of Mississippi, all the states have some form of education clause in their respective state constitutions. Plaintiffs in the second wave cases generally argued that the existence of an education clause in a state constitution meant that education was a "fundamental right" and that any impingement of that right was subject to "strict scrutiny" under standard equal protection analysis.

Levittown was one of the cases in this second wave, and it was among the majority of cases that found that unequal funding of school districts did not violate state equal protection clauses.

Commentators point to three cases decided in 1989 by the highest courts of Montana, Kentucky, and Texas as the beginning of the third wave (*see Heise, op. cit.,* 68 Temple L. Rev. at 1162). With some exceptions, third wave cases de-emphasize equal protection analysis and rely instead solely on education clauses in state constitutions (*e.g. Abbeville Co. School Dist. v. State of South Carolina,* 335 S.C. 58, 515 S.E.2d 535 [1999]; *McDuffy v. Secretary of the Executive Office of Education,* 415 Mass. 545, 615 N.E.2d 516 [1993]; *cf. Brigham v. State,* 166 Vt. 246, 692 A.2d 384 [1997] [post-1989 case employing equal protection analysis to strike down school funding scheme]).

Although the third wave cases contain greater diversity in legal reasoning than some commentators suggest, these cases are for the most part characterized by an emphasis on adequacy rather than equality. Plaintiffs in the initial two waves of school funding cases tended to emphasize reducing spending disparities and focused on input measures like per-pupil spending. Plaintiffs in third wave cases concentrate instead on the sufficiency of school funding and postulate that there is a constitutional floor of minimally adequate education to which public school students are entitled.

Where courts have found that the education afforded public school students falls below this constitutional floor, they have found violations of their state constitutions (*see Abbeville Co. School Dist. v. State of South Carolina,* 335 S.C. 58, 515 S.E.2d 535 [1999]; *DeRolph v. State Of Ohio,* 78 Ohio St.3d 193, 677 N.E.2d 733 [1997]; *McDuffy v. Secretary of the Executive Office of Education,* 415 Mass. 545, 615 N.E.2d 516 [1993]; *Rose v. The Council For Better Education,* 790 S.W.2d 186 [Ky.1989]).

In third wave cases courts are called on to give content to education clauses that are composed of terse generalities. For example, in Ohio the relevant constitutional provision requires the state legislature to secure "a thorough and efficient system of common schools" (Ohio Const. art. VI, § 2). In South Carolina the relevant constitutional provision provides only that the legislature "shall provide for the maintenance and support of a system of free public schools open to all children in the State".

In *Rose v. The Council For Better Education,* 790 S.W.2d 186, the Supreme Court of Kentucky placed a detailed gloss upon that state's typically vague education clause. The court held that the constitutional mandate that the state "provide for an efficient system of common schools throughout the State" (at 205) meant that it must create a school system that has as its goal "each and every child['s]" development of seven "capacities" (at 212).

The goals articulated in _Rose_, though relatively detailed and ambitious, have been followed by at least three states in defining their own education clauses (see _Claremont School Dist. v. Governor of N.H._, 142 N.H. 462, 474, 703 A.2d 1353, 1359 [1997]; _McDuffy v. Secretary of the Executive Office of Education_, 415 Mass. 545, 617, 615 N.E.2d 516, 554 [1993]; _Opinion of the Justices_, 624 So.2d 107 [Ala.1993] [advisory opinion directing state legislature to follow order of trial court]).

III. THE LEGAL STANDARD FOR EVALUATING PLAINTIFFS' EDUCATION ARTICLE CLAIM

The Education Article of the New York State Constitution provides simply:

The legislature shall provide for the maintenance and support of a system of free common schools, wherein all the children of this state may be educated.

(N.Y. Const. art. XI, § 1.)

The Court of Appeals has interpreted this article to require the provision of "a sound basic education." (_Levittown, supra_, 57 N.Y.2d at 48, 453 N.Y.S.2d 643, 439 N.E.2d 359.)

In its 1995 decision the Court of Appeals directed this court to undertake a three-part inquiry in evaluating plaintiffs' Education Article claim. First, this court must define what constitutes a sound basic education. Second, the court must determine whether New York City school children are provided with the opportunity to obtain a sound basic education in the City's public schools. Third, if New York City public school children do not have the opportunity to obtain a sound basic education, the court must determine whether there is a "causal link" between this failure and the State's system for funding public schools (86 N.Y.2d at 317-18, 631 N.Y.S.2d 565, 655 N.E.2d 661).

In this section the court provides a definition of sound basic education. In section IV the court will determine whether New York City public school students are provided with a sound basic education. In section V, the court will address the causation issue.

In its 1995 decision, the Court of Appeals stated:

We do not attempt to definitively specify what the constitutional concept and mandate of a sound basic education entails. Given the procedural posture of this case, an exhaustive discussion and consideration of the meaning of a "sound basic education" is premature. Only after discovery and the development of a factual record can this issue be fully evaluated and resolved. Rather, we articulate a template reflecting our judgment of what the trier of fact must consider in determining whether defendants have met their constitutional obligation. The trial court will have to evaluate whether the children in plaintiffs' districts are in fact being *11 provided the opportunity to acquire the basic literacy, calculating and verbal skills necessary to enable them to function as civic participants capable of voting and serving as jurors. The Court of Appeals also made it clear that the State must assure that certain essential inputs are provided to public school students.

Children are entitled to minimally adequate physical facilities and classrooms which provide enough light, space, heat, and air to permit children to learn. Children should have access to minimally adequate instrumentalities of learning such as desks, chairs, pencils, and reasonably current textbooks. Children are also entitled to minimally adequate teaching of reasonably up-to-date basic curricula such as reading, writing, mathematics, science, and social studies, by sufficient personnel adequately trained to teach those subject areas.

A. The Education Article Requires a Sound Basic Education, Not One That is State of the Art

The defendants are correct when they argue that the Court of Appeals 1995 decision did not call for the provision of a "state of the art" education. The Court clearly intended that a sound basic education should not be defined in a way that incorporates the highest aspirations of educators. The Court repeatedly used the terms "adequate," "basic," and "minimally adequate" to describe the education to be provided to the State's public school students. The Court of Appeals did not, as other states' high courts have done, adopt the ambitious "minimum goals" for an adequate education first set forth by Kentucky's Supreme Court in _Rose v. The Council For Better Education, 790 S.W.2d 186, 212._

Further evidence that the Court of Appeals did not set the constitutional floor by reference to a state of the art education is the Court's statement that because many of the [State Board of Regents' State-wide educational standards] exceed notions of a minimally adequate or sound basic education-some are also aspirational prudence should govern utilization of the Regents' standards as benchmarks of educational adequacy. Proof of noncompliance with one or more of the Regents'...standards may not, standing alone, establish a violation of the Education Article.

(86 N.Y.2d at 317, 631 N.Y.S.2d 565, 655 N.E.2d 661.)

After the Court of Appeals 1995 decision the New York State Board of Regents promulgated more rigorous educational standards. Therefore, contrary to plaintiffs' argument, these new standards _a fortiori_ cannot constitute the definition of a sound basic education.

The new standards, called the Regents Learning Standards, were adopted in 1996 after more than a decade of development. The standards embrace seven areas of study. In each of these subject areas, four or five basic standards are set forth. Each standard is then applied at three levels (elementary, intermediate and commencement). Examples of student work that demonstrate mastery of the standards accompany the standards. Some of the Regents Learning Standards set forth in general terms basic skills and areas of knowledge that fall well within a sound basic education.

However, it is clear when looking at examples of student work that satisfy the standards that some of the standards require work that exceeds a sound basic education. Accordingly, the court must heed the Court of Appeals' direction to use the new standards with "prudence."

Even if the new Regents Learning Standards were not more rigorous than the old, this court would reject using the new standards to embody the definition of sound basic education. Admittedly it would be tempting to use the Regents Learning Standards to provide content· for the sound basic education standard as the plaintiffs urge. The Standards' specificity would probably help the court take the measure of the education provided New York City public school students, just as they help the Regents do the same.

However, this approach would essentially define the ambit of a constitutional right by whatever a state agency says it is. This approach fails to give due deference to the State Constitution and to courts' final authority to "say what the law is." (*Marbury v. Madison*, 1 Cranch [5 U.S.] 137, 177, 2 L.Ed. 60; *Schieffelin v. Komfort*, 212 N.Y. 520, 530-31, 106 N.E. 675.)

Finally, the Court of Appeals left undisturbed *Levittown*'s holding that inequalities in school funding among school districts do not run afoul of the State Constitution. Accordingly, defendants are correct that differences in spending among school districts do not, standing alone, establish that any of the lower-spending districts receive less than a sound basic education.

B. A Sound Basic Education Instills the Skills Students Need to Become Productive Citizens

While it is important to recognize the limits of the sound basic education standard set forth by the Court of Appeals, this court rejects defendants' contention that the Court of Appeals gave a final definition of sound basic education and that that definition is limited to an education sufficient to allow high school graduates simply to serve as jurors and voters.

First, the portion of the Court of Appeals decision quoted above makes clear that the Court did not "definitively specify what the constitutional concept and mandate of a sound basic education entails." (86 N.Y.2d at 317, 631 N.Y.S.2d 565, 655 N.E.2d 661.) Instead the Court held that "only after discovery and the development of a factual record can this issue be fully evaluated and resolved." (*Id.*)

Second, the Court of Appeals described its summary of a sound basic education as a "template." A template is a guide for constructing something; it is not the thing itself.

Finally, the statutory requirements for voting and for serving on a jury are low. With some minor exceptions, New York State law provides any United States citizen residing in the State who is 18 years of age or older, who is not mentally incompetent, who is not an incarcerated felon or previously incarcerated felon with an unexpired sentence or parole term, and who has not offered to sell his vote or buy that of another, may register to vote (*see* Election Law §§ 5-100, 5-102, 5-104, 5-106; New York Jurisprudence 2d *Elections* §§ 84-123). Similarly, jury service is open to anyone eighteen years or older who is a citizen of the United States and resident of the relevant county, who can understand and communicate in the English language, and who has not been convicted of a felony. (Judiciary Law § 510.) Clearly the Court of Appeals' template describes qualities above these low thresholds.

The Court of Appeals invoked voting and jury service as synecdoches for the larger concept of productive citizenship (*see* 86 N.Y.2d at 316, 631 N.Y.S.2d 565, 655 N.E.2d 661 [sound basic education should consist of skills necessary to enable children "to eventually function productively as civic participants capable of voting and serving on a jury").

Productive citizenship means more than just being *qualified* to vote or serve as a juror, but to do so capably and knowledgeably. It connotes civic engagement. An engaged, capable voter needs the intellectual tools to evaluate complex issues, such as campaign finance reform, tax policy, and global warming, to name only a few. Ballot propositions in New York City, such as the charter reform proposal that was on the ballot in November 1999, can require a close reading and a familiarity with the structure of local government.

Similarly, a capable and productive citizen doesn't simply show up for jury service. Rather she is capable of serving impartially on trials that may require learning unfamiliar facts and concepts and new ways to communicate and reach decisions with her fellow jurors. To be sure, the jury is in some respects an anti-elitist institution where life experience and practical intelligence can be more important than formal education.

Nonetheless, jurors may be called on to decide complex matters that require the verbal, reasoning, math, science, and socialization skills that should be imparted in public schools. Jurors today must determine questions of fact concerning DNA evidence, statistical analyses, and convoluted financial fraud, to name only three topics.

Defendants argue that passage of the Regents Competency Tests-which measure the reading, writing and math competency required of eighth to ninth graders-is a sufficient indicator that a student is capable of voting or serving on a jury. Defendants' expert witness, Professor Herbert Walberg, a professor of education and psychology at the University of Illinois-Chicago, testified that most media coverage of elections is pitched at an eighth to ninth grade level of reading comprehension and that therefore any student who passes the Regents Competency Tests is a productive citizen capable of voting or sitting on a jury. The court was not persuaded by this testimony. This argument implies that the Court of Appeals believed that the State Constitution requires only that graduates of New York City's high schools receive a ninth-grade education.

Beyond voting and jury service, productive citizenship implies engagement and contribution in the economy as well as in public life. Defendants make much of the fact that the Court of Appeals 1995 decision contains no explicit reference to public schools' duty to give students the foundational skills they need to obtain productive employment or pursue higher education. The court finds that this duty is inherent in the Court of Appeals' admonition that students must be prepared to become productive citizens.

Any other interpretation of the 1995 decision would ignore a universally understood purpose of public education. Plaintiffs presented un-rebutted expert testimony that preparing students for employment has traditionally been one of the rationales for public education. This point has been recognized by the New York State Education Department and in papers generated by national conferences on public education.

The Supreme Court has long recognized that public education is meant to assist students to become "self-reliant and self-sufficient participants in society." (*Wisconsin v. Yoder*, 406 U.S. 205, 221, 92 S.Ct. 1526, 32 L.Ed.2d 15 [1972].) Most state courts that have examined the substantive right to education under the education clauses of their constitutions have recognized both civic participation and preparation for employment as the basic purposes of public education.

Finding that a sound basic education encompasses preparation for employment begs the question: what level of employment? The Court of Appeals 1995 opinion does not explicitly address this issue. It is reasonable to assume that the Court of Appeals did not intend that the City's high school graduates need only be prepared for low-level jobs paying the minimum wage.

On the other hand, the Court's use of the "minimally adequate" standard indicates that a sound basic education does not require that most of the City's public school graduates be accepted into elite four-year colleges and universities in preparation for lucrative careers. Some middle ground between these two extremes comports with the Court of Appeals' emphasis on preparation for productive citizenship and its eschewal of a state of the art standard.

The Court of Appeals' emphasis on productive citizenship connotes an education that contributes to society's economic needs as well as high school graduates'. An emphasis on the economic needs of society requires that this court look at the current and projected labor needs of the State of New York in general and the needs of New York City in particular. However, the labor needs of the City and State must be balanced with the needs of high school graduates.

For example, while the greatest expansion in the local labor market might be composed of low level service jobs, such jobs frequently do not pay a living wage. A sound basic education would give New York City's high school graduates the opportunity to move beyond such work.

This analysis necessarily rests upon a dynamic interpretation of the Education Article. That the definition of sound basic education must evolve is axiomatic. If the meaning of the Education Article were to be frozen as of 1894, when it was added to the State Constitution, the Article would cease to have any relevance. It is undeniable that the level of skills necessary to obtain employment in today's economy exceeds those required in 1894. "The Constitution is to be construed...to give its provisions practical effect, so that it receives 'a fair and liberal construction, not only according to its letter, but also according to its spirit and the general purposes of its enactment.' " (*Ginsberg v. Purcell*, 51 N.Y.2d 272, 276, 434 N.Y.S.2d 147, 414 N.E.2d 648 [1980], *quoting Pfingst v. State of New York*, 57 A.D.2d 163, 165, 393 N.Y.S.2d 803 [1977].)

The remaining portion of this subsection constitutes findings of fact concerning the labor needs of New York City and State.

The un-rebutted evidence presented at trial demonstrates that New York City has experienced a contraction of its manufacturing sector and a concomitant rise of its service sector. Stated in broad terms, jobs that pay a living wage in the service sector require a more rigorous formal education than jobs that have historically paid a living wage in the City's manufacturing sector. The plaintiffs submitted substantial evidence that there is a consensus among educators, labor experts, and business and government leaders around the nation that, as stated in the policy statement of the 1996 National Education Summit:

Today's economy demands that all high school graduates, whether they are continuing their education or are moving directly into the workforce, have higher levels of skills and knowledge.

The educational demands of New York City's current economy were recently summarized by the Mayor's Advisory Task Force on the City University of New York ("CUNY"). The CUNY Task Force was created by Mayor Giuliani to examine issues faced by CUNY, including the extensive need for remedial education for matriculating students-many of whom are graduates of New York City public schools. The Task Force was chaired by Benno Schmidt, formerly President of Yale University and, before that, Dean of the Columbia University School of Law. The Task Force retained both PricewaterhouseCoopers and the RAND Corporation to investigate CUNY's current operations.

The CUNY Task Force's final report, issued in June 1999, states that the minimum skills necessary to compete successfully for good jobs are "high-level academic skills."

Opportunities for less-educated workers are likely to keep declining, while continued increases in the service sector will bring more good jobs to people with computer skills who are literate, can write, and are well-grounded in science and mathematics.

Plaintiffs' expert Professor Henry Levin, who has conducted research and published numerous papers concerning the economics of education, testified that between 1969 and 1998, the earnings of high school dropouts and high school graduates have declined relative to those of college graduates. Dr. Levin also found that the earnings of high school graduates, adjusted for inflation, declined during that time. The court finds Dr. Levin's findings to be credible and well-founded.

The Governor's most recent Executive Budgets have stressed the increasing importance to the State of its high technology sector. However, there is a disconnect between the skills of the State's and City's labor forces and the needs of the high technology sector. Indeed, the myriad high-technology companies that have sprung up in the last five years in New York City's Silicon Alley must often go outside the City and State for personnel with appropriate skills.

In sum, this court finds that a sound basic education consists of the foundational skills that students need to become productive citizens capable of civic engagement and sustaining competitive employment.

C. Plaintiffs' Standing

Almost as an afterthought, defendants raise the issue of plaintiffs' standing in a one-and-a-half-page section near the end of their memorandum of law. Defendants do not explain why they raise this issue for the first time at this late juncture, after extensive motion practice raising other issues of justiciability and a seven-month trial. Plaintiffs, apparently unaware that defendants would raise this issue, do not mention it in their post-trial submissions.

Standing is a core requirement that a party requesting relief from a court have an injury in fact that is redressable by a judicial resolution (see Community Board 7 of Manhattan v. Schaffer, 84 N.Y.2d 148, 154-5, 615 N.Y.S.2d 644, 639 N.E.2d 1 [1994]). An organization may have standing if one or more of its members would have standing to sue, if the claims it brings are germane to the organization's purposes, and if neither the claim nor the remedy necessarily requires the participation of the individual members of the organization (The Society of the Plastics Indus. v. County of Suffolk, 77 N.Y.2d 761, 775, 570 N.Y.S.2d 778, 573 N.E.2d 1034 [1991]).

Standing vel non is a threshold determination that, "when challenged, must be considered at the outset of any litigation." (Id. at 769, 570 N.Y.S.2d 778, 573 N.E.2d 1034.) However, this court is compelled to reach the issue even though defendants herein raise it only at the eleventh hour. Standing, unlike capacity to sue, concerns this court's jurisdiction and may not be waived (*City of New York v. State of New York*, 86 N.Y.2d 286, 292, 631 N.Y.S.2d 553, 655 N.E.2d 649; *cf. Santoro v. Schreiber*, 263 A.D.2d 953, 695 N.Y.S.2d 443, *lv. dismissed* 94 N.Y.2d 817, 701 N.Y.S.2d 708, 723 N.E.2d 564 [1999]).

Defendants argue that none of the plaintiffs established injury in fact at trial. The court disagrees. Lead plaintiff Campaign for Fiscal Equity (CFE) is an organization comprised, *inter alia*, of school-parent organizations. As discussed below, the children of these parents who attend public school in New York City have established an injury in fact which is redressable by this court. Pursuant to CPLR 1201 children must appear in court via their parent or guardian. Accordingly, CFE has members who have suffered an injury in fact redressable by this court. The other requirements of organizational standing are easily satisfied. CFE is an organization founded to reform school funding in New York State, so its mission is clearly related to the claims it asserts in this action. Finally, the participation of its members was not necessary to prosecute this action nor to devise a remedy.

IV. THE EDUCATION PROVIDED TO NEW YORK CITY'S PUBLIC SCHOOL STUDENTS

The following constitute the court's findings of fact regarding the New York City School District and the education it provides its students.

A. Summary of the Structure of New York City's Public Schools

New York City's public school system is the largest school district in the United States, comprised of approximately 1100 schools serving a student population of 1.1 million. In the 1999-2000 school year New York City's public schools employed over 135,000 people, including approximately 78,000 teachers, 19,000 teachers' aides, and 13,000 other administrators and pedagogical employees.

1. School Governance

Overall supervision of the New York City public school system is vested in the central Board of Education ("BOE") which has seven members. Each of the five Borough Presidents appoints one BOE member and the remaining two members are appointed by the Mayor. BOE appoints a Chancellor (currently Harold Levy) who is responsible for the operation of the school system.

The system is divided into 32 geographically based school districts to provide elementary and middle school education and six high school districts for secondary school education. Each district is supervised by a district superintendent who, as of 1996, is responsible to the

Chancellor for the operation of all the schools within their respective districts. Community school districts are also supervised by elected community school boards. High school districts are not supervised by community school districts and report only to the Chancellor. In addition to these geographically based districts there are four non-geographical districts in New York City.

In 1996, changes in State law altered the structure of the City's school system. The authority of community school boards to control and operate elementary and middle schools was revoked by the State legislature. The legislature gave the Chancellor the authority to appoint community school district superintendents from a list of candidates proffered by the community school boards, and the authority to terminate superintendents. These changes have increased the Chancellor's authority over community school district superintendents. Under this new governance statute, superintendents, rather than community school boards, have basic operating authority over how resources are used in the various districts.

Under New York State law, BOE is subject to the jurisdiction of the Board of Regents and the New York State Education Department ("SED"). The Board of Regents is composed of sixteen individuals, one from each of the State's twelve judicial districts, and four from the State at large, each of whom is elected to a five-year term by concurrent resolutions of both houses of the legislature. In any area where the legislature has not enacted specific statutes regarding educational policy, the policies issued by the Regents serve as the policies of the State. In practice, the Regents have broad legislative authority over the State's educational system and are charged with overseeing SED and choosing the State's Commissioner of Education. The Regents determine the standards by which all state elementary and secondary schools shall operate.

While the Regents have no authority to determine school financing, the Regents, along with the Commissioner of Education, make annual finance recommendations to the State legislature. Funding proposals are also contained in the Governor's Executive Budget, which states the Governor's opening position in subsequent negotiations with the legislature. The legislature eventually enacts an annual budget bill which is signed into law by the Governor.

SED is the Regents' administrative arm. Together with the Commissioner of Education, SED is charged with the general management and supervision of the State's public schools. Subject to specific statutory mandates and the general control of the Regents, the Commissioner of Education possesses supervisory authority over all aspects of the public schools.

The Commissioner's authority includes the power to promulgate regulations, to examine and inspect school facilities and curricula, and to advise and guide school officers and other public officials in all districts and cities in the State with regard to their duties and the general management of the schools (Education Law §§ 215, 305[2]). SED is not responsible for the day-to-day operation of public schools, but it does influence the operation of the schools by specifying the nature of the curricula, determining teaching standards, and issuing regulations pertaining to the rights of students.

2. Demographic Profile of New York City Public School Students

The students served by the New York City public schools come from varied backgrounds. Approximately 37% of students are Latino; 35% are African-American; 15.5% are White; 11.5% are Asian; and less than 1% are American Indian or Alaskan Native.

Close to 180 languages and dialects are spoken by students as their native tongue. BOE classifies approximately 16% of City public school students as "Limited English Proficient" ("LEP"), a designation given to students who score below the 40th percentile on a language assessment test. The large number of English Language Learners ("ELLs") in New York City is not surprising given that almost one in eleven students is a recent immigrant.

A defining characteristic of the New York City public school system is its high concentration of students from poor and low income families. In the 1998-99 school year, approximately 442,000 children-out of a total student attendance that year of 1,093,071-came from families receiving Aid to Families with Dependent Children. In the 1997-98 school 73% of students from kindergarten through 6th grade were eligible to participate in the free lunch program, compared with 5% in the rest of the State.

A large number of New York City public school students have special needs that require them to attend full-time or part-time special education programs. As of December 1, 1997, the most recent figure submitted in evidence, more than 135,000 students were enrolled in such programs.

The intersection of factors such as students' poverty, immigration status, and limited English language proficiency means that New York City has a high proportion of students "at risk" for academic failure. In the Regents' formulation "at risk" students are defined as: those students whose social, economic or personal circumstances are not supportive of successful schooling...They are at-risk of not completing high school, and, as a result, will be denied future opportunities for future participation in and contribution to the economic, social, cultural and civic life of their communities.

The correlation between high poverty and low academic performance is well documented in numerous State publications, and was confirmed by fact and expert witnesses for both defendants and plaintiffs. The evidence points to several causes of the depressed academic achievement of poor children. Plaintiffs' experts testified that children in poverty are often educationally disadvantaged by domestic environments that do not encourage, and sometimes impede, academic endeavor. Parents in low-income families frequently work long hours and often do not have much formal education themselves.

Thus they frequently lack the time to engage in activities to bolster their children's education. Additionally, family income must be spent on food and shelter and frequently there is little money left over for books or other educational tools. For most low-income families a home computer remains unaffordable. However, even if money were available, low-income parents with little formal education may not appreciate the need for educational enrichment via books, educational toys or a computer. Children of low income families typically start school without such skills as knowledge of the alphabet, sound/symbol relationships, familiarity with counting and numbers, and vocabulary and concept development. All the disadvantages summarized in this paragraph may be compounded in poor single-parent families.

Other factors that often attend poverty, such as homelessness, frequent change of residence, teen pregnancy, and poor health, have negative effects on educational achievement.

Low income students frequently live in areas and attend schools with high concentrations of poverty, which limits their contact with higher achieving students from more privileged backgrounds. Isolation of low-income students from higher achieving peers can reinforce negative attitudes toward schooling.

Minority status is another socioeconomic indicator that is negatively correlated with student achievement, in part because it is linked with poverty. According to SED, minority students are "more likely than white students to attend public schools with concentrated poverty" where "concentrated poverty" is defined as more than 40% of students' families on public assistance. The evidence indicates that race and ethnicity are not pure proxies for poverty, however. Plaintiffs' expert Dr. David Grismer conducted a study of academic achievement by minorities in which he controlled for poverty status, parents' education and family income.

Dr. Grismer found that race and ethnicity can be correlated with lower academic performance. The cause of this phenomenon has yet to be determined by social scientists. Explanations include the legacy of historic discrimination inflicted upon African-Americans and Latinos, and the rise of an anti-academic "oppositional" culture among some Blacks and Latinos that equates working hard in school with "acting White." It is not necessary to resolve this question in order to decide the issues presented by this lawsuit.

Recent immigrants also face formidable obstacles to academic success. They are plagued by the same factors, discussed above, that attend poverty. Lack of proficiency in English and unfamiliarity with American culture can also all have a negative effect on the academic performance of the children of recent immigrants.

As discussed in section V below, poverty, race, ethnicity, and immigration status are not in themselves determinative of student achievement. Demography is not destiny. The amount of melanin in a student's skin, the home country of her antecedents, and the amount of money in the family bank account are not the inexorable determinants of academic success. However, the life experiences summarized above that are *correlated* with poverty, race, ethnicity, and immigration status do tend to depress academic achievement.

The evidence introduced at trial demonstrates that these negative life experiences can be overcome by public schools with sufficient resources well deployed. It is the clear policy of the State, as formulated by the Regents and SED, that all children can attain the substantive knowledge and master the skills expected of high school graduates. The court finds that the City's at risk children are capable of seizing the opportunity for a sound basic education if they are given sufficient resources.

B. Measuring a Sound Basic Education by Inputs and Outputs

In its 1995 decision the Court of Appeals directed this court to evaluate whether New York City public school students are receiving a sound basic education by examining both "inputs," the resources available in public schools, and "outputs," measures of student achievement, primarily test results and graduation rates.

The inputs listed by the Court of Appeals fall into three large categories:

1. "minimally adequate teaching of reasonably up-to-date basic curricula such as reading, writing, mathematics, science, and social studies, by sufficient personnel adequately trained to teach those subject areas";

2. "minimally adequate physical facilities and classrooms which provide enough light, space, heat, and air to permit children to learn"; and

3. "minimally adequate instrumentalities of learning such as desks, chairs, pencils, and reasonably current textbooks."

Teacher quality and curriculum are discussed in subsections C-E, below. The adequacy of school facilities and classrooms is discussed in subsections F-G. The adequacy of "instrumentalities of learning" is discussed in subsection H, below. Educational outputs are discussed in subsection I below.

Relevant educational inputs and outputs must be examined over multiple years. The evidence at trial demonstrates the obvious proposition that education is cumulative. Primary and secondary school students acquire mastery of subjects by building on an expanding base of knowledge. A student's result on a sixth grade reading examination reflects her experience in grades one through five, and not merely of what she has learned in sixth grade.

C. Measures of Teacher Quality

The evidence demonstrates the validity of the intuitive conclusion that quality of teaching has a direct effect on student outcomes. This finding is confirmed by SED studies, by the empirical studies of plaintiffs' experts, and by the observations of numerous BOE district superintendents who testified at trial. Even defendants' experts agreed that quality teaching plays a role in effective education, though they differed with plaintiffs on the extent of that role and the correct measures of teacher quality.

There are several probative measures of teacher quality, including the number of uncertified teachers teaching in New York City public schools, teachers' scores on certification exams, and the quality of teachers' undergraduate education.

By each of these measures, the quality of New York City's public school teachers-in the aggregate-is inadequate. The court hastens to add that there are many excellent and dedicated teachers employed in New York City public schools-many of whom foster learning under extremely adverse conditions. It is not hyperbolic to describe some New York City public school teachers as heroes. However, there are too many ill-trained and inexperienced teachers to meet the difficult challenges presented in the New York City public schools.

1. Certification

As part of its effort to ensure that qualified teachers are employed in the State's public schools, the State created a system of certification. New York City has an overlapping system of license requirements for teachers. Under the current system in effect until 2003, the State has two categories of certification and a third category for uncertified teachers called temporary license. In 2003 the Regents will impose more rigorous certification standards.

It is possible for an uncertified teacher to be an effective pedagogue. However, the evidence at trial demonstrates that lack of certification is generally an indicator that a teacher falls below minimal adequacy. The court also finds that the converse is not true. Numerous BOE personnel, including district supervisors, testified that certification standing alone is no guarantee of teacher quality. The court finds this testimony to be credible.

For the last decade, approximately 10% to 14% of New York City's public school teachers have lacked certification in any given school year. The specific percentage of uncertified teachers listed as employed in a given district at a specific time is dependent upon which persons are counted as teachers, the definition of certification used, and the time in the school year that certification is assessed. Although figures from various sources differ slightly, they demonstrate that there is a high percentage of uncertified teachers working in New York City's public schools.

Plaintiffs' expert Professor Hamilton Langford, a professor of economics and public policy at the State University of New York at Albany, defined as uncertified any teacher who does not teach a single course in a subject area for which he is certified. (Such individuals may be certified in another subject.) Dr. Langford's research demonstrates that in the 1997-98 school year, the last year for which data were available, 13.7% of New York City's public school teachers were not certified in any subject they taught, as compared with only 3.3% in the rest of the State.

Using a slightly different standard, SED issued a report that found that in 1997-98 17% of New York City's public school teachers taught more than 20% of their time in a subject in which they lack state certification, compared with a statewide average (which includes New York City) of 9%. Statistics from BOE demonstrate that the percentage of uncertified teachers has fluctuated between 11.4% and 13.3% between the 1991-92 and 1999-2000 school years.

The highest percentage of uncertified teachers in New York City high schools tend to be in math and sciences. BOE records show that as of October 1, 1999, 476 uncertified teachers taught high school biology, 152 taught high school chemistry, and 435 taught high school mathematics. Using the conservative assumptions that each teacher instructs five classes a day of 25 students each (most high school classes are larger), and that these uncertified teachers were not replaced by certified ones, last year 59,500 students were taught high school biology by an uncertified teacher, 19,000 students were taught high school chemistry by an uncertified teacher, and 54,375 students were taught high school mathematics by an uncertified teacher.

Defendants contend that these shortages are in subjects in which there is a nationwide shortage of teachers. However, in New York State localities other than New York City experience nowhere near the shortages seen in the City.

Uncertified teachers tend to be concentrated in New York City's lowest performing schools. Such schools often present the most difficult working conditions, such as poor physical plants, large class sizes, and locations in high-crime neighborhoods. To some degree, this concentration of uncertified teachers in low performing schools is enabled by the teachers' collective bargaining agreement with BOE.

With some restrictions, experienced teachers are able to transfer out of such schools pursuant to a contract provision that gives senior teachers priority in filling vacant positions in other schools. It is understandable that many, though not all, experienced teachers faced with the poor working conditions of many low performing schools would take the opportunity to transfer to schools in safer neighborhoods with better working conditions. This phenomenon is likely to increase in the coming years as retirements increase (for reasons described below) providing more opportunities for the remaining experienced teachers to transfer from low performing schools.

Indeed BOE has failed to employ sufficient certified staff in its very worst schools, known as Schools Under Registration Review ("SURR, despite a mandate from SED that it hire only certified teachers in such schools as of September 1, 1999. The Regents have mandated that all schools shall have only certified teachers by 2003. The evidence suggests that BOE will have great difficulty fulfilling this mandate.

Special education programs have a high proportion of uncertified teachers. In District 75, which comprises all of the self-contained special education schools for severely and profoundly disabled children, 25% of the teachers are uncertified. In bilingual special education classes, nearly 50% of the teachers are uncertified.

The Regents' decisions to remove uncertified teachers from SURR schools, and from the system entirely by 2003, are evidence that uncertified teachers are less able to provide New York City public school children with a sound basic education.

2. Passage Rates on Certification Examinations

The probative evidence at trial demonstrates that passage rates on certification examinations are predictive of teacher performance. Such evidence included expert testimony by Professor Ronald Ferguson of the Kennedy School of Government at Harvard University. Using voluminous data collected in Texas during the 1980s, Dr. Ferguson convincingly demonstrated a strong positive relationship between teacher quality as measured by certification test scores and student achievement.

Defendants' expert, Professor Eric Hanushek of the Economics Department at the University of Rochester, drew an opposite conclusion from Texas data concerning teacher test scores. Apparently this data was from more recent years than those studied by Dr. Ferguson, but Dr. Hanushek's testimony on this matter was terse. Dr. Hanushek testified that data from Texas tends to show teachers with higher test scores do not affect student outcomes. As Dr. Hanushek set forth only his conclusion regarding the data without any discussion of his methodology, his testimony does not rebut Dr. Ferguson's.

Plaintiffs' expert Dr. Langford demonstrated that New York City public school teachers have a much higher failure rate on the State's certification examinations than do public school teachers in the rest of the State. For teachers employed in 1997-98, the first-time failure rate of the New York City public school teaching force on the basic Liberal Arts and Science Test ("LAST"), which is now required for all teachers, was 31.1%, compared with 4.7% for teachers elsewhere in the State.

The average first score on the LAST for City teachers was 236.3 (220 is a passing score) while the average first score on the test for teachers in the rest of the State was 261.6. New York City teachers employed as of 1997-98 also did poorly on their first attempts on the Elementary and Secondary Assessment of Teaching Skills Written Tests ("Elementary ATS" and "Secondary ATS"). Nearly 27% of New York City teachers failed the Elementary ATS, compared with 3% of their peers in the rest of the State; 25.7% failed the Secondary ATS, compared with 3.5% in the rest of the State.

On many of the content or subject matter examinations, which test teachers' knowledge of their particular subject, New York City teachers' failure rates were even higher. For example 42.4% of the math teachers currently teaching in New York City's public schools failed the math content examination at least once.

Dr. Langford's testimony was undercut somewhat by one of defendants' experts, Professor Michael Podgursky, Chair of the Economics Department at the University of Missouri. Dr. Podgursky testified that Langford's comparison of City teachers' test scores with those of teachers in other parts of the State may have been marred by incomplete data. In particular, Dr. Langford's data appeared to have a disproportionate number of test scores for New York City compared with other areas in the State.

Plaintiffs opine that this may have been a result of the admittedly higher amount of turnover in New York City schools, which would result in more teachers taking the tests in the City, but this was not established as a fact. Additionally, because of the unavailability of test scores for teachers who were hired prior to the mid-1980s, Dr. Langford's test score analysis covers about 40% of New York City's teachers. Despite these valid criticisms of his study, Dr. Langford's testimony concerning teacher test scores is some evidence that New York City teachers are in general less qualified than those in the rest of the State.

3. Experience

The un-rebutted evidence validates the unremarkable proposition that teachers, like any professionals, frequently require several years' experience to achieve competency. The court finds that teaching experience of two years or less is correlated with poor teacher quality.

New York City public school teachers tend to have fewer years' experience than teachers in the remainder of the State. The attrition rate of new teachers is more than 50% in their first six years according to BOE data. In addition to negatively affecting teacher quality, high turnover can negatively affect a school's cohesiveness and ability to create cooperative effort among teachers. The large number of inexperienced teachers-who, like uncertified teachers, are disproportionately assigned to the schools with the greatest number of at risk students-makes it more difficult for New York City public schools to meet the needs of their students.

4. College or University Attended and Degree Obtained

Finally, plaintiffs presented probative evidence that the average New York City public school teacher attended a less competitive college than the average public school teacher in the rest of the State. For this analysis, plaintiffs ranked colleges using: 1) Barron's college rankings, 2) the average SAT scores and grades of admitted high school seniors, and 3) the average scores on State certification exams of the colleges' graduates. According to Dr. Langford's findings, which are based on State data, in 1997-98 45% of New York City's public school teachers held undergraduate degrees from CUNY institutions, and 48.8% held master's degrees from CUNY institutions. BOE data show somewhat smaller, though still significant, percentages of New York City teachers who have received undergraduate and master's degrees from CUNY.

Dr. Langford's analysis also demonstrates that, in addition to hiring teachers from less competitive institutions, New York City tends to hire its teachers from the less qualified graduates of any given undergraduate institution.

The Regents and SED have found that the quality of undergraduate teacher programs can have an effect on public school student outcomes. Prompted by a report of its Task Force on Teaching, the Regents have recently heightened the requirements for teacher education programs in New York State. The findings of SED and the Regents are strong evidence that student outcomes are affected by teacher quality as measured by undergraduate institution attended.

As measured by the percentage of teachers with at least a master's degree, New York City's public school teachers again compare unfavorably with those in the rest of the State. In 1997-98, 16% of New York City's teachers held only a bachelor's degree or less, compared with 10.9% of teachers in the rest of the State. The sole measure by which City public school teachers compare favorably with the teachers from the rest of the State is that a higher percentage of City teachers have a master's degree plus 30 credits. However, there was no evidence at trial that the additional 30 credits is a measure of teacher quality. The 30 credits may be in subjects wholly unrelated to the subject(s) taught by a teacher.

5. Professional Development

Professional in-service training, commonly known as professional development, involves the teaching of many skills to new and experienced educators. It includes teaching everyday teacher responsibilities such as classroom management, discipline, attendance taking and lesson planning. It also includes training to keep staff knowledgeable regarding content in specific subjects. Finally, it includes the teaching of instructional strategies, such as methods for determining whether students have mastered course material.

Both SED and BOE have recognized the positive effects of professional development programs on both new and experienced teachers. The Regents have stated that professional development is particularly crucial to help teachers deal with the needs of at-risk students. The substantial inadequacies of the New York City public school teaching force enhance the need for effective professional development programs.

Professional development is essential in training and maintaining qualified teachers. Among other benefits effective professional development can ameliorate the shortcomings of new teachers, keep teachers current in their subject areas, and disseminate techniques for teaching at-risk students. The evidence demonstrates that professional development is most effective when it is ongoing, tailored to a school's local needs, and conducted in schools themselves rather than at remote locations. Community School District 2, one of the most effective school districts in New York City, has placed special emphasis on such intensive, school-based professional development. District 2's success in fostering a well-qualified corps of teachers is evidence of the benefits of professional development.

Plaintiffs put on the stand SED personnel and several district superintendents all of whom testified that the professional development currently being provided to New York City public school teachers is inadequate, particularly given the number of at-risk students that attend the City's public schools. Districts with the greatest proportion of at-risk students often spend the least on professional development. Because of the larger proportion of uncertified math and science teachers, the need for professional development in these areas is particularly acute. The court finds that this testimony was credible.

For their part, defendants recite the litany of professional development resources that BOE makes available to its teachers, and argue that the results of an internal BOE survey, the Performance Assessment in Schools Survey ("PASS"), demonstrate that teachers are satisfied with these offerings. For the reasons set forth in the next section the PASS survey is not probative. After weighing the evidence offered by both sides on this issue, the court finds that the professional development currently provided to New York City public school teachers is inadequate.

6. BOE's Internal Ratings and Surveys Regarding Teacher Quality

Defendants argue that the most accurate measures of teacher quality are two internal rating mechanisms used by BOE. The court disagrees and finds that these two internal mechanisms, referred to herein as "U ratings" and "PASS reviews," are not reliable.

Each year, New York City teachers are reviewed by their principals and receive either a "U" for unsatisfactory or an "S" for satisfactory. BOE records demonstrate that very few New York City teachers receive Us. Defendants argue that this small number of unsatisfactory ratings is evidence that the City's public school teachers are qualified to teach.

The court finds credible the testimony of numerous current and former BOE personnel who stated that unsatisfactory ratings, in the words of former district superintendent Granger Ward, are "really reserved for those people who were the worst of the worst, those people who are actually-endangering students in what they were doing in the classroom." Mr. Ward described the system as "almost a system of triage. You are focusing on the worst, the absolute worst, and trying to get those individuals out of classroom settings. If you had people who were mediocre or not the absolute worst, you didn't put energy into trying to remove them."

The reasons why the U ratings have become a system for triage and not for accurate measurement of teacher quality were clearly set forth at trial. First, given the shortage of qualified teachers principals are aware that it may be difficult to replace a teacher rated unsatisfactory with a more effective teacher. If no replacement is found a principal must cobble together coverage by relying on substitute teachers and/or by assigning extra classes to permanent teachers who already have a full class load.

Such improvised solutions strain a school's resources and rarely provide students with adequate instruction. Second, the administrative process required to rate a teacher unsatisfactory is arduous. A substantial record of the teachers' inadequacies and of the administration's attempts to intervene and remediate must be developed. Each documented item is potentially subject to the grievance procedure set forth in the teachers' contract. Third, the teachers' contract also restricts transfers of unsatisfactory teachers to other schools. Therefore, a principal who succeeds in rating a teacher unsatisfactory must retain that teacher on her employee roster.

The PASS ("Performance Assessment in Schools Survey") results are also not reliable measures of teacher quality. Under SED regulations, a school that performs poorly, even if not at the SURR level, must prepare a Comprehensive Education Plan ("CEP"). In an effort to help schools in this self-assessment BOE developed the PASS questionnaire. The PASS questionnaire is designed around the attributes of model, exemplary schools. The elements of such schools are used as a benchmark for self-assessment and the results of the PASS survey provide an organized basis for preparation of a CEP. A PASS review team is comprised of administrators, parents and teachers from the school, and an outside observer from BOE. The team completes the PASS review on a consensus basis.

The original purpose of the PASS review became obscured as schools began to worry that PASS reviews would be used by BOE for evaluating and comparing schools. According to Robert Tobias, the head of BOE's Division of Assessment and Accountability, school administrators' concern that the PASS survey would be used as an accountability mechanism causes them to paint a rosy, rather than a realistic, picture of their schools. Instead of engaging in internal assessment, schools use PASS for public relations.

Additionally, there is credible evidence that many PASS reviewers fail to apprehend the true measures of an exemplary school, and therefore grade schools by a lower standard. Most of the district superintendents who testified agreed that PASS reviews are not objective measures of school quality.

Defendants' expert who testified regarding PASS reviews, Dr. Christine Rossell, a Professor of Political Science at Boston University, appeared to have little knowledge about how the reviews were actually conducted. Dr. Rossell apparently misunderstand the reviews' scoring system in attempting to aggregate the results of the reviews. Accordingly, her testimony is not probative.

D. Competition for Qualified Teachers

New York City's lack of a sufficient number of qualified teachers is in large measure a function of its lack of competitiveness in the relevant labor market. Unless steps are taken to improve New York City's competitiveness as compared to neighboring school districts, this problem will only get worse in the years to come.

New York City competes in a common labor market for teachers and other college-educated individuals with Westchester, Nassau, Suffolk, Rockland, and, to a lesser extent, Orange and Putnam Counties. New York City is at a competitive disadvantage in this labor market, principally because New York City school teachers make substantially less and generally labor under more difficult working conditions than their suburban counterparts.

Figures ranging from 20% to 36% were used by State and BOE officials to quantify the difference in teacher salaries between New York City and its suburbs. The range on these figures arises from differences in both the experience levels of the teachers being compared as well as the suburbs included in the comparisons. Plaintiffs' expert Dr. Langford conducted an independent analysis which confirms that average salaries of New York City teachers lag substantially behind those of Nassau, Rockland, Suffolk and Westchester Counties for teachers at all levels of experience.

Salary differentials are consistently mentioned in SED and BOE documents as the primary reason qualified teachers choose to work in suburban rather than City schools. These findings were echoed in the testimony of BOE personnel most knowledgeable about hiring. Additionally, Dr. Ferguson's analysis of the Texas data establishes a clear statistically significant association between the performance of students within a school district and the salaries paid to teachers within that school district. Salary differentials hurt New York City in its search for qualified teachers.

New York City's public schools' lack of competitiveness in the relevant labor market can be seen by comparing the qualifications of New York City's public school teachers with those who work in public schools in the counties near New York City.

Dr. Langford conducted a study that suggests that New York City attracts, on average, the least qualified teachers in the relevant labor pool. He compared the qualifications of teachers residing in the City who teach in New York City public schools with those who reside in the City but teach in public schools in surrounding counties. The latter category was in the aggregate more qualified as measured by certification rates and by failure rates on the LAST certification examination.

He also compared the qualifications of teachers residing in surrounding counties who teach in New York City with those who both reside and teach in the surrounding counties. Again, the teachers in this study who taught in the surrounding counties were more qualified on average than those who commuted into the City to teach in public schools.

Dr. Langford also found that, while teachers in both New York City and its surrounding suburbs earn less on average than other college-educated workers, the gap between teachers and other college-educated employees in the City is substantially greater than the gap between teachers and other college-educated workers in the suburbs. The court credits Dr. Langford's findings as the result of a well-designed study based on accurate data.

In addition to losing out in the competition for hiring teachers seeking employment, New York City has experienced a small but persistent annual "brain drain" of some of its most experienced teachers to the public schools of surrounding counties.

Plaintiffs presented a number of witnesses who testified that New York City's competitiveness is also hurt by crumbling school infrastructure (discussed in subsection F, below), the location of some schools in high crime areas, the perception of teachers that New York City public schools are unsafe, and large class sizes. The court finds that this testimony is credible.

New obstacles faced by BOE in the coming years in attracting a sufficient number of qualified teachers will include increased attrition in its workforce and the imposition of higher certification standards.

Between the 2000-01 and 2003-04 school years, BOE predicts that it will need 41,105 new teachers due to normal rates of attrition. Additionally, BOE predicts a wave of retirements over the next five years as a large cohort of teachers known as Tier 1 eligibles reach their twentieth year of employment. Tier 1 eligibles may retire after twenty years with a pension totaling 50% of their salary. Adding the predicted retirements of Tier 1 eligibles to normal attrition rates swells the projected number of teacher slots to be filled in the next four years to approximately 54,000. The need to fill between 41,000 and 54,000 slots in four years means that BOE will have to hire between 8,000 and 14,000 new teachers a year, far more than the approximately 6,200 teachers hired annually between 1993-94 and 1999-2000.

BOE will have to fill these teacher slots at a time when it will be trying to reduce the number of uncertified teachers working in its SURR schools and, by 2003, end its dependence on uncertified teachers entirely. As already noted the Regents have mandated that all schools have only certified teachers on staff by 2003.

Plaintiffs also submitted probative evidence that BOE has increasingly been unable to fill principal, assistant principal and other administrative positions with adequately qualified individuals because of low salaries and poor working conditions. The evidence demonstrates that these administrators play a crucial role in building and maintaining effective schools.

Defendants' attempts to rebut plaintiffs' evidence concerning New York City's competitiveness are not persuasive. First, defendants argue that the relevant salary comparison was not between New York City and the counties surrounding it, but rather between New York City and other large metropolitan areas. By this measure New York City teachers are better paid than their peers in many, though not all, large cities in the United States.

This analysis is of limited probative value. The analysis fails to account for cost of living differences among cities. It also assumes a national labor market for teachers. While it is true that BOE recruits out of state (and does a small amount of recruiting in a few foreign countries) no evidence was presented at trial concerning the extent of a national market for teachers.

Defendants also argue that New York City public school salaries are actually competitive in comparison with the surrounding suburbs because New York City teachers' contracts allow them to work shorter hours than their suburban peers. According to charts presented by Dr. Podgursky, a New York City teacher's workday is shorter than that of a representative sample of

16 other school districts in the State. Dr. Podgursky testified that when the shorter day is considered New York City's per hour teacher pay falls in the middle of these 16 districts.

Dr. Podgursky's analysis is based on the working hours specified in collective bargaining agreements governing the relevant school districts. These collective bargaining agreements were apparently obtained by counsel and there was no testimony at trial that the work hours specified therein have not been superseded or modified by side agreements or amendments.

Even assuming that the collective bargaining agreements relied upon by Dr. Podgursky are accurate, an analysis based purely on hours at school is incomplete. Dr. Podgursky's study does not examine how suburban schools deploy teachers during this longer workday. Moreover, as discussed below, New York City class sizes are higher than those in the surrounding suburbs, which suggests that New York City public school teachers have more students to follow and homework to grade. Finally, with respect to the approximately 68% of New York City public school teachers who reside in the City, Dr. Podgursky's analysis does not account for the City's greater cost of living. In all events, the allegedly shorter workday of New York City's public school teachers has not provided the City an advantage in the competition for qualified teachers, as the evidence discussed above demonstrates.

Finally, defendants criticize BOE's recruitment efforts and argue that BOE's poor outreach is in part to blame for any shortage of qualified teachers. For example, BOE has lost opportunities to hire qualified teachers by late recruiting. The court finds that, given lower salaries and often difficult working conditions, BOE has done an adequate job in recruiting new teachers. While BOE's efforts prior to 1997 were sometimes haphazard and even counterproductive, it has since engaged in a number of initiatives designed to attract new teachers to its schools. The problem is not BOE's sales pitch, but its product.

E. Curricula

BOE has in place "reasonably up-to-date basic curricula" for the provision of a sound basic education. (86 N.Y.2d at 317, 631 N.Y.S.2d 565, 655 N.E.2d 661.) The problem is not with the content of the curricula, but rather with its implementation. Inadequate teaching and, as discussed below, inadequate school facilities and instrumentalities of learning have hampered the delivery of curricula.

The failure to assure the delivery of core curricula has been exacerbated by a chronic defunding over the last twenty years of two non-core subjects that can play an important supporting role in preparing students to become productive citizens: arts and physical education.

The Court of Appeals' definition of sound basic education does not mention arts instruction or physical education. The court interprets this omission-in conjunction with the Court of Appeals' emphasis on a "minimally adequate" education-to mean that arts instruction and physical instruction for their own sake are not part of a sound basic education under the State's Education Article.

However, arts instruction and physical education are important means of supporting the teaching of other subject areas that are part of a sound basic education.

For English language learners and other at risk students visual and performing arts provide a means of expression and achievement which foster self-confidence and positive attitudes about school. A well run arts program can induce students to attend school. Additionally, in the hands of an imaginative teacher the arts can provide a jumping off point for the discussion of important aspects of contemporary society. Examples are numerous and self-evident. Without being too reductive, the production of plays such as *Inherit the Wind, Richard II,* or *A Doll's House* can be used to provoke discussion among students concerning the importance of dissent, the organization of government, and the role of women in society.

While merely reading the play in a class may enable such discussions, a production seen by students in other classes would likely add to the didactic impact. Visual art with political content such as Francisco Goya's, Honore Daumier's, and Hans Haacke's can also be used to enhance learning. Arts from non-Western societies can be an effective means of introducing the belief systems of such societies to students in the United States.

All these pedagogic uses of the arts can assist schools in molding students into productive citizens. Finally, it is worth noting that an impressive amount of homegrown artistic talent has passed through New York City's public schools. Nurturing such talent may go beyond a sound basic education but certainly it is a public good.

Physical education can have similar effects in supporting a sound basic education. Sports can aid students in acquiring important socialization skills such as cooperation, good sportsmanship, and the importance of practice as a means of achieving mastery. A good sports program may increase school attendance of at risk students.

Both arts and physical education were severely defunded after New York City's fiscal crisis in the mid-1970s. Budget cutbacks affected every aspect of the arts curriculum until the initiation of Project ARTS in 1997. Project ARTS is a collaborative project between the City and BOE through which the City has contributed $150 million to restoring arts education in New York City. Project ARTS, while a step in the right direction, cannot restore the arts curriculum overnight after 20 years of neglect.

School space formerly dedicated to the arts has been converted to other purposes, as arts programs atrophied and the City's public schools became increasingly overcrowded. The restoration of an adequate physical education program faces similar obstacles. Over the last twenty years gymnasiums and playgrounds were allowed to deteriorate and/or were converted into instructional space due to overcrowding. The credible evidence at trial demonstrated that arts and physical education need their own dedicated spaces within a school.

The dilapidated state of the City's public school buildings is described in the next section.

F. School Facilities and Classrooms

The second "input" set forth in the Court of Appeals 1995 decision concerns the physical plant in which a sound basic education is to take place. "Children are entitled to minimally adequate physical facilities and classrooms which provide enough light, space, heat, and air to permit children to learn." (*Campaign for Fiscal Equity v. State of New York*, 86 N.Y.2d at 317, 631 N.Y.S.2d 565, 655 N.E.2d 661.)

A substantial number of BOE's approximately 1100 facilities require major infrastructural repair to items such as roofs and facades. Many more facilities are plagued by overcrowding, poor wiring, pock-marked plaster and peeling paint, inadequate (or non-existent) climate control, and other deficiencies that speak of a history of neglect.

Though it would appear to be self-evident that such conditions would impede, rather than facilitate, the delivery of a sound basic education, this proposition is difficult to prove or disprove. For the reasons set forth below the court finds that there is a causal link between New York City's poor school facilities and the performance of students, though the strength of that link is difficult to measure.

1. The Condition of City Public Schools

For more than a decade, the parlous physical state of New York City's approximately 1100 public school buildings has been recognized in written pronouncements of the State legislature, SED and BOE. The credible testimony at trial confirmed the bleak picture.

In 1988, the State legislature created the New York City School Construction Authority ("SCA"), a separate authority for the construction of schools, based on legislative findings that decried the "deplorable" condition of the City's schools.

The legislature hereby finds and declares that the elementary and secondary schools of the city of New York are in deplorable physical condition. Many of the schools are overcrowded, unsafe, unhealthy and unusable. The physical deterioration of the schools is a serious impediment to learning and teaching. If the quality of education in New York City is to be improved, the city's schools must be modernized, expanded and restored to a state of good repair.

a. SED and BOE Documents

The creation of SCA did not succeed in shoring up City public schools' crumbling infrastructure. The lack of progress is documented in a series of Master Plans and five-year capital plans developed by BOE during the past decade. In 1989 the Board of Education developed its Year 2000 Master Plan to "determine the level of effort required to restore the New York City public school system to a state of good repair and to modernize and expand it by the year 2000." The Year 2000 Master Plan concluded that "the estimated cost for completely upgrading and modernizing the school system by the 21st Century is $17 billion in current dollars." BOE did not come close to spending this amount by the close of 1999.

When it prepared the Year 2000 Master Plan, BOE also prepared a five year capital plan for the period 1990-94. Unlike Master Plans, which identify all the needs of the system over a ten-year period, the five year capital plans identify only those items that require urgent attention and can be reasonably funded and fixed within a five year period.

Four years later, BOE again reviewed the state of public school facilities in its Year 2003 Master Plan. As then-Chancellor Fernandez wrote: "The year 2003 Master Plan is a comprehensive needs assessment based on all available technical data and information...." The Year 2003 Master Plan stated that the total cost for meeting the system's needs by 2003 was $25 billion in 1992 dollars. The Plan noted that though the previous Master Plan had called for over $17 billion to be spent over ten years, the first five-year capital plan had been funded at only $4.3 billion. The Year 2003 Master Plan reflects a system unable to maintain even an inadequate status quo. The Plan notes:

Deterioration is occurring at a rate faster than we can save systems, and much of what needed repair back in 1988, as predicted, now needs replacement. The buildings that required modernization back in 1988 that were not modernized in the current capital plan are a tremendous drain on the lump sum and maintenance budgets leaving no funding for the other 500 buildings in need of capital work.

The Year 2003 Master Plan found that 85% of the system needed some kind of capital work, with 424 buildings requiring modernization. The Plan identified a severe impediment to maintaining, modernizing and replacing schools which is discussed at greater length below: overcrowding in New York City public schools.

The next BOE five year capital plan (covering fiscal years 1995-99) described a "crisis on three fronts". On the first front, the capital plan noted that "today practically every building in the system is plagued by disrepair." The second front described in the plan was a worsening capacity crisis driven by explosive growth in enrollment. The third front was antiquated building interiors inadequate to support current educational needs. While BOE called for $7.5 billion in "barebones" funding, this five year plan was originally budgeted at $3.4 billion, an amount later increased to $4.9 billion.

BOE concluded that the inadequate funding of the plan would cause the overall condition of the schools to get worse, not better. Additionally, many of the major modernizations of new schools originally funded for design back in the previous five-year plan were not scheduled for construction during the 1995-99 plan.

In June 1995 a commission appointed by then-Chancellor Cortines issued "A Report of the Commission on School Facilities and Maintenance Reform," known as the Levy Commission Report after its Chair, Harold Levy. The Levy Commission found that the condition of New York City public school facilities constituted "a school infrastructure crisis." The Levy Commission discovered "shocking conditions in our schools, such as collapsing building facades, thoroughly rusted structural beams, falling masonry, precariously hung windows, and roof gables held together with wire."

It found more than 760 buildings had serious problems with their heating and ventilation systems and 424 buildings required wholesale modernization. The Levy Commission also decried the fact that more than a quarter of all public schools, 343 buildings, had coal burning *42 boilers-a form of heating apparently that is extinct or nearly so in the rest of the City.

These findings were echoed in reports issued by the Regents and SED in 1996 and 1997. The Regents determined that facilities' needs in New York City were greater in dollar figures than those of the rest of the State combined.

b. The United Federation of Teachers' Lawsuit

In 1994, the United Federation of Teachers sued BOE over the conditions of New York City's public school facilities. The late Justice Friedman's 1998 decision notes that BOE did not contest the deplorable conditions in the City's schools. The decision cited a BOE memorandum that found 237 school buildings had immediately hazardous exterior conditions in need of repair.

This list of 237 did not include nearly 150 buildings that had defective roofs or other building code violations. The court ordered the parties to settle a judgment providing for a safety plan. The plan adopted involved the extensive use of temporary scaffolding to safeguard people but did not involve the actual repair of defective conditions. As a result of this judgment close to one third of all school buildings in New York City at the time of trial had sidewalk shedding around their exteriors-simply to ensure minimal safety, not in preparation for remedial measures.

c. Building Condition Assessment Survey

The most recent comprehensive survey of the condition of New York City public school buildings is the Building Condition Assessment Survey ("BCAS"), conducted between late 1997 and mid-1998. Outside engineers and architects conducted visual inspection of approximately 340 building components identified by BOE. Each component was given a numerical rating: 1 (good), 2 (good to fair), 3 (fair), 4 (fair to poor) or 5 (poor).

Because not all components of a building are of equal importance, the outside engineers also assigned two additional ratings to each component: "purpose of action" and "urgency of action."

The "purpose of action" ratings give some sense of the importance of a component's condition. In other words a building's parapet wall-though it may be rated "3" (fair condition) overall-could have a portion that is severely cracked. Such a wall might be considered a greater priority because of safety concerns than, say, lighting in a gym that is rated "5" (poor condition). The most important purpose of action rating is "life safety" which describes a situation where the physical safety of the children and teachers who use the building is at risk. The second most important is "structural" which means that the condition affects the building's structural integrity. The third category, "regulation code," denotes a condition that is in violation of applicable building codes and regulations. The remaining categories describe less severe conditions.

The "urgency of action" categories describe the time frame within which work should be done based on the rate of deterioration of the component.

The BCAS results demonstrate that hundreds of New York City public school buildings have serious structural deficiencies. Two hundred thirty-one school buildings were identified as having three to four major exterior components ranked with a 3, 4 or 5 coupled with a life safety or structural "purpose of action" rating. BOE has determined that such scores require complete overhauls of these exteriors and there was no evidence at trial tending to cast any doubt on that conclusion. An additional 114 buildings have roofs that must be replaced. Still more buildings have severe problems with their windows and external masonry. Each of these problems concerns the integrity of buildings' external "envelopes" which the evidence demonstrates is a prerequisite to buildings' physical health.

Defendants agree that BCAS is the most probative measure of the condition of New York City public school buildings, but they differ in their interpretation of BCAS data. Defendants offered an interpretation of BCAS by their expert witness, Robert O'Toole, who was for ten years the Chief Fiscal Officer in charge of the Tucson, Arizona, School District where one of his duties was oversight of school facilities. Mr. O'Toole conducted two analyses based on BCAS data designed to gauge the health of New York City school facilities.

In his first analysis, Mr. O'Toole examined the average scores of 251 of the approximately 350 building components examined in the BCAS survey. According to Mr. O'Toole these 251 components embraced all the components in the architectural, electrical and mechanical categories, which he described as the most basic categories. He found that the average score among all school buildings for 83.6% of the 251 components was greater than "3," or fair. Only 41 of the components had an average score of 3 or less.

Mr. O'Toole's second analysis attempted to ascertain a per square foot cost for the repairs indicated by BCAS. This study encompassed 921 of the approximately 1400 school structures surveyed in BCAS. Using the cost estimates included in the BCAS, Mr. O'Toole derived square foot costs for repairs in each of the 921 structures. The actual calculation of this per square foot cost, and the person who performed the calculation, were not described by Mr. O'Toole or by any of defendants' other witnesses. Apparently, the figure was arrived at by dividing a school building's square footage by BCAS cost estimates. While this calculation would appear to be a plausible method for deriving a per square foot repair cost, it did not receive the imprimatur of Mr. O'Toole or any other expert at trial. Relying on BCAS, Mr. O'Toole opined that per square foot costs of $100 or less indicated a building that was in "fair" condition. Eighty-nine percent of the buildings in his survey by this measure were in fair condition.

Mr. O'Toole concluded that these two analyses reinforce each other in supporting his ultimate conclusion that the vast majority of New York City public school buildings are in fair condition, requiring at most only preventive maintenance.

Mr. O'Toole's analyses are not persuasive.

Crucially, Mr. O'Toole's first analysis made no distinction among the 251 components measured. It made no attempt to weight each component's centrality to a school's functioning and does not attempt to account for BCAS' "purpose of action" and "urgency of action" ratings. It did not reveal which 41 components had an average less than three. An analysis based on the averages of components, standing alone, is of no probative value. Numerous schools have at least some components that score below the average. Depending on the components in question, a school with a handful of components below "fair" may have a severely compromised infrastructure. The crucial analysis, which *was* presented by plaintiffs, is what BCAS reveals about individual schools, not about individual components.

With respect to Mr. O'Toole's second analysis, plaintiffs point out that his cost per square foot exercise is based upon only 921 of the approximately 1400 structures included in BCAS. Mr. O'Toole testified that he collected these 921 structures by cross-referencing BOE and SED files regarding cost and square footage, respectively, and that the failure to match all the buildings in the BCAS survey was a function of the incongruence of the two files, not of any selection on his part.

From this he concluded that his sample of school buildings was random. Plaintiffs offered no evidence to rebut this conclusion. Nonetheless, the incompleteness of Mr. O'Toole's survey does cast some doubt on his analysis. There was no testimony that gaps in discovery create a random sample. It is at least plausible that the lack of congruence between BOE and SED files may have been caused by some factor that was not random.

Another weakness of this analysis was that the actual calculation of the repair cost per square foot for each building was not set forth explicitly by defendants.

Finally, Mr. O'Toole's "cost per square foot" analysis was compromised by his reliance on cost estimates included in the BCAS, rather than on more accurate refinements to those cost estimates later generated by BOE for inclusion in its 2000-2004 five year plan.

d. Old Buildings and Changing Needs

In addition to the major structural deficiencies described above, New York City public school buildings contain antiquated science laboratories and wiring, heating, and air conditioning systems. In large measure this is a function of the buildings' age. Most City school buildings were built in an era when there was no need for computers, summer school, or more than rudimentary laboratory equipment. More than half of the buildings in the system are more than 58 years old.

Science labs are often obsolete or absent altogether in City public schools. According to BOE figures a minimum of 31 high schools lack a science lab of any description, leaving over 16,000 high school students without access to this crucial resource. In schools that do have labs, a single lab must be used for biology, chemistry and physics classes. Each subject area involves different equipment, and the near-constant use of labs in schools can restrict the complexity of experiments performed in the lab.

Inadequate wiring can impede a school's ability to offer computer education and other initiatives. Computers also require air conditioning to work properly during the warmer months.

The lack of air conditioning can also take its toll on teachers and students during the summer session recently inaugurated by BOE. Only 7344 out of approximately 35,000 classrooms in the system have air conditioning. In addition, there was credible evidence that existing air conditioning units often do not function properly.

The evidence demonstrates that New York City's public schools have a substantial backlog of interior repairs. New York City's schools are plagued by the disrepair of such basic amenities as lights, toilets, plaster and paint.

Finally, as discussed in subsection G below, overcrowding in the City's public schools is both a cause of facilities' deterioration and an impediment to remedial measures. Overcrowding has necessitated the use of important resources such as libraries, music and art rooms, and gymnasiums as classrooms. Overcrowding makes it difficult to conduct proper repairs without severe displacement of students.

2. The Causal Link between Inadequate School Facilities and Student Outcomes

Plaintiffs argue that there is no need to inquire into the causal link between inadequate school facilities and student outcomes, arguing that minimally adequate school facilities are an entitlement under the Court of Appeals 1995 decision. This court disagrees. The Court of Appeals 1995 decision states that the adequacy of school facilities is to be measured by whether they "permit children to learn." (*Campaign for Fiscal Equity v. State of New York*, 86 N.Y.2d at 317, 631 N.Y.S.2d 565, 655 N.E.2d 661.) Accordingly, this court must examine the effect of poor physical conditions on students' ability to learn.

The State legislature, SED and BOE have all concluded that the City's decaying and decrepit school facilities impede learning but have not attempted to quantify the negative effect of crumbling school buildings on student performance.

Plaintiffs presented numerous SED and BOE witnesses who testified that the physical plant of a school can have a marked effect upon learning. In the case of absent or obsolete science labs the connection is obvious. Students cannot learn a subject without the requisite tools to do so. Similarly, computer science classes, and the use of computers to support other subjects, cannot happen in schools that have antiquated wiring. The evidence is conclusive that the numerous City school buildings with these deficiencies impede learning.

Plaintiffs also offered probative evidence that the totality of conditions in crumbling facilities can have a pernicious effect on student achievement. As former SED Commissioner Thomas Sobol testified:

If you ask the children to attend school in conditions where plaster is crumbling, the roof is leaking and classes are being held in unlikely places because of overcrowded conditions, that says something to the child about how you diminish the value of the activity and of the child's participation in it and perhaps of the child himself. If, on the other hand, you send a child to a school in well-appointed or [adequate facilities] that sends the opposite message. That says this counts. You count. Do well.

The court finds that this evidence is credible as it is based on the experience and intuition of knowledgeable educators. However, this evidence does not attempt to gauge the magnitude of the effect of school facility condition upon student performance.

Unlike plaintiffs, defendants attempted to measure empirically the effect (or lack there-of) that school facilities have on student performance. Defendants offered statistical analyses performed by their expert, Dr. Hanushek, which purport to show no link between a school's disrepair and the test score performance of its students.

Dr. Hanushek first examined whether school building conditions, as measured by repair costs per square foot, in high and moderate poverty schools were related to student scores on standardized reading and math tests. This analysis tended to show that higher-performing students in elementary and middle schools are clustered in schools with high per square foot repair costs, i.e. those in worse condition. Dr. Hanushek thus concluded that facility repair needs do not cause performance differences among students.

Dr. Hanushek further analyzed all New York City public elementary schools using, among other variables, per square foot repair costs and something called "facility scores" allegedly derived from the BCAS rating system. In these regression analyses Dr. Hanushek attempted to control for socio-economic deficits of a school's students by accounting for various factors in each of the schools including the median income of parents, the Limited English Proficiency rate for students, and rate of special education participation. He again reached the conclusion that facility disrepair is not causing negative student performance.

Dr. Hanushek's statistical analyses on this question are of limited probative value. First, the underlying data regarding per square foot repair costs and facility scores is questionable. Dr. Hanushek testified that he did not compile this data, and the court admitted these analyses subject to the establishment of a foundation by another witness. Defendants' attempts to do so were both convoluted and incomplete.

Defendants at least arguably established that the per square foot repair costs were calculated at the direction of Mr. O'Toole and then provided to Dr. Hanushek through defendants' counsel and another defense expert. However, no witness laid a foundation for the facility scores data. Accordingly, to the extent that they rely on facility scores Dr. Hanushek's regression analyses have no probative value. It appears that facility scores are compilations of BCAS scores (1-5) for building components, without any weighting assigned to the various components. Therefore, for the reasons discussed in subsections above, even if the court were to consider them, facility scores would not adequately measure facility conditions.

The per square foot repair costs used by Dr. Hanushek are compromised to an unknowable degree by Mr. O'Toole's use of cost estimates included in the BCAS, rather than on more accurate refinements to those cost estimates later generated by BOE for inclusion in its 2000-2004 five year plan. Less important, but still a source of doubt, is defendants' failure to set forth how they calculated per square foot costs. This calculation appears to have been a simple division of a building's square footage by its BCAS repair cost estimates, but defendants failed to establish the validity of this calculation.

Dr. Hanushek's regression analysis is hampered by its time frame, which encompassed a single school year. As stated above, education is a cumulative undertaking. A student's performance cannot be measured by the resources he was provided in a single year, but rather should be measured by the resources provided over a number of years. Accordingly, longitudinal studies of student performance over a period of years are more probative than one-year snapshots.

Perhaps it could be argued that because Dr. Hanushek's analyses concerning school facilities encompassed the performance of all the students in a given school, it thereby provided a kind of compressed longitudinal study wherein the performance of students in different grades in a given school stands in for a study of a cohort of students as they progress through grades over multiple years. However, defendants did not make this argument and the court finds no support for it in the record.

For the reasons stated, the physical condition of New York City's schools has a negative effect upon the academic performance of the City's public school students. However, the magnitude of that effect is unclear from the evidence at trial.

G. Overcrowding and Class Size

The poor physical state of New York City public school facilities coupled with an influx of new students into the system in the late 1980s and the first half of the 1990s has resulted in severe overcrowding in many of its schools. Overcrowding, which exists at every level, is most severe in elementary and high schools. Overcrowding has a negative effect on student achievement.

Public school enrollment grew rapidly in the 1950s and 1960s and peaked in 1971 at approximately 1,150,000 students. Between 1971 and 1982, enrollment shrank by approximately 220,000, though some districts did experience expansion during this period. New York City's fiscal crisis in the mid-1970s caused the City to shed a number of school buildings, decrease the money spent on maintaining school facilities, and slow the creation of new schools.

Thus the City was ill-prepared when enrollment began to increase in 1983 and exploded in 1989. In the five years from October 1988 to October 1993, enrollment grew by close to 80,000 students and reached a total of 1,016,000 students. Rapid growth continued until 1996, when it slowed somewhat. Enrollment in the 1999 2000 school year was 1,102,000. The credible evidence at trial indicates that steady growth of the system will continue.

While projections generated by the Grier Partnership, consultants to BOE, indicate that enrollment will level off and begin to drop in the middle of the current decade, recent data on birth rates and immigration that post-dates the Grier Partnership report cast doubt on its predictions. In any event, the evidence indicates that system capacity lags far behind existing enrollment.

BOE measures building utilization annually in its Enrollment Capacity Utilization ("ECU") report. The most recent ECU report in evidence was for the 1998-99 school year. The report describes the formulas by which BOE determines the capacity of each school. Because buildings are used differently based on level and type of schooling, BOE uses different formulas to determine the capacities of elementary schools, middle schools, high schools and citywide special education.

The utilization numbers reflect widespread overcrowding. Almost 60% of all elementary schools, serving 63% of the City's elementary school students, and 67% of high schools, serving 70% of the City's high school students, are overcrowded under the formula used by the ECU report. Overall, the numbers indicate that approximately 59% of New York City public school students attend over-utilized schools. Overcrowding tends to plague certain school districts more than others. For example all of the Queens school districts are over-utilized, and five of seven are operating in excess of 110% of capacity.

Overcrowding is even worse than indicated above because the ECU formulas actually overstate schools' capacity. This inflation occurs because the formulas adjust for overcrowding by adding to schools' capacity non-classroom space if such space is in fact used for classrooms.

For example if a crowded school is forced to convert its gymnasium or auditorium into classroom space, the capacity formula indicates increased capacity. Second, there was credible testimony that the amount of space allocated to each pupil is too small, failing to allow sufficient room for a teacher's desk, for a set-back for student desks sufficient for all students to view the backboard, or for space for educational tools such as computers. Additionally, the formula assumes class rosters larger than what is optimal from a pedagogical standpoint as measured by State and federal goals.

Overcrowding has numerous negative consequences for students. Specialized spaces in school, such as gymnasiums, science labs, libraries and art rooms must be taken over for full-time classroom space thereby depriving students of the programs intended for those rooms. Marginal spaces in a school building, including undersized offices, hallways, and storage space, have been converted to classrooms.

Many school administrators have had to resort to the use of trailers and other temporary structures. Such structures outside the main school building isolate teachers and students from the rest of the school and often occupy much-needed playground space. The students taught in the temporary structures still must use the main school building's cafeteria and gymnasium. Temporary structures are often difficult to heat and they frequently lack sufficient power for computers.

Some schools, particularly in Queens, have been forced to employ extended day and multi shift schedules to relieve overcrowding. SED has granted waivers to seven Queens schools, with a total enrollment of approximately 25,000 students, to operate two shifts of six periods a day, instead of the State-mandated seven. This response reduces students' school day, obviously a less than optimal solution. Students at risk in particular often need a *longer* than usual school day-more "time on task" in current educational jargon. School buildings become extremely crowded during the overlap of the two shifts, and the educational program is distorted, resulting in anomalies such as 150-student gym classes.

Overcrowding often necessitates the creation of multiple lunch shifts. There was credible testimony that such staggered lunch shifts over the day can have a negative effect on students who must take lunch early in the morning or late in the afternoon. It would not be news to generations of school teachers that hungry students find it difficult to focus in the classroom.

For these reasons increased utilization of existing school facilities is not a satisfactory solution to overcrowding.

1. Class Size

The most significant negative impact of overcrowding is its effect on class size. In schools that are bursting at the seams there is little or no room to allocate the necessary space to reduce the number of students per class.

The evidence demonstrates that class size has an effect on student outcomes, and that smaller class size can boost student achievement, particularly among at risk children. The advantages of small classes are clear. A teacher in a small class has more time to spend with each student. Fewer students mean fewer administrative tasks for each teacher. Student discipline and student engagement in the learning process improve in smaller classes.

The federal government, SED, and BOE all agree that smaller class sizes help students to learn, and all have initiated programs to reduce class size. Although the federal and State programs differ slightly in the specifics and methods of implementation (the federal program seeks to lower class size in grades 1-3 to an average of 18 students, while the State program seeks to lower class size in grades K-3 to an average of 20 students) their goals are similar: to reduce class size in the lower grades to 20 students or fewer. The court also finds credible the testimony of the numerous New York City district superintendents called by plaintiffs who were unanimous in their assessment of the advantages of smaller classes.

The positive effect of smaller classes on student outcomes is also documented by statistical evidence. Plaintiffs' expert Jeremy Finn, a professor of statistics at SUNY Buffalo, testified at length about the Tennessee Student Teacher Achievement Ratio ("STAR") project, a landmark study of the effect of class size on student achievement.

The STAR project was conducted in Tennessee with cohorts of students in 79 schools. The students were randomly divided into three types of classes: 1) small classes of between 12 and 17 students with one teacher, 2) regular-sized classes of between 22 and 26 students with one teacher and 3) regular-sized classes with one teacher and one teacher's aide.

Teachers were randomly assigned to the classes. The controlled part of the study followed the students that started kindergarten in 1985 through their graduation from third grade. Students enrolled in the STAR program were tested at grades K-3. The students were tracked after they left third grade to see how they performed as they moved through elementary and secondary school. Nearly 50% were receiving free lunch, an indicator of low economic status, and approximately one-third were minority, almost entirely African-American.

The STAR project demonstrated that there is a significant causal relationship between reducing class size and improving student achievement. The effects were positive and durable, particularly for students who started in the smaller classes in kindergarten and stayed in them for 3-4 years. Such students continued to perform at a higher level on average than those students in the large class sizes. To articulate these differences, Dr. Finn used a measure called "months of schooling," which, as its name suggests, equates a child's achievement level to the number of months of schooling a child with that achievement level normally would have. In each analysis, the children in small classes outperformed the students in the large classes by this measure.

Dr. Finn noted that the presence of teachers' aides was found not to affect student performance in the larger classes. However, he noted that the teachers' aides in the STAR study were persons-parents mostly-who signed on only for the duration of the study. He opined that teachers' aides with better training and a higher degree of professionalism could have a positive effect on student performance.

The benefits enjoyed by the children in the smaller class sizes in K-3 continued even after the STAR program ended in third grade. Of the thirty statistical analyses of STAR students taking tests in grades 4 through 8, 29 yielded statistically significant differences between the children who had been in small classes compared to the children in the large classes. Significantly, the advantages to minority students were greater than those exhibited by all students.

The STAR project is considered especially probative by experts in the field because it was conceived as an experiment, rather than as a simple observation. Researchers are able to draw conclusions regarding the causal relationship between class size and student performance because of the STAR project's random assignment of children and teachers, and because of its isolation of two variables: class size-and, to a lesser extent, the presence of teachers' aides.

The STAR project has been invoked by New York State and the federal government as justification for their efforts to reduce class size in the early grades.

Defendants' expert, Dr. Hanushek, presented some evidence that the value of the STAR project was undercut by student transfers in and out of the schools participating in the project and by some schools leaving the project altogether. Dr. Hanushek conceded on cross examination that these transfers did not demonstrate that the STAR results were unreliable.

The court finds that Dr. Hanushek did not demonstrate that the transfers undermine Dr. Finn's conclusions regarding the STAR data. Dr. Hanushek did provide some probative evidence from California that that state's attempt to reduce class size in a very short time frame actually hurt student performance. According to Dr. Hanushek California may have hired too many unqualified teachers in order to speed the reduction of class sizes. This evidence does not undermine the STAR results. At most, it suggests that class size reduction must be carefully planned and coordinated with the hiring of qualified teachers.

New York City's class sizes have been consistently higher than the State average and higher than the 18-20 student maximum that experts regard as the ceiling necessary to obtain the benefits seen in the STAR project. Dr. Finn presented the most comprehensive description of class sizes in New York City. As of October 31, 1998, average general education class sizes in New York City were: 23.8 for kindergarten, 25.12 for first grade, 24.97 for second grade, 25.46

for third grade, 27.34 for fourth grade, 28.05 for fifth grade, 27.62 for sixth grade, 28.13 for seventh grade, and 28.72 for eighth grade.

These averages of course mean that a significant portion of New York City's school children are in much larger classes than the average. Thus, 27.1% of all students in classes K-3 (or 89,139 children) were in classes of 28 or more; 66.6% of all students in fourth and fifth grades (or 102,347 children) were in classes of 28 or more; and 72.3% of the students in sixth through eighth grades (or 148,869 children) were in classes of 28 or more.

New York City class sizes are consistently higher than the State averages at every level, including high school, for every year that data are available for the last 20 years. This data is contained in the April 1999 "655 Report," the annual report submitted by the Regents to the governor and the legislature (*see* Education Law § 215-a). For example from 1980-81 to 1997-98 the average kindergarten sizes in the City fluctuated between 24.2 and 25.4, while the statewide average (including New York City) fluctuated between 21.3 and 22.4, an average difference of at least 3 students.

In the same time span, class size for grades 1-6 ranged between 27 and 28.3; statewide the range (including New York City) was between 23.5 and 24.2, a difference of nearly four students. Similar averages obtain for middle and high school classes. Obviously, the statewide averages quoted in the 655 Report are inflated by the inclusion of New York City's students. The differences are stark when the City is compared to the rest of the State.

In sum, large class sizes in New York City's public schools have a negative effect on student performance. Conversely, smaller class size-particularly classes with a maximum of 18-20 students in grades K-3-can have a positive effect on student performance, particularly that of at risk students.

Defendants argue that class size results from the way BOE deploys its teachers, and they argue that this deployment is beset by inefficiencies. Defendants point out that New York City's public school teacher student ratio in the 1999-2000 school year was one teacher for every 14.1 students. This figure is substantially lower than the average for large school districts around the nation. The City's teacher student ratio has declined in recent years, from 1 to 16.5 in 1997-98, to 1 to 15.3 in 1998-99, to 1 to 14.1 in 1999-2000. Defendants also argue that BOE employs thousands of school-based certified professionals, such as principals, assistant principals, attendance teachers, school psychologists, guidance counselors and social workers who may assist teachers in the instructional program.

Defendants assert that these teachers and potential teachers could be put to more efficient use. Defendants claim that currently only approximately 3 hours, 45 minutes of the 6 hour, 20 minute teacher workday is spent on classroom instruction. It is true that the teachers' current contract provides that high school teachers must teach 25 of the 35 periods per week that they are expected to be present in school. For the remaining ten periods teachers are assigned non-instructional activities. According to defendants, City teachers' workday is shorter than the average workday in a sample of 16 other school districts in New York State, and in several large cities scattered around the country. Finally, defendants argue that BOE has a large number of teachers' aides on payroll who add little or nothing to student productivity, and that money spent to pay these workers could be better used to pay for the salaries of more teachers.

The court finds that teacher student ratios are not the relevant benchmark of adequacy. No matter how many teachers are on staff, class size cannot be reduced without expanding classroom space. Defendants propose that school days can be extended in order to accommodate more classes. As noted above, this "solution" has not worked in the schools where it has been tried. Another solution proposed by defendants is to place two teachers in overcrowded classrooms. The evidence at trial was equivocal as to whether this staffing model has any effect on student outcomes.

That said, defendants' evidence concerning BOE's inefficient deployment of teachers and other personnel has some validity. It is no secret that some personnel in the public school system are not working as hard or as efficiently as they could. Both the City Comptroller and the Citizens Budget Commission conducted analyses in the last five years arguing that BOE can and should insist on productivity gains from the City's public school teachers.

While space constraints might make it difficult to utilize underused teaching staff to reduce class size, there are certainly other arguments for productivity gains. More efficient use of teachers' time could in theory reduce the number of teachers needed to cover all classes. Additionally, while in theory teachers'aides could assist student productivity, there was evidence that frequently these jobs are sources of patronage filled by individuals who add little to education. Personnel costs are BOE's single largest budget item and savings in this area could be used to address the system's chronic needs in other areas.

On the other hand, legitimate questions about the magnitude of this inefficient deployment are raised by the evidence. Neither the Comptroller's nor the Citizens Budget Commission's analyses offered by defendants account for the greater amount of time that New York City School teachers must spend grading work and completing administrative tasks because of larger class sizes. Additionally, as discussed at length below, there are a variety of factors that have increased student placements into special education, especially into its most restrictive (and heavily staffed) settings. This phenomenon is caused in part by factors outside BOE's control. Smaller class sizes are mandated in special education classes, creating a lower teacher student ratio. Excluding special education teachers, the general education teacher student ratio in 1997-98 was 1 to 18.04; in 1998-99 it was 1 to 17.03.

Finally, New York City has had a difficult time competing with neighboring school districts for qualified teachers with the currently configured New York City public school work day. In the next few years, as the rate of retirements among City public school teachers is likely to increase, the competition for qualified teachers is likely to go up as well. If defendants are correct that the City's public school teachers have a shorter workday, that fact plausibly may be a competitive advantage that BOE may use to attract teachers. Conversely, a longer workday could plausibly hurt the City's competitiveness.

H. Instrumentalities of Learning

The third "input" set forth by the Court of Appeals 1995 decision is "minimally adequate instrumentalities of learning such as desks, chairs, pencils, and reasonably current textbooks." (*Campaign for Fiscal Equity v. State of New York*, 86 N.Y.2d 307, 317, 631 N.Y.S.2d 565, 655 N.E.2d 661, *supra*.) Given the Court of Appeals' insertion of "such as" this court interprets this list to be non-exhaustive.

The evidence demonstrates that for nearly two decades BOE has struggled to provide adequate instrumentalities of learning to its students.

1. Textbooks

BOE has not maintained systematic records of the textbooks used by its students from year to year. However, there was probative evidence that at least since the early 1980s New York City has endured a chronic shortage of adequate textbooks. In recent years, primarily because of an influx of funds from the New York City Council, BOE has been able to significantly upgrade City public school textbooks. Beginning in 1996-97, the City Council allocated $50 million over four years. Community school districts actually were unable to spend all of their textbook funds in the ensuing three school years.

At the present time the quantity and quality of textbooks used by students in the City's schools satisfy minimal adequacy. However, education is cumulative, each year building upon the last. While the present textbook allocation is adequate, it cannot remedy the negative effects of past shortages. Moreover, there is no structural funding mechanism that gives any assurance that the recent spike in textbook funding will continue.

The primary source of State funding for textbooks is the New York State Textbook Law ("NYSTL"). In the 1995-96 school year the NYSTL allocation was $35 per student, an amount that the New York City Comptroller found in a 1996 report to be inadequate. Two years later, in 1997-98, the allocation was increased by $1 per student to $36. The allocation crept up to $41 per student in 1999-2000. The NYSTL must cover the costs of numerous types of instructional materials, not just hardcover textbooks. While the evidence at trial demonstrated that hardcover textbooks must be replaced every 3-4 years, other materials known as "consumables" are used up in a year. The NYSTL allocation is inadequate to cover the cost of all these materials.

2. Library Books

The books in New York City public school libraries are inadequate in number and quality. New York City has historically lagged behind the rest of the State in the number of library books per student. The State's allocation for library materials-which includes books, software, periodicals and videotapes-has been $4 per pupil since 1994, despite SED's requests for higher funding. This allocation is insufficient to assure adequate libraries in the City's public schools.

3. Classroom Supplies and Equipment

Plaintiffs presented substantial evidence that New York City public schools have in the last two decades suffered from inadequate classroom supplies and equipment. Science classes have suffered from a shortage of lab supplies such as beakers, Bunsen burners, beam balances, and microscopes. In the same period schools have suffered from a lack of basic supplies such as chalk, paper, art supplies, and, in some schools, desks and chairs. There was little except anecdotal evidence concerning the current state of such supplies. Accordingly, the court cannot make a finding concerning whether New York City public schools are at present providing a minimally adequate supply of such materials.

4. Instructional Technology

For at least a decade it has been the position of SED that instructional technology-computers, related hardware such as printers and modems, and appropriate software-is an essential resource for students. Similarly BOE has concluded that "[o]ur schools must prepare all students to succeed and prosper in the information age and the new global economy, where access to information and ownership of knowledge will be defining characteristics of 'the competitive edge.'

The omnipresence of computer technology in the economy undergirds SED's and BOE's emphasis on instructional technology. While computer proficiency is an important skill that can lay a foundation for a career, it also allows students to use an array of instructional software and research tools to enhance their study of other subjects. In addition to their importance to the economy, computers and the Internet have become important conduits of public discourse. Today the Internet has taken its place besides other media outlets as a resource used by voters. For these reasons instructional technology is a core "instrumentality of learning" embraced by the Court of Appeals' template.

For the last decade New York City public schools have failed to provide adequate instructional technology to their students. This inadequacy has been thoroughly set forth in SED documents, particularly the 655 Reports. In 1997, districts in the State outside of New York City had twice as many computers per 100 students as did the City. New York City has fewer computers than districts in the rest of the State, and its computers tend to be older and less capable of handling sophisticated educational software.

As noted above, the age and antiquated wiring of New York City's school buildings has impeded the introduction of computers into the classroom. An additional impediment has been inadequate professional development to help teachers understand and use new instructional technology.

Defendants correctly point out that in the last three years there has been an infusion of funds devoted to increasing schools' use of instructional technology. However, these funds have failed to remedy New York City public schools' technological deficit. Moreover, it is unclear whether funding for technological improvements in New York City public schools will continue.

During the 1997-98 and 1998-99 school years, the City's public schools received $150 million in City and private funding for instructional technology under a program called Project Smart Schools. Project Smart Schools was intended to lower the student to computer ratio in elementary, middle, and high schools. Only the needs of middle schools were addressed by the time the money ran out. A large portion of Project Smart Schools funding had to be spent on rewiring old school buildings. As of the time of trial, there were no funds under this program available to address the needs of high schools, elementary schools, or special education classes. In recent years BOE has also received funding for technological improvements from the City Council. However, this funding is not reliable as it is wholly dependent on revenues from the recently robust City economy.

The City has also seen an influx in federal funding in recent years, primarily through the "Universal Service Fund," known as the "E-Rate" program. E-Rate is a spend-to-get program which provides discounts to schools for certain telecommunication charges. It does not provide discounts for computers or software; it solely provides discounts for the purchase of telecommunication infrastructure. The E-Rate program has assisted BOE in increasing schools' ability to connect to the Internet. However, because it only addresses telecommunications technology, it is not a panacea for all of the public schools' technology woes. Additional E-Rate discounts have shifted in ways that have impeded BOE's planning.

Defendants also argue that a survey of the quantity of computers updated in March or April 1999 showed a ratio of one computer for every ten students, which compares favorably with nationwide ratios. However, Elspeth Taylor, BOE's Chief Information Officer from 1996 through 1999, testified that this survey found that approximately 20,000 of the total of 109,341 computers in New York City public schools were essentially obsolete and that an additional number of aged "486s" and Apple Computers were too weak to power recent operating platforms, Internet, or CD-ROM applications.

While defendants argue that these two categories of computer are both described as "new generation" by SED's 1999 655 Report, this definition appears to be used in the 655 Report for assessing computers as of fall 1997. Fall 1997 to March/ April 1999 is a very long time in the annals of computer technology.

I. Outputs: Graduation/Dropout Rates and Test Scores

Previous sections have set forth the shortcomings of the "inputs" provided to students in New York City's public schools, such as the quality of teachers, the condition of facilities, and the amount and nature of the "instrumentalities of learning" available in the schools. In its 1995 decision, the Court of Appeals also directed this court to examine the "output" of public schools, *i.e.* student performance.

The most telling measures of student performance are the percentage of students who actually graduate and the bundle of knowledge and skills that they possess on the day that they graduate. Accordingly, the court examines below evidence concerning: 1) how many students graduate on time, 2) how many drop out, 3) the nature of the degrees graduates receive, and 4) the performance of those who pursue higher education at the campuses of the City University of New York.

The court also finds that the results of State and City evaluative exams taken from grades K-11 are of some probative value in measuring whether New York City's schools are imparting the requisite minimum educational skills that undergird a sound basic education. However, the court's analysis of these test results is informed by the Court of Appeals' admonition that test results should be used "cautiously as there are a myriad of factors which have causal bearing on test results."

By each of these output measures New York City public schools fail to provide a sound basic education.

1. Graduation/Dropout Rates

In recent years, more than 60,000 students enter ninth grade in New York City public schools annually. Consistently since the late 1980s, approximately 30% of these students drop out and do not receive either of the two types of diplomas conferred by SED. Many who do graduate take more than four years to do so. Only 50% of New York City Public School students who entered ninth grade in 1996, and who stayed in school, made it to twelfth grade in four years.

Since the late 1980s, approximately ten percent of ninth graders ultimately received a general equivalency degree ("GED"). The evidence at trial demonstrated that a GED recipient has not received a sound basic education. The requirements for a GED are too minimal to provide any assurance that a student has been prepared for the duties of productive citizenship. Plaintiffs' expert, Dr. Henry Levin, testified concerning studies of the earning rates of GED recipients compared to those of high school graduates and dropouts.

He concluded that "the job prospects and lifetime earnings of the GED certificates is considerably less than the high school graduate. In fact, it is equal or close to that of high school dropouts." Dr. Levin also testified that the armed services do not accept GED recipients, and he noted that GED recipients who attend college have a completion rate of approximately 2%. Dr. Levin's testimony is credible. For purposes of evaluating the effectiveness of the City's schools, GED recipients are the functional equivalents of dropouts.

The remaining 60% of ninth graders who are able to graduate in four to seven years receive one of the two diplomas recognized by SED: 1) a "local" diploma, and 2) a Regents diploma. Students choose whether to take the examinations for one or the other of these diplomas. A local diploma is awarded to students who pass a series of Regents Competency Tests ("RCTs") which represent the minimum statewide requirements for graduation. As originally conceived the purpose of the RCTs was to identify those in need of remediation. Passing the RCT in reading requires only reading comprehension at the eighth to ninth grade level. The math examination tests approximately sixth grade mathematics.

Defendants argue that a graduating student's passing grade on the RCTs is the surest indication that he received a sound basic education. The court rejects this contention. The RCTs do not test the basic literacy, calculating and verbal skills that should be imparted to all high school graduates.

Because of the low level of academic achievement measured by the RCTs, SED has decided to phase out the local diploma option by 2004. As of 2001, all would-be graduates must take an expanding number of the five Regents examinations necessary to receive the second type of diploma, the Regents diploma. These examinations are more rigorous than the RCTs and measure whether students have met the new Regents Learning Standards.

Historically, of the approximately 60% of ninth graders who ultimately received a Regents or local diploma, the vast majority received a local diploma. In recent years, less than 12% of all ninth graders have eventually received a Regents diploma. The following data are illustrative:

	1994	1995	1996
Local Diploma	50.2%	47.4%	46.7%
Regents Diploma	9.9%	11.3%	11.7%
GED	10.5%	11.2%	10.8%
Drop Out	29.4%	30.0%	30.7%

The class of 1996 was the last class for which complete data were available at trial, given the possibility that students entering the ninth grade may receive a diploma in four to seven years. However, the proportion of students who received local and Regents diplomas has remained relatively constant. From 1996 through 1999, the number of local diplomas awarded every year has hovered between 20,928 and 22,211. The number of Regents diplomas awarded to City public school students has been between 7,134 and 8,795, though the trend has been toward a slightly higher proportion of Regents diploma recipients.

In sum, in recent years approximately 30% of ninth graders in New York City public schools did not receive a high school diploma of any kind by the time they reached 21 years of age. Roughly ten percent of ninth graders obtained a GED-a certificate that is conferred upon a demonstration of marginal skills.

Approximately 48% ultimately received a local diploma-which measures the skills expected of sixth to ninth graders, not those of high school graduates. The remaining 12% or so obtained a diploma that actually demonstrates that they have received a sound basic education. This evidence depicts a public school system that is foundering.

Defendants argue that they cannot be blamed if students choose to drop out. It is certainly true that in individual cases there is little that can be done to keep a troubled child in school. However, when 30% of students drop out without obtaining even a GED serious questions arise about system breakdown.

It could also be argued that students have historically been given a choice whether to seek a local or a Regents diploma, and that students who choose the less rigorous battery of examinations may well be capable of more advanced work. While this argument is impossible to test, the experience of City public school graduates at the campuses comprising the City University of New York is instructive. In recent years approximately 80% of City public school graduates who entered CUNY required remedial help in such basic areas as reading and mathematics. Roughly 50% needed remedial help in more than one area.

Defendants also argue that the State is required only to provide the *opportunity* for a sound basic education, that it has done so, and that students' failure to seize this opportunity is a product of various socio-economic deficits experienced by the large number of at risk students in New York City public schools. The court agrees that the State must only provide the opportunity for a sound basic education, but this opportunity must be placed within reach of all students. The court rejects the argument that the State is excused from its constitutional obligations when public school students present with socio-economic deficits.

Finally, defendants speculate that the poor progress of the City's ninth graders is caused at least in part by students who enter the New York City public school system for the first time in the ninth grade. If such students are ill-prepared when they enter the system, that lack of preparation obviously cannot be blamed on the New York City public schools. This argument has as its premise one that is shared by the court: that education is cumulative, and that a student's performance in high school is affected by what he learned in elementary and middle school. Defendants are correct that the evidence at trial did not include any data on the percentage of drop-outs, GED recipients, and local diploma recipients who had not attended public school in New York City prior to ninth grade.

However, City public school students' scores on standardized tests in elementary and middle school evince the poor performance of City public schools before high school as well. Accordingly, the slow and incomplete progress of the City's ninth graders as they make their way through high school cannot be attributed solely to new students. Student performance on standardized tests is discussed in the next section.

2. Standardized Tests

The results of evaluative tests administered by the State and by BOE to elementary and middle school students-"cautiously" analyzed per the Court of Appeals' admonition-are probative evidence of the poor quality of education provided by New York City public schools.

The first test given youngsters entering New York City public schools before the third grade is the Early Childhood Learning Assessment ("ECLAS"). The ECLAS is not intended to be an achievement test. It is more of a diagnostic tool to see what children know and where they need help. The results of the ECLAS demonstrate what has been noted above: students entering New York City public schools lack such skills as knowledge of the alphabet, sound/symbol relationships, familiarity with counting and numbers, and vocabulary and concept development.

Achievement tests begin in the third grade. Throughout elementary and middle school students take an array of such tests, some of which are given statewide and are administered by SED and some of which are City-specific and administered by BOE. Both SED and BOE rely on commercially available tests that have been modified to some extent for New York City.

a. State Tests

New York State gives two sets of standardized tests, the Pupil Evaluation Program ("PEP") and the Program Evaluation Test ("PET"). The PEP measures individual achievement in reading and mathematics. By contrast, the PET is meant to measure the general effectiveness of a school in teaching science and social studies. It is not intended to measure the achievement of individual students.

During the period 1990-98 SED used a commercially prepared test called the Degrees of Reading Power ("DRP") for its PEP reading test. Before the 1998-99 school year, this test was designed to test whether students have achieved an extremely low level of reading skills, measured in reference to a particular score known as the State reference point ("SRP").

As such, the DRP test was only effective at differentiating students at the lowest end of the reading achievement spectrum, and was designed to identify children in need of remedial help. A similarly low SRP was set for State achievement examinations in mathematics. The State reading and math tests were given in 3rd and 6th grades.

SED requires that school districts have at least 90% of their students scoring at or above the SRP in reading and math. For the years that data is available, nearly all school districts outside of New York City have been able to achieve this low threshold of achievement. The City has not.

In the years 1990-91 through 1997-98, New York City did poorly in bringing its students over the low achievement threshold represented by the SRP. Its students did particularly poorly on the reading PEP. On the third grade reading examination, the range of students scoring over the SRP varied from 59%-69%. Sixth graders scoring above the SRP for reading ranged from 63%-74%. In math, 92% of third graders scored above the SRP in 1996-97.

In other years, New York City's third graders ranged from 81%-89% above the math SRP, with a general upward trend from 1994-95 through 1997-98. City sixth graders scored at 91% above the math SRP in 1997-98. In other years the range was 79%-88% above the SRP, with a general upward trend in the later years. These percentage scores are an average for the entire City and thus include extremely poor performances in numerous districts within the City.

In 1998-99, concerned about the poor evaluative properties of the DRP, SED switched to a new more rigorous commercial test that measures student performance across a wider spectrum. The test was keyed to the Regents' new learning standards. Instead of a single criterion (the SRP), student achievement was measured by reference to four stepped criteria, with level one being the lowest and level four the highest. Students in levels one and two are characterized by requiring extra help to meet the Regents' new academic standards. The examinations were given to fourth and eighth graders. In reading tests given in 1998-99, 21.3% of City fourth graders scored in level one, the lowest level, while only 5.8% of fourth grade students in the rest of the State scored in level one. In the same year 17% of eighth graders scored in level one for reading, compared with 5% in the rest of the State.

Similar results were recorded for math tests with City's eighth graders performing particularly poorly. On none of the tests did more than half of the City's students score in levels three and four, the higher levels that demonstrate that students are on track to meet the Regents' standards.

School performance on SED's PET tests, which concern science and social studies, was similarly low. In the period 1990-96, the City's average scores were in the lowest 25% for the science examinations and never higher than the 16th percentile for the social studies tests.

b. City Tests

Since 1969 BOE has given standardized tests of its own in reading and math to students in grades three through eight, separate and apart from the State's PEP and PET tests. Beginning in 1998-99 the City adopted the commercial examinations used by SED with some modifications. That same year, BOE determined that it would not do its own testing in fourth and eighth grades, relying instead on the new State examinations for those grades.

Until 1999-2000, and in contrast to the State, BOE scored its tests on a curve using "norm-based scoring." A student's performance on the examination was graded by comparison to the performance of a sample of students from around the country assembled by the test publisher. Norms are usually reported in percentiles which represent the number of students in the sample that scored at or below a particular score. For example, a score at the "50th percentile" indicates that 50% of the sample group of students scored at or below that level.

Defendants argue that New York City public school students are getting a sound basic education because City students typically score at just below the 50th percentile on City reading tests and above the 50th percentile on the math tests. Defendants argue that these scores show that New York City students score at the "national average" or at "grade level."

The court finds the terms "grade level" or "national average" inapplicable to BOE's norm-based exams. These examinations do not assess performance by fixed criteria concerning what a student should know in a given grade, but rather by the performance of the sample. Therefore the term "grade level" is misleading. Similarly, the so-called "national average" is not set by tallying scores on an examination given around the country.

This would be impossible, as different school districts around the country use different examinations created by different publishers. Rather, the percentile ranks are set by reference to a relatively small sample. While the commercial publishers of the tests attempt to make the sample statistically representative of the nationwide student population, the evidence at trial demonstrated that they are not entirely successful in that endeavor.

Defendants also argue that the sample has a smaller proportion of at risk students than does New York City, and that a school system with so many at risk students must be providing a minimally adequate education if it is able to keep pace with a sample of students from proportionately more privileged backgrounds. While this argument has some merit, it is overcome by a careful examination of the performance of the City's public school students.

First, it must be remembered that while the City's public schools have a large proportion of at risk students, they also have a significant minority of students who are extremely accomplished. These high-achieving students push up the City's average scores and can offset to a degree the poor performance of at risk students.

Second and more significant is the fact that City public schools every year decide not to promote a substantial proportion of students. Over 40% of all 9th graders do not enter the 10th grade on time. In Queens and Manhattan, two of the higher performing high school districts, over 25% of students are overage for their grade. In Manhattan, a majority of students entering ninth grade will have scores above the 50th percentile in reading and math standardized tests given in the eighth grade.

Yet over 25% of ninth graders then go on to fail English and math courses. These figures demonstrate that a class' performance at the 50th percentile of the City's standardized tests does not equal performance at grade level. City students' poor performance on the State's new examinations also undercuts any optimism caused by their scoring at the 50th percentile in the City's tests.

These and other shortcomings of norm-referenced standardized tests, and a desire to ensure that students are meeting the Regents' new standards, led BOE to replace norm based tests with criterion-based tests beginning in the 1999-2000 school year.

In sum, City public school students' graduation/dropout rates and performance on standardized tests demonstrate that they are not receiving a minimally adequate education. This evidence becomes overwhelming when coupled with the extensive evidence, discussed above, of the inadequate resources provided the City's public schools. The majority of the City's public school students leave high school unprepared for more than low-paying work, unprepared for college, and unprepared for the duties placed upon them by a democratic society. The schools have broken a covenant with students, and with society.

In the next section, the court examines whether the failure of the New York City public schools is attributable to the State's actions.

V. CAUSATION

The following constitute the court's findings of fact regarding the causal link between the State's public school funding system and educational opportunity.

In its 1995 decision the Court of Appeals directed this court to determine whether plaintiffs demonstrated this causal link:

In order to succeed in the specific context of this case, plaintiffs will have to establish a causal link between the present funding system and any proven failure to provide a sound basic education to New York City school children.

(*Campaign for Fiscal Equity v. State of New York*, 86 N.Y.2d at 318, 631 N.Y.S.2d 565, 655 N.E.2d 661.)

The establishment of such a causal link might appear to be fairly straightforward. If it can be shown that increased funding can provide New York City with better teachers, better school buildings, and better instrumentalities of learning, then it would appear that a causal link has been established between the current funding system and the poor performance of the City's public schools.

Defendants brought forth evidence at trial which they assert invalidates this assumption.

First, defendants offered expert testimony that educational resources do not have an effect on student outcomes. If these experts are correct, then lack of resources cannot be a "cause" of students' failure to receive a sound basic education. According to defendants' experts the crucial determinants of student performance are students' socio-economic characteristics, and enhanced resources can do little to overcome the educational deficits that at risk children bring to school.

While the court is not persuaded by this argument it cannot reject it out of hand. Beginning with the publication of the seminal Coleman Report in 1966, there has been a significant body of educational research that purports to show that variations in school resources have, at best, small and uncertain effects on student achievement.

Defendants' expert Dr. Hanushek is one of the leading exponents of this school. There is, of course, a significant body of research that purports to demonstrate that resources *do* matter.

It is not the court's job to resolve this long-running academic debate but rather to decide the issue as it pertains to New York City public schools based on the evidence introduced at trial.

Accordingly, the first order of business in examining causation is to evaluate the parties' evidence regarding whether resources affect student outcomes.

A causation analysis is also complicated by the fact that public school funding in New York State-in common with most states-is a joint undertaking of the State, local, and, to a lesser extent, federal governments. Currently New York State school districts receive 56% of their funding to support educational programs from local revenues, 40% from the State, and 4% from other sources, including the federal government. The relative mix of State, local and federal revenue has fluctuated over time and among districts. For example, State revenue over the last decade has ranged from 38% to 43% of total education spending. The percentage of federal spending has consistently been in the low single digits.

Defendants argue that the State's funding mechanism provides more than enough resources to assure New York City public school students the opportunity for a sound basic education, and that any failure to provide such an education is due to BOE's alleged mismanagement of the resources available to it.

Additionally defendants argue that any funding shortfall that exists must be blamed on the inadequate financial contribution of New York City to its own public schools. The court discusses these contentions in the following sections.

A. The Analyses of Defendants' Experts that Purport to Show that Resources Do Not Affect Student Outcomes

Defendants presented two expert witnesses who testified concerning analyses they performed to determine whether educational resources could boost student achievement. Some of the analyses of one of these experts, Dr. Hanushek, are discussed above in section IV(F). Defendants' other expert in this area was Professor David Armor, a Sociology Professor at George Mason University. According to defendants these experts' analyses demonstrate "the lack of any systematic relationship between spending and achievement, both in New York City and the State."

Before discussing these experts' analyses, the court notes that the State's own Education Department, and the Board of Regents, has long taken an opposing view. Both SED and the Regents have long pressed for more resources for New York City's public schools, and both have unequivocally stated that all students can learn with sufficient resources. While SED and the Regents have acknowledged that socioeconomic disadvantages create a high probability of lower academic performance, they have taken the position that such disadvantages may be overcome by sufficient, targeted resources.

1. Dr. Armor's Testimony

Dr. Armor offered his regression analyses as proof that socioeconomic background is such a crucial factor in student success that student performance is essentially unaffected by school funding.

Dr. Armor first compared the City's scores on the State PEP tests with the rest of the State's. He attempted to adjust test scores for the 1997-98 school years according to students' socioeconomic status. Dr. Armor used individual student data regarding whether a student received free lunch and was classified as LEP (Limited English Proficient). He also incorporated 1990 census data that concerned individual school districts as a whole, including the average household income in a district, the percentage of adults with baccalaureate degrees in a district, and a composite variable designed to capture the number of at risk families in a district.

For the State PEP test scores for general education students in math and reading, Dr. Armor performed a regression that predicts the scores of general education students based on their socioeconomic status. He then used this analysis to "level the playing field" between New York City, with its high percentage of at risk students, and the rest of the State, with its significantly lower percentage of such students. Once he removed the effect of the socioeconomic factors on student test scores Dr. Armor found that there was almost no difference between City and State general education students on the sixth and third grade PEP reading and math tests.

Dr. Armor also looked at City general education public school students' scores on State and City tests in the 1996-7 and 1997-8 school years to determine if they bore any relation to five school resource measures: 1) teacher experience, as defined by five or more years on the job, 2) teacher education as defined by the percentage of teachers with a master's degree or better, 3) teacher certification, 4) pupil-teacher ratio, and 5) per pupil spending. He analyzed single-year performance of four cohorts of students: 1) fifth grade students in the 1996-97 school year, 2) sixth grade students who in 1997-98 attended schools that went from kindergarten to sixth grade, 3) eighth graders in 1997-98, and 4) sixth graders in 1997-98 who had attended schools that went from kindergarten to fifth grade. He again adjusted student test scores by their socioeconomic status in an attempt to level the playing field for a comparison of student test scores. He concluded that there was little or no statistically significant causal relation between student test scores and the five school resource measures.

Finally, Dr. Armor conducted a series of regressions in which he found that there were no statistically significant correlations between per pupil spending and the levels of teacher certification, teacher education or teacher experience in New York City's public schools. According to Dr. Armor each of these measures of teacher quality relied upon by plaintiffs do not increase when funding increases.

Dr. Armor's analyses are not persuasive. First, all of Dr. Armor's studies are flawed by their reliance on analyses of single years of data. As noted above, education is a cumulative enterprise, and student outcomes are dependent not just on the resources that they receive in a single school year, but on the resources that they receive over years of schooling. Dr. Armor's analyses are not probative because they rest on the premise that student test results in a single year can be compared to the resources available to the student in that single year to gauge the effectiveness of resources.

The court also finds that all of Dr. Armor's results are skewed by his decision to "level the playing field" by adjusting test scores to account for socioeconomic characteristics of at risk students. This decision rests on the premise that was not established at trial: that at risk students' educational potential is immutably shaped by their backgrounds. This is not the position of SED or the Regents, and it is contrary to the evidence at trial. Defendants argue that BOE has made similar adjustments in its official rankings of schools. However, BOE has done this primarily to compare schools with similar demographic characteristics; it has not taken the position that the demographic characteristics of a school's student body excuse poor performance.

Dr. Armor's analyses of resources failed to track the effect of resources provided to individual students. For example, dollars spent on a Reading Recovery program in a given school would be attributed to a school's budget, but very few students would actually receive that benefit. Studies that examine overall spending on student achievement are of limited probative value. Rather, an accurate measurement of spending effectiveness must examine the particular inputs upon which money is spent.

Even if overall spending were a probative measure, Dr. Armor's spending data were incomplete. The data failed to account for variance in school costs and resources depending on such factors as the size of the school, whether its space was owned or leased, transportation costs, and whether it received private funding.

Finally, some of Dr. Armor's resource variables were not well-chosen to measure the effect of inputs on student performance. For example, the evidence at trial indicated that teachers with two years' or less experience were particularly correlated with lower student outcomes. Dr. Armor measured the supposed effect of teachers with five years of experience or less. Additionally, although the percentage of teachers with a master's degree is sometimes used by experts to measure teacher quality, the evidence indicated that it is not the strongest such measure.

2. Dr. Hanushek's Testimony

Dr. Hanushek also testified concerning the alleged disconnect between student achievement and school resources.

Dr. Hanushek began by examining spending and performance trends in the United States as a whole. He presented charts which demonstrated that nationwide student performance on the SAT tests declined in the mid-1960s to the early 1980s. After a slight increase thereafter, student performance has remained essentially flat since 1985. This decline and plateau persisted during this period despite decreases in teacher-student ratios, and steady increases in per pupil spending and teacher experience as measured by teachers with an MA and years teaching. Dr. Hanushek noted a similar trend for National Assessment for Educational Progress ("NAEP") tests, though this data does not reach back into the 1960s.

Dr. Hanushek also presented data concerning nationwide labor market outcomes based on 1990 census data, in which he found that school funding levels do not generally have an effect on individuals' subsequent earnings. The one group for which there *was* a statistically significant positive correlation was black women. However, the effect observed was very small. By contrast, Dr. Hanushek found that the parental education level did have a strong effect on their children's adult earnings levels.

Dr. Hanushek then sought to examine the effect of spending on New York City public schools. He first examined 619 New York school districts outside of the City to see if the number of students who received Regents, as opposed to local, diplomas was affected by funding levels. He examined the number of students who received Regents diplomas for a single year, 1996-97. In his final analysis, he sought to account for students' socioeconomic status. After accounting for socioeconomic status, Dr. Hanushek found that there was in fact a *negative* relationship between spending and the number of students who received Regents diplomas.

Dr. Hanushek then turned his attention to New York City to examine whether elementary students' test performances in 1997-98 bore any relation to district spending. He isolated "high poverty" schools-those with over 90% of students receiving free lunch-and determined whether those schools scoring above the mean on nationally normed City tests ("high-performing schools") spent more or less per pupil than schools scoring less than the mean ("low-performing schools"). He found that the high-performing schools receive less funding than the low-performing schools. This result was statistically significant. He observed the same patterns for "moderate poverty schools" with 75% of their students receiving free lunch.

Dr. Hanushek performed similar analyses for other inputs. His analysis of school facilities is discussed in section IV(F), above. He also determined that pupil-teacher ratio and "computer availability" are not related to student performance.

Dr. Hanushek also performed parallel analyses for middle schools, again using the "high poverty" and "moderate poverty" and "high performing" and "low performing" typology. The results were essentially the same as those for elementary schools. Dr. Hanushek again found a statistically significant negative correlation between per pupil spending and student performance. He also found no correlation between student performance and "computer availability." The result was equivocal for the relationship between student performance and pupil-teacher ratios in high poverty schools.

Finally, Dr. Hanushek conducted regression analyses for all schools, looking at the effect, or lack thereof, of the inputs discussed above. He controlled for students' socioeconomic status. His results were consistent with those of the analyses discussed above.

In summing up his testimony Dr. Hanushek stated that he believed that poor students can improve their academic performance, and that teacher quality, at least, can make a difference in student outcomes. However, he testified that he felt that school systems are not using correct criteria in identifying, or compensating, better teachers. He recommended tying teacher compensation to outcomes. He concluded that New York City has sufficient resources at present to improve student outcomes without any influx of new funds.

Dr. Hanushek's analyses suffer from some of the same shortcomings as Dr. Armor's. Crucially, his State-specific analyses studying the effect of resources on students are snapshots of single years, and do not measure the effect of resources over time. Like Dr. Armor's, those of his analyses which focus only on gross per pupil spending are of limited value 5 absent an examination of the effects of particular inputs. His calculations of per pupil spending also do not account for variations in costs among schools, and for private funding received by some schools.

Dr. Hanushek's studies concerning students' receipt of Regents diplomas are not probative. These studies do not incorporate far more relevant information concerning student progress, including drop-out rates, GED rates, and the number of years it takes to graduate. Moreover, the problems discussed above with respect to limiting statistical analyses to a single year of inputs and outcomes increase when the year studied is the students' last year of education.

As plaintiffs' expert Dr. Grismer explained, studying Regents diploma rates where the only educational inputs considered are those to which the child is exposed in her last year of education "leaves out 12 years of investment or 11 years of investment that have been made that we all know affect a particular test score in high school."

Finally, Dr. Hanushek's use of computers per pupil as a resource measure was compromised, as he acknowledged on direct examination, by the fact that this resource measure and student test scores were culled from different years. Additionally, the analysis does not capture any information about the age and quality of computers and whether they were actually in use.

For these reasons, Dr. Hanushek's analyses of State and City data are not persuasive. Dr. Hanushek's testimony regarding national trends casts some doubt on the proposition that spending more money will inevitably raise student outcomes. However, as discussed below the evidence demonstrates that increased spending on certain inputs can positively affect student outcomes.

B. The Effect of Additional Resources on Student Achievement

Contrary to defendants' argument, increased educational resources, if properly deployed, can have a significant and lasting effect on student performance. There is a causal link between funding and educational opportunity.

Many of the subsidiary findings of fact that form the foundation for this finding have been recited above. To summarize, the court has already found, *inter alia,* that:

> Effective teachers and school administrators can boost student performance. New York City's school administrators and teaching force, particularly in its neediest districts, are inadequate.

> Smaller class sizes can have a marked positive effect on student performance, particularly in early grades. At present New York City's school buildings are too overcrowded to effectively address this problem.

> New York City's school buildings are in many cases so dilapidated or antiquated as to impede learning. Conversely, better school facilities can boost student achievement by providing students with the resources they need, such as up-to-date science labs, adequate climate control, and sufficient electrical capacity for computers and other instructional aids.

The evidence demonstrates that other resources also have a substantial positive effect on student outcomes.

Plaintiffs convincingly demonstrated that New York City's public school population, with its high percentage of at risk students, requires what BOE terms an "expanded platform" of programs that will allow students to spend "more time on task." In other words, at risk students need specially tailored programs, and more time spent on all aspects of academic endeavor, in order to increase their academic achievement. Initiatives that have been shown to positively affect student performance in New York City include pre-kindergarten programs, summer programs, and increased hours at school via after school and Saturday programs. None of these extended time programs have been fully implemented in New York City public schools.

Literacy programs are particularly important for at risk students. The array of programs provided by BOE under the umbrella of the Project Read initiative has had a positive effect on the students who have participated in the programs. Project Read was established in 1997 to provide assistance to students who are at risk of never achieving literacy.

The program is targeted to first through third graders. It is comprised of three components: an Intensive School Day Program, which provides individual or small group instruction to permit teachers to spend more time working with each student; an After-School Program, which provides more instructional time; and a Family Literacy Program, which helps parents better support their children's education.

Defendants cite BOE studies, which, while acknowledging the effectiveness of the After-School Program, cast some doubt on the results of the Intensive School Day Program. These BOE studies were undercut by Robert Tobias, head of BOE's Division of Assessment and Accountability, who testified that they were based on incorrect data provided in error by a testing company. Additionally, because of insufficient funds, Project Read services are rationed to only the neediest students.

The control groups for evaluative purposes were comprised of higher-functioning students from the waiting list. There is evidence that this disparity between participants and students in the control skewed the comparison. In all events, there is substantial evidence that certain of the programs offered during the Intensive School Day Program, including Success for All and Reading Recovery, have been extremely effective. These two programs are also among the most expensive under the Project Read umbrella.

SED and BOE have long recognized that summer school can be an important resource for low performing students. Particularly with BOE's cessation of "social promotion" and the advent of the Regents' new standards, summer school has become an important source of additional instructional support for New York City's at risk public school students.

1. The Potential Costs of Increased Educational Resources

Increasing the resources available to New York City school children will require substantial additional funding. It may well be, as defendants argue, that additional resources may be realized by more efficient use of BOE's existing funding. However, the court finds as a matter of fact that financial resources in addition to those already available will be required to lift the City's public schools from their current abysmal state.

The following outline of the potential costs for bringing the New York City public schools in compliance with the State Constitution is not exhaustive and is for illustrative purposes only. As described in section VII below, the choice of measures designed to remedy the constitutional violation described herein lies in the first instance with the State legislature informed by the expertise of the Governor, SED, BOE and the Regents. At this juncture, the court does not prescribe the precise spending measures that must be taken. The following examples are given to sketch the breadth and depth of the public schools' needs.

a. Better Teachers and Administrators

If the New York City public schools are to compete successfully with surrounding suburban schools for qualified teachers and administrators, more resources will have to be made available to increase salaries and improve working conditions. Given that New York City has approximately 78,000 teachers, even a modest increase in teachers' salaries will be costly.

If the average raise were $5,000-which would be a good deal less than the current average wage differential between the City and its suburbs-the annual increase in teacher pay (not including benefits) would amount to $390 million. Other initiatives to attract teachers and administrators, such as subsidized housing, loan forgiveness, or moving stipends, would require additional funds.

Professional development is an important and effective means of improving the performance of existing teachers. The experience of District 2 demonstrates that effective professional development requires a significant financial commitment. BOE requested $34.1 million in additional professional development funds for the 1999-2000 school year. Credible evidence indicates that this request understated actual need in order to be "politically acceptable." Only about $14.1 million of this request was provided.

b. Improved School Buildings

Remedying the disrepair and overcrowding that plague New York City's public schools may require billions of additional dollars. As described above the State has consistently underfunded BOE's capital and maintenance needs.

Because BOE is currently doing only emergency repairs to its buildings, it is difficult to determine exactly how much more maintenance spending is necessary to repair existing buildings. A conservative estimate can be gleaned from the 2000-04 Proposed Plan, which sought $327 million annually in order to establish a regular and reliable cycle of preventive maintenance. However, the credible testimony at trial indicated that even this amount was too low.

BOE also lacks sufficient capital funds. Again a conservative estimate can be gleaned from the 2000-04 Proposed Plan, which sought $11.2 billion for capital spending during the Plan period. The credible evidence at trial demonstrated that this amount was insufficient to address all of the City public schools' capital needs. As in past plan periods, State funding has lagged far behind BOE's capital needs.

c. Other Resources

Other potential costs are harder to quantify based on the record produced at trial but are nonetheless real. For example BOE needs additional funding for library books, school supplies, and instructional technology. Substantial funds are necessary to provide the expanded platform of educational resources necessary to boost the achievement of all at risk children.

While many of BOE's programs for at risk children have shown to produce positive results, only a fraction of New York City's public school children have access to such programs. The State has mandated that Universal Pre-kindergarten be made available to all eligible children by 2004. However, while this initiative has been well-funded compared to other programs in the expanded platform, it has still lagged behind the amount necessary to ensure that New York City meets the deadline.

Project Read has thus far been funded entirely by the City and the amount allocated has been insufficient to reach all the students who need such services in order to achieve literacy. Similarly, BOE is able to make summer school available only to the neediest of the needy, leaving the majority of at risk students un-served.

C. Causation and the Hierarchy of Governmental Actors

Defendants offer two additional arguments in support of their assertion that no causal link exists between inadequate State funding and the failure to provide New York City public school students with a sound basic education.

First, defendants assert, as their counsel phrased it in closing argument, that "the money is there," *i.e.* that the State's funding of public education is adequate to provide all students with the opportunity for a sound basic education. Any failure to provide such an opportunity, according to defendants, is caused by BOE's inefficient spending of the funds available to it. Defendants point out that New York State's per pupil expenditures are the third highest among the states. The New York City school district has consistently been among the highest spending large school districts in the nation.

Second, defendants argue that the City of New York's local contribution to its own public school district is lower than the statewide average and argue that any failure to provide a sound basic education must be attributed to the City's failure to adequately fund its schools.

Defendants presented evidence that New York City's provision of local revenues is about $4000 per pupil, while the State average is approximately $6200 per pupil. Defendants further argue that the State has increased its contribution to the City's public schools in recent years while the City's local effort has declined since 1986. Defendants decry this decline, particularly in light of the City's recent budget surpluses and tax cuts.

The short dispositive answer to both of these arguments is that the State Constitution reposes responsibility to provide a sound basic education with the State, and if the State's subdivisions act to impede the delivery of a sound basic education it is the State's responsibility under the constitution to remove such impediments. As the Court of Appeals explained in sustaining the complaint in this case, "We recognized in *Levittown* that the Education Article imposes a duty upon the *Legislature* to ensure the availability of a sound basic education to all the children of the State." (*Campaign for Fiscal Equity v. State of New York*, 86 N.Y.2d at 315, 631 N.Y.S.2d 565, 655 N.E.2d 661 [emphasis added].)

The State's power over education is plenary.

The State prescribes the architecture of governance in the State's school districts. For example, in 1969 the State decentralized the New York City School District, devolving significant power to the City's community school boards (*see* L. 1969, Ch. 330). In 1996, after decentralization-at least as practiced in the City-had long proven to be a failure, the legislature radically reduced the power of community school boards and concomitantly increased the power of the Chancellor and the central board (*see* Education Law §§ 2590-d-2590-j).

Other examples of the State's plenary powers over educational governance can be seen by such diverse actions as the creation of the New York City School Construction Authority in 1988 (*see* L. 1988, 738 § 1) and the imposition of a "Maintenance of Effort Law" requiring the City to maintain education funding at a specified portion of the City's budget (*see* L. 1976, 132; *Board of Education of the New York City School District v. City of New York*, 41 N.Y.2d 535, 542-3, 394 N.Y.S.2d 148, 362 N.E.2d 948 [1977]).

The State prescribes the means by which municipalities and school districts raise revenue for education. Pursuant to State law, all but five of the State's approximately 682 school districts are "independent" districts which raise local revenue for education through taxes levied by their boards of education on residential and commercial properties within the boundaries of each district. For the independent school districts, such property taxes provide nearly 90% of local education funding.

By contrast the legislature dictates that the school districts of the State's five largest cities (New York, Yonkers, Buffalo, Syracuse, and Rochester) shall have no independent revenue generating authority. Because they are not allowed to levy taxes to fund their school budgets, these "Big 5" school districts are known as "dependant school districts." The dependant school districts must depend on the local municipal government and citywide taxes for the local component of their school budgets.

The State Constitution gives the State broad authority to create and modify local governments and their functions, including their tax structures and limitations on their tax rates and debt capacity. (N.Y. Const. Arts. III, § 1, XVI, § 1.) Local governments, such as New York City, may incur debt and levy, collect and administer local taxes only where consistent with the laws of the legislature. The Court of Appeals has ruled that:

Under our form of State government, the exclusive power of taxation is lodged in the State Legislature…. A corollary to this basic rule is that municipalities such as the City of New York have no inherent taxing power, but only that which is delegated by the State…. Moreover, the delegation of State taxing power to a municipality must be made in express terms by enabling legislation.

(*Castle Oil Corp. v. City of New York*, 89 N.Y.2d 334, 338-9, 653 N.Y.S.2d 86, 675 N.E.2d 840 [1996].)

The State regularly dictates or approves changes in the City's tax structure. For example, the City has enacted at least 14 different tax cuts in the last several years, as part of its tax reduction plan. New York State has authorized or approved a majority of these cuts. The State has also acted unilaterally to repeal or restrict New York City taxes.

The State's causation arguments run athwart the argument it successfully made in seeking the dismissal of the companion case of *City of New York v. State of New York.* There the State argued, and the Court of Appeals agreed, that the City lacked capacity to bring a suit against the State asserting virtually the same claims as those asserted by the plaintiffs herein.

Constitutionally as well as a matter of historical fact, municipal corporate bodies-counties, towns and school districts-are merely subdivisions of the State, created by the State for the convenient carrying out of the State's governmental powers and responsibilities as its agents. Viewed, therefore, by the courts as purely creatures or agents of the State, it followed that municipal corporate bodies cannot have the right to contest the actions of their principal or creator affecting them in their governmental capacity or as representatives of their inhabitants.

As "creatures or agents of the State" both BOE and the City are subject to the State's control. Whatever authority they exercise over education is authority delegated by the State. The State Constitution explicitly provides that the State's control over educational matters is not subject to the home rule powers granted local governments (*see* N.Y. Const. art. IX, § 3[a][1]).

Defendants point out that the State's public schools have traditionally been funded from State and local sources. From this inarguable fact, they proceed to assert that the State has "surrendered" a portion of its sovereign powers to school districts (and, in the case of the "Big 5," to municipal governments), as if this "surrender" were irrevocable. To the contrary, the cases cited by defendants for this proposition make it clear that the State's delegation of powers is revocable (*see Board of Education of Buffalo v. City of Buffalo*, 32 A.D.2d 98, 100, 302 N.Y.S.2d 71 [1969]; *Hirshfield v. Cook*, 227 N.Y. 297, 301, 309-10, 125 N.E. 504 [1919]).

This holding, that the State is ultimately responsible for assuring the provision of a sound basic education, does not carry with it a correlative finding that BOE's management of the New York City School District is entirely adequate, or that the City's contribution to its own schools is sufficient. In fact evidence introduced at trial, summarized in subsection F below, suggests that both BOE and the City have contributed to the schools' current crisis.

However, even if this court were to hold that the failures of the City and BOE were not the ultimate responsibility of the State, the State's own funding mechanism for distributing aid to schools would remain a substantial cause of the public schools' malaise. The State's system for allocating aid to public schools is discussed in the next section.

D. The State Aid Distribution System

The State's school aid distribution system has for over a decade prevented the New York City public school system from receiving sufficient funds to provide its students with a sound basic education. As SED, the Regents, and numerous State-appointed blue ribbon commissions have repeatedly reported to the State legislature, the State aid distribution system does not provide adequate funding to all districts.

As recently stated by SED: "resources are not aligned with need. Those schools with the greatest need frequently have the fewest fiscal resources.... The situation in New York City illustrates this point."

The evidence demonstrates that the State aid distribution system is unnecessarily complex and opaque. It is purportedly based on an array of often conflicting formulas and grant categories that are understood by only a handful of people in State government. Even the State Commissioner of Education testified that he does not understand fully how the formulas interact.

However, more important than the formulas' and grants' needless complexity is their malleability in practice. The evidence at trial demonstrated that the formulas do not operate neutrally to allocate school funds-at least with respect to annual increases in State aid. Rather the formulas are manipulated to conform to budget agreements reached by the Governor, the Speaker of the State Assembly, and the State Senate Majority Leader.

The court emphasizes that a process in which the final allocations to the State's school districts is determined by three elected officials is not inherently unconstitutional. Rather, it is the fact that the State's school funding mechanism has failed for more than a decade to align funding with need-and thus has failed to provide a sound basic education to New York City's school children-that runs afoul of the Education Article.

1. State Funding Formulas and Categorical Grants

In 1999-2000 New York State used approximately 50 different formula-based aids and categorical grant programs to distribute the $12.5 billion allocated to the State's public schools by the legislature. As in past years, the formula-based aids constituted approximately 95% of State aid, while categorical grants constituted the remaining five percent.

The individual formulas generally consist of several components that may include a base amount, a student count, a weighting factor and additional multipliers. For each type of aid, these components are combined together, with one or more mathematical calculations, to determine the amount of aid generated for each district. Such formulas exist for each type of aid. As a result the entire State aid distribution is extremely complicated. SED's description of all the formulas extends to 59 pages. The State Division of the Budget's explication of a single formula can require several pages of dense calculations.

Basic Operating Aid, the largest State aid program, illustrates the complexity and arbitrariness of the State aid formulas. SED's description of the Basic Operating Aid formula requires three and a half pages of single spaced text and mathematical formulas. Operating Aid is distributed according to a complex formula which involves four components: 1) a "fixed sum" for calculating the maximum district expenditure for which State aid will be calculated, 2) a "ceiling adjustment," which permits a small second tier of aid above the basic expenditure ceiling, 3) a "state operating ratio" and 4) a "selected total aidable pupil unit (TAPU)" for payment.

TAPU, which is a weighted student count, appears in several State aid distribution formulas. It begins with an attendance-based student count and adds "weights" for additional student characteristics. For example TAPU includes a weight of .25 for a category of at risk students called "Pupils with Special Education Needs." There was no evidence in the record that the TAPU weightings bear any relation to actual student need. In addition, TAPU is based on a district's attendance, rather than its enrollment figures. Since districts with large numbers of at risk students will have higher absentee rates, this aspect of TAPU harms schools with high concentrations of poor and minority students.

Even State aid formulas that purport to address specific needs do not in fact attempt to measure or prioritize the needs of different districts or the actual costs of addressing these needs. For example, Class Size Reduction Aid for 1999-2000 includes a complex formula that estimates the number of kindergarten classes needed as "the positive result of 1995-96 full-day and half-day enrollment divided by 20 minus such enrollment divided by a district's 1993-94 average kindergarten class size." The basic grant per classroom uses the 1994-95 median teacher salary. New York City is phased in using a lower percentage (0.187) than either the other Big Five school districts (0.333) or school districts in the rest of the State (0.400). There is nothing in the record that demonstrates that any of these factors is related in any way to the actual cost of reducing class size.

So-called "transition adjustments" also distort the operation of State aid formulas. Transition adjustments are used either to increase or decrease the amount of aid that a district is entitled to receive pursuant to the terms of a particular formula. There are two types: (1) "caps" that limit any increase in funds to a fixed percentage determined independently of the operation of any particular aid formula, and 2) "hold harmless" provisions that prevent districts from losing State aid from one year to the next through operation of the aid formulas. Transition adjustments have had an impact on the distribution of State aid.

In 1997-98 SED determined that due to caps or hold harmless adjustments, only 12.8% of districts in the State received the aid that they would have been entitled to under the formulas in the absence of the transition adjustments.

Defendants are correct that in recent years fewer aid categories have been subject to transition adjustments. Defendants' expert James Guthrie, a Professor of Public Policy and Education at Vanderbilt University, demonstrated that transition adjustments amount to less than 6% to 7% of total State aid. Nonetheless transition adjustments have a significant impact on yearly increases in State aid and permit the State to direct millions of dollars in resources without regard to its aid formulas.

Defendants defend the State aid distribution system by stating that it serves several legitimate State purposes. Principally, defendants claim that the distribution of aid is equalized, so that relatively poor districts receive more aid than relatively wealthy districts. Additionally, defendants claim that the system is responsive to student need.

Defendants are correct that the State aid distribution system is equalizing in that aid is generally distributed in inverse relation to wealth. As measured by the State's Combined Wealth Ratio ("CWR"), which gauges a district's income and property wealth, New York City is a relatively wealthy district and for this reason sees its share of state funding somewhat depressed.

By definition, a CWR of 1.0 identifies a district of "average" wealth, but the index number would not fairly disclose where a district in fact lies within the distribution of all districts in the State. In 1995-96 only 232 school districts out of 683 in New York State had CWRs of 1.0 or greater-in other words the school district wealth distribution is so skewed that only about one third of the State's districts were of average or greater wealth. New York City's CWR of .985 for 1995-96 ranked it 237th, wealthier than 65% of the districts in the State.

However the evidence indicates that CWR overstates New York City's wealth. First, CWR and other formula components that purport to account for district wealth fail to take into account regional costs. School districts face significant variation in costs to deliver educational services, which in turn affects their ability to pay for various educational inputs.

In 1999, SED noted the longstanding recommendations made by various blue ribbon panels to include regional cost estimates in the State aid formulas and concluded that "[t]he failure to explicitly recognize geographic cost differences within the major operating aid formulas has led to formula allocations which are inequitable." SED has quantified these differences in regional costs. New York City's regional cost ratio is the highest in the State, which means that a dollar buys fewer educational resources in New York City than anywhere else in the State.

Second, the CWR's wealth equalization is undermined to a degree by the State's STAR program. Under STAR, qualified households receive a partial school property tax exemption, thereby reducing their school property tax bill. The State then reimburses local school districts for the foregone tax revenue due to property tax cuts and thereby shifts a portion of local education taxes from individual school districts to the State.

The un-rebutted evidence at trial indicates that New York City receives less STAR aid than localities in the rest of the State. The Independent Budget Office estimates that New York City homeowners received an average reduction in tax liability of $323 per participating household, while those in the rest of the State received an average reduction of $926. The State Comptroller has predicted that when the STAR program is fully implemented, New York City will fare even worse vis-a-vis the rest of the State. Defendants' assertion that "STAR is property tax relief, not school aid" does not comport with the practices of SED or the State Division of Budget, which include STAR tax relief in their evaluations of school aid.

Finally, even though State aid distribution formulas are grossly wealth equalizing, they do not appear to be particularly responsive to changes in district income. From 1988-89 through 1997-98, measures of New York City's property wealth varied considerably. During 1994-98, New York City's actual value of taxable real property per "Total Wealth Pupil Units" in thousands dropped from $260.3 to $215.7, a loss in value of 17.2%. In contrast the average value in the rest of the State dropped by 1.9%. Despite these differences, during each of these years New York City received virtually the same percentage share increase in State aid.

For the above stated reasons, the wealth equalization effects of the State aid formulas do not accurately reflect New York City's wealth and ability to pay for education.

More importantly, defendants' other primary defense of the State aid distribution system-that it is driven in large measure by student need-is almost completely negated by the record. It is true that the State aid formulas contain factors such as TAPU that are weighted to a degree by a district's percentage of at risk children. Additionally, some State aid formulas, such as "Extraordinary Needs Aid" and "Limited English Proficiency Aid," are purportedly designed to send more money to districts with large numbers of at risk children. However, these formulas and weightings do not accurately account for the costs of education caused by large numbers of at risk students in a single district.

The State Education Department has long documented this misalignment of resources in its Needs/Resource Capacity Index, a measure of a district's ability to meet the needs of its students with local resources. Based on a comparison of districts according to their Needs/Resource Capacity Index ratios, SED has determined that New York City receives substantially less State aid than districts with similar needs.

For example in 1996-97 the City received $3562 per pupil in State aid, between $1500 and $1800 less than districts with similar Needs/Resource Capacity Index ratios. This analysis is substantiated by other SED analyses using different methods that demonstrate that New York City receives substantially less State aid than districts with similar numbers of at risk students. Indeed, the City receives less State aid than many districts with substantially smaller proportions of at risk students.

Even if the State aid formulas were designed to allocate education aid more fairly, it would be difficult to change the orientation of State education funding because any annual *increase* in State aid has historically been divided without reference to the formulas. The evidence at trial demonstrated that the formulas and grant categories are not allowed to operate neutrally but rather are manipulated during the State's annual budget negotiations by State officials to produce consistent funding allocations of aid increases among school districts around the State. The evidence at trial demonstrated clearly what the State Comptroller has found:

It is well known that the formulas are annually "worked backwards" until the politically negotiated "share" for the City schools is hit in the calculations. In this context, the data feeding into the school aid formulas for New York City is really of no practical consequence whatsoever-the City will get the negotiated share of aid regardless of what data they report.

The evidence supported the Comptroller's conclusion that annual increases in State education aid are allocated pursuant to an agreement struck by the Governor and the leaders of the State Assembly and the State Senate as part of the overall annual budget negotiations.

These negotiations produce a general agreement on the overall amount to be spent on education and how it is to be distributed across the State which is then ratified by the legislature. This phenomenon is commonly referred to as "three men in a room."

If there are "three" men in a room, and the Comptroller is not among them, one may reasonably query how the Comptroller is able to speak authoritatively regarding this process. The answer is that the process is an open secret in Albany. The means for effectuating the agreement to provide a fixed share of State aid increases are contained in State software and documents. The documents and software relied upon by the court do not reveal any deliberations of individual legislators. Rather, they simply confirm how the process of allocating increases in State school aid works. Confirmation of the process is also seen in New York City's consistent "share" of any annual State aid increase.

The State has created computer software, called the "State aid modeling system," to enable governmental personnel to evaluate the distributional impact on school districts of changes to the State's public school funding formulas. The State aid modeling system includes thousands of variables that the State has devised as part of approximately 50 State aid formulas and categorical grant programs that it uses to fund public schools in New York State.

The State aid modeling system is used by staff from SED, the Division of the Budget ("DOB") and members and staff of both houses of the legislature. In order to manipulate data using the State aid modeling system, personnel from SED, DOB and the legislature fill out a form entitled "Confidential State Aid Data Form" in which they indicate the changes to the formula or formulas they wish to test. The form permits users to specify numerous very precise changes in formulas.

The blank Confidential State Aid Data Form includes a section entitled "goals" that lists several factors, including "% increase for NYC." No other school district is listed on the form. The existence of this "goal" is evidence that confirms the Comptroller's assessment that the City's annual increases in State aid is determined during budget negotiations, and not by neutral operation of the State's funding formulas.

State budget documents reflect that New York City receives a fixed percentage share of any annual increase in State aid for education. The target has been 38.86%, and the State has hit or come very close to this percentage over the last 13 years. This percentage share is reflected in the final computer runs that SED generates at the conclusion of the budget process. These are the most reliable measures of intended allocations of State aid increases. These runs reflect that an array of manipulations of computerized State aid formulas-and in some years, other types of State aid-were used from year to year to reach this percentage. It is inconceivable that this recurring percentage share could randomly recur year after year.

Defendants correctly point out that the actual amounts eventually allocated to school districts have varied somewhat from the amounts set forth in SED's computer runs. The process discussed above determines changes in the formulas. However, some of the data inputs used in the formulas may change before the State school aid is paid out, which in turn may change the percentage increase afforded New York City.

The fact remains that the formulas have been altered to effect a particular distribution of State aid and not for any reason keyed to the educational goals supposedly embodied in the formulas. Moreover, the total increase in aid actually received by the City is generally consistent with the amounts predicted in SED's computer runs.

Plaintiffs' evidence on this issue does not concern impermissible "legislative motive," as defendants argue. The First Department has cautioned this court to protect against any evidence that would violate the speech and debate clause of the State Constitution or the correlative common law privilege that protects executive branch officials acting in a legislative capacity (*Campaign for Fiscal Equity v. State of New York*, 271 A.D.2d 379, 707 N.Y.S.2d 94 [2000]).

The speech and debate clause and the common law legislative privilege protect governmental officials as they deliberate and weigh policy and legislation. The evidence discussed above is not concerned with legislative deliberations or motives but rather with what the legislature ultimately does when it modifies State aid formulas to achieve certain annual percentage allocations of increases in school aid.

E. Funding Comparisons and Recent BOE Surpluses as Evidence of Adequacy

Defendants frequently state in their papers that New York State is the third highest-spending State on education, and that New York City spends more per pupil than most large urban school systems. They argue that these figures alone demonstrate that the State provides enough resources for a sound basic education. Defendants also cite recent increases in State spending as evidence that the State is meeting its constitutional obligation. These facts in isolation are of no probative value. Among other failings, gross spending amounts do not take into account local costs and do not reveal whether the money is spent effectively. Fundamentally, spending comparisons cannot erase the facts discussed above which demonstrate-as measured by the inputs and outputs included in the Court of Appeals' template-that New York City public school students are not receiving a sound basic education. A sound basic education is gauged by the resources afforded students and by their performance, not by the amount of funds provided to schools.

The State's recent increases in school funding can only begin to address longstanding problems in New York City's public schools. These increases have been enabled by unprecedented budget surpluses. They have not been coupled with the structural reform necessary to assure that adequate resources are provided to New York City's public schools on a sustained basis. Since there has been no fundamental change in the structure and operation of the State education finance system, there is no guarantee that recent increases are sufficient or will be sustained.

Defendants also urge the court to compare the City's public schools with Catholic schools in the City. They argue that the City's Catholic schools meet the educational needs of their students and achieve better results than New York City's public schools despite Catholic schools' larger student-to-teacher ratio, larger class sizes, lower paid teachers and lower per-pupil spending. It is true that the City's Catholic schools consistently outperform public schools on State-wide tests, have a lower dropout rate, a higher percentage of students graduating high school in four years, and substantially more students attending four-year colleges upon graduation.

While the City's Catholic schools do an admirable job, the comparison between the two systems is not apt. The student bodies of the two systems are markedly different. Catholic schools have far fewer students eligible for free lunch, or who are Limited English Proficient. The City's public school students are approximately 84% minority, compared with approximately 56% of Catholic school students. Catholic schools enroll very few special education children. They also are able to expel from the system any students who are disruptive. Finally, the vast majority of Catholic school teachers are not unionized, and there was credible evidence in the record that many choose lower pay in order to work in a religious environment.

Defendants point to recent BOE annual budget surpluses as evidence that the funds provided to BOE are sufficient or that BOE is unable to spend the money given to it because of its hopeless inefficiency. Defendants quote from a letter from plaintiffs' counsel to a BOE official in which he states "How do we defend these [BOE] surpluses...and plead poverty?"

The evidence demonstrates that these surpluses are the product of sound budgeting practices and not signs of abundance. The practice allows for rational long-term financial planning and enables extra and ongoing funding of high-priority projects. Indeed, defendants defend transition adjustments on similar grounds, arguing that school districts need to provide for ongoing expenses.

F. The Actions of the City and BOE as Additional "Causal Links"

The court has already held that the State's method for financing education is a substantial cause of the failure to provide New York City public school students with the opportunity for a sound basic education. Under the State Constitution the State is ultimately responsible for the delivery of a sound basic education, and any failure to do so may not be blamed on the actions of its subdivisions BOE or the City.

Even if the State Constitution did not place upon the State this ultimate responsibility for the provision of a sound basic education, the State's distribution system for its own funding, in isolation, remains a cause of this constitutional violation. The law recognizes that there may be many "causal links" to a single outcome, and there is no reason to think that the Court of Appeals 1995 opinion mandates a search for a single cause of the failure of New York City schools. For this reason, even if the State were not ultimately responsible for the actions of BOE or the City, its own actions expose it to liability.

1. Defendants' Assertions Regarding BOE

Defendants alleged at trial that BOE wastes vast sums of money through fraud, corruption and waste.

The evidence demonstrates that decentralization of the governance of the New York City School District led to inefficiency, mediocrity and corruption in some of the City's community school districts. Pursuant to the broad decentralization law passed by the legislature in 1969, community school boards were given control of elementary and middle schools in their respective districts. This power included the power to hire an array of school personnel, from district superintendents to principals to school aides. The central board retained control of City high schools, special education and a variety of city-wide programs.

In many of the City's school districts, community school board members were more concerned with their own political advancement (and in some cases, with their enrichment) than they were with education. Board members used their hiring power to find jobs for supporters and relatives. Some board members received kickbacks in return for the provision of jobs. Theft of school supplies was common in certain corrupt school districts. Some of the worst community school boards had jurisdiction over schools in the City's poorest neighborhoods.

The evidence did not show that large sums were lost to corruption and fraud. The most important results of corrupt or inept community school boards were demoralization of school staff and inattention to educational issues. The evidence indicates that student performance in some districts inevitably suffered as a result of poor governance by community school boards. There was no probative evidence measuring the magnitude of this negative effect, however.

Moreover, the failings of community school boards cannot be blamed on BOE. The decentralization law gave BOE limited powers to oversee the boards. To the extent that defendants allege that corruption and waste by community school boards had a negative effect on student outcomes, the blame must lie with the State for perpetuating a form of school governance that generated corruption and waste. Though problems with decentralization became clear by the early 1980s, the State did not diminish the powers of community school boards until 1996.

This legislation, however belated, appears to have reduced malfeasance in the City's public schools. In addition, BOE is subject to extensive financial reporting rules and regulations. It is also served by an active Special Commissioner for Investigation who is charged with investigating corruption, fraud, conflicts of interest and other forms of unethical conduct. Both of these are checks on widespread illegality.

Defendants presented some probative evidence that BOE does not make the most effective use of all the money provided to it. However, BOE's record of waste is not so grim as defendants allege.

As discussed in section IV(G), above, defendants provided some evidence that BOE's personnel could be more effectively managed. However, the issues of productivity gains and incentive pay are two of many that must be considered in contract negotiations with the relevant unions. Any cost savings realized by productivity gains would likely be offset by the costs of improving working conditions and increasing teacher salaries in order to attract and retain better teachers.

Defendants are correct that BOE's methods for evaluating teachers and improving their performance are currently ineffective. However, as discussed above these failings are to some degree a function of inadequate funding. Because of a dearth of qualified teachers willing to work in the City's public schools, supervisors are often unwilling to take steps to replace ineffective teachers. Additionally, professional development that could help underperforming teachers is currently underfunded in the City's public schools.

Defendants presented little evidence concerning BOE's allegedly wasteful spending on administration. Plaintiffs point out that BOE spends a smaller percentage of its budget on its central administration than the statewide average. The most recent estimates introduced at trial indicate that New York City spends 1.8% of its budget on central administration, compared with 1.9% statewide (an average that includes New York City).

Additionally, BOE spends 77.8% of its funds on instruction, a greater proportion than the 76.1% statewide average. These figures do not reveal that the funds they encompass were spent *effectively*, but the comparison does cast some doubt on BOE's reputation as a top-heavy bureaucracy.

Defendants did not provide convincing evidence that BOE is responsible for failure to conduct preventive maintenance on the City's public school buildings. Rather, the evidence shows that BOE lacks sufficient funds to conduct all necessary preventive maintenance, and must devote the lion's share of its limited resources to fixing major structural problems at the schools.

Defendants' claims that BOE is profligate in its new construction spending are also not supported by the record. The credible evidence demonstrates that construction of new schools will have to be part of any plan to deal with overcrowding. As discussed in section IV above, the defendants' proposals to simply increase the utilization of existing school buildings would overtax these buildings and impede students' access to the educational resources they need for a sound basic education.

Additionally, defendants' claim that the schools built by BOE are educational "Taj Mahals" is not supported by the record. The evidence indicates that, with a few exceptions, BOE and the School Construction Authority are building functional schools without unnecessary amenities. The record does establish that some inefficiencies have been created by the State-imposed division of authority between BOE and the School Construction Authority. However, the Authority was created by the State. To the extent that it has hampered school construction in New York City, the responsibility must lie with the State.

The most serious evidence of BOE's inefficient spending concerns special education. However, fixing the problems of special education will cost money which will largely offset any cost savings realized by reform.

In New York City, approximately 135,000 students are enrolled in full-time or part-time special education programs, almost 20,000 of whom are students with severe and profound disabilities. BOE spends over $2.5 billion annually, more than 25% of its total budget, on special education.

Applicable federal and State laws require each school district to provide a continuum of educational services for students who have been recommended for special education services. The services on the continuum range from those that are "less restrictive" (i.e. involve contact with students who are not disabled) to those which are "more restrictive" (i.e. involve less contact with students who are not disabled). By State and federal law special education students should be educated to the greatest extent possible in the least restrictive environment.

A recent task force convened by Mayor Giuliani, which included then City Schools Chancellor Rudy Crew, concluded that "tens of thousands" of students who are not disabled are placed in special education classes in New York City. Studies conducted in the early 1990s in part by one of plaintiffs' experts, Dr. Mark Alter, found that more than 80% of students classified by the City's special education system as learning disabled did not meet the threshold criteria for learning disability. The over placement in special education of students erroneously classified as learning disabled is significant because approximately 59% of all special education students are so classified.

Compared to the rest of the State and to the rest of the nation, New York City's public schools have a higher proportion of special education students enrolled in separate classes or in programs in separate educational settings-in other words, in the more restricted end of the placement continuum. According to the most recent SED annual report, 58% of the City's special education children are in restrictive placements. Such placements are expensive and often can cause inappropriately referred students tangible educational harm.

The evidence demonstrates that the primary causes of New York City's over-referral and over-placement in restrictive settings are a lack of support services in general education and State aid incentives that tended until recently to encourage restrictive placements. With respect to State aid, the State funding formula was amended in 1999 to provide greater financial incentives to place students in less restrictive settings.

However, it remains true that the disproportionate number of New York City students placed in special education is directly related to the lack of educational and support services in the general education environment. This finding has consistently been reaffirmed by SED and BOE studies. Defendants cite a portion of a study conducted by Dr. Alter which appears to reach the opposite conclusion. Properly placed in context the passages relied upon by defendants do not support their argument.

The cause of over-referral is not hard to trace: given large class sizes in general education and comparatively smaller class sizes in special education, teachers and parents who believe a student's learning needs are not being met in general education will often attempt to obtain more individualized instruction by referral to special education. Placement in special education for these children is facilitated by the flexible definition of "learning disability" under applicable State regulations.

The fiscal implications of over-referral and over-placement are significant. According to BOE documents, the budgeted cost of educating even a part-time special education student in 1998-99 was approximately twice the cost for a general education student ($14,405 vs. $7,225). The average budgeted cost to serve a full-time special education student ($24,313) was over three times the general education cost.

These numbers suggest the potential for significant cost savings. Defendants' expert, Dr. Daniel Reschley, Chairman of the Department of Special Education at Peabody College at Vanderbilt University, conducted studies which generally support the conclusion that special education reform could save significant amounts of money. Dr. Reschley testified that, even without reducing the total number of students receiving special education services, BOE would reduce its annual expenditures by $300 to $335 million if students with disabilities were placed in less restrictive settings according to the national average. Once these figures are adjusted for the reduction in State reimbursement that would occur, the BOE could still save somewhere between $105-185 million per year, depending on the assumptions made. Additional savings would be realized by moving students out of special education entirely.

Plaintiffs point out that BOE has recently taken steps to decrease the over-referral of students to special education, and the over-placement of special education students in restrictive settings. Plaintiffs assert that students removed from special education will continue to have problems that will have to be addressed by services in addition to those currently available in general education classes.

Plaintiffs are correct that the cost savings projected by defendants would be offset by the cost of providing to students removed from special education an array of necessary educational and support services in general education. Additional preventive resources would be necessary to staunch the flow of inappropriate referrals to special education. Finally, special education currently has several significant deficiencies that will cost money to fix, such as too-large class sizes and too many uncertified teachers. New and successful models of least restrictive placements have also proven to be expensive.

Despite these offsets, the evidence introduced at trial indicates that tens of millions of dollars annually could be saved by special education reforms. The evidence concerning cost savings above that range is equivocal.

2. Defendants' Assertions Regarding the City

Defendants correctly point out that the City, despite a higher proportion of at risk students, spends substantially less on education than other localities around the State. Defendants' expert, Dr. Michael Wolkoff, Deputy Chairman of the Department of Economics at the University of Rochester, provided data tending to show that New York City's effort has lagged behind that of other districts in the State at least since 1991.

In 1996-97, the latest year for which comparative data are available, New York City raised only about $4000 per pupil from local resources, while school districts in the rest of the State raised on average about $6200. Dr. Wolkoff testified that New York City's local education contribution per student is exceeded by every member of the wealthiest quartile of districts, by nearly every district in New York City's own quartile (the second wealthiest), by many districts in the second poorest quartile and even by one district in the poorest quartile.

Defendants argue that the State-local partnership in school funding allows a local district to choose to spend more than the average local contribution, but the State is not required to lift up laggard districts. Defendants argue that New York City in recent years has tried to buck this principle by reducing its contribution as the State has increased its contribution to education.

The evidence at trial supports this assertion. Based on data compiled by the State Comptroller's Office, the share of school district spending represented by State aid grew over the period 1986-97 from slightly over 37% to more than 42% for New York City, while in the rest of the State the share of State on average spending decreased from over 41% to below 37%. Over the same period, the City's local share of education funding decreased from over 52% to below 48%. BOE has noted this phenomenon in official documents.

Plaintiffs do not dispute Dr. Wolkoff's testimony on this issue, but point out that New York City collects more tax revenue per capita than the State average and argues that this demonstrates that the disparity in education funding is a result of the extraordinary burdens placed upon the City's fiscal resources by the need to provide extensive and expensive municipal services.

The evidence confirms that New York City's combined property and income tax burden is above the New York State average. In February 2000, the Independent Budget Office published an analysis demonstrating that City residents' combined property and personal income tax burden averaged $7.26 per $100 of income, compared to averages of $6.90 per $100 in the City's suburban counties and $6.78 in upstate counties.

In addition to this higher-than-average tax burden, various structural characteristics impede New York City's ability to fund education at a constant and more generous level.

Outside of New York City, local school districts rely principally on property taxes to finance school budgets. By contrast, local education funding in New York City is derived from municipal revenues. Approximately 37% of these municipal revenues are raised from property taxes. Twenty-one percent of municipal revenues come from personal income tax, 16% from sales taxes and 26% from all other taxes, including a variety of business taxes. Income, sales, and business taxes are particularly susceptible to changes in the local economy. New York City's economy has come to rely to a great degree on cyclical business sectors, namely finance, insurance and real estate, creating a tax base sensitive to the vagaries of the economy.

In addition to the instability created by a tax base particularly sensitive to business cycles, New York City's municipal finance system is subject to an extraordinary array of demands for services. The per capita costs of providing these services are increased by higher demand in New York City and higher regional costs. Some of the demand is amplified by State requirements. For example, the State has imposed a matching requirement for Medicaid and public assistance funding which forces City taxpayers to pay nearly $300 more per capita for Medicaid and $70 more for public assistance than residents in the rest of the State. New York City also has a heavy debt burden that reduces its ability to support education.

In addition to these impediments to increased City funding, the City is also under no legal compulsion to maintain its funding at a given level. The evidence at trial demonstrated that the State's "Maintenance of Effort Law," which is ostensibly designed to stabilize the City's education funding, is ineffective.

This law, referred to as "the Stavisky-Goodman bill," requires New York City to appropriate an amount of funds to BOE from the total budget equal to average proportion of the total budget appropriated for the Board in the three preceding fiscal years. Because this law applies to all funds within the City budget, not just local revenues, the City is generally not forced to spend more of its own funds. The Regents and SED have repeatedly and in vain called for the legislature to strengthen Stavisky-Goodman.

In sum, the court finds that the City's ability to contribute to education is hampered by its diversified tax base, its higher costs for other municipal services, and by its debt burden. However, as discussed below, it is the legislature's duty in the first instance to reform how education is financed in New York State in conformance with the strictures of the Education Article of the N.Y. Constitution. This duty entails evaluation of a variety of policy choices. If the legislature determines that the City, despite the substantial impediments described above, should fund education more consistently and generously, it has the power to force it to do so, *inter alia,* by tightening its maintenance of effort law.

Having found that the State's system of school funding violates the Education Article of the N.Y. Constitution, the court now addresses plaintiffs' claim arising under federal law.

VI. TITLE VI REGULATIONS CLAIM

Plaintiffs' second claim arises from implementing regulations promulgated pursuant to Title VI of the Civil Rights Act of 1964 (42 USC § 2000d). Section 601 of Title VI provides that:

[n]o person in the United States shall, on the ground of race, color, or national origin, be excluded from participation in, be denied the benefits of, or be subjected to discrimination under any program or activity receiving federal financial assistance.

(42 USC § 2000d.)

The Supreme Court has ruled that a plaintiff must make a showing of intentional discrimination to succeed on a Title VI claim (*Guardians Assn. v. Civil Service Commission of the City of New York,* 463 U.S. 582, 610-11, 103 S.Ct. 3221, 77 L.Ed.2d 866 [Powell, J., concurring], 639-42 [Stevens, J., dissenting] [1983]).

Plaintiffs make no claim of intentional discrimination here. Instead plaintiffs rely on regulations promulgated by the U.S. Department of Education ("DOE") pursuant to Title VI. Section 602 of Title VI (42 USC § 2000d-1) expressly authorizes federal agencies to promulgate rules and regulations to effectuate its provisions.

The DOE regulations relied on by plaintiffs incorporate a disparate impact standard of liability. The U.S. Supreme Court has held that federal agencies have the authority to promulgate regulations pursuant to § 602 that prohibit recipients of federal funds from taking any action that results in a disparate impact or produces discriminatory effects on the basis of race, color or national origin (see *Guardians Assn., supra,* 463 U.S. at 584 n. 2, 591-2, 623 n. 15, 103 S.Ct. 3221). As the Court of Appeals has already held in this case, "under Title VI's implementing regulations, proof of discriminatory intent is not a prerequisite to a private cause of action against governmental recipients of Federal funds." (*Campaign for Fiscal Equity v. State of New York,* 86 N.Y.2d at 322, 631 N.Y.S.2d 565, 655 N.E.2d 661.)

The DOE regulations provide, *inter alia,* that recipients of federal funding may not utilize criteria or methods of administration which have the effect of subjecting individuals to discrimination because of their race, color, or national origin, or have the effect of defeating or substantially impairing accomplishment of the objectives of the program as respect individuals of a particular race, color, or national origin.

(34 C.F.R. § 100.3[b][2].)

Although the Supreme Court has not yet ruled on the issue, the vast majority of courts have agreed that the parties' respective burdens in a Title VI disparate impact case should follow those used in Title VII employment discrimination cases (see *Powell v. Ridge,* 189 F.3d 387, 393-4, *cert. denied* 528 U.S. 1046, 120 S.Ct. 579, 145 L.Ed.2d 482 [1999]; *New York Urban League v. State of New York,* 71 F.3d 1031, 1036 [1995]; *Sharif v. New York State Educ. Dept.,* 709 F.Supp. 345, 361-62 [1989] [Title VII burden shifting analysis applied in Title XI case]).

Thus, a plaintiff in a Title VI regulation disparate impact case bears the initial burden of establishing a prima facie case that a facially neutral practice has had an adverse and disparate impact upon a protected class of people (see *New York City Environmental Justice Alliance v. Giuliani,* 214 F.3d 65, 69 [2000]). If the plaintiff meets that burden then the defendant must demonstrate a "substantial legitimate justification" for the practice.

In the education context, the defendant must demonstrate that the challenged practice is justified by "educational necessity" (see *Board of Education v. Harris,* 444 U.S. 130, 151, 100 S.Ct. 363, 62 L.Ed.2d 275 [1979]; *Georgia State Conf. of Branches of NAACP v. State of Georgia,* 775 F.2d 1403, 1418 [1985]; *Sharif, supra* 709 F.Supp. at 361-2). If the defendant meets its rebuttal burden, then the plaintiff must establish either that the defendant overlooked an equally effective alternative with less discriminatory effects or that the proffered justification is no more than a pretext for racial discrimination (*see Powell v. Ridge, supra,* 189 F.3d at 394).

In analyzing this claim, the court relies on much of the fact finding set forth above. In order to avoid needless repetition, the following findings of fact refer wherever possible to previous relevant findings.

A. Plaintiffs' Prima Facie Case

Plaintiffs argue that they have made out a prima facie case of disparate impact by per capita funding comparisons and by regression analyses performed by their expert, Dr. Robert Berne, a Professor of Public Administration at New York University. They also rely upon certain findings of defendants' expert Dr. Wolkoff.

The court agrees with an implicit premise of plaintiffs' analyses: that money is a crucial determinant of educational quality, and that receipt of less educational funding by minority students is an adverse disparate impact within the purview of DOE's Title VI regulations.

Stating this premise in the abstract is easier than applying it to the facts of this case. Plaintiffs must first prove the existence of a disparate adverse impact felt by minority students. Tracking the educational funding spent on minority and non-minority students in New York State is not a straightforward exercise. The State's school funding system provides money to districts, not to individual students, and it does so for the most part according to "weighted pupil units," not by a simple nose count of pupils. Under Title VI and DOE's regulations, the disparate impact complained of must fall on individuals, not upon governmental entities such as school districts.

The filtering of school funding through localities also requires that some attention be paid to causation. Plaintiffs must prove that the State's school funding mechanism *caused* the alleged disparate impact.

1. Per Capita Funding Comparisons

Plaintiffs' per capita funding comparisons are based on the following facts: 1) 73% of the State's minority public school students are enrolled in New York City's public schools, 2) minority students make up approximately 84% of New York City's public school enrollment, and 3) New York City receives less funding per capita, on average, than districts in the rest of the State. From these facts plaintiffs ask the court to conclude that the State's funding mechanism has a disparate adverse impact upon a super-majority of the State's minority student population.

The court finds that where, as is the case here, 73% of a state's minority students are concentrated into a single district, then comparisons of that district's funding with average district funding in the rest of the State can be an accurate indicator of the presence (or absence) of a disparate impact based on race. This is particularly true here where approximately 84% of the City's public school children are members of minority groups. The size of this percentage obviates the need to break the huge New York City school district into its constituent community school districts in order to investigate disparate funding of minorities and non-minorities within New York City.

An analysis that relies on comparisons of district funding for purposes of determining the presence or absence of a disparate impact is endorsed in the Court of Appeals 1995 decision (86 N.Y.2d at 324, 631 N.Y.S.2d 565, 655 N.E.2d 661). The Third Circuit Court of Appeals has endorsed a similar analysis in an action challenging Pennsylvania's school funding system. In that action, in which plaintiffs rely on the same DOE regulations invoked here, the Third Circuit held that plaintiffs stated a viable claim by alleging that Pennsylvania's educational funding system gives school districts with high proportions of white students on average more Commonwealth treasury revenues than school districts with high proportions of non-white students, where the levels of student poverty are the same.

A similar analysis comparing funding of geographic units was used to find liability under a disparate impact theory in _Meek v. Martinez_, 724 F.Supp. 888 [1987], a case involving a challenge to funding under the Older Americans Act of 1965 (42 U.S.C. § 3021). In _Meek_, plaintiffs claimed that Florida's formula for allocating funds to senior citizens pursuant to the Act discriminated against minority seniors. The court compared the effects of the State's allocation formula with a stripped down version of the State's formula that excluded certain elements that plaintiffs claimed favored White seniors. Under the statute, funds were distributed to geographically defined districts, known as Planning and Service Areas ("PSAs").

The court found a disparate impact when it compared the amount of funding directed under the two formulas to the four highest and four lowest percentage minority PSAs in Florida. The high percentage minority PSAs received less funding under the State's formula than they did under the alternate formula (_Meek_, 724 F.Supp. at 906). The _Meek_ court ultimately found that this disparate impact could not be justified by any valid state policy and so held that Florida's distribution of funds under the Older Americans Act violated Title VI regulations promulgated by the U.S. Department of Health and Human Services.

Plaintiffs' complaint herein frames their Title VI regulation claim by reference to the State education financing system as a whole, alleging that "the State education financing scheme" causes a disparate impact on minority students. However, plaintiffs' post-trial submission attempts to demonstrate disparate impact by focusing entirely on evidence of disparities solely in the allocation of State aid. Plaintiffs may have focused solely on the State portion of school funding in recognition that both the Supreme Court and the Court of Appeals have held that disparate funding caused by wealthier, higher spending, school districts within the State is an inevitable-and constitutionally permissible-consequence of a state-local partnership in education funding (*San Antonio, supra,* 411 U.S. at 50-51, 93 S.Ct. 1278; *Levittown, supra,* 57 N.Y.2d at 45-6, 453 N.Y.S.2d 643, 439 N.E.2d 359).

Focusing then entirely on the State component of education funding, the court finds that from 1994-95 to 1999-2000, New York City has consistently received less total State aid than its percentage share of enrolled students. In those years, New York has approximately 37% of the State's enrolled students and has received a percentage of total State aid ranging from 33.98% to 35.65%. This is evidence of disparate impact. Defendants' argument that transportation aid and building aid should be omitted from this analysis is without foundation. These two funding components are obviously essential in delivering core educational services.

Defendants also argue that since State aid is generally awarded according to average student attendance, not enrollment, the correct comparison is to measure State aid by the City's attendance, not by its enrollment. Because City schools tend to have greater problems with truancy, their average attendance tends to be a smaller portion of total enrollment than that of other schools around the State. Accordingly, comparing State funding to a student roster measured by average attendance would tend to decrease the City's historic pro rata shortfall.

The court holds that disparate impact may be measured by comparing funding to enrollment figures and that the data presented by plaintiffs demonstrates a disparate impact in this case. Defendants' policy justifications for distributing funding by attendance are more appropriately considered in the second stage of the disparate impact burden-shifting analysis mandated by Title VI regulations. In other words, when the burden of proof shifts to defendants, the court will consider their argument that using an average attendance measure to distribute funds is supported by a "substantial legitimate justification."

The parties' other non-statistical evidence concerning disparate impact in State aid distribution is not persuasive.

Plaintiffs' expert, Dr. Berne, examined a weighted student unit, " State Aid per TAPU for expense," a unit that is used annually by SED to compare funding among districts in New York City. He found that New York City received less State aid per this pupil unit than the average in the rest of the State. In 1997-98 New York City received approximately $3007 in State revenue per TAPU for expense. The average for the rest of the State was approximately $3325 per TAPU for expense.

By this measure, the City receives approximately $318 less per pupil unit. Dr. Berne did not testify as to whether this disparity was subject to a test of statistical significance. Such a test would provide some indication whether the observed disparity was explainable by chance. By contrast, defendants' expert Dr. Wolkoff, in his study of statewide per capita funding disparities, which is described below, did conduct tests of statistical significance of the comparatively small disparities he observed using a difference of means test.

Dr. Berne's analysis of TAPU per expense funding disparities is undercut by his failure to address whether the disparity observed in funding allocated by TAPU per expense was attributable to chance. Additionally, Dr. Berne's failure to conduct a similar analysis in other school years limits the probative value of the conclusion that he drew from this single year's disparity.

On the other hand, Dr. Berne's analysis may be considered to be conservative in that it ignores two factors that would tend to exacerbate disparate funding. First, it does not take into account New York City's higher regional costs in providing educational services. As noted above, New York City's higher regional costs depress its buying power for educational services.

When examining funding disparities among geographic districts, differences in costs within those geographic districts are relevant in a disparate impact analysis (see _New York Urban League, supra_ 71 F.3d at 1038). Second, it does not account for the higher proportion of STAR tax relief afforded school districts outside the City. As noted above, the STAR program has the effect of directing more education dollars to districts outside the City.

Plaintiffs also attempt to rely on certain data introduced during the testimony of defendants' expert Dr. Wolkoff. This data purportedly compares New York City's per pupil spending with the rest of the State excluding New York City. However, the exhibits relied upon by plaintiffs for this point all contain statewide averages that _include_ New York City. In neither his direct testimony nor his cross examination did Dr. Wolkoff break this data out into a statewide average that excluded New York City. During cross examination, plaintiffs showed Dr. Wolkoff a Memorandum of Law submitted by defendants in support of a pre-trial motion for summary judgment that purported to perform this division between the City and the rest of the State for data from 1995-96. However, the relevant portion of the memorandum cites an affidavit submitted by Dr. Wolkoff which does not contain this calculation. The court was unable to ascertain whether the calculation contained in the memorandum received the imprimatur of any expert. Accordingly, the court declines to rely on this evidence proffered by plaintiffs.

To disprove disparate impact defendants relied on statewide per capita funding comparisons conducted by Dr. Wolkoff. For two school years, 1995-96 and 1996-97, Dr. Wolkoff examined the per pupil (unweighted) expenditures of all of the State's school districts, and then made the assumption that minority students in each district are funded at the district average.

By averaging minority and non-minority per pupil expenditures in all districts across the State, Dr. Wolkoff found that average State aid per minority pupil as measured by attendance was $4097 in 1995-96 while average State aid per non-minority student in attendance was $4019. In other words, as measured by students in attendance, minority students in the State actually received an average of $78 more per pupil more than non-minority students. In the same year, Dr. Wolkoff found that aid per enrolled minority student was $3615, compared with $3767 per enrolled non-minority student.

In other words, as measured by students enrolled in public schools statewide, Dr. Wolkoff found that minority students received $152 less than non-minority pupils. The differences between enrolled and attending students reflected a lower attendance rate by minority students compared with their non-minority peers. Dr. Wolkoff showed similar results for the 1996-97 school year.

Dr. Wolkoff found that these differences in average per-pupil expenditures statewide between minority and non-minority students were too small to be statistically significant.

Dr. Wolkoff's per capita analysis fails to account for regional cost differences, which, as discussed above, are highest in New York City. He also made no effort to account for the relative advantages that districts outside of New York City enjoy because of STAR tax relief. Additionally, his analysis does not account for the concentration of minority students in New York City and his minority averages appear to have been driven up by a few high spending districts.

In all, the court is not persuaded by either Dr. Berne's or Dr. Wolkoff's per capita analyses of the distribution of State aid.

2. Dr. Berne's Regression Analyses

Dr. Berne's regression analyses are probative evidence of disparate impact and provide independent proof of disparate impact.

Dr. Berne conducted a statistical regression analysis for the 1995-96 and 1996-97 school years to determine whether minority and non-minority students attending similar districts receive the same level of aid. His analysis used five different pupil "units" used by the State to distribute or analyze the State school finance system. He analyzed operating aid, the largest aid category, in isolation, and he analyzed all aid distributed by computerized formulas, which accounts for approximately 95% of all State aid.

Based on his review of the State's justifications for its present funding system, and upon a review of the national literature concerning school finance, he selected a number of independent variables to determine their effect on the distribution of State aid. These variables included: 1) property and income as measured by the combined wealth ratio, 2) effective tax rates, 3) levels of student poverty as measured by the provision of free and reduced-price school lunch, 4) the number of ELL students, 5) district attendance rates, 6) district size, 7) percentage of non-minority students, and 8) the number of students with disabilities (this data was available for 1996-97 only).

Dr. Berne conducted thirty regressions for each of the two years studied. Regardless of the variables, weighting, and student counts applied, Dr. Berne determined that the State aid system had a disparate racial impact on minority students across the State in every regression. Fifty-eight of the 60 regressions were statistically significant. Dr. Berne's regressions tend to show that minority students receive less State aid as their overall concentration increases in a particular district.

Dr. Wolkoff leveled several critiques against Dr. Berne's regression analyses and reworked several of the regressions by adding his own variables. Dr. Wolkoff testified that the failure to include non-formula aid (i.e. the five percent of State aid that is not distributed by formulas) may have skewed Dr. Berne's results. Dr. Wolkoff noted that a number of these non-formula aids funnel money by criteria that often sends the aid to the State's minority public school students. For example, categorical reading aid goes only to the Big Five school districts, which of course contain the vast majority of the State's minority students. Dr. Wolkoff, though he replicated many aspects of Dr. Berne's regressions, did not attempt to quantify the effect the inclusion of these categorical aids would have on the regressions. Given the relatively small total dollar amount of categorical aids, and the fact that many do not appear on their face to direct a higher proportion of aid to high minority districts, this criticism does not undermine the validity of Dr. Berne's regressions.

Dr. Wolkoff also correctly points out that Dr. Berne did not account for the fact that the operating aid formula contains a "floor," by which all districts, no matter how wealthy, receive at least $400 per pupil in operating aid. Dr. Berne instead assumed an entirely linear relation between wealth and the distribution of operating aid, where the two were inversely related. Dr. Wolkoff attempted to account for this non-linearity in his regressions. When he did so he found no statistically significant results that tended to show that non-minority students receive more State aid than minority students.

The court notes that this result is highly counter-intuitive. Accounting for the $400 floor that is guaranteed even the richest districts-which generally have low percentages of minority students-would appear to exacerbate, not ameliorate, the funding disparities favoring low-minority districts observed by Dr. Berne.

In all events, Dr. Berne adequately justified his decision not to model the $400 floor in his regressions. The regression analyses were not meant to exactly replicate the computer aid formulas run by the State. Minority status is obviously not an explicit factor in the State aid formulas. The point of the regression analyses is to see if minority status of students is, *sub rosa*, a factor that determines the distribution of State aid. This factor cannot be measured if the funding formulas are simply recreated verbatim.

For the reasons stated the evidence demonstrates the existence of a disparate adverse impact on minority students caused by the State's school funding system.

With respect to the causation issue, the facts in this case demonstrate that disparate funding of school districts in the State has had a real effect on individual students. The court has already found, in ruling on plaintiffs' claim under the Education Article, that lack of sufficient district funding has had a negative effect on student performance. While defendants demonstrated that there is some inefficiency, waste and corruption in the New York City School District, these factors do not break the chain of causation between disparate funding distributed by the State school finance system and poor student performance.

B. Defendants' Asserted "Substantial Legitimate Justifications"

The plaintiffs having made out a prima facie case, the burden of persuasion now shifts to defendants to demonstrate a substantial legitimate justification for its system of distributing school funding. As noted above, the State's justification must be related to "educational necessity," that is it must bear a "demonstrable relationship to classroom education." (*Georgia State Conf. supra*, 775 F.2d at 1417-18.)

Defendants articulate four broad justifications for the disparate impact caused by the distribution of State school aid. First, defendants argue that school funding formulas are wealth-equalizing and New York City is a relatively more affluent school district. Second, they argue that directing funding according to districts' average attendance, rather than to enrollment, is related to the State's legitimate objectives of encouraging districts to keep attendance up and discouraging their inflation of enrollment figures.

It is undisputed that the City is harmed by using attendance, rather than enrollment, as the benchmark, because it has a higher than average truancy rate. Third, defendants argue that distributing transportation and building aid on a reimbursement basis, which has historically harmed the City, is justified. Fourth, defendants argue that their formulas take student need into account.

This final justification may be disposed of summarily. The court has already found that New York City does not receive State aid commensurate with the needs of its students and that it in fact receives less State aid than districts with similar student need.

Defendants claim that wealth equalization is "the principal explanation for NYC's receipt of lower aid per enrolled student than the average in the rest of the State." The court finds that wealth equalization, when properly implemented, can be a valid goal for State school aid. By attempting to compensate for differences in district wealth, wealth equalization may be an important component of a school funding scheme that assures the delivery of a sound basic education.

However, as implemented, the State's efforts at wealth equalization do not further this substantial legitimate purpose. There are two principal reasons why this is so.

First, wealth equalization can do actual harm, where, as is the case in New York State, it is not coupled with funding mechanisms that effectively take account of differences in districts' student need. It may be generally true that a district's wealth is inversely correlated with its percentage of at risk students, but that generalization does not hold for New York City. New York City, though it is treated by State funding formulas as a relatively wealthy district, has a very high concentration of at risk students.

Its public schools serve a relatively small proportion of middle- to upper-class children. Most of its students come from poor and working class families, and many of these children are at risk of academic failure. The State's school funding system does not adequately account for the needs of such children. This is one of the great failings of the State school financing system. The State Education Department has long documented the misalignment of resources in its Needs/Resource Capacity Index, which is discussed above. Based on a comparison of districts according to their Needs/Resource Capacity Index ratios, SED has determined that New York City receives substantially less State aid than districts with similar needs.

Second, as described above, defendants' measure of wealth is inaccurate because it does not account for differences in regional costs. School districts face significant variation in costs incurred in delivering educational services, which in turn affects their ability to pay for various educational inputs. In 1999, SED noted the longstanding recommendations made by various blue ribbon panels to include regional cost estimates in the State aid formulas and concluded that "[t]he failure to explicitly recognize geographic cost differences within the major operating aid formulas has led to formula allocations which are inequitable." SED has quantified these differences in regional costs. New York City's regional cost ratio is the highest in the State, which means that a dollar buys fewer educational resources in New York City than anywhere else in the State. This failure to include estimates of regional costs in its assessment of wealth compromises the State's wealth equalization scheme.

For these reasons, defendants have demonstrated that wealth equalization in school funding, in the abstract, is related to legitimate educational objectives. However, plaintiffs have demonstrated that this objective is not served in practice by the State's current school funding mechanism. It would be more effectively served by an alternate school funding mechanism that accounts more completely for student need and regional costs.

Defendants' defense of basing State funding on districts' average attendance, rather than enrollment, suffers from similar flaws. The State argues that keying State funding to attendance encourages districts to keep attendance levels high. The goal is laudable; the State's implementation of the goal is counterproductive or worse.

There is no question that a student's regular attendance at school is a prerequisite to a sound basic education. As SED has repeatedly recognized:

Attendance is critical to teaching and learning. Poor attendance is statistically linked to low achievement. Schools with low attendance rates tend to be in urban areas, have large numbers of students on free or reduced lunch and high minority composition.

Poor attendance is often a signal that a student is disengaging from involvement in school. This disengagement can begin with not paying attention in class, can move to class cutting, and can end up in truancy. It can be caused by low self-esteem, poor instructional programs, fear for personal safety and lack of meaningful activities or relationships with others. Family environment and lack of parental encouragement can also contribute to attendance problems, as can health-related conditions, such as asthma.

The evidence demonstrates that at risk students have much higher rates of truancy. Accordingly, New York City, with its high percentage of at risk students, has a lower average attendance rate than most districts in the rest of the State. Lower attendance rates do not reduce New York City's obligations, however. The City is still required to provide space and staff to serve all enrolled pupils. This is a source of disparate impact.

The State's choice to base school funding on districts' average attendance is unnecessarily punitive. It creates a perverse direction of State aid by directing aid away from districts with large numbers of at risk students. The evidence at trial demonstrates that at risk students require a higher level of intervention to ensure attendance. As is clear from the facts recited in this opinion, the vast majority of the City's at risk students do not receive such services and instead are placed in schools lacking basic resources necessary for a sound basic education. In part because of the State's insistence on attendance as a guiding measure of school aid distribution, the City is denied the resources it needs to provide a sound basic education.

Modifying State aid formulas to give some consideration to enrollment and at risk factors would result in less racial disproportionality than the current system. SED has recommended such a modification. The State has other options to increase attendance, such as directing adequate funding to programs that help assure higher attendance levels, such as arts, physical education, and school-based health services.

Defendants argue in passing that the reimbursement principles embodied in building and transportation aid send proportionally more dollars to districts in the rest of the State than to New York City. Defendants do not elaborate on this argument, which is contained in a footnote in their memorandum of law. They do not quantify the effects of building aid and transportation aid, nor set forth how their reimbursement principles bear a demonstrable relationship to classroom education.

There was little evidence at trial concerning the distribution of transportation aid. The evidence concerning building aid demonstrates that the State's system for allocation of this aid category actually harms the City. Unlike most types of State aid, building aid does have a multiplier for regional costs. However, this multiplier understates New York City's costs. The capital needs of New York City's public schools have been drastically underfunded. Accordingly, this argument is not persuasive.

For the foregoing reasons, the court finds unpersuasive defendants' justifications for the adverse disparate racial impact caused by the distribution of state aid. Plaintiffs have established a violation of the relevant Title VI implementing regulations.

VII. REMEDY AND ORDER

New York State has over the course of many years consistently violated the Education Article of the N.Y. Constitution by failing to provide the opportunity for a sound basic education to New York City public school students. In addition, the State's public school financing system has also had an unjustified disparate impact on minority students in violation of federal law.

The court will not at this time prescribe a detailed remedy for these violations. Rather it is the legislature that must, in the first instance, take steps to reform the current system.

The legislature must be given the first opportunity to reform the current system for several related reasons. First, the Court of Appeals held in its 1995 decision that the State Constitution "imposes a duty on the Legislature to ensure the availability of a sound basic education to all the children of the State" (86 N.Y.2d at 315, 631 N.Y.S.2d 565, 655 N.E.2d 661). Second, this action has focused principally on how the current system affects New York City, but any remedy will necessarily involve the entire State.

The legislature is in a better position to gauge the effects of reform on the State as a whole. Third, the legislature is better positioned to work with the Governor and other governmental actors who have a role in reforming the current educational system. In particular, the Regents, SED and BOE have far greater expertise than this court in crafting solutions to the educational problems discussed in this opinion. This expertise should guide the State as it reforms the current system. There is no need, at least at this time, for the court to supersede the legislature, the Governor, the State Education Department, and the Regents, in imposing a remedy.

That said, the court's deference to the coordinate branches of State government is contingent on these branches taking effective and timely action to address the problems set forth in this opinion. The parlous state of the City's schools demands no less. The court will not hesitate to intervene if it finds that the legislative and/or executive branches fail to devise and implement necessary reform.

Because the State is ultimately responsible for the provision of a sound basic education this court rejects defendants' contention that the City and BOE are necessary parties that must be joined in this litigation before any remedy may issue. The court recognizes that reform of the system of State funding for schools may also require concomitant reorganization of school governance to ensure that funds are spent effectively. However, the State has the statutory power to change districts' management structure to ensure the more effective spending of education funding.

The following parameters must guide defendants' reform of the current system.

This court has held that a sound basic education mandated by the Education Article consists of the foundational skills that students need to become productive citizens capable of civic engagement and sustaining competitive employment. In order to ensure that public schools offer a sound basic education the State must take steps to ensure at least the following resources, which, as described in the body of this opinion, are for the most part currently not given to New York City's public school students:

1. Sufficient numbers of qualified teachers, principals and other personnel.

2. Appropriate class sizes.

3. Adequate school buildings with sufficient space to ensure appropriate class size.

4. Sufficient and up to date books, supplies, libraries, technology and laboratories.

5. Suitable curricula to help students by giving them "more time on task."

6. Adequate resources for students with extraordinary needs.

7. A safe orderly environment.

In the course of reforming the school finance system, a threshold task that must be performed by defendants is ascertaining, to the extent possible, the actual costs of providing a sound basic education in districts around the State. Once this is done, reforms to the current system of financing school funding should address the shortcomings of the current system by, *inter alia*:

1. Ensuring that every school has resources for providing a sound basic education.

2. Taking into account variations in local costs.

3. Providing sustained funding to promote long-term planning by school districts.

4. Providing transparency so that the public may understand how the State distributes school aid.

5. Ensuring a system of accountability to measure whether the reforms actually provide a sound basic education.

Finally, the court directs defendants to examine the effects of racial isolation on many of the City's school children. There is significant social science research that indicates that this isolation has a negative effect on student achievement. There is also some nascent research that indicates that steps to increase racial and socio-economic integration may be more cost effective in raising student achievement than simply increasing funds allocated to high percentage minority schools (*see* James Ryan, *Schools, Race & Money*, 109 Yale L. J. 249).

The court hereby declares that defendants' method for funding education in the State of New York violates plaintiffs' rights under the Education Article of the New York State Constitution (Article XI, Section 1); and

The court further declares that defendants' method for funding education in the State of New York violates plaintiffs' rights under regulations passed by the U.S. Department of Education pursuant to Title VI of the Civil Rights Act of 1964 (42 U.S.C. § 2000d; 34 C.F.R. § 100.3[b] [1], [2]); and

The court orders that the defendants shall put in place reforms of school financing and governance designed to redress the constitutional and regulatory violations set forth in this opinion. Defendants shall have until September 15, 2001 to implement these reforms. The parties shall appear before the court on June 15, 2001 to describe the progress of these reforms. The court will retain jurisdiction over this matter for as long as necessary to ensure that the constitutional and statutory/regulatory violations set forth herein have been corrected.

The court thanks all the attorneys, paralegals, and support staff involved in litigating this action. Given the enormous amount of relevant material and the sometimes novel legal issues, the attorneys for both sides tried the case intelligently, economically, and with a minimum of acrimony. Both sides fought hard, but they fought fair. The parties' written submissions were excellent.

END OF DOCUMENT

OPINION #5

Supreme Court, Appellate Division, First Department, New York

295 A.D.2d 1

CAMPAIGN FOR FISCAL EQUITY, INC., et al., Plaintiffs-Respondents

v

The STATE of New York, et al., Defendants-Appellants

June 25, 2002

Students, parents, and organizations concerned with education issues brought action challenging state's funding of New York City's public schools. Following remand, 86 N.Y.2d 307, 631 N.Y.S.2d 565, 655 N.E.2d 661, the Supreme Court, New York County, Leland DeGrasse, J., 187 Misc.2d 1, 719 N.Y.S.2d 475, entered judgment in favor of plaintiffs. State appealed. The Supreme Court, Appellate Division, Lerner, J., held that:

(1) public school children were receiving opportunity for sound basic education, as mandated by Education Article of Constitution;

(2) ability to "function productively" should be interpreted as ability to get a job, support oneself, and not be a charge on public;

(3) evidence was insufficient to prove that inadequate school facilities deprived students of opportunity to acquire skills of sound basic education;

(4) city schools had minimally adequate instrumentalities of learning;

(5) city schools had minimally adequate teaching;

(6) evidence was insufficient to prove that deficiencies in city schools were caused by state funding system; and

(7) implementing regulations for Title VI did not confer federal right as would support § 1983 claim.

Reversed.

Tom, J.P., filed concurring opinion.

Saxe, J., filed opinion dissenting in part.

Implementing regulations for Title VI, promulgated by Department of Education, did not flesh out content of statutory right, but rather created new right not indicated in statute, and thus could not confer federal right as would support § 1983 claim against city based on alleged disparate impact of state public school funding system on minority students. 42 U.S.C.A. § 1983; Civil Rights Act of 1964, § 602, 42 U.S.C.A. § 2000d-1.

PETER TOM, J.P., DAVID B. SAXE, JOHN T. BUCKLEY, JOSEPH P. SULLIVAN, and ALFRED D. LERNER, JJ.

LERNER, J.

The "sound basic education" standard enunciated by the Court of Appeals in *Campaign for Fiscal Equity, Inc. v. State of New York*, 86 N.Y.2d 307, 631 N.Y.S.2d 565, 655 N.E.2d 661 requires the State to provide a minimally adequate educational opportunity, but not, as the IAS court held, to guarantee some higher, largely unspecified level of education, as laudable as that goal might be. Since the court, after a trial of the issues, applied an improper standard, we reverse.

Plaintiffs, students, parents and organizations concerned with education issues, commenced this action in May 1993 for a declaratory judgment and injunctive relief, on the ground that the State's public school financing system violated the Education Article of the State Constitution (N.Y. Const. art. XI, § 1), the equal protection clauses of the Federal and State Constitutions (U.S. Const., 14th Amend; N.Y. Const. art. I, § 11), the anti-discrimination clause of the State Constitution (N.Y. Const. art. I, § 11), Title VI of the Civil Rights Act of 1964 (42 USC § 2000[d], *et seq.*), and the implementing regulations there under issued by the United States Department of Education (34 CFR 100.3[B][2][p]).

The State moved to dismiss the complaint for failure to state a cause of action, and ultimately the Court of Appeals ruled that plaintiffs had stated causes of action under the State Constitution's Education Article and the Title VI implementing regulations (*Campaign for Fiscal Equity, Inc. v. State of New York*, 86 N.Y.2d 307, 631 N.Y.S.2d 565, 655 N.E.2d 661 [" *CFE I* "]). The Court ruled that the Education Article requires the State Legislature to offer all children "the opportunity of a sound basic education" (*id.* at 316, 631 N.Y.S.2d 565, 655 N.E.2d 661).

Although the Court declined to "definitively specify what the constitutional concept and mandate of a sound basic education entails," since this would be premature and would require the development of a factual record in order to be "fully evaluated and resolved," it did state that such an education "should consist of the basic literacy, calculating, and verbal skills necessary to enable children to eventually function productively as civic participants capable of voting and serving on a jury" (*id.* at 316-318, 631 N.Y.S.2d 565, 655 N.E.2d 661).

According to the court, the State must ensure that certain resources are made available under the present system in order to provide minimally acceptable essential facilities and services so that children may obtain a sound basic education (*id.* at 314-316, 631 N.Y.S.2d 565, 655 N.E.2d 661).

Specifically, children are entitled to "minimally adequate physical facilities and classrooms which provide enough light, space, heat, and air to permit children to learn," as well as "access to minimally adequate instrumentalities of learning such as desks, chairs, pencils, and reasonably current textbooks," and "minimally adequate teaching of reasonably up-to-date basic curricula such as reading, writing, mathematics, science, and social studies, by sufficient personnel adequately trained to teach those subject areas" (*id.* at 317, 631 N.Y.S.2d 565, 655 N.E.2d 661). Nevertheless, the Court cautioned that "proof of noncompliance with one or more of the Regents' or Commissioner's standards may not, standing alone, establish a violation of the Education Article," since such standards often exceed notions of a minimally adequate or sound basic education and are sometimes merely aspirational (*id*).

Similarly, performance on standardized competency examinations established by the Regents and the Commissioner "[is] helpful," but should be used "cautiously as there are a myriad of factors which have a causal bearing on test results" (*id.*).

In order to prevail in the instant case, plaintiffs would have to prove a causal link between the present funding system and any proven failure to provide a minimally adequate educational opportunity (*id.* at 318-319, 631 N.Y.S.2d 565, 655 N.E.2d 661). However, the Court of Appeals concluded that, at the pleading stage, plaintiffs had stated a cause of action, since the fact-based allegations of the "failure to provide the opportunity to obtain such fundamental skills as literacy and the ability to add, subtract and divide numbers would constitute a violation of the Education Article" (*id.* at 319, 631 N.Y.S.2d 565, 655 N.E.2d 661).

Although the Court of Appeals dismissed the claim under Title VI, since there was no showing of intentional discrimination, the Court of Appeals reinstated the claim for violations of Title VI's implementing regulations, which merely require proof of discriminatory *effect*, not discriminatory *intent*, for a private cause of action (*id.* at 321-322, 631 N.Y.S.2d 565, 655 N.E.2d 661).

The Court of Appeals dismissed the cause of action under the Federal and State equal protection clauses, on the ground that: (1) education is not a fundamental constitutional right and therefore a rational basis test applies; and (2) any disparities in funding arising from the State's financing scheme are reasonably related to the legitimate State interest in preserving and promoting local control of education (*id* at 319-321, 631 N.Y.S.2d 565, 655 N.E.2d 661).

Upon remand, a non-jury trial was held during which 75 witnesses testified, generating 23,000 pages of transcript, and 4300 documents were received in evidence.

New York City's public school system is the largest in the United States, with 1,189 schools, 1.1 million students, and over 135,000 employees (including 78,000 teachers, 19,000 teacher aides, and 38,000 others). Overall supervision of the City schools is vested in the Board of Education ("BOE"), which is composed of seven members, one appointed by each of the five borough presidents and two by the mayor.

In turn, BOE appoints a Chancellor, who is responsible for the school system's operation. The City school district is divided into 32 geographically based elementary and middle school community school districts ("CSD's") (each of which has, its own elected board, which does not exercise executive or administrative authority, and a superintendent appointed by the Chancellor), and six high school districts, overseen by a superintendent. In addition, there are four non-geographically based school districts for: (1) students with serious academic and other problems; (2) severely disabled children; (3) extremely low-performing districts; and (4) anomalous schools.

BOE and the other school districts throughout the State are subject to the jurisdiction of the State Education Department ("SED"), which is overseen by the Board of Regents (the "Regents"). This board is made up of 16 individuals who are elected by the State Legislature, and who in turn select the Commissioner of SED. Absent a specific State statute, the Regents dictate official State education policy. They also certify teachers and set educational standards, such as the subjects and units of study which are required to be taught and must be passed for graduation.

The Regents and SED make budgetary recommendations to the Governor and the Legislature which, for the 2000-2001 school year, appropriated $13.6 billion for public education statewide, a $1.1 billion increase over the previous year. In fiscal year 2000, BOE received a total of $10.4 billion from Federal, State, City and private sources, or about $9,500 per student. From 1994 to 2000, the State's share of the City's education budget increased from 47% to 51%, while the City's share decreased from 54% to 49%.

The State Constitution requires the Legislature to "provide for the maintenance and support of a system of free common schools, wherein all the children of this state may be educated" (N.Y. Const art XI, § 1). As noted *supra*, the Court of Appeals has ruled that the Education Article charges the Legislature to offer all children the "opportunity of a sound basic education," defined as "the basic literacy, calculating, and verbal skills necessary to enable children to eventually function productively as civic participants capable of voting and serving on a jury" (*CFE I*, 86 N.Y.2d at 316, 631 N.Y.S.2d 565, 655 N.E.2d 661). The "failure to provide the opportunity to obtain such fundamental skills as literacy and the ability to add, subtract and divide numbers" constitutes a violation of the constitutionally mandated "minimally adequate educational opportunity" (*id.* at 319, 631 N.Y.S.2d 565, 655 N.E.2d 661).

The Court of Appeals wrote that the exact meaning of a "sound basic education" could only be "evaluated and resolved" after discovery and the development of a factual record (*id.* at 317, 631 N.Y.S.2d 565, 655 N.E.2d 661). In response, the IAS court interpreted the "skills necessary to enable children to eventually function productively as civic participants capable of voting and serving on a jury" (*CFE I*, 86 N.Y.2d at 316, 631 N.Y.S.2d 565, 655 N.E.2d 661) as requiring more than just enabling children to *qualify* for jury service and voting, since one need only be 18 years or older, a U.S. citizen residing in New York, and not incarcerated or on parole in order to vote, and one need only be 18 years or older, be able to understand English and not convicted of a felony in order to serve on a jury (187 Misc.2d 1, 13-14, 719 N.Y.S.2d 475).

Rather, the IAS court believed that an education must be provided which enables people to evaluate complex campaign issues, such as tax policy, global warming and charter reform, and to have the "verbal, reasoning, math, science, and socialization skills" necessary to determine questions of fact on such matters as DNA evidence, statistical analyses, and convoluted financial fraud (*id.* at 14, 719 N.Y.S.2d 475).

Contrary to the State's assertions, the IAS court did not rule that high school graduates must actually be experts in those various specialized fields, but only that they be able to understand such matters(by listening and reading), to communicate thoughts to fellow jurors, and to reach decisions. This is a reasonable formulation, since merely being able to find the jury assembly room or to pull a lever on a voting machine cannot be deemed "civic participation" (*CFE I*, 86 N.Y.2d at 316, 631 N.Y.S.2d 565, 655 N.E.2d 661) or the "skills, knowledge, understanding and attitudes necessary to participate in democratic self-government" (*id.* at 319, 631 N.Y.S.2d 565, 655 N.E.2d 661).

The Court of Appeals had referred to the need for educating children to "function productively as civic participants" (*id.* at 318, 631 N.Y.S.2d 565, 655 N.E.2d 661). The IAS court interpreted "function productively" as meaning to engage in "competitive employment," which the IAS court defined as something more than "low-level jobs paying the minimum wage" but not what would constitute preparation for acceptance into "elite four-year" (187 Misc.2d at 14-18, 719 N.Y.S.2d 475). The term "function productively" does imply employment. It cannot be said, however, that a person who is engaged in a "low-level service job" is not a valuable, productive member of society. In reaching the contrary conclusion, the IAS court was influenced by its opinion that such jobs "frequently do not pay a living wage" (*id.* at 16, 719 N.Y.S.2d 475).

Aside from the fact that that observation is unsupported by any statistics, the IAS court, by substituting the concept of "competitive employment" for "productive functioning," expanded the already complex scope of the instant case to include such issues as minimum wage, housing costs and the capitalist system in general.

Moreover, the IAS court acknowledged that the greatest expansion in the local labor market would largely consist of low-level service jobs, with which assessment plaintiffs' expert, Henry Levin, agreed. Thus, the IAS court went too far in stating that a sound basic education must prepare students for employment somewhere between low-level service jobs and the most lucrative careers. Rather, the ability to "function productively" should be interpreted as the ability to get a job, and support oneself, and thereby not be a charge on the public.

Society needs workers in all levels of jobs, the majority of which may very well be low level. The IAS court's aspirational standards, therefore, are inconsistent with the Court of Appeals' declaration that the Constitution only requires the " *opportunity* " for a "sound *basic* education" or a " *minimally adequate.* education" (86 N.Y.2d at 316-317, 631 N.Y.S.2d 565, 655 N.E.2d 661 [emphasis added]).

Thus, a "sound basic education" should consist of the skills necessary to obtain employment, and to competently discharge one's civic responsibilities. The State submitted evidence that jury charges are generally at a grade level of 8.3, and newspaper articles on campaign and ballot issues range from grade level 6.5 to 11.7 (based more on the publisher than on the issues reported). Plaintiffs' expert disagreed, but did not quantify the level needed.

Thus, the evidence at trial established that the skills required to enable a person to obtain employment, vote, and serve on a jury, are imparted between grades 8 and 9, a level of skills which plaintiffs do not dispute is being provided. The IAS court rejected this evidence solely on the ground that the State Constitution should require something more than a ninth-grade education (187 Misc.2d at 14, 719 N.Y.S.2d 475).

Nevertheless, the IAS court failed to posit an alternative level of skills; nor does the dissent enunciate a level other than something more than eighth-grade reading and sixth-grade arithmetic. The absence of a clearly articulated level helps explain why neither the IAS court nor the dissent is able to determine what programs or what amounts of funding are needed, and why they can only say that more money will lead to a better educational system.

However, that is not the constitutional standard, and a statement that the current system is inadequate and that more money is better is nothing more than an invitation for limitless litigation. Moreover, as long as the State has "provide[d] children with the opportunity to obtain the [ ] essential skills, the State will have satisfied its constitutional obligation" to furnish a minimally adequate education (CFE I, 86 N.Y.2d at 316, 631 N.Y.S.2d 565, 655 N.E.2d 661), even though a higher level of education is extremely desirable.

There was no evidence that students are unable to perform basic mathematical calculations, and allowing that some amount of history and civics, and science and technology, are components of a sound basic education, there was no evidence concerning what that amount should be or what amount is actually being provided.

Accordingly, plaintiffs have failed to establish that the New York City public school children are not receiving the opportunity for a sound basic education. That is not to say that the State should not strive for higher goals; indeed, as the IAS court recognized, the new Regents Learning Standards, adopted in 1996, exceed any notions of a basic education (187 Misc.2d at 12, 719 N.Y.S.2d 475).

It bears contemplation that the State's obligation is to provide children with the *opportunity* to obtain the fundamental skills comprising a sound basic education. That not all students actually achieve that level of education does not necessarily indicate a failure of the State to meet its constitutional obligations.

The opportunity to obtain the fundamental skills is established by the provision of: (1) "minimally adequate physical facilities and classrooms which provide enough light, space, heat, and air to permit children to learn"; (2) "minimally adequate instrumentalities of learning such as desks, chairs, pencils, and reasonably current textbooks"; and (3) "minimally adequate teaching of reasonably up-to-date basic curricula such as reading, writing, mathematics, science, and social studies, by sufficient personnel adequately trained to teach those subject areas" (CFE I, 86 N.Y.2d at 317, 631 N.Y.S.2d 565, 655 N.E.2d 661). The IAS court adopted that outline, and advanced seven categories of resources, which essentially fall within the three areas set forth by the Court of Appeals: (1) sufficient numbers of qualified teachers, principals and other personnel; (2) appropriate class sizes; (3) adequate and accessible school buildings with sufficient space to ensure appropriate class size and implementation of a sound curriculum; (4) sufficient and up-to-date books, supplies, libraries, educational technology and laboratories; (5) suitable curricula, including an expanded platform of programs to help at-risk students by giving them "more time on task"; (6) adequate resources for students with extraordinary needs; and (7) a safe orderly environment (187 Misc.2d at 114-115, 719 N.Y.S.2d 475).

Minimally Adequate Facilities

At trial, various superintendents gave anecdotal evidence concerning the condition of certain schools with leaky roofs, deficient heating, and other problems. Plaintiffs stressed that the State Legislature enacted the New York City School Construction Authority Act (Public Authorities Law § 1725, *et seq.*) in 1988 to create an agency exempt from local laws and regulations to repair, modernize and expand the City's schools, after a finding that "the elementary and secondary schools of the City of New York are in deplorable physical condition" in that "[m]any of the schools are overcrowded, unsafe, unhealthy and unusable."

Such conditions, it was said, had been brought about largely due to "inefficient bureaucratic practices and lengthy review and approval processes" of BOE (L.1988 c. 738 § 1). However, Lewis Spence, the Deputy Chancellor of Operations for the City schools, and Patricia Zedalis, the Chief Executive of the Division of School Facilities, testified at trial that all immediately hazardous conditions had been eliminated, and all buildings had been made watertight at least by interim repairs

The evidence at trial indicated that progress is being made in other areas. For example, 343 schools were heated by inefficient coal-burning boilers in 1995, whereas only 125 still had such boilers by 1999. Although there was evidence that some schools have no science laboratories, music rooms or gymnasia, there was no proof that these conditions are so pervasive as to constitute a system-wide failure, much less one that was caused by the school financing system, or one that can be cured only by a reformation of that system.

This point was effectively conceded by the IAS court in its observation that plaintiffs failed to even try to measure the empirical effect of school facilities on student performance and that "the magnitude of [the perceived negative] effect is unclear from the evidence at trial" (187 Misc.2d at 47-49, 719 N.Y.S.2d 475).

BOE records indicate that in 1997 there was an overload of 35,800 students in the City high schools and 28,000 in 11 elementary school districts, though it is unclear what the overall utilization rate would be if the remaining 21 districts were considered. While enrollment is projected to increase until 2004, it is also projected to drop by about 66,000 students by 2008. Overcrowding, which can be addressed through new construction, can also be dealt with by less expensive means, such as transferring students between schools, extending the school day or providing year-round education.

Plaintiffs' complaint that busing will move students outside their neighborhoods is at odds with their allegation of racial segregation, and the long history of busing to address this condition. Contrary to plaintiffs' further assertion, the State does not prohibit year-round education.

The evidence established that class sizes average between 23.8 to 28.72 students per class for kindergarten through grade 8. While plaintiffs' experts and witnesses testified that students perform better in a class of 20 or fewer pupils, there was no indication that students cannot learn in classes consisting of more than 20 students, and plaintiffs concede that the City's Catholic schools have larger classes yet outperform public schools.

Thus, the IAS court's implication that classes of over 20 students are unconstitutional is unsupported.

In sum, while no witness described the condition of the City schools' facilities as perfect, neither was there sufficient proof that the facilities are so inadequate as to deprive students of the opportunity to acquire the skills that constitute a sound basic education.

Minimally Adequate Instrumentalities of Learning

Plaintiffs concede that recent funding increases have relieved a textbook shortage, but nevertheless complain that there is no assurance that the recent spike in textbook funding will continue. They also wonder whether "the recent influx of dedicated technology funding will continue," and argue that 9.2 computers per 100 students (in 1997) is inherently inadequate, while 18.2 computers per 100 students (the ratio in the rest of the State) is sufficient. Thus, plaintiffs concede that recent funding has relieved the previous alleged inadequacies. Moreover, a mere comparison with the rest of the State reveals little about the constitutional mandate and, granting that some of the City's computers cannot run the most advanced systems or connect to the Internet, plaintiffs never explained why they cannot be used for introductory classes.

Thus, plaintiffs failed to establish that those instrumentalities of learning are inadequate, and as the IAS court observed, there was little except anecdotal evidence concerning the amount of supplies such as chalk, paper, desks, chairs, and laboratory supplies.

Contrary to the IAS court's findings, the twin facts that the average number of books per student in the City's schools lags behind that of the rest of the State, and that the State allocates only $4 per student for library materials, do not demonstrate that the City's libraries are inadequate. Furthermore, the IAS court's finding that the books are inadequate in quality appears to be predicated solely on certain superintendents' opinions that most of the books were "antiquated," in that they were "not current in terms of...the multicultural themes our children should be exposed to." However, we believe that such a yardstick is not determinative. Surely, a library that consists predominantly of classics should not be viewed as one that deprives students of the opportunity of a sound *basic* education.

Minimally Adequate Teaching

The IAS court ruled that, in general, the teachers in the City's public schools are not qualified, as determined by a comparison with the rest of the State's teachers on teacher certification status, scores on certification tests, experience, turnover rate, quality of the institutions the teachers themselves attended, and the percentage of teachers with a Master's Degree or higher.

Board of Education records indicate that from 1991 to 1999, the percentage of uncertified teachers in the City has ranged from 11.4% to 13%; in 1999, 12.8% of the 78,162 teachers were uncertified. Richard Mills, the Commissioner of Education, testified that there is a "clear pattern" that the lowest performing schools tend to have the highest proportion of uncertified teachers. Although the IAS court believed that certification standing alone is no guarantee of teacher quality, Thomas Sobol, Education Commissioner from 1987 to 1996, asserted that certification assures a minimal level of competence and ability to teach. He further maintained that although the quality of an uncertified teacher is uncertain, the lack of certification does not necessarily mean a teacher is incompetent. In any event, the Regents have required that all schools have only certified teachers by 2003.

As of the 1997-1998 academic year, 31.1% of City public school teachers had failed the basic certification test (the Liberal Arts and Sciences Test or LAST) at least once, and the mean score for first time takers was 236.3 (on a test where 220 is passing). Outside the City, 4.7% of public school teachers had failed it once and had a mean first time score of 261.6. There was a similar divergence on other tests: 21.1% of City teachers failed English Content at least once while 2.2% outside the City failed; 47.3% of City teachers failed the Math Test while 21.1% outside the City failed; 19.6% of City teachers failed the Social Studies Test while 5.9% outside the City failed; 37.0% of City teachers failed the Biology Test while 11.9% outside the City failed; and 24.1% of City teachers failed the Chemistry Test while 15.4% outside the City failed. Dr. Ronald Ferguson, plaintiffs' expert, stated that, based on his study conducted from 1986 to 1990 in Texas, students scored higher on State examinations in districts where teachers scored higher on State certification examinations, although he conceded that some other factors could possibly account for the student results.

In the 1997-1998 academic year, 14% percent of City public school teachers had two years' or less experience, compared with 9.7% in the rest of the State. Although various plaintiff witnesses testified that teachers with more than two years of experience are generally better, the median experience for City teachers is 13 years.

With respect to the academic credentials of City teachers: 16.0% have only a Bachelor's Degree, 40.4% have a Master's and 43.5% have a Master's Degree plus 30 credits or a Doctorate. For teachers in the rest of the State, the numbers are 10.9%, 64.1% and 25.0%, respectively. It was undisputed that the City's teaching force, in general, comes from less competitive undergraduate institutions than does that of the rest of the State.

The mere fact, however, that the City's teachers have lower qualifications than those in the rest of the State does not establish that the City's teachers are inadequate, as the IAS court reasoned. The IAS court gave insufficient weight to the evidence that from 1995 through 1998, only 523 teachers, or less than 1% of the 78,000 employed, received "unsatisfactory" ratings on annual performance reviews filled out by principals.

Although various superintendents asserted that "unsatisfactory" ratings are generally reserved for the "worst of the worst," and are rarely given to underperforming teachers because of the additional paperwork involved and the prospect of unknown replacements, nevertheless, there was no testimony from principals, the ones who actually fill out the forms.

We find that reviews of teaching ability, completed by principals in daily contact with teachers, are more indicative of a teacher's ability to instruct than is a teacher's curriculum vitae, or a superintendent's supposition that deficiencies are unreported due to sloth or fear.

Although certain superintendents and Education Department employees testified that professional development to help train teachers is lacking, they did not specifically state why the $3,000 per teacher spent on professional development is insufficient.

In support of its finding that the State has failed to provide a sound basic education or minimally adequate facilities, teachers, and supplies, the IAS court cited various "outputs" or results.

For example, from 1986 to 1996, about 30% of City students failed to obtain any diploma, 10% received GED diplomas, 48% obtained "Local Diplomas," and 12% achieved "Regents Diplomas." In order to obtain a "Local Diploma," a student must pass all required courses and a series of Regents Competency Tests ("RCT's") which test students at an eighth-to-ninth-grade reading level and a sixth-to-eighth-grade math level; students are also tested in United States history and government, science, and global studies.

In order to obtain a "Regents Diploma," a student must pass a series of Regents Exams based on "Regents Learning Standards" ("RLS's"), which test at a tenth-to-eleventh-grade reading level. Prior to 1996, students had a choice of whether to take the RCT's or the Regents Exams, but the Board of Regents is phasing out the RCT's and plans to eliminate them completely by 2005. While plaintiffs' expert, Dr. Richard Jaeger, testified that the RCT's do not test at a level sufficient to demonstrate the skills needed to understand jury charges or ballot propositions, the State's expert, Dr. Herbert Walberg, disagreed. Plaintiffs concede that students who have passed the RCT's may have been capable of passing the Regents Exams, which, plaintiffs agree, demonstrates that a student has obtained a sound basic education.

The IAS court attacked the RCT's on the ground that a CUNY task force determined that most graduates of City high schools need remediation in one or more basic skills. However, a "sound basic education" consists only of those skills necessary to enable children to "eventually function productively as civic participants capable of voting and serving on a jury," not to qualify them for advanced college courses or even attendance at a higher educational institution.

Furthermore, by effectively adopting the RLS standards as the measure of a sound basic education, the IAS court disregarded the Court of Appeals' exhortation to use performance levels on standardized examinations "cautiously" (*id.* at 317, 631 N.Y.S.2d 565, 655 N.E.2d 661). In any event, the RCT's will be completely phased out by 2005, and thus any deficiency in their usage will be eliminated.

Although plaintiffs would most likely disagree with the characterization, their position is essentially a form of *res ipsa loquitur:* the fact that 30% of City students drop out and an additional 10% obtain only a GED must mean that the City schools fail to offer the opportunity of a sound basic education, which is ultimately the State's responsibility (pursuant to the Education Article), and therefore the State's funding mechanism must be the cause of the problem. However, the proper standard is that the State must offer all children the *opportunity* of a sound basic education, not *ensure* that they actually receive it.

Thus, the mere fact that some students do not achieve a sound basic education does not necessarily mean that the State has defaulted on its obligation. Notably, the standard is a "sound basic education," not graduation from high school; nor can the State be faulted if students do not avail themselves of the opportunities presented.

Although there was evidence that the failure to obtain a high school diploma (and to some extent possession of only a GED) limits one's ability to obtain high-paying jobs, there was no evidence that such a person is *ipso facto* an unproductive citizen incapable of intelligently voting or serving on a jury. In short, there was no evidence quantifying how many drop-outs fail to obtain a sound basic education, let alone were denied the opportunity to get one.

In fact, for 1997-1998, 90% of the City's 11th graders achieved graduation competency status in English and mathematics by passing either the RCT's or the Regents examinations in those fields. It is unclear how many students dropped out of school (never to return) before that point or why a large number of them did not obtain a degree (i.e., whether for failing an examination in another discipline such as global studies or failing to obtain sufficient credits in some other course of study).

The IAS court also failed to give proper weight to nationally normed reading and math tests, which are used by more than one-third of school districts across the United States. Indeed, from 1996 to 1999, for grades three through eight, it was demonstrated that City public school children scored at or close to the national average. The IAS court dismissed that statistic as insignificant, since it merely compares City students to students elsewhere in the nation, notwithstanding the court's reliance on comparisons between City students and pupils from the rest of the State to demonstrate inadequacy.

However, we do not confine our analysis only to comparisons between students from the City and the rest of the State. Instead, we look at the nation as a whole, to the extent that such comparisons are indicative of the provision of the opportunity for a sound basic education.

To the extent that the State relies on Performance Assessments in Schools System wide ("PASS") reviews to demonstrate that schools are "close to being exemplary," they were properly rejected by the IAS court, since they are generally used as self-assessment reports by schools having a natural interest in rating themselves highly.

Even if we were to assume that the schools in the City do not provide a sound basic education, plaintiffs failed to prove that deficiencies in the City's school system are caused by the State's funding system. The IAS court conceded as much by relying on a standard that "[i]f it can be shown that increased funding can provide New York City with better teachers, better school buildings, and better instrumentalities of learning, then it would appear that a causal link has been established between the current funding system and the poor performance of the City's public schools" (187 Misc.2d at 68, 719 N.Y.S.2d 475). However, the constitutional question is not whether more money can improve the schools, but whether the current funding mechanism deprives students of the opportunity to obtain a sound basic education.

Both parties agree that the City students' lower test results in comparison with the rest of the State are largely the result of demographic factors, such as poverty, high crime neighborhoods, single parent or dysfunctional homes, homes where English is not spoken, or homes where parents offer little help with homework and motivation. Although there was evidence that certain "time on task" programs, such as specialized reading courses, tutoring and summer school, could help such "at-risk" students, nevertheless, plaintiffs' own expert, Dr. David Grissmer, conceded that investing money "in the family" rather than the schools "might pay off even more." That is not to say that this circumstance lessens the State's burden to educate such students. But it is indicative of the fact that more spending on education is not necessarily the answer, and suggests that the cure lies in eliminating the socio-economic conditions facing certain students.

There was also significant evidence that sizeable savings could be reaped through more efficient allocation of resources by BOE, which would then make available large sums of money for programs which are purportedly underfunded, such as "time on task" programs. For example, the IAS court recognized that merely placing disabled students in the least restrictive environment possible (a position *Amici* Association for the Help of Retarded Children and similar entities support, and which conforms with Federal requirements [20 USC § 1412; 34 CFR 300.550]), would yield a savings of somewhere between $105 million and $335 million. The court also acknowledged that "tens of thousands" of the 135,000 students in special education have been improperly placed there, and indeed that over 80% of students classified as learning disabled do not meet that standard. Since BOE expends $2.5 billion annually, or over 25% of its budget, on special education, the savings created by returning improperly referred students to the general school population (where the cost is 50% to 75% less per student than special education) would amount to hundreds of millions of dollars, if not one billion dollars, even after accounting for the cost of redirecting students to the general population.

The IAS court failed to consider this fact or otherwise dismissed it as "equivocal" in any amount above "tens of millions of dollars." Similarly, the dissent opines that any savings are merely "wishful thinking." In the absence of any proof to support such suppositions, however, the IAS court and the dissent are effectively applying a presumption of unconstitutionality to the Legislature's funding laws, the reverse of the standard that must be applied (*see, Hymowitz v. Eli Lilly and Co., 73 N.Y.2d 487, 515, 541 N.Y.S.2d 941, 539 N.E.2d 1069, cert. denied sub. nom. Rexall Drug Co. v. Tigue 493 U.S. 944, 110 S.Ct. 350, 107 L.Ed.2d 338*).

Indeed, it is plaintiffs' burden to demonstrate that the current funding scheme is unconstitutional and that the only way to allocate sufficient resources to the programs they desire is to annul the entire funding mechanism. Plaintiffs have failed to demonstrate that the proper placement of students will not generate the savings mentioned herein, and as amply supported at trial, or that such amounts will not be able to finance the "time on task" programs they deem necessary.

To support their case, plaintiffs rely to a great extent on the fact that less money is expended per student in the City than the rest of the State. Not only is this an impermissible equality, rather than adequacy, claim, foreclosed by *Levittown, supra*, but plaintiffs then inconsistently argue that it is meaningless to consider that the City is among the highest spenders compared to the rest of the country or other large urban school districts. Plaintiffs' claim that it costs more to educate students in New York City than elsewhere in the State is based, to a large extent, on a cost of living index which factors in salaries of non-educators, and is thus irrelevant to the cost of educating a student.

Notably, the dissent agrees that students who are not "at risk" are receiving a sound basic education, but argues that "at-risk" students are being deprived of the opportunity. The dissent then goes on to categorize almost the entire City student population as "at risk." This implicates the system of education, not the system of funding. If all "at-risk" students need "time on task" programs, and almost all students are "at risk," then the pedagogic system should be geared towards such students. That is to say, more classes should utilize "time on task" or other effective methods. As noted *supra*, significant numbers of students have been improperly placed in restrictive settings or special education classes where they do not belong, and where they are not receiving the education they need. Once again, this is a problem of the educational system, not the funding system. In fact, proper placement will yield large amounts of money which can be reinvested into "time on task" programs.

The dissent's primary complaint with the adequacy of the teaching staff, that the neediest students are assigned the least qualified teachers, is an argument which does not involve the funding system. As the dissent admits, the assignment of experienced, i.e., senior, teachers is the product of collective bargaining agreements, not the manner in which the State funds the City's schools.

Although the State cites instances of fraud and/or waste in construction, such work is now mostly controlled by the State School Construction Authority, rather than BOE, and thus the State bears responsibility, though it does not necessarily implicate the State's funding mechanism. We also reject the State's contentions that: (1) any inadequacy in funding is the fault of the City, which has reduced its percentage of overall educational funding over the last few years, and that (2) it would be unfair to essentially allow the City to dictate how much the State spends. Joint funding of education by the State and the localities has been acknowledged to be reasonably related to the legitimate State interest in preserving and promoting local control over education (*Levittown*, 57 N.Y.2d at 44, 453 N.Y.S.2d 643, 439 N.E.2d 359).

However, the State must "assure" that some essentials are provided, and thus it is indeed ultimately responsible for providing students with the opportunity for a sound basic education (*see, CFE I, 86 N.Y.2d at 316-317, 631 N.Y.S.2d 565, 655 N.E.2d 661)*. Moreover, the State exerts extensive control over the City, including taxes that may be levied and debts that may be incurred. Nevertheless, requiring the State to write out a check every time the City underfunds education is not the only possible means of redress; rather, the State could require the City to maintain a certain level of education funding.

In fact, Education Law § 2576 (5), the "Stavisky Goodman Law," requires the City to spend at least the average of the prior three years' expenditure on education. While plaintiffs and the IAS court complain that the law has not been enforced, the remedy is to seek compliance with that statute, rather than to annul the entire State funding system.

The IAS court also found that the State's funding system has a disparate impact on minority students, in contravention of the Title VI implementing regulations, promulgated by the U.S. Department of Education ("DOE"). Section 601 of Title VI, codified at 42 USC § 2000d, provides:

No person...shall, on the ground of race, color, or national origin, be excluded from preparation in, be denied the benefits of, or be subjected to discrimination under any program or activity receiving Federal financial assistance.

Section 602 of Title VI, codified at 42 USC § 2000d-1, authorizes Federal agencies to "effectuate the provisions of section [2000d of this title]...by issuing rules, regulations, or orders of general applicability." Pursuant to that authority, DOE has promulgated a regulation prohibiting a recipient of Federal financial assistance from "utilizing criteria or methods of administration which have the effect of subjecting individuals to discrimination because of their race, color, or national origin" (34 CFR 100.3 [b][2]).

As noted *supra*, Title VI itself only prohibits intentional discrimination (of which there is no allegation in the instant case), and plaintiffs concede that, under the recent U.S. Supreme Court decision in *Alexander v. Sandoval*, 532 U.S. 275, 121 S.Ct. 1511, 149 L.Ed.2d 517 there is no private right of action under the implementing regulations, since the empowering statute reveals no Congressional intent to create one. Nevertheless, plaintiffs argue that they may still enforce the regulations through 42 USC § 1983, which provides a cause of action for "the deprivation of any rights, privileges, or immunities secured by the Constitution and laws" by anyone acting "under color of any statute, ordinance, regulation, custom, or usage, of any State." As the dissent by Justice Stevens in *Sandoval* made clear, the plaintiffs in that case did not allege a § 1983 claim.

The cases determining whether a Federal "law" gives rise to a § 1983 claim have generally interpreted that term as applying to "statutes" (see, e.g., *Maine v. Thiboutot, 448 U.S. 1, 100 S.Ct. 2502, 65 L.Ed.2d 555; Blessing v. Freestone,* 520 U.S. 329, 117 S.Ct. 1353, 137 L.Ed.2d 569), and the contrast between the language "Constitution and laws" and "statute, ordinance, regulation, custom, or usage" in § 1983 demonstrates that Congress distinguished between statutes and regulations, and that regulations, standing alone, are not "laws" within the meaning of § 1983 (see, *Mungiovi v. Chicago Housing Auth., 98 F.3d 982, 984 [7th Cir.]).*

In *Chrysler Corp. v. Brown,* 441 U.S. 281, 301-303, 99 S.Ct. 1705, 60 L.Ed.2d 208, decided in the context of the Trade Secrets Act (18 USC § 1905), which prohibits the disclosure of information "not authorized by law," and not 42 USC § 1983, the Court did state that a regulation may have the "force and effect of law" if: (1) it is substantive (a legislative-type rule that affects individual rights and obligations, rather than interpretive, a general statement of policy or a procedural agency rule); (2) it is promulgated by an agency pursuant to a Congressional grant of quasi-legislative authority; and (3) the promulgation of the regulation conforms with any procedural requirements imposed by Congress. Although the Supreme Court in *Wright v. City of Roanoke Redevelopment and Hous. Auth.*, 479 U.S. 418, 107 S.Ct. 766, 93 L.Ed.2d 781 approvingly cited *Chrysler Corp*, at 431-432, 99 S.Ct. 1705, it found a viable § 1983 claim based on a *combination* of a statute (the Brooke Amendment to the Housing Act of 1937, 42 USC § 1437a, which imposed a ceiling for "rents" in public housing projects) *and* the implementing regulations thereunder of the Department of Housing and Urban Development (which defined "rent" as including a reasonable amount for utilities), which the Court later made clear in *Suter v. Artist M.*, 503 U.S. 347, 361 n. 13, 112 S.Ct. 1360, 118 L.Ed.2d 1.

Thus, *Wright, supra,* did not hold that a regulation, standing alone, is a "law" enforceable via § 1983. In other words, "so long as the statute itself confers a specific right upon the plaintiff, and a valid regulation merely further defines or fleshes out the content of that right, then the statute-'in conjunction with the regulation'-may create a Federal right as further defined by the regulation" (*Harris v. James*, 127 F.3d 993, 1009 [11th Cir.] [citing *Suter*, 503 U.S. at 361 n. 13, 112 S.Ct. at 1369 n. 13]; *see also, Mungiovi, 98 F.3d at 984* [7th Cir.]; *Smith v. Kirk*, 821 F.2d 980, 984 [4th Cir.] ["[a]n administrative regulation...cannot create an enforceable § 1983 interest not already implicit in the enforcing statute"]). As the Eleventh Circuit noted in *Harris,* the touchstone of the Supreme Court's decision in *Wright, supra,* was the Congressional intent to create a particular Federal right (*Harris,* 127 F.3d at 1007-1008).

The DOE implementing regulations at issue in the instant case fail under that analysis, since the regulations do not flesh out the content of a statutory right, but rather contradict the statute. Although the Court in *Sandoval* assumed, without deciding, that the regulations "may validly proscribe activities that have a disparate impact on racial groups, even though such activities are permissible under § 601" and noted that five justices (in three separate opinions) voiced that view in *Guardians Assn. v. Civil Serv. Com'n of New York City,* 463 U.S. 582, 103 S.Ct. 3221, 77 L.Ed.2d 866, as did dictum in *Alexander v. Choate,* 469 U.S. 287, 294 n. 11, 105 S.Ct. 712, 83 L.Ed.2d 661, such statements were "in considerable tension" with the Court's holding in other cases that 42 USC § 601 forbids only intentional discrimination (*Sandoval,* 532 U.S. at 281-282, 121 S.Ct. 1511). To the extent that the dissent in *Sandoval* posited that merely referencing § 1983 enables litigants to enforce Title VI enabling regulations (*id.* at 300, 121 S.Ct. 1511, Stevens, J., dissenting), the majority cautioned that the silence of a majority on an issue raised in a concurring or dissenting opinion does not imply agreement (*id.* at 285 n. 5, 121 S.Ct. 1511).

The Circuits which have determined that regulations alone can support a § 1983 claim either assume so without any analysis or rely on an interpretation of *Wright,* which for the reasons discussed *supra,* should be rejected (*Loschiavo v. City of Dearborn,* 33 F.3d 548, 551 [6th Cir.], *cert. denied* 513 U.S. 1150, 115 S.Ct. 1099, 130 L.Ed.2d 1067), or they have stated it in dictum (*DeVargas v. Mason & Hanger-Silas Mason Co., Inc.,* 844 F.2d 714, 724 n. 19 [10th Cir.]).

Other Circuits, while expressing the same broad principle, have actually decided cases based on a regulation in conjunction with the authorizing statute (*Buckley v. City of Redding*, 66 F.3d 188 [9th Cir.]; *Samuels v. District of Columbia*, 770 F.2d 184 [D.C.Cir.]). The Second Circuit has declined to address whether a regulation, standing alone, is sufficient to create a Federal right upon which a § 1983 claim can be based (*King v. Town of Hempstead*, 161 F.3d 112, 115 [2d Cir.]; *Rodriguez v. City of New York*, 197 F.3d 611, 617 [2d Cir.], *cert. denied* 531 U.S. 864, 121 S.Ct. 156, 148 L.Ed.2d 104), and the District Courts within the Second Circuit are split on the issue (*see, DaJour v. City of New York, 2001 WL 830674 at n. 7, 2001 U.S. Dist Lexis 10251 at n. 7 [S.D.N.Y.]* [and cases cited therein]).

The only Court to decide the specific issue as applied to Title VI implementing regulations after *Sandoval* has determined that there is no cause of action under section 1983 for a violation of the Title VI implementing regulations, since they do not merely define a right Congress already conferred by statute, but rather "give the statute a scope beyond that Congress contemplated" (*South Camden Citizens in Action v. New Jersey Dept. of Envtl. Protection*, 274 F.3d 771, [3d Cir.]).

We agree that DOE's implementing regulations do not merely "flesh out" a Federal right created by Congress in Title VI, but rather, create a new right, not indicated in the statute. Section 602 of Title VI, codified at 42 USC § 2000d-1, only authorizes Federal agencies to "effectuate the provisions of section [2000d of this title]…by issuing rules, regulations, or orders of general applicability," not to create new rights, and accordingly, the implementing regulations, standing alone, do not create a Federal "right" upon which a claim can be brought under § 1983 (*see, Sandoval, 532 U.S. at 286-291, 121 S.Ct. 1511).*

Accordingly, the order and judgment (one paper) of the Supreme Court, New York County (Leland DeGrasse, J.), entered January 31, 2001, which, following a non-jury trial, declared that the State's method of funding education violates the Education Article of the State Constitution and the United States Department of Education's ("DOE") implementing regulations under Title VI of the Civil Rights Act of 1964, and directed the State to implement various "reforms of school financing and governance," should be reversed, on the law and the facts, without costs, a declaration made in favor of the State of New York that the State's educational funding system does not contravene the constitutional Education Article, and the claim under the DOE implementing regulations and 42 USC § 1983 dismissed.

Order and judgment (one paper), Supreme Court, New York County (Leland DeGrasse, J.), entered January 31, 2001, reversed, on the law and the facts, without costs, a declaration made in favor of the State of New York that the State's educational funding system does not contravene the constitutional Education Article, and the claim under the Department of Education implementing regulations and 42 USC § 1983 dismissed. Motions seeking leave to file *amicus curiae* briefs granted.

All concur except TOM, J.P. who concurs in an Opinion and SAXE, J. who dissents in part in an Opinion.

TOM, J.P. (concurring).

I agree with the majority's conclusion that the State's method of funding education does not violate the Education Article of the New York State Constitution and the United States Department of Education's implementing regulations under Title VI of the Civil Rights Act of 1964. Moreover, many of the points raised by plaintiffs and the *amici* parties, and articulated by the decision of the IAS court, are issues that relate to how the New York City school system is administered.

The administration of the system appears to be a substantial contributing factor in the failings of our public school system. On this basis, I also disagree with Justice Saxe's dissent, though he makes a persuasive argument on behalf of "at-risk" students. However, a constitutional challenge to the funding of the school system must view the system as an entirety rather than parse its parts, and especially not be fixed only on particular programs. For constitutional purposes, once we as judges start micro-managing how a school system as vast and complicated as this one is to be administered, and how funding is to be distributed to ensure that portions of the student body are better served, we are really traversing a very problematic region that is quintessentially administrative and perhaps even political in nature.

We should do so only with the greatest circumspection. Our task is not to evaluate how this municipal school system is administered, but to determine whether the level of State funding is depriving students of an opportunity for a sound basic education. Plaintiffs have failed to carry their burden of proving that link.

However, one cannot dispute that a nascent educational crisis has been growing over the years, with roots decades deep, but with consequences that are taking on a new urgency. As the record reflects, approximately 30% of high school students drop out and fail to obtain a degree. Approximately 10% of high school students obtain only a general equivalency diploma (GED), for which the requirements are so low that GED recipients who attend college have only a 2% completion rate. Of the remaining 60% of students who do graduate, only about 12% apt to take the examinations qualifying for a "Regents diploma," while the remaining 48% apt for a "local diploma," which merely requires that students pass tests for reading comprehension at the ninth-grade level and math at the sixth-grade level.

The record further reflects that 80% of City public school graduates who enter the City University of New York require remedial help in basic areas such as reading and math, and 50% require remedial help in more than one area. As noted, however, plaintiffs have failed to prove a causal link between the State's funding mechanism and the deficiencies of City schools.

The growing crisis, such as it is, results from a matrix of administrative, demographic, and economic factors which, one may fairly judge from the appellate record, are not presently resolvable by increased State spending. That is a short-term expedient rather than a realistic long-term solution to numerous problems which are not necessarily related to each other, and some of which may even be intractable from the standpoint of State funding.

One may reasonably take from plaintiffs' as well as the State's positions the apt point that the very complexity of the system requires either that its many problems be directly and inno-vatively addressed, or, alternatively, that a complete overhaul be undertaken. I offer no opinion on this, but only observe that State funding, itself, is not a magic bullet. Mere budgetary fixes, extracted from the State rather than from the City or even by shifting resources within the sys-tem itself, are not going to achieve a system-wide functionality that has evaded prior budgetary infusions and half-hearted administrative reforms over the years. If the system contains serious flaws within the managerial level, one must worry whether an infusion of funding will only be absorbed into the system with minimal or no improvement in raising the educational achieve-ments of students. Moreover, one must seriously wonder how a system that seems historically mismanaged and chronically unaccountable financially-accepting for the moment some of the characterizations in the record-is going to become miraculously better managed and more financially accountable just because more attractive funding can be extracted from Albany. Such a quick-fix approach seems better described as a two-dimensional numbers game being played out in a multi-dimensional system.

These are administrative and logistical problems and, to some extent, demographic chal-lenges. One may even posit that at some fundamental level they are political issues, either in terms of necessary legislation, or in terms of greater State oversight, or deciding what should be the appropriate relationship between the system's administration and the Mayor, or the role, if any, to be played by local school boards, or even the obvious questions of how and why personnel have been hired over the years and who should be hired in the future and why a purportedly flawed administrative structure still remains.

Some of these matters, especially the role of the Mayor, are, in fact, being addressed now. Many of these issues are not presently justiciable, and others are not before us. We are review-ing only the constitutional issue and, as I stated, I concur with the majority's conclusion that plaintiffs have not demonstrated, on this record, a present constitutional violation.

However, this is not to say that if current trends continue, there are no future constitu-tional consequences. In this regard, I focus on the personnel of the school system who, in the final analysis, must be seen as the most important elements from a purely pedagogical stand-point-the teachers. Administrators may come and go. But it strikes me as being beyond serious dispute that the quality of the teachers will necessarily and directly affect the educational process and whether educational standards can be satisfied. Justice DeGrasse very appropriately made this point.

It should also be beyond dispute that the teaching quality necessary to provide an opportunity for an adequate education itself depends on the simultaneous presence of several discrete qualities: educational credentials, teaching experience, communicative skills, a nurturing temperament, and a pedagogical mission. The logic seems inescapable that the input of these factors necessarily affects the educational output: the students' level of knowledge and the intellectual rigor they will be able to bring to the decisions of everyday life. Again, the trial court's analysis seems to me to reflect very good common sense, and I especially share its concern for the number of uncertified teachers in the system though, as he notes, more rigorous certification requirements have been scheduled by the Regents, effective after 2002.

However, there remains the problem of ensuring that sufficient numbers of teachers actually certified will remain for the foreseeable future and that new teachers are willing to work in the New York City School system. If the system cannot attract or retain qualified educators, then students will not receive a sound, basic education, as that standard has been constitutionally applied.

Notwithstanding the many complexities being forced into the constitutional question before us, I would suggest that this correlation seems very simple: the system must attract and retain qualified teachers if it is to produce qualified students. I would further venture that teacher compensation, coupled with work environment, the predictability of advancement, job satisfaction, job location and all the other variables that are factored into employment decisions, play a role in where qualified educators choose to start and spend their careers.

Hence, at some level, how the school system is funded, and where the funding is distributed, and how teacher compensation is coupled with rigorous State standards, relates to the quality of the students' education. To the extent that the adequacy of the education made available by the New York City school system, in its many parts, is impaired by the system's inability to attract and retain qualified teachers, a constitutional issue, then, may be presented.

I accept for present purposes the State's data as to teachers' compensation, class size, spending-per-student ratios, and the like, and also accept that we may use national comparable as well as State comparable as units of measurement. However, on the question whether the system can attract and retain sufficient qualified teachers as to offer a sound basic education, the record demonstrates some disturbing trends.

The trial court points out that uncertified teachers will be removed from the system by 2003, and that the Board of Education has not been allowed to hire uncertified teachers since 1999. Considered in isolation, this would seem to be a beneficial goal in terms of anticipated pedagogical results. Yet, what if these gaps cannot be filled by qualified teachers-with qualifications evaluated by certification plus such other factors that enhance the effectiveness of the teaching? The trial court's decision sets forth statistics indicating that New York City teachers have had difficulties in getting certified. The system seems to have trouble attracting competitive numbers of potential teachers who can even meet the requirement of certification. The issue then becomes not whether the system can get the best of the best, an ideal goal that is not likely achievable in the immediate future, but whether there will be adequate qualified replacements as experienced teachers retire or, in many schools, transfer.

A healthy educational system, it seems, should be able to rely on competition among more than enough qualified candidates for teaching positions, so that a system that faces chronic shortages of such candidates would be, almost by definition, unhealthy. Undoubtedly, at some point, the functioning of an unhealthy system spirals downward as desirable personnel, facing increasing responsibilities but decreasing satisfaction, continue to leave in response to their work environment.

It does not take extraordinary imagination to conclude that such a system at some point cannot provide even a basic education. The issue then becomes not just certification of some teachers, per se, which, as noted, is being addressed administratively, but whether sufficient numbers of qualified teachers can even be attracted and retained to prop up the system as new classes of students enter and leave. This is not a problem that can be easily deferred as a solution is devised. Before long, the problem is not so much that some programs are being inadequately funded, or some schools are favored over others within the larger system, which, I think, is central to Justice Saxe's concern, but that the system as a whole totters. That, I think, would certainly get closer to the heart of the constitutional issue.

From here, the analysis then turns to why the school system may face such a deficiency in its core pedagogical mission. Again, Justice DeGrasse's decision, and the appellate record, fairly state the case that ideal teaching candidates have already been going elsewhere to pursue their careers, a trend that does not seem to be abating, and other qualified candidates seem to be joining that trend. Certainly, and as noted above, work environment and career opportunities, are weighed in such individual and perhaps even idiosyncratic decisions, but the sharp disparity in annual compensation (and, inevitably, in the consequences for pensions) may well be dispositive in a critical mass of cases.

Those teachers leaving the system for other educational employment and those considering entering the teaching profession, but elsewhere, are not necessarily relocating to other regions. They are looking to the New York City suburbs for employment, where, as the State's and BOE's own evidence indicates, they may receive 20% to 36% more in compensation while working in a generally more favorable school environment. Here, competition severely disfavors the New York City system.

I will not pretend to know the magic number that will reverse this trend, and I have no intention of suggesting results that are more appropriate to collective bargaining. The argument may even be made that compensation should be linked with increased productivity. Nor am I suggesting that the teacher's union is entitled to a windfall as a consequence of the present litigation. My concern is with the students, and not the teachers. Rather, it is the trend itself, and its impact on the basic soundness of the education being offered to New York City students, in the aggregate, that concerns me.

As Justice DeGrasse points out, a fact supported by the record, normal attrition between 2000 and 2004 will require the replacement of some 41,105 teachers. Anecdotally, though perhaps plausibly in view of retirement factors, one is given to understand that the number of experienced teachers leaving the system may well exceed this estimate over the next few years. These retirements, to the extent that they occur as is estimated, will be straining the teaching resources of the system during a period of time that the system is also shedding uncertified teachers. Yet, teachers who would be suitable replacement candidates seem to be looking not very far afield at suburban school districts and their better pay and working conditions.

Though we are deciding a constitutional challenge rather than merely stating educational preferences, I am still concerned with that apparent trend, and what it portends for the pedagogical integrity of the system. It may be an ironic result that as the State and BOE, commendably, move to enforce higher standards on teacher hiring and retention, the numbers of qualified teachers in the system may shrink proportionately, unless some missing variable provides a solution. Otherwise, an administrative crisis may well take on stronger constitutional overtones. That is where school funding and especially the State contribution will likely become a critical component of a renewed constitutional challenge. Hence, while I join the majority in its conclusions and part of its analysis, I would not yet close the door on plaintiff's claims that funding decisions at some level, specifically in the impact on hiring and retention of qualified teachers, may trigger a State constitutional violation.

SAXE, J. (dissenting in part).

The Education Article of the New York State Constitution (N.Y. Const., art. XI, § 1), mandates that every public school student be provided with the opportunity to obtain a sound basic education (see, *Campaign for Fiscal Equity v. State of New York*, 86 N.Y.2d 307, 315, 631 N.Y.S.2d 565, 655 N.E.2d 661, citing *Board of Educ., Levittown Union Free School Dist. v. Nyquist*, 57 N.Y.2d 27, 48, 453 N.Y.S.2d 643, 439 N.E.2d 359, *appeal dismissed* 459 U.S. 1138, 103 S.Ct. 775, 74 L.Ed.2d 986). The trial court, after hearing over 100 days of testimony from over 70 witnesses, essentially found that the New York City school system is not receiving sufficient funding to offer all of its students the required opportunity for a sound basic education. While I, like my colleagues, take issue with certain of the trial court's conclusions and directives, there was more than ample support for the central finding that the City's "at-risk" students, amounting to a large segment of its student population, are unable to obtain the education to which they are entitled. Further, evidence supports the trial court's conclusion that it is deficiencies in the programs, personnel, tools and instrumentalities of learning provided by the City schools that prevent these at-risk students from obtaining an education, and that these deficiencies are due to a lack of funds needed to provide the needed programs, personnel and training.

Of course, this Court has authority as broad as that of the trial court to review the evidence and make different findings of fact (see, *Northern Westchester Professional Park Assoc. v. Town of Bedford, 60 N.Y.2d 492, 499, 470 N.Y.S.2d 350, 458 N.E.2d 809*). However, the evidence here so strongly supported the trial court's fundamental conclusions with regard to the education being provided to "at-risk" students that the trial court can only be reversed by ignoring either much of the evidence or the actual circumstances of the City's student population.

The Relevance of the Needs of the City's "At-Risk" Students

New York City's 1.1 million public school students include a large percentage of children at serious risk of academic failure due to poverty and other socioeconomic and demographic factors. It was established that in past years, 73% of New York City students have been eligible for the Federal free lunch program offered to low-income students, over 40% have come from families receiving Aid to Families with Dependent Children, and that 84% of its students are from a racial minority group. Over 90% of the State's recent immigrants live in New York City, and over 80% of the State's students with limited proficiency in English live here as well.

Generally, the "at-risk" label has been applied where several factors affect a child's education: as the trial court recognized, poverty, race, ethnicity, and immigration status are not in themselves determinative of student achievement, but the life experiences that are correlated with those factors tend to create barriers to academic achievement. In addition, children from impoverished families may experience further hurdles if they attend a school filled with similarly disadvantaged children, schools with "concentrated poverty." Further, children from poor immigrant families may also experience problems with limited English language proficiency.

The State protests that these statistics have no applicability to this case, contending that deficiencies in student performance that are attributable to socioeconomic conditions extrinsic to the education system are not relevant to assessing whether schools are meeting constitutional standards.

It takes the position that once socioeconomic factors are factored out, spending has no significant impact on students obtaining an education. Stated another way, this argument limits the State's responsibility to that of providing whatever educational experience would be necessary for some theoretical student, without any socioeconomic disadvantages, to obtain the requisite education. In a related argument, the State suggests that the City's expenditure of an average of $9,500 per year per student must necessarily provide the required opportunity for a minimally adequate education.

I do not accept the State's position. First of all, the question of whether a minimally adequate education is being offered to New York City's public school students cannot be answered by considering whether it would be adequate if it were being provided to a theoretical student body consisting only of privileged children. In that case, the form and content of the education currently being offered generally in New York City might be deemed adequate, despite its many deficiencies. Indeed, there are currently many students in New York City public schools who are obtaining far better than a merely adequate education. However, many of these students are in the City's special academic programs, or are in schools in wealthier districts that receive additional funds from outside corporate and family sources, which districts are more likely to contain families whose members assist and provide support for their children's studies.

To properly weigh whether a minimally adequate education is being offered to New York City's public school students, the actual circumstances and needs of all the students must be considered. It is not enough that a portion of the City's students can obtain an adequate education, where it is demonstrated that another large segment of students is unable to do so, especially when this inability is caused by the school system's failure to provide the necessary programs, facilities and educational approaches due to a lack of sufficient funding.

Nor does the City's average expenditure of approximately $9,500 per student in and of itself establish that a "minimally adequate education" is being offered. As the trial court properly found, this figure is misleading. In fact, given the sums the City schools are required to spend for special education, and the disproportionate number of students receiving special education services, the real amount available to be spent for a non-special education student is far lower.

The City's average per-pupil spending is lower than the average of New York State school districts, and is even low in comparison to the amount spent per student by other large municipal school districts, including Newark, Boston and Buffalo. This disparity is attributable in part to the City's lower contribution, but it is also explained by the State's providing less aid to New York City than it does to many districts with similar needs, even those with substantially smaller proportions of at-risk students. Indeed, the State's "wealth equalization" approach to school funding, by which less affluent districts receive greater funding, actually serves to *decrease*

New York City's share of the State's education funding, despite the City's extremely high concentration of students requiring extra assistance.

None of this is to say that the State is answerable where students decline to take the opportunity to learn. The mere fact that many students have failed to obtain even a minimally adequate education does not alone demonstrate that the City schools failed to offer these students the opportunity to obtain an education; in and of itself, it could simply mean that all those students failed to take advantage of that opportunity.

Nevertheless, plaintiffs' point is that the failure of the New York City school system is not solely attributable to unwilling or uninterested students; they have demonstrated that a large portion of the student population of New York City has been *unable* to obtain an adequate education because of shortcomings in what is offered and how it is offered, due in large part to a lack of funds necessary to successfully provide those New York City students with that which they need in order to obtain a sound basic education.

Once it is recognized that the needs of actual students must be considered in determining whether the requisite education is being offered, the question becomes whether the evidence warrants the conclusion that (1) a substantial segment of the students of the New York City public schools has been unable to obtain a sound basic education, and (2) these students would be able to successfully obtain the education to which they are entitled if the State ensured that the City was able to spend sufficient funds.

What Constitutes a Sound Basic Education

The State argues that despite the poor test results touted by plaintiffs, a sound basic education is being made available since the level of education required by the Education Article amounts to the ability to read and perform arithmetic calculations.

While the Court of Appeals insisted that it did not intend a full definition of what constitutes a sound basic education, it explained the concept generally as consisting of "the basic literacy, calculating, and verbal skills necessary to enable children to eventually function productively as civic participants capable of voting and serving on a jury" (*see, Campaign for Fiscal Equity, 86 N.Y.2d 307, 316, 631 N.Y.S.2d 565, 655 N.E.2d 661, supra*).

It went on to explain that the concept requires "minimally adequate teaching of reasonably up-to-date basic curricula such as reading, writing, mathematics, science, and social studies, by sufficient personnel adequately trained to teach those subject areas" (*id.* at 317, 631 N.Y.S.2d 565, 655 N.E.2d 661). Also required are "minimally adequate physical facilities and classrooms which provide enough light, space, heat, and air to permit children to learn," and "access to minimally adequate instrumentalities of learning such as desks, chairs, pencils and reasonably current textbooks" (*id.*).

The trial court heard and considered vast quantities of evidence and found, based upon that evidence, that while "the City's at-risk children are capable of seizing the opportunity for a sound basic education *if* they are given sufficient resources," the resources those at-risk children need in order to successfully obtain an education are currently not being provided. Specifically, these children need an "expanded platform" of programs that will allow them to spend "more time on task," including the availability of pre-kindergarten, so-called "extended time programs" such as after-school and summer programs, and literacy programs such as "Reading Recovery" and "Success for All." They also need competent teachers adequately trained to teach their subject areas, which, particularly in such difficult circumstances, means teachers who receive ongoing professional development to assist them with instructional strategies.

The conclusion that this large segment of the City's public school students is not, in fact, being given the opportunity to receive even a minimally adequate education, was well supported by the data offered at trial.

Year after year, an extraordinary percentage of New York City public school students demonstrate a lack of basic skills. For instance, large percentages were unable to achieve even the very low competency threshold set for the standardized reading and math tests required by the State for third and sixth graders until 1998, which low thresholds were designed to identify students in need of remedial assistance. Since 1998 the State Education Department has used more rigorous standardized tests keyed to the New York State Regents' new learning standards; on these tests, New York City public school students scored substantially worse than the rest of the State's students.

The State protests that the trial court applied too elevated a standard for defining the elements of a sound basic education. While I, like the majority, would reject the trial court's definition of "functioning productively as civic participants" to include the possession of such skills as are necessary to obtain employment paying a "living wage," there is no need to entirely reject the trial court's findings based upon that disagreement. The findings of fact, made upon overwhelming evidence, reflect an educational process that fails to offer far more than merely the skills to get a high-paying job; it fails to offer a large segment of its students the opportunity to obtain sufficient skills to "function productively as civic participants" in any sense of those words.

I do not accept the proposition that providing students with instruction by which they may achieve sixth-grade arithmetic skills and an eighth-grade reading level is sufficient to satisfy the constitutional requirement that the State provide children with the opportunity to obtain "the basic literacy, calculating, and verbal skills necessary to enable children to eventually function productively as civic participants capable of voting and serving on a jury" (*see, Campaign for Fiscal Equity v. State of New York, 86 N.Y.2d 307, 316, 631 N.Y.S.2d 565, 655 N.E.2d 661*).

Even defendants agree that the skeletal framework set out by the Court of Appeals requires not only competency at reading, writing, and mathematics, but essentials of reasoning and analysis as well. I also note that if the State's constitutional mandate under the Education Article is satisfied by providing students with low-level arithmetic and reading skills, then logically, it has no meaningful obligation to provide any high school education at all.

Accordingly, while I disagree with the trial court's suggestion that to be "minimally adequate" an education must prepare a student for more than a "low-level job[ ] paying the minimum wage" (187 Misc.2d 1, 15, 719 N.Y.S.2d 475), the facts established by plaintiffs demonstrate a failure to satisfy even the basic parameters set out by the Court of Appeals, which requires "the basic literacy, calculating, and verbal skills necessary to enable children to eventually function productively as civic participants capable of voting and serving on a jury" (*see, Campaign for Fiscal Equity v. State of New York, 86 N.Y.2d 307, 316, 631 N.Y.S.2d 565, 655 N.E.2d 661, supra*).

I disagree with the majority's suggestion that the evidence "implicates the system of education, not the system of funding." To assert that the problem is with the pedagogy, not the amount of funding, fails to acknowledge plaintiffs' showing that programs proven to succeed with at-risk students have repeatedly needed to be cut back or eliminated *because of a lack of sufficient funds to provide those programs in addition to the basic, "no frills" classroom education in crowded classrooms with large student-teacher ratios, insufficient professional development and poor supplies.*

The majority also interprets my views as suggesting that "almost the entire City student population is 'at risk,' " and reasons that if this is so, the obvious answer is to completely redirect the funding to the type of programs needed by at-risk students. Of course, this line of reasoning is disingenuous. The City school system has a wide variety of students, one large segment of which needs, and is not getting, a type of focused assistance that the school system has found to be too expensive to provide to all who need it.

Causation

I disagree with the majority's view that plaintiffs failed to prove a causal link between the State's inadequate funding of the New York City public schools and the inability of so many City public school students to obtain an education.

There was substantial evidence that at-risk students who have received the type of resources proposed by plaintiffs have made impressive academic progress. In New York City, 99% of the students who completed the Reading Recovery program were able to read at grade level by the end of the school year, even though they began the year significantly below grade level;

a comparison group of at-risk students who did not receive Reading Recovery support only achieved this level for 38% of the group.

Another illustration can be found in the so-called "Chancellor's District," created from the worst performing schools, the successes of which also demonstrate how providing extra funds can dramatically improve the education being obtained by the worst-performing students. The program has taken "discretionary" funds from other parts of the Chancellor's budget and given those schools extra supervision and extra resources, such as implementation of the "Success for All" literacy program. The result in the lower grades was that the students' reading scores climbed faster than in most other New York City schools.

The majority points out that plaintiff's expert "conceded" that investing money in the family rather than the schools "might pay off even more." This assertion, even if true, adds nothing to the analysis. It is the job of the schools to provide all students with the opportunity to obtain at least a basic education, and it is the responsibility of the State to provide enough funding for it to do so. It is irrelevant that other, and perhaps greater accomplishments could be achieved by investing the same funds to provide other kinds of support to those children's families.

The evidence demonstrates that the failure of the New York City public schools to provide a large portion of its students with an education is the direct result of insufficient resources. The lack of funds results not only in insufficient programs for the at-risk students who require extra programs in order to successfully learn, but additionally, *inter alia*, in insufficient numbers of qualified, properly certified teachers as well as insufficient support for teachers. For instance, as a direct result of lower teacher salaries than those offered in surrounding districts, as well as worse teaching conditions, New York City is unable to attract the necessary number of qualified, certified teachers.

Further, the neediest students, who require the most assistance from their teachers if they are to succeed at obtaining a basic education, are assigned the system's least qualified teachers, since the poorest, neediest students generally reside in the poorer, more dangerous neighborhoods, and, by collective bargaining, teachers with seniority are entitled to transfer into open positions in districts. These less qualified and less experienced teachers then in turn receive insufficient support and supervision, caused in part by the absence of funds in these districts to provide for ongoing professional development of the type most useful in assisting new teachers in succeeding with difficult students.

Chronic underfunding, although interspersed with some years of greater funding, has also led to deterioration of school buildings, overcrowding, inadequacy of textbooks, library materials, laboratory supplies and basic classroom supplies, and, in some schools, even an insufficient number of desks and chairs.

The majority concludes that it is not the State's underfunding, but rather, the Board of Education's misuse of funds, that is the cause of the City schools' inability to fund the necessary programs. This approach fails to recognize that re-directing the already allocated funds from one program to another would simply create other problems caused by underfunding to spring up elsewhere.

Notably, the majority does not accept the State's argument that the Board of Education is actually chargeable with waste or abuse of funds. Rather, it emphasizes the testimony that millions of dollars could be saved by reassignment into the general school population of students who were improperly assigned to special education programs.

There was evidence indicating that possibly tens of thousands of the 135,000 students in special education were improperly placed there, and that a majority of students classified as learning disabled do not meet the definition of that term. I agree with the proposition that students ought to be placed in the least restrictive educational environment.

However, we cannot assume that if these students were to be removed from their special education programs they would be reabsorbed within the general student population at no further additional expense to the Board of Education. This is not to suggest that there would be no savings at all if all students were properly placed in the least restrictive environment. It should be acknowledged, though, that whether or not the students at issue fall within the formal definition of "learning disabled" or "special education students," most of them were diagnosed and/or placed as they were precisely because the standard teaching approach, used for the general student population, was not successful with those students. Consequently, changing their placement would not necessarily result in the extent of savings the majority so optimistically suggests.

The trial court therefore appropriately concluded that although there would be substantial savings (between $105 million and $335 million) in the sums directly funneled to the special education program if all students were properly placed, it also correctly recognized that nevertheless, much of this amount would *not* then become available to be spent on the type of programs demonstrably needed here.

In sum, the evidence demonstrates that which the trial court found, namely, that New York City's large number of at-risk students are not receiving the "sound basic education" to which they are entitled, that in order for at-risk students to have the opportunity for academic success, they must be provided with sufficient resources and programs with which they currently are not being provided, and that this deficiency is caused by insufficient resources resulting from inadequate funding. No "presumption of unconstitutionality" is being applied here. Rather, the evidence amply supports the conclusion that the level of funding provided to the

New York City public school system is at a level so low as to violate the Education Article of the New York State Constitution.

Accordingly, I would affirm to the extent that the trial court found that defendants have violated the Education Article of the New York State Constitution by failing to provide a substantial portion of its students with the opportunity to obtain a sound basic education.

In view of this, I would affirm the provision of the judgment which directs the State to determine the actual cost of providing City public schools with the programs they need in order to be able to give all their students the opportunity to obtain an education. Such costs would include the extended platform of programs needed by at-risk children, and the type of teacher development programs that assist new and inexperienced teachers develop the skills they need to successfully educate their students.

The State must then ensure that those necessary funds are provided. To the extent the State believes it is the City's responsibility to provide additional funds, under the Education Article, the State has the responsibility to enact and enforce the legislation to bring that about.

However, those provisions of the judgment requiring defendants to alter the State wide funding mechanisms go beyond the relief sought. Laudable a goal as that may be, the purpose of this lawsuit was to ensure sufficient funding for the New York City public schools, and any other relief, no matter how beneficial, is uncalled for. Finally, I agree with the majority's rejection of plaintiff's claims under Title VI's implementing regulations.

END OF DOCUMENT

OPINION #6

Court of Appeals of New York

100 N.Y.2d 893

CAMPAIGN FOR FISCAL EQUITY, INC., et al., Appellants

v

STATE of New York et al., Respondents

June 26, 2003

Background: Students, parents, and organizations concerned with education issues brought action challenging state's funding of New York City's public schools. Following remand, 86 N.Y.2d 307, 631 N.Y.S.2d 565, 655 N.E.2d 661, the Supreme Court, New York County, Leland DeGrasse, J., 187 Misc.2d 1, 719 N.Y.S.2d 475, entered judgment in favor of plaintiffs, and State appealed. The Supreme Court, Appellate Division, 295 A.D.2d 1, 744 N.Y.S.2d 130, reversed, and plaintiffs appealed.

Holdings: The Court of Appeals, Kaye, Chief Judge, held that:

(1) lower, grade-specific level of skill was not proper measure of a sound basic education required under New York Constitution;

(2) plaintiffs established causation element of prima facie case that state funding system failed to provide a sound basic education to city's school children in violation of New York Constitution; and

(3) state would be required to initially determine the actual cost of providing a sound basic education in city and enact reforms accordingly.

Affirmed as modified and remitted.

Smith, J., filed concurring opinion.

Read, J., filed dissenting opinion.

OPINION OF THE COURT

KAYE, Chief Judge.

We begin with a unanimous recognition of the importance of education in our democracy. The fundamental value of education is embedded in the Education Article of the New York State Constitution by this simple sentence: "The legislature shall provide for the maintenance and support of a system of free common schools, wherein all the children of this state may be educated" (N.Y. Const., art. XI, § 1).

Plaintiffs claim that the State has violated this mandate by establishing an education financing system that fails to afford New York City's public schoolchildren the opportunity guaranteed by the Constitution. Plaintiffs additionally claim that the State's method of school funding in New York City violates their rights under United States Department of Education regulations pursuant to title VI of the Civil Rights Act of 1964 (42 USC § 2000d et seq.).

This case does not arrive before us on a blank slate. On June 15, 1995-precisely eight years ago-we denied the State's motion to dismiss plaintiffs' claims, thereby resolving three issues of law that now become the starting point for our decision (*Campaign for Fiscal Equity v. State of New York*, 86 N.Y.2d 307, 631 N.Y.S.2d 565, 655 N.E.2d 661 [1995] [*CFE*]).

First, echoing *Board of Educ., Levittown Union Free School Dist. v. Nyquist*, 57 N.Y.2d 27, 453 N.Y.S.2d 643, 439 N.E.2d 359 [1982] [*Levittown*], in *CFE* we recognized that by mandating a school system "wherein all the children of this state may be educated," the State has obligated itself constitutionally to ensure the availability of a "sound basic education" to all its children. (86 N.Y.2d at 314, 631 N.Y.S.2d 565, 655 N.E.2d 661.)

Second, we made clear that this Court is responsible for adjudicating the nature of that duty, and we provided a template, or outline, of what is encompassed within a sound basic education. And third, we concluded from the pleadings that plaintiffs had alleged facts that, if proved, would constitute a violation of the State's constitutional duty as well as the federal regulations.

The actual quality of the educational opportunity in New York City, the correlation between the State's funding system and any failure to fulfill the constitutional mandate, and any justification for claimed discriminatory practices involve fact questions. For that reason, we remitted the matter to the trial court for development of the record. Extensive discovery ensued. Trial commenced on October 12, 1999 and the last witness left the stand seven months later, on May 15, 2000.

Based on the testimony of 72 witnesses and on 4,300 exhibits, the trial court on January 9, 2001 determined that the State over many years had consistently violated the Education Article of the Constitution. In keeping with our directive, the trial court first fleshed out the template for a sound basic education that we had outlined in our earlier consideration of the issue. To determine whether the State actually satisfied that standard the court then reviewed the various necessary instructional "inputs" we had identified, and concluded that in most of these the New York City schools were deficient.

The trial court further held that the "outputs"-test results and graduation rates-likewise reflected systemic failure and that the State's actions were a substantial cause of the constitutional violation. Finally, the court found a violation of title VI, and directed defendants to put in place systemic reforms.

A divided Appellate Division reversed, on the law and facts. The majority rejected the trial court's definition of a sound basic education, as well as the bulk of Supreme Court's findings of fact concerning inputs, outputs and causation. Lastly-and on this point the panel was united-the Appellate Division concluded that plaintiffs' title VI claim failed in light of _Alexander v. Sandoval,_ 532 U.S. 275, 121 S.Ct. 1511, 149 L.Ed.2d 517 [2001], which postdated the trial court's decision. Plaintiffs appealed to us as of right on constitutional grounds.

Plaintiffs' appeal presents various questions of law, but one is paramount: whether the trial court correctly defined a sound basic education. Further-in light of the Appellate Division's express and implicit substitution of its findings of fact for those of the trial court regarding the inputs, outputs and causation-we must determine which court's findings more nearly comport with the weight of the credible evidence (_see_ CPLR 5501[b]).

We now modify, affirming for reasons stated by the Appellate Division so much of the decision as dismissed plaintiffs' title VI claim, and otherwise reversing the Appellate Division's order (_see, by contrast, Paynter v. State of New York,_ 100 N.Y.2d 434, 765 N.Y.S.2d 819, 797 N.E.2d 1225 [2003]).

I. Overview

At the time of trial, the New York City public school system comprised nearly 1,200 schools serving 1.1 million children and employing a staff of over 135,000, including 78,000 teachers (_see generally_ 187 Misc.2d 1, 19-23, 719 N.Y.S.2d 475 [2001], 295 A.D.2d 1, 5-6, 744 N.Y.S.2d 130 [2002]). Some 84% of City schoolchildren were racial minorities; 80% were born outside the United States; and 16% were classified as Limited English Proficient (LEP-persons who speak little or no English)-most of the state's students in each of these categories. Upwards of 73% were eligible for the federal free or reduced price lunch program; 442,000 City schoolchildren came from families receiving Aid to Families with Dependent Children; and 135,000 were enrolled in special education programs.

The New York City public school system was and is supervised by the Board of Education and its Chancellor (_see_ Education Law § 2590-b [1]; §§ 2590-g, 2590-h). The system is divided into 32 geographically-based community school districts to provide elementary and middle school education; six geographically-based high school districts; and four non geographical districts. At the time of trial, elected community school boards supervised the community school districts, and had done so since 1969. Statewide, oversight of the public school system is vested in the Regents of the University of the State of New York (_see_ N.Y. Const., art. XI, § 2; Education Law § 207). The State Education Department (SED) and Commissioner of Education supervise and manage the State's public schools, promulgating regulations and determining teaching standards and curricula, among other things.

Neither the Regents nor the SED is responsible, however, for the day-to-day operation of the schools or for their funding. Rather, a combination of local, state and federal sources generates school funding. Almost half of the state aid component consists of operating aid, which is allocated using a complex statutory formula that apportions various categories of aid based on a district's combined wealth ratio-which measures its ability to generate revenue-and student attendance (*see* Education Law § 3602).

The statute contains extensive prescriptions regarding how districts may use funds, and it is perhaps the proliferation of highly specific aid categories that most differentiates the current section 3602 from its shorter, simpler predecessors (*see e.g.* L. 1962, ch. 657, § 3).

Every year, pursuant to Education Law § 215-a, the Board of Regents and the SED submit a report to the Governor and Legislature on the educational status of the State's schools. The most recent of these "655 Reports" at the time of trial-that of April 1999-provides a comprehensive statistical view of the funding system as of the 1996-1997 school year, the last year for which the record provides such a complete picture. That year, statewide, the State provided 39.9% of all public school funding-$ 10.4 billion out of a total of $26 billion-while districts provided 56% and the federal government four percent.

These figures represented an investment of $9,321 per pupil, $3,714 of it by the State. Per-pupil expenditures in the New York City public schools, at $8,171, were lower than in three quarters of the State's districts, including all the other "large city" districts, as classified by the SED. The State's dollar contribution to this figure was also lower, at $3,562, than its average contribution to other districts; and the City's, at about $4,000, was likewise lower than the average local contribution in other districts.

II. The Standard

In *CFE* we equated a sound basic education with "the basic literacy, calculating, and verbal skills necessary to enable children to eventually function productively as civic participants capable of voting and serving on a jury" (86 N.Y.2d at 316, 631 N.Y.S.2d 565, 655 N.E.2d 661). We thus indicated that a sound basic education conveys not merely skills, but skills fashioned to meet a practical goal: meaningful civic participation in contemporary society. This purposive orientation for schooling has been at the core of the Education Article since its enactment in 1894. As the Committee on Education reported at the time, the "public problems confronting the rising generation will demand accurate knowledge and the highest development of reasoning power more than ever before " (2 Documents of 1894 N.Y. Constitutional Convention No. 62, at 4).

In keeping with this core constitutional purpose and our direction further to develop the template, the trial court took evidence on what the "rising generation" needs in order to function productively as civic participants, concluding that this preparation should be measured with reference to the demands of modern society and include some preparation for employment (187 Misc.2d at 16, 719 N.Y.S.2d 475).

The Appellate Division also recognized that our "term 'function productively' does imply employment" (295 A.D.2d at 8, 744 N.Y.S.2d 130), and we agree with both parties and both lower courts that an employment component was implicit in the standard we outlined in *CFE.* Nevertheless, the parties dispute the nature of the employment-and of civic participation generally-for which a sound basic education should prepare children, as well as the nature of the instruction necessary to achieve such preparation. We address each of these areas of dispute in turn.

First, as to employment, the Appellate Division concluded that the trial court "went too far" in construing the ability to "function productively" as the ability to obtain "competitive employment" or, indeed, as anything more than "the ability to get a job, and support oneself, and thereby not be a charge on the public" (295 A.D.2d at 8, 744 N.Y.S.2d 130).

More is required. While a sound basic education need only prepare students to compete for jobs that enable them to support themselves, the record establishes that for this purpose a high school level education is now all but indispensable. As plaintiffs' education and economics expert Dr. Henry Levin testified, manufacturing jobs are becoming more scarce in New York and service sector jobs require a higher level of knowledge, skill in communication and the use of information, and the capacity to continue to learn over a lifetime.

The record showed that employers who offer entry-level jobs that do not require college increasingly expect applicants to have had instruction that imparts these abilities, if not a specific credential.

Second, as to other aspects of civic participation, the difference between the trial court and the Appellate Division centers on our statement in *CFE* that a sound basic education should leave students "capable of voting and serving on a jury" (86 N.Y.2d at 316, 631 N.Y.S.2d 565, 655 N.E.2d 661). The State's expert on educational psychology, Dr. Herbert Walberg, testified that pattern jury instructions and newspaper articles typically feature vocabulary and sentence length comparable to those of texts eighth-graders are expected to be able to read.

Based on this testimony, the Appellate Division concluded that the skills necessary for civic participation are imparted between eighth and ninth grades (295 A.D.2d at 8, 744 N.Y.S.2d 130). The trial court, by contrast, concluded that productive citizenship "means more than just being *qualified* to vote or serve as a juror, but to do so capably and knowledgeably" (187 Misc.2d at 14, 719 N.Y.S.2d 475 [emphasis in original])-to have skills appropriate to the task.

We agree with the trial court that students require more than an eighth-grade education to function productively as citizens, and that the mandate of the Education Article for a sound basic education should not be pegged to the eighth or ninth grade, or indeed to any particular grade level. In *CFE* we pointed to voting and jury service because they are the civic responsibilities *par excellence*. For reasons founded in the American historical experience, the statutory requirements for participation in those activities are aimed at being inclusive.

Indeed, the latest amendment of Judiciary Law § 510-the juror qualification statute-removed requirements based on jurors' literacy (*see* L. 1995, ch. 86, § 3). Yet it cannot reasonably be supposed that the demands of juror service, and any related demands on the City schools, have become less rigorous, or that the concept of a sound basic education would not include literacy.

Finally, with these goals in mind, we come to the dispute over the kind and amount of schooling children need in order to be assured of the constitutional minimum of educational opportunity. In *CFE* we refrained from addressing this problem in detail, simply setting forth the "essentials":

"Children are entitled to minimally adequate physical facilities and classrooms which provide enough light, space, heat, and air to permit children to learn. Children should have access to minimally adequate instrumentalities of learning such as desks, chairs, pencils, and reasonably current textbooks. Children are also entitled to minimally adequate teaching of reasonably up-to-date basic curricula such as reading, writing, mathematics, science, and social studies, by sufficient personnel adequately trained to teach those subject areas" (86 N.Y.2d at 317, 631 N.Y.S.2d 565, 655 N.E.2d 661).

As we further explained, many of the more detailed standards established by the Board of Regents and Commissioner of Education "exceed notions of a minimally adequate or sound basic education," so that proof that schools do not comply with such standards "may not, standing alone, establish a violation of the Education Article" (*id.*).

The trial court, accordingly, declined to fix the most recent, and ambitious, statement of educational goals-the Regents Learning Standards, adopted in 1996-as the definition of a sound basic education (187 Misc.2d at 12, 719 N.Y.S.2d 475). As the trial court observed, so to enshrine the Learning Standards would be to cede to a state agency the power to define a constitutional right.

Although some amici nevertheless urge us to adopt the Learning Standards as the definition of a sound basic education, plaintiffs make no such request. Rather, they contend that children are entitled to a meaningful high school education, one that provides the essentials we listed.

Defendants maintain that plaintiffs are trying to set the requirements for a high school diploma as the constitutional floor, and thereby to make mastery of the Learning Standards-which are being phased in as the basis for a high school diploma (*see* 8 NYCRR 100.5)-the test of a sound basic education after all. We do not construe plaintiffs' arguments as a request for a rule tied to whatever diploma requirement the Regents promulgate, however high; nor do plaintiffs need such a rule to prevail.

The issue to be resolved by the evidence is whether the State affords New York City school-children the opportunity for a meaningful high school education, one which prepares them to function productively as civic participants. This is essentially the question the trial court addressed, and we conclude that the Appellate Division erred to the extent that it founded a judgment for defendants upon a much lower, grade-specific level of skills children are guaranteed the chance to achieve.

III. The Evaluation

To determine whether New York City schools in fact deliver the opportunity for a sound basic education, the trial court took evidence on the "inputs" children receive-teaching, facilities and instrumentalities of learning-and their resulting "outputs," such as test results and graduation and dropout rates. This organization of the facts follows naturally from our summary of the "essentials" in *CFE* and was not disputed by the Appellate Division.

While the State urges an affirmance based on what it considers good outputs, the dissent-relying on *Paynter*-suggests that there is something "inconsistent" about even discussing them (dissenting op. at 952 n. 5, 769 N.Y.S.2d at 144 n. 5, 801 N.E.2d at 364 n. 5). *Paynter* holds that proof of inadequate inputs is *necessary* for an Education Article claim, not that such proof is *sufficient* for such a claim. Thus, our discussion of outputs is consistent with both *Paynter* and *CFE*-which contemplated cautious use of output evidence-as well as responsive to an argument the State made.

A. Input

Teaching. The first and surely most important input is teaching. The trial court considered six measures of teacher quality-including certification rates, test results, experience levels and the ratings teachers receive from their principals-and concluded that the quality of New York City schoolteachers is inadequate, despite the commendable, even heroic, efforts of many teachers. The Appellate Division reached a contrary conclusion based on its perception that principals' reviews of the teachers they supervise are the best indication of teaching ability (295 A.D.2d at 14, 744 N.Y.S.2d 130).

But plaintiffs' expert on the labor market for teachers, Dr. Hamilton Lankford, testified authoritatively regarding other factors that are probative of teacher quality, and several experienced administrators testified that principals' reviews tend to conceal teacher inadequacy because principals find it difficult to fire bad teachers and to hire better ones. In our view, the Appellate Division improperly narrowed the inquiry here. Considering all of the factors, we agree with the trial court's findings and its conclusion that the teaching is inadequate.

The 1999 655 Report noted that schools with the highest percentages of minority children "have the least experienced teachers, the most uncertified teachers, the lowest-salaried teachers, and the highest rates of teacher turnover." The same report showed that well over half of the State's minority children attended New York City schools; that 84% of New York City schoolchildren were minorities; and that most of these children are poor. Taken together, these and other facts and statements in the 655 Report amount to an admission by the state agencies responsible for education that-with respect to teacher experience and retention, certification and pay-New York City schools are inferior to those of the rest of the state.

To be sure, the Education Article guarantees not equality but only a sound basic education (*see* <u>Levittown, 57 N.Y.2d at 48, 453 N.Y.S.2d 643, 439 N.E.2d 359)</u>. But as Judge Levine observed in his concurrence in <u>CFE,</u> "the constitutional history of the Education Article shows that the objective was to 'make it *imperative* on the State to provide *adequate* free common schools for the education of *all* of the children of the State' and that the new provision would have an impact upon 'places in the State of New York where the common schools are not adequate' " <u>(86 N.Y.2d at 327, 631 N.Y.S.2d 565, 655 N.E.2d 661</u> [Levine, J., concurring], quoting 3 Revised Record of Constitutional Convention of 1894, at 695 and adding emphasis).

The 655 Report indicates a mismatch between student need in New York City and the quality of the teaching directed to that need, and it is one authoritative source of facts showing the extent of the mismatch. The report, for instance, shows that in 1997 17% of New York City public schoolteachers either were uncertified or taught in areas other than those in which they were certified. The trial court noted this fact and evidence that uncertified and inexperienced teachers tend to be concentrated in the lowest performing schools.

Notably, Dr. Lankford demonstrated not only that New York City schools had the largest percentage of teachers with two or fewer years' experience but also that this percentage was greatest-at 17.9%-in the quintile of City schools with greatest student need. Classifying teachers who either were uncertified or had less than three years' experience as novice teachers, Dr. Lankford testified that nearly a quarter of all City teachers, and nearly a third of the teachers in the neediest quintile of City schools, were novices. And he reviewed the colossal failure rates of City teachers on the State's certification content-specialty tests, which rise above 40% in mathematics, even for math teachers currently teaching in New York City public schools.

As the trial court's decision shows, the record contains many more facts proving a serious shortfall in teacher quality in New York City schools, proving that this shortfall results from those schools' lack of competitiveness in bidding for and retaining personnel, and proving that better teachers produce better student performance (*see* 187 Misc.2d at 25-36, 719 N.Y.S.2d 475).

On this last point the testimony of Dr. Ronald Ferguson is particularly revealing. Using data from Texas-where all teachers are tested-Dr. Ferguson demonstrated that in districts where teachers perform badly on teacher certification tests, student performance declines as student grade level rises-and, conversely, that where teachers test well, student performance at higher grade levels surpasses student performance at lower grade levels.

Thus, the longer students are exposed to good or bad teachers, the better or worse they perform. Based on evidence offered by Dr. Lankford, Dr. Ferguson projected that the same correlation would apply in New York. Defendants' expert, Dr. Eric Hanushek, challenged Dr. Ferguson's conclusions, but the trial court rejected this challenge and the Appellate Division-though it referred to Dr. Ferguson's testimony-did not rest any of its own contrary findings on Dr. Hanushek's testimony.

In sum, we conclude that the Appellate Division erred in relying solely on principals' evaluations, and we agree with the trial court's holdings that teacher certification, test performance, experience and other factors measure quality of teaching; that quality of teaching correlates with student performance; and that New York City schools provide deficient teaching because of their inability to attract and retain qualified teachers.

School Facilities and Classrooms. As we noted in *CFE,* children are entitled to "classrooms which provide enough light, space, heat, and air to permit children to learn" (86 N.Y.2d at 317, 631 N.Y.S.2d 565, 655 N.E.2d 661). The trial court divided this further-considering first the physical plant of New York City schools, and then the specific problem of overcrowding and class size-and concluded that New York City schools are deficient. The court conceded, however, that the harmful effect of physical deficiencies of the first kind on student performance is difficult to measure.

The Appellate Division took note of this concession, dismissed as "anecdotal" plaintiffs' evidence of "leaky roofs, deficient heating, and other problems," and credited testimony that "all immediately hazardous conditions had been eliminated" (295 A.D.2d at 10, 744 N.Y.S.2d 130).

Eliminating immediate hazards is not the same as creating an environment conducive to learning, and the record contains much evidence about deficient school infrastructure. Nevertheless, on this record it cannot be said that plaintiffs have proved a measurable correlation between building disrepair and student performance, in general.

On the other hand, plaintiffs presented measurable proof, credited by the trial court, that New York City schools have excessive class sizes, and that class size affects learning. Even in the earliest years-from kindergarten through third grade-over half of New York City schoolchildren are in classes of 26 or more, and tens of thousands are in classes of over 30. As the trial court noted, federal and state programs seek to promote classes of 20 or fewer, particularly in the earliest years, and plaintiffs' experts testified on the advantage of smaller classes. As the 1999 655 Report shows, New York City elementary school classes average five more pupils than those of other schools statewide excluding Buffalo, Rochester, Syracuse and Yonkers.

Although the Appellate Division found "no indication that students cannot learn in classes consisting of more than 20 students" (295 A.D.2d at 11, 744 N.Y.S.2d 130), plaintiffs' burden was not to prove that some specific number is the maximum class size beyond which children "cannot learn." It is difficult to imagine what evidence could ever meet a burden so formulated; nothing in _CFE_ required plaintiffs to do so. Rather, plaintiffs alleged "fact-based inadequacies" in educational inputs, and we held that the State's failure to provide the opportunity to obtain "fundamental skills" would constitute a violation of the Education Article (86 N.Y.2d at 319, 631 N.Y.S.2d 565, 655 N.E.2d 661). Accordingly, plaintiffs had to show that insufficient funding led to inadequate inputs which led to unsatisfactory results.

Plaintiffs' education evaluation statistics expert Dr. Jeremy Finn showed-on the basis of the Tennessee Student Teacher Achievement Ratio (STAR) project and related research-that, holding other variables constant, smaller class sizes in the earliest grades correlate with better test results during those years and afterwards (187 Misc.2d at 52-53, 719 N.Y.S.2d 475). The trial court found that the State's expert Dr. Hanushek failed to rebut these conclusions, and the Appellate Division, mistakenly addressing a nonexistent claim "that classes of over 20 students are unconstitutional" (295 A.D.2d at 11, 744 N.Y.S.2d 130), set forth no acceptable basis to disturb the trial court's finding. We conclude that plaintiffs' evidence of the advantages of smaller class sizes supports the inference sufficiently to show a meaningful correlation between the large classes in City schools and the outputs to which we soon turn. In sum, the Appellate Division erred in concluding that there was not "sufficient proof" (295 A.D.2d at 11, 744 N.Y.S.2d 130) that large class sizes negatively affect student performance in New York City public schools.

Instrumentalities of Learning. The final input is "instrumentalities of learning," including classroom supplies, textbooks, libraries and computers. The courts below agreed that the textbook supply is presently adequate and the evidence on classroom supplies is inconclusive. On the other hand, evidence including the latest 655 Report showed that New York

City schools had about nine library books per student-half as many as schools statewide excluding the City, and just under half the number recommended by the American Library Association.

In light of _Levittown,_ the intrastate inequality does not prove anything in itself, and a library association might be expected to advocate book purchases at levels exceeding the constitutional floor. But in holding that the library books in New York City schools are "inadequate in number and quality" (187 Misc.2d at 57, 719 N.Y.S.2d 475) the trial court clearly relied on the abundant testimony on the adequacy of the books for pedagogical purposes rather than on purely numerical intrastate comparisons.

The un-rebutted testimony indicated that the books in City school libraries are old and not integrated with contemporary curricula. The Appellate Division suggested that school libraries simply consist of "classics" rather than "multicultural" books (295 A.D.2d at 12, 744 N.Y.S.2d 130), but the record contains not one scintilla of evidence that antiquated books in City school libraries are "classics." The Appellate Division thus gave no factual basis for its disagreement with the trial court that the library books in New York City schools are inadequate in quality.

The record concerning computers is similar, establishing that some exposure to them has become essential and that City schools not only have about half as many computers per student as all other New York schools, but also have aging equipment that, in some cases, simply cannot support presently-available software. The Appellate Division speculated that old equipment might be used "for introductory classes" (295 A.D.2d at 11, 744 N.Y.S.2d 130), but this possibility was not even advocated by the State and, like the "classic" outdated library books, has no record support at all. While we hesitate to overstate the importance of libraries and computers relative to other inputs, we conclude that as to these two instrumentalities of learning the trial court's findings again better comport with the weight of the evidence, and support its conclusion that the New York City schools are deficient in instrumentalities of learning.

In sum, considering all of the inputs, we conclude that the trial court's findings should be reinstated, as indicated, and that the educational inputs in New York City schools are inadequate. There are certainly City schools where the inadequacy is not "gross and glaring" (_Levittown,_ 57 N.Y.2d at 48, 453 N.Y.S.2d 643, 439 N.E.2d 359). Some of these schools may even be excellent. But tens of thousands of students are placed in overcrowded classrooms, taught by unqualified teachers, and provided with inadequate facilities and equipment. The number of children in these straits is large enough to represent a systemic failure. A showing of good test results and graduation rates among these students-the "outputs"-might indicate that they somehow still receive the opportunity for a sound basic education. The showing, however, is otherwise.

B. Outputs

School Completion. Concerning the first output, school completion, the proof revealed that of those New York City ninth graders who do not transfer to another school system, only 50% graduate in four years, and 30% do not graduate or receive a general equivalency degree (GED) by the age of 21, when they cease to be eligible for free public education. This rate of school completion compares unfavorably with both state and national figures, and the trial court considered it symptomatic of "system breakdown" (187 Misc.2d at 63, 719 N.Y.S.2d 475). The Appellate Division concluded that "there was no evidence quantifying how many dropouts fail to obtain a sound basic education" (295 A.D.2d at 15, 744 N.Y.S.2d 130).

That conclusion follows from the Appellate Division's premise that a sound basic education is imparted by eighth or ninth grade. A sound basic education, however, means a meaningful high school education. Under that standard, it may, as a practical matter, be presumed that a dropout has not received a sound basic education. In any event the evidence was unrebutted that dropouts typically are not prepared for productive citizenship, as the trial court concluded.

The Appellate Division would have required a precise quantitative division between those dropouts who somehow are adequately prepared and those who are not, but such a requirement is nowhere to be found in *CFE.*

The State argues nonetheless that it is responsible only to provide the opportunity for a sound basic education and cannot be blamed if some students-perhaps those who enter New York City schools after years of schooling in another country-do not avail themselves of the opportunity it provides. As the trial court correctly observed, this opportunity must still "be placed within reach of all students," including those who "present with socioeconomic deficits" (187 Misc.2d at 63, 719 N.Y.S.2d 475).

This observation follows from the constitutional mandate to provide schools wherein all children may be educated, and is consistent with the official position of the Regents and Education Department, as set forth in the 655 Report for 1999, that "all children can learn given appropriate instructional, social, and health services."

The evidence on why students drop out suggested mainly that the choice to drop out correlates with poor academic performance and, as noted in the 655 Report for 1999, racial minority status and concentrated poverty. The Report further indicated that "dropout rates serve as useful measures of schools' abilities to motivate learning," supporting the commonsense proposition that large dropout rates reflect problems with the schools as well as the students.

The trial court properly considered both possibilities and declined to pin the blame solely on the deficits a "troubled child" brings to school (*see* 187 Misc.2d at 63, 719 N.Y.S.2d 475). There was certainly no proof that dropout rates are high because inordinate numbers of recent immigrants enter the ninth grade unable ever to graduate, though such students may take longer to graduate. Moreover, as the trial court properly observed, "education is cumulative," and the State's hypothesis that poor completion rates stem from the educational deficits of teenage immigrant students does not jibe with the significant evidence that New York City schoolchildren begin to accumulate learning deficits well before high school (187 Misc.2d at 63, 719 N.Y.S.2d 475).

Test Results. The State's main answer to the proof of graduation and dropout rates in City schools consists of evidence that, in any event, test results are not bad-and this is also where the Appellate Division concentrated its discussion of outputs (295 A.D.2d at 15-16, 744 N.Y.S.2d 130).

The State's reliance on some favorable standardized test results fails to take into account the full record on examination evidence. In particular, that evidence related to elementary school tests administered statewide and intended to present results with reference to the content appropriate to their grade level: the Pupil Evaluation Program (PEP), which measures individual achievement in reading and mathematics, and the Program Evaluation Test (PET), which measures performance in other subjects. As the trial court explained, the PEP measures student performance relative to a particular score, the state reference point (SRP) (187 Misc.2d at 65, 719 N.Y.S.2d 475). The particular examination used for the PEP reading test during most of the 1990s was the Degrees of Reading Power (DRP).

The DRP was replaced in 1998 because it was considered too elementary, in that over 90% of children outside New York City scored above the SRP, so that the exam was inadequate as a means of distinguishing fair from good and good from excellent students. As a means, however, of identifying students in need of remedial attention, the DRP was adequate: a score below the SRP signaled need for improvement.

Between 1994 and 1998, the undisputed evidence showed that upwards of 30% of New York City sixth graders scored below the SRP in reading. Among third graders, 35 to 40% scored below the SRP, while in the rest of the state about 90% scored above. The evidence showed that at the third grade level-when children are expected to have learned to read-a score at the SRP means a child is barely literate, and hence that over a third of City schoolchildren were functionally illiterate. PET scores in science and social studies showed New York City fourth, sixth and eighth graders invariably in the lowest quartile statewide, and generally between the 10th and 16th percentile.

The trial court attached significance to these low PEP and PET scores (187 Misc.2d at 65-66, 719 N.Y.S.2d 475). It also properly recognized that-as always-City-wide averages reflect a process of aggregation wherein some successful schools and districts balance others where even larger numbers of pupils score below the SRP (*id.*). The Appellate Division set forth no basis to challenge the trial court's analysis of this output, other than its belief that courts should "look at the nation as a whole," rather than to test result comparisons within New York State (295 A.D.2d at 16, 744 N.Y.S.2d 130). We reject this exclusive focus on national comparisons because the record provides no information on how many students receive a sound basic education nationwide.

The State does rely partly on tests administered statewide. In particular, it cites student performance on the Regents Competency Tests (RCTs), which have historically been administered to 11th graders as a prerequisite for graduation. In 1997-1998, 90% of the New York City schoolchildren who reached 11th grade demonstrated competency in reading and mathematics by passing either the RCTs or the more challenging Regents examinations-a figure not far behind the statewide and suburban averages.

Although the RCTs are no longer used to measure readiness to graduate, this fact alone does not disqualify them as a measure of whether students have received a sound basic education. Nevertheless, as both parties agree, the RCTs assess achievement at only an eighth or ninth grade level in reading and a sixth-to-eighth grade level in math. Thus, while passing the RCTs may show that students have received a sound basic education as defined by the Appellate Division, it does not prove that they have received a meaningful high school education, as the trial court concluded (187 Misc.2d at 61, 719 N.Y.S.2d 475).

Additionally, according to the 655 Report for 1999, City students who took the RCTs in 1997-1998 actually passed at a much lower rate than 90%; 51% passed in math and 72% in English. The Report explains that City schools had adopted a new policy of administering the examinations to ninth rather than 11th graders, and this may account for some of the difference. Since the exams are a diagnostic tool for measuring skills taught in middle school, these results, at most, cast doubt on the results middle schools accomplish, rather than proving that students have received a meaningful high school education. Further, the 1997-1998 11th grade class with the 90% qualification rates consisted of only about 40,000 students, compared to a ninth grade enrollment of over 90,000.

Thus the state's RCT passage rates-aside from proving nothing about high school achievement-would surely be lower, but for the alarming number of students who fall behind or drop out and so do not take the exam. This fact illustrates the need to be cautious in relying on test results, a point we made in *CFE* even as we recognized that such results have some value (86 N.Y.2d at 317, 631 N.Y.S.2d 565, 655 N.E.2d 661). The trial court properly exercised such caution in its discussion of test results, noting that the failure of many students to be promoted diminishes the value of evidence that students test at grade level (187 Misc.2d at 67, 719 N.Y.S.2d 475).

Apart from the RCTs, the State relies on results from an assortment of commercially-available nationally normed reading and math tests administered to children in City elementary schools, notably the CTB-Reading (CTB-R) and California Achievement Test (CAT). As the State points out, just under half of all City schoolchildren score at or above the 50th percentile in reading, and a larger number do so in math. Plaintiffs counter that these exams are "norm-referenced"-they present information only on how students perform relative to other students-in contrast to "criterion-referenced" exams, which are informative about how students master content they are expected to know at a given level. Further, plaintiffs argue that national comparisons are irrelevant to the issue of whether New York City public school students have received a sound basic education. The Appellate Division rejected this argument (295 A.D.2d at 16, 744 N.Y.S.2d 130).

As we have already suggested, the New York Constitution ensures students not an education that approaches the national norm-whatever that may be-but a sound basic education. Moreover, _CFE_ makes clear that the measure of a sound basic education is educational content-the set of "basic literacy, calculating, and verbal skills" children acquire and its fit with the goal of productive citizenship (86 N.Y.2d at 316, 631 N.Y.S.2d 565, 655 N.E.2d 661).

Of course, results on a national norm-referenced exam may be translatable into a measure of the skills students must master to have a sound basic education, and we have no cause to doubt that the CTB-R and CAT are designed, as the State argues, to measure mastery of curricula considered important in New York as well as nationally.

But during the years reflected in the record, the scores of City schoolchildren on these exams were reported-as the State admits-with reference to a norm rather than to achievement levels. The State has not shown how to translate these results into proof that the schools are delivering a sound basic education, properly defined. Thus, while we cannot say that the CTB-R and CAT exam results have no place in the mix of information on outputs, on this record the Appellate Division erred in according primacy to these results.

In sum, the Appellate Division improperly relied on the RCTs in that they measure a level of proficiency far below a sound basic education, and, as to exams administered to younger children, it erred in relying on national norm-referenced exam results without evidence tying these results to the constitutional standard.

We conclude that the trial court's assessment of exam results, like its assessment of completion rates, better comports with the weight of the credible evidence, and supports its conclusion that, whether measured by the outputs or the inputs, New York City schoolchildren are not receiving the constitutionally-mandated opportunity for a sound basic education.

IV. Causation

As we noted in _CFE,_ in order to prevail plaintiffs must "establish a correlation between funding and educational opportunity a causal link between the present funding system and any proven failure to provide a sound basic education to New York City school children" (86 N.Y.2d at 318, 631 N.Y.S.2d 565, 655 N.E.2d 661). The trial court reasoned that the necessary "causal link" between the present funding system and the poor performance of City schools could be established by a showing that increased funding can provide better teachers, facilities and instrumentalities of learning (187 Misc.2d at 68, 719 N.Y.S.2d 475). We agree that this showing, together with evidence that such improved inputs yield better student performance, constituted plaintiffs' prima facie case, which plaintiffs established.

That the trial court's "Causation" section is largely devoted to the State's rebuttal arguments, rather than to plaintiffs' prima facie case, is insignificant, in that the court had already incorporated much of the correlation evidence in its discussion of inputs and outputs, as we have done. The trial court, for instance, concluded that teacher certification rates are one valid measure of teaching quality and are too low in New York City, and it founded these conclusions on evidence establishing the correlation between teacher certification and performance (187 Misc.2d at 26-27, 719 N.Y.S.2d 475).

The Appellate Division speculated about the significance of certification and noted that more certified teachers will be hired "[i]n any event" (295 A.D.2d at 12, 744 N.Y.S.2d 130), but its only clear holding about the quality of instruction-which we reject-was that principals' ratings of teachers should be the preeminent measure of pedagogical quality and, implicitly, that by this measure the teaching input is adequate (_id._ at 13-14, 744 N.Y.S.2d 130). The Appellate Division did nothing to undermine the rest of the trial court's syllogism: that better funded schools would hire and retain more certified teachers, and that students with such teachers would score better. The same is true with respect to class size and instrumentalities of learning.

We thus have no occasion to repeat the evidence establishing plaintiffs' prima facie case regarding the causal connection between better funding, improved inputs and better student results.

The State nevertheless makes several further arguments concerning the correlation between its funding scheme and the educational results. Most of these points, however, more properly concern the apportionment of responsibility among various government actors than causation. In any event, the trial court interpreted _CFE_ correctly when it said that the "law recognizes that there may be many 'causal links' to a single outcome, and there is no reason to think that the Court of Appeals 1995 opinion mandates a search for a single cause of the failure of New York City schools" (187 Misc.2d at 92, 719 N.Y.S.2d 475).

Socioeconomic Disadvantage. The State argues that poor student performance is caused by socioeconomic conditions independent of the quality of the schools and better remedied with investment in other resources. The Appellate Division agreed, reasoning that because of "demographic factors, such as poverty, high crime neighborhoods, single parent or dysfunctional homes, homes where English is not spoken, or homes where parents offer little help with homework and motivation more spending on education is not necessarily the answer, and the cure lies in eliminating the socioeconomic conditions facing certain students" (295 A.D.2d at 16, 744 N.Y.S.2d 130). This is partly an argument about why students fail, which we have rejected in the discussion of outputs. But it is also a distinctly constitutional argument in the sense that choosing between competing beneficial uses of funds is a legislative task.

This is, in fact, the argument that Judge Simons made in his solitary dissent in CFE, 86 N.Y.2d at 342-343, 631 N.Y.S.2d 565, 655 N.E.2d 661. Had we accepted the argument, we would have saved everyone considerable effort and expense by dismissing the case on the spot. We did not do so. Decisions about spending priorities are indeed the Legislature's province, but we have a duty to determine whether the State is providing students with the opportunity for a sound basic education. While it may be that a dollar spent on improving "dysfunctional homes" would go further than one spent on a decent education, we have no constitutional mandate to weigh these alternatives. And, again, we cannot accept the premise that children come to the New York City schools ineducable, unfit to learn.

Comparative Spending. The State next argues that per-student expenditures in the New York City schools compare favorably with the average in the United States generally and in other large cities such as Los Angeles, a fact purportedly incompatible with finding "gross and glaring inadequacy" in education (see Levittown, 57 N.Y.2d at 48, 453 N.Y.S.2d 643, 439 N.E.2d 359). The premise is that some expenditure level, if high enough relative to figures nationwide, simply must be "enough," without reference to student need, local costs, and the actual quality of inputs and outputs. This premise, also, is compatible with the interpretation of Levittown endorsed by the dissent in CFE, 86 N.Y.2d at 337-338, 631 N.Y.S.2d 565, 655 N.E.2d 661 and apparently also today's dissent (dissenting op. at 954, 769 N.Y.S.2d at 145-146, 801 N.E.2d at 365-366). We reject it for much the same reason we rejected exclusive reliance on nationally-normed tests-the record discloses no information on whether those students are receiving a sound basic education.

City Mismanagement. The State's most sustained arguments on causation, however, are based on evidence that the Board of Education mismanages New York City schools and the City itself fails to devote a sufficient part of its revenues to them. The State reasons that if either proposition is true, then the cause of any shortage of educational inputs in City schools is not the state funding system but City bureaucracy.

Specifically, the State argues first that fraud and corruption in the community school boards and City school construction spending, rather than the funding system, are the cause of any shortage of inputs. The trial court rejected these arguments (187 Misc.2d at 92, 94, 719 N.Y.S.2d 475) and the Appellate Division likewise rejected the point about construction spending (295 A.D.2d at 18, 744 N.Y.S.2d 130) while saying nothing about the community school boards. We thus have no occasion to review either argument.

The State argues second that, corruption aside, the Board of Education mismanages the schools, particularly by referring too many students to special education and placing too many of these children in costly full-time segregated settings. The trial court credited evidence that better special education practices could save City schools between $105 and $185 million annually, though some of these savings would be offset by the greater cost of instructing children with special education needs in a mainstream environment (187 Misc.2d at 96-97, 719 N.Y.S.2d 475). The Appellate Division saw the possible savings mounting to "hundreds of millions of dollars, if not $1 billion" (295 A.D.2d at 17, 744 N.Y.S.2d 130)-a figure exceeding even the $335 million claimed by the State's expert, Dr. Daniel Reschly.

We are thus constrained to accept that some saving on special education is possible, a fact that to some extent undermines plaintiffs' argument that the school funding system is unconstitutional because it leaves New York City schools with insufficient funds to provide a sound basic education. But the magnitude of the savings is in dispute. The Appellate Division appears to have arrived at its "billion" simply by taking the number of full-time special education students, assuming that 80% could be moved to part-time settings, and multiplying the number of students subject to this move by the $10,000 difference between the cost of full-time and part-time placement. No witness for the State sponsored any such calculation, and there was thus no opportunity to test the Appellate Division's assumptions on which it is based.

The available evidence-based conclusions are that over-referral to special education costs City schools somewhere between tens of millions and $335 million. Even the lower of these figures would reflect both resources squandered and the likelihood that many children are badly served and perhaps stigmatized by segregated placements in the special education system in City schools. But, conversely, even savings approaching the higher figure would not necessarily translate dollar-for-dollar into funds free for investment in better inputs, much less into an investment sufficient to relieve the existing systemic educational crisis. In any event, the State points us to no evidence on how much of any savings on special education would be invested in more productive inputs in City schools.

We need not speculate further on the possible saving from special education placement, however, for the State's argument on Board of Education mismanagement fails for a more basic reason. As the trial court and Appellate Division recognized (187 Misc.2d at 81-82, 719 N.Y.S.2d 475, 295 A.D.2d at 18-19, 744 N.Y.S.2d 130), both the Board of Education and the City are "creatures or agents of the State," which delegated whatever authority over education they wield (*City of New York v. State of New York*, 86 N.Y.2d 286, 289-290, 631 N.Y.S.2d 553, 655 N.E.2d 649 [1995]). Thus, the State remains responsible when the failures of its agents sabotage the measures by which it secures for its citizens their constitutionally-mandated rights.

As our ensuing discussion of remedy shows, various reforms unrelated to financing-some already in the works-may be part of the package of legislative and administrative measures necessary to ensure a sound basic education to New York City schoolchildren. The requirement stated in *CFE*, however, was for plaintiffs to "establish a causal link between the present funding system and any proven failure" (86 N.Y.2d at 318, 631 N.Y.S.2d 565, 655 N.E.2d 661), not to eliminate any possibility that other causes contribute to that failure.

Moreover, in every instance where the State has relied on purported political or managerial failings of the City or the Board of Education, closer inspection of the details casts doubt on whether the City could eliminate the failing without the State's help or would have developed the failing without the State's involvement. The issue of special education is illustrative. The trial court held that "the primary causes of New York City's over-referral and over-placement in restrictive settings are a lack of support services in general education and State aid incentives that tended until recently to encourage restrictive placements" (187 Misc.2d at 95, 719 N.Y.S.2d 475). This conclusion is supported by the record and was not disturbed by the Appellate Division. Thus, the State cannot blame over-referral on the institutional culture of the Board of Education and City schools without acknowledging that this culture has evolved to its present condition partly in response to the funding system. At the very least, under *CFE*, this problem does not constitute a cause sufficiently independent from the State's funding system to overcome plaintiffs' case.

Similar reasoning disposes of the State's argument that the Board of Education's inefficient management of personnel is the supervening cause that, rather than the funding system, accounts for deficiencies in the teaching input. The State points to disturbing evidence that thousands of City schoolteachers do not teach; others teach under contracts that limit their classroom time to under four hours a day; and all are paid according to the same salary schedule, regardless of whether a more flexible system of incentives might be needed, for instance, to induce senior teachers to remain in troubled schools.

The Appellate Division characterized such evidence as "the product of collective bargaining agreements, not the manner in which the State funds the City's schools" (295 A.D.2d at 18, 744 N.Y.S.2d 130). But as the trial court found, "the allegedly shorter workday of New York City's public school teachers has not provided the City an advantage in the competition for qualified teachers" (187 Misc.2d at 36, 719 N.Y.S.2d 475). Such considerations, as well as the simple constitutional principle that the State has ultimate responsibility for the schools, counsel us against the State's rebuttal arguments on causation.

Local Funding. Of the State's rebuttal arguments, one more requires special attention. The State argues that the City actually has a greater capacity to fund education from local revenues than many local governments statewide, yet fails to make anything like the same "tax effort" that other localities make. Indeed, the State marshals evidence that when the State injects funds pursuant to formulas intended to compensate for inequalities in local school funding, the City deducts proportionately from its own contribution, leaving the school budget unimproved.

The trial court found evidence to support this assertion; noted unique pressures on the City budget and other factors that account for some of the difference in tax effort; and concluded that the ultimate responsibility to address this problem still lay with the State (187 Misc.2d at 97-99, 719 N.Y.S.2d 475). The Appellate Division expressly rejected the State's contention that "any inadequacy in funding is the fault of the City," noting that "the State exerts extensive control over the City, including taxes that may be levied and debts that may be incurred," but reflecting that the remedy, rather than "requiring the State to write out a check every time the City underfunds education" may be for the State to "require the City to maintain a certain level of education funding" (295 A.D.2d at 18, 19, 744 N.Y.S.2d 130).

Here, therefore, there is next to no dispute. If the State believes that deficient City tax effort is a significant contributing cause to the underfunding of City schools, it is for the State- through a combination of enforcing existing laws such as the Stavisky-Goodman Law (Education Law § 2576 [5-a]) and new legislation-to consider corrective measures. This possibility pertains to the remedy, not to the definition of plaintiffs' burden of proof on causation or-what amounts to the same thing in practice-to the determination of whether plaintiffs' cause of action is viable.

In CFE Judge Simons argued otherwise, citing declining City contributions to the school budget as part of his reason why plaintiffs' claim should have been dismissed (86 N.Y.2d at 334, 340-341, 631 N.Y.S.2d 565, 655 N.E.2d 661). The State essentially tries to revive this argument, contending that plaintiffs must lose because they have not shown why their grievance could not be addressed by measures less drastic than constitutional adjudication: greater effort by the City, whether voluntary or statutory.

The analysis we have already outlined regarding responsibility for special education placement and teacher employment practices applies here again. Relative to the State, the City has "absolutely no control" over the school funding system (City v. State, 86 N.Y.2d at 295, 631 N.Y.S.2d 553, 655 N.E.2d 649) and while any failings may be considered in determining the remedy, they do not constitute a supervening cause sufficient to decide the case for the State. Plaintiffs have established the causation element of their claim.

V. The Remedy

Challenging as the previous issues are, in complexity they pale by comparison to the final question: remedy. Pointing to a long history of State inaction despite its knowledge of the inadequacy of the education finance system, plaintiffs ask us to initiate a legislative/judicial dialogue by issuing guidelines to the Legislature for restructuring the system and directing with strict timetables-that the necessary resources be provided. The State, by contrast, urges that, should a constitutional violation be found, the Court simply direct the proper parties to eliminate the deficiencies.

Both extremes are problematic. We are, of course, mindful-as was the trial court-of the responsibility, underscored by the State, to defer to the Legislature in matters of policymaking, particularly in a matter so vital as education financing, which has as well a core element of local control. We have neither the authority, nor the ability, nor the will, to micromanage education financing. By the same token, in plaintiffs' favor, it is the province of the Judicial branch to define, and safeguard, rights provided by the New York State Constitution, and order redress for violation of them. Surely there is a remedy more promising, and ultimately less entangling for the courts, than simply directing the parties to eliminate deficiencies, as the State would have us do.

The trial court ordered the State first to ascertain the actual cost of providing a sound basic education statewide, and then reform the system to (1) ensure that every school district has the resources necessary to provide a sound basic education; (2) take into account variations in local costs; (3) provide sustained and stable funding in order to promote long-term planning by school districts; (4) provide "as much transparency as possible so that the public may understand how the State distributes school aid"; and (5) ensure a system of accountability to measure the effect of reforms implemented (187 Misc.2d at 115, 719 N.Y.S.2d 475). We take it that the fourth, "transparency" requirement would relate to the process by which funds are allocated in Albany, while the fifth, "accountability" requirement relates to the evaluation of schools and of programs designed to improve them.

The State objects to each of these guidelines on various grounds, but a common theme is that existing reforms already address existing problems. Indeed, ongoing federal, state and City programs-several initiated after the close of trial-likely constitute the most ambitious education reform in recent years. Starting at the federal level, the No Child Left Behind Act of 2001 (Pub L. 107-110, 115 U.S. Stat. 1425 [2002]), amending the Elementary and Secondary Education Act of 1965 (20 USC § 6301 et seq.), now requires states to establish mechanisms to identify schools where student performance does not meet standards set by each state. To qualify for federal education funding, states must give children who attend such schools remedial options, such as tutoring or the right to transfer to a better school.

As part of a statewide procedure to identify schools in need of improvement, a number of City schools have been designated as Schools Under Registration Review (SURR) (*see* 8 NYCRR 100.2[p]). This SURR list consists of those schools the Commissioner of Education deems farthest from meeting accountability criteria tied to the Learning Standards (8 NYCRR 100.2[p] [4], [7]). Such schools are required to implement a "corrective action plan" and undergo monitoring; if they do not improve, they may be declared "unsound" (8 NYCRR 100.2[p] [5]).

In New York City, some SURR schools are removed from their community school district and absorbed into a special "Chancellor's District," where they receive greater resources and supervision. City schools constituted 94 of the 98 SURR schools statewide in 1997-1998, the last year for which the record discloses the number of SURR schools.

In addition to federal and state measures directed at identifying and improving bad schools, significant legislation reorganizing City school governance has been passed since the trial (*see* L. 2002, 91; *cf.* L. 2003, 6, 15). The legislation enhances the powers and duties of the Mayor of New York City and persons accountable to the Mayor-notably the Chancellor-to manage school finances and the School Construction Authority, and select and supervise district superintendents and other staff (*see* Legis. Rep. of City of N.Y., 2002 McKinney's Session Laws of N.Y., at 1718-1719).

Further, through an ongoing process of reform, the Regents have sought to reduce the employment of uncertified teachers and fortify the requirements for certification (*see e.g.* 8 NYCRR 80-3.4, 80-5.10[j]). Likewise, regulations adopted with the Learning Standards and intended to improve the rigor of instruction statewide are close to being fully phased in; for instance, students who entered ninth grade in the 2001-2002 school year no longer had the option to take a "local diploma" (*see* 8 NYCRR 100.5).

All of these initiatives promise, but await, demonstrable outcomes. We are, of course, bound to decide this case on the record before us and cannot conjecture about the possible effect of pending reforms, at least when determining whether, on the evidence gathered over four years and presented during the seven-month trial, a constitutional violation exists. To the extent that recent reforms enable more students to receive a sound basic education, the State will have the opportunity on remittal to present evidence of such developments.

For similar reasons, we cannot join the dissent in attaching significance to state budget figures showing that in 2002-2003, "the City enrolled 37% of the State's public school population and was allocated 37% of the combined major aid enacted" (dissenting op. at 955, 769 N.Y.S.2d at 146-147, 801 N.E.2d at 366-367). Presumably the dissent cites this figure as proof that any inequalities in the funding system have been remedied since trial. But under *Levittown* and *CFE*, plaintiffs have a right not to equal state funding but to schools that provide the opportunity for a sound basic education.

Aside from this, even assuming the 2002-2003 figures-which were not part of the record-were properly before us, the dissent misstates their significance. They are based on total aidable pupil units (TAPU) (Education Law § 3602[8] [ii]) and thus would demonstrate not that the City's funding share equaled its *enrollment* share, but that its funding share equaled its *attendance* share-a significant difference given evidence that City schools are beset by truancy. Further, the figures do not reflect STAR tax relief, a $2.7 billion program in the year on which the dissent has focused (*see* New York State Division of the Budget, Education Unit, Description of 2002-03 New York State School Aid Programs, at 30, table II-B). STAR enables homeowners to pay lower property taxes to fund the school system, and enables districts to make up the difference with state funds (*see* Education Law § 3609-e; RPTL 425).

As the trial court said, "New York City receives less STAR aid than localities in the rest of the State" (187 Misc.2d at 86, 719 N.Y.S.2d 475). Finally, of course, the record reflects that a dollar does not go so far in New York City as it goes elsewhere in the State. Thus, even if interdistrict equality were the issue, the 2002-2003 figure cited by the dissent would be far from decisive. We do not explore this point to discredit any choices the Legislature may have made in recent budgets to increase the City's relative allocation of state aid, but simply to emphasize why we focus on record facts whose significance has been properly tested in litigation.

Given all of the jurisprudential constraints discussed above, we begin our review of the trial court's directives by rejecting the provision that the remedy be statewide, and that variations in local costs be taken into account. Courts deal with actual cases and controversies, not abstract global issues, and fashion their directives based on the proof before them. Here the case presented to us, and consequently the remedy, is limited to the adequacy of education financing for the New York City public schools, though the State may of course address statewide issues if it chooses.

Second, we recognize that mechanisms in place, including No Child Left Behind and the SURR process, may already to some extent function as a system of accountability. They are not foolproof, and neither is tied to the definition of a sound basic education. Nevertheless, the State should be able to build on existing criteria to identify the schools in greatest need and set measurable goals for their improvement.

Third, we are not prepared to say as a constitutional matter that a new system must ensure the City "sustained and stable funding." The language of this directive may appear unobjectionable, but in the context of the trial court's decision it implies a need for fundamental change in the relationship between New York City schools and their local tax base. The school districts in New York City, Buffalo, Yonkers, Syracuse and Rochester-unlike every other district in the State-are "fiscally dependent": they lack the authority to levy property taxes to support education.

As the trial court observed, City schools are dependent on municipal revenues, largely from other kinds of taxes more susceptible to the vagaries of the business cycle (187 Misc.2d at 98, 719 N.Y.S.2d 475). It may well be that this susceptibility hinders City schools from developing a more stable budgetary plan-and that any plan to improve City schools that required better local tax effort, in particular, would need to address this matter. At the same time, the State has suggested that reforms tending to concentrate responsibility with the Mayor of New York City may prove beneficial, and we do not know that a "sustained and stable funding" requirement addressing fiscal dependency would necessarily fit together with such reforms. Accordingly, while the trial court's directive is understandable, we do not make it mandatory.

Fourth, as the foregoing implies, the trial court properly indicated that reforms may address governance as well as the school funding system. Various factors alleged by the State as causes of deficiencies in the schools-and rejected by us on the ground that the State has ultimate responsibility for the conduct of its agents and the quality of education in New York City public schools-may be addressed legislatively or administratively as part of the remedy. We do not think such measures will obviate the need for changes to the funding system, but they may affect the scope of such changes.

Finally, we know of no practical way to determine whether members of the political branches have complied with an order that the funding process become as transparent as possible, and we therefore decline to incorporate such a directive into our order. No one, however, disputes the trial court's description of the existing education funding scheme as needlessly complex, malleable and not designed to align funding with need (187 Misc.2d at 82-90, 719 N.Y.S.2d 475). The causes are worth considering.

As _Levittown_ indicates, the justification for a school funding system based on local taxation is "the preservation and promotion of local control of education" (57 N.Y.2d at 44, 453 N.Y.S.2d 643, 439 N.E.2d 359). Conversely, the purposes of state aid to schools are, according to the SED, to assist school districts in providing an effective education; maintain a state-local partnership in public education; equalize school revenues by providing state aid in inverse proportion to each school district's ability to raise local revenues; and encourage model programs to address the needs of the school community. Clearly these purposes reflect a recognition that inputs should be calibrated to student need and hence that state aid should increase where need is high and local ability to pay is low.

In the case of New York City, student need is high, as is the local ability to pay, as measured by the State's Combined Wealth Ratio. Thus, as the trial court observed, the equalizing elements of the state aid formula do not operate to the advantage of City students, the more so in that the system does not take into account the high cost of running schools in the City (187

Misc.2d at 85-86, 719 N.Y.S.2d 475). And the record supports the trial court's conclusion that funding components that might channel funds to meet the needs of City students fail to make a difference in the end: New York City regularly receives a fixed share-just under 39%-of any funding increase (187 Misc.2d at 89, 719 N.Y.S.2d 475).

Thus, the political process allocates to City schools a share of state aid that does not bear a perceptible relation to the needs of City students. While we do not join the trial court in ordering that the process be made as transparent as possible, we do agree that the funding level necessary to provide City students with the opportunity for a sound basic education is an ascertainable starting point. Once the necessary funding level is determined, the question will be whether the inputs and outputs improve to a constitutionally acceptable level. Other questions about the process-such as how open it is and how the burden is distributed between the State and City-are matters for the Legislature desiring to enact good laws.

In view of the alternatives that the parties have presented, we modify the trial court's threshold guideline that the State ascertain "the actual costs of providing a sound basic education in districts around the State" (187 Misc.2d at 115, 719 N.Y.S.2d 475). The State need only ascertain the actual cost of providing a sound basic education in New York City. Reforms to the current system of financing school funding and managing schools should address the shortcomings of the current system by ensuring, as a part of that process, that every school in New York City would have the resources necessary for providing the opportunity for a sound basic education. Finally, the new scheme should ensure a system of accountability to measure whether the reforms actually provide the opportunity for a sound basic education.

The process of determining the actual cost of providing a sound basic education in New York City and enacting appropriate reforms naturally cannot be completed overnight, and we therefore recognize that defendants should have until July 30, 2004 to implement the necessary measures.

VI. Conclusion

We offer these concluding thoughts, against the backdrop of the dissent.

Courts are, of course, well suited to adjudicate civil and criminal cases and extrapolate legislative intent (dissenting op. at 959, 769 N.Y.S.2d at 149, 801 N.E.2d at 369). They are, however, also well suited to interpret and safeguard constitutional rights and review challenged acts of our co-equal branches of government-not in order to make policy but in order to assure the protection of constitutional rights.

That is what we have been called upon to do by litigants seeking to enforce the State Constitution's Education Article. The task began with *Levittown* 's articulation of the constitutional right to a sound basic education-not at all a "catchphrase for an inferred constitutional guarantee" (dissenting op. at 948-949, 769 N.Y.S.2d at 141, 801 N.E.2d at 361), but this Court's careful judgment 21 years ago as to what is meant by our State Constitution's promise in the Education Article. *CFE* built on our definition of the constitutional requirement, adding to the law a determination that the complaint stated a cause of action, and that-if plaintiffs proved their assertions, as they have-they would establish a violation.

Nor is the Court's standard of a sound basic education, articulated both in *Levittown* and *CFE,* "illusory" for failing to fix the moment when a meaningful high school education is achieved (dissenting op. at 948-954, 769 N.Y.S.2d at 141-146, 801 N.E.2d at 361-366). As the dissent itself exemplifies by "of course" rejecting the eighth (or ninth) grade test of the Appellate Division *and offering no other,* a constitutional standard of sound basic education need not pinpoint a date with statutory precision, so long as it defines the contours of the requirement, against which the facts of a case may then be measured. Indeed, a sound basic education back in 1894, when the Education Article was added, may well have consisted of an eighth or ninth grade education, which we unanimously reject. The definition of a sound basic education must serve the future as well as the case now before us.

Finally, the remedy is hardly extraordinary or unprecedented (dissenting op. at 958, 769 N.Y.S.2d at 148, 801 N.E.2d at 368). It is, rather, an effort to learn from our national experience and fashion an outcome that will address the constitutional violation instead of inviting decades of litigation. A case in point is the experience of our neighbor, the New Jersey Supreme Court, which in its landmark education decision 30 years ago simply specified the constitutional deficiencies, beginning more than a dozen trips to the court (dissenting op. at 958 n. 11, 769 N.Y.S.2d at 148-149 n. 11, 801 N.E.2d at 368-369 n. 11), a process that led over time to more focused directives by that court (*compare Robinson v. Cahill,* 63 N.J. 196, 198, 306 A.2d 65, 66 [1973] *with Abbott v. Burke,* 119 N.J. 287, 385-391, 575 A.2d 359, 408-411 [1990]).

In other jurisdictions, the process has generated considerably less litigation, possibly because courts there initially offered more detailed remedial directions, as we do (*see e.g. Rose v. Council for Better Educ., Inc.,* 790 S.W.2d 186, 215-216 [Ky.1989]). We do not share the dissent's belief that in New York any constitutional ruling adverse to the present scheme will inevitably be met with the kind of sustained legislative resistance that may have occurred elsewhere.

Nor is it certain that plaintiffs' success will necessarily inspire a host of imitators throughout the state (dissenting op. at 956, 769 N.Y.S.2d at 147, 801 N.E.2d at 367). Plaintiffs have prevailed here owing to a unique combination of circumstances: New York City schools have the *most* need in the state and the *highest* local costs yet receive some of the *lowest* per-student funding and have some of the *worst* results. Plaintiffs in other districts who cannot demonstrate a similar combination may find tougher going in the courts.

We trust that fixing a few signposts in the road yet to be traveled by the parties will shorten the already arduous journey and help to achieve the hoped-for remedy.

Accordingly, the order of the Appellate Division should be modified and the case remitted to Supreme Court for further proceedings in accordance with this opinion, and as so modified affirmed, with costs to plaintiffs.

SMITH, J. (concurring).

I concur in and join the decision of the Chief Judge and the decision to modify the order of the Appellate Division. I write separately in order to focus on several aspects of this litigation. I conclude that (a) the Regents Learning Standards provide students with the minimum skills required by a sound basic education, (b) the remedy should be statewide in scope and (c) the remedy should include the reformulation of the present formula for allocating state funds. All the children of New York are constitutionally entitled to the opportunity of a high school education-up to the 12th grade-that imparts the skills necessary to sustain competitive employment within the market of high school graduates, acquire higher education, and serve capably on a jury and vote.

The Importance of a Sound Basic Education

It is commonly said that education is the State's most important responsibility. Education is just one of the many responsibilities of the State. Only a few of the responsibilities involving the provision of certain services are actually mentioned in the State Constitution. These include the incarceration of criminals, helping the needy and providing housing for the poor and the elderly.

Of the three, only the section dealing with helping the needy contains the mandatory "shall," although it then gives the Legislature the discretion to determine "from time to time" how the help to those it classifies as needy is to be provided.

There is no discretion, however, in the statement, "The legislature shall provide for the maintenance and support of a system of free common schools, wherein all the children of this state may be educated". The only discretion is in the hands of parents who do not have to send their children to public schools. Since education is the most important responsibility of the State, it follows, a priori, that building schools that provide children with a sound education is more important than building jails to incarcerate criminals, shelters to house the homeless, and low income housing for the poor.

This order of priorities recognizes that a child who has an opportunity for a sound education is less likely to become a criminal or be homeless.

Sound Basic Education Equals A High School Education

Throughout this litigation, the State has ferociously clung to the argument that a sound basic education consists of the ability to read, write, and do math at a rudimentary level. Since these skills are generally acquired by the eighth or ninth grade, the State then argues that this is the constitutional minimum. The view of the State is essentially that of the concurring opinion of Judge Levine in *Campaign for Fiscal Equity v. State of New York*, 86 N.Y.2d 307, 324, 631 N.Y.S.2d 565, 655 N.E.2d 661 [1995] [*CFE I*], who concluded that "what legitimately might be called an education are the basic literacy (reading and writing) and computational skills and, in a public educational system, citizenship awareness. A public educational system failing to provide the opportunity to acquire those basic skills would not be worthy of that appellation" (*id.* at 331, 631 N.Y.S.2d 565, 655 N.E.2d 661).

Judge Levine disagreed with the holding of the majority that a sound "education should consist of the basic literacy, calculating, and verbal skills necessary to enable children to eventually function productively as civic participants capable of voting and serving on a jury" (*id.* at 316, 631 N.Y.S.2d 565, 655 N.E.2d 661). The majority in *CFE I* also stated that this definition did not "definitively specify what the constitutional concept and mandate of a sound basic education entails," which would take place "after discovery and the development of a factual record" (*id.* at 317, 631 N.Y.S.2d 565, 655 N.E.2d 661). At this point, the discovery has taken place, and the factual record has been developed.

The record establishes what would strike many as an obvious truth: a high school education is today as indispensable as a primary education was in 1894. Children in the 21st century need the opportunity for more than a ninth grade education to be productive citizens. Back in the 19th century, a high school education was not needed to obtain a good job. Now, a high school education is a prerequisite to most good jobs. Those who lack a high school education and have obtained good jobs have done so in spite of, not because of, the lack of a high school education. While it may be true that there will always be menial low-skills jobs, and thus a need for people to fill them, it should not be the purpose of the public schools to prepare students for those jobs, which are limited in number and dwindling.

Dr. Linda Darling-Hammond, a professor at Stanford University and Executive Director of the National Commission on Teaching and America's Future, testified that "preparing students for employment has been part of the rationale for public education since the beginning of public education in this country." She also testified that the findings of abundant research in this area are "that students today need much higher levels of technical skills and knowledge than they did in the past; that that set of skills includes the ability to manage and comprehend complex text and information to manage resources. About 90 percent of the jobs that are in the economy today are jobs that require at least a high school education and a level of technical skill in managing technology, text, and various kinds of content specific competencies that we used to expect of only about 50 percent of the employees in 1950."

Even one of defendants' experts, John Murphy, the President of Education Partners, testified, "I would think that a school system has a responsibility to prepare all of its children to compete in this society, yes." He then agreed with the statement that to "compete in society means to get a good, productive job."

It is worth noting that although a secondary education was not as prevalent at the time the Education Article was adopted as it is today, free public education included a high school education. It was in 1853, almost 40 years before the adoption of the Education Article, that the Legislature began allowing districts to form union districts, which could establish a high school. Thus, the public school system that the Education Article constitutionalized included a system that provided a free high school education.

A sound education also connotes the necessary preparation to acquire higher education. In connection with the second section of the Education Article, which constitutionalized the Regents, the Constitutional Convention committee on education stated that "higher education here, as in every other civilized country, has been the chief factor in developing the elementary and secondary schools" (2 Documents of 1894 N.Y. Constitutional Convention No. 62, at 6). Primary and secondary schools and colleges were thus perceived as interdependent, in the same way that they are perceived today. At the time, the common schools primarily prepared students for high school, and only a few went on to college. Now that a high school education has taken the place of a primary education, it should prepare students for higher education.

Thus, the Education Article requires the opportunity for a sound high school education that should prepare students for higher education, or to compete in the employment market of high school graduates.

The Legislature has prescribed that the Regents "shall exercise legislative functions concerning the educational system of the state, determine its educational policies, and, except, as to the judicial functions of the commissioner of education, establish rules for carrying into effect the laws and policies of the state, relating to education" (Education Law § 207). The 16 members of the Regents are elected by concurrent resolutions of both houses of the Legislature, and they in turn appoint the Commissioner of Education who is the head of the State Education Department (SED) (N.Y. Const., art. XI, § 2; Education Law §§ 202, 101). The SED carries out the policies enacted by the Regents, and is responsible for the general management and supervision of all of the public schools in the state (Education Law § 101).

Pursuant to their delegated authority, the Regents establish the requirements students must satisfy in order to obtain a high school diploma. In the past, students could obtain a local high school diploma by passing the Regents Competency Tests (RCTs). Plaintiffs offered unchallenged testimony that the RCTs measured eighth grade reading skills and sixth grade math skills. Students who wished to obtain a Regents diploma were required to pass more rigorous tests. That system is being phased out, and a new system is being phased in.

Under the new system, students are required to pass five State-administered Regents examinations in four subject areas (English, mathematics, social studies and science) that are aligned with new Learning Standards. Students can obtain a Regents diploma evincing higher levels of achievement in mathematics, science, and foreign language by successfully completing eight Regents examinations.

The State argues that the Learning Standards are aspirational and "world-class." That the minimum requirements in order to obtain a high school diploma are aspirational, which connotes striving for something that is not necessarily achievable, may actually come as a surprise to high school students who must satisfy them. If these tests are aspirational, then the tests for an advanced high school diploma must be ultra aspirational. While some witnesses described the Learning Standards as "high" and "rigorous," all the witnesses testified that they represent the minimum students need in order to be productive citizens. It is clear that in comparison to the RCTs, the Learning Standards are indeed rigouous.

In addition, they are rigorous to the extent the Regents and the SED have determined that being a productive citizen requires learning the skills the Learning Standards impart. The record clearly supports the view that the Learning Standards satisfy the minimum required by the Education Article. In any event, even if the Learning Standards offered more than the minimum required by the Education Article, the State has a constitutional responsibility to ensure that students have the opportunity to meet those standards, since they are a prerequisite to a high school diploma (*see* 8 NYCRR 3.35, 100.1[g], [t]; 100.2[e]; 100.5).

The record establishes that the RCTs did not meet the constitutional minimum because at the high school level, they prepared students to read at an eighth grade level or perform sixth grade mathematics. As a result, students who obtained a local diploma were not assured that they received a high school education. They might have graduated from high school, but the education offered was effectively primary. It is not surprising then, that, as found by the Mayor's Advisory Task Force on the City University of New York, a majority of CUNY freshmen, about half of whom were graduates of New York City high schools, required remedial courses (The City University of New York: An Institution Adrift, at 21-22 [June 7, 1999]).

It is this Court's constitutional responsibility to review the educational standards established by the Regents and determine whether they meet the constitutional minimum. A finding that the Learning Standards meet the constitutional minimum does not somehow constitute an abdication of this Court's responsibility to interpret the Education Article. On the contrary, it would be the failure to review the educational policies of the State to determine if they satisfy the requirement of the Education Article that would constitute a dereliction of this Court's duty to say what the law is.

To conclude that courts should not question what the Legislature, through the Regents, determines is a sound basic education is to conclude that this Court should play no role in interpreting the Education Article. It is the responsibility of the State to offer the opportunity of a sound basic education, and it is the responsibility of this Court to determine whether the State is fulfilling its responsibility to the plaintiffs.

The Formulas Do Not Equal A Sound Basic Education

New York's public education system is supported and maintained by funds from three sources: localities (about 56%), the State (about 40%), and the federal government (about four percent). The Legislature has given most boards of education the authority to raise local funds by imposing taxes on residential and commercial properties within each district. In addition, the boards have no constitutional tax limits. The so-called Big 5 cities (Buffalo, New York City, Rochester, Syracuse, and Yonkers), on the other hand, have constitutional tax limits that apply to the total municipal budget. In addition, the boards of education of the Big 5 lack the authority to levy taxes, making them fiscally dependent. Rather, their appropriations are part of the overall budget, which is funded through citywide taxes, including property taxes, sales taxes, and income taxes. As stated by Dr. Robert Berne, Vice-President for Academic Development and professor of public administration at New York University, this means that "within the confines of the City budget process, education competes directly for other municipal services as opposed to being separate in an independent school district." According to the SED, the "fiscal dependence on these school districts is fraught with problems related to level and stability of funding and the effective use of education dollars."

One obvious problem for districts in the Big 5 is that during a fiscal crisis, local appropriations for schools may fall dramatically, affecting their ability to provide the opportunity for a sound education. The same is not necessarily the case in fiscally independent districts since property values tend to be stable, and in fact, may rise during difficult economic times. In the words of Dr. Berne, "Compared to the resources say in New York City where it is a combination of all of the general resources, the property tax is less, economically less sensitive and more predictable tax." Another problem is that in addition to having limits in the amount that they can borrow, there are also State-imposed limits in the amount of taxes cities may levy.

The State uses a system comprised of about 54 formulas to distribute about $13 billion of state aid. Historically, New York City has received close to 34% of the total of state aid. For 1999, New York City's Board of Education had a budget of $9.8 billion. The average per-pupil expenditure for that year was $8,957. The roughly 1.1 million public school students in New

York City make up 37% of the total state student population. About 73% of New York City students qualify for the federal government's free or reduced price lunch program that is targeted to poor students. About 72% are African-American or Hispanic. About 80% of all state students with limited English proficiency attend New York City public schools.

A substantial number of New York City students are said to be at risk of doing poorly in school because of socioeconomic disadvantages, including poverty, race and limited English proficiency. The record establishes that these students need more help than others in order to meet educational goals, such as extended school programs, remedial instruction, and support services.

The most important category of formulas is termed basic operating aid, which distributes $5 to $6 billion of state aid based on weighted attendance and wealth of school districts. Although we held in *Board of Educ., Levittown Union Free School Dist. v. Nyquist,* 57 N.Y.2d 27, 453 N.Y.S.2d 643, 439 N.E.2d 359 [1982] that the Education Article does not require equality of educational resources, operating aid seeks to have a wealth equalizing effect by giving more to low-value property districts and less to high-value property districts. Operating aid also distributes flat grants to each district regardless of the level of wealth.

New York City receives about 36% of operating aid. Mr. Kadamus testified that operating aid treats New York City as an average wealth district, overlooking the high concentration of poverty. Thus, it is "impossible for that particular aid formula to drive a lot of additional money into New York City, so, therefore, you have to use other parts of the formulas to do that and so far those parts of the formulas have not been particularly well-funded compared to the operating aid formula."

The State did make an attempt to ensure that high-need districts have adequate resources by adopting an Extraordinary Needs Aid (ENA) formula in 1993. About 93% of New York City students fall within the ENA formula. Thus, New York City received most of the funding allocated to ENA. Despite this, however, New York City's total state aid allocation hardly changed after ENA was phased in, largely because ENA only accounts for about five percent of the total state aid. Mr. Kadamus testified that ENA fails to provide districts with high-need students with the needed funds. The former Director of the State Division of the Budget, Robert L. King, testified that the central budget office had not determined whether the amount allocated under ENA provided schools with the necessary funds to educate at-risk children. In the same vein, the Division has not sought to determine whether school districts have sufficient resources to provide students with an adequate education.

Year after year the formulas have consistently failed to measure the actual costs necessary to provide New York City students with a sound education. Rather, New York City's share of state aid has been close to 34% regardless of the City's actual education needs. The record supports Dr. Berne's opinion that "it is well known that the share of New York City's increase in aid is determined first in the legislative process and then the formulas are actually driven backwards to get that share to come out."

The Paper Trail

The ineffectiveness of the formulas has been documented by the Regents. While the Regents are responsible for establishing educational policy in the State, they have no equivalent power with respect to funding. That power is in the hands of the Governor and the Legislature.

However, the Regents, along with the Commissioner of Education, suggest to the Legislature the amount of spending they believe is necessary to meet the educational goals they have established. Each year, the Regents and the SED submit to the Governor and the Legislature an annual report containing a great deal of information about the state of the education system, which is designed to ensure greater correlation between student outcomes and expenditures (Education Law § 215-a).

In addition, the Regents and the SED regularly appoint formal committees and task forces to study educational issues. Virtually every document in the record prepared by the Regents or the SED dealing with funding has been critical of the formulas. For example, the Regents' Proposals on School Aid for 1993-1994 and 1994-1995 state that the formulas:

• do not provide adequately for all students, especially the most needy

• are unduly complicated, with 53 separate formulas governing the distribution of aid

• inhibit local flexibility, since many kinds of aid require specific programs whether or not such programs are the best use of the money

• entail no accountability for results, because districts continue to receive the money no matter what

• do not deal adequately with local differences in wealth and cost

• do not adequately support needed improvements in teaching and learning

• lack public credibility for all of these reasons

The preface to the 1999 annual report prepared by the Regents and the SED finds that:

"With few exceptions, the formulas do not consider the extra help in achieving the standards needed by children placed at risk by poverty and limited proficiency in English. Thus, because New York City's property and income wealth per pupil is close to the State average, its State aid allocation per pupil is also close to the State average. The fact that the City's percentage of students eligible for free lunches exceeds the State average by 28 percentage points (73 compared with 45 percent) does not substantially increase their State aid allocation."

A 1999 Discussion Paper prepared by the SED for the Regents Subcommittee on State Aid (Moving Toward Adequacy, Recognizing High Cost Factors In the Financing of Public Education) concluded the formulas did not take into account regional cost differences in professional service costs and the number of high need pupils. The Paper made several proposals, which it noted,

"recognize and correct the fundamental unfairness of allocating $3,000 in State Aid per pupil to districts which are *identical in fiscal capacity*. One district is located in a high cost area of the State where this $3,000 has a purchasing power of only $2,250 and 80 percent of the students live in households that fall below poverty. The second district is in a low cost area of the State where the purchasing power equivalent of this $3,000 is $3,500 per pupil and only 10 percent of its student body is poor."

The Paper also reaffirmed the conclusion of substantial prior research that "as the concentration of children in poverty increased at the school building level, achievement decreased. These negative achievement effects were not trivial but dramatic." As to the relationship between funding and student need, the Paper found that 93% of New York City students fell within the ENA formula, and that this percentage:

"was almost three times greater than the comparison percentage of other districts similar to New York City in their wealth. Since State Aid is highly equalizing with respect to wealth, but less well equalized with respect to the concentration of disadvantaged pupils, the unusually high concentration of disadvantaged pupils places it at a funding disadvantage."

Although the distribution of $10.4 billion in state aid "was found to be highly wealth equalized" when it was "recalculated on a poverty-weighted pupil basis, the desired equalization of the current aid distribution diminished significantly."

The same observation was made in the forward to the Regents' Proposal on State Aid to School Districts for the School Year 2000-2001. According to its foreword:

"At a time when the Regents have imposed higher standards for graduation throughout the State's public schools, it is important that State aid to school districts must be better targeted on those districts with the highest costs and the farthest to go to meet the standards.

"Throughout history, State Aid to education has not been distributed in a manner that both recognized student need and provided incentives for academic improvement. In addition, schools and districts were not held accountable for the results of education spending. Rather, State Aid has been distributed based primarily on the wealth of a district as measured by its real estate assessments and income of residents (the lower the value of its combined wealth, the more the aid) and its student attendance. Accordingly, State Aid has been distributed on a district's theoretical capacity to pay for education, with limited regard to educating its students to desired levels.

"The New York City School District has been affected by this process with its near-average wealth and high student need. The result is that the district has never enjoyed State Aid increases that reflect the costs of educating all students to levels accepted in the rest of the State. Student results have shown that many schools have great difficulty in meeting student needs. The State and the nation must face the exorbitant costs for public assistance, criminal justice and lost productivity that such education failure requires."

The then-current Chancellor of the Regents, Dr. Hayden, was asked, "Do you believe that you have a thorough understanding of the state aid formula system?" He replied, "I do not." When asked why not, he said, "I think it defies scrutiny Quite frankly, I think there are very few people in the State of New York who understand the state aid formula and how it works I believe the public is at an extreme disadvantage when it cannot follow the way in which the money moves." The same sentiment was expressed by Dr. Sobol. He testified that the complexity of the formulas "made it more difficult to direct the aid where we thought it was most needed, namely, with those students who were not now enjoying the benefits of the resources needed to require the sound basic education."

Under his helm, the SED was concerned with disparities in wealth and cost across the State "not only because of the inequality, but because of the inadequacy, because, in some situations, it makes it impossible for local schools or school districts to provide the conditions that students need if they were to obtain the sound, basic education under the constitution." New York City was one of these school districts.

The current Commissioner, Dr. Mills, testified that he did not have a deep understanding of how the formulas work, and that only "very few people" do. Dr. Berne, who is one of those few people, testified that the formulas are extremely complex, making it "hard for most people in the State to understand and easier for manipulation." The shares agreement "negates the general factors that are shown in the formulas that are supposedly driving resources to children in school districts." The complexity of the formulas and the decision to predetermine the amount New York City students need are the culprit for the lack of "alignment between educational goals and the components of the school finance system." Defendant Governor Pataki has called the formulas "incomprehensible," "convoluted," and destined for the "ash heap of history."

<u>Remedies</u>

The formulas have consistently failed to provide New York City schools with the funds necessary to allow them to provide a sound education for their students. Despite constant fine tuning, the formulas have impeded the duty of the Legislature to maintain and support an effective system of public schools in New York City. In fact, their Byzantine complexity makes it possible for aid to be distributed in an arbitrary manner that bears no relationship between educational goals and costs associated with meeting those needs. Consequently, the formulas are incompatible with the Legislature's duty to provide a sound education to New York City students.

Since the formulas are used to distribute aid to all the schools in the state, the remedy must necessarily affect the entire interdependent school system. In place of the formulas, the Legislature should institute a scheme that: (1) eliminates the current state formula for distributing aid to New York City; (2) determines, to the extent possible, the actual costs of the resources needed to provide the opportunity for a sound basic education in all school districts in the state; and (3) ensures that at a minimum every school district has the necessary funds to provide an opportunity for a sound basic education to all of its students.

While the foregoing may not guarantee that the opportunity of a basic education will be available to all the children in the state, they are necessary steps in that direction. In sum, I join the decision of the Chief Judge, but the Constitution requires the State to do even more than is stated to ensure a sound basic education for all students.

<u>READ</u>, J. (dissenting).

This case is not about whether education is important for the vitality of our democracy-of course, it is. This case is not about whether the children who attend New York City's public schools require more than an eighth-grade education to meet the demands of today's world-of course, they do. This case is not about whether New York City's public schools have too often failed to furnish our children the learning opportunities that they deserve-of course, they have. These are obvious truths, universally acknowledged, which have lately spurred the most significant education reform effort in the history of the New York City public school system.

Rather, this case is about whether the perceived shortcomings of New York City's public schools are constitutional infirmities under the Education Article attributable to inadequate state funding. On a more fundamental level, this case is about whether the courts or the Legislature and the Executive should set education policy for our public schools. Because the constitutional standard crafted by the majority to define a "sound basic education" is illusory, because the causal connection between the level of state aid and any deficiencies in New York City's public schools is not proven, and because the majority's proposed remedy exceeds the prudential bounds of the judicial function, I respectfully dissent.

<u>Sound Basic Education</u>

The New York Constitution does not mandate an educational system of a certain quality in express terms. The relevant constitutional text simply reads: "The legislature shall provide for the maintenance and support of a system of free common schools, wherein all the children of this state may be educated" (<u>N.Y. Const., art. XI, § 1</u>). The words "sound basic education," which have become the catchphrase for an inferred constitutional*949 guarantee of an education of a certain quality, first appeared in our decision in *Board of Educ., Levittown Union Free School Dist. v Nyquist,* 57 N.Y.2d 27, 48, 453 N.Y.S.2d 643, 439 N.E.2d 359 [1982] [*Levittown*].

The plaintiffs and intervenors in *Levittown* sought a declaration that the State's school financing system, then as now comprised of local taxation and state aid, violated the Equal Protection Clauses of the State and U.S. Constitutions and the State Constitution's Education Article because of the funding disparities between wealthier and poorer school districts. We rejected the equal protection claims on the ground that the State had demonstrated a rational basis for its school financing system: " the preservation and promotion of local control of education" (*id.* at 44, 453 N.Y.S.2d 643, 439 N.E.2d 359).

We further observed that the Education Article focuses on a "State-wide system assuring minimal acceptable facilities and services," not a system assuring equal educational facilities and services throughout the State (*id.* at 47, 453 N.Y.S.2d 643, 439 N.E.2d 359). We recognized that the State undeniably had in place a system of free schools and a statutory framework requiring minimum days of school attendance, specific courses, textbooks and qualifications for teaching and nonteaching staff. Accordingly,

"if what is made available by this system (which is what is to be maintained and supported) may properly be said to constitute an education, the constitutional mandate is satisfied.

"Interpreting the term education, as we do, *to connote a sound basic education,* we have no difficulty in determining that the constitutional requirement is being met in this State, in which it is said without contradiction that the average per pupil expenditure exceeds that in all other States but two" (*id.* at 48, 453 N.Y.S.2d 643, 439 N.E.2d 359 [emphasis added]).

We were careful to register our reluctance to interfere with the Legislature's funding allocations among competing imperatives by mandating an even higher priority for education funding "in the absence, possibly, of gross and glaring inadequacy" (*id.*).

The suggestion in _Levittown_ of a possibly justiciable claim became a reality in _Campaign for Fiscal Equity v. State of New York_, 86 N.Y.2d 307, 631 N.Y.S.2d 565, 655 N.E.2d 661 [1995] [_CFE I_]. Because the case came to us in the procedural posture of a motion to dismiss, all the complaint's averments were deemed true (_see CFE I_, 86 N.Y.2d at 318, 631 N.Y.S.2d 565, 655 N.E.2d 661). We did not, however, measure the allegations of gross and glaring inadequacy against the constitutional standard to determine if the complaint stated a cause of action under the Education Article. In fact, we refused to "attempt to definitively specify what the constitutional concept and mandate of a sound basic education entails" (_id._ at 317, 631 N.Y.S.2d 565, 655 N.E.2d 661). Instead, we crafted a "template" ("the basic literacy, calculating and verbal skills necessary to enable [children] to function as civic participants capable of voting and serving as jurors") for the trial court to utilize to establish the meaning of a "sound basic education" after discovery and trial (_id._ at 317-318, 631 N.Y.S.2d 565, 655 N.E.2d 661).

Thus was a constitutional standard transformed into the end product of a trial at which experts aired differing views of what is required for minimal educational proficiency and employment success in a competitive urban society. The trial court would be left with policy choices to make, not factual contentions to resolve. The trial court would have to fashion "the constitutional concept and mandate of [what] a sound basic education entails" on the testimony of competing experts (_id._ at 317, 631 N.Y.S.2d 565, 655 N.E.2d 661).

· The risks inherent in this novel approach to constitutional adjudication have now been realized. The trial court modified the "template" to reflect a "dynamic" understanding of the constitutional imperative that must "evolve" with the changing demands of a modern world (187 Misc.2d 1, 16, 719 N.Y.S.2d 475 [2001]). A sound basic education was expanded to require an "engaged, capable voter" who has the "intellectual tools to evaluate complex issues, such as campaign finance reform, tax policy, and global warming" (_id._ at 14, 719 N.Y.S.2d 475). Furthermore, the trial court understood our "template" to encompass the opportunity to obtain "productive employment or pursue higher education" (_id._ at 15, 719 N.Y.S.2d 475).

The template was transmuted from a constitutional minimum into "the aspirational, largely subjective standards expressed by the lower courts and the dissent in _Levittown_, representing what typically one would desire as the outcome of an entire public education process-to produce useful, functioning citizens in a modern society" (_CFE I_, 86 N.Y.2d at 329, 631 N.Y.S.2d 565, 655 N.E.2d 661 [Levine, J., concurring]).

Today the majority defines a "sound basic education" as "a meaningful high school education, one which prepares [young people] to function productively as civic participants" (majority op. at 908, 769 N.Y.S.2d at 112, 801 N.E.2d at 332). While unimpeachable, what exactly does this supposed refinement of a "sound basic education" mean? Does a "meaningful high school education" entail a high school diploma, requiring completion of the 12th grade? Evidently not, because the majority notes that "a sound basic education should not be pegged to the eighth or ninth grade, or indeed to any particular grade level" (majority op. at 906, 769 N.Y.S.2d at 111, 801 N.E.2d at 331).

This begs the question of how the courts (or the other branches) are expected to figure out whether the majority's constitutional minimum (i.e., a "sound basic education" defined as a "meaningful high school education" that prepares students "to function productively as civic participants") has been met if completion of the 12th grade and graduation are irrelevant.

Similarly, the majority observes that a "high school level education is now all but indispensable" for employment (majority op. at 906, 769 N.Y.S.2d at 111, 801 N.E.2d at 331), without suggesting how a job applicant establishes that level of competence absent a diploma. Further, if the majority means to imply that some quantum of high school education short of graduation comprises a "meaningful high school education," how is this measured other than by relating it to completion of some grade level lower than the 12th?

The requirements for a high school diploma are defined by the State Education Department (8 NYCRR 100.5 [2003]). Students who entered ninth grade in 2001-2002 and those thereafter (except students with disabilities) will only be eligible for a high school diploma upon satisfactorily meeting Regents Learning Standards (RLSs) (8 NYCRR 100.5[a][3] [2003]). Thus, if a "meaningful high school education" does, in fact, mean a high school diploma, the majority's standard "cede[s] to a state agency the power to define a constitutional right" (majority op. at 907, 769 N.Y.S.2d at 112, 801 N.E.2d at 332)-a result it emphatically rejects.

Although the majority resists adopting the Regents Learning Standards to define a "sound basic education" or a "meaningful high school education," the Board of Regents is, in fact, the constitutionally designated education policymaking body in our state. "The adoption of regulations with respect to graduation requirements, including basic competency examinations, to establish a standard that would make a high school diploma in this State a meaningful credential of the graduate, is clearly within the authority and power of [the Board of Regents and Commissioner of Education]" (*Matter of Board of Educ. of Northport-E. Northport Union Free School Dist. v. Ambach*, 90 A.D.2d 227, 231-232, 458 N.Y.S.2d 680 [3d Dept.1982], *affd.* 60 N.Y.2d 758, 469 N.Y.S.2d 669, 457 N.E.2d 775 [1983]).

Further, the majority offers no objective reference point as an alternative to the Regents Learning Standards. In order to determine whether "inputs" are sufficient to avoid a constitutional violation, the majority must look to "outputs" correlated to an objective reference point. All traditional education ends in assessment: an examination result, grade advancement, or graduation. In short, the majority has articulated a constitutional standard without any way to measure whether it has been (or may be) met.

The "outputs" section of the majority opinion underscores the problematic nature of the constitutional standard of its devising. First, my colleagues "presume[ ] that a dropout has not received a sound basic education" and rely on evidence to support this presumption (majority op. at 914, 769 N.Y.S.2d at 117, 801 N.E.2d at 337). They then observe that between a quarter and half of all dropouts leave after completing four years of high school (majority op. at 915 n. 7, 769 N.Y.S.2d at 117 n. 7, 801 N.E.2d at 337 n. 7).

If dropouts by definition do not receive a "meaningful high school education," then it logically follows that the recipient of a high school diploma is the only student who does. Students either graduate from high school or drop out-there is no middle ground where a "meaningful high school education" makes any sense.

Next, the majority criticizes the probative value of test results offered by the State on "an assortment of commercially available nationally-normed reading and math tests administered to children in City elementary schools" because the results were referenced to a norm rather than to achievement levels (majority op. at 918, 769 N.Y.S.2d at 119, 801 N.E.2d at 339).

Even though New York City's elementary school students rank in the middle nationally in terms of the reading and mathematical skills of their peers, the majority views these tests results as irrelevant because "[t]he State has not shown how to translate these results into proof that the schools are delivering a sound basic education, *properly defined*" (majority op. at 918, 769 N.Y.S.2d at 120, 801 N.E.2d at 340 emphasis added). I fail to grasp why scores reflecting proficiency for New York City students which is equal to, or better than, that of half of their peers nationally still falls short of a constitutional minimum.

Lastly, the majority discounts the Regents Competency Tests (RCTs), the state prerequisite for a "local" high school diploma, because the RCTs assess "an eighth or ninth grade level in reading and a sixth-to-eighth grade level in math" and thus do "not prove that [students] have received a meaningful high school education" (majority op. at 917, 769 N.Y.S.2d at 119, 801 N.E.2d at 339). But students who receive a local diploma have successfully completed the twelfth grade. They simply have not taken Regents exams in their courses.

The indispensable nature of the "outputs" in determining whether the New York City public school system currently or prospectively provides the opportunity for a "meaningful high school education" cannot be overstated. Here, the majority definitively specifies only what the acceptable educational "output" is *not*. It is definitely not the RCTs, which are being phased out in favor of the RLSs, because they are insufficiently ambitious to comport with modern-day understandings of what a sound basic education encompasses (and, if measured by the RCTs, the New York City public school system does not violate the quality standard of the Education Article). But the majority also balks at adopting the RLSs, which represent too ambitious a minimum at present for the ever-evolving constitutional principle at stake. In any event, the

RLSs are not a proper constitutional standard because they may bend, grow or retreat at the will of a state agency.

The majority's dilemma is easy to appreciate. Recognizing the Judiciary's limitations as an education policymaker, my colleagues are reluctant to create a detailed quality standard by which to define the State's obligation under the Education Article. But they are also unwilling to cede to the Board of Regents and the State Education Department the power to define (and, in the future, redefine) what is claimed to be a constitutional principle (albeit a dynamic one), not an education policy decision.

As a result, the standard that the majority has created-a "meaningful high school education" that prepares students "to function productively as civic participants"-is illusory. It surely is no more definite than the template enunciated for a "sound basic education" in *CFE I,* unless, of course, the majority, in fact, intends to equate a "meaningful high school education" with a high school diploma. In that event, my colleagues have, as a practical matter, adopted the RLSs and the Regents diploma as defining the constitutional minimum-for the present.

Causation

In *Levittown,* we had "no difficulty in determining that the constitutional requirement [was] being met" by virtue of the State's substantial financial contribution to education alone, which placed New York third among the states in per-pupil expenditures (*see Levittown,* 57 N.Y.2d at 48, 453 N.Y.S.2d 643, 439 N.E.2d 359). New York still spends more on state aid for education than all but two states in the nation, although New York has lost its rank as the second most populous state in the 20 years since *Levittown.*

In 2002-2003, the Legislature disbursed $12.3 billion from the General Fund for public education statewide. This represented almost 31% of all General Fund disbursements for the fiscal year. Moreover, the State's contribution to the New York City school system has markedly increased over the past several years, from $3.1 billion in fiscal year 1993-1994 to $4.5 billion in fiscal year 1999-2000 to more than $5 billion in fiscal year 2002-2003. As the State's contributions have increased, the City has not kept pace. As a result, from fiscal year 1994-1995 to fiscal year 1999-2000, the State's share of the City's combined state and local education funding increased from 47% to 51% (approximately 10% of the City's education budget consists of federal funds). Concomitantly, the City's share decreased from 53% in 1995-1996 to 49% in 1999-2000.

In 1999-2000, the school year during which the trial in this case ended, the Board of Education received more than $10.4 billion from all sources to operate New York City's public schools, amounting to $9,500 per pupil. Between 1997, when the Board's budget was $8.1 billion, and 2000, pupil spending increased by 20% even after adjusting for inflation. The City reports its current school year overall budget to have risen to $12.4 billion, or $11,300 per enrolled student. In addition to its operating budget, the Board's capital plan at the time of trial provided over $7 billion in funding for new school facilities and repairs to existing facilities.

In short, very substantial sums are spent on New York City's public schools. If it were counted as a state, New York City would rank fifth in per-pupil expenditures; it would rank ninth if spending were adjusted for cost-of-living differences. Again, the State contributes about half of these very substantial sums.

The plaintiffs originally complained that New York City's public schools were necessarily underfunded by the State because they enrolled 37% of the State's public school population but received slightly less than 35% of the total state aid distributed. Addressing this point in _CFE I,_ Judge Simons in his dissent pointed out that "[t]here is no constitutional requirement that the State maintain exact parity in the financial aid distributed to the several thousand school districts" (_CFE I,_ 86 N.Y.2d at 340, 631 N.Y.S.2d 565, 655 N.E.2d 661). In any event, for the 2002-2003 school year, the City enrolled 37% of the State's public school population and was allocated 37% of the combined major aid enacted (_see_ New York State Division of the Budget, Education Unit, Description of 2002-03 New York State School Aid Programs, at 35, table II-E).

In this lawsuit, plaintiffs assert that the Education Article establishes a particular quality standard, and that New York City's public schools do not offer students the opportunity for an education that meets this quality standard. Plaintiffs then argue that the reason for this failure is necessarily inadequate state funding, even though the New York City public school system receives substantial school aid and has benefitted from huge increases in school aid over the life of this litigation. Plaintiffs' proof of a causal link amounts to nothing more than an article of faith: the New York City public school system is not what we would like it to be or what it needs to be, and more money is always better; therefore, the system's shortcomings are attributable to inadequate funding, for which the State is necessarily responsible because of the obligation placed upon it by the Education Article.

As the Appellate Division recognized, this is not proof of a causal connection, it is a recipe for "limitless litigation" (295 A.D.2d 1, 9, 744 N.Y.S.2d 130 [2002]). Moreover, I would not expect this "limitless litigation" to be confined to litigants concerned about New York City's public schools. The success of plaintiffs' theory here will no doubt inspire a host of future litigants representing other communities and school districts throughout the State.

In fact, of course, educational deficiencies are not always attributable to the lack of money or necessarily cured by the infusion of more funds. A wide variety of nonfinancial factors (not to mention socioeconomic factors) may contribute to academic failure, including mismanagement, excessive administration, mis-assigned teachers, misplaced spending priorities, outright corruption, and an improper emphasis on some programs.

For example, the majority points to excessive class size as a measurably deficient "input." Certainly, the Board of Education might hire more teachers if increased funds were made available for this purpose. Class size, however, is also a function*957 of how the Board deploys its teachers. Before their recently negotiated collective bargaining agreement, the City's teachers had a shorter contractual teaching day than was the case in any other school district in the state or in other large urban districts across the nation.

New York City has one teacher for every 14.1 students, placing it in the top 10% of large districts across the nation. By comparison, Los Angeles, the second largest school system in the nation, has one teacher for every 20.8 students.

Further, the Board of Education employs thousands of teachers who are not assigned classroom teaching duties. Thus, although the City employs roughly the same number of teachers per student as the rest of the state, its class sizes are much larger.

Nor does additional funding for more teachers or increased teacher pay neatly translate into the assignment of more qualified teaching staff to the "worst" schools. For example, the record clearly established that the most inexperienced teachers are routinely placed in the "worst" schools. This situation is likely to persist, regardless of the number of teachers or their pay, so long as the collective bargaining agreement between the teachers' union and the school district allows more experienced teachers to opt out to "better" schools.

Remedy

The majority first directs the State to determine the actual cost of a "sound basic education" and to ensure that every school in New York City has the necessary funding to meet the standard, and sets a deadline. The funding level must reflect the cost of a "sound basic education" that is not tied to anything other than a "meaningful high school education." The majority also remands the case to the trial court to review the Legislature's efforts to determine if under the new funding scheme "inputs and outputs improve to a constitutionally acceptable level" (majority op. at 930, 769 N.Y.S.2d at 128, 801 N.E.2d at 348).

This remedy is extraordinary, if not unprecedented. Having determined that the State is not satisfying its constitutional obligation with respect to the education of New York City's public schoolchildren, we should-as the State requests-simply specify the constitutional deficiencies. It is up to the Legislature, as the entity charged with primary responsibility under the Education Article for maintaining the State's system of public education, and the Executive, who shares responsibility with the Legislature, to implement a remedy.

This lawsuit should be at an end. Instead, the majority, observing that "the political process allocates to City schools a share of state aid that does not bear a perceptible relation to the needs of City students" (majority op. at 930, 769 N.Y.S.2d at 128, 801 N.E.2d at 348), casts the courts in the role of judicial overseer of the Legislature. This disregards the prudential bounds of the judicial function, if not the separation of powers.

Moreover, as soon as the trial court is called upon to evaluate the cost and effectiveness of whatever new programs are devised and funded to meet the needs of New York City's school-children, the education policy debate will begin anew in another long trial followed by lengthy appeals. The success of the new funding mechanism will then be tested by outputs (proficiency levels). This dispute, like its counterparts elsewhere, is destined to last for decades, and, as previously noted, is virtually guaranteed to spawn similar lawsuits throughout the state.

Our remedy also signals the demise of local control, a key component to the constitutionalization of New York's public school system. Long before the Education Article's adoption in 1894, New Yorkers were free to require their local schools to provide more than a minimal education. As _Levittown_ instructs, this may be done without offending the Constitution. Nonetheless, by constitutionalizing what we would like our children to learn and making the State solely responsible for ensuring that this standard is met, we have severely undercut local control. We have centralized responsibility for educational competence (not constitutional compliance) in the courts and their anticipated "dialogue" with the Legislature.

Conclusion

Trial judges and appellate courts are well suited to assess criminal responsibility in accordance with prescribed procedures; to assign liability for breaches of duty; to extrapolate legislative intent; or to interpret commercial agreements. Each dispute is based on fact and law. They are not, however, well suited to make the subtle judgments inherent in education policymaking, or to assess how the State of New York may best allocate its limited resources to meet its citizens' educational and other pressing needs.

Of course, the majority sincerely sees itself as interpreting constitutional commands, a proper and solemn judicial function, not as making policy choices and value judgments constitutionally committed to the other branches of government. In my view, however, by this decision, the majority has allowed its deep sympathy for educational excellence to overwhelm its sense of the proper and practical limits of the judicial function.

Accordingly, I would affirm the decision of the Appellate Division, and dismiss plaintiffs' complaint.

Judges SMITH, CIPARICK and ROSENBLATT concur with Chief Judge KAYE.

Judge SMITH concurs in a separate concurring opinion.

Judge <u>READ</u> dissents in another opinion.

Judge <u>GRAFFEO</u> taking no part.

Order modified, etc.

END OF DOCUMENT

OPINION #7

Court of Appeals of New York.

8 N.Y.3d 14

CAMPAIGN FOR FISCAL EQUITY, INC., et al., Appellants-Respondents

v

STATE of New York et al., Respondents-Appellants

Nov. 20, 2006

Background: Students, parents, and organizations concerned with education issues brought action challenging state's funding of New York City's public schools. The Supreme Court, New York County, <u>162 Misc.2d 493, 616 N.Y.S.2d 851,</u> dismissed claims under equal protection clauses and Title VI but denied motion to dismiss claims under Education Article. On appeal, the Supreme Court, Appellate Division, <u>205 A.D.2d 272, 619 N.Y.S.2d 699,</u> granted motion to dismiss remaining claims. On appeal, the Court of Appeals, <u>86 N.Y.2d 307, 631 N.Y.S.2d 565, 655 N.E.2d 661,</u> ruled that complaint stated cause of action for violation of Education Article. On remand, the Supreme Court, New York County, <u>187 Misc.2d 1, 719 N.Y.S.2d 475,</u> entered judgment for plaintiffs. State appealed.

The Supreme Court, Appellate Division, <u>295 A.D.2d 1, 744 N.Y.S.2d 130,</u> reversed. Plaintiffs appealed. The Court of Appeals, <u>100 N.Y.2d 893, 769 N.Y.S.2d 106, 801 N.E.2d 326,</u> directed State to ensure that schools had resources necessary to provide opportunity for sound basic education. On remand, the Supreme Court, New York County, <u>Leland DeGrasse</u>, J., confirmed referees' report and directed implementation of funding plan for school district. State appealed. The Supreme Court, Appellate Division, <u>29 A.D.3d 175, 814 N.Y.S.2d 1,</u> affirmed in part and vacated in part. Plaintiffs appealed, and State cross-appealed.

Holdings: The Court of Appeals, <u>Pigott</u>, J., held that:

(1) trial court should not have confirmed referees' report which calculated anew the cost of providing sound basic education in New York City schools;

(2) Governor's proposed calculation was reasonable; and

(3) part of Appellate Division order that required capital improvement plan was unnecessary.

Affirmed as modified.

<u>Rosenblatt</u>, J., filed concurring opinion.

<u>Kaye</u>, Chief Judge, filed opinion concurring in part and dissenting in part.

OPINION OF THE COURT

<u>PIGOTT</u>, J.

In this third appeal by plaintiffs Campaign for Fiscal Equity, Inc. (CFE), et al., we address the cost of providing children in New York City's public schools with a sound basic education. The State estimated this cost to include a minimum of $1.93 billion, in 2004 dollars, in additional annual operating funds. We conclude that this estimate was a reasonable one and that the courts should defer to this estimate, appropriately updated.

More than a decade ago, we held that the Education Article of the New York State Constitution requires the State "to offer all children the opportunity of a sound basic education" (<u>Campaign for Fiscal Equity v. State of New York</u>, 86 N.Y.2d 307, 316, 631 N.Y.S.2d 565, 655 N.E.2d 661 [1995] [<u>CFE I</u>]). Plaintiffs had sought a declaratory judgment against the State, claiming that students in New York City public schools were not receiving a basic education and that the State's public school financing system was unconstitutional.

Mindful of the fundamental value of education in our democratic society, we agreed with plaintiffs' interpretation of the Education Article. The State must ensure that New York's public schools are able to teach "the basic literacy, calculating, and verbal skills necessary to enable children to eventually function productively as civic participants capable of voting and serving on a jury" <u>(86 N.Y.2d at 316, 631 N.Y.S.2d 565, 655 N.E.2d 661).</u> In assessing adequacy of education, this standard is the constitutional minimum or floor that we had acknowledged earlier, in <u>Board of Educ., Levittown Union Free School Dist. v. Nyquist,</u> 57 N.Y.2d 27, 47-48, 453 N.Y.S.2d 643, 439 N.E.2d 359 (1982). Accordingly, we held that plaintiffs' cause of action under the Education Article survived a motion to dismiss (86 N.Y.2d at 318-319, 631 N.Y.S.2d 565, 655 N.E.2d 661), reminding plaintiffs that they would "have to establish a causal link between the present funding system and any proven failure to provide a sound basic education to New York City school children" (86 N.Y.2d at 318, 631 N.Y.S.2d 565, 655 N.E.2d 661).

Plaintiffs succeeded in establishing that causal link, in a 1999-2000 trial concerning the 1997-1998 school year. In 2003, we decided that this trial record supports the conclusion that, because of inadequate funding for their public schools, children in New York City "are not receiving the constitutionally-mandated opportunity for a sound basic education" (*Campaign for Fiscal Equity v. State of New York*, 100 N.Y.2d 893, 919, 769 N.Y.S.2d 106, 801 N.E.2d 326 [2003] [*CFE II*]). In *CFE I*, we had understood a sound basic education as teaching skills that enable students to undertake civil responsibilities meaningfully. In *CFE II*, we defined "sound basic education" more exactly, as the "opportunity for a meaningful *high school* education, one which prepares [children] to function productively as civic participants" (100 N.Y.2d at 908, 769 N.Y.S.2d 106, 801 N.E.2d 326 [emphasis added]).

We determined that New York City public schools provided inadequate teaching, because they were unable to attract and retain qualified teachers (100 N.Y.2d at 909-911, 769 N.Y.S.2d 106, 801 N.E.2d 326). They were deficient in at least two instrumentalities of learning: libraries and computers (100 N.Y.2d at 913, 769 N.Y.S.2d 106, 801 N.E.2d 326). Moreover, although plaintiffs had not proven "a measurable correlation between building disrepair and student performance, in general" (100 N.Y.2d at 911, 769 N.Y.S.2d 106, 801 N.E.2d 326), they sufficiently demonstrated "that large class sizes negatively affect student performance in New York City public schools" (100 N.Y.2d at 912, 769 N.Y.S.2d 106, 801 N.E.2d 326).

Whether measured by "inputs" or by "outputs," i.e. school completion rates and test results (100 N.Y.2d at 914-919, 769 N.Y.S.2d 106, 801 N.E.2d 326), New York City schoolchildren, we determined, were not receiving the opportunity for a sound basic education. Finally, we concluded that plaintiffs had established the causation element of their claim by showing that increased funding can provide better teachers, facilities and instrumentalities of learning, and that such improved inputs in turn yield better student performance (100 N.Y.2d at 919-925, 769 N.Y.S.2d 106, 801 N.E.2d 326).

Accordingly we directed the State to ensure, by means of "reforms to the current system of financing school funding and managing schools…that every school in New York City would have the resources necessary for providing the opportunity for a sound basic education" (100 N.Y.2d at 930, 769 N.Y.S.2d 106, 801 N.E.2d 326). Noting that "the political process allocates to City schools a share of state aid that does not bear a perceptible relation to the needs of City students" (*id.*), we instructed the State to ascertain the actual cost of providing a sound basic education in New York City, rather than the state as a whole (*id.*). We also held that "the new scheme should ensure a system of accountability to measure whether the reforms actually provide the opportunity for a sound basic education" _(id.)._ We gave the State a deadline of July 30, 2004 by which to implement the necessary measures _(id.)_ and remitted to Supreme Court for further proceedings in accordance with our opinion (100 N.Y.2d at 932, 769 N.Y.S.2d 106, 801 N.E.2d 326).

Within a matter of weeks, Governor Pataki issued an executive order creating the New York State Commission on Education Reform, charged with recommending, to the Executive and the Legislature, education financing and other reforms that would ensure that all children in New York State have an opportunity to obtain a sound basic education. The Commission, chaired by Frank G. Zarb, published its final report on March 29, 2004.

The Zarb Commission retained Standard and Poor's (S & P) School Evaluation Services to calculate the additional spending required to provide a sound basic education directing S & P to use a "Successful Schools" model that studies the expenditures of school districts with a proven track record of high student performance. The method had been used by the New York State Board of Regents in its Proposal on State Aid to School Districts for 2004-05.

The Zarb Commission developed three alternative criteria for identifying successful school districts. One option was based on New York's 2007-2008 performance standard set in accordance with the federal No Child Left Behind Act of 2001. Another was similar to the first but substituted the 2006-2007 performance standard. The third criterion was the same approach to identifying successful schools that the Board of Regents had used; it picked out school districts-281 of 699-in which at least 80% of the students performed at or above a proficient level, over a three-year period, in seven tests required by the Board of Regents: two fourth-grade examinations and five examinations required for high school graduation.

Reasoning that not all successful schools operate in a manner that is economical, the Zarb Commission instructed S & P to apply a cost-effectiveness filter: once successful school districts were identified by the methods just described, they were to be ranked according to expenditures and those in the lower-spending half were to be used to create an average. The Board of Regents had noted the necessity for applying such an efficiency filter, because "districts that perform at high levels often enjoy a very substantial wealth base, and therefore also spend at very high per pupil levels".

Drawing on an extensive review of pertinent research literature, S & P applied three weightings to the resulting base expenditures, in order to take into account the greater spending required for students with special needs. The coefficients by which the base expenditures were multiplied were 2.1 for students with disabilities, 1.35 for economically disadvantaged students, and 1.2 for students with limited English proficiency. S & P cautioned that it was not in a position to recommend explicitly the set of weightings it applied.

Adjustments were also made to account for the local purchasing power of the dollar, using two, alternative cost indices, the New York Regional Cost Index (NYRCI), provided by the New York State Education Department and based on differences in labor market costs, and the Geographic Cost of Education Index (GCEI), provided by the National Center for Education Statistics. The latter index was developed by Jay Chambers, one of the principal authors of the New York Adequacy Study, a cost analysis project cosponsored by plaintiff CFE in 2003-2004. The GCEI attempts to measure the attractiveness of employment within a particular district, one of the key determinants of the cost of providing education. S & P used what was then the most recent, publicly available version of the GCEI, a 1997 update by Chambers. Finally, amounts were adjusted for inflation to reflect January 2004 purchasing power.

S & P thus calculated "sound basic education" spending estimates for each school district, using the two regional cost indices and the four alternative criteria for identifying successful school districts. The spending estimates did not include capital, debt or transportation costs. Finally, these figures were compared with amounts actually spent in 2002-2003, in order to identify "spending gaps."

Applying the GCEI, the estimated spending gaps for New York City ranged from $1.93 billion to $2.53 billion and the statewide spending gaps from $2.45 billion to $3.39 billion, depending on which criterion for successful school districts was used. (New York City's spending gap thus comprised 74% to 79% of the State's total gap.) When the NYRCI was applied, the estimated spending gaps were larger, ranging from $4.05 billion to $4.69 billion for New York City, and $4.61 billion to $5.57 billion statewide. Applying the GCEI and the Board of Regents approach to identifying successful schools, the spending gap for New York City, in 2004 dollars, was $1.93 billion.

Governor Pataki convened the Legislature in extraordinary session on July 20, 2004, and proposed a program bill to the Senate, incorporating the Zarb Commission's methodology. The Senate passed an amended version of the bill. Ultimately, the legislation was not enacted. In both versions of the bill, the Legislature would have found that the actual costs of providing a sound basic education should be determined using the Board of Regents approach to identifying successful schools (which had picked out 281 of 699 school districts), the S & P weightings for students with special needs, the GCEI, and the cost-effectiveness filter (see 2004 Extraordinary Session N.Y. Senate Bill S 1-A, § 1, at 2 [July 20, 2004]; 2004 N.Y. Senate Bill S 7684-B, § 2, at 2 [July 20, 2004]).

In other words, Governor Pataki and the Senate endorsed the approach that generated a minimum figure of $1.93 billion as the estimated spending gap in operating expenses for New York City. In his State Education Reform Plan, submitted in the course of this litigation, the Governor concluded that "the S & P analysis as adopted by the Zarb Commission and by State defendants determined that $2.5 billion in additional revenues statewide (equating to

$1.9 billion in New York City) was a valid determination of the cost of providing a sound basic education in New York City" (State Education Reform Plan, at 14 [Aug. 12, 2004]).

In his program bill memorandum, Governor Pataki made it clear that he intended New York City schools to receive additional funding that exceeded the minimum cost of a sound basic education. Proposals for a Dedicated State Fund for Sound Basic Education and for a New York City local state aid match would, when coupled with projected increases in state school aid and federal aid, generate "approximately $4.7 billion in additional support over the next five years" (Governor's Program Bill Mem. in Support of 2004 Extraordinary Session N.Y. Senate Bill S 1-A, at 4). As noted, the proposed legislation was not enacted. The Legislature, however, passed a bill on August 10, 2004, providing $300 million in additional education aid to New York City.

Once the deadline of July 30, 2004 we had set in *CFE II* had passed, Supreme Court set out to determine whether the measures we had declared necessary had been carried out. It appointed a blue-ribbon panel of referees "to hear and report with recommendations" on whether the steps taken by the State brought compliance with *CFE II*.

The Referees conducted numerous hearings, in which they heard from many witnesses, including the Mayor of New York City, the Chancellor of the New York City School District, and representatives of the New York State Division of the Budget and Education Department. They received extensive written submissions, including four compliance plans: the Governor's State Education Reform Plan, drawing on the Zarb Commission; plaintiffs' Plan for Compliance, which included the New York Adequacy Study, a cost analysis conducted by the American Institutes for Research (AIR) and Management Analysis and Planning, Inc. (MAP); the Regents Proposal on State Aid to School Districts for 2004-05; and a proposal from the City of New York.

Although they accepted the "successful school districts" methodology of the Zarb Commission, the Referees rejected its cost-effectiveness filter, used a 1.5 weighting for economically disadvantaged students in place of the S & P coefficient of 1.35, and insisted on the use of an updated GCEI prepared for plaintiff CFE's New York Adequacy Study. They concluded that the spending gap in New York City was $5.63 billion in 2004-2005 dollars, rejecting the State's contention that additional funding in the amount of $1.93 billion would ensure the opportunity for a sound basic education in New York City's public schools.

The Referees adopted CFE's capital funding program, "Building Requires Immediate Capital for Kids" (BRICKS), recommending that the State be required to ensure that $9.179 billion in 2004-2005 dollars would be available as funding for capital improvements over the following five years. Additionally, the Referees recommended that costing-out studies be carried out every four years, supervised by the Board of Regents, "until it becomes clear that reforms to the State's education finance formulas have rendered such studies no longer necessary to assure all New York City students the opportunity for a sound basic education" (Report and Recommendations of the Judicial Referees, at 39).

On the question of accountability, the Referees concluded that existing state systems, identifying schools that perform poorly and sanctioning failing schools, already provide adequate accountability, and that no new Office of Educational Accountability should be created. They recommended, however, that the current system should be enhanced by the development of a comprehensive "sound basic education" plan by the New York City Department of Education.

Supreme Court confirmed the Judicial Referees' Report and Recommendations. The Appellate Division vacated that confirmation (29 A.D.3d 175, 814 N.Y.S.2d 1 [2006]). It found support in the record for the State's "cost-effectiveness" approach, as well as for its weighting for economically disadvantaged students. Noting that record support, the Appellate Division observed that

"Supreme Court should not have substituted the Referees' opinion for that of the State... [and] converted a factor that was arguable and reasonable for the Legislature and Governor to consider into an incontrovertible fact. As long as the State's choices remained within the range of professionally accepted practices in determining the costs of a sound basic education, Supreme Court should have left the conclusions for legislative and gubernatorial consideration and determination." (29 A.D.3d at 184, 814 N.Y.S.2d 1.)

Citing Governor Pataki's proposal to increase funding of the New York City School District by $4.7 billion (over a period of five years), the Appellate Division directed the Governor and Legislature to appropriate at least $4.7 billion in additional operating funds (phased in over four years). The Appellate Division also directed the Governor and Legislature to "implement a capital improvement plan that expends $9.179 billion over the next five years or otherwise satisfies the city schools' constitutionally recognized capital needs" (29 A.D.3d at 191, 814 N.Y.S.2d 1).

Plaintiffs CFE et al. appeal pursuant to CPLR 5601(a) and (b) (1). The state defendants cross-appeal under CPLR 5601(b)(1).

The Judicial Referees' Report, dated November 30, 2004, commands our attention as well as our respect; it is likely that much of value may be learned from the Referees' careful consideration of methods of ascertaining the cost of a sound basic education and reforms to the current system of public school financing. Nevertheless, we hold that Supreme Court erred by, in effect, commissioning a de novo review of the compliance question. The role of the courts is not, as Supreme Court assumed, to determine the best way to calculate the cost of a sound basic education in New York City schools, but to determine whether the State's proposed calculation of that cost is rational. Supreme Court should not have endorsed an examination in which the cost of a sound basic education in New York was calculated anew, when the state budget plan had already reasonably calculated that cost. In this respect, we agree with the Appellate Division. It was error to confirm the Referees' Report.

We differ from the Appellate Division, however, in two respects. First, we observe that the state plan found that the cost of providing a sound basic education in New York City was $1.93 billion in additional annual operating funds, and that Governor Pataki's proposal to provide $4.7 billion in additional funding amounted to a policy choice to exceed the constitutional minimum. Second, in light of recently enacted legislation designed to allow the State to remedy inadequacies in New York City schools facilities, we reject as unnecessary the Appellate Division's directive regarding capital improvement.

Therefore, we modify the order of the Appellate Division, in two ways. We declare that the constitutionally required funding for the New York City School District includes, as demonstrated by this record, additional operating funds in the amount of $1.93 billion, adjusted with reference to the latest version of the GCEI and inflation since 2004. We vacate the requirement that the Governor and the Legislature implement a capital improvement plan that either expends $9.179 billion over the following five years "or otherwise satisfies the city schools' constitutionally recognized capital needs." As modified, we affirm.

In _CFE II_, we expressed the necessity for courts to tread carefully when asked to evaluate state financing plans. On the one hand, the Judiciary has a duty "to defer to the Legislature in matters of policymaking, particularly in a matter so vital as education financing, which has as well a core element of local control. We have neither the authority, nor the ability, nor the will, to micromanage education financing." (100 N.Y.2d at 925, 769 N.Y.S.2d 106, 801 N.E.2d 326.) On the other hand, "it is the province of the Judicial branch to define, and safeguard, rights provided by the New York State Constitution, and order redress for violation of them" (_id._).

The need for deference, where appropriate, is no less important for this Court than it is for the Judiciary as a whole. We are the ultimate arbiters of our State Constitution (_see e.g. Cohen v. State of New York_, 94 N.Y.2d 1, 11, 698 N.Y.S.2d 574, 720 N.E.2d 850 [1999]). Yet, in fashioning specific remedies for constitutional violations, we must avoid intrusion on the primary domain of another branch of government. We have often spoken of this tension between our responsibility to safeguard rights and the necessary deference of the courts to the policies of the Legislature. "While it is within the power of the judiciary to declare the vested rights of a specifically protected class of individuals, in a fashion recognized by statute...the manner by which the State addresses complex societal and governmental issues is a subject left to the discretion of the political branches of government" (_Matter of New York State Inspection, Sec. & Law Enforcement Empls., Dist. Council 82, AFSCME, AFL-CIO v. Cuomo_, 64 N.Y.2d 233, 239-240, 485 N.Y.S.2d 719,

475 N.E.2d 90 [1984] [citations omitted]). When we review the acts of the Legislature and the Executive, we do so to protect rights, not to make policy.

Our deference to the Legislature's education financing plans is justified not only by prudent and practical hesitation in light of the limited access of the Judiciary "to the controlling economic and social facts," but also by our abiding "respect for the separation of powers upon which our system of government is based" (*Matter of 89 Christopher v. Joy*, 35 N.Y.2d 213, 220, 360 N.Y.S.2d 612, 318 N.E.2d 776 [1974]). We cannot "intrude upon the policy-making and discretionary decisions that are reserved to the legislative and executive branches" (*Klostermann v. Cuomo*, 61 N.Y.2d 525, 541, 475 N.Y.S.2d 247, 463 N.E.2d 588 [1984]).

Deference to the Legislature is especially necessary where it is the State's budget plan that is being questioned. Devising a state budget is a prerogative of the Legislature and Executive; the Judiciary should not usurp this power. The legislative and executive branches of government are in a far better position than the Judiciary to determine funding needs throughout the state and priorities for the allocation of the State's resources.

We have therefore spoken of the "formidable burden" of proof imposed on "one who attacks the budget plan" (*Wein v. Carey*, 41 N.Y.2d 498, 505, 393 N.Y.S.2d 955, 362 N.E.2d 587 [1977]). Indeed, the burden is

"realistically, impossible as to some categories of estimates. But there are some estimates that could be demonstrated on their face to be unreasonable. An extreme example would be a tripling of the estimates of personal income tax revenue, without a change in the tax rate, in a period in which the economy appears to be on a plateau or in decline." The illustrations we gave in *Wein v. Carey*, while extreme, were meant to show how patently *irrational* a state financing plan must be, before judicial deference will give way. Judicial intervention in the state budget "may be invoked only in the narrowest of instances."

When we remitted in *CFE II*, we did so in order that Supreme Court would determine, when our deadline had passed, whether the State had implemented the reforms we required-legislation that would ensure that New York City schools have the resources necessary for providing the opportunity for a sound basic education and that would ensure accountability. *CFE II* called for the State to present evidence of its reforms, both predating *CFE II* (see 100 N.Y.2d at 927, 769 N.Y.S.2d 106, 801 N.E.2d 326) and following *CFE II*, and for Supreme Court to determine whether they satisfied our directives.

In light of our language in *CFE II* and our jurisprudence as a whole concerning deference to the Legislature in matters of policymaking, it was incumbent upon Supreme Court to begin by making a finding as to whether the State's estimate of the cost of providing a sound basic education in New York City was a *reasonable* estimate. Then the court should have proceeded to determine whether the state plan, as of July 30, 2004, incorporated that sound basic education expenditure in its proposed budget and would, if enacted, ensure a system of accountability. Supreme Court should not have provided a panel of referees with a mandate to make *recommendations* as between compliance proposals-the State's, the plaintiffs', the City's, the Regents'. The State, not Supreme Court, was ordered to ascertain the cost of a sound basic education in New York City.

We do not believe that Governor Pataki's proposed State Education Reform Plan was unreasonable. In particular, we do not find irrational the Governor's acceptance of the Board of Regents approach to identifying successful schools, the S & P weightings for students with special needs and the cost-effectiveness filter (2004 Extraordinary Session N.Y. Senate Bill S 1-A, § 1, at 2 [July 20, 2004]). As a result, we do not find unreasonable the assertion that "$2.5 billion in additional revenues statewide (equating to $1.9 billion in New York City) was a valid determination of the cost of providing a sound basic education in New York City" (State Education Reform Plan, at 14 [Aug. 12, 2004]). There is substantial record support for that statement.

First, the use of the cost-effectiveness filter is rationally defensible. The variation in spending between New York school districts is very large. As S & P explained, averaging the expenditures of *all* successful schools would "mask a considerable range of per-pupil spending among the individual districts...If the concept of 'adequacy' means spending no less, but not necessarily more, than is necessary to produce high achievement levels, then there is reasonable cause to adjust the base expenditure by a measure of *cost effectiveness.* This can be done by ranking the successful districts under each scenario by their base expenditure, and computing the average of the lowest 50% (in terms of spending), which is the same approach used by the New York Board of Regents in its recent study of educational costs. An analysis of the average achievement levels of the lower-spending half of districts shows that they closely resemble the average achievement levels of the upper-spending half of districts.

The essential premise of the cost-effectiveness filter is that the higher-spending half of the successful districts is spending more than the constitutional minimum-either because those districts spend less efficiently than some others or because they have chosen to do more for their students than the Constitution requires. The State, in adopting S & P's approach, implicitly concluded that New York City could attain minimal constitutional standards while spending less than this higher-spending group of successful districts. The premise and conclusion are no doubt debatable, but we cannot say they are irrational, and they are therefore entitled to deference from the courts.

The S & P weightings for children with special needs also have record support. While S & P did not recommend any particular weighting over another, the coefficients that S & P applied were drawn from an extensive review of relevant research. Indeed the pertinent footnote to S & P's Resource Adequacy Study cites no fewer than 37 articles, reports and other scholarly works (Standard & Poor's Resource Adequacy Study for the New York State Commission on Education Reform, n. 16, at 89-92 [Mar.2004]).

The S & P calculations-applying a 2.1 weighting for students with disabilities, 1.35 for economically disadvantaged students, and 1.2 for students with limited English proficiency, and reaching the conclusion that the spending gap for the New York City School District is $1.93 billion-were reasonable. Although we recognize that legitimate arguments can be made for raising the coefficient for economically disadvantaged students to 1.5, we do not believe that the figure of 1.35 lacks grounding in prudent reason.

Accordingly, we declare that the constitutionally required funding for the New York City School District includes additional operating funds in the amount of $1.93 billion, adjusted with reference to the latest version of the GCEI and inflation since 2004.

Turning to capital improvements, we emphasize again, as we did in *CFE I*, that New York's public schoolchildren "are entitled to minimally adequate physical facilities and classrooms which provide enough light, space, heat, and air to permit children to learn" (86 N.Y.2d at 317, 631 N.Y.S.2d 565, 655 N.E.2d 661). The Appellate Division directed the Governor and the Legislature to implement a capital improvement plan that either expends $9.179 billion over the following five years "or otherwise satisfies the city schools' constitutionally recognized capital needs" (29 A.D.3d at 191, 814 N.Y.S.2d 1). In choosing its words thus, the Appellate Division was perhaps mindful of the fact that in *CFE II* we did not expressly require the State to calculate the amount of capital funding necessary to remedy deficiencies in facilities, with the result that the State did not carry out a costing-out study for capital funding needs in the way it did for operating costs.

The part of the Appellate Division order that requires a capital improvement plan should be vacated as unnecessary. In 2006, the Legislature set forth a capital construction program totaling $2.6 billion, that includes $1.8 billion for the New York City School District (L. 2006, 58, part A-2; L. 2006, 61, part I). Crucially, the Legislature increased the cap for the New York City Transitional Finance Authority by $9.4 billion to help fund the cost of capital improvements, and permitted New York City to pledge future state building aid in order to repay borrowed funds (L. 2006, 58, part A-3). We are of course bound to decide this case on the record before us. But since the parties now agree that the funds envisaged by the Legislature this year would be sufficient to remedy facilities deficiencies, we believe that there is no need for further judicial direction.

Finally, insofar as the Appellate Division vacated Supreme Court's order confirming the Referees' Report, it struck Supreme Court's call for state costing-out studies every four years and its requirement that the New York City Department of Education prepare a comprehensive "sound basic education" plan, to ensure accountability. We agree with these results. In particular, we agree with the City of New York, an amicus in this case, that a new and costly layer of city bureaucracy is not constitutionally required. It is undisputed that there are minimally adequate accountability mechanisms now in place for the evaluation of New York schools (including the Schools Under Registration Review process and the state standards required by the federal No Child Left Behind Act of 2001).

Accordingly, the order of the Appellate Division should be modified, without costs, by granting judgment declaring in accordance with this opinion and, as so modified, affirmed.

ROSENBLATT, J. (concurring).

I join the majority in its rationale and result, but write separately to emphasize that my vote should not be construed as concluding that $1.93 billion, as adjusted, is necessarily the proper additional budgetary amount to provide New York City schools, or that $2.45 billion is the amount that should be budgeted statewide. These figures were determined by a commission designated by the State as reflecting the constitutional *minimum* for a sound basic education. I join the majority because I agree that Supreme Court should not have directed the referees' recalculation, considering that the state budget plan had already calculated the amount in a way that, as a matter of law, was not arbitrary or irrational.

That does not mean that the State is limited to the minimum, or "floor," of what it takes to provide a sound basic education. Judging by Governor Pataki's higher budgeting and the similarly heartening indications that Governor-elect Spitzer will continue in a direction higher than the minimum, there is every indication that the amounts dedicated will be well above the constitutional floor. When it comes to educating its children, New York State will not likely content itself with the minimum. Indeed, after this suit was initiated the State provided for an additional $9 billion investment in capital improvements for the City's schools. How much more it can and should spend, however, is a matter for the political branches, which will be free to avail themselves of the valuable work performed by the distinguished panel of referees.

I also emphasize, most importantly, that this lawsuit has consequences beyond New York City and that there are, no doubt, other school districts that should benefit from increased budgets. This requires a statewide approach that is also best left to the Executive and Legislature.

Chief Judge KAYE (concurring in part and dissenting in part).

Recognizing that we have neither the authority, nor the ability, nor the will to micromanage education financing, in *Campaign for Fiscal Equity v. State of New York*, 100 N.Y.2d 893, 925, 769 N.Y.S.2d 106, 801 N.E.2d 326 (2003) (*CFE II*) the Court demarcated standards that must be met, but left it to defendants to come into compliance, affording them more than a year to do so. Regrettably, our trust was misplaced. Today, more than three years later-and more than 13 years after this litigation began-defendants still have failed to fund the New York City public schools adequately. Having failed to satisfy their responsibility, defendants now compel this Court to determine the specific steps that must be taken to remedy the undisputed constitutional violation. Also regrettably, I must dissent because the majority does not resolve the inadequate funding of the New York City public schools and reaches a result that is well below what the governmental actors themselves had concluded was required.

Although the dollar differences that separate the majority and dissent are great, our actual points of difference are only two: first, the deference owed, and second, the rationality of two factors used by defendants to calculate the cost of a sound basic education.

I. *The Issue of Deference*

The heart of the majority writing is that substantial deference is owed to the executive and legislative branches of government, particularly in matters of budgeting and policymaking (*see* majority op. at 28-30, 828 N.Y.S.2d at 243-245, 861 N.E.2d at 58-60). I agree wholeheartedly. When the Executive and the Legislature have acted together on matters within their particular province, the courts should indeed tread lightly.

That, however, is not what happened here. There is no state budget plan for bringing the schools into constitutional compliance; that is precisely the problem. When, as here, the Executive and the Legislature are specifically at odds as to the cost of providing the opportunity for a sound basic education to New York City schoolchildren, the approach of a single branch, rejected by another, cannot legitimately be considered "the State's estimate" (majority op. at 29, 828 N.Y.S.2d at 243-244, 861 N.E.2d at 58-59), and is entitled to no special weight.

In *CFE II* we directed defendants to ascertain the actual cost of providing a sound basic education in New York City; to ensure that every city school have the resources necessary to provide the opportunity for a sound basic education; and to ensure a system of accountability to measure whether the reforms actually provide the opportunity for a sound basic education. Although there is no dispute that defendants failed to comply with our second directive, I cannot agree with the majority that they complied with our first.

To be sure, the Governor, in undertaking to determine the cost of a sound basic education, and in proposing $4.7 billion in increased annual funding for the New York City public schools, took important steps toward that objective. And in most cases, of course, we can assume that the Governor, in whom the executive*35 power is vested, speaks for the State. But not so here. The enactment of an appropriation bill that ensures adequate educational funding requires agreement among the Governor and both houses of the Legislature, and plainly that has not occurred.

As the deadline for compliance approached, defendants advised the trial court, to which we had remitted the case, of the actions they had by then undertaken to satisfy this Court's order. Based on defendants' failure to fulfill the *CFE II* mandate, the court appointed three referees "to hear and report with recommendations on what measures defendants have taken to follow the *[CFE II]* directives and bring this State's school funding mechanism into constitutional compliance insofar as it affects the New York City School System. The referees shall also identify the areas, if any, in which such compliance is lacking."

Even today, it is hard to see what alternative the court had. The Executive and Legislature were at loggerheads-there was no agreed amount to be implemented.

The majority faults the trial court and referees for undertaking to determine the actual cost of a sound basic education, believing instead that calculations proffered by certain of the defendants should have been beyond question. For more than 200 years, however, it has been the province and duty of the judicial branch to enforce compliance with constitutional norms, including (when necessary) as against the other branches of government. Defendants' continued failure to cure the violation properly obligated the courts to determine the extent of noncompliance and to direct a remedy.

When courts undertake to resolve a controversy that others have brought before them, they appropriately resort to the tools of the judicial trade-testimony, evidence and fact-finding. The referees thus conducted seven days of evidentiary hearings on the primary question before them-the actual cost of a sound basic education for New York City schoolchildren. Based on the testimony of 15 witnesses, expert evidence, and extensive briefing and argument, they rationally determined that the actual cost of providing a sound basic education in New York City required an annual increase in operational funding of $5.63 billion, calculated in 2004-2005 dollars. The Appellate Division, too, determined that constitutional compliance required additional annual expenditures of between $4.7 billion and $5.63 billion. The majority, however, rejects the findings of the referees, and indeed the very process undertaken by the courts, and instead accepts at face value $1.93 billion as sufficient to satisfy the Education Article.

The origins of that number are instructive. In response to our decision in *CFE II*, the Governor established the New York State Commission on Education Reform-the Zarb Commission-charged with, among other things, "studying and making recommendations regarding...[t]he actual cost of providing all children the opportunity to acquire a sound basic education in the public schools of the State of New York" (Executive Order [Pataki] No. 131 [9 NYCRR 5.131]). The Commission, in turn, retained Standard & Poor's School Evaluation Services, which produced a lengthy Resource Adequacy Study offering a wide variety of possible amounts of education spending, each based on different assumptions and variables as to the desired level of educational achievement and the costs required to attain it.

Inasmuch as the Commission was asked to study statewide costs, even though this Court's mandate had been limited to New York City, Standard & Poor's used each scenario to calculate both statewide amounts and their citywide equivalents. With respect to New York City, Standard & Poor's calculated resource gaps-defined as the difference between the amount actually spent in the most recently completed fiscal year and the amount that would be required to fund the particular scenario-ranging from $1.93 billion to $7.28 billion in core operating expenditures. In so doing, however, Standard & Poor's itself repeatedly made clear that it "does not recommend any spending level or the adoption of any particular achievement scenario" (Standard & Poor's School Evaluation Services, Resource Adequacy Study for the New York State Commission on Education Reform, at 23 [2004]).

Relying on the Resource Adequacy Study, and specifically endorsing the "cost effectiveness" variable considered by Standard & Poor's, the Commission similarly reported a wide range to the Governor-that is, from $2.45 billion to $5.57 billion statewide, which translated to between $1.93 billion and $4.69 billion for the City-concluding that "[t]he State's elected leaders should make a choice of funding within this range" (New York State Commission on Education Reform, Final Report, at 24 [2004]).

Even defendants did not recommend these numbers. Rather, defendants, through the Attorney General, submitted to the referees an "education plan prepared by Governor Pataki setting forth his proposal for complying with the June 23, 2003 decision of the Court of Appeals in this action." The Governor's plan proposed additional annual operating funds for New York City of $4.7 billion, and $8 billion statewide. As the Attorney General wrote in a letter to the referees:

"Governor Pataki is a named defendant in this action, and this office therefore is presenting the plan prepared by the Governor, as his counsel, and a description of that plan as prepared by the Governor's office. We also note, however, that the decision of the Court of Appeals requires the enactment of legislation by the State of New York, and this office is the institutional counsel for the State.

"Unfortunately, the two houses of the Legislature and the Governor have not been able to agree upon a single unified plan for submission to this panel."

On this record, the $1.93 billion figure is not entitled to special deference.

II. *The Issue of Rationality*

The $1.93 billion now embraced by the majority is, moreover, based on two unsustainable factors. When those factors are properly adjusted, the resultant cost of a sound basic education, as calculated by Standard & Poor's, is identical to that reached by the referees and accepted by the trial court-a determination that should therefore be upheld as rationally based.

In conducting its study, Standard & Poor's, as instructed by the Commission, utilized the "successful schools and districts" model for calculating per-pupil expenditures-one of three distinct methodologies typically used by experts in education policy and finance. No party disputes the legitimacy of the successful schools method as a means for determining the cost of a sound basic education. By using this method, Standard & Poor's was able to calculate a range of numbers that varied according to choices made as to four distinct factors-first, the standard for measuring a successful school district; second, the additional expenditures necessitated by special needs students; third, the use of a cost filter; and fourth, the manner of converting "standardized" education dollars into New York City dollars.

With respect to the first factor, Standard & Poor's made a set of calculations using four different academic achievement standards for identifying a successful school district, and again the parties agree, and the referees found, that satisfaction of the Regents Criteria provides an appropriate standard for measuring a successful school. Nor is there any dispute as to the fourth factor-the proper conversion of state education dollars into New York City dollars. Inasmuch as the purchasing power of a dollar varies across the state, and the successful schools method examined all of the school districts in the state, Standard & Poor's offered two alternative regional cost adjustment indices to determine the cost in New York City dollars: (1) the "New York Regional Cost Index," provided by the State Education Department; and (2) the "Geographic Cost of Education Index" (GCEI), provided by the National Center for Education Statistics. The referees found, and the parties agree, that use of the GCEI was appropriate.

The difference-a huge dollar difference-centers on the second and third factors: the proper weighting adjustments for special needs students, and the use of a 50% cost reduction filter.

A. *The Low-Income Weighting*

A successful schools analysis produces "base expenditures," which are estimated costs per pupil. However, such base expenditures must then be multiplied by "weightings" for students with special needs, who require such costly accommodations as differentiated curricula, smaller class sizes, assistive technology and classroom aides. Standard & Poor's assigned a weighting of 2.1 to students with disabilities (special-education students); 1.35 to economically disadvantaged students; and 1.2 to students with limited English proficiency. Although the parties and referees agree that the special-education and English-language weightings were appropriate, the record reflects that the 1.35 low income weighting applied by Standard & Poor's-according to which $1.35 must be allocated to students in poverty for every dollar spent on a student not in poverty-was irrational and cannot be sustained.

Defendants' principal rationale for choosing this weighting-a choice that drew considerable criticism from the witnesses and amici-was that the Standard & Poor's study had identified 1.35 as the proper adjustment for educating economically disadvantaged students. But Standard & Poor's had in fact emphasized that 1.35 was simply a figure that it had "drawn from a review of research literature on the coefficients that education agencies tend to use in practice," and that "insufficient empirical evidence exists in New York to determine how much additional funding is actually needed for different categories of students with special needs to consistently perform at intended achievement levels" (Standard & Poor's School Evaluation Services, Resource Adequacy Study for the New York State *40 Commission on Education Reform, at 8-9 [2004]). As a result, Standard & Poor's made clear that its study "does not explicitly recommend a particular set of weightings." (*Id.*)

Unlike Standard & Poor's, the Regents, in determining that a higher poverty weighting was required, had focused on the specific circumstances of New York City schools, including an especially heavy concentration of high-needs students, very low graduation rates, large classes and a disproportionate number of schools in need of improvement, and thereby determined that the appropriate low-income weighting for New York City was 1.8. With respect to the state as a whole, the Regents recommended weightings for low-income students ranging from 1.5 to 2.0, depending on the concentration of poverty in the district.

Because the Standard & Poor's weighting of 1.35 for low-income students was not focused on the specific circumstances of New York City schools, its use to determine the actual cost of providing a sound basic education to economically disadvantaged New York City students was irrational, as the referees found. The referees thus properly determined that a poverty weighting of at least 1.5-the lower end of the range proposed by the Regents-must instead be used.

B. *The 50% Cost Filter*

Finally, as endorsed by the Zarb Commission, Standard & Poor's applied a "cost effectiveness filter" of 50% in an alleged effort to screen out successful school districts that either spent money inefficiently or spent more than was necessary to provide the opportunity for a sound basic education. Under that approach, Standard & Poor's considered the average expenditures of only the lower-spending half of successful school districts in New York State, thereby excluding from the analysis 140 of the 281 successful school districts meeting the Regents Criteria standard.

Multiple witnesses and amici heavily criticized this filter. Indeed, several testifying witnesses criticized the use of *any* cost reduction filter, and others would have used an approach substantially different from the one adopted by defendants, such as simply eliminating the highest- and lowest-spending 5% of districts as "outliers." Defendants' own expert, Dr. Robert

M. Palaich, testified that his own firm would not use the 50% filter, and there was no evidence offered that this filter is generally accepted by experts in educational finance or, more fundamentally, that the higher-spending districts that were excluded from defendants' analysis by the cost filter were in fact inefficient.

Inasmuch as defendants made no attempt to determine why some successful schools spent less per pupil than others, the assumption that this must have been because the lower-spending schools were more efficient is utterly speculative. Indeed, certain expert amici posited that the lower spending in the selected schools might instead have been due to low wage costs and a low concentration of disadvantaged students, not to efficiency.

Only one decision maker anywhere in the country-the New Hampshire Legislature-has ever implemented a 50% cost reduction filter. But as even defendants acknowledge, "in New Hampshire it appears that the efficiency factor was selected to drive costs down" to a predetermined amount; it was not based on the expertise of any education finance experts. The 50% number not only is wholly arbitrary, but also has the effect of eliminating most of the school districts in Westchester and Nassau, the two counties that border New York City and thus most resemble the City in the concentration of students who are not English proficient and in the higher regional costs, particularly in hiring and retaining capable teachers. Accordingly, the 50% cost filter was properly rejected by the referees.

Defendants nevertheless defend the use of the 50% filter on the ground that the State Board of Regents also used it in its own budget proposal, submitted to the referees. But if deference to the Regents is called for with respect to the cost filter, surely it must also be shown with respect to the appropriate poverty weighting. The Regents, as noted, recommended a weighting for New York City low-income students of 1.8. Application of a 1.8 low-income weighting-even with the 50% cost filter-would result in a resource gap of $5.25 billion, almost identical to the $5.26 billion gap found by the referees.

Notably, the Governor proposed additional annual New York City spending of $4.7 billion; the Regents proposed $4.7 billion from the State, plus $0.9 billion from the City, for a total of $5.6 billion; and New York City proposed $5.3 billion. Plainly, every governmental actor knew what the referees and the Appellate Division here concluded: A sound basic education will cost approximately $5 billion in additional annual expenditures.

Judges ROSENBLATT, READ and SMITH concur with Judge PIGOTT.

Judge ROSENBLATT concurs in a separate opinion.

Chief Judge KAYE concurs in part and dissents in part in another opinion in which Judge CIPARICK concurs.

Judge <u>GRAFFEO</u> taking no part.

Order modified, etc.

END OF DOCUMENT

OPINION #8

Supreme Court, Appellate Division, First Department, New York

29 A.D.3d 175

CAMPAIGN FOR FISCAL EQUITY, INC., et al., Plaintiffs–Respondents

v

The STATE of New York, et al., Defendants–Appellants

Alliance for Quality Education, Brennan Center for Justice at New York University School of Law, City of New York, and United Federation of Teachers Amici Curiae

March 23, 2006

Background: Students, parents, and organizations concerned with education issues brought action challenging state's funding of New York City's public schools. Following remand, <u>86 N.Y.2d 307, 631 N.Y.S.2d 565, 655 N.E.2d 661,</u> the Supreme Court, New York County, <u>187 Misc.2d 1, 719 N.Y.S.2d 475,</u> entered judgment in favor of plaintiffs, and State appealed. The Supreme Court, Appellate Division, <u>295 A.D.2d 1, 744 N.Y.S.2d 130,</u> reversed, and plaintiffs appealed. The Court of Appeals, <u>100 N.Y.2d 893, 769 N.Y.S.2d 106, 801 N.E.2d 326,</u> affirmed as modified and remitted for further proceedings. The Supreme Court, New York County, <u>Leland DeGrasse,</u> J., confirmed referees' report and directed implementation of funding plan for school district. State appealed.

<u>Holding:</u> The Supreme Court, Appellate Division, <u>Buckley</u>, P.J., held that order directing state to take specific steps to adequately fund school district violated separate of powers doctrine.

Affirmed in part, vacated in part, and remanded.

<u>Saxe</u>, J., dissented and filed opinion in which <u>Tom</u>, J., joined.

JOHN T. BUCKLEY, P.J., PETER TOM, DAVID B. SAXE, JOSEPH P. SULLIVAN, BERNARD J. MALONE, JR., JJ.

BUCKLEY, P.J.

This is the third appeal to this Court arising from plaintiffs' challenge to the State's funding of the New York City school system under the Education Article of the New York Constitution (art. XI, § 1).

We hold that the State, in enacting a budget for the fiscal year commencing April 1, 2006, must appropriate the constitutionally required funding for the New York City schools. Our disagreement with the dissent lies only in our adherence to well-established constitutional doctrine that it is for the Governor and the Legislature, not the courts, to adopt a dollar-specific budget.

The record establishes a range of between $4.7 billion and $5.63 billion, a difference of $930 million, in additional annual operating funds, that would satisfy the State's constitutional education funding obligations. We disagree with the dissent that the courts can usurp the budgetary and educational powers of the Governor and the Legislature and preclude them from making that determination.

In calling for periodic, judicially supervised reviews of the amount of education funding, the dissent implicitly acknowledges that ascertaining the cost of the constitutionally mandated education is not susceptible to mathematical certitude, but rather depends, to a significant extent, on estimates.

The dissent does not reconcile that basic fact of educational budgeting with its proposed directive that there is one and only one scientifically precise amount of funding and that the State cannot consider any evidence to the contrary. As a unanimous Court of Appeals has stated:

"Assuming it were feasible to convert a courtroom into a super-auditing office to receive and criticize the budget estimates of a State with an $11 billion budget, the idea is not only a practical monstrosity but would duplicate exactly what the Legislature and the Governor do together, in harmony or in conflict, most often in conflict, for several months of each year" (Wein v. Carey, 41 N.Y.2d 498, 504–505, 393 N.Y.S.2d 955, 362 N.E.2d 587 [1977]).

History of the Case

The Education Article of the New York Constitution (art. XI, § 1) states, in full: "The legislature shall provide for the maintenance and support of a system of free common schools, wherein all the children of this state may be educated."

At the conclusion of the first appellate round, the Court of Appeals declared that the Education Article "requires the State to offer all children the opportunity of a sound basic education," consisting of "the basic literacy, calculating, and verbal skills necessary to enable children to eventually function productively as civic participants capable of voting and serving on a jury," as well as "minimally adequate physical facilities and classrooms which provide enough light, space, heat, and air to permit children to learn," "minimally adequate instrumentalities of learning such as desks, chairs, pencils, and reasonably current textbooks," and "minimally adequate teaching of reasonably up-to-date basic curricula such as reading, writing, mathematics, science, and social studies, by sufficient personnel adequately trained to teach those subject areas" (*Campaign for Fiscal Equity v. State of New York*, 86 N.Y.2d 307, 316–317, 631 N.Y.S.2d 565, 655 N.E.2d 661 [1995] [*CFE I*]).

On the second appeal, the Court of Appeals held that "the opportunity of a sound basic education" means "the opportunity for a meaningful high school education," though not pegged to any particular grade level, Board of Regents standard, or high school diploma eligibility requirement (*Campaign for Fiscal Equity v. State of New York*, 100 N.Y.2d 893, 906–908, 769 N.Y.S.2d 106, 801 N.E.2d 326 [2003] [*CFE II*]).

The Court of Appeals upheld the trial court's findings that various "inputs" (teaching, school facilities, classrooms, and instrumentalities of learning) and "outputs" (school graduation rates and test results) demonstrated that New York City schoolchildren were not receiving the opportunity for the constitutional sound basic education, and that there was a causal link between the State's current funding system and such failure (*see id.* at 909–925, 769 N.Y.S.2d 106, 801 N.E.2d 326).

With respect to the remedy, the Court of Appeals acknowledged that the judiciary should "defer to the Legislature in matters of policymaking, particularly in a matter so vital as education financing," and that the courts "have neither the authority, nor the ability, nor the will, to micromanage education financing" (*id.* at 925, 769 N.Y.S.2d 106, 801 N.E.2d 326). The Court of Appeals also noted various Federal, State, and City education reforms initiated after the close of trial that might provide the opportunity for a sound basic education to more students and thus affect the scope of needed changes to the school funding system (*see id.* at 926–927, 769 N.Y.S.2d 106, 801 N.E.2d 326).

The Court directed the State to "ascertain the actual cost of providing a sound basic education in New York City," to reform the current system of school funding and management to furnish every school in the City with the resources necessary for providing the opportunity for a sound basic education, and to "ensure a system of accountability to measure whether the reforms actually provide the opportunity for a sound basic education" (*id.* at 930, 769

N.Y.S.2d 106, 801 N.E.2d 326). The Court of Appeals set a deadline of July 30, 2004, a little more than one year after the date of the decision, for defendants "to implement the necessary measures" (id.).

Despite the Legislature's thereafter having been called into extraordinary session and passing a budget in 2004 increasing statewide school funding by $740 million, of which $300 million would go to the New York City schools, the deadline passed without an agreement on additional court-ordered funding for New York City schools.

In August 2004, Supreme Court appointed three Referees "to hear and report with rec-ommendations on what measures defendants [had] taken" to follow the directives of the Court of Appeals.

The Defendants' Proposals:

At the Referees' hearing defendants submitted a State Education Reform Plan, which proposed $4.7 billion in additional annual funds for the City schools, phased in over five years, plus various accountability reforms. That plan largely drew upon the report of the New York State Commission on Education Reform, the "Zarb Commission," appointed by the Governor in 2003.

The Zarb Commission had identified three methods of determining the actual cost of providing City school children with the opportunity for a sound basic education: (1) the "econometric method," which uses a statistical model to estimate the costs associated with dif-ferent levels of school district performance; (2) the "professional judgment method," which uses panels of education professionals to determine the scholastic elements needed to attain certain goals and then assigns costs to those elements; and (3) the "successful schools method," which examines the expenditures of school districts that meet or exceed performance stan-dards. The Zarb Commission rejected both the econometric method, since it had not been used by any other state, and the professional judgment method, which is based only on hypo-thetical constructs. The Commission selected the successful schools method as the most reli-able, because it is based on actual data from school districts with a proven record of success, and is used by the State Board of Regents.

The Commission retained Standard & Poor's School Evaluation Services, which, using the successful school districts method, calculated an annual spending gap for the City schools ranging from $1.93 billion to $4.69 billion, depending on the standard for measuring a suc-cessful school district, the additional expenditures necessitated by special needs students, and the manner of converting "standard" education dollars into New York City dollars.

Standard & Poor's used four different academic achievement standards for identifying a successful school district: (1) the "top performers," that is, the top 25 percent of the State's school districts as measured by an "Index of Multiple Performance Measures," which is comprised of scores on various State examinations, graduation rates, and high school enrollment retention rates; (2) the State school districts meeting the Federal No Child Left Behind Act's performance targets on various examinations for the year 2006; (3) the State school districts meeting the No Child Left Behind Act's performance targets for the year 2008; and (4) the State school districts meeting the "Regents Criteria," where at least 80 percent of the students demonstrated proficiency on seven Regents examinations.

The successful school analyses produced "base expenditures," which are estimated costs per student. Base expenditures were multiplied by "weightings" for students with special needs. Relying on research literature, Standard & Poor's assigned a weighting of 2.1 to students with disabilities, 1.35 to economically disadvantaged students, and 1.2 to students with limited English proficiency.

Because the purchasing power of a dollar varies across the State, and the successful schools method examined all of the school districts in the State, Standard & Poor's offered two alternative regional cost factors to determine the cost in New York City dollars: (1) the "New York Regional Cost Index," provided by the State Education Department; and (2) the "Geographic Cost of Education Index," provided by the National Center for Education Statistics.

Finally, Standard & Poor's applied a "cost effectiveness filter" of 50%, the same method used by the New York State Board of Regents, to screen out successful school districts that either spent money inefficiently or spent more than was necessary to provide the opportunity for a sound basic education. Under that approach, Standard & Poor's used the average expenditures of the lower spending half of successful school districts. Since the average achievement levels of the lower spending half of successful school districts closely resembled the achievement levels of the higher spending half of successful school districts, Standard & Poor's concluded that there was little evidence that the additional spending by the higher half led to meaningfully higher achievement levels.

The Zarb Commission found Standard & Poor's methodologies to be valid and recommended increased annual spending within the ranges of that study, phased in over five years. The Commission declined to endorse a specific dollar amount, believing that the decision should be left to the State's elected officials.

In July 2004, the Governor proposed legislation that would adopt the Zarb Commission's recommendations and, using the New York State Regents Criteria as the measure of a successful school district, would increase funding of the City school districts by $4.7 billion annually, phased in over five years. However, that legislation was not enacted.

In August 2004, as noted, the Legislature passed, and the Governor signed, a bill to provide $300 million more to the City schools than had been appropriated the previous year.

<u>The Proposals of Plaintiffs, the City, and the Board of Regents:</u>

Plaintiffs submitted to the Referees a report by the American Institutes for Research (AIR) and Management Analysis and Planning, Inc. (MAP), which recommended additional annual expenditures of $5.63 billion. The AIR/MAP study used the professional judgment method (rather than the successful schools method, used by Standard & Poor's), and the Regents Learning Standards as the academic **6 achievement standard (rather than the Regents Criteria).

The City submitted a plan calling for $5.3 billion in additional annual funds and $13.1 billion in capital improvements. The Board of Regents, using the successful schools method, the Regents Criteria as the measure of success, a cost efficiency filter of 50%, the New York Regional Cost Index, and poverty weightings ranging from 1.5 to 2, recommended an increase in annual funding of $4.7 billion, phased in over seven years.

The Referees' Recommendations

In November 2004, the Referees issued their report, recommending additional annual funds of $5.63 billion, phased in over four years, and capital improvements of $9.179 billion over a five-year period. They accepted the Zarb Commission's use of the "successful schools method," and the "Regents Criteria" as the appropriate achievement standard, but rejected the 50% cost effectiveness filter (or any cost effectiveness filter), recommended a weighting of 1.5 for low income students rather than 1.35, and proposed modifications to the Geographic Cost of Education Index calculations.

The Referees recommended a costing-out study every four years, "until it becomes clear that reforms to the State's education finance formulas have rendered such studies no longer necessary to assure all New York City students the opportunity for a sound basic education." The studies would be designed and supervised by the Board of Regents, with an opportunity for the parties to be heard, and would incorporate both the successful schools method and the professional judgment method. Similarly, there would be a facilities review every five years. The Referees recommended against the State's proposed Office of Educational Accountability, but endorsed the parties' agreed-upon accountability enhancements. Finally, the Referees recommended leaving to the State the decision of how much of the additional funding should be paid by the City. Supreme Court confirmed the Referees' report. We conclude that the confirmation should be vacated.

The Referees determined that the "Regents Criteria," the achievement standard utilized by the State and the Board of Regents, was an appropriate measure of student success, and not the "Regents Learning Standards," which had been found to exceed a sound basic education by *CFE II*, 100 N.Y.2d at 907–908, 769 N.Y.S.2d 106, 801 N.E.2d 326.

The Referees rejected the 50% cost effectiveness filter as "both unsupported and arbitrary." However, there was no evidence to support the Referees' apparent assumption that every successful school district spends only the minimum amount necessary to succeed under the Regents Criteria. On the other hand, the Board of Regents based their adoption of the identical cost-efficiency factor upon "a careful examination of characteristics of these two groups of successful school districts," which demonstrated that the higher spending districts had "chosen to offer more than a sound basic education." More importantly, the record establishes that the academic performance of the successful school districts in the lower spending half was nearly the same as that of the higher spending half of successful school districts, which in itself indicates that the efficient use of funds produces results. In recommending a multi-year phase-in to enable the "efficient planning to use prudently the additional funding," the Referees acknowledged that efficiency is a legitimate concern.

Although several testifying witnesses criticized the use of any cost efficiency filter, and others would have used a formula different from the one adopted by the State, the Board of Regents, to whom the Referees deferred as experts in other matters, used the same 50% filter. The Referees were also concerned that the filter has the effect of eliminating most of the school districts in Westchester and Nassau, counties that border New York City and thus resemble the City in the concentration of students who are not English proficient and in the higher regional costs, particularly in hiring and retaining capable teachers. However, the weightings (representing extra funding) for students with limited English proficiency and the geographical cost indexes are designed to address just such factors.

The Referees found "only limited support in the record" for the weighting of 1.35 for low income students, because it was not focused on the specific circumstances of the City schools. The Referees attached "much greater probative value" to the weighting recommended by the Board of Regents and implicit in the AIR/MAP study, on the ground that they purportedly were focused on New York City. But as the Referees recognized, by their own characterization, the State's weighting assessment had record support. In such circumstances, as with the cost effectiveness filter, Supreme Court should not have substituted the Referees' opinion for that of the State on an issue that was clearly debatable. As a consequence, Supreme Court converted a factor that was arguable and reasonable for the Legislature and Governor to consider into an incontrovertible fact. As long as the State's choices remained within the range of professionally accepted practices in determining the costs of a sound basic education, Supreme Court should have left the conclusions for legislative and gubernatorial consideration and determination.

The Referees accepted the use of the Geographic Cost of Education Index to convert statewide costs to New York City costs, but recommended the use of a more updated version and the calculation of costs in 2004–2005 dollars, rather than January 2004 dollars, to account for inflation. Defendants do not contest that modification.

The Standard of Review and Constitutional Requirements

Plaintiffs argue that the Referees' factual findings are owed deference if supported by the record. Concededly, there is evidence in the record to support the Referees' findings with respect to the actual annual cost of providing the opportunity for a sound basic education in the City. There is also, however, a respectable body of evidence to support the State's plan, as found by the Board of Regents, Standard & Poor's, and the Zarb Commission, and as proposed by the Governor. The "burden of proof...is on one who attacks the [State's] budget plan" and "[i]t is a formidable burden" (*Wein*, 41 N.Y.2d at 505, 393 N.Y.S.2d 955, 362 N.E.2d 587). That burden has not been met.

Insofar as the Referees derived "comfort" from the "relative convergence" of the yearly additional funding levels recommended by plaintiffs, the City, and the State (as modified by the Referees), they should find repose in the nearly exact correspondence of the calculations of the Board of Regents and the State's unmodified plan. Indeed, one of the most crucial facts established by the record is that reasonable minds can differ as to the actual cost of providing the opportunity for a sound basic education within the City schools. Where there is sufficient evidence to support a range of numbers, it ill behooves the Court to dictate the result; at that point, more than ever, the issue becomes a matter of policy for the other branches of government to determine.

As the Court of Appeals observed in the context of undisputed, serious gaps in rent-control legislation, "ultimate resolution requires correction at the legislative level...and not at the judicial level. The courts have limited access to the controlling economic and social facts. They are also limited by a decent respect for the separation of powers upon which our system of government is based" (*Matter of 89 Christopher Inc. v. Joy*, 35 N.Y.2d 213, 220, 360 N.Y.S.2d 612, 318 N.E.2d 776 [1974]). Although that case did not entail a constitutional challenge, the salient point is that, "because of the significant policies involved," i.e., the conservation of necessary housing, the well-being of residents, and the property interests of building owners, "they should be resolved by legislative action" (*id.*), and "it is not the province of the courts to direct the legislature how to do its work" (*People ex rel. Hatch v. Reardon*, 184 N.Y. 431, 442, 77 N.E. 970 [1906], *affd.* 204 U.S. 152, 27 S.Ct. 188, 51 L.Ed. 415 [1907]).

The doctrine of the separation of powers is so fundamental to our system of government that the Legislature is precluded from enacting legislation charging the judiciary with the mandatory performance of non-judicial duties (see _Matter of Richardson_, 247 N.Y. 401, 160 N.E. 655 [1928] [the Governor and the Legislature may not instruct a Justice of the Supreme Court to investigate and prosecute a public official pursuant to a provision of the Public Officers Law]). Just as the other branches of government may not compel the judiciary to perform non-judicial functions of government, the courts must refrain from arrogating such powers to themselves. Indeed, the New York Constitution prohibits members of the judiciary from holding "any other public office or trust" (N.Y. Const. art. VI, § 20[b] [1]), which embodies a policy "to conserve the time of the judges for the performance of their work as judges, and to save them from the entanglements, at times the partisan suspicions, so often the result of other and conflicting duties" (_Matter of Richardson_, 247 N.Y. at 420, 160 N.E. 655). As pointed out by the Court of Appeals in _CFE II_: "in a budgetary matter the Legislature must consider that any action it takes will directly or indirectly affect its other commitments" (100 N.Y.2d at 930 n. 10, 769 N.Y.S.2d 106, 801 N.E.2d 326).

Thus, without the ability or the authority to review the entire State budget, "it is untenable that the judicial process...should intervene and reorder priorities, allocate the limited resources available, and in effect direct how the vast [City and State] enterprise[s] should conduct [their] affairs" (_Jones v. Beame_, 45 N.Y.2d 402, 407, 408 N.Y.S.2d 449, 380 N.E.2d 277 [1978]). "While it is within the power of the judiciary to declare the vested rights of a specifically protected class of individuals..., the manner by which the State addresses complex societal and governmental issues is a subject left to the discretion of the political branches of government" (_Matter of New York State Inspection, Sec. and Law Enforcement Employees_, 64 N.Y.2d 233, 239–240, 485 N.Y.S.2d 719, 475 N.E.2d 90 [1984] [declining to fashion a remedy that would "embroil the judiciary in the management and operation of the State correction system"]).

The principle is well stated in _Klostermann v. Cuomo_, 61 N.Y.2d 525, 475 N.Y.S.2d 247, 463 N.E.2d 588 [1984], relied on by plaintiffs. In _Klostermann_, the plaintiffs, patients and former patients of State psychiatric hospitals, claimed that their constitutional and statutory rights had been violated when they were released into the community without residential placement, supervision, and care, under the least restrictive conditions suitable to their condition (see _id._ at 531–532, 475 N.Y.S.2d 247, 463 N.E.2d 588). The Court of Appeals held that it had the authority to compel the State to exercise its mandatory duties, even if those duties are to be executed through discretionary means, but lacked the power to direct the State to act in a particular manner (see _id._ at 540, 475 N.Y.S.2d 247, 463 N.E.2d 588).

The Court could compel the State to perform a legal duty, but not direct how it should perform that duty, since "[t]he activity that the courts must be careful to avoid is the fashioning of orders or judgments that go beyond any mandatory directives of existing statutes and regulations [and constitutional provisions] and intrude upon the policy-making and discretionary decisions that are reserved to the legislative and executive branches" (*id.* at 541, 475 N.Y.S.2d 247, 463 N.E.2d 588).

Thus, the Court could direct the State to prepare plans and programs to provide suitable treatment (a mandatory duty), which would also necessarily require the expenditure of funds, but not dictate the specific manner in which such plans and programs operated (discretionary and policy decisions for the Governor and Legislature) (*see id.* at 539–541, 475 N.Y.S.2d 247, 463 N.E.2d 588).

In the Court of Appeals' most recent decision concerning the Constitution's Education Article, *New York Civil Liberties Union v. State of New York,* 4 N.Y.3d 175, 791 N.Y.S.2d 507, 824 N.E.2d 947 [2005], the plaintiffs challenged the failure of the State Commissioner of Education to take affirmative action to determine the causes of failure in their schools and rectify them by classifying them Schools Under Registration Review (SURR) (*see id.* at 182–183, 791 N.Y.S.2d 507, 824 N.E.2d 947).

The Court refused to compel the Commissioner, "because the administrative action of deciding which and how many schools to place under registration review involves an exercise of judgment and discretion by the Commissioner" (*id.* at 184, 791 N.Y.S.2d 507, 824 N.E.2d 947). Even after a school is placed on the SURR list, the specific actions to be taken rest within the Commissioner's expertise, judgment and discretion *(id.).* The act of choosing among different reasonable funding plans is no less a matter of discretion, and therefore one that does not belong in the courts.

It is not for the courts to make education policy (*see CFE II,* 100 N.Y.2d at 931, 769 N.Y.S.2d 106, 801 N.E.2d 326). The judiciary must take "a disciplined perception of the proper role of the courts in the resolution of our State's educational problems," since "primary responsibility for the provision of fair and equitable educational opportunity within the financial capabilities of our State's taxpayers unquestionably rests with that branch of our government [the Legislature]" (*Board of Educ., Levittown Union Free School Dist. v. Nyquist,* 57 N.Y.2d 27, 49 n. 9, 453 N.Y.S.2d 643, 439 N.E.2d 359 [1982], *appeal dismissed* 459 U.S. 1138, 103 S.Ct. 775, 74 L.Ed.2d 986 [1983]). Indeed, the Constitution expressly states that "*the legislature* shall provide for the maintenance and support of a system of free common schools" (N.Y. Const., art. XI, § 1 [emphasis added]). For that reason:

"The determination of the amounts, sources, and objectives of expenditures of public moneys for educational purposes, especially at the State level, presents issues of enormous practical and political complexity, and resolution appropriately is largely left to the interplay of the interests and forces directly involved and indirectly affected, in the arenas of legislative and executive activity. This is of the very essence of our governmental and political polity. It would normally be inappropriate, therefore, for the courts to intrude upon such decision-making" (*Levittown,* 57 N.Y.2d at 38–39, 453 N.Y.S.2d 643, 439 N.E.2d 359).

The criticism of the dissent herein of an adherence to separation of powers principles ignores the guidelines of *Levittown,* as set forth *supra,* and draws an erroneous inference from the interplay of the majority, concurring, and dissenting opinions in *CFE I* and *CFE II, supra.* The majority in *CFE I* did not reject the doctrine of the separation of powers as a vital component of our governmental structure or hold that the courts can or should conduct independent budgetary hearings, choose among different reasonable estimates, or dictate precise *188 dollar amounts of appropriation.

Rather, the majority in *CFE I* expressly stated that its decision "does not extend the State's funding obligations" and that "any discussion of funding or reallocation [of resources] is premature," since " [t]he question of remedies is not before the Court" (86 N.Y.2d at 316 n. 4, 631 N.Y.S.2d 565, 655 N.E.2d 661). In *CFE II,* the majority respected the separation of powers doctrine by declining the plaintiffs' request "to initiate a legislative/judicial dialogue" and by limiting its remedy to remanding to the Legislature and Governor to ascertain the cost of providing the opportunity for a sound basic education in the City schools (100 N.Y.2d at 925, 930, 769 N.Y.S.2d 106, 801 N.E.2d 326). The rationale for such forbearance was that the courts must "defer to the Legislature in matters of policymaking, particularly in a matter so vital as education financing," since the courts have "neither the authority, nor the ability, nor the will, to micromanage education financing" (*CFE II,* 100 N.Y.2d at 925, 769 N.Y.S.2d 106, 801 N.E.2d 326).

Moreover, after *CFE II,* the Court of Appeals squarely addressed the budgetary process in *Pataki v. New York State Assembly,* 4 N.Y.3d at 97, 791 N.Y.S.2d 458, 824 N.E.2d 898, declaring: "to invite the Governor and the Legislature to resolve their disputes in the courtroom might produce neither executive budgeting nor legislative budgeting but judicial budgeting—arguably the worst of the three." Although there was a concurring and a dissenting opinion in that case, both stressed the importance of the separation of powers (*see id.* at 100, 791 N.Y.S.2d 458, 824 N.E.2d 898 [Rosenblatt, J., concurring]; *id.* at 107, 791 N.Y.S.2d 458, 824 N.E.2d 898 [Kaye, C.J., dissenting]). Under the New York Constitution, " 'the executive and legislative branches of government...are the sole participants in the negotiation and adoption of [a] budget' " (*Saxton v. Carey,* 44 N.Y.2d 545, 550, 406 N.Y.S.2d 732, 378 N.E.2d 95 [1978] [quoting *Hidley v. Rockefeller,* 28 N.Y.2d 439, 445, 322 N.Y.S.2d 687, 271 N.E.2d 530 [1971]] [Breitel, J., dissenting]).

The fact that certain legislators might hope that the courts will take control of educational budgeting, as reported in various newspapers cited by the dissent herein, is of no moment. The allocation of budgetary powers set forth in the Constitution is not "a requirement which may be waived if the executive and legislative branches agree on it" (*New York State Bankers Assn. v. Wetzler,* 81 N.Y.2d 98, 104, 595 N.Y.S.2d 936, 612 N.E.2d 294 [1993]). To the contrary:

"The object of a written Constitution is to regulate, define and limit the powers of government by assigning to the executive, legislative and judicial branches distinct and independent powers. The safety of free government rests upon the independence of each branch and the even balance of power between the three. It is not merely for convenience in the transaction of business that they are kept separate by the Constitution, but for the preservation of liberty itself" (*id.* at 105, 595 N.Y.S.2d 936, 612 N.E.2d 294 [quoting *People ex rel. Burby v. Howland,* 155 N.Y. 270, 282, 49 N.E. 775 [1898]]).

For the foregoing reasons, the Court should not substitute its own budgetary calculations for those of the other branches.

It is undisputed that the State has failed to appropriate an adequate amount of funding to meet its educational mandate as outlined in *CFE II*. However, that neglect does not give the Court the authority to participate in budget negotiations or, absent a constitutional failing, to exercise a veto power over the State's calculations of the cost of a sound basic education. The fact that the other two branches of government have not remedied constitutional failings in the past does not authorize the courts to commit their own constitutional violations now.

Mindful of these constitutional and institutional constraints, the Court of Appeals in *CFE II* was careful to seek a "less entangling" remedy (*CFE II,* 100 N.Y.2d at 925, 769 N.Y.S.2d 106, 801 N.E.2d 326). By requiring judicial approval of the educational budget plan currently at issue, and periodic reviews, Supreme Court would ensure the "decades of litigation" that the Court of Appeals has cautioned against (*id.* at 931, 769 N.Y.S.2d 106, 801 N.E.2d 326). Thus, while the Legislature should consider the Governor's proposal to increase annual funding by $4.7 billion, together with the Referees' recommendation that $5.63 billion per year is the preferable amount to expend, in the final analysis it is for the Governor and the Legislature to make the determination as to the constitutionally mandated amount of funding, including such considerations as how the funds shall be raised, how the additional expenditures will affect other necessary appropriations and the economic viability of the State, and how the funding shall be allocated between the State and the City.

Contrary to the dissent's repeated characterization, this directive does not merely urge the Governor and the Legislature to consider taking action. They are directed to take action. The matter for them to consider is whether $4.7 billion or $5.63 billion, or some amount in between, is the minimum additional annual funding to be appropriated for the City schools.

Although the State's proposal originally projected a five-year phase-in, the passage of time since the plan was presented indicates that a four-year period would now be in accord. A judicial decree enjoining the Legislature to spend the higher of the two reasonable figures is all the more unwarranted in light of the fact that the increased spending is to be phased in over the course of several years, which thus enables the Governor and the Legislature to revisit the issue and adjust the amount upward or supplement it in future sessions, should they determine, in the exercise of their constitutional responsibilities, that more is needed.

Plaintiffs' reliance on _Montoy v. State,_ 279 Kan. 817, 112 P.3d 923 [2005] for the proposition that the courts should review legislative funding determinations is misplaced. In that case, the Supreme Court of Kansas directed the State Legislature to implement an increase in annual school funding of $285 million, and rejected the State's appropriation of $142 million as inadequate, because: there was no study or other evidence to support the State's amount; the higher amount was derived from a study commissioned by the Legislature itself to determine the actual costs of a constitutional education; that study was the only evidence submitted to the Court; and the Kansas State Department of Education supported the study (_see_ 279 Kan. at 829–830, 839, 844–845, 112 P.3d at 931–932, 937, 940). By contrast, in the instant matter, New York State's proposed annual funding amount has substantial record support, including the studies of the Zarb Commission and Standard & Poor's, as well as the New York State Board of Regents.

The Referees adopted plaintiffs' proposed $9.179 billion five-year capital improvement plan to address overcrowding, reduce class sizes, provide computers and other technology, and create libraries, laboratories, and auditoriums. Defendants have neither presented evidence concerning the expected cost of capital projects nor outlined a basic plan. Rather, defendants maintain that all of the City's needs will be satisfied by a project-by-project assessment under the existing building aid program, together with some accountability reforms. That assurance, considered in conjunction with the City's endorsement of plaintiffs' plan and the State's failure to refute it or offer an alternative, indicates that the finding of Supreme Court with respect to a capital plan was not erroneous.

As the Referees found, the accountability system of the Board of Regents is widely recognized as one of the best in the nation, and an Office of Educational Authority may well be an unnecessary bureaucratic expense, but to the extent Supreme Court's order may be read as prohibiting the State from establishing such an entity, it exceeded its authority. Such a ban would be based not on any constitutional clause, operation of law, or strong public policy, but only on Supreme Court's personal view as to the preferable allocation of resources and administrative responsibilities.

Defendants are directed to act as expeditiously as possible to implement a budget that allows the City students the education to which they are entitled. Accordingly, the order of the Supreme Court, New York County (Leland DeGrasse, J.), entered on or about March 16, 2005, which, inter alia, granted plaintiffs' motion to confirm the Referees' report, denied defendants' cross motion to reject the report in part, and directed defendants to implement a funding plan to provide the New York City School District with at least $5.63 billion in additional annual operating funds, phased in over four years, to conduct quadrennial reviews of the cost of providing the opportunity for a sound basic education to all public school students in New

York City, to expend a minimum of $9.179 billion on capital improvements over the next five years, to conduct capital improvement funding studies every five years, to enhance the current system of educational accountability by developing a comprehensive plan setting forth the precise management reforms and instructional initiatives that the Department of Education will undertake to improve student achievement, and to ensure that the Department of Education issues an annual Sound Basic Education Report, tracking additional spending and student performance, should be modified, on the law and the facts, to vacate the confirmation of the Referees' report; to direct that, in enacting a budget for the fiscal year commencing April 1, 2006, the Governor and the Legislature consider, as within the range of constitutionally required funding for the New York City School District, as demonstrated by this record, the proposed funding plan of at least $4.7 billion in additional annual operating funds, and the Referees' recommended annual expenditure of $5.63 billion, or an amount in between, phased in over four years, and that they appropriate such amount, in order to remedy the constitutional deprivations found in *CFE II*, and that, in enacting such budget, the Governor and the Legislature implement a capital improvement plan that expends $9.179 billion over the next five years or otherwise satisfies the City schools' constitutionally recognized capital needs, and otherwise affirmed, without costs.

Order, Supreme Court, New York County (Leland DeGrasse, J.), entered on or about March 16, 2005, modified, on the law and the facts, to vacate the confirmation of the Referees' report; to direct that, in enacting a budget for the fiscal year commencing April 1, 2006, the Governor and the Legislature, consider, as within the range of constitutionally required funding for the New York City School District, the proposed funding plan of at least $ 4.7 billion in additional annual operating funds, and the Referees' recommended annual expenditure of $ 5.63 billion, or an amount in between, phased in over four years, and that they appropriate such amount, in order to remedy constitutional deprivations, and that, in enacting such budget, the Governor and the Legislature implement a capital improvement plan that expends $ 9.179 billion over the next five years or otherwise satisfies the City schools' constitutionality recognized capital needs, and otherwise affirmed, without costs.

All concur except <u>TOM</u> and <u>SAXE</u>, JJ. who dissent in an Opinion by <u>SAXE</u>, J.

<u>SAXE</u>, J. (dissenting).

The majority views the separation of powers doctrine as precluding the IAS court from affirmatively directing the Legislature to take the specific steps necessary to carry out the previous mandate of the Court of Appeals (*see Campaign for Fiscal Equity v. State of New York [CFE II],* 100 N.Y.2d 893, 905, 769 N.Y.S.2d 106, 801 N.E.2d 326 [2003], *modfg.* 295 A.D.2d 1, 744 N.Y.S.2d 130 [2002], *revg.* 187 Misc.2d 1, 719 N.Y.S.2d 475 [2001]). In this way, it allows a festering constitutional problem of enormous dimension to continue indefinitely.

While it accepts that the shortfall in the funds needed by the New York City public schools in order to provide all its students with the opportunity to obtain a sound basic education comes to at least $4.7 billion, if not $5.63 billion, the majority limits itself to asserting that in enacting a budget for the fiscal year commencing April 1, 2006, the State "must appropriate the constitutionally required funding" and directing the Governor and the Legislature to "consider" a funding plan in that range.

Remanding this matter back to the Legislature and Governor with the general and inadequate directive that they now "appropriate the necessary funding" is insufficient at this juncture. First, given our executive budgeting system (*see Pataki v. New York State Assembly*, 4 N.Y.3d 75, 791 N.Y.S.2d 458, 824 N.E.2d 898 [2004]), it is not clear exactly what the majority's direction to appropriate funding requires: is it the Governor's proposal of an appropriation bill, the Legislature's enactment of such a bill, or both? Second, in the face of the Legislature's proven inability to agree upon the level of appropriation it was willing to enact in order to comply with *CFE II*, the fact-finding ordered by the IAS court, and the exact finding made, was clearly necessary. The appropriate step now is for this Court to uphold the confirmation of the Referees' findings and the affirmative direction that defendants enact legislation making the specified allocation in their budget.

It bears emphasis that the Court of Appeals, in *CFE II, supra,* directed that by July 30, 2004, the Legislature and the Governor were to not only ascertain the cost of providing the opportunity for a sound basic education in the City schools, but also to *ensure, through "enacting appropriate reforms," "that every school in New York City would have the resources necessary for providing the opportunity for a sound basic education"* (100 N.Y.2d at 930, 769 N.Y.S.2d 106, 801 N.E.2d 326 [emphasis added]). It was only when that deadline had come and gone without compliance that plaintiffs asked the court to do, or order, that which defendants seemingly could not. The IAS court therefore, through the appointment of Referees, itself ascertained the cost of providing the opportunity for a sound basic education in the City schools, and then defined the exact terms of the legislative reform which would, if enacted, ensure "that every school in New York City would have the resources necessary for providing [it]"

The majority asserts that "in the final analysis it is for the Governor and the Legislature to make the determination as to the constitutionally mandated funding." However, the majority ignores the fact that the deadline for making that determination has already passed without the Legislature successfully enacting such legislation. Indeed, the Legislature has proven itself unable to either agree upon the necessary level of constitutionally mandated funding or to make provision for its allocation, and its failure has continued both during and after the period of time that the Court of Appeals allotted for it to act. The majority's directive, aside from pointing to the numbers that have been in defendants' possession for over a year, in effect accomplishes no more than what the Court of Appeals already did when it directed the enactment of appropriate reforms providing that the schools be given the necessary financial resources.

Even the majority's apparently definitive "holding" that the State must "appropriate the constitutionally required funding," is in effect illusory. The Governor has already proposed such an appropriation to the Legislature in July 2004. The Legislature showed itself to be unwilling or unable to enact the bill. In now telling the Legislature to "appropriate the constitutionally required funding," the majority assumes that the Legislature will, upon that direction, be capable of agreeing internally, and with the Governor, on an amount, when it has already demonstrated that it is unable to do. The range of amounts specified by the majority does not change anything; this is the same information the Legislature had before it in 2004.

The majority's "direction," at this juncture, leaves the students of the New York City public schools without any more of a remedy for this substantial constitutional violation than they had on July 31, 2004, the day noncompliance with the Court of Appeals' prior directive was clear. I am unable to read the majority's decretal paragraph as containing the type of clear and exact directive that, if ignored, may be the subject of enforcement proceedings. Without that type of clarity, it merely amounts to a suggestion to consider taking action, an illusory and possibly unenforceable remedy.

The majority also asserts that the failure of the other two branches of government to remedy constitutional failings "in the past" does not authorize this Court to commit what it terms constitutional violations of our own. But, the "constitutional failings" of which we speak are current and ongoing, not simply "in the past," and there is no indication that they will be remedied unless and until those branches of our state government have a clear and exact directive as to what they must do to rectify the violation. By framing the discussion, and the purported remedy, as it does, the majority is consigning the schoolchildren of New York to further constitutional violations and neglect. Under these circumstances, where the legislative and executive branches of government have repeatedly failed to confront and solve a problem of state constitutional dimension, it is the obligation of the judiciary to assert its historic role.

The order of the Supreme Court, which confirmed the Referees' findings and directed the implementation of a funding program in accordance with those findings, was in all respects fully supported and proper, and ought to be affirmed.

In the prior appeal, the Court of Appeals upheld the finding that many of the 1.1 million children attending public schools in the City of New York were not receiving the opportunity to obtain a "sound basic education" as required by Article XI of the New York Constitution (*see CFE II,* 100 N.Y.2d at 905, 769 N.Y.S.2d 106, 801 N.E.2d 326). The Court, while aware of the need to defer to the Legislature in matters of policymaking, nevertheless recognized the need to ensure a meaningful remedy for the constitutional violation (*id.* at 925, 769 N.Y.S.2d 106, 801 N.E.2d 326). It therefore directed the State to (1) "ascertain the actual cost of providing a sound basic education in New York City," (2) "address the shortcomings of the current system by ensuring...that every school in New York City would have the resources necessary for providing the opportunity for a sound basic education," and (3) "ensure a system of accountability to measure whether the reforms actually provide the opportunity for a sound basic education" (*id.* at 930, 769 N.Y.S.2d 106, 801 N.E.2d 326). The Court imposed a deadline of July 30, 2004 (*id.*).

Attempts were made to comply with these directives, particularly on the part of the Governor. In September 2003, the Governor appointed the State Commission on Education Reform (Zarb Commission). On March 29, 2004, the Zarb Commission released its final report, indicating that a funding increase in the "range of $2.5 billion to $5.6 billion is a good place to start." In July 2004, the Governor proposed legislation contemplating a total increase of up to $4.7 billion over five years; this bill provided that $2 billion would be contributed by the State, with the remainder made up of New York City funds and an expected increase in federal and state aid. The State Assembly also proposed a bill which called for an increase of $6.1 billion in operating funds and $1.3 billion as the State's share of a $2.6 billion capital fund.

However, although the Governor called the State Legislature into extraordinary session in an effort to take the action directed by the Court of Appeals, the Court's July 30, 2004 deadline passed without the Legislature's enactment of either the Governor's proposal or any other bill.

In consequence of defendants' failure or inability to comply with the prior order, upon an application by plaintiffs, the IAS Court properly appointed a panel of three distinguished Referees to hear and report with recommendations on the areas in which compliance with *CFE II* was lacking. After extensive hearings, the Referees made six key recommendations, including a four-year phase-in of operational increases totaling $5.63 billion, a review of operational funding in 2008 and every four years thereafter, and a five-year phase-in of capital funding totaling $9.179 billion.

The Referees arrived at the $5.63 billion figure for the necessary operational funds increase by applying the so-called "successful school district" methodology employed by defendants' expert to the particular circumstances presented here. However, they declined to use three adjustment factors suggested by defendants: (1) a 50% "cost efficiency filter," which the Referees properly considered to be insufficiently supported by either the evidence or experts in education finance, (2) a poverty weighting figure based on national, rather than local, data, and (3) an out-of-date regional cost of living index.

Defendants continue to assert on appeal that a sound basic education can be provided for an additional $1.93 billion, but fail to provide support for that number. Indeed, that number is merely part of the calculations contained in the Standard & Poor's study intended to set out a range of "spending gap" calculations, specifically, the part of the analysis in which is calculated the average of the bottom-spending 50% of successful school districts. Nowhere did S & P claim that a sound basic education could be provided with the addition of this particular sum, nor did any defendants' witness explain how this sum would successfully do so. Therefore, the majority correctly ignores that suggested amount.

As to the Referees' findings that an increase of $9.179 billion in capital funding is necessary in order for the City schools to provide the opportunity for a sound basic education, I agree with the majority that these findings are fully supported by the record. At the hearing, defendants took the position that the Court of Appeals' decision required *no* increase in capital funding; accordingly, they presented no evidence on the issue. In contrast, plaintiff submitted an extensive capital funding plan, designed by a 22–person expert task force focused on addressing the particular capital funding issues raised by the decision, such as overcrowding, excessive class sizes, and an absence of laboratories, libraries, and computer equipment.

"The rule is well settled that where questions of fact are submitted to a referee, it is the function of the referee to determine the issues presented, as well as to resolve conflicting testimony and matters of credibility, and generally courts will not disturb the findings of a referee 'to the extent that the record substantiates his findings and they may reject findings not supported by the record' " (*Kardanis v. Velis*, 90 A.D.2d 727, 455 N.Y.S.2d 612 [1982], quoting *Matter of Holy Spirit Assn. for Unification of World Christianity v. Tax Commn.*, 81 A.D.2d 64, 71, 438 N.Y.S.2d 521 [1981], *revd. on other grounds* 55 N.Y.2d 512, 450 N.Y.S.2d 292, 435 N.E.2d 662 [1982]).

Based upon the extensive testimony presented in support of the Referees' plan, including the acknowledgment of defendants' expert that the methodology and general conclusions of the plan were sound, the Referees' findings were fully supported by the evidence before them, and therefore properly confirmed by the IAS court (*see Merchants Bank of N.Y. v. Dajoy Diamonds*, 5 A.D.3d 167, 772 N.Y.S.2d 521 [2004]). The majority's vacatur of the IAS court's confirmation of the Referees' findings, implicitly disaffirming their report and recommendations, is contrary to the applicable, well-settled rule. While CPLR 4403 allows a court to reject a referee's findings or make new findings upon the evidence presented to a referee, this Court merely vacates the confirmation of the Referees' findings. If we are to infer from this result that the entire fact-finding reference was improper, the majority should explain the appropriate action for the IAS court to have taken when faced with defendants' inaction.

Moreover, in regard to the majority's reliance upon *Wein v. Carey*, 41 N.Y.2d 498, 505, 393 N.Y.S.2d 955, 362 N.E.2d 587 [1977] to hold that plaintiffs have not met the "formidable" burden placed on one who attacks the State's budget plan, I merely note that since the State's budget plan failed to include the court-ordered reforms providing for the necessary funds, plaintiffs' right to relief has been well established.

Defendants' bare assertion on appeal that the State's building aid program, as enhanced by recent legislation, will produce compliance with the Court of Appeals' directive, is not only too late, but vague and unsubstantiated, and cannot serve to alter the Referees' findings in this regard. Yet, rather than confirming the finding to at least that extent, the majority directs that in enacting the 2006 budget, "the Governor and the Legislature implement a capital improvement plan that expends $9.179 billion over the next five years or otherwise satisfies the City schools' constitutionally recognized capital needs." Here, too, where all the evidence before the Referees supported their findings, instead of upholding the confirmed report and recommendations in order to provide an enforceable solution, the majority phrases its relief so as to leave open the possibility of more years of disagreements and fruitless negotiations.

We should reject defendants' argument that the only appropriate judicial remedy is a declaratory judgment. A declaratory judgment is meant to settle disputes at the outset, before a "wrong" has occurred (see _Klostermann v. Cuomo,_ 61 N.Y.2d 525, 538–539, 475 N.Y.S.2d 247, 463 N.E.2d 588 [1984]). Here, the "wrong" is an established violation by the State of the constitutional rights of New York City's schoolchildren, and as the IAS court noted, it "has been ongoing for more than a decade." It is long past time to order redress of this longstanding constitutional violation, where those in a position to take action have shown no signs of readiness to do so.

More importantly, however, it is simply misguided to set aside the Referees' well-supported findings and vacate the court's directives in a show of judicial deference to the executive and legislative branches. The necessary deference was shown to the other branches of government when the Court of Appeals gave them over a year to determine what needed to be done and how to do it. Not only did the State Legislature fail to comply with the Court of Appeals' mandate with regard to funding, but it made no efforts to take the other steps required by the Court. Moreover, even defendants' brief acknowledges that the political branches remain "badly divided" concerning the issue of how much money is necessary to provide the opportunity for a sound basic education to New York City schoolchildren.

Commentators have discussed at length the ongoing legislative impasse that pervades New York State's governmental process (see Benjamin, _Reform in New York: The Budget, the Legislature, and the Governance Process,_ 67 Alb. L. Rev. 1021, 1025 [2004]). Indeed, news reports indicate that key legislators believe that the current political stalemate regarding school funding can only be resolved by a direct order from the courts (see _Passing the Buck,_ Journal News (Westchester County, N.Y.), May 2, 2004, at 8B; Rothfeld, _School Funding Solution on Hold,_ Newsday, March 22, 2005, at A24). Under the circumstances, no further deference is appropriate.

The majority expresses its belief that the separation of powers doctrine precludes us from directing the Legislature to make the appropriation necessary to comply with the findings. However, at this late stage of the process, when the Legislature's unwillingness or inability to enact the necessary legislation is well established, to preclude a specific court directive to the Legislature on the grounds of separation of powers is to virtually preclude enforcement of the Court of Appeals' decision in *CFE II*.

I recognize that in the ordinary course of governmental operations, the process of funding and appropriation is strictly in the hands of the Governor and the Legislature; I do not disagree with the majority's view of the vitality and importance of the separation of powers doctrine (*see* <u>N.Y. Const., art. VII, §§ 2</u>, <u>3</u>, <u>4</u>; *see also* <u>*Pataki v. New York State Assembly*, 4 N.Y.3d at 81–86, 791 N.Y.S.2d 458, 824 N.E.2d 898)</u>. Of course, our constitutional scheme does not contemplate the judiciary determining or directing appropriations in the normal course of government.

Nevertheless, these standard procedures must give way once it has been determined that (1) the level of spending by the Governor and the Legislature on public school education is so insufficient that it results in a violation of constitutional dimension, and (2) the coordinate branches of government have shown themselves to be unable to remedy the violation in the absence of a court directive. If, as defendants suggest, the judiciary is not permitted to direct the coordinate branches to exercise their appropriation authority so as to remedy the violation, we are left with a potentially un-resolvable severe constitutional violation.

The recent case of <u>*New York Civil Liberties Union v. State of New York*, 4 N.Y.3d 175, 791 N.Y.S.2d 507, 824 N.E.2d 947 [2005],</u> cited by the majority, does not stand for the proposition that the court may not take action to remedy the uncorrected unconstitutional level of funding. The Court there affirmed the dismissal of a proceeding seeking to compel the Commissioner of Education to designate certain schools as "Schools Under Registration Review" and to take corrective action with respect to those schools; the Court held these tasks to be discretionary in nature and therefore not amenable to article 78 review. The majority here, in asserting that "the act of choosing among different reasonable funding plans is no less a matter of discretion, and therefore one that does not belong in the courts," fails to take into account that a constitutional violation has already been established, and legislative remediation directed, and that the Legislature had a full opportunity to "choose among reasonable funding plans," but failed to do so.

To the extent the majority seeks to imply that once several reasonable funding plans have been presented, only the Legislature may decide which plan to adopt, this would have been true if the Legislature had actually made such a decision. For instance, had the Legislature enacted a funding increase of $4.7 billion, based upon a reasonable analysis and assessment of the facts and circumstances, it would have been inappropriate for the court to conduct its own assessment of the evidence and come to a different factual conclusion, unless it first determined that the assessment adopted by the Legislature was irrational or unreasonable. But, the Legislature's failure to act created the need for the Court to step into the breach and conduct the analysis and make the findings the Legislature should have made.

At each step of the way in this litigation, the Court of Appeals has considered the concerns expressed by dissenting justices who protested that the majority rulings would result in a violation of the separation of powers doctrine (*see CFE I*, 86 N.Y.2d at 341, 631 N.Y.S.2d 565, 655 N.E.2d 661 [Simons, J., dissenting]; *CFE II*, 100 N.Y.2d at 958, 769 N.Y.S.2d 106, 801 N.E.2d 326 [Read, J., dissenting]).

In reasoning that the cause of action should be dismissed at the outset, Judge Simons emphasized that "[t]he courts have the power to see that the legislative and executive branches of government address their responsibility to provide the structure for a State-wide school system and support it but we have no authority, except in the most egregious circumstances, to tell them that they have not done enough" (86 N.Y.2d at 342, 631 N.Y.S.2d 565, 655 N.E.2d 661). He went on to point out that directing increased State aid requires either cutting other programs' aid, reallocating funds at the expense of other school districts, forcing an increase in local taxes, and "encroaching on the Legislature's power to order State priorities and allocate the State's limited resources" (*id.* at 343, 631 N.Y.S.2d 565, 655 N.E.2d 661). The majority declined to follow this reasoning.

Then, following the determination at trial that the constitutional mandate had been violated, when the Court of Appeals upheld the trial court's findings and directed the State to take action, Judge Read protested in her dissenting opinion that "[i]t is up to the Legislature, as the entity charged with primary responsibility under the Education Article for maintaining the State's system of public education, and the Executive, who shares responsibility with the Legislature, to implement a remedy" (100 N.Y.2d at 958, 769 N.Y.S.2d 106, 801 N.E.2d 326). Nevertheless, the majority of the Court of Appeals mandated that the State provide its public school students with the opportunity to obtain a sound basic education, and upheld the determination that the State's appropriations have been insufficient to provide such an education to New York City schoolchildren.

Despite the misgivings of these dissenting judges, the determinations already made by a majority of the Court of Appeals necessarily assume that it is the obligation of the courts, under such circumstances, not only to detect the existence of constitutionally inadequate school funding, but to direct its remediation. While the Court gave the coordinate branches of government the opportunity to determine for themselves both the extent of the violation and the appropriate remedy, their failure to effectively take action requires the court to exercise its equitable power to ensure that the necessary action is taken.

Notwithstanding the importance of the separation of powers doctrine, when a coordinate branch of government, given the opportunity to remedy a constitutional violation, has shown itself unable and unwilling to take the necessary action to do so, there is ultimately no other option than for the court to ensure that the necessary steps are taken. It is too late for this Court to limit our determination to simply espousing our view as to the range of amounts that would be constitutionally adequate, and directing that an allocation in such a range be "considered" by the Legislature, without actually directing any definitive action.

It is true, as the majority points out, that in initially reinstating the complaint the Court of Appeals observed that—at that point—"any discussion of funding…is premature" (CFE I, 86 N.Y.2d at 316 n. 4, 631 N.Y.S.2d 565, 655 N.E.2d 661), and that in reinstating the trial court's findings of a constitutional violation after trial, the Court limited its remedy to giving the executive branch time to decide upon and enact remedial measures (CFE II, 100 N.Y.2d at 925, 930, 769 N.Y.S.2d 106, 801 N.E.2d 326). However, when the Legislature let the deadline pass without enacting any legislation to remediate the constitutional violation, the circumstances fundamentally changed. Without any reason to believe that the Legislature would comply with the Court of Appeals' order, plaintiffs properly sought the assistance of the IAS court, which properly proceeded to take the steps that the Legislature should have taken. This legislative paralysis has now brought us to the point in this litigation when an order directing the remediation of the constitutional violation has become necessary. In view of the ongoing, persistent legislative inaction, we *must* have the authority to direct the enactment of legislation, rather than merely direct that the Legislature consider taking action; otherwise, there could be no enforceable remedy for a legislative failure to correct its constitutionally deficient expenditure.

Defendants cite to other school funding cases in which, they contend, the courts have abided by the separation of powers doctrine to decline to direct specific spending. However, the cases they cite do *not* preclude such court directives based upon the separation of powers doctrine. Moreover, review of school funding cases in litigation around the country reflects that many courts have specifically considered and rejected this separation of powers argument, where—as here—the coordinate branches of government have demonstrated an unwillingness or inability to make the necessary changes in their education funding to remedy the constitutional violation.

In *Hancock v. Commissioner of Educ.*, 443 Mass. 428, 430, 822 N.E.2d 1134, 1136–1137 [2005], one of the cases cited by defendants, the Massachusetts court merely declined to adopt the conclusion of the assigned trial-level judge who held that the Commonwealth was still not meeting its constitutional obligations.

Notably, the concurring judge emphasized the trial court's findings that in the 12 years since the Court had initially declared that Massachusetts was failing to fulfill its educational obligation (see *McDuffy v. Secretary of Exec. Office of Educ.*, 415 Mass. 545, 617, 615 N.E.2d 516, 554 [1993]), the state had "radically restructured the funding of public education across the Commonwealth based on uniform criteria of need, and dramatically*202 increased the Commonwealth's mandatory financial assistance to public schools" and "spending gaps between districts based on property wealth have been reduced or even reversed" (443 Mass. at 432–433, 822 N.E.2d at 1138 [Marshall, C.J., concurring]).

Accordingly, it was not the separation of powers, but the successful remedial action taken by the coordinate branches of government that obviated the need for the court in *Hancock* to take directive action. And, in *Idaho Schools for Equal Educ. Opportunity v. State*, 140 Idaho 586, 97 P.3d 453 [2004] and *Butt v. State*, 4 Cal.4th 668, 842 P.2d 1240 [1992], both of which were cited by defendants, the courts actually indicated their approval of the implementation of remedial measures by courts "when the Legislature...failed to take appropriate action" *(Idaho Schools*, 140 Idaho at 589, 97 P.3d at 456).

As to *Hoke County Bd. of Educ. v. State*, 358 N.C. 605, 599 S.E.2d 365 [2004], relied upon by defendants for the court's remark upon the judicial branch's "limitations in providing specific remedies for violations committed by other government branches in service to a subject matter, such as public education, that is within their primary domain" (358 N.C. at 645, 599 S.E.2d at 395), the only remedial directive reversed by the court there was the order requiring the expansion of pre-kindergarten educational programs so that they would reach and serve all qualifying "at-risk" students (358 N.C. at 609, 599 S.E.2d at 373). That directive was held to "infringe on the constitutional duties and expectations of the legislative and executive branches of government."

The decision affirmed, however, the directive that the state "assume the responsibility for, and correct, those educational methods and practices that contribute to the failure to provide students with a constitutionally-conforming education". There is no reason to believe that if faced with total inaction following this directive, the North Carolina court would assume itself to be powerless to make any further direction. In fact, it is particularly noteworthy that the defendants there began acting to remedy the constitutional violation immediately after the trial court's decision, and continued to allocate increasing amounts to their high-need districts. There is no indication in that decision that the Legislature was viewed as having failed to take the contemplated actions.

In contrast, where courts in other states have observed insufficient progress in the remediation of educational funding failures, they have uniformly made the necessary directives active remediation by judiciary appropriate "(a)s long as such power is exercised only after legislative noncompliance.

Defendants' argument that the State's actions over the past decade show an increasing commitment to the State's system of public education and to New York City's schools completely fails to take into account the strong showing that in many respects it is a lack of funding, in amounts reaching billions of dollars, that is largely the cause of the lost opportunity for millions of schoolchildren. Putting in place comprehensive standards, an accountability system, an overhaul of the teacher certification process, and management reforms, as important as they are, cannot reduce class sizes and provide the needed resources.

The Referees appointed by the IAS court devoted their exceptional abilities to arrive at a carefully reasoned conclusion as to exactly what must be done to correctly remedy the established constitutional violation. The IAS court then carefully and fully considered the same evidence, and the Referees' reasoning, and properly confirmed their findings. It then took the absolutely necessary step of directing defendants to implement such a plan, including periodic reviews and studies and the development of a comprehensive plan for reforms and initiatives. Nothing in the court's measured directives overstepped the bounds of accomplishing only that which was necessary. Both the confirmed findings, and the affirmative directives, should be upheld.

Chapter 2
Substantive Law and Analytical Writing

Chapter Learning Objectives:

Upon completing this chapter and the related assignments students will be able to:

- Master the legal interoffice memorandum by :

    Learning the basic large scale organization and structure of a memorandum.

    Practicing how to effectively communicate ideas and analysis of statutes and cases as they relate to a specific client problem or fact pattern.

- Understand the elements of cases and statutes in order to:

    Be able to brief a case.

    Be able to synthesize case law to draw a predictive conclusion about a legal issue.

    Become familiar with statutes and the elements thereof.

    Enhance legal analysis and case synthesis abilities.

- Build upon the basic formulas for legal thought and expression and transition from skills relative to objective, predictive writing to the basic skills of persuasive writing.

Overview of Search and Seizure Substantive Law

The Fourth Amendment to the United States Constitution forbids "unreasonable searches and seizures." This overview does not cover the entire body of law devoted to this constitutional principle. This overview outlines the general principles of analyzing search and seizure claims.

When an unreasonable search or seizure takes place, an attorney will write, file and argue a motion to suppress the evidence obtained. A motion to suppress physical evidence can be case dispositive. A motion to suppress evidence, with a corresponding memorandum of law, argues every possible ground for suppression. Such a motion will allege relevant facts (and cite relevant law) which justify the suppression of the seized evidence.

If, when the prosecution answers your motion, its version of the facts differs from those you have set forth, the court will hold a suppression hearing. In addition to alleging facts of an illegal search or seizure, you must also allege facts which indicate that your client has _standing_ to contest the violation. Standing is defined as sufficient interest in the area searched or item seized to challenge the police action.

One goal of the suppression argument will be to get the relief a defense attorney is requesting without giving up too much information about his overall strategy, in case that matter goes to trial. While he must allege all possible legal grounds for suppression, he will allege just enough facts to win the argument.

Why Move to Suppress?

A defense attorney always has the goal of winning a suppression motion and gaining a significant, and sometimes case-dispositive, victory for his client. At a suppression hearing the attorney will also be able to learn a great deal about the prosecution's case, see and hear the witnesses who will testify against his client at trial, and lock those witnesses into testimony that they will have to repeat at trial. The entire suppression hearing is recorded, word for word, by a court stenographer. So if a witness tries to change his testimony at trial, he will be found out.

General Principles of Search and Seizure

The Fourth Amendment's limitations on unreasonable searches and seizures governs state prosecutions by incorporation into the Due Process Clause of the Fourteenth Amendment, Mapp v Ohio, 367 US 643; 81 SCt 1684; 6 LEd2d 1081 (1961).

Searches which were "conducted outside the judicial process, without prior approval by a judge or magistrate, are per se unreasonable under the Fourth Amendment. There are some exceptions, however." Katz v United States, 389 US 347, 357; 88 SCt 507; 19 LEd2d 576 (1967). Those exceptions are:

1. When a search takes place as a result of valid consent of an authorized person; or incident to a valid arrest; or under exigent circumstances; or when certain motor vehicle stops are made; or when objects are in plain view; or

2. Where the intrusion was minimal, or where, as a practical matter, the police could not have obtained a warrant. Terry v Ohio, 392 US 1, 20; 88 SCt 1868; 20 LEd2d 889 (1968).

Your client must have standing, or a sufficient interest in the area searched or item seized, to challenge the police action.

And there is also a procedural question of whether, when a search or seizure <u>was</u> unconstitutional, the prosecution may nevertheless use the evidence at trial because it is not viewed as "tainted" by the unlawful search or seizure. If the evidence would have been ultimately or inevitably discovered by lawful means, it is not subject to the exclusionary rule. <u>Nix</u> v <u>Williams</u>, <u>467 US 431</u>; 104 SCt 2501; 81 LEd2d 377 (1984). Once the defendant has alleged an illegal search or seizure, it is the prosecution's burden to establish the legality of the police action.

<u>State Constitutional Protections and Statutory Provisions</u>

It is very important when writing a memo of law to cite both the state and federal constitutional grounds for your motion to suppress tangible evidence. All of the cases I have cited above are federal cases. While the state Constitution cannot provide your client with less constitutional protections, there may be areas where it provides your client with greater protections.

<u>How to Analyze Search and Seizure Issues</u>

When you consider the possibilities for arguments to suppress physical evidence, it is often helpful to work through a check-list of possible avenues for relief and the bases for them. This checklist should not be considered exhaustive, but rather a beginning for you to organize your Fourth Amendment claims.

If your client was stopped, arrested or taken into custody by the police—consider what took place in slow chronological order. View the arrest as a film in freeze-frame as each action takes place. Break down the police action as much as possible in this manner. If police intrusion escalated during an encounter consider whether the police have an articulable basis for each escalation. Your suppression challenge to what the police did may be multifaceted.

If what the police did was a stop, was it warranted? Did the police have the authority to make such a stop? What facts will the police use to justify the stop? You must try to argue those same facts as equally consistent with innocence. This is your opportunity to describe the facts in your client's favor.

For example, if your client (Larry) was found by the police with a note in his pocket that read, "Dear Larry: I will come by your house later today to deliver the drugs you purchased." You would argue that the "drugs" could be heart worm medicine for Larry's dog and thus not indicative of any wrongdoing. If after the stop the police also frisked your client, where they entitled to do so under the circumstances?

Then, if an arrest was made, did the police have probable cause to make the arrest? An arrest is a seizure of the person requiring probable cause. Under the criminal law probable cause is the standard by which an officer has grounds to make an arrest, to conduct a personal or property search, or to obtain a warrant for arrest. This term comes from the Fourth Amendment of the United States Constitution: "The right of the people to be secure in their persons, houses, papers, and effects, against unreasonable searches and seizures, shall not be violated, and no Warrants shall issue, but *upon probable cause*, supported by Oath or affirmation, and particularly describing the place to be searched, and the persons or things to be seized".

The best-known definition of probable cause is "a reasonable belief that a person has committed a crime". Another common definition is "a reasonable amount of suspicion, supported by circumstances sufficiently strong to justify a prudent and cautious person's belief that certain facts are probably true". With regard to search warrants, the *Oxford Companion to American Law* defines probable cause as "information sufficient to warrant a prudent person's belief that the wanted individual had committed a crime (for an arrest warrant) or that evidence of a crime or contraband would be found in a search (for a search warrant)". "Probable cause" is a stronger standard of evidence than a reasonable suspicion, but weaker than what is required to secure a criminal conviction.

<u>Some additional related cases to consider are:</u>

<u>Terry v. Ohio</u>, 392 U.S. 1 (1968) held that a "stop and frisk" may be made upon *reasonable suspicion* when an officer believes a crime has been committed, is, or soon will be committed with a concealed weapon.

<u>Illinois v. Gates</u> 462 U.S. 213 (1983) lowered the threshold of probable cause by holding that a "substantial chance" or "fair probability" of criminal activity could establish probable cause.

<u>New Jersey v. T. L. O.</u>, 468 U.S. 1214 (1985) set a special precedent for searches of students at school. The Court ruled that school officials act as state officers when conducting searches, and do not require probable cause to search students' belongings, only <u>reasonable suspicion</u>.

In <u>O'Connor v. Ortega</u>, 480 U.S. 709 (1987), the Court relied on *T.L.O.* to extend the reasonable suspicion standard to administrative searches of public employees' belongings or workplaces when conducted by supervisors seeking evidence of violations of workplace rules rather than criminal offenses.

<u>Georgia v. Randolph</u>, 547 U.S. 103 (2006) the Supreme Court held that when officers are presented with a situation where two parties, each having authority to grant consent to search premises they share, but one objects over the other's consent, the officers must adhere to the wishes of the non-consenting party.

If the police did not consider your client under "formal" arrest until another point during the encounter is not dispositive of the legal question of whether the police seized your client in such a way that they needed probable cause to do so. The test to apply is whether a reasonable person would not feel free to leave the police encounter as it took place. If not, it was an arrest. Was your client searched after he was arrested?

Did the police search any sealed containers (purses, suitcase, briefcases, etc.) that were in your client's possession?

If the police search your clients house or apartment (or any place where your client has standing to expect privacy) did they have a valid search warrant? Was the warrant, even if valid, executed properly? Did the police limit their search to that specified in the warrant or did they go beyond the scope of the warrant? If someone other than your client consented to a search, did that person have the authority to do so? For example, if your client went out of his house to buy some food, did his babysitter have authority to allow the police to search the house while he was gone? (No.) The police are not allowed to coerce (force) consent. They cannot threaten to arrest a person for refusing to consent to a search.

It is not necessarily true that a member of the same household as your client has the authority to consent to a search of the entire household. Parents cannot give a valid consent to a search of their children's rooms. Co-tenants cannot give lawful consent to a search a roommate's room.

Were items seized by the police in "plain view"? The plain view doctrine provides that objects perceptible by an officer who is rightfully in a position to observe them can be seized without a Search Warrant and are admissible as evidence. The U.S. Supreme Court developed the plain view doctrine over time. In Coolidge v. New Hampshire, 403 U.S. 443(1971), the Court ruled that the seizure of two automobiles in plain view during the arrest of the defendant, along with later findings of gunpowder, did not violate the defendant's Fourth Amendment rights.

In Arizona v. Hicks, 480 U.S. 321(1987), the Court held that no seizure occurred when a police officer who was called to the scene of a shooting recorded the serial numbers of stereo equipment he observed in plain view, which he believed had been stolen. The Court held that the officer's actions in moving the equipment to find the serial numbers constituted a search; the officer had a "reasonable suspicion" that the equipment had been stolen, but it was not supported by Probable Cause.

If the police stopped your client's car, was it a valid stop for a real traffic infraction or was that used as a pretext? For example, your client was minding the speed limit. All of his car lights were properly working. He had his seat belt on. But hc is pulled over by the police and told, "You were drifting, sir, and I am just checking to see if you're okay". Your client may have been the victim of a tactic known as a pretext stop. If the police ordered your client to get out of his car, what took place to escalate the initial stop?

In 1997 the Supreme Court of the United States ruled that police officers may order passengers out of the cars they stop for routine traffic violations, even in the absence of any reason to suspect that the passenger has committed a crime or presents a threat to the officer's safety.

The 7-to-2 decision, adopting a position long advocated by police organizations, was an extension of a 1977 Supreme Court decision permitting police officers to order the driver out of the car in a routine traffic stop.

Chief Justice Rehnquist reasoned for the majority of the bench, "On the public interest side of the balance, the same weighty interest in officer safety is present regardless of whether the occupant of the stopped car is a driver or passenger." The two dissenting Justices, Stevens and Kennedy, objected that the decision marked a substantial contraction of the Fourth Amendment right to be free of unreasonable searches and seizures. "The Court takes the unprecedented step of authorizing seizures that are unsupported by any individualized suspicion whatsoever," Justice Stevens said. Justice Kennedy said the result would be to place "tens of millions of passengers at risk of arbitrary control by the police."

Did the police search your client's car upon an arrest? Was the arrest valid? Was the search of the car properly limited in scope? The scope (extent) of the search is limited by the object of the search. Did the police have probable cause to search the car? Probable cause to believe that an automobile contains contraband or evidence or is transporting individuals who have committed, are committing or are about to commit a crime permits the police to search every part of the vehicle and any items in it which may conceal the object of the search.

The motor vehicle exception was first established by the United States Supreme Court in 1925, in <u>Carroll v. United States</u>. The motor vehicle exception allows a police officer to search a vehicle without warrant if he has probable cause to believe that evidence is located in the vehicle. This exception is based on the idea of a lower expectation of privacy in motor vehicles.

The scope of a car search is limited to only the area the officer has probable cause to search. This area can be the entire car including the trunk. The motor vehicle exception also allows officers to search any containers found inside the vehicle that could contain the evidence being searched for. The objects searched do not need to belong to the owner of the vehicle. In <u>Wyoming v. Houghton</u>, the U.S. Supreme Court ruled that the ownership of objects searched in the vehicle is irrelevant to the legitimacy of the search. In addition, some state constitutions require officers to show there was <u>not</u> enough time to obtain a warrant. With the exception of states with this requirement, an officer is not required to obtain a warrant even if it is possible to get one.

The motor vehicle exception does not only apply to automobiles. The U.S. Supreme Court in <u>California v. Carney</u> found the motor vehicle exception can apply to a motor home. The court did make a distinction between readily mobile motor homes and parked mobile homes. In <u>United States v. Johns</u>, the motor vehicle exception was applied to trucks. In <u>United States v. Forrest</u> it was applied to trailers pulled by trucks. <u>United States v. Forrest</u> applied the exception to boats and in <u>United States v. Hill</u> to house boats. In <u>United States v. Nigro</u> and <u>United States v. Montgomery</u> the motor vehicle exception was found to also include airplanes.

Was your client's car impounded and searched as an "inventory" search? If so, was the search performed according to standard procedures? What are those procedures? The following Supreme Court (7th Circuit, 12/29/2010) decision discusses inventory car search issues and the Inevitable Discovery Rule:

<u>United States of America v. Dewayne Cartwright, No. 10-1879</u>

Police pulled Dewayne Cartwright over for a traffic violation, arrested him when he failed to produce a driver's license and gave a false name, then searched the car incident to his arrest, locating a gun in the back seat.

Charged with possessing a firearm as a felon, *see* 18 U.S.C. § 922(g)(1), Cartwright moved to suppress the firearm, relying on *Arizona v. Gant*, 129 S. Ct. 1710 (2009), a decision that came down subsequent to his arrest and which narrowed the scope of a permissible automobile search incident to arrest. The district court held an evidentiary hearing, then denied the motion, concluding that the police would have inevitably discovered the firearm pursuant to an inventory search of the car.

Cartwright entered a conditional guilty plea, and the district court sentenced him to 84 months in prison. Cartwright now appeals the denial of his motion to suppress, arguing that the district court erred in applying the inevitable discovery doctrine. We affirm.

On August 12, 2008, at about 9:00 p.m., Officer Richard Stratman of the Indianapolis Metropolitan Police Department ("IMPD"), while on routine patrol, noticed a vehicle without an illuminated rear license plate, a violation of Indiana law. *See* Ind. Code § 9-19-6-4(e). Stratman stopped the vehicle, which pulled into a grocery store parking lot, stopping between two rows of parking spaces but not in a designated spot. The car was occupied by the driver, Cartwright; a front seat passenger, Ciera Golliday, who owned the car; and in the back seat, Golliday's two- or three-year-old child.

Stratman asked Cartwright for his driver's license, but Cartwright replied that he did not have one in his possession. Stratman asked the driver for his name, and Cartwright gave a name Stratman could not confirm. Based on Cartwright's nervous demeanor and refusal to identify himself, Stratman removed him from the car, handcuffed him, and placed him under arrest.

In the meantime, Officer James Barleston arrived on the scene and removed Golliday and her child from the car. Subsequent to Cartwright's arrest, Barleston searched the back seat and found a loaded Ruger semi-automatic pistol. After removing and securing the gun, Barleston completed a search of the car, finding nothing other than old clothes.

Pursuant to IMPD policy, Stratman had the car towed, as Cartwright was under arrest and Golliday did not have a driver's license. Also pursuant to IMPD policy, Barleston performed an inventory search of the car prior to its impoundment, finding nothing of value, and filled out a tow slip, listing the reason for the tow as "arrest." However, contrary to IMPD policy, Barleston failed to list all of the car's contents, only the keys. He testified that, although he usually lists the inventory of a vehicle on the tow slip, he did not do so in the present case because he found nothing of importance.

Golliday testified that upon learning the car would be towed she asked the officers to allow her to have someone else move it, but they refused.

At the time of this encounter, our circuit allowed police to search a vehicle incident to the driver's arrest even after having removed and secured the driver. *See, e.g., United States v. Sholola,* 124 F.3d 803, 817-18 (7th Cir. 1997). However, in *Gant,* the Supreme Court narrowed the rule, holding that:

Police may search a vehicle incident to a recent occupant's arrest only if the arrestee is within reaching distance of the passenger compartment at the time of the search or it is reasonable to believe the vehicle contains evidence of the offense of arrest. When these justifications are absent, a search of an arrestee's vehicle will be unreasonable unless police obtain a warrant or show that another exception to the warrant requirement applies.

In response to Cartwright's motion to suppress below, the government acknowledged that *Gant* made a search incident to arrest improper but argued that the police would have inevitably discovered the gun pursuant to the inventory search. The district court agreed and denied the motion.

II. Discussion

    1.   Standard of Review

We apply a dual standard of review to a district court's denial of a suppression motion, reviewing legal conclusions de novo and findings of fact for clear error. *United States v. Jackson*, 598 F.3d 340, 344 (7th Cir.), *cert. denied*, 131 S. Ct. 435 (2010). In the context of an inventory search, we review for clear error a district court's conclusion that the police followed standard impoundment procedures, but our review of the reasonableness of the inventory search and seizure is plenary. *United States v. Cherry*, 436 F.3d 769, 772-73 (7th Cir. 2006).

    1.   Inevitable Discovery

Under the inevitable discovery doctrine, if the government can establish that the evidence at issue, even though unlawfully obtained, would have inevitably been discovered through lawful means, then the deterrence rationale animating the exclusionary rule has so little basis that the evidence should be admitted. *Nix v. Williams*, 467 U.S. 431, 444 (1984). To obtain the benefit of the doctrine, the government must show a chain of events that would have led to a warrant or some other justification independent of the unlawful search. *United States v. Brown*, 64 F.3d 1083, 1085 (7th Cir. 1995).

Inventory searches constitute a well-recognized exception to the warrant requirement and are reasonable under the Fourth Amendment. *See South Dakota v. Opperman*, 428 U.S. 364, 376 (1976). In *Opperman*, the Supreme Court noted that local police departments routinely inventory and secure the contents of impounded automobiles. Doing so protects the police from potential danger, protects the owner's property while it remains in police custody, and protects the police against claims of lost, stolen, or dam aged property. *Id.* at 369.

An inventory search is lawful if (1) the individual whose possession is to be searched has been lawfully arrested, and (2) the search is conducted as part of the routine procedure incident to incarcerating an arrested person and in accordance with established inventory procedures. *United States v. Jackson*, 189 F.3d 502, 508-09 (7th Cir. 1999). "Both the decision to take the car into custody and the concomitant inventory search must meet the strictures of the Fourth Amendment." *United States v. Duguay*, 93 F.3d 346, 351 (7th Cir. 1996). "[T]he decision to impound (the `seizure') is properly analyzed as distinct from the decision to inventory (the `search')." *Id.*

In the present case, the district court found that, pursuant to IMPD policy, the officers towed the vehicle from the scene because Golliday, the passenger/owner, did not have a driver's license and Cartwright was under arrest. The district court further noted that under IMPD policy the police conduct inventory searches prior to impounding a vehicle.

The district court found that the police conducted such a search in the present case and concluded that had they not already found the gun, they would inevitably have done so.

Cartwright argues the district court ignored Golliday's testimony that she could have found someone to move the car, making impoundment unnecessary. He relies primarily on *Duguay*, in which we found unreasonable the decision to impound a car in which the defendant was a passenger because the defendant's girlfriend, the driver, could have moved it.

We said that: "The decision to impound an automobile, unless it is supported by probable cause of criminal activity, is only valid if the arrestee is otherwise unable to provide for the speedy and efficient removal of the car from public thorough-fares or parking lots." *Duguay*, 93 F.3d at 353. This case is nothing like *Duguay*, and we find that the officers acted reasonably in impounding the car here.

As we have noted, the police followed IMPD policy in deciding to tow the car. While that fact is important, it is not dispositive for purposes of the Fourth Amendment. The existence of a police policy, city ordinance, or state law alone does not render a particular search or seizure reasonable or otherwise immune from scrutiny under the Fourth Amendment. *See Sibron v. New York*, 392 U.S. 40, 61 (1968) ("The question in this Court upon review of a state-approved search or seizure is not whether the search (or seizure) was authorized by state law. The question is rather whether the search was reasonable under the Fourth Amendment

Unlike the police department in *Duguay*, which had no standardized procedure, *see id.* at 352, the IMPD has a comprehensive towing and impoundment policy, which the government introduced at the evidentiary hearing below. The policy sets forth the circumstances under which the police may tow a car, establishes the procedures officers must follow in calling for a tow, requires an inventory search whenever an officer takes a vehicle into custody, and specifically forbids inventory searches "motivated by an officer's desire to investigate and seize evidence of a criminal act.

Because Golliday was unlicensed and Cartwright under arrest, the policy permitted impoundment in the present case. *See United States v. Velarde*, 903 F.2d 1163, 1166 (7th Cir. 1990) (upholding police impoundment where neither driver nor passenger had a valid driver's license). The IMPD policy is sufficiently standardized, the district court committed no clear error in finding that the officers followed the policy, and, for the reasons that follow, we find the officers' actions reasonable under the circumstances.

Unlike *Duguay*, where the officers impounded the car despite the presence on the scene of a licensed driver readily able to move it, 93 F.3d at 353, the record in this case shows that the unlicensed Golliday had no means of ensuring the "speedy and efficient" removal of her car from the parking lot.

The Fourth Amendment does not require that the police offer these sorts of alternatives to impoundment. *See Colorado v. Bertine,* 479 U.S. 367, 373-74 (1987) (holding that the police need not give a motorist "an opportunity to make alternative arrangements" that avoid impoundment and inventory); *United States v. Clinton,* 591 F.3d 968, 972 (7th Cir.) ("That Clinton's girlfriend, the owner of the car, could have been called to take possession of the car, is irrelevant."), *cert. denied,* 131 S. Ct. 246 (2010). Moreover, no one could have lawfully driven Golliday's car from the scene, as (the car) did not have the functional license plate lamp required by Indiana law. Ind. Code § 9-19-6-4(e).

Finally, Cartwright argues that Barleston did not conduct the inventory search properly, failing to make a complete list of the property he found in Golliday's car. While Cartwright correctly points out that IMPD policy required Barleston to make such a list, Barleston's failure to do so does not undermine the proposition that the police would inevitably have found the gun through a lawful inventory search.

In the end, the district court found, based on the evidence and the IMPD policy, that an inventory search would have been conducted and that the gun would have been found pursuant to such a search. The evidence supports that conclusion. In any event, we have held that minor deviations from department policy do not render an inventory search unreasonable. *See United States v. Lomeli,* 76 F.3d 146, 148-49 (7th Cir. 1996).

III. Conclusion

For the foregoing reasons, we AFFIRM Cartwright's conviction.

Moving on to another suppression issue here, did the police act to conduct a search because they relied on information received from informants? Were the informants anonymous? Were they a reliable source of information?

The Aguilar-Spinelli Test:

The Aguilar–Spinelli test was set by the U.S. Supreme Court for evaluating the validity of a search warrant based on information provided by a confidential informant or an anonymous tip. The Supreme Court abandoned the Aguilar–Spinelli test in Illinois v. Gates, 462 U.S. 213 (1983), in favor of a rule that evaluates the reliability of the information under the "totality of the ircumstances." However, Alaska, Massachusetts, New York, Tennessee, Vermont, and Washington have retained the Aguilar–Spinelli test, based on their own state constitutions.

The two "prongs" of the test are that, when law enforcement seeks a search warrant, a judge must sign the warrant and:

The judge must be informed of the reasons to support the conclusion that such an informant is reliable and credible.

The judge must be informed of some of the underlying circumstances relied on by the person providing the information.

This information provided to a judge allows him to make an independent and objective evaluation as to whether probable cause exists that a crime has been or will be committed.

In the past, even if the police made an illegal search and seizure, evidence thus obtained could often be used against a defendant in a criminal trial regardless of its illegality.

But in <u>Weeks v. United States</u>, 232 U.S. 383 (1914), the Supreme Court created the "exclusionary rule" which declared that, in most circumstances, evidence obtained through an illegal search and seizure could not be used as admissible evidence in a criminal trial. This decision created the rule only on the federal level. <u>Mapp v. Ohio</u>, 367 U.S. 643 (1961) held that the exclusionary rule was binding on the states as well.

As a result, the defense in criminal trials attempted to prove that a search warrant was invalid, thus making the search illegal and hence the evidence obtained through the search inadmissible in the trial. The problem with that was that there were no hard guidelines defining the legality of a search warrant and it was difficult for a judge to decide upon a warrant's validity.

In order to get a search warrant an officer must appear before a judge (or magistrate) and affirm that he has probable cause to believe that a crime has been (or will be) committed. The officer is required to present his evidence and an affidavit setting forth his evidence. The affidavit must show a substantial basis for determining the existence of probable cause. Thus, the officer must present his evidence, not just conclusions. Sufficient information must be shown to allow the judge to determine probable cause; his action cannot be a mere ratification of the bare conclusions of others.

In <u>Johnson v. United States</u>, 333 U.S. 10 (1948), the Court said:

"The point of the Fourth Amendment, which often is not grasped by zealous officers, is not that it denies law enforcement the support of the usual inferences which reasonable men draw from evidence. Its protection consists in requiring that those inferences be drawn by a neutral and detached magistrate instead of being judged by the officer engaged in the often competitive enterprise of ferreting out crime."

Development of the two-pronged test took place in <u>Aguilar v. Texas</u>, 378 U.S. 108 (1964), when the Court held that:

"The judge must be informed of some of the underlying circumstances relied on by the person providing the information and some of the underlying circumstances from which the affiant concluded that the informant, whose identity was not disclosed, was creditable or his information reliable".

In <u>Spinelli v. United States</u>, 393 U.S. 410 (1969), the Court went further by requiring that a judge must be informed of the "underlying circumstances from which the informant had concluded" that a crime had been committed.

The two-pronged test was abandonment in <u>Illinois v. Gates</u>, 462 U.S. 213 (1983) when the Supreme Court abandoned the two-pronged rule in favor of the totality of the circumstances rule. According to Justice Rehnquist:

"The rigid two-pronged test under Aguilar and Spinelli for determining whether an informant's tip establishes probable cause for issuance of a warrant is abandoned, and the "totality of the circumstances" approach that traditionally has informed probable-cause determinations is substituted in its place.

Even though the Gates decision abandoned the "two-pronged test" it did not expressly overturn the Spinelli decision itself and it did not overrule the Aguilar decision at all. The two-pronged test still survives under some state laws, however. Individual states can provide more rights under their own laws than the Federal Constitution requires. Alaska, Massachusetts, New York, Vermont and Tennessee have rejected the Gates rationale and have retained the two-prong Aguilar–Spinelli test .

<u>Fruit of the Poisonous Tree Doctrine</u>

The Fruit of the Poisonous Tree doctrine prohibits the use of secondary evidence at trial that was obtained directly from primary evidence derived from an illegal Search and Seizure.

The doctrine is an offspring of the *exclusionary rule* which mandates that evidence obtained from an illegal arrest, unreasonable search, or coercive interrogation must be suppressed and excluded from trial. Under this doctrine, evidence is excluded if it was gained through evidence uncovered in an illegal arrest, unreasonable search, or coercive interrogation. Like the exclusionary rule, the fruit of the poisonous tree doctrine was established to deter police from violating rights against unreasonable searches and seizures.

The name *fruit of the poisonous tree* is a metaphor. The <u>poisonous tree</u> is evidence illegally seized by law enforcement. The <u>fruit</u> of this poisonous tree is evidence discovered later as a direct result of knowledge gained from the first illegal seizure. It is important to remember that both the poisonous tree and the fruit are both subject to suppression.

For example, if an officer searches a car stopped for a minor traffic violation, and the traffic violation is the only reason the officer conducts the search (nothing indicates that the driver is impaired by drugs, alcohol, etc.) and there is no evidence of a crime, then it is an unreasonable search under the Fourth Amendment to the U.S. Constitution. If that the officer finds drugs in the car and charges the driver with possession of a controlled substance and the case goes to trial, the drug evidence obtained from this search is excluded from trial under the exclusionary rule, and the criminal charges are dropped for lack of evidence.

But suppose that <u>before</u> the original charges are dismissed, the police ask a judge for a warrant to search the car owner's house. The evidence used as a basis, or probable cause, for the warrant the drugs found in the unlawful car search. The Judge, unaware that the drugs were found as a result of an unlawful search and seizure, approves the warrant for a house search. The officers search the driver's house and discover stolen jewelry. Under the fruit of the poisonous tree doctrine, the jewelry must be excluded from any trial on theft charges because the search of the house was based on evidence obtained in the illegal search of the car.

The term *fruit of the poisonous tree* was first used in <u>Nardone v. United States</u>, 308 U.S. 338 (1939). In Nardone, the defendant appealed his convictions for smuggling and concealing alcohol. In an earlier decision, the Court ruled that an interception of Nardone's telephone conversations by government agents violated the Communications Act of 1934 (47 U.S.C.A. § 605). The issue before the Court was whether the trial court erred in refusing to allow Nardone's lawyer to question the prosecution on whether, and in what way, it had used information obtained in the illegal wire tapping.

In reversing Nardone's convictions, the Court held that once a defendant has established that evidence was illegally seized, the trial court must give opportunity to the accused to prove that a substantial portion of the case against him was a fruit of the poisonous tree. The fruit of the poisonous tree doctrine was first held applicable to Fourth Amendment violations in the landmark case <u>Wong Sun v. United States,</u> 371 U.S. 471 (1963).

The Court in Wong Sun also set forth a test for determining how closely derivative evidence must be related to illegally obtained evidence to warrant exclusion. In Wong Sun, federal narcotics agents arrested Hom Way on suspicion of narcotics activity. Although the agents had been watching Way for six weeks, they did not have a warrant for his arrest. Way was searched, and the agents found heroin in his possession. After the arrest Way stated that he had bought heroin from Blackie Toy, the owner of a laundry.

Even though Way had never been an informant for the police, the agents visited the laundry. The agents remained out of sight while Agent Wong rang the bell. When Toy answered the door, Wong said he was there for laundry and dry cleaning. Toy answered that he did not open until 8:00 A.M. and started to close the door. Wong then identified himself as a federal narcotics agent. Toy slammed the door and began to run down the hallway to his bedroom, where his wife and child were sleeping. Without a warrant, Wong and the other agents broke open the door, followed Toy, and arrested him. A search of the premises uncovered no illegal drugs.

While Toy was in handcuffs, one of the agents told him that Way had said Toy sold narcotics. Toy denied it, but said he knew someone who did sell drugs, am man named "Johnny." Toy told the officers that "Johnny" lived on Eleventh Avenue, and then he described the house. Toy also said that "Johnny" kept an ounce of heroin in his bedroom, and that he and "Johnny" had smoked heroin the night before. The agents located the house on Eleventh Avenue. Without a search or an arrest warrant, they entered the home, went to the bedroom, and found Johnny Yee. After a discussion with the agents, Yee surrendered less than one ounce of heroin.

The same morning, Yee and Toy were taken into custody. Yee stated that he had gotten the heroin about four days earlier from Toy and another person he knew as "Sea Dog." The agents then asked Toy about "Sea Dog," and Toy identified "Sea Dog" as Wong Sun. Some of the agents took Toy to Sun's neighborhood, where Toy pointed out Sun's house. The agents walked past Sun's wife and arrested Sun, who had been sleeping in his bedroom.

A search of the premises turned up no illegal drugs. Toy and Yee were arraigned in federal court and Sun was arraigned the next day. All were released without bail. A few days later, Toy, Yee, and Sun were interrogated separately at the Narcotics Bureau by Agent Wong. Sun and Toy made written statements but refused to sign them.

Sun and Toy were tried jointly on drug charges. Way did not testify at the trial. The government offered Yee as its principal witness, but Yee recanted his statement to Agent Wong. With only four drug items in evidence, Sun and Toy were convicted by the court in a bench trial. The Court of Appeals for the Ninth Circuit affirmed the convictions (*Wong Sun*, 288 F.2d 366 (9th Cir. 1961)). Sun and Toy appealed to the U.S. Supreme Court.

The Supreme Court accepted the case and reversed the convictions. The Court confirmed that the arrests of both Sun and Toy were illegal. The issue was whether the four items in evidence against Sun and Toy were admissible despite the illegality of the arrests. According to the Court, the arrest was illegal because the agents had no evidence supporting it other than the word of Way, an arrestee who had never been an informer for law enforcement. The officers did not even know whether Toy was the person they were looking for. Furthermore, Toy's flight did not give the officers probable cause to arrest Toy: Agent Alton Wong had first posed as a customer, and this made Toy's flight ambiguous and not necessarily the product of a guilty mind. Thus, under the exclusionary rule, the oral statements made by Toy in his bedroom should not have been allowed at trial.

The Court then considered the drug evidence seized from Yee. The Court, in deference to *Nardone*, stated, "We need not hold that all evidence is 'fruit of the poisonous tree.'" Instead, the question in such a situation was "'whether, granting establishment of the primary illegality, the evidence has been come at by exploitation of that illegality or instead by means sufficiently distinguishable to be purged of the primary taint."

According to the Court, the drugs in *Wong Sun* were indeed come at by use of Toy's statements. Toy's statements were the only evidence used to justify entrance to Yee's bedroom. Since the statements by Toy were inadmissible, the drugs in Yee's possession were also inadmissible, as fruit of the poisonous tree. The conviction was overturned.

In determining whether evidence is fruit of a poisonous tree, the trial court judge must examine all the facts surrounding the <u>initial</u> seizure of evidence and the <u>subsequent</u> gathering of evidence. This determination is usually made by the judge in a suppression hearing held before trial. In this hearing, the judge must first determine that an illegal search or seizure occurred and then decide whether the evidence was obtained as a result of the illegal search or seizure.

In conclusion, fruit of an illegal police action may be physical evidence (such as drugs), statements (such as confessions) or identification procedures. But what happens if the fruit would have been discovered <u>*anyway*</u> by lawful means? Inevitable discovery is a doctrine in criminal procedure that allows evidence of a defendant's guilt that would otherwise be considered inadmissible under the exclusionary rule to be admitted into evidence in a trial. The doctrine was first adopted in 1984 by the United States Supreme Court in <u>Nix v. Williams</u>. The Court held that evidence unlawfully obtained is admissible in court if it can be shown that normal police investigation would have led to the discovery of the evidence anyway.

Thinking through these, and other legal issues, about the police action that led to the recovery of the evidence that you are seeking to suppress will help you decide how to write a suppression memo.

<u>Miranda Warnings: Suppression of Confessions</u>

Confessions are not admissible if obtained by coercion. The due process clause of the Fourteenth Amendment to the United States Constitution and Article I bars the use of involuntary confessions against a criminal defendant. (See Jackson v. Denno, 378 U.S.368, 1964). A confession is involuntary if it is not "the product of a rational intellect and a free will." (Mincey v. Arizona, 437 U.S. 385, 1978). The test is whether defendant's will was overborne at the time he confessed.

The question is whether the police used force or psychological tactics which are so coercive that they produce an involuntary statement which is unreliable. The test is <u>objective</u>. Subjective <u>factors</u> will be considered in determining whether a suspect's will was overborne, but only if police coercion is present. Whether a statement is involuntary depends upon the totality of the circumstances surrounding the interrogation.

An involuntary confession is one extracted by any sort of threats or violence, or obtained by any direct or implied promises, however slight, or by the exertion of any improper influence (Hutto v. Ross, 429 U.S.28, 1976). Relevant factors include the police coercion, the length of the interrogation, its location, its continuity, as well as the defendant's maturity, education, physical condition, and mental health. (Withrow v. Williams (1993) 507 U.S. 680, 1993).

A confession obtained when a defendant is in custody is subject to suppression under the Fifth Amendment if the defendant was not adequately advised of his Miranda Rights. In Miranda v. Arizona, 384 U.S. 436, 1966, the Supreme Court held that in order to protect a defendant's constitutional right against self-incrimination guaranteed by the Fifth Amendment, the police must inform a defendant in custody of certain rights. If police fail to do so, the confession obtained will be suppressed.

The Miranda rights are well known. Police must tell a person in custody he or she has the right to remain silent, that anything said will be used against her or him in court, that the person has the right to consult with a lawyer and have a lawyer present during questioning, and that if the person cannot afford a lawyer one will be appointed to represent her or him. If the defendant indicates <u>in any manner</u>, at <u>any time</u> prior to or during questioning, that he wishes to remain silent, the interrogation must cease. Any physical evidence which is the fruit of a Miranda violation must also be suppressed.

The Miranda rights only apply to custodial interrogations. Interrogation is custodial when "a person has been taken into custody or otherwise deprived of his freedom of action in any significant way." (Miranda v. Arizona, 384 U.S. 436, 1966). The test is objective. The subjective views of the police and the suspect are not relevant. The ultimate inquiry is simply whether there is a 'formal arrest or restraint on freedom of movement' of the degree associated with a forma arrest." (California v. Beheler, 463 U.S. 1121, 1983). Where no formal arrest has taken place, the pertinent question is "how a reasonable man in the suspect's position would have understood his situation." (Berkemer v. McCarty, 468 U.S. 420, 1984).

Further, Miranda warnings are only required if there is interrogation (Rhode Island v. Innis, 446 U.S. 291, 1980). Interrogation under Miranda refers not only to express questioning, but also to any words or actions on the part of the police (other than those normally attendant to arrest and custody) that the police should know are reasonably likely to elicit an incriminating response from the suspect. In Innis, interrogation took place when police, with the arrested in the police car, began saying they hoped to find a shotgun, which witnesses had said the suspect was carrying, before kids at a nearby handicapped school found it.

Volunteered statements are admissible, since they are not the product of interrogation. Statements volunteered when not in response to an interrogation are admissible against a defendant, even after an initial assertion of the right to remain silent. There is no interrogation when police provide the opportunity for a suspect to talk with a third party. For example, if police allow a defendant to talk with his sister, and he makes incriminating statements, there is no Miranda violation because defendant's statements were not the produce of interrogation. The common police practice of putting defendants together and taping their conversation is not a Miranda violation.

The Miranda warnings must be <u>understood</u> and do not have to be given in any <u>perfect</u> language. In Miranda v. Arizona, supra, the court stated the warnings had to be given in the absence of a fully effective equivalent. For example, in California v. Prysock, 453 U.S. 355, 1981, the Supreme Court held that if the rights are effectively communicated, the *exact words* used by the police are not important. In Duckworth v. Eagan, 492 U.S. 195, 1989, the defendant was told, "We have no way of giving you a lawyer, but one will be appointed for you, if you wish, if and when you go to court." The Supreme Court held that this did not invalidate the defendant's confession.

Police cannot ask questions until they get a confession, and <u>then</u> give Miranda rights. A second confession given after Miranda advisements and waiver is not admissible when police employ this "question first, advise later," tactic. In Missouri v. Seibert, 542 U.S. 600, 2004, the court condemned the "question first" tactic, an intentional effort to bypass Miranda strictures.

A waiver of Miranda rights must be <u>knowing and intelligent</u>, and the government has a "heavy burden" to establish a valid waiver (Miranda v. Arizona). The waiver may be implied by the defendant's conduct. An express oral or written waiver is not necessary (North Carolina v. Butler, 441 U.S. 369, 1979). The courts must presume that a defendant did not waive his rights; the prosecution's burden is great; but in at least some cases waiver can be clearly inferred from the actions and words of the person interrogated.

In determining whether the prosecution has met its burden of establishing a valid waiver, the court must consider the particular facts and circumstances surrounding that case, including the background, experience, and conduct of the accused. Thus, the court must consider the individual's defendant's ability to understand the warnings and what he or she is giving up. Factors such as age, IQ and language proficiency should be considered.

For example, in determining whether a juvenile's waiver of his Miranda rights is voluntary courts should consider the juvenile's age, experience, education, background, and intelligence, and whether he has the capacity to understand the warnings given him, the nature of his Fifth Amendment rights, and the consequences of waiving those rights.

Finally, what happens if a defendant is questioned <u>after</u> he has invoked his right to remain silent? The general rule is that once a defendant has invoked his right to counsel, he is not subject to further interrogation by the authorities until counsel has been made available to him, unless the accused himself initiates further communication, exchanges, or conversations with the police (Edwards v. Arizona, 451 U.S. 477, 1981).

The Purpose of an Interoffice Memo of Law

If you work as a paralegal or law clerk you will spend some of your time researching and writing objective memoranda, or interoffice memos. Typically, an attorney asks you to provide an analysis of the law as it applies to the facts of a client's case. The purpose is to inform—not persuade. That is because an interoffice memo of law stays <u>in the office</u> (inter office). Anything negative about the client's case is not seen by the court or by opposing counsel. You should consider which conclusion favors your client, also keep in mind that you will represent the client most effectively by being objective and realistic.

The attorney will use the information contained in the memo to advise the client and may use it to prepare a document that will ultimately be filed in court, such as a memorandum in support of a motion to suppress evidence.

A dispassionate discussion of the issues and the applicable law is the <u>central purpose</u> of the memorandum. Use the analysis section to predict the answers that a court would give if it were faced with your facts and under the pertinent law.

Basic Interoffice Memorandum Outline

A simple interoffice memorandum of law is a relatively short legal document (between 5 and 20 pages) in which no more than two or three client issues of moderate complexity are researched, analyzed and discussed. For your memo of law, use the following format:

- Heading
- Statement of Assignment
- Issue(s) (aka Questions Presented)
- Brief Answer(s)
- Facts
- Analysis (aka Discussion)
- Conclusion
- Recommendations

The *Heading* contains basic information about the writer and the memo. It is centered at the top of the page stating that it is, for example, an interoffice memorandum of law. The heading must include the following:

- Supervising Attorney's name and your name (the memo writer)
- Date
- Name of Case or Client
- Office File Number
- Court Docket Number (if applicable)
- Subject Matter

Here is a sample Heading:

To:	John Smith, Esq.—Senior Partner
From:	Mary Smith, Esq.—Associate Attorney
Date:	February 15, 2011
Case:	People v. Barbara Anderson
File #:	123-456
Docket #:	C-1234567
Re:	Petty Larceny Charges

The *Statement of Assignment* states what you have been asked to do / the purpose of the memo. For example: I was asked to research the criminal case against our client Barbara Anderson to determine if we should accept a plea bargain or proceed to trial.

The *Issues* are the questions that must be analyzed and answered. The issues should be expressed as complete statements. They should take into account your client's objectives and their legal issues.

The *brief answers* answer the issues above concisely. The *brief answers* may also be used to begin the analysis section (see below).

The *Facts* will include a concise statement of your client's entire case. This section should be concise, leaving out any irrelevant facts. This section of a memo must be very accurate and well organized.

The *Analysis* section of the memo <u>begins</u> with a conclusion / recap which provides an answer to each issue raised. This is called the *Brief Answer*. The full analysis section follows in which you present your full analysis and arguments. You explain which side of the litigation you believe will prevail—and why. You also cite relevant case law and statutory law, and set out potential counterarguments.

In the *Recommendations* section of the memo you explain what the next steps in the litigation and /or discovery process should be and why.

WRITING AN INTEROFFICE MEMORANDUM OF LAW

1. Heading

2. Issue(s) (or Question Presented): states the question(s) that the memorandum must resolve. The Issue also itemizes the few facts that you predict to be crucial to the answer. The reader should understand the question without having to refer to the facts.

3. Brief Answer(s): the writer's prediction, summarizes concisely *why* the prediction is likely to happen. It refers to determinative facts and rules.

4. Facts: set out the facts on which the prediction is based.

5. Analysis: is the longest and most complex part of memo. It proves the conclusion set out in brief answer. A highly detailed or complicated memo that analyzes several issues should be broken down into subheadings.

6. Conclusion and Recommendations: Explain what the next steps in the litigation and /or discovery process should be and why.

Sample Memo Outline:

INTEROFFICE MEMORANDUM

TO: Senior Partner or Professor

FROM: You

DATE: Submission Date

RE: Case Name and / or Issues Label

File #   123-4567

Docket #   C—896785

ISSUES(S)

Phrased as a question and ending with a question mark, state the specific issue or issues you will address. Use short single sentences that include relevant facts and applicable law. Start the question with the word "Does". For example,

"Does the underlying felony have to be proven before a defendant can be found guilty of felony murder?"

BRIEF ANSWER(S)

You asked a question above. Answer it here. Your Brief Answer follows the same formula as your Question Presented. The Brief Answer should include a brief *answer* (yes or no) plus a statement of your reasons beginning with the word "Because." For example,

"Yes. Because a conviction for felony murder is predicated upon a corresponding conviction for an underlying felony, a conviction for felony murder must be dismissed where the underlying felony count was dismissed".

The brief answer follows the issues presented and a statement of facts. The brief answer is best written *after* you've written the full body of the memorandum because you will have a better idea of the issues once you have completely analyzed the facts, issues and law.

FACTS

Give all relevant facts in chronological order. A relevant fact is a fact upon which the outcome will depend. It is a fact that will affect the outcome in one way or another. Include all relevant times, dates, and places. As you write an interoffice memo you must remain objective—so omit legal argument. Instead, use very neutral language. Include both favorable and unfavorable facts.

Set out all of the important facts in your case. If there is a dispute over the facts, set out both versions. Be as brief as possible and set the facts out chronologically or by another logical method. One study on judges' opinions of memo briefs listed <u>inadequate statement of facts</u> as the major problem with legal memoranda.

ANALYSIS

This is the most challenging part of a memo. In this section you must explain the law and apply it to the facts. Your must distil the cases and extract a common rule of law. A common mistake is to just list case law without applying it directly to the facts of your case. To avoid this mistake, begin your thesis paragraph with a sentence that anticipates your conclusion. Tell the reader where you are headed with your analysis.

Then, discuss one point at a time. State the legal rule(s) that apply. Use proper citation. Next, explain what the law or legal rule means. Next, **A**nalyze (explain) how the relevant facts fit (or do not fit) the legal standard.

Use a style or format that works best for your particular argument. But virtually every aspect of every legal argument must contain a:

1) Statement of Applicable Law;

2) Analysis of the law and how it applies to your relevant facts; and

3) Possible counterarguments (contrary law) and a conclusion for each issue.

Your statement of applicable law should include applicable statutory provisions. If the statutes are long, you may cite and paraphrase them. Your statement of applicable law should also include relevant, primary law precedents that govern your set of facts (are on point with your set of facts). You do not need to include a history of the case law you select to use. Just use the most recent and definitive cases.

Know your audience and use the method of legal analysis that your professor or your employer prefers. Be patient; learning how to synthesize statutes, cases and secondary sources and presenting them in a clear, concise, and logical manner takes time and much practice.

Provide a fuller explanation of your brief answer at the beginning of the analysis. If your conclusion is negative, or will disappoint your client, you may lead up to it gradually and save the answer until a later point. It may also help to explain the policy behind the law, which is having the negative effect on your client.

CONCLUSION AND RECOMMENDATIONS

Conclude and recommend the best solution for the problems that your client is facing.

Additional Analysis Section Suggestions

Always discuss contrary authority—do not ignore it. Are there cases that go against your position? Subsequent *counterargument* paragraphs could open with: "But, in Alfred v. Stern, the court held that a father did not have a valid cause of action for negligent infliction of emotional distress." Then tell the reader why the court won't follow or give much weight to this contrary authority (e.g., the facts are different).

General Style Issues:

Verb Tense: You should state facts and court decisions in the past tense and legal rules in the present tense.

Choice of Wording: Express your conclusions based on logic and avoid phrases like:

"I believe…" "I feel…" "I suppose…"

If there are some missing facts, or there is something you do not know, say so. Say that you are still investigating it and add it to the recommendations section of the memo. State honestly if you speculate based on a given set of assumptions, or that you need to further investigate facts before you can form a certain opinion.

Avoid Legalese: Legalisms such as Latin phrases or abbreviations are commonly used in legal writing. But they can sound pretentious and are unnecessary and cause readability to suffer. Like frequent exclamation marks, legalisms serve as crutches when plain English would suffice.

Legalisms which do not amplify a thought have no place in modern memo writing. Some legalisms, such as case citations, are unavoidable. In legal memorandums, do not allow case cites to interfere with your analysis. Avoid long case law introductory phrases in your sentences.

It is better to let a citation stand alone at the end of a sentence or paragraph. Avoid string citations and cite only the leading case in the text of your memo. If you need to cite three or four related cases, put the citations in a footnote. Or use endnotes at the back of your memo. No one reads a long string of citations. The eye just skips over text. Finally, get the citation right.

Footnotes: Excessive footnote use is a common mistake among legal writers. Anything which is essential to understanding the text of the memo should be in the text itself, not in footnotes.

Quotations: Legal writers are prone to using too many quotations. Avoid quotes unless the way the writer expressed a thought is a gem you cannot equal. When referring to case law, summarize or paraphrase when possible. If you must quote at least be precise in deciding what must be used and what can be left out.

Memo of Law in Support of a Motion:

A memo written to support a motion is different from an inner office memo of law in that it does not discuss the pros and cons of a client's case, but rather it strongly advocate's on behalf of the client's interests—only. The negative or weak aspects of your client's case are the responsibility of opposing counsel to argue. A <u>motion</u> brings contested issues before a court for a decision. A motion is a formal request to a judge to make a decision about the case. Motions may be made at any point in litigation. The party requesting the motion is called the movant, or the moving party. The party opposing the motion is the non-movant or nonmoving party.

Motions may be made in the form of an oral request in court, and are granted or denied orally. Most motions are decided after oral argument preceded by the filing and service of legal papers. There, the movant is required to serve advance written notice along with a written legal argument (memo of law) justifying the motion.

The legal argument is in the form of a memo of points (issues) and authorities (case law and statutes) supported by affidavits or declarations. The non-movant may file and serve opposition papers. Most jurisdictions allow extra time for the movant to file reply papers rebutting the points made in the opposition papers. The court serves all parties with its decision or may serve only the winner and order the winner to serve everyone else in the case.

Here are some sample motions.

Motion to Dismiss:

A "motion to dismiss" asks the court to decide that a claim, even if true as stated, is not one for which the law offers a legal remedy. If granted, the claim is dismissed without any evidence being presented by the other side.

Motion for Summary Judgment:

A "motion for summary judgment" asks the court to decide that the available evidence, even if taken in the light most favorable to the non-moving party, supports a ruling in favor of the moving party. This motion is usually only made when sufficient time for discovering all evidence has expired. For summary judgment to be granted in most jurisdictions, a two-part standard must be satisfied: (i) no genuine issue of material fact can be in dispute between the parties, and (ii) the moving party must be entitled to judgment as a matter of law.

Motion In Limine:

A "motion in limine" asks the court to decide that certain evidence may or may not be presented to the jury at the trial. A motion in limine generally addresses issues which would be prejudicial for the jury to hear in open court, even if the other side makes a timely objection which is sustained, and the judge instructs the jury to disregard the evidence.

There are 3 types of Motions in Limine 1. Inclusionary—asks the court to have something included in the trial. 2. Exclusionary—asks the court to have something excluded in the trial. 3. Preclusionary—asks the court to have something precluded in the trial.

Motion for a Directed Verdict:

A "motion for a directed verdict" asks the court to rule that the plaintiff or prosecutor has not proven the case, and there is no need for the defense to attempt to present evidence. This motion is made after the plaintiff has rested its case, and prior to the defense presenting any evidence. If granted, the court would dismiss the case.

Motion for New Trial:

A motion for new trial asks to overturn or set aside a court's decision or jury verdict. It is brought by a party who is dissatisfied with the result of a case. This motion must be based on some vital error in the court's handling of the trial, such as the admission or exclusion of key evidence, or an incorrect instruction to the jury.

Motion to Set Aside Judgment:

Asks the court to nullify a judgment and/or verdict. Motions may be made at any time after entry of judgment, and in some circumstances years after the case has been decided by the courts.

Motion to Compel:

Asks the court to order the opposing party (or a third party) to take some action. This sort of motion most commonly deals with discovery disputes, when a party who has requested discovery to either the opposing party or a third party believes that the discovery responses are insufficient.

SAMPLE MEMO OF LAW IN SUPPORT OF MOTION TO SUPPRESS

Note: Once again, take careful notice that the format for an out-of-office memorandum of law is different from that of an inner (or inter) office memorandum of law. When you write a memo of law assignment you must use the inner office memo of law format.

Law Office of Robert Jones, P.C.
25 Bamberger Lane
Williamsville, New York 14202
(716) 234-5678

Attorney for John Smith

IN THE SUPREME COURT OF THE STATE OF NEW YORK FOR ERIE COUNTY

STATE OF NEW YORK

v

JOHN SMITH, Defendant

CASE No. 12345

MEMORANDUM OF LAW IN SUPPORT OF

MOTION TO SUPPRESS EVIDENCE

SUMMARY OF ARGUMENT

Trooper X lawfully stopped Mr. Smith in his car for speeding. During the traffic infraction stop, Trooper X obtained probable cause of another crime committed by Smith—possession of marijuana. Trooper X completed his traffic stop investigation, including issuing a citation for the marijuana infraction, when

he returned to Smith's car. Rather than give Smith his driver's license and citations, he unlawfully extended the stop by asking about possible criminal conduct not supported by reasonable suspicion. Trooper X request to search Smith's car was conditional, he said, "let me search your vehicle, then I will give you the citations and you can leave."

Smith said "sure" but it was submission to a show of authority and not voluntary consent. Trooper X also obtained consent by using the unlawfully extended stop. Smith and his car were unlawfully seized when Trooper X told him to exit the car Trooper X searched the car. The seizures of Smith and his car were not supported by probable cause, warrant or voluntary consent. The Trooper's search of Smith's car was without probable cause, warrant or voluntary consent. During the search of the car, Trooper X took and searched Smith's briefcase without asking for consent, without probable cause, or warrant. The seizure and search of the briefcase exceeded the scope of his initial request to search the vehicle, assuming that Smith consented to that initial request. Smith did not voluntarily consent to opening his briefcase, but rather submission to a show of authority. All of this was in violation of Fourth and Fourteenth Amendments to the United States Constitution.

MEMORANDUM OF LAW

1. <u>Remedy for Violation</u>: Exclusion of evidence is the proper remedy for a violation of a person's constitutional rights. The good faith of the police officers in seizing evidence may not be considered with regard to the reasonableness of any search or seizure. The reason for the exclusionary rule under the Constitution is to protect the privacy interests of its citizens and not simply to deter police misconduct.

2. <u>What Constitutes a "Stop"?</u>: A "stop" occurs when a person is approached by a law enforcement officer who demands and retains a person's identification. During these encounters a person cannot refuse to cooperate and walk away (Brown v. Texas, 443 US 47, 99 S Ct 2637, 1977). The test is whether the police, through some "show of authority," restrained a person's liberty so a reasonable person would not feel free to refuse to cooperate or leave the scene of the investigation.

3. <u>Reasonable Suspicion Required</u>: A stop of a person is reasonable when the officer has facts providing a reasonable suspicion that a crime has been committed. An officer may broaden the scope of the investigation of a traffic infraction if there is a reasonable suspicion that a defendant has committed illegal acts other than the traffic infraction. A reasonable suspicion is defined as an objective test that requires an officer to point to specific facts giving rise to a reasonable inference that the defendant committed a crime. An officer's subjective belief that the stopped person is committing a crime fails to establish reasonable suspicion if that belief is not objectively reasonable.

4. <u>Prolonged Stop Was Unlawful</u>: Even if the initial traffic stop of a defendant was reasonable, his continued detention by law enforcement officers may be excessive, becoming an unlawful stop, unless supported by reasonable suspicion that the defendant is committing a crime. An officer's authority to retain a person's driver's license ends when the officer has all the evidence needed to issue a citation. An excessive stop constitutes a seizure of the person; prolonged detention may constitute an illegal arrest if not based on probable cause (Dunaway v. New York, 442 US 200, 1979).

5.   Evidence Obtained by Exploiting Unlawful Stop Must be Excluded: Any and all evidence obtained as the result of an illegal stop must be suppressed as "fruit of the poisonous tree." This includes any and all oral derivative evidence. If consent was illegally obtained, a subsequent consent does not purge the taint of the illegally received consent.

6.   Fourth Amendment Law: Under the Fourth Amendment, a seizure occurs whenever there is a "meaningful interference, however brief, with an individual's freedom of movement." According to United States v. Jacobsen, 466 US 109, 1984, a person is seized when the officer, by means of physical force or show of authority has in some way restrained the liberty of a citizen. In Michigan v. Chesternut, 486 US 567, 1988, a person is considered seized if a reasonable person in that situation would have believed that he was not free to leave.

7.   Probable Cause To Search: Probable cause requires articulable facts that must lead a reasonable person to believe that evidence of a crime will probably be found in the location to be searched. This is the more-likely-than-not requirement. A well warranted suspicion is not probable cause because a suspicion, no matter how well-founded, does not rise to the level of probable cause.

8.   What Constitutes a "Search"?: Police conduct a search when the officer opens the door of the vehicle to inspect the interior compartment of the vehicle for evidence. Likewise, a search occurs when an officer inserts his head into an open car window. Police conduct a search within the meaning of the Fourth Amendment when they move an item to check for a serial number (Arizona v. Hicks, 480 US 321 (1987), or when they physically manipulate a carry-on bag aboard a bus (Bond v. United States, 529 US 334, 2000). No search can be conducted without probable cause. When Trooper X began handling and moving McGhee's briefcase around inside the car, he effected a search of the briefcase before asking for Smith's consent to search.

9.   Probable Cause and Exigent Circumstances Required To Search Briefcase: No probable cause and exigent circumstances justified the warrantless search of any closed container belonging to the defendant. Exigent circumstances include, among other things, situations in which immediate action is necessary to prevent the disappearance, dissipation, or destruction of evidence.

10.   Voluntary Consent: Defendant did not consent to any search and/or seizure. Mere acquiescence to lawful authority is not consent and does not justify any search and/or seizure. To be an effective consent, the consent cannot be obtained after the search has commenced. If a person feels that he/she had no choice but to grant the officers request to search, there is no consent.

11. <u>Scope of Consent Limits Scope of Lawful Search</u>: The scope of permissible searches is limited to the consent given. When the state relies on consent to support a search, it must prove by a preponderance of the evidence that officials complied with any limitations on the scope of the consent. The scope of a person's consent does not turn on what the person subjectively intended. Rather, it turns on what a reasonable person would have intended. The specific request that the officer made, the stated object of the search, and the surrounding circumstances all bear on a court's determination of the scope of a person's consent.

12. <u>Standards for Determining Validity of Consent</u>: The burden of proving lawful consent to search and/or seize is on the State. The prosecution must show that the consent was voluntarily given and that proof must be by a preponderance of the evidence. Although the totality of circumstances approach is to be applied in testing consents given after illegal police conduct as well as in testing consents given where police conduct has been proper, the burden on the State to show voluntariness when consent occurs after illegal conduct is greater than when no illegality has occurred.

<u>Remedy for Unlawful Search or Seizure</u>

Any and all evidence derived from an unreasonable search and/or seizure must be suppressed as "fruit of the poisonous tree." (Dunaway v. New York, 442 US 200 (1979).

DATED: July 22, 2011

ROBERT JONES, Esq., ATTORNEY FOR DEFENDANT

END OF DOCUMENT

Memo Writing Lessons (MFC 334 Web: Legal Research & Writing)

Lesson 1: Basic Citations

There are several different forms of citation depending upon the jurisdiction you are in, but for the purposes of this paper, you are required to use the Harvard Law convention, which is found in the Blue Book: A Uniform System of Citation. The majority of your authority in a memorandum of law will consist of case law. The following is a typical example of what you will encounter as you do your research:

People v. Briscoe, 99 N.Y.2d 596 [2003]

The first part of the citation is the title (People v. Briscoe), which identifies the primary parties involved in the case. The next information (99), is the volume number of the reporter in which the case appears. This number is traditionally found on the binding of the book. Next we find the Reporter in which the case appears. In this instance, the case appears in N.Y.2d which is the official reporter of the New York State Court of Appeals (Highest Court in New York).

The second number is the page where the case first appears, in this situation that is page 596. Finally, the number in parenthesis is the year that the case was decided. In summary, the case of *People v. Briscoe* can be found in volume 99 of the New York second series (N.Y.2d) at page 596. Additionally, we know that the case was decided in 2003 before the New York State Court of Appeals.

The rules concerning case citations are found in Chapter 10 of your Blue Book. It is important to remember that citations are extremely technical. Underlining, typeface, spacing and punctuation are all essential elements of a proper cite. In trial practice many of the rules get cast aside, however, for your memo, citation form must be strictly complied with. (The sample memo was written using the New York conventions for citation and thus are not in Blue Book form).

Parallel Citations:

Most states use more than one reporter. However, only one reporter is the "Official Reporter" and when drafting memorandum of law in NY, only the "Official Reporter" cite is given. To determine which reporter is the "Official Reporter" for a given state, refer to table T.1. Thus your memo should only contain one cite per case reference. That does not mean that you do not have to re-cite case when they are referred to subsequently in your paper, but rather at each specific cite only one reporter should appear.

Short Forms for Citations:

When a case has been previously cited within the course of a memorandum, frequently, a short form citation may be used in lieu of a complete citation. Usage and forms are discussed in your Blue Book under "Short Forms for Cases".

Point Cites:

When the information cited (i.e. a quote) comes from a specific point in the case, the pages upon which the information appears is included in your citation. Thus, for example if a quote from *People v. Johnson*, 81 N.Y.2d 828 [1993] is put in your memo, and the original cite is found on page 831, the citation would look as follows: *People v. Johnson*, 81 N.Y.2d 828, 831 [1993]. If the original quote appeared on pages 831 and continued on 832, the citation would read: *People v. Johnson*, 81 N.Y.2d 828, 831-32.

Statutory Citation:

The second most common citations you will use and encounter will be statutes or rules. The premise for such citations is similar to that of a case, however the information is somewhat different. For example, taking the citation, Comprehensive Environmental Response, Compensation and Liability Act, 42 U.S.C. §§ 9601-9675 (1988), we see that the first part of the citation is still the title, or name of the statute (Comprehensive Environmental Response, Compensation and Liability Act), the second part is the title number, in this case 42, the third part is the abbreviated code title, here being U.S.C. (United States Code) and we have the section in the code where the statute is found, §§ 9601-9675, and lastly we have the date of the code which is cited.

When we compare the case citation to the above citation, we see that the caption title, *People v. Briscoe*, is analogous to the statute title, Comprehensive Environmental Response, Compensation and Liability Act, that the volume number, 99, is analogous to the title number, 42, the reporter title, U.S. is analogous to the code title and the starting page number, 596, is analogous to the section number.

Lesson 2: Reading a Case: ARAC

In general, legal writing and the comprehension of legal writing follows a specific pattern: ARAC. This acronym is extended into:

> Answer
> Rule
> Analysis
> Counterarguments and Conclusion

Written decisions are the individual court's resolution of issues, which then serve as precedent for future courts that encounter the same issue. Thus, when reading a case, the first question you must ask is "What issue or issues are being resolved?" Most cases have one or two primary issues in question which often lead to several sub-issues. To illustrate the steps utilized in identifying the issues I have provided (below) the cases of <u>People v. Hill</u> and <u>People v. Singh.</u>

Supreme Court, Appellate Division, Fourth Department, New York

PEOPLE of the State of New York, Plaintiff-Respondent

v

Gregory HILL, Defendant-Appellant.

March 21, 2001

Defendant was convicted in the Erie County Court, Drury, J., of burglary in the second degree, and he appealed. The Supreme Court, Appellate Division held that:

(1) notice of intent to use defendant's prior statement was not required where rebuttal testimony is offered solely for the purpose of impeachment;

(2) defendant's counsel was not ineffective; and

(3) court properly precluded defense counsel from questioning the arresting officer concerning self-serving exculpatory statements made by defendant at the time of his arrest.

Affirmed.

Defendant appeals from a judgment convicting him after a jury trial of burglary in the second degree (Contrary to the contention of defendant, he received effective assistance of counsel. Defendant failed to show that, had counsel moved for a Huntley hearing, his statements would have been suppressed (see, The court did not abuse its discretion in admitting in evidence a videotape of the crime scene (see, <u>People v. Scutt, 254 A.D.2d 807, 807-808, 679 N.Y.S.2d 489,</u> lv. denied<u>92 N.Y.2d 1038, 684 N.Y.S.2d 503, 707 N.E.2d 458).</u>

The People established an adequate foundation for the admission of the videotape through the complainant's testimony that it accurately depicted the crime scene except for the fact that the videotape was made during the daytime and the burglary occurred at night. <u>People v. Middleton, 247 A.D.2d 713, 714, 669 N.Y.S.2d 82,</u> lv. denied<u>92 N.Y.2d 856, 677 N.Y.S.2d 87, 699 N.E.2d 447;</u> see also, <u>People v. Weston, 249 A.D.2d 496, 671 N.Y.S.2d 518,</u> lv. denied<u>92</u>

N.Y.2d 931, 680 N.Y.S.2d 473, 703 N.E.2d 285; People v. Riddick, 229 A.D.2d 453, 454, 645 N.Y.S.2d 80, lv. denied 88 N.Y.2d 993, 649 N.Y.S.2d 400, 672 N.E.2d 626).

We reject defendant's contention that the statements were not offered for the truth of the matter asserted therein but to show the arresting officer's state of mind. The statements were irrelevant unless offered to prove the truth of the matter asserted therein (see, People v. Reynoso, 73 N.Y.2d 816, 818-819, 537 N.Y.S.2d 113, 534 N.E.2d 30; People v. Starostin, 265 A.D.2d 267, 698 N.Y.S.2d 6, lv. denied 94 N.Y.2d 885, 705 N.Y.S.2d 17, 726 N.E.2d 494; People v. Middleton, 143 A.D.2d 1053, 1055, 533 N.Y.S.2d 893). Finally, the verdict is not against the weight of the evidence (see, People v. Bleakley, 69 N.Y.2d 490, 495, 515 N.Y.S.2d 761, 508 N.E.2d 672). People v. Leeper, 254 A.D.2d 754, 678 N.Y.S.2d 554, lv. denied 93 N.Y.2d 973, 695 N.Y.S.2d 59, 716 N.E.2d 1104; see also, People v. Walker, 234 A.D.2d 962, 963, 652 N.Y.S.2d 441, lv. denied 89 N.Y.2d 1042, 659 N.Y.S.2d 873, 681 N.E.2d 1320).

Indeed, the statements made by defendant at the time of his arrest were exculpatory and were not used by the People as evidence-in-chief. Counsel's alleged failure to seek discovery does not constitute ineffective assistance of counsel in the absence of any showing by defendant that there was additional discovery material that was not received by defendant (see generally, People v. Walker, supra, at 963, 652 N.Y.S.2d 441). Penal Law § 140.25[2]). Contrary to defendant's contention, County Court did not err in allowing the rebuttal testimony of the arresting officer despite the failure of the People to disclose that testimony on their CPL 710.30 notice. The complainant testified that he heard intruders in his house and went downstairs to investigate. Two men ran out of his home, and he chased them down the street. He caught up with one of the men, whom he identified as defendant. The police arrived and arrested defendant.

At the close of the People's case, the prosecutor informed the court that, if defendant testified that he was not in the area of the complainant's residence on the night of the burglary, he would recall the arresting officer to testify that she observed defendant and a man who fit the description of the second perpetrator in the area of the burglary earlier that same evening. The court properly held, over defendant's objection, that the proposed rebuttal testimony of the arresting officer was proper. A prosecutor may impeach the testimony of a defendant through rebuttal testimony (see, People v. Harris, 57 N.Y.2d 335, 345, 456 N.Y.S.2d 694, 442 N.E.2d 1205, cert. denied 460 U.S. 1047, 103 S. Ct. 1448, 75 L.Ed.2d 803).

Although the People failed to disclose on the CPL 710.30 notice that they had "testimony regarding an observation of the defendant either at the time or place of the commission of the offense or upon some other occasion relevant to the case" (CPL 710.30[1][b]), the People did not offer that testimony as evidence-in-chief. A CPL 710.30 notice is not required where the rebuttal testimony is offered solely for the purpose of impeachment (see generally, People

v. Rigo, 273 A.D.2d 258, 258-259, 709 N.Y.S.2d 571, lv. denied95 N.Y.2d 937, 721 N.Y.S.2d 614, 744 N.E.2d 150; People v. Skinner, 251 A.D.2d 1013, 674 N.Y.S.2d 883, lv. denied 92 N.Y.2d 930, 1038, 680 N.Y.S.2d 472, 684 N.Y.S.2d 503, 703 N.E.2d 284, 707 N.E.2d 458; People v. Spinks, 205 A.D.2d 842, 844, 613 N.Y.S.2d 288, lv. denied 84 N.Y.2d 833, 617 N.Y.S.2d 153, 641 N.E.2d 174). 110k419(1.5) Most Cited Cases110k413(1) Most Cited CasesU.S.C.A. Const.Amend. 6.110k444 Most Cited CasesU.S.C.A. Const.Amend. 6.110k641.13(6) Most Cited CasesMcKinney's CPL § 710.30.110k641.13(6) Most Cited Cases110k629(1) Most Cited Cases110k412(4) Most Cited Cases410k319 Most Cited Cases110k683(1) Most Cited Cases

Judgment unanimously affirmed.

END OF DOCUMENT

The People of the State of New York, Respondent

v

Gurdip Singh, Appellant

Supreme Court, Appellate Division, Second Department, New York

(October 2, 2000)

Appeal by the defendant from a judgment of the Supreme Court, Queens County (Finnegan, J.), rendered October 15, 1998, convicting him of murder in the second degree, upon a jury verdict, and imposing sentence.

Ordered that the judgment is affirmed.

Viewing the evidence in the light most favorable to the prosecution (see,

People v Contes, 60 NY2d 620), we find that it was legally sufficient to establish the defendant's guilt of depraved indifference murder beyond a reasonable doubt. Three eyewitnesses testified at trial that, while the defendant's friend engaged the victim in a fistfight, the defendant retrieved a gun from a van across the street and fired one shot into the air, shattering the window of a room full of people. He then shot the victim once in the thigh at close range as the victim lay on the ground.

Thereafter, when the defendant was being restrained, he struggled to free himself and stated that he wished to fire another shot. This evidence established that "under circumstances evincing a depraved indifference to human life, [the defendant] recklessly engage[d] in conduct which create[d] a grave risk of death to another person" (Penal Law § 125.25 [2]). More-over, upon the exercise of our factual review power, we are satisfied that the verdict of guilt was not against the weight of the evidence (see, CPL 470.15 [5]).

The Supreme Court erred in admitting into evidence prior consistent statements made by the People's witnesses to the police regarding their identification of the defendant as the shooter. While prior consistent statements are admissible to rehabilitate a witness whose testi-mony has been attacked as a recent fabrication (see, People v McDaniel, 81 NY2d 10; People v Davis, 44 NY2d 269), the prior consistent statements at issue were elicited by the prosecutor on his direct examination of these witnesses, making any rehabilitation premature (see, People v McDaniel, supra). Moreover, the theory of the defense was that the witnesses' motive to fabri-cate arose before the prior consistent statements were made (see, People v Davis, supra; People v Rogers, 193 AD2d 822). However, in light of the overwhelming evidence of the defendant's guilt presented at the trial, the error in the admission of the prior consistent statements was harmless (see, People v Crimmins, 36 NY2d 230).

The defendant's remaining contentions are either unpreserved for appellate review or without merit.

O'Brien, J. P., Altman, Krausman and Schmidt, JJ., concur.

END OF DOCUMENT

When we consider the first paragraph in *Singh* we see that the Court is concerned with whether the evidence before the jury was legally sufficient to allow for a guilty verdict. This issue is identified in the first sentence "we find that it [the evidence] was legally sufficient to establish the defendant's guilt of depraved indifference murder beyond a reasonable doubt."

As a sub-issue arising out of the legal sufficiency of the evidence, the Court addresses its factual review of the evidence indicating that the verdict was not against the weight of the evi-dence. Thus, the first paragraph deals with two issues: (1) the legal sufficiency of the evidence and (2) the factual sufficiency of the evidence.

The second paragraph identifies the second primary issue, whether the trial court erred in admitting a prior consistent statement as an exception to the hearsay rule. This issue is identified in the first sentence, second paragraph where the Appellate Court tells us where the lower court erred; "the Supreme Court erred in admitting into evidence prior consistent statements made by the People's witnesses to the police regarding their identification of the defendant as the shooter."

Every case which you review must be considered with an eye towards isolating the issue because the issue sets the rule and it is the rule you want. If the issue in your case varies significantly from the issue discussed in the opinion you've found, then the rule iterated in the opinion is of little utility.

Using the *Singh* case as our example, we see that the second issue is the admissibility of a prior consistent statement and *Singh* gives us the rule "prior consistent statements are admissible to rehabilitate a witness whose testimony has been attacked as a recent fabrication". If we have the same issue in our case than this rule is useful and this case can be cited. If our issue differs from the one addressed in Singh, such as the admissibility of third party testimony concerning a witness' out-of-court identification, then the rule in Singh does us no good.

The rule is the ultimate gem from each case. However, it is not the only useful information. Frequently, when a court opines on an issue it provides an analysis of how the rule works in application. For instance, in *Singh* the Court gives us the above rule concerning the admissibility of prior consistent statements, pointing that such statements are admissible to disprove a claim of recent fabrication.

The Court goes on to apply the rule to its facts deciding that although admissible to disprove claims of recent fabrication, such was not its proffer in this case as the defendant had not yet made a claim of recent fabrication at the time that the statements were elicited and even when the witness was confronted, the defendant's claim was that the witness's motive to fabricate existed before the consistent statement. This case analysis can be extremely useful depending on how closely it mirrors the facts in your case. If the facts are similar or analogous, you can adopt the court's rationale and incorporate their argument in your memo.

It is the court's conclusion which based upon its application will often dictate whether a case is chosen. Opinions which state the rule you want, as well as the results you desire, are preferable to a case which states the rule but comes out negative to your position because such cases frequently contain an argument which cuts against your position. For instance, a case which concludes that a prior consistent statement is admissible because the facts demonstrate that the proffer is made to counter a claim of recent fabrication is preferable to *Singh* if you are the party offering the prior consistent statements in your case.

Lesson 3: Outlining A Memo

The basic outline form in a persuasive memorandum is ARAC:

Answer (to Issues)—Rule(s)—Analysis—Counterarguments and Conclusion

Issue Presentation

Before you can make an argument, you must identify what it is that you are trying to prove. Often this is dictated to you, for instance the Court will tell you what issues it wants fleshed out, or precedent will mandate the issues to be addressed. In this case, the primary issues are set by the moving party, the defendant. Thus, our primary issues are:

1. Whether the weapon is admissible, and

2. Whether victim's statement is admissible.

Understanding that these are our points of interest, we have to decide whether they can be better addressed as sub-issues. In this case again we find that the defendant has set the parameters of initial sub-issues, setting forth two grounds for each issue.

Issue 1. Admissibility of the Weapon

      a. Is the search illegal?

      b. Is the scope of the search too broad?

Issue 2. Admissibility of the victim's statement

      a. Is it hearsay?

      b. Does it violate the right of confrontation?

These sub-issues may in turn have sub-sub-issues depending on how you address . Let us look at the example memo (See the attachment in the web course materials for lesson/assignment #3). In the example there is a single primary issue, and it appears as a "point heading":

THE COURT MUST DENY THE DEFENDANT'S MOTION FOR THE SUPPRESSION OF WITNESS IDENTIFICATION TESTIMONY BECAUSE THE SHOW-UP IDENTIFICATION PROCEDURE USED BY THE BUFFALO POLICE WAS REASONABLE AND NOT UNDULY SUGGESTIVE

When reconfigured into a question, we see that the issue before the court is whether the witness' testimony concerning the identification of the defendant will be admissible. The prosecution has further narrowed the scope of the issue as to whether the testimony will be admissible based on the propriety of the show-up identification procedure.

In response to this issue the People proffered two grounds (sub-issues) for admission:

1. The show-up procedure was legal (legal in theory)

2. The application of the procedure was not prejudicial (legal in application)

If there were no sub-issues, the body of the argument would follow without sub-headings, however, when there are sub-headings, before the first heading, the general rule pertaining to both sub-issues is presented. Therefore, a working outline of the example memo would look like this up to this point:

I. Facts

        a. Fact 1

        b. Fact 2 etc

Argument: The identification testimony of the witness is admissible because . .

        1. Procedure was followed

        2. Application was not unduly prejudicial

Rule(s):

The rules are normally defined by statute or case law. When developed from statute, the presentation in your memo is relatively straight forward. For example:

§ 160.10(1) Robbery in the Second Degree:

"A person is guilty of robbery in the second degree when he forcibly steals property and when he is aided by another person actually present". However, when the rule is generated from case law, the process is frequently more complex because you must detail the evolution of your rule through a series of pronouncements often times made in a series of different cases. Using the example memo:

"The general rule pertaining to show-up identifications is that they are permissible, even without exigent circumstances, as long as the police procedures employed are reasonable and not unduly suggestive. (See People v.Brisco, 99 NY2d 596 [2003]).

Crime scene witness identifications are no longer "presumptively infirm" as indicated by the courts' increasing willingness to allow show-ups if they survive careful scrutiny. (See People v. Duuvon, 77 NY2d 541, 543-544 [1991]; See also People v.Ortiz, 90 NY2d 533, 537 [1997])."

Our rule is "[t]he general rule pertaining to show-up identifications is that they are permissible, even without exigent circumstances, as long as the police procedures employed are reasonable and not unduly suggestive." which comes from the case of People v. Brisco, 99 NY2d 596 [2003].

However, this is an evolution from the preceding rule that crime-scene identification were "presumptively infirm" as evidenced by the decisions in Duuvon and Ortiz.

Most rules can be broken down, whether it be into elements, legal concepts or term definition. For instance, the robbery statute has two elements:

1. Forcible stealing, and

2. Aided by another person actually present

Analysis (or Application):

The application of the rule to the facts is the most important part of your paper. You need to look at the natural logic of your rule. First you set out the elements of your rule. Then you define any specific or specialized terms in your elements. Thirdly, you will take your facts and show how they meet each of the requirements of the rule.

For example in our memo we see the rule that show-up identifications are permissible when done in close geographic and temporal proximity to the crime. The elements are thus (1) geographic proximity, and (2) temporal proximity. In the example memo, the rationale for the rule is presented to put a context to the elements. Thereafter, we are presented with the definition of the scope of temporal proximity (How much time is too much?), and since there is no bright-line test, the facts are applied by analogy (In case X 2 hours was OK and in this case there was only an hour so therefore in applying the rule to these facts, our time frame is OK). This process is then repeated for the second element, geographic proximity, and the same process is used.

Counterarguments and Conclusion (With Recommendations):

Your conclusion, especially in a legal document, is a succinct statement of your position. It is also known as your "prayer for relief". Let us look at an outline for the sample memo:

Issue: Is the Identification Testimony Admissible?

Rule: Testimony is admissible after proper show-up (People v. Brisco)

    1. Proper procedure (element 1)

        a. Temporal Proximity < 2hrs People v. Boyd (sub-element 1)

        b. Geographic proximity < 12 blocks People v. Cannon (sub-element 2)

    2. Proper application People v. Ortiz (element 2)

        a. Handcuffs People v. Clark (sub-element)

        b. Information given to witness pre-ID "possible suspect" People v. Jolley (sub-element)

        c. Police presence People v. Ponder (sub-element)

Analysis:

    1. Proper procedure

        a. Time apprx 1 hr. T. 14-15, 41 (located in facts)

        b. Distance apprx 1 block T. 14-15, 41

    2. Proper application

        a. Hands not exposed T. 19

        b. No evidence of communication regarding suspect with victim

        c. Limited police presence

The more detailed you make your outline, the less work you will have to do to put your paper together and the less time you will waste doing unnecessary research.

Lesson 4: Point #1—The Stop

The Issues: The first issue we must address is whether the stop of the vehicle was lawful. Therefore, our first step is to lay out all of the facts which go to the stop. Normally, and in this case, such analysis follows the chronology of the event. Let us look at the facts known prior to the stop:

-    11:45 Costantino and Martin see the violation.
-    The vehicle is identified by make/model and plate's State of origin.
-    Officers identify last known direction of travel.

- Officers make estimate as to number of occupants.
- Trooper (Trp) Edwards has the above information prior to seeing the suspect vehicle.
- Six minutes elapses between time Trp. gets info and time vehicle is reacquired.
- Trp. confirms make/model and license plate (as to State of origin).
- Trp observes three occupants.
- Trp observes behavior of rear occupant, looking nervous.
- Vehicle stops.

Those are the facts known to us occurring before the stop. Any information gained after the stop is irrelevant to this issue. Your next question is "so what?" To answer that question we must identify what issues surround the stop of an automobile. To determine the issues we need to know a little about the law.

First, when can an officer make a lawful MV stop? The answer to this question is found in *People v. Ingle*. Thus, you need to go back and read *Ingle*. Ultimately, we are told "]ll that is required is that the stop be not the product of mere whim, caprice, or idle curiosity. It is enough if the stop is based upon 'specific and articulable facts which, taken together with rational inferences from those facts, reasonably warrant [the] intrusion'. (*People v. Ingle* 36 N.Y.2d 413, 420 [1975]).

Our inquiry does not end there, because some, if not all of the facts which may lead to an articuable basis to stop were not actually observed by the officer who made the stop. Thus, as a secondary issue we must also consider the "fellow officer" rule which is found in *People v. Ramirez-Portoreal*, (88 N.Y.2d 99 [1996]).

After we address the issue of the stop, we turn to the issue of the search. Even if you are the defendant and you argue that the stop is no good, you must nevertheless argue in the alternative that even if the stop is good, the search is not.

Your next inquiry is what additional facts develop post-stop and pre-search.

- Rear passenger hands off dark object
- Rear passenger looks nervous
- Officers confirm vehicle is one they saw
- Trp confirms registrations
- Trp learns that Driver's license is suspended
- None of the other occupants has a license
- Officers and Trooper converse and conclude that it would be safe to leave the car
- Officers and Trooper decide that they want to check the glove box to look for the object
- Officers and Trooper decide to conduct inventory search in order to look in glove box.

- Occupants are removed from vehicle and placed in police vehicles
- Not handcuffed, but unable to get out without outside help.
- Search is done pursuant to NYSP inventory policy
- Trp find knife in glove compartment.

So our next question is, "when may the police search a vehicle after a traffic stop?" For that answer we start with <u>People v. Johnson</u>, (1 N.Y.3d 252 [2003]) and the inventory search. There may be other arguments in regards to the authority to search and I will give extra credit to students who search them out and integrate them in the argument, but I am only requiring each party to deal with the issue of the inventory search.

Nevertheless, there is a secondary issue to the question of the inventory search and that is since the police had discretion not to impound the vehicle and the true motive was to search the car, does pre-text negate lawful authority to search? Here we turn to <u>People v. Robinson</u>, (97 N.Y.2d 341 [2001]), which although dealing with a different set of circumstances, discusses the ramifications of a pre-textual stop. It will be your job to analogize, or distinguish *Robinson* from this case.

<u>The Rules:</u>

I have given you a baseline of cases and they will be sufficient to argue your point, however, the cases are not exhaustive, and I strongly recommend that you supplement them with other cases which may be legally and factually analogous. The advantage is that often times, these cases will already have the arguments you wish to adopt, thus cutting down on your need to reinvent the wheel.

To recap:

<u>People v. Ingle</u> gives you the rules about when a stop can be made

<u>People v. Ramirez-Portoreal</u> contains the "fellow officer" rule.

<u>People v. Johnson</u> talks about inventory searches

<u>People v. Robinson</u> is the rule on pre-text stops.

<u>Analysis:</u>

Armed with the issues and the rules, you must now take the facts listed above or any others you can glean from the problem (do <u>not</u> make-up your own facts) and apply them to the rules.

For instance, if the law said that a show-up I.D. must be made in close geographical proximity to the crime and the facts were that the I.D. was three blocks from the crime, one could apply the rule by saying "since the identification procedure happened three blocks from the crime scene, it was conducted in close proximity, thus satisfying the requirement that the identification procedure be done in close geographic proximity to the crime." The argument in the above example develops from whether three blocks is in fact a close proximity and that is where the bulk of the argument would develop.

<u>Counterarguments and Conclusion (With Recommendations):</u>

The above example not only demonstrates application of rules to facts, but also give a preliminary conclusion (i.e. the requirement was satisfied). The same type of conclusion will present itself with each rule. Either it is met based on the facts or it is violated based on the facts, ultimately that is what your paper is about.

To summarize the next step in your Memo:

- You will argue that either the police did or did not have authority to stop the vehicle.
- You will argue whether the trooper could rely on the info from other police and to what extent.
- You will argue whether the police could conduct an inventory search
- You will argue what effect pre-text has on the possible validity of the search.

Before you do this however, you must do an <u>outline of your argument</u>. And that is the next assignment.

Lesson 5: Point #2—The Statements

Issues:

Once we have dealt with the weapon we must turn to the statement of the last victim. Before we can speak about a statement we need to know the rules. First: hearsay rule. Hearsay is an out-of-court declaration, offered for the truth of the matter asserted. Generally, hearsay is inadmissible. The statement at issue is clearly hearsay.

It was made out of court and it is to be offered for the truth of the matter asserted. As with almost everything in the law, there are exceptions to the hearsay rule. For the purposes of our analysis we are going to look at the excited utterance exception. There may be other exceptions and certainly you can get extra credit dealing with those exceptions, but for our purposes we are going to deal with the "excited utterance" exception. An excited utterance is one that is made under the stress or influence of a startling event, dealing with the event.

For instance, a woman watches her daughter hit by a truck. The police arrive on the scene in minutes and the woman describes a blue dump truck with yellow writing on the side speeding down the street. She describes the driver as man with blonde hair and light skin, wearing sunglasses.

At the time that the woman is giving her statement she is holding back sobs, she cries at times when discussing the event and seems to be more concerned with her daughter than the officers. This is the prototypical excited utterance. The issues surrounding an exciting utterance are:

1.   The event must be of a startling nature.

2.   The witness/declarant must have observed/experienced the event.

3.   The witness/declarant must be under the influence of the event.

    a.   Declarant has not had time to reflect on the events to the degree that such reflection has affected declarant's memory.

    b.   Declarant still shows physical manifestations of trauma.

Let's break down the example: Is the event startling? I doubt that anyone can say that seeing your daughter hit by a truck is anything but traumatic. Thus, issue one is satisfied. Did the declarant see or experience the event? In this case, she saw the event. A person in a car accident may not have seen the collision, but that type of witness would be said to have experienced the event.

Is the declarant still under the influence of the event? This is usually the most difficult issue. Time lapse is certainly a factor, but it is not determinative. A person who watches an old man fall off a curb and get injured may be disturbed for a shorter time then the witness in our problem. Additionally, the degree that a person is affected by an event differs from person to person. For instance, a surgeon who watches a person get injured in a football game, may be less affected than the parent of the player.

In general, you are going to be required to rely on common sense. What is the witness' relationship to the event? What is the person's involvement to the event? What is the nature of the event? How much time has passed? What is the witness' demeanor when the statement is given?

In your memo, you will need to go through all of the steps outlined above and either conclude that they are met (the prosecution) or that one or more criteria are lacking (the defense).

Rules (applicable case law):

People v. Johnson, (1 N.Y.3d 302 [2003]) illustrates the rule in New York State. The ultimate question is whether the statement was made before the declarant had an opportunity to reflect on the event, such that the answer is affected by the biases and prejudices of studied reflection.

People v. Gantt, (—- A.D.3d—-, 848 N.Y.S.2d 156 [1st Dept. 2007])- An extrajudicial statement will be admitted under the excited utterance exception to the hearsay rule when it relates to a startling event and is made while declarant remains under the stress of excitement caused by the startling event. Test for admission of a statement pursuant to the excited utterance exception to the hearsay rule is whether the declarant was so influenced by the excitement and shock of the event that it is probable that he or she spoke impulsively and without reflection. Testimony of three witnesses, that victim, while lying seriously wounded on the sidewalk almost immediately after the shooting, identified defendant as the one who shot him, was admissible, in prosecution for second-degree murder, under the excited utterance exception to the hearsay rule, even though one of the statements was made in response to a question from a police officer; identifications were made under circumstances that did not allow for studied reflection, and they were not testimonial in nature. (Since this case is new, there is no official cite (A.D.3d) therefore, you use the national reporter system (N.Y.S.2d)).

People v. Caviness, (38 N.Y.2d 227 [1975])- Spontaneous declarations made by a participant while he is under the stress of nervous excitement resulting from an injury or other startling event, while his reflective powers are stilled, and during the brief period when considerations of self-interest could not have been brought fully to bear by reasoned reflection and deliberation, are admissible as true exceptions to the hearsay rule.

There are additional cases available which may be more illustrative of our scenario and will allow you to make easier analogies. However, the above cases are sufficient to deal with the issue.

Analysis:

As noted from the above cases, you will need to analyze the facts to answer the following:

1.   Did the witness experience an excitable event?

2.   Was the witness still under the influence of the trauma?

3.   Were her answers spontaneous and without regard to self interests?

Counterarguments and Conclusion (With Recommendations):

If your answers to the above questions were yes, then the statements were excited utterances. If your answer to any of the above questions was negative, then the statements were not excited utterances and are therefore inadmissible hearsay.

Issue 2

If you conclude that the statements are excited utterances, your inquiry must continue. Also, if you decide that the statements are not excited utterances, you must nevertheless argue in the alternative. That is, the second question, is does the admission of the statement violate the defendant's right of confrontation.

In general, the 6th Amendment of the United States Constitution guarantees the accused to be confronted with the witnesses against him. (U.S.C.A. Const. Amend. VI-Jury Trials).

Thus, hearsay is generally inadmissible. The rationale is that only upon through cross-examination, can the accuracy of a witness' testimony be tested. Hearsay is not subject to cross examination and therefore, its reliability is questionable. However, there are exceptions which have generally been recognized as situations where the reliability of a statement is assumed.

Excited utterances are considered reliable because they are spontaneous and not the product of studied reflection.

In 2004, the Supreme Court held that hearsay exceptions only apply when the statements are not the testimonial in nature. (*Crawford v.* Washington, 541 U.S. 36 [2004]) Thus, the Supreme Court added another layer to the issue. Now, instead of simply deciding whether a statement meets one of the hearsay exceptions, you must then decide whether the statement is testimonial in nature.

Rules (applicable case law):

Crawford v. Washington, (541 U.S. 36 [2004])- The Confrontation Clause, providing that accused has right to confront and cross-examine witnesses against him, applies not only to in-court testimony, but also to out-of-court statements introduced at trial, regardless of admissibility of statements under law of evidence. Out-of-court statements that qualify as testimonial, and thus that are not admissible, under the Confrontation Clause, unless witness is unavailable and defendant had prior opportunity to cross examine witness, include at a minimum prior testimony at preliminary hearing, before a grand jury, or at a former trial, and statements elicited during police interrogations.

Davis v. Washington, (547 U.S. 813 [2006])- Statements taken by police officers in the course of an interrogation are "nontestimonial," and not subject to the Confrontation Clause, when they are made under circumstances objectively indicating that the primary purpose of the interrogation is to enable police assistance to meet an ongoing emergency. Statements taken by police officers in the course of interrogation are "testimonial," and subject to the Confrontation Clause, when the circumstances objectively indicate that there is no ongoing emergency, and that the primary purpose of the interrogation is to establish or prove past events potentially relevant to later criminal prosecution.

People v. Bradley, (8 N.Y.3d 124 [2006])- The admission of a statement made out of court does not violate a defendant's Confrontation Clause rights unless the out-of-court statement is testimonial.

People v. Nieves-Andino, (9 N.Y.3d 12 [2007])-

Shooting victim's statement to first officer on scene that he had had an argument with defendant and that defendant had shot him three times, made in response to officer's question of "what happened," was not "testimonial," and thus admission of statement did not violate defendant's right of confrontation, in second-degree murder prosecution; primary purpose of officer's inquiry was to find out nature of attack, so that he could decide what action was necessary to prevent further harm, not to investigate for future criminal prosecution.

Analysis:

Simply put, you have to persuade the reader that the statements of the witness are either testimonial (the defense) or that they are not testimonial (the prosecution).

Counterarguments and Conclusion

If the statements are testimonial, then they must be excluded as in violation of the 6th Amendment. If the statements are not testimonial, and the statements are excited utterances, then they are admissible as a hearsay exception.

Lesson 6: Counterarguments and Conclusions

We are close to reaching the end. However, that is not all that conclusions are about. Remember, you will have conclusions in each segment of your memo. For every issue you identify, you must have a conclusion. Thus, if you identify that time is an issue in the determination of an excited utterance, then after you assert the rule, apply the rule to the fact, you must give the reader the conclusion you believe must be made.

Continuing with our time issue, if you determine that the appropriate rule is that there is a bright line test setting time at two hours (please do not draw conclusions from this example), and the facts show that the statement was given four hours after the startling event, then when you apply the rule to the facts, the reader must determine that the statement is not an excited utterance because it was made beyond two hours of the startling event. You must have the conclusion identified in your paper, do not leave it to the reader, regardless of how obvious you think the answer is.

Issues in the law rarely have one correct answer. If the issue is "black and white" then the good advocate moves to an area of "gray". Thus, the basic form of legal writing looks like this (ARAC):

Answer (to Issues)

Rule(s)

Analysis

    Reason in Favor of Argument

    Reasons Against Argument

Conclusion

Lesson 7: Statement of Facts

Although it may seem counter-intuitive, the statement of facts (SOF) is usually the last step in the process of synthesizing your memorandum. This is because you need to know what facts are material to your argument in order to properly present them in the SOF.

However, in order to know what facts are material and how they affect your argument, you must write the argument. Thus, it is not until you are done with that step, that you can properly address the SOF. To help you along, I have attached an example memo, which I reference in the below steps. The memo was created and saved in MSWord and should be available to anyone with Word 2000 or better. If you have a problem opening the attachment, please call me and I will endeavor to rectify the situation.

Many scholars believe that the introduction (statement of facts) to a memorandum is the most important aspect of the paper. The theory is that the introduction sets the theme and that the impression made during the presentation of facts colors the reader's perspective throughout the rest of the argument. With that in mind there are three concepts that you need to integrate into your fact pattern.

First: Simple is Better

What facts are essential to your argument? And perhaps more importantly what facts are not? In order to answer these questions, you must be familiar with your argument, which you should have developed in preparing your outline.

You want to avoid putting in facts which are unnecessary to prove your point because these facts often distract your reader and result in the reader getting confused and off point.

For instance, using the example memo we see that the issue concerns identification evidence and each paragraph deals with some element of the identification, whether it be the witness' ability to perceive the assailant (first paragraph) or the actual procedure utilized by the police in conducting the show-up, absent from the discussion is any fact concerning the statements given to the police after the identification was completed.

This is not say that such statements were not important to the case, but rather they are not the subject of the argument. In the same vein, you need to include all facts which are going to be discussed in your argument. You do not want your reader to be hearing about a fact for the first time two-thirds of the way through because it calls in to question the credibility of such a fact since if it was so important that you relied on it in your argument why did you omit it from your intro, "are you try to hide this fact?", if so "Why?". Also, it reflects poorly on your organizational skills, as it looks as is you are coming up with your argument as you go along. In either case, it detracts from the persuasiveness of your argument.

Second: The Attention Step

In legal writing this concept is less exciting then the title indicates. Your first sentence must set the foundation for your argument. That is, what you want from the Court. Additionally, you are starting the art of persuasion, thus you also want your first sentence to convey the strength of your argument. In this case, the example memo is a bad example as it only deals with your prayer. However, the example in chapter 14 CELW gives a good example of an effective first sentence. As the commentators point out, the sentence asserts three of the defendant's main arguments and sets the tone for the entire argument.

Third: Chose Your Words Wisely

Good legal writing avoids adjectives and "qualifiers" whenever possible. Thus, you will want to take advantage of the fact that the English language almost always gives you more than one word or phrase to express and idea. For instance, an immigrant's rights group wants to extend voting rights to undocumented foreigners, and a group of federalists oppose. In this scenario, the petitioner (the immigrant's rights group) presents the issue as: "The Government Should Grant Undocumented Workers The Right To Vote Because…" contrary, the respondent (the federalists) phrases the issue as: "The Government Should Deny Illegal Aliens The Right To Vote Because " In this example we see the subject described two different ways "undocumented workers v illegal aliens" each accurately describing the group, but also carrying very different connotations. This is the art of "spin" at work and as lawyers, this is your job.

Qualifiers" are cheating! Words and phrases such as: clearly, obviously, without question, only an idiot would believe, etc., are the tools of the pundit and are used to shut down argument when one lacks the skills to defend his position. Frequently, these words and phrases are superfluous and they can always be replaced, or omitted. If your position is so obvious that it cannot be legitimately challenged then such should be obvious to the reader without you telling her.

Critical readers often find that when such qualifiers are utilized, they often signal that the opposite is true, the issue is not clear, the conclusion is not obvious and I am not an idiot. Therefore, do not insult your reader, rather write your paper in such a fashion that the reader has no questions without being told that he has no questions.

Lesson 8: Editing and Proof Reading

I want to take this opportunity to do an overall review of the memo. We need to look both at the purpose and structure of the memo.

Purpose

The purpose of the memo is to convince the trial court of your position. If you are the prosecution, your goal is to convince the court that both the weapon and the victim's statement are admissible at trial. As the defense, you want to convince the court that the opposite is true.

1. The Weapon

There are two questions surrounding the admissibility of he weapon. First, is the stop authorized? Second, is the search legal?

In regards to the stop, there are two sub-questions. Do the police have "reasonable suspicion" to stop the car? If the answer is yes, can the secondary trooper rely on the information conveyed by fellow officers, invoking the "fellow officer" rule. As the defendant you must deal with both sub-issues regardless of your answer. The defendant must deal with the issues in the alternative. That is, assuming for the sake of argument, the first police had reasonable suspicion to stop the car, the trooper nevertheless lacked authority to stop the vehicle.

Once you have dealt with the stop, you must address the search. The issue concerns the legality of the inventory search. There are alternative theories for the authorization to search the vehicle, and I will give extra credit for those students who deal with any of these other theories. However, you will get full credit for addressing the inventory issue.

2. The Victim's Statement

There is little question that the victim's statement is hearsay. The prosecution is offering the out-of-court statements of the victim for the truth of the matter. Thus, the issue is whether the statement is an exception to hearsay. In this case, the exception in question is the "excited utterance".

In addressing the issue, the ultimate concern is whether the declarant had time to make reflective thought so as to render the statement the product subject to the biases and prejudices of the witness rather than the spontaneous declaration carrying the ring of veracity.

Regardless of your conclusion, both parties must address the second issue, and that is whether the statement is testimonial in nature. This is *Crawford* issue. In this case, the prosecution will argue that the statement is non-testimonial. While the defense will try to convince the court, that regardless of whether the statement meets one on the hearsay exceptions, it is nevertheless testimonial and therefore violates the defendant's confrontation right.

For the prosecution you must conclude that the stop is legal and the search is authorized. You must also conclude that the statement meets a hearsay exception and the statement is non-testimonial.

For the defendant, you must find that either the stop or the search is illegal. Additionally, the defendant must conclude that the statement is either hearsay without a valid exception, or that the statement is testimonial.

EDITING

Editing consists of two parts. First you edit for substance. You are looking to make sure that your rules are supported by case law or statutes. Then you need to read to make sure that your argument makes sense. Is each paragraph a complete thought? Have you intertwined two unrelated issues? Can your argument be simplified?

Once you have read each paragraph looking at the above issues, you need to make sure that the paragraphs are in the proper order. Think about whether the argument follows a logical sequence.

Once you have completed your editing for substance, you must turn to editing for form. Here is where you check spelling, grammar, tense and syntax.

- Is your sentence a complete thought?
- Is your sentence two distinct thoughts (run-on)?
- Do you have undefined or ambiguous pronouns?

My suggestion is that after you proof for substance, you should put down your paper for a day, and then read for form.

The Problem: "Monsters Among Us" Fact Pattern

The case at issue is People v. Lehman. Ari Lehman is charged with seven counts of Murder in the First Degree and one count of Criminal Possession of a Weapon in the Fourth Degree. For the purposes of the problem, the case happened in the City of New Scotland which is located in the 4th Department in the State of New York. The case is being tried in New York State Supreme Court and all issues of standing have been

The defendant has moved for the suppression of a knife found in the car he was riding in, as well as the statement given by one of the victims to the New York State Police. In lieu of a suppression hearing both sides have stipulated to the following facts:

On October 23rd, 2007, at approximately 11:45 pm, Ofc. Cosantino and Ofc. Martin, members of the New Scotland Police Department (NSPD), while on foot patrol, observed a blue Ford Mustang with Michigan plates make an illegal left turn, heading the wrong way down a one way street. Ofc. Cosantino immediately engaged in the following radio communication (Cosantino is C-140):

Time	Caller	Broadcast
2345:43	C-140	C-140 to dispatch, over.
2346:02	Disp	Go ahead C-140
2346:06	C-140	We just observed a blue Ford Mustang with Michigan plates make an illegal left turn south bound on Causeway Ave. in the direction of Fowler Street. We were unable to get any num bers off the plate. Observed at least 2 passengers. Over.
2346:51	Disp	Copy that C-140. (General Broadcast Starts) Attention all patrols! Be on the look-out for a blue Ford Mustang with Michigan plates. NSPD reports car last seen driving wrong-way, south bound, on Causeway toward Fowler. Car has at least 2 occupants. Will advise on DMV. Over.

Six minutes after hearing the above dispatch, New York State Trooper Tracy Edwards sees a blue Ford Mustang with Michigan plate, CCH-6869, westbound on Fowler St., heading away from

Causeway Ave.

Trooper Edwards activates her lights and while in pursuit sees that there are 3 occupants in the vehicle, driver, front-seat passenger and rear-seat driver's side passenger. Rear passenger continues to look back at Trooper as she pursues the vehicle.

After apprx. 15 seconds, the vehicle stops on the side of the road. As Trp. Edwards approaches the vehicle, she observes the rear-seat passenger pass a dark object off to the front-seat passenger and then look back "nervously" at Trp. Edwards.

Driver is an Anthony Perkins, who shows a New York State Driver's license and claims that the car is registered to his mother, who runs a motel in Michigan. Trooper Edwards returns to her vehicle to check the registration and while waiting for a reply is joined by officers Cosantino and Martin, who confirm that the vehicle is the one they saw turn onto Causeway.

The DMV check confirms that the vehicle is registered to Perkins' mother, but also shows that Perkins' license has been suspended for failure to pay child-support.

Trooper Edwards informs Cosantino and Martin about the passing of the dark object and the three law enforcement agents return to the car. Upon informing Perkins that he cannot continue to drive because of the license suspension, Trp. Edwards inquires of the front-seat passenger, one Nick Castle, if he has a valid license. Castle informs Edwards that he has recently been released from a psychiatric center and does not have a license. Ofc. Martin then asks the rear passenger, Ari Lehman, whether he has a license. In response, Lehman tells Martin that he left his license in a canoe at the camp he works at.

The three officers then discuss the situation and although they could leave the vehicle on the side of the road, decide that they want to check the glove compartment. Trooper Edwards calls for a tow truck and the three occupants are taken out and put in Trp. Edwards' & the NSPD police cars. None of the three are handcuffed, but they are unable to get out of the vehicles without assistance, as the doors are locked from the outside.

Pursuant to the written policy of the New York State Police (NYSP), Trp. Edwards commences and inventory search of the vehicle. Upon opening the glove compartment, she finds a large butcher's knife with what appears to be blood around the handle.

When confronted with the knife, all three occupants deny any prior knowledge of its existence. Perkins' adds that Lehman had been using the car earlier that day and had his own set of keys.

The three voluntarily accompany the officers back to the NSPD Detective offices. While waiting for the detectives, Trp. Edwards gets a call that six bodies have been discovered at Camp Crystal Lake, and that Lehman's wallet & driver's license was found with one of the bodies in a canoe. She is also informed that there is one survivor at New Scotland Medical Center (NSMC), who is in critical condition.

Leaving the three suspects with the NSPD, Trp. Edwards goes to NSMC to interview the witness. Upon her arrival she is informed that the witness' condition is dire. The witness' name is Alice Hardy, and she is visibly upset, bordering on hysterical when the trooper interviews her. Trooper Edwards' tape recording shows the following dialog:

Edwards: Alice, my name is Tracy Edwards, and I am with the State Police.

Hardy: Is he here?

Edwards: Is who here Alice?

Hardy: Him .. the killer! He's fu .. . crazy! He is still out there, I know it!

Edwards: You're safe here…

Hardy: Bull…, he's crazy! He'll kill you! He'll kill all of us!

Edwards: Who will kill all of us?

Hardy: Ari!

Edwards: Who is Ari?

Hardy: He was one of the kids at the camp! He went crazy, grabbed a butchers knife and just started hacking everyone up! I thought he was dead and then he just jumped out of the water and stabbed me with that goddamn knife!

Edwards: Alice. I need you to go slower and describe what happened.

Hardy: (unresponsive)

Edwards: Alice…Alice…Oh Sh**! Nurse get a doctor now!

The knife recovered in the car was swabbed for genetic material.

Analysis of the swab showed that the blood came from Alice Hardy, who never regained consciousness and was pronounced dead 12 hours after the interview with Edwards. Cause of death was cardiac arrest brought on by internal bleeding resulting from a stab wound to Hardy's liver.

Further analysis showed that the lethal wounds to the other six decedents were made with a blade with characteristics similar to the knife recovered.

Note: <u>You may choose either the defense or the prosecution.</u>

As the defendant you are seeking to suppress the weapon as the result of an unlawful search and seizure. Your first claim is that the stop of the vehicle was unlawful. Assuming that the initial stop of the vehicle was lawful, the subsequent search of the vehicle was unlawful.

The defendant is also seeking to have the court exclude the witness' statement to the police. First, the defendant claims that the statement is inadmissible hearsay. Second, it is claimed that even if the statement meets a hearsay exception, its admission violates the defendant's right of confrontation. The prosecution takes the converse positions.

Your memorandum should be in the form of a memorandum of law (aka a memo of points and authorities) submitted to the trial court prior to the commencement of jury selection.

Citations (relevant case law):

People v. Robinson, 97 N.Y.2d 341 [2001]-Court holds that pre-text stops are OK so long as police have reasonable suspicion to believe that an offense or violation has occurred.

People v. Ramirez-Portoreal, 88 N.Y.2d 99 [1996]- People sufficiently established by circumstantial evidence that officer conducting surveillance of defendant directed arrest of defendant or communicated to arresting officer information which gave probable cause to arrest, so that arrest could be upheld under "fellow officer" rule even though arresting officer lacked personal knowledge sufficient to establish probable cause, where officers were engaged in single assignment, they were together on roof during surveillance, they proceeded together to arrest defendant, and arresting officer alighted from car and immediately detained defendant despite having no personal knowledge of defendant's activity, appearance, or precise location.

People v. Ingle, 36 N.Y.2d 413 [1975]- The stop of automobile on highway is a limited seizure within meaning of constitutional limitations and, if unreasonable, the subsequently discovered evidence would constitute derivative evidence obtained by an illegal seizure. It should be emphasized that, in the context of a motor vehicle inspection 'stop', the degree of suspicion required to justify the stop is minimal. Nothing like probable cause as that term is used in the criminal law is required.

People v. Johnson, 1 N.Y.3d 252 [2003]- Following a lawful arrest of the driver of an automobile that must then be impounded, the police may conduct an inventory search of the vehicle.

The specific objectives of an inventory search, particularly in the context of a vehicle, are to protect the property of the defendant, to protect the police against any claim of lost property, and to protect police personnel and others from any dangerous instruments.

People v. Johnson, 1 N.Y.3d 302 [2003]- An out-of-court statement is properly admissible under the excited utterance hearsay exception when made under the stress of excitement caused by an external event, and not the product of studied reflection and possible fabrication. In determining whether an out-of-court statement is admissible under the excited utterance hearsay exception, the test is whether the utterance was made before there has been time to contrive and misrepresent, i.e., while the nervous excitement may be supposed still to dominate and the reflective powers to be yet in abeyance.

Crawford v. Washington, 541 U.S. 36 [2004]- he Confrontation Clause, providing that accused has right to confront and cross-examine witnesses against him, applies not only to in-court testimony, but also to out-of-court statements introduced at trial, regardless of admissibility of statements under law of evidence. Out-of-court statements that qualify as testimonial, and thus that are not admissible, under the Confrontation Clause, unless witness is unavailable and defendant had prior opportunity to cross examine witness, include at a minimum prior testimony at preliminary hearing, before a grand jury, or at a former trial, and statements elicited during police interrogations.

People v. Gantt,—- A.D.3d—-, 848 N.Y.S.2d 156 [1st Dept. 2007]- An extrajudicial statement will be admitted under the excited utterance exception to the hearsay rule when it relates to a startling event and is made while declarant remains under the stress of excitement caused by the startling event. Test for admission of a statement pursuant to the excited utterance exception to the hearsay rule is whether the declarant was so influenced by the excitement and shock of the event that it is probable that he or she spoke impulsively and without reflection. Testimony of three witnesses, that victim, while lying seriously wounded on the sidewalk almost immediately after the shooting, identified defendant as the one who shot him, was admissible, in prosecution for second-degree murder, under the excited utterance exception to the hearsay rule, even though one of the statements was made in response to a question from a police officer; identifications were made under circumstances that did not allow for studied reflection, and they were not testimonial in nature. (Since this case is new, there is no official cite (A.D.3d) therefore, you use the national reporter system (N.Y.S.2d)).

People v. Caviness, 38 N.Y.2d 227 [1975]- Spontaneous declarations made by a participant while he is under the stress of nervous excitement resulting from an injury or other startling event, while his reflective powers are stilled, and during the brief period when considerations of self-interest could not have been brought fully to bear by reasoned reflection and deliberation, are admissible as true exceptions to the hearsay rule.

Davis v. Washington, 547 U.S. 813 [2006]- Statements taken by police officers in the course of an interrogation are "non-testimonial," and not subject to the Confrontation Clause, when they are made under circumstances objectively indicating that the primary purpose of the interrogation is to enable police assistance to meet an ongoing emergency. Statements taken by police officers in the course of interrogation are "testimonial," and subject to the Confrontation Clause, when the circumstances objectively indicate that there is no ongoing emergency, and that the primary purpose of the interrogation is to establish or prove past events potentially relevant to later criminal prosecution.

People v. Bradley, 8 N.Y.3d 124 [2006]- The admission of a statement made out of court does not violate a defendant's Confrontation Clause rights unless the out-of-court statement is testimonial.

People v. Nieves-Andino, 9 N.Y.3d 12 [2007]-

Shooting victim's statement to first officer on scene that he had had an argument with defendant and that defendant had shot him three times, made in response to officer's question of "what happened," was not "testimonial," and thus admission of statement did not violate defendant's right of confrontation, in second-degree murder prosecution; primary purpose of officer's inquiry was to find out nature of attack, so that he could decide what action was necessary to prevent further harm, not to investigate for future criminal prosecution.

Chapter 3
Legal Research, Briefing Cases and Lawyerly Writing

Chapter Learning Objectives:

Upon completing this chapter and the related assignments students will be able to:

- Read, understand and use cases to construct legal arguments.

- Read, understand and use statutes to solve legal problems and construct legal arguments.

- Predict the probable judicial resolution of simulated legal disputes using hypothetical fact patterns as a basis for legal analysis.

- Write an inner office memorandum of law predicting the probable judicial resolution of a similar legal dispute in a form that conforms to basic professional conventions.

- Recognize excellent writing in and about the law and to learn techniques for improving one's own legal writing.

AN INTRODUCTION TO LEGAL RESEARCH

Section A Skill Objectives—Students will be able to:

- Understand basic legal research terminology.
- Understand basic legal research methodology.
- Use online research databases and resources.

Section A Outline:

- Introduction and Important Definitions
- Finding The Law
- Relevant Law: A Case "On Point"
- Legal Research Process Overview & Flowchart
- Legal Research Guides & Online Research Resources

The only true wisdom is in knowing you know nothing.

Unknown Author

Introduction

Legal research is defined as the process of identifying and finding legal information needed to support legal analysis. Legal research is practiced by lawyers, law librarians, para-legals and anyone seeking legal information. Legal information can be researched in books, legal research websites and free information portals, or for a membership fee from data providers such as LexisNexis and Westlaw.

Legal research involves:

- Finding primary authority (cases, statutes, regulations)
- Finding secondary authority on a specific legal topic
- Finding non-legal sources for supporting information.

Before you learn how to brief case law and to understand statutes, you have to learn how to find case law and statutes. Before I begin to discuss how to go about doing legal research, I need to provide a few important definitions.

Common Law: In the U.S. our legal system is an evolving body of law created by judges when they decide cases. Their decisions (opinions) are printed and are legally binding.

<u>Statutes</u>: Federal and state legislative bodies pass statutes (laws), which are also legally binding.

<u>Administrative Law</u>: A third source of law created by administrative agencies such as the department of environmental protection. These laws are like statutes and are binding on all those to whom they apply. NB: The above three sources of law are called <u>primary sources of law</u> because they are all legally binding.

<u>Precedent</u>: Cases that have been previously decided. Lower courts in the same jurisdiction must adhere to the rules of law opinioned previously by higher courts. Decisions from the same jurisdiction, binding on lower courts in that jurisdiction, are called *mandatory authority*. Decisions from courts in other jurisdictions are not binding and are called *persuasive authority*. This means a case decided by an outside court <u>may</u> be used to reach a similar holding (conclusion).

<u>Case Law</u>: The written opinions of appellate courts that decide contested legal issues raised during litigation of cases (civil & criminal) at the trial courts.

<u>Stare Decisis Doctrine</u>: A doctrine that mandates that precedent cases must be followed. Under this doctrine, similar cases are decided in a similar manner so that judgments are consistent. This way, attorneys may predict the outcome of a case based on prior holdings in similar cases. When attorneys research the law they are looking for prior similar cases decided in their jurisdiction.

<u>Primary Sources of Law—Chronological Publication</u>: Primary sources of law, such as case law and statutes, are published chronologically, along a timeline. Without regard to content or substance, case opinions and statutes are published in the order they were decided or enacted. This makes find law by *subject* very hard. One must use research resources such as encyclopedias and digests. Primary sources of law are published officially and commercially.

Statutes are printed as *codes* according to subject, are printed chronologically and compile statutes within a jurisdiction (New York) into a code (examples: New York Penal Code, New York Vehicle and Traffic Code). An *annotated code* lists statutes plus abstracts of judicial opinions along with citations to those opinions.

<u>Shepard's Citations</u>: A listing of every case that cites to (or is related to) a previous case. It also lists any changes to statutes and case law that is related to the statute. Shepardizing can tell you if a case has been overruled.

<u>Secondary Sources of Law</u>: Are not legally binding. Examples include legal periodicals, legal encyclopedias, legal texts and legal treatises. Secondary sources of law help attorneys to under-

stand a problem or legal issue and often direct the attorney to relevant primary sources of law. These explain legal concepts and help the attorney to understand the primary sources of law.

Legal Encyclopedias—Organized alphabetically by topic, explain legal doctrine. A good way to find citations but not considered persuasive authority because of the broad analysis they contain. Two examples of national legal encyclopedias are Corpus Juris Secundum (West Publishing) and American Jurisprudence 2d (Lawyers Co-operative Publishing).

State Legal Encyclopedias—Arranged like the national encyclopedias described above but specific to the law of one particular state. For example, in New York we use an encyclopedia called New York Jurisprudence 2d (Lawyers Co-op. Publishing).

Legal Texts—Summaries, guides and commentaries for understanding developing legislation and case law. Some trace legal history. Others offer a general overview of a legal subject, such as torts (see West's Hornbook and Nutshell series). Hornbooks offer a single volume overview of the law on a legal subject, such as contract law.

These are used by law students to see how course material is broken down or organized. Hornbooks are written by experts in a given field of law. Nutshells are small paperback volumes published by West that explain single legal subjects, just like hornbooks, but these are much shorter and more concise.

Legal Periodicals—Secondary sources of law which contain citations to and analysis of primary sources of law. These include the following:

Academic Law Reviews—Produced at major law schools and provide a complete discussion new legal developments and issues regarding case law and statutes. Law review journals are edited by law students.

Bar Association Literature & Periodicals—Devoted to particular areas of practice.

Commercial Journals—Subject specialized as law specialization has increased, published commercially or by public interest groups. These focus on recent developments in the law of specific legal areas. Used by busy attorney practitioners, these are brief and lack deep analysis. *Legal Newsletters in Print* (Infosources) describes hundreds of specialized journals & newsletters and how to subscribe to them.

More Secondary Sources of Law:

Treatises—An exhaustive discussion of an area of law in narrative form. Some treatises are many volumes in length and they include so much highly detailed information that they are not useful for law students. Treatises are written by legal experts for attorneys and judges in a particular field of practice. Hornbooks (discussed earlier) are like mini treatises. They are useful for law students because they offer a concise and direct discussion of the law. My favorite hornbook in law school was *Prosser on Torts*.

Legal Outlines—Commercially created, usually soft cover, booklets that summarize (outline) one law school course, such as torts for example. I do not recommend that you rely on these outlines instead of creating your own course outlines (more on this later).

Canned Briefs—Like outlines, case brief books are commercially created and sometimes correspond to specific law text books (case books). I do not recommend that you rely on these instead of briefing your own cases. If you are called on in class to discuss a case, and your familiarity with the case came from a canned brief, you will be unprepared to answer deep analytical questions regarding that case. Commercially written briefs sometimes miss central issues and are so brief that they may explain very complicated legal issues in a manner that is too superficial or vague.

Computer Research—Lexis and Westlaw are the two main systems for conducting legal research.

Issues of Fact: Determined at the trial court level by the trier of fact (judge or jury). Facts determined may not be appealed unless there was a problem with the fact finding process.

Issues of Law: Decided by the trial judge and can be appealed to an intermediate level court of appeals, then to a higher court of appeals, and then the highest level of appeals (the court of last resort). At each level of appeal the issues raised are considered by appeal judges who then write and publish opinions (case law). These opinions usually contain a holding which is a declaration that sums up the opinion of the court on one or two sentences. The holding is binding on similar future cases because it is precedent.

How Decisions Are Published:

Not all published decisions are formatted in the exact same way. But some components are relatively standard, such as the following:

Caption—Names the parties to the case and case cite (Smith v. Jones, 188 AD2 90).

Syllabus—Summary of relevant facts containing head notes related to different points or issues that were decided by the court.

Names of Judge(s)

Brief Opinion—The holding, with concurrences and dissents (agreements and disagreements among the judges who decided the case).

Case Facts & Law

Holding—The court's answer as to the issues presented for review.

Reasoning—The court's reasoning for the holding. May be omitted.

Dissents Elaborated—Any judges who did not agree with the majority decision may elaborate on their own view of the facts and law, and why they would reach a different holding. A dissent is not part of the final ruling and is not considered precedent language.

The following case opinion illustrates how a decision is commonly published.

The PEOPLE of the State of New York, Respondent,

v.

Eddie MATOS, Appellant

Court of Appeals of New York

83 N.Y.2d 509 (1994)

OPINION OF THE COURT

CIPARICK, Judge.

The issue to be considered in this appeal is under what circumstances a fleeing felon's actions cause another's death for purposes of Penal Law § 125.25(3), the felony murder statute.

There was evidence at trial that, in the early morning hours of October 17, 1989, defendant, Eddie Matos, and two accomplices broke into a McDonald's restaurant on Seventh Avenue and 40th Street in Manhattan by shattering the glass door with a sledgehammer. Once inside, Matos and his accomplices rounded up the employees at gunpoint. A maintenance worker, however, managed to escape and then returned to the restaurant with three police officers. As they approached the restaurant, they saw Matos run toward the back of the [p. 511] restaurant. The officers ran into the restaurant in time to see Matos climb up a ladder that led to the roof. Police Officer Dwyer hurriedly climbed up the ladder right behind Matos. About 10 seconds later, another officer, Sergeant Flanagan, proceeded up the ladder to the roof and later discovered Dwyer lying on his back about 25 feet down an airshaft. It took emergency services personnel about 45 minutes to rescue Dwyer from the airshaft, but he was later pronounced dead at Bellevue Hospital.

The Appellate Division affirmed the conviction of murder in the second degree, burglary in the second degree and attempted robbery. The Court concluded that the elements of felony murder were established, 191 A.D.2d 383, 595 N.Y.S.2d 207. A Judge of this Court granted leave to appeal and we now affirm.

It is well established that in order for criminal responsibility to attach, a defendant's actions must have been an actual contributory cause of death (People v. Stewart, 40 N.Y.2d 692, 697, 389 N.Y.S.2d 804, 358 N.E.2d 487). It must be shown that the defendant sets in motion the events which ultimately result in the victim's death (People v. Kibbe, 35 N.Y.2d 407, 362 N.Y.S.2d 848, 321 N.E.2d 773). However, the defendant's acts need not be the sole cause of death (Matter of Anthony M., 63 N.Y.2d 270, 280, 481 N.Y.S.2d 675, 471 N.E.2d 447).

Here, defendant's conduct set in motion and legally caused the death of Police Officer Dwyer. Had defendant not first committed an armed violent felony and then attempted to escape by way of the roof, the officer would not have pursued him onto the roof, thereafter plunging to his death in the airshaft.

The trial court stressed to the jury that "but for" causation was only one step in determining cause in the criminal context, an aspect defendant-appellant does not dispute. Additionally, the jury was told that it must also find that defendant's conduct was a sufficiently direct cause of the ensuing death before it could impose criminal responsibility. The defendant's conduct qualifies as a sufficiently direct cause when the ultimate harm should have been reasonably foreseen (People v. Kibbe, 35 N.Y.2d, at 412, 362 N.Y.S.2d 848, 321 N.E.2d 773, supra).

The accused need not commit the final, fatal act to be culpable for causing death. In Kibbe, the fatal act was inflicted by a passing truck driver who struck and killed the victim. The defendants were held to have caused his death, for the event was a directly foreseeable consequence of their own earlier act of abandoning the victim on the shoulder of a [p. 512] highway. In People v. Kern, 75 N.Y.2d 638, 555 N.Y.S.2d 647, 554 N.E.2d 1235, the "Howard Beach" defendants were held to have caused their victim's death even though he was actually killed by the intervening act of a passing motorist.

In People v. Hernandez, 82 N.Y.2d 309, 604 N.Y.S.2d 524, 624 N.E.2d 661, this Court held that the defendants initiated or participated in the chain of events that led to an officer's death by attempting to rob an undercover officer in a failed drug transaction. Since, in initiating a gun battle, they should have foreseen that someone's bullet might go astray, their conduct was a sufficiently direct cause of a backup officer's death even though the shot which killed him was fired by another officer. The Court held (supra, at 319, 604 N.Y.S.2d 524, 624 N.E.2d 661) that "immediate flight and attempts to thwart apprehension are patently within the furtherance of the cofelons' criminal objective," citing People v. Gladman, 41 N.Y.2d 123, 390 N.Y.S.2d 912, 359 N.E.2d 420. The Court further noted that foreseeability does not mean that the result must be the most likely event.

In the instant case, the jury was correctly given the issue as to whether it was foreseeable that upon defendant's attempt to escape by way of the roof, he would be pursued by an officer. In those circumstances it should also be foreseeable that someone might fall while in hot pursuit across urban roofs in the middle of the night.

Accordingly, the order of the Appellate Division should be affirmed.

KAYE, C.J., and SIMONS, BELLACOSA, SMITH and LEVINE, JJ., concur.

TITONE, J., taking no part.

END OF DOCUMENT

Legal Research Process Overview

1. Decide on the question or issue to be researched.

2. Research the broad subject area—legal encyclopedias, hornbooks, nutshells, codes.

3. Find related case law (cites) and statutes (code)—to find the answer to your question.

4. Stop research—upon finding the answer, all related authority or when cost exceeds benefit.

The Issue or Question:

You must determine how the courts look at the issue at hand to see which cases are ultimately relevant. You must find out how the courts in <u>your jurisdiction</u> have evaluated your set of facts and what legal rules they have applied to those facts. The case law and statutes are organized by big categories (contracts, criminal law, torts, wills) with countless subcategories.

So, be certain that you are looking up the correct legal issue or question. If you start researching the wrong issue you will find cases that are NOT relevant to your facts. When starting research it is best to cast a wide net and then narrow your scope as you go along. But stay focused on the right issue(s). Keep firmly in your mind what the issue is.

Next, go to secondary authority (such as legal encyclopedias, treatises, restatements of law, WestLaw, Lexis) to get an overview of the issue you are researching. Such sources have great footnotes and millions of cites to decided cases. Secondary sources of law are not "law". They are summaries of the law and are never controlling precedent, but they will lead you to primary sources of law.

Next, you must look for legally and factually similar cases using cites found. This means that you must find, read and analyze many, many cases. You sift through them to find the few cases that are controlling and on-point.

Then take the controlling cases and go backwards in time by finding and reading earlier opinions that are used as precedent by the court who wrote the original opinion. By doing this you may find earlier cases that are relevant to your issue. If you find earlier cases that are relevant you must repeat the process for the precedent cases cited therein.

ust as you checked for earlier relevant cases, you must next look for subsequent relevant cases—you must go forward. To do this use Shepard's to see if later courts have cited back to the relevant cases you found. You then take those relevant cases and read all precedent cases contained therein. Shepardizing is important as well because it shows if a case you found has been overruled or if the holding has been limited or expanded.

You must go backwards and forward for every relevant case. It is time consuming and tedious but crucial. There will rarely be just one answer to your original question. Every opinion will be slightly different from the facts of your hypothetical as no two cases are identical. Like snowflakes. The law is never so clear that the one opinion that you did NOT find will hold the perfect answer to your question. You will never know for certain that you have found all relevant law. At some point you will have to stop researching. As your legal research skills develop, you will know better when to stop. If you start seeing the same opinions over and over again, with no new cases arising, you are very close to finding all of the opinions that are out there relevant to your question.

What Does "Relevant" Mean?

Two levels of relevance are legal relevance and factual relevance. You need both. A great opinion is one with your same legal question/issue and facts that are very similar to the ones in your fact pattern. If you do not find a case with almost identical facts, look for one with analogous facts. If your case involves a house destroyed by flames try to use a case where a house was destroyed by a flood, or a boat destroyed by flames. If you do not find an opinion that contains a legal issue exactly like yours, try to find one with an analogous legal issue. It is easier to find legally relevant cases than to find factually similar cases.

Legal Relevance—if the legal issue is different than your issue the case is probably not relevant. If a case is not discussing the same legal issue that your facts implicate, it is not legally relevant. For example, if a case issue is criminal assault but your issue is a tort assault then the opinion is not legally relevant.

Factual Relevance—If a case you find involves a similar or analogous set of facts to the ones in your fact pattern, it is factually relevant. The more similarities exist between your set of facts and the ones discussed in a decided case, the more likely that the decided case will predict your problem's outcome.

To be useful, a decided case must address BOTH the legal and factual issues in your fact pattern. If it does not, under the doctrine of stare decisis it is not considered precedent or binding.

You will get better at legal research the more you practice doing it. As you gain more experience you will learn which methods of finding the law works best for you. It is very important to keep organized so that you will not waste time looking for and re-reading opinions that you have already read—and possible dismissed as irrelevant.

Most importantly, you must take the time to actually read and re-read (as needed) the decided opinions. You may need to make notes and outlines to understand the case. Diagram the facts if needed. Legal research and understanding opinions are skills which best developed by practice.

After you find relevant cases, think carefully about what they say. Read cases in chronological order to see how the law developed. Read the entire case and not just the part that addresses your issue. Decide of the opinions are favorable or unfavorable to your fact pattern. If they are unfavorable you must find factual distinctions to argue that there should be a different result in your dispute. You must argue how your case is like the cases with good results, and how it is different from the cases with bad results.

There are many different approaches to doing legal research. Here is a basic guide that may be generally followed when doing research:

Legal Research Flowchart

- select topic by identifying relevant facts & legal issues (questions)
- define your topic keywords
- decide which law resources to use (secondary & primary authority)
- start search
- find relevant material
- read and evaluate materials and refine/continue search as needed
- stop searching
- organize research materials
- outline an assessment that addresses the legal issues

Legal Research Methodology

This book offers a general overview of legal research fundamentals. The best way to become familiar with legal research is to have a law librarian or law instructor guide you through the process the first time.

Secondary Sources Are Good Starting Points

Legal encyclopedias are a good first source if you are unfamiliar with law and legal concepts. They combine primary and secondary sources to provide overviews of the law, and they provide citations to relevant authority. The two major legal encyclopedias are: *Corpus Juris Secundum* (*CJS*) and *American Jurisprudence* (*AmJur*), 2nd edition.

Legal Treatises

Are good sources for general information on substantive law. Consulting a treatise on a specific subject will yield background information and citations to statutory or case law.

Identifying Index Terms

When consulting legal treatises, encyclopedias, periodicals, digests, and codes, *index terms* are used to research legal issues. For example, some index terms for dog bite cases are: "dog," "canine," and "domestic animal". The best way to search an index is to begin with a narrow term. Searching under antonyms, synonyms, and associated words of all kinds may lead to useful information.

<u>Next Step: Understanding the Major Types of Law and Jurisdiction</u>

Once you have become familiar with a legal topic from reading about it in a legal encyclopedia, treatise, or other secondary source, you must research it further in a primary legal sources. Before doing so, let us review the three major types of law and the importance of jurisdiction.

The word *law* is often used generically, but there <u>are three categories of law</u>:

<u>Common law or case law</u>: created by a judicial body, such as a Court of Appeals or a Supreme Court.

<u>Statutory law</u>: created by a legislative body, such as the U.S. Congress.

<u>Regulatory law</u>: created and enforced by an administrative body, such as the U.S. Department of Labor.

To complicate matters, these types of laws are created by government bodies in different *jurisdictional entities*, such as:

- federal
- state
- regional
- county
- city

Each jurisdictional entity has government bodies that create common, statutory, and regulatory law. Some legal issues are handled at the federal level, while other issues are the domain of the states. For example, civil rights, immigration, interstate commerce, and constitutional issues are subject to federal jurisdiction. Issues such as property, contracts and criminal laws are generally governed by states, unless there is federal preemption. State laws and terminology will vary from state to state, and there are few comparative guides available.

<u>How To Read Legal Citations</u>

Most primary sources are chronologically arranged. To find them, you use legal citations. In citations, the number preceding the name of the source refers to a volume number. The number following the name of the source refers to the page number on which the cited material begins.

Tables of abbreviations will help you identify an abbreviation. Legal dictionaries, dictionaries of legal abbreviations, and the *Bluebook: A Uniform System of Citation* provide commonly used abbreviations and acronyms.

Recommended Readings:

Cohen, Morris L., and Kent C. Olson. *Legal Research in a Nutshell.* 7th ed. St. Paul: West Publishing Co., 2000.

Jacobstein, J. Myron, Roy M.. Mersky, and Donald J. Dunn. *Fundamentals of Legal Research.* 7th ed. Westbury, N.Y.: The Foundation Press, 1998.

BASIC LEGAL RESEARCH STEPS

Step 1: Preliminary Analysis

A.   Gather & analyze facts.

B.   Identify & arrange legal issues in a logical order.

C.   Prioritize work & research the most important issues first.

Step 2: Start with Secondary Sources: For most legal research it is best to start with a secondary source before going to the primary authorities because you will:

- obtain background information
- learn terms of art
- focus your research
- learn black letter law (basic statutory and case law)
- obtain citations to primary authorities

Step 3: Find and Read Primary Authorities

Primary authorities include court decisions, statutes, regulations, municipal ordinances, and court rules. They are either mandatory/binding or persuasive in terms of their authoritativeness. It is important to understand which authorities are mandatory for your research issues and which are only persuasive.

Sources for finding primary authority are:

Digests: useful for finding case law using topics and key numbers.

Statutory Codes: try to use the annotated versions of the codes, since they often contain cites to related cases, regulations, and/or secondary sources.

Regulations: can be found through (1) indexes to regulatory codes, (2) tables of statutory authorities, or (3) references obtained from annotated statutory codes.

Step 4: Update Your Research

Updating is necessary to 1) ensure the validity of the primary authorities you located, and 2) identify subsequent developments or new authority. Update Sources: pocket parts, supplements, Shepard's, and KeyCite.

Final Tips to Remember for Legal Research

- Prioritize work and research discrete questions separately.

- Always look for relevant statutes / regulations. Case law is not the end all and be all of legal research. Find mandatory authority if it exists.

- Be flexible and creative with respect to your search terms when searching indexes and digests.

- Read the primary authorities yourself—do not rely on secondary source descriptions.

- Consider the law librarian as a resource to consult for assistance, guidance, and suggestions.

LEGAL RESEARCH GUIDES

Legal Research Guides: There are a variety of research guides that are valuable when doing general and specific legal research. Below is a list.

National Research Guides:

Fundamentals of Legal Research (8th edition) by R. Mersky and D. Dunn (Foundation Press 2002)

Legal Research in a Nutshell (9th edition) by M. Cohen et al. (Thomson/West 2007)

Finding the Law (12th edition) by R. Berring and E. Edinger (Thomson/West 2005)

FREE ONLINE LEGAL RESEARCH SOURCES

Legal Portals: Portals are websites that provide links to other informational sources. Below is a list of portals that will link you to free legal websites:

Findlaw.com (for the Legal Professional)—http://lp.findlaw.com/

Cornell Law School's Legal Information Institute—www.law.cornell.edu

The Public Library of Law—http://www.plol.org

Online Databases: There are many free online databases that allow access to primary law. Below are a few:

<u>Case Law</u>: Google Scholar (via an Advanced Search provides published opinions from Federal and state courts)

http://scholar.google.com/advanced_scholar_search?hl=en&as_sdt=2000

<u>Statutes, Legislation, and Court Rules</u>: FDsys (A website of the Government Printing Office that provides access to various federal primary laws.) http://www.gpo.gov/fdsys/search/home.action

<u>THOMAS (Library of Congress)</u>: http://thomas.loc.gov/

<u>U.S. Courts</u>: Includes federal court rules and links to local court rules.

http://www.uscourts.gov/rules/index.html

<u>Administrative Law</u>: FDsys http://www.gpo.gov/fdsys/search/home.action

ADDITIONAL SOURCES OF LAW

Law by State

http://www.law.cornell.edu/states/ny.html

Primary Legal Sources

http://firestone.princeton.edu/law/statutory.php

Secondary Legal Resources

http://www.loc.gov/law/help/secondary-rsrcs.php

New York State Laws

http://www.legallawhelp.com/state_law/New_York

CASE LAW AND BRIEFING CASES

Section B Skill Objectives—Students will be able to:

- Read and understand legal opinions.

- Brief case law.

Section B Outline:

- What Is A Case Brief?
- Why Study Legal Opinions?
- Why Brief Cases?
- Important Parts of a Case Opinion
- Basic Case Law Formula
- Sample Case: Annie Nilan v. Richmond County Gas Light Company (1 AD 235)

The Best Brief Is A Brief Brief.

Judge Richard Posner

What Is A Case Brief?

A case brief is defined as a summary of a reported case that concisely outlines the elements of that case. Those elements are:

-   the parties involved in the case
-   the history of the case (level of appeal and prior outcomes)
-   the issue / question that the present court must address
-   the rules (precedent, primary law) that the court apply to reach a decision
-   how the court applies the rules to the unique facts of the case (legal analysis)
-   the *holding* or resolution that the court reaches regarding the issue

These elements are formatted into the following parts of a case brief:

- case history (procedure)	- governing law (rules)
- relevant facts	- legal analysis / reasoning
- the issue (argument or dispute)	- disposition / holding

Note that case briefs never contain your personal opinions about a case. The only opinion that matters is that of the reviewing court. The most relevant facts are those that are stressed by the court. By relevant I mean that they are important to the overall understanding of the case itself.

Case briefs distill and simplify reported case law. Case law itself is written by judges in a simple format that contains essential components. Case briefs contain the same components in a format that mirrors the format used by courts to record decisions.

Why is this important: because to "write like a lawyer" on final exams you have to use a similar format—ARAC (discussed later in detail).

Why Study Legal Opinions?

During your first few weeks in law school you will start to read, brief and discuss case law (also known as legal opinions). By doing so, you will develop an important skill required by practicing attorneys. Attorneys must be able to apply the law to the unique situations presented by clients (legal analysis). Sometimes, a rule that seems fairly clear may become unclear in application.

For example, a law may state that there is "No Sleeping Allowed in the Park". That law may have been adopted to prevent homeless people from camping out and sleeping on park benches. You client tells you that he was issued a citation for violating that rule when he dozed off for a few minutes, on a park bench, sitting upright, while reading a newspaper.

As you study legal rules, you must train yourself to be creative and to imagine how a law applies, where it is unclear and how that may lead to unexpected results. The case study method and hypothetical exams will train you to think like a lawyer. To learn to look at the law the way attorneys do, like judges do, you must study actual cases—AKA case law, AKA legal opinions—AKA precedent cases.

Why Brief Cases (when you can buy them already briefed or "canned") ?

When you brief a case you write your own summary of it. Briefing cases will help you to understand how judges and lawyers analyze fact patterns in light of the law. Briefing cases will also condense long cases into "brief" summaries that are easier to use when studying for exams and when writing memorandums of law or appellate briefs.

Briefing case opinions also helps you to read cases efficiently and effectively—with greater understanding. None of the above will be true if you only copy the court's language without carefully analyzing what happened in the case. Briefing cases is an important skill that you must master in law school.

As you break down case opinions into briefs, you will develop a greater and permanent understanding of the decision. If you use commercially prepared case brief study aids instead of briefing your own cases, you will not fully understand the case and you will forget it much sooner.

When you brief a case, put the following elements into *your own words*:

- case history (procedure)   - governing law (rules)

- relevant facts   - legal analysis / reasoning

- the issue (argument or dispute)   - disposition / holding

I recommend briefing cases out in full for the first few weeks of law school. After that, you should brief cases using highlighters or with margin notes. The time you save not briefing out cases in full can be better spent reading and reasoning out the law. Stop copying it over—use the time to understand it better. NB: Brief cases using the particular format your professor suggests.

Briefing cases is usually part of a larger research project, such as writing a memorandum of law.

Important Parts Of A Case Opinion

When you read case law you should focus on the facts, arguments, disposition, holding and reasoning of the case. The law is highly *fact sensitive*. Hypothetical law exams are likewise highly fact sensitive. Your professors will devote a great deal of class time to discussing the specific facts of assigned cases.

The **ARGUMENT** is the question that the attorneys to a dispute present to a judge for resolution. A judge must resolve very specific points of disagreement. You must understand the argument(s) posed by opposing attorneys.

The **DISPOSITION** of a case is the action taken by the court. For example, an appellate judge may *reverse* the disposition of a lower court. The judge may *affirm* the decision of the court below (agree with the lower court's opinion). The lower court's decision may likewise be *vacated* (this disposition erases the lower court's decision from the records). Finally, the case at bar (the case being decided) may be *remanded* (sent back down to the court below for additional proceedings).

Judges use different types of law to justify an opinion. They rely on statutes, the Constitution, precedent cases and the common law. The *common law* refers to case law decisions based on the law in England prior to 1776. That early law was brought to the States by the colonists.

Judge's decisions are bound by established precedent. Precedent cases are those that have already been decided by past courts and which involve similar facts and issues. *Stare decisis et non quieta movere* means "Maintain what has been decided and do not alter that which has been established." This concept is abbreviated as stare decisis.

Judges may also reason out a decision based on public policy issues and fairness. A judge will use any or all of these justifications to reach a holding. A holding is any ruling or decision by a court / judge / bench of judges. It is a clear rule set out by the deciding court which has the effect of resolving the argument or issue that was presented to the court. The court's opinion may also contain extra language or remarks that are not needed to resolve the case. These remarks are known as dicta or mere dicta (mere words, filler or "yadda-yadda").

A dissent is a statement of disagreement between the majority of judges on an appellate bench and the minority of judges on that bench. Judges do not always agree as to the holding. The dissent does not affect the holding. Only the holding becomes new precedent law.

Not all judicial opinions / case law are well written and clear. Some may be vague and confusing. Some may be poorly written with no clearly stated holding. You may have to re-read a case several times to understand it. Sometimes you do understand the opinion but do not agree with it. It is valuable to learn how to think independently regarding holdings and opinions. If all holdings were correct there would be no need for our system of appeals. Some decisions are just *plain wrong* and they get overturned upon appeal to a higher court.

NB: Buy a legal dictionary and look up every word that you do not understand while reading case law.

Basic Case Law Formula

Case law / judicial opinions tend to follow the same formula, format or layout. That format is the outcome of *centuries* of judicial thought, practice and history. Most cases contain an introduction followed by the full body of the opinion. Here is the basic format of a case opinion:

Caption: Includes the title of the case with information about the litigants.

Example: People v. Clyburn (This is a criminal case brought by The People of the State of New York against defendant Clyburn.

Cite: The deciding court, official reporter (book) in which the opinion is published and the volume and page number where the opinion is found.

Example: 46 NY2d 109 New York Court of Appeals, vol. 46 p.109

Author: Name of judge(s) who wrote the opinion. (NB: "J" = judge.)

Example: Anderson, J.

History:

The procedural history of the case which includes hearings, motions trials and sentences that have already taken place.

Facts:

The relevant facts of the case. These may be discussed in great detail or in very little detail by the court.

Issue:
Issue: The question presented to the court for analysis and resolution. There may be more than one issue. Each issue is expressed as one sentence and as a question or as a statement that begins with the word "whether".

<u>Law (Rules)</u>: A discussion of precedent related to the case at bar. This background information will support the court's holding. The law referenced will also be applied to the facts of the case (legal analysis).

<u>Holding</u>: The court's answer to the issues. Each issue is answered.

<u>Dissent</u>: While many appellate decisions are unanimous, many are the opinion of the majority of the judges deciding the case. If one or more of the judges in the minority wish to, they may write a dissent to express how they would have decided the case differently. Sometimes a judge agrees with the outcome but for different reasons. In that case he writes a *concurring* opinion to explain his own rational for the holding.

When I first read a case law it was like reading a foreign language that was only similar to English. I recognized the words but could not translate them into clear meaning. That is because I had not yet acquired the ability to think like a lawyer. The cases contained unfamiliar terms (some in Latin) and technical legal jargon. The older cases were especially difficult to understand because the judges used complicated wording that has been replaced in newer cases with more simple writing.

The following is a simple case decided in 1896 by the Second Department Appellate Division by Judge Willard Bartlett.

Assignment: Read the following case and try to highlight each opinion section discussed above.

Annie Nilan, as Administratrix, etc. of James Nilan, Deceased, Appellant v. Richmond County Gas Light Company, Respondent.

1 AD 235

Negligence—a gas company's employee throwing dirt out of a trench which frightens passing horses.

In an action brought to recover damages resulting from the death of the plaintiff's intestate, caused as alleged by the negligence of the defendant, a gas company, it appeared that the defendant was lawfully constructing a trench in the street in which it intended to lay a service gas pipe; that the trench did not extend entirely across the street, and that there was room enough left between it and the curb for the passage of a four horse wagon, loaded with beer kegs, upon which the plaintiff's intestate was riding; that the driver of this wagon had his horses under control; that the leading horses, when opposite the trench, shied at the earth thrown out by the laborers in the trench; that the driver pulled them over again, when the rear part of the wagon slewed against the curb towards which the ground slanted, whereupon "the kegs and everything came down," and the deceased and the driver were thrown off.

Held, that the only possible ground of recovery must be based upon the fact that earth was thrown out of the trench while the team was passing, and that such act did not constitute negligence.

Motion by the plaintiff, Annie Nilan, as administratrix, etc. of James Nilan, deceased, for a new trial on a case containing exception orders to be heard at the Appellate Division in the first instance, upon the dismissal of the complaint directed by a court after a trial at the Richmond Circuit before the court and a jury. Also, an appeal by said plaintiff from an order entered in the office of the clerk of the County of Richmond on the 30th day of September, 1985, denying the plaintiff's motion to set aside said dismissal of the complaint for a new trial.

Charles A. B. Pratt and *Edward A. Hibbard*, for the plaintiff and appellant.

Sidney F. Rawson, for the defendant and respondent.

Willard Bartlett, J.:

This action was brought to recover damages for the alleged negligence of the defendant corporation in so carelessly excavating a trench upon a highway in Richmond County as to cause the plaintiff's intestate to be thrown from a wagon in which he was riding and suffer injuries which resulted in death. The accident occurred on Central Avenue in the town of Castleton on the afternoon of December 31, 1984.

The defendant, through his servants and agents, was engaged in constructing a trench across a portion of Central Avenue, in which to law a gas pipe. This trench left space enough between it and the curb on one side of the avenue for the passage of the wagon in which the plaintiff's intestate rode. This wagon was a beer truck drawn by four horses. It was capable of carrying ninety four quarter kegs of beer, and was laden with a considerable number at the time. The driver testifies that as he approached the trench he did not see the men working in it, as he could not see how deep it was until he came right opposite, when it seemed to be from five and a half to six feet deep. Coming down the avenue he had on the brakes as tight as they could be held and he had his horses under full control when he passed the trench.

The manner in which the accident occurred is thus described by his witness: "In passing the trench, my lead horses were right opposite the trench when a man in the trench threw out some earth which made my horses shy and they swerved to the left side of the sidewalk and I pulled them over again, in pulling them over the rear part of the wagon slewed against the curb and the first thing I knew I was thrown over the horses, and the kegs and everything came down and Nilan was thrown over."

The driver further testified that the space over which he tried to drive slanted toward the curb, having a fall of about six inches; that his horses were half way past the excavation when they shied; that the horses were under full control and did not run at all until he was thrown off; and that after the leaders shied he still had them under control.

It is plain from this statement of facts (which seem to me as favorable to the plaintiff as the evidence will justify), that the sole ground on which any negligence could be imputed to the defendant is suggested by the seventh request of plaintiff's counsel, in which he asked to go to the jury on the question whether the throwing of the dirt from the excavation while the horses were passing constituted negligence.

There is no evidence that the defendant was not authorized to do the work that it was engaged in doing. The excavation did not prevent vehicles from passing to and fro, for, as a matter of fact, there was sufficient space left for the passage of this beer truck, and it actually did pass, inasmuch as, according to the driver's testimony, he was about ten feet beyond the excavation when he was thrown out of the wagon.

He knew the situation perfectly—just where the trench was and just what space he had to drive through—and it is manifest from what he says about the condition of the brakes and his control over his horses that he could not have had them better in hand if he had been expressly informed in advance that a few shovelfuls of earth would be thrown from the ditch as he approached the excavation.

This brings the case right down to the question whether negligence can be predicated of such an act as simply shoveling soil out of a trench in the course of work properly being performed on a public highway, merely because horses may be caused thereby to shy.

There is no suggestion that anything struck any of the horses, or that there was anything extraordinary in the way of throwing the earth. The learned trial judge evidently thought that to pronounce the conduct of the defendant negligence, even under the most favorable view of the circumstances for the plaintiff, would be to impose too onerous a burden of care upon those engaged in work of this character. I

In this conclusion I think he was right. It would be practically impossible to guard against the happening of every event which might chance to frighten a timid team.

It seems unreasonable to require the exercise of exceptional care simply because it sometimes happens that a very trifling occurrence will occasionally induce a sensitive horse to shy. In my opinion, the proof failed to make our any negligence on the part of the agents of the defendant leading to the injury to the plaintiff's intestate, and hence the complaint was properly dismissed.

For these reasons I think that the plaintiff's exceptions should be overruled and the order denying the motion for a new trial should be affirmed.

Exceptions overruled and motion for a new trial denied, with costs. Judgment directed to be entered in accordance with the direction of the trial court.

END OF DOCUMENT

ADDITIONAL READING:

How to Brief A Case

http://www.lib.jjay.cuny.edu/research/brief.html

Lear How to Write A Case Brief

http://www.4lawschool.com/howto.htm

How to Brief A Case

http://www.4lawschool.com/howto.htm

LEGAL ANALYSIS:

LOGICAL REASONING AND LAWYERLY WRITING

Section C Skill Objectives—Students will be able to:

- Appreciate the origin of the law and legal theories which have given rise to current definitions of law.

- Identify the features of case law and statutory law and the objectives of law in society.

- Understand legal reasoning in the judicial (case law) and legislative processes (statutes).

- Apply case and statutory law in an analytical framework utilizing the principles of analogies, distinctions, and canons of construction to write an objective legal memorandum.

Section C Outline:

- The Reasoning Behind the Method
- Sample (Simple) Hypothetical Fact Pattern: Dog Bite Law
- What Is Legal Analysis?
- Sample Legal Analysis In A Hypothetical Parrot Case

Law school taught me one thing; how to take two situations that are exactly the same and show how they are different.

Hart Pomerantz

The Reasoning Behind the Method

Why must law students study case law? To study case law is to study the <u>process of legal analysis</u>. In published case opinions, judges and their law clerks apply existing law (precedent cases and statutes) to the particular set of facts presented in the case at bar. "At bar" means the case presently before the bench. "The bench" means the panel of judges deciding the case at bar. The judges must apply the law to the facts of the case at bar to so as to reach a fair decision (or *holding*) that aligns with policy. The judges are aware that their decision (opinion, holding) will become new precedent that will influence and shape future case analysis and future court decisions.

The <u>reason</u> that you must master the skill of legal analysis on law school exams is that you will need to use that skill to <u>pass the bar exam</u>. You will also apply that skill as a practicing attorney when a potential client walks into your office. But let us not put the cart before the horse. The bar exam comes first. Remember, you do not practice law in law school. You practice legal *skills* that you will use to pass the bar exam. If you do not pass the bar exam later practice will be out of the question. The following is an overview of typical law school learning progression:

1. Learn to understand case law by briefing cases and becoming skilled at recognizing the important elements of those cases (relevant facts, relevant parties, issues, precedent and the holding). NB: On an exam you will be examining a dense fact pattern and not an appellate case. Legal analysis is not the same thing as case analysis.

2. Learn to understand statutory law by breaking it down into basic elements that you later prove or disprove on an exam by applying the facts of a hypothetical to those elements. Learn the scope of application for each element.

3. Take law school exams by using #1 and #2 above to develop and sharpen your <u>legal analysis</u> and <u>writing skills</u> to reach your own "holding" on exams. NB: Appellate holdings are often long, convoluted and elaborate reasoning structures. On a law exam you will not have time for that type of writing. There will be many more issues packed into a fact pattern than are examined in a typical appellate case.

4. Pass the bar exam essay portion by applying legal analysis and writing skills gained from taking law exams. Pass the multiple choice aspect of the bar exam based on the law you have studied during law school classes.

5. THEN practice law by using the above skill rehearsal and training to analyze potential cases brought to you by prospective clients. When a new client comes into your office seeking help, he does not know the law. You do. The client will tell you his story (his set of facts just like in a hypothetical) and you must be able to apply the law

learned in law school to his facts to extract the important underlying legal issues (like issue spotting on a law exam). As a lawyer you will ask the client questions, consider evidence and conduct legal research to decide whether to accept the case and how to best represent the client.

Legal Analysis of a Simple Hypothetical Fact Pattern

During any law school semester students are taught the substantive law and they examine related case law and statutes. For example, during 1L students learn contract law and brief cases relating to offer, acceptance and consideration. At the end of the semester the students are presented with a hypothetical fact pattern final exam. "Hypothetical" means imaginary or theoretical. These fact patterns mimic the set of facts which may be presented to an attorney by a client for legal analysis.

Law students prepare for real legal practice by analyzing final exam fact patterns. They apply all of the law learned during the semester to the fact pattern. For example, students apply everything learned in contracts class to a contract based final exam. For our purposes, I will introduce you to the law of dog bites.

Overview of law regarding liability for damages suffered in a dog attack.

When we learned to tame wild animals they became "domesticated". The Restatement (Second) of Torts defines a domestic animal as:

"An animal that is by custom devoted to the service of mankind at the time and in the place where it is kept."

Domestication meant that wild animals came in closer contact with man and society. Man then made laws to govern animals. Since ancient times, the law makes owners of animals responsible for damage that his animals cause. Until recently, most domesticated animals were used for farming and herding purposes.

The common law is founded in this agricultural use of animals. Those animals had rare interaction with city people. After the Industrial Revolution, farming was a smaller sector of the economy, resulting in increasing exposure of city people to animals. This resulted in the evolution of the laws which relate to wild and domesticated animals. According to the common law, there are three theories of liability that can be raised against the owners of animals to make them responsible for the damage done by their animals.

I. Strict Liability for Trespass

The owner of an animal is strictly liable for the damage caused by his animal's trespass on someone else's land, including damage to crops.

II. Strict Liability for Injury Caused by Dangerous Animals

Society has decided that the risk of harm from wild or dangerous animals outweighs the social use or benefit of the animal. Thus, the owner of an animal with <u>known dangerous propensities</u> is strictly liable for the injuries which the animal causes.

The possessor of a <u>wild animal</u> (example: Lion) is <u>strictly liable</u> for harm arising from the dangerous propensities <u>characteristic of wild animals of its class</u>, whether or not the owner believes the animal is safe or free from those propensities. However, if a <u>domesticated animal's</u> owner <u>knows</u> that his domesticated animal has dangerous propensities, with "dangerous" meaning "likely to inflict serious injury", the owner is responsible for the injuries caused by those dangerous propensities—according to the Restatement (Second) of Torts, Section 509 which reads:

(1)   A possessor of a domestic animal that he knows or has reason to know has dangerous propensities abnormal to its class, is subject to liability for harm done by the animal to another, even though he has used the utmost care to prevent it from doing harm.

(2)   This liability is limited to harm that results from the dangerous propensity of which the owner knows or has reason to know.

III. Negligence

At common law the owner of a <u>domestic animal</u> is not liable for injuries caused by the animal unless the injuries were the result of a <u>vicious propensity</u> of which the owner <u>had notice or knowledge of</u>. Liability for foreseeable harm is imposed only after proof that the particular animal:

(1)   demonstrated a dangerous propensity that
(2)   caused the plaintiff's injury and
(3)   that the defendant had actual or constructive knowledge of that propensity

<u>Proving Actual or Constructive Knowledge</u>

There are three ways to prove prior knowledge:

1.   By establishing a history of the dog's prior attacks or other injurious behavior which permits a reasonable person to draw the inference that the dog is likely to engage in

such behavior again. One or two prior bites may not be enough to prove dangerous propensity. One must consider the circumstances surrounding the prior bites. For example, a dog stung by a bee that is frightened and in pain, may bite as a natural reaction to those circumstances without exhibiting a vicious propensity.

2.   A second way to prove knowledge is when the owner has seen or heard enough to convince him of his animal's inclination to commit the injury charged against it. The old English common law maxim, ``A dog is entitled to a first bite (one free bite rule),'' is still true in states that have not enacted statues to the contrary.

3.   A third way to prove knowledge is by using circumstantial evidence and/or the testimony of expert witnesses to prove the commonly understood dangerous propensities of the dog in question. Example: reputation in the neighborhood, the purpose for keeping the dog (pet v. watch dog), posted warnings, etc.

Negligence liability may arise from any type of dog attack, even one which does not result in a "bite" or "tearing" of the skin. Example: liability against a dog owner for injuries caused when the dog jumped on plaintiff and knocked her to the ground causing her to break a leg.

Animal Injury Defenses

Claims may be denied or recovery diminished by the actions of the plaintiff which are termed:

"assumption of risk"

"contributory" or "comparative" fault / negligence

Assumption of the risk is a person's voluntary action which means that he has waived any duty of due care owed to him by other people. For example, this absolute defense generally arises in the voluntary participation in a sporting event. But it may also be applicable in a dog injury case.

More frequently, the defense of "contributory" or "comparative" negligence is used. This is plaintiff's own negligence which contributed to his injuries. In most states a jury determines a percentage of responsibility of the defendant and of the plaintiff, and will make the defendant responsible only for his share of liability. The most common example of contributory negligence is when the plaintiff has provoked the dog into attacking him. Provocation is defined as "something that arouses anger or animosity".

When a plaintiff has intentionally excited a dog, he is partially at fault when the dog reacts in a normal or expected manner. Many states have found the following conduct as the basis of holding a plaintiff partially or wholly at fault for a dog attack:

Coming into contact with the dog; touching; striking; petting, stroking, handling; pulling or pushing the dog's chain or an object in the dog's mouth; hugging; straddling or attempting to ride; carrying; kicking or pushing with foot; stepping on or falling over; throwing objects at; Spraying with a hose; coming into the proximity of the dog; approaching the dog nearing a fence which is restraining the dog, putting body parts through the fence; approaching the dog in a yard, porch, or in a building; presence in the home where the dog lives; opening the door of the house with the dog behind it; encountering a dog on the street, either walking or riding; encouraging the dog to enter the plaintiff's own house or yard; other actions directed at or near the dog; waiving objects or hands; getting involved in a dog fight; attempting to restrain the dog; shouting, yelling, stamping, jumping, staring at the dog or the dog's owner; interacting with the dog despite knowledge of the dog's vicious propensities or history of prior bites.

Our Parrot Fact Pattern:

Mary purchased a parrot from a parrot breeder. The parrot was kept as a pet in a large metal cage kept in the living room. The cage door was secured with a combination lock. Mary's parrot was hand raised in a gentle fashion by the breeder and by Mary so it was very tame. The parrot had never bitten Mary before. It only used its powerful beak to break open nut shells, to climb and to groom. It would often climb up Mary's arm or leg by holding onto the fabric of her shirt or pants. The parrot would also sometimes take food directly from Mary's hand. One night during a violent thunderstorm, a loud crack of thunder frightened the parrot and it bit Mary, but did not break the skin. It just left a bruise.

While the parrot was still with the breeder it was frightened by the breeder's husband when he clapped his hands loudly near the parrot to get its attention. The parrot bit the breeder's husband and he needed 3 stitches to close the wound. The breeder did not tell Mary about the incident.

On July 22, 2010 Mary invited her friend John to her house to pick up some books that he wanted to borrow. Mary let John into the house through the back door directly into the dining room. She asked him to wait there while she got the books. John got bored while waiting and walked into the living room. He saw the parrot cage and walked up to it. He wanted to touch the parrot but saw the lock on the cage. So he put his finger inside the cage. When the parrot came over to investigate his finger, John said in a loud voice so that Mary might hear him, "OMG Mary, what a beautiful bird!" This freaked out the parrot and it tried to bite off his finger. John was fast and he pulled his finger out of the cage just in time. However, John lost his balance, fell backwards and cut his head open when it hit the nearby coffee table.

We represent Mary as a client as she has been sued by John for his injuries.

What Next?

After you have a set of facts you must do legal research to determine applicable case law and statutory law. The previous general discussion covered the general law regarding dog bites, but now we must consider specific case law and statutes on the subject. The following New York statute defines "domestic animal": (New York Agriculture & Markets Article 7 Section 8 Definition 7.)

"Domestic animal" means any domesticated sheep, horse, cattle, fallow deer, red deer, sika deer, whitetail deer which is raised under license from the department of environmental conservation, llama, goat, swine, fowl, duck, goose, swan, turkey, confined domestic hare or rabbit, pheasant or other bird which is raised in confinement under license from the state department of environmental conservation before release from captivity, except the varieties of fowl commonly used for cock fights shall not be considered domestic animals for the purposes of this article."

The Restatement (Second) of Torts defines a domestic animal as: "An animal that is by custom devoted to the service of mankind at the time and in the place where it is kept."

Three cases to read and consider when evaluating the parrot fact pattern are provided below:

Supreme Court, Allegany County, New York

Patricia O'BRIEN, Plaintiff

v

Mark AMMAN and Carol Amman, Defendants.

Oct. 20, 2008

JAMES E. EUKEN, J.

The uncontroverted allegations before the court are that the defendants own three Labrador Retrievers, and that on August 2, 2007, in the Village of Andover, one of them bit the plaintiff. Plaintiff had just left her home for her early morning jog and was walking down Fairview Avenue. She then encountered the Defendant, Carol Amman, who was walking her three dogs on the opposite side of the street. For some reason, the three dogs pulled Mrs. Amman across the street and one of them, which one is not known, bit the plaintiff's right wrist. Plaintiff received medical treatment for her wounds and was then hospitalized when they became infected. This case is now before the court on defendants' motion for summary judgment.

The parties do not disagree about the law: dog owners are <u>not liable</u> for injuries caused by their dogs, unless the owners had prior knowledge of their vicious propensities; see, <u>Collier v. Zambito, 1 NY3d 444 (2004)</u>; <u>Bard v. Jahke, 6 NY3d 592 (2006)</u>. The oft-repeated aphorism "every dog gets a free bite" is not true. Though a dog may never have bitten anyone, still, if its owner knew it to be vicious, then even its first bite is not free. The reason is that it is the knowledge of the dog's propensity to bite, not just the proof of it, that gives rise to the owner's duty to take precautions.

In this case, the defendants claim that they are entitled to summary judgment for two reasons. First, defendants claim that plaintiff has no proof that the defendants knew, or should have known, that any of their three dogs had vicious propensities. Absent proof of such actual or constructive knowledge, defendants rightfully argue, they cannot be held liable. Second, defendant states that the plaintiff cannot prove which one of the defendants' three dogs bit her, and that in the absence of such particularized proof, plaintiff's case against them must fail.

The plaintiff has responded that the defendants knew or should have known that their three dogs showed vicious propensities. Ms. Orr's affidavit states that she resided in the Village of Andover from August of 2006, to September of 2007, and that she personally was familiar with the defendants' three dogs, describing them as "chocolate-colored Labrador Retrievers." Ms. Orr further avers that "on many occasions" prior to August 2, 2007, the "defendants' dogs lunged at me inappropriately as they were walked past me by Mrs. Amman."

On this basis of materiality, the court will dispose of the defendant's contention that the plaintiff is required to show which of the defendants' three dogs bit her. That all three dogs were owned by the defendants is uncontroverted. That one of these three dogs bit the plaintiff is also uncontroverted. According to the affidavit of Mattea Orr, all three dogs, on many occasions, lunged at her inappropriately. If such "lunging inappropriately" demonstrates a dog's vicious propensities, then the defendants would be liable no matter which dog bit the plaintiff. And if the reverse were true, that "lunging inappropriately" does not show a dog's vicious propensities, then the defendants would not be liable, no matter which dog bit the plaintiff. Therefore, the issue of which one of the defendants' three dogs bit the plaintiff is not one upon which defendants' liability depends. Since this issue is not material, plaintiff need not point to a triable issue of that particular fact in order to defeat this part of defendants' motion for summary judgment.

The defendants' second argument—that a dog's having "lunged inappropriately" at a person is insufficient to raise an issue of fact about the dog's viciousness—is more difficult to resolve.

Fortunately, the Court of Appeals has recently explored the issue of what kinds of canine behavior demonstrate viciousness, and may impute to the dog's owner actual or constructive knowledge of its vicious propensities. The Court held that the plaintiff need not show the dog had bitten someone else before. The proverbial "one free bite" is, according to the Court, a "misnomer." Mere evidence that the dog has "been known to growl, snap or bare its teeth" may raise a triable issue of fact as to viciousness.

Alternatively, a showing "that a dog previously barked at people" has never been sufficient to create an issue of fact about the dog's viciousness. Such canine behavior is not "threatening or menacing," just typical. "Barking and running around are what dogs do."

"Lunging" would appear to fall within a lacuna on this continuum of canine behavior, perhaps less vicious than biting, snapping or growling but more threatening than barking. To "lunge" according to Webster, is "to thrust or propel (as a blow) ." The word connotes aggression. As for the act itself, at least one appellate court has found that a dog's lunging, *inter alia,* was "sufficient to raise a question of fact" as to the dog's vicious propensities, see *Sorel v. Iacobucci,* 221 A.D.2d 852 (3rd Dept.1995). Orr's allegation that the defendants' dogs "lunged" at her "on many occasions" allows the inference that that the dogs' behavior was consistently and purposefully aggressive.

Viewing the issue in a light most favorable to the plaintiff, the court cannot hold, as a matter of law, that a dog's repeated lunging at another person is not "threatening or menacing" behavior that is indicative of vicious propensities.

Accepting as true Ms. Orr's allegation that the dogs lunged at her while being walked by Carol Amman, the court finds an issue of fact whether this defendant had actual or constructive knowledge of the dogs' vicious propensities. Therefore, the court must deny the defendants' motion.

Supreme Court, Nassau County, New York

Stephen BUDWAY and Lisa Amorin-Budway, Plaintiffs

v

Adelaide J. McKEE, Defendant.

Jan. 29, 2010

Background: Pedestrian, who was allegedly attacked and bitten by owner's dog, brought action against owner. Owner moved for summary judgment. Holdings: The Supreme Court, Nassau County, <u>Daniel R. Palmieri</u>, J., held that:

(1) there was no evidence that would give rise to strict liability upon owner for dog bite sustained by pedestrian, but

(2) fact issues precluded summary judgment on claim for medical costs.

Motion for summary judgment granted.

DANIEL R. PALMIERI, J.

Plaintiff Stephen Budway alleges that on March 4, 2005, while walking his dog on Wellington Street, Mineola, New York, he was attacked and bitten by defendant's dog, a cocker spaniel named Casey.

With respect to cases involving injuries by reason of the action of domestic animals, the law is: "That owners of domestic animals could be held strictly liable for harm caused by an animal, where it is established that the owner knew or should have known of the animal's vicious propensities and harm is caused as a result of those propensities. The strict liability rule can be traced back to the 1816 case of <u>*Vrooman v. Lawyer*, 13 Johns 339.</u>

Knowledge of vicious propensities may be established by proof of an animal's attacks of a similar kind of which the owner had notice, or by an animal's prior behavior that, while not necessarily considered dangerous or ferocious, nevertheless reflects a proclivity to place others at risk of harm. Factors to be considered in determining whether an owner has knowledge of a dog's vicious propensities include 1) evidence of a prior attack, 2) the dog's tendency to growl, snap or bare its teeth, 3) the manner of the dog's restraint, 4) whether the animal is kept as a guard dog, and 5) a proclivity to act in a way that puts others at risk of harm." <u>*Petrone v. Fernandez,* 53 A.D.3d 221, 225, 862 N.Y.S.2d 522 (2d Dept.2008)</u>.

In *Petrone, supra,* the Court of Appeals in reversing, held that liability of an owner is determined *solely* by application of the above rule, and emphasized that the cause of action is not based on a theory of negligence but on a rule of strict liability. Rejected as irrelevant was the plaintiff's claim that negligence should be applied where an owner violates a local leash law.

Except for the claim that Casey was noted to be barking while at the window of the defendant's home, there is a complete lack of evidence of any prior conduct, behavior or actions on his part that would give rise to the imposition of strict liability upon defendant.

Based on the foregoing, plaintiff's common law cause of action and his spouse's derivative claim are dismissed.

Supreme Court, Appellate Division, Third Department, New York

William J. LAGODA, an Infant Under the Age of 14 Years, by William Lagoda His Guardian ad litem et al., Appellants

v

George DORR et al., Respondents

Nov. 3, 1967

Action by infant bicyclist and his father for injuries sustained by bicyclist when he was jumped on and knocked down by defendants' dog while riding on a highway.

On appeal, the Supreme Court, Appellate Division, Gabrielli, J., held that evidence was sufficient to authorize finding that the dog possessed propensities essential to impose liability and that the owner knew of them, in view of disclosures that on day of accident, the dog had been chained to a garage, had freed himself and was again chained, and that the dog had been trained and used as a watch dog, and that defendants knew he had jumped on people prior to accident, and that the dog had chased the injured boy on previous occasions.

GABRIELLI, Justice.

In this negligence action, the court, following a jury trial, granted the defendants' motion to dismiss the complaints and set aside verdicts (1) in favor of the infant plaintiff in the sum of $1.00 and (2) in favor of the father in his derivative action in the sum of $1,689.64, being the exact amount of the special damages consisting entirely of medical expenses.

While riding his bicycle on the highway, the infant plaintiff was injured when a German Shepherd dog owned by the respondents ran out from their home, jumped on the boy knocking him to the ground, from which he sustained serious injuries of considerable duration, resulting in a permanent defect.

In entering judgment in favor of the defendants, the trial court erroneously predicated his decision on the ground that there was insufficient evidence as to previous acts by the dog from which an ordinarily prudent person might conclude that the dog would act in a manner injurious to persons or property.

The testimony showed that on the day of the incident, the dog had been chained to the garage, had freed himself and was again chained; that he had been trained and used as a watchdog; that the respondents knew he had jumped on people prior to the occurrence in question and that it had chased the injured boy on previous occasions.

Respondents quite properly urge that an owner of a domestic animal is liable to one injured by the animal only if it is established that the owner has knowledge of its vicious propensities (Stevens v. Hulse, 263 N.Y. 421, 189 N.E. 478), but it is likewise true that the vicious propensities which go to establish liability include a propensity to do any act which might endanger another (Shuffian v. Garfola, 9 A.D.2d 910, 195 N.Y.S.2d 45) and it has been held that these propensities may include jumping on people (Shain v. Crausman, 3 N.Y.2d 764, 163 N.Y.S.2d 990, 143 N.E.2d 532).

The doctrine that every dog is entitled to 'one free bite', if it ever prevailed in this State, is no longer followed (Kennet v. Sossnitz, 260 App.Div. 759, 23 N.Y.S.2d 961). The gravamen of the action is the knowledge of the owner that the dog was possessed of vicious or mischievous propensities (Lier v. Bloomingdale Bros., Inc., 274 App.Div. 918, 83 N.Y.S.2d 465).

That the danger was foreseeable is clear from the dog's conduct prior to the unfortunate event (Shain v. Crausman, supra). Here the jury was entitled to reach the conclusion that the dog possessed the propensities essential to impose liability and that the owner knew of them. Moreover, the circumstance that the owner found it necessary to keep the dog tied up and took precautions to restrain it, is further evidence of knowledge of the dog's propensities (Brice v. Bauer, 108 N.Y. 428, 432, 15 N.E. 695, 696; Hahnke v. Friederich, 140 N.Y. 224, 35 N.E. 487).

In the infant's case, however, the verdict for damages was shockingly contrary to the weight of the evidence as inadequate to the extent hereinafter indicated. Here the issues of liability and damages were not so entwined or interwoven as to require a new trial on both issues. The jury by a general verdict determined the liability issue in favor of plaintiffs and there is no meaningful reason to believe that a jury, on a retrial of the issue of liability, would properly reach a different result. The power of the court is to be exercised in the interests of justice and when, in the exercise of sound discretion, such interests so require, the retrial should be had solely on the damage issue.

The order which granted defendants motion to set aside the verdicts and to dismiss the complaint should be reversed and verdicts reinstated. The judgment should be reversed and a new trial, limited to the issue of damages to the infant plaintiff.

GIBSON, P.J., and HERLIHY and AULISI, JJ., concur; REYNOLDS, J., concurs in the result.

END OF DOCUMENT

<u>What Is Legal Analysis?</u>

Now that we have the (previously discussed) general law, statutory law and case law to apply to the fact patter, <u>legal analysis</u> requires elaboration on all of the following:

1) <u>Issue</u>—what is being debated

2) <u>Rule(s)</u>—what legal rule(s) governs the issue (and elements thereof)

3) <u>Facts</u>—what are the *relevant facts* that apply to the rule(s)

4) <u>Analysis</u>—application of the rules to the relevant facts (add counterarguments—weigh both sides of the issue)

5) <u>Conclusion</u>—after applying the rules to the facts—reach a fair / logical outcome

<u>Legal Analysis Explained Using Our Parrot Example</u>

1) <u>Issue</u>

The "issue" is the legal issue. It is not just an interesting question. It asks whether existing law has anything to say about a topic. An example of this is whether a parrot is a domestic animal. We know that a cow and horse are domestic animals, as are cats and dogs. But what about a parrot, or a monkey or a pet alligator?

2) <u>Rule(s)</u>—State the applicable rule(s).

At common law the owner of a domestic animal is not liable for injuries caused by the animal unless the injuries were the result of a <u>vicious propensity</u> of which the owner <u>had notice or knowledge of</u>. Liability for foreseeable harm is imposed after proof that the animal:

    (1)   possessed a dangerous propensity that
    (2)   caused the plaintiff's injury and
    (3)   that the defendant had actual or constructive knowledge of that propensity

⁓⁓

The <u>Restatement (Second) of Torts</u> defines a domestic animal as: "An animal that is by custom devoted to the service of mankind at the time and in the place where it is kept."

New York Agriculture & Markets Article 7 § 108 Definition 7: "Domestic animal" means any domesticated sheep, horse, cattle, fallow deer, red deer, sika deer, whitetail deer which is raised under license from the department of environmental conservation, llama, goat, swine, fowl, duck, goose, swan, turkey, confined domestic hare or rabbit, pheasant or other bird which is raised in confinement under license from the state department of environmental conservation before release from captivity, except the varieties of fowl commonly used for cock fights shall not be considered domestic animals for the purposes of this article."

b) Cite case law:

Lagoda v Dorr, 28 A.D.2d 208, 284 N.Y.S.2d 130 (1967)

O'Brien v Amman, 21 Misc.3d 1118(A), 873 N.Y.S.2d 513 (2008)

Budway v McKee, 27 Misc.3d 316, 893 N.Y.S.2d 766 (2010)

3) Relevant Facts

There are many facts that make up a client's story. For the purpose of legal analysis, we look for relevant facts (aka: material facts). These are the facts that prove or disprove the elements of the rule.

So, in the parrot example, we first need to look at the elements—need to know:

- if the parrot is a domestic or a wild animal
- if the owner of the parrot had prior notice of vicious propensities
- that caused the plaintiff's injuries

*** All three elements here are "at issue". That means that there is no clear answer (no black & white answer) and that counterarguments exist. ***

4) Analysis

In the analysis we have to argue each of the three elements (above) from the perspective of Mary's attorney and John's attorney. We must then take the judge's perspective to weigh out the arguments on both sides. Since John brought this law suit, the burden of proving each element is his.

Thus, to win the case, John's attorney must prove that a parrot is a wild animal (not domestic therefore strict liability applies) or, <u>in the alternative</u>, that even if the parrot is considered a domestic animal, that Mary had prior notice of its vicious propensities and she is thus liable for John's injuries.

It is always best to map out both sides of the argument before you begin to write out a full analysis. Below I have listed the arguments that may be made by the attorneys in our parrot case.

<u>Arguments Made by John's Attorney</u>	<u>Arguments Made by Mary's Attorney</u>

As to the <u>first element</u> (wild v. domestic):

A parrot is not listed as a domestic animal under Ag. & Markets Law Art 7. If not "wild" why keep it in a cage with padlock—circumstantial evidence. Not "devoted to the service of mankind" as per the Restatement of Torts definition.	Neither are dogs which are clearly a domestic species. It is a *partial* list. To protect the parrot, and keep it from flying out of an open window. Parrots are "companion animals" and their service is companionship.

As to the <u>second element</u> (prior notice):

It bit breeder's husband.	Breeder did not tell that to Mary.
It bit Mary and left a bruise.	Caused by shocking thunder (fear). Parrots are not required to be licensed, like dogs, thus not deemed dangerous as a species.

As to the <u>third element</u> (vicious propensity):

All pet birds bite at one time or another. "	Propensity" is defined as a tendency not a one-time event; Mary was bit once. Not a tendency.

(foreseeability)

Large powerful beak is used as a weapon.	Beaks are a parrot's hands and are used for every purpose (climbing, grooming, feeding young, etc.) Parrot did not even bite John!

His injuries were caused by his fall. (proximate cause) Other arguments: assumption of risk and contributory negligence on John'spart when he stuck his finger in the cage.

5) Conclusion

Now that we have considered the arguments on both sides, we must take the judge's perspective to decide which argument should prevail—and why it should prevail. The judge cannot just base a decision on what is best for Mary or what is best for John. The decision must be based on precedent (past established laws) and with an eye toward future ramifications of a decision for either party.

For example, if the judge holds that a parrot is a "wild" animal, then a major ripple effect would result throughout the state of jurisdiction. If the state is New York, for example, then the holding would affect New York pet shops, parrot owners, avian vets, insurance companies and parrot breeders. If parrots are deemed "wild" then New York becomes a strict liability state, like California, with regards to all parrots.

A conclusion must be fair and logical. It must be rooted it the law. It must address the specific and material facts of the case at bar. A judicial decision may take into account evidence such as the testimony of expert witnesses.

WEB Sources of Information Can be Useful Too

In addition to researching the law, it is wise to do some web research on the topic to see if you can find expert's information. Such articles are not binding law but they can help an attorney develop useful case arguments and strategies.

What To Do After Legal Analysis of a Fact Pattern:

After analyzing a fact pattern you have to (1) write out your analysis as an essay using a format (such as ARAC) and (2) using a lawyerly writing *style*.

On a final law exam you are expected to do a fact pattern analysis and write an answer essay under time constraints (usually three hours). That added stress may fog your thinking if you have not practiced thoroughly beforehand. The more you practice the more confident you will be when you take a final exam.

Remember: read the facts carefully

articulate applicable law

address elements at issue from different viewpoints

offer a fair and logical conclusion

write answer essay using a format (such as ARAC)

use a lawyerly writing style

FACT PATTERN HYPOTHETICAL EXAMS

CRITICAL READING AND CRITRICAL WRITING

Section D Skill Objectives—Students will be able to:

- Understand the structure and purpose of essay type law exams.

- Develop a strategy for taking essay law exams.

- Use proper essay answer structure and format.

Section D Outline:

- Four Basic Types of Law exams
- The Fact Pattern Hypothetical Exam
- The Tradition of Hypothetical Exams: Pros and Cons

If you think that law exams are a drag, wait until you see your grades.

O.A. Posse

<u>There are four basic types of law school exams:</u>

fact pattern issue spotting exams—aka essay exams—aka hypothetical exams

multiple choice exams

take home exams

short answer exams

No two law exams are alike and a few exams may mix of any or all of the four categories listed above. In this chapter I will discuss fact pattern hypothetical exams and how they are graded.

I will focus on the fact pattern issue spotting category because it is the most common, difficult, and most foreign to law students. These "issue spotting" tests usually contain three to five fact patterns but *may* also include one big fact pattern and/or shorter policy questions, multiple choice or short answer questions.

In issue spotting exams your main job is to spot every legal issue. What does this entail? You are tested on your ability to:

- read the fact pattern

- identify legal claims

- identify defenses and policy issues

- apply the law to the facts

- make a clear and well reasoned argument to reach a conclusion as to the issues

- evaluate all counter arguments—CRITICAL!

    a)   try to offer a counter argument for every position

    b)   show that you can see the argument from both sides

    d)   if there is no counter argument ask yourself if you have spotted a real issue or if you have analyzed the facts carefully enough

Remember, you are not being tested on how well you memorized the law. It is presumed that you have mastered the law as a starting point. If you only know the law but cannot apply it you may earn a grade of C (or worse). You are not being tested on how well you can memory dump your outline into your analysis. That is, you attempt to use everything you learned / memorized during the semester to answer the exam, whether or not it is relevant to the facts. You must limit your analysis to the issues actually present in the fact pattern.

Your final exam is only three hours long and may not cover 60% of the class material. Thus, not every subject will be on the test. Never include a subject just because you know a lot about it. Only raise issues that are reasonably brought up by the facts. Do not read too much into the fact pattern—no not make things up or add facts to show off how much you know about a subject. The issues being tested have been limited by your professor.

When you read a fact pattern you must decide what the question is asking you to do. This means that you must determine the <u>role</u> you are playing in the fact pattern (defense or prosecution, judge, legislator, etc.). Thus, you should limit your claims to those that involve your client if you are a lawyer. If the exam calls for you to write a memorandum of law, do NOT use a memo format. That is, do not write a heading, question presented or brief answer. Just write the answer using whatever exam format you favor (such as ARAC).

<u>System</u>: Develop and use a system that works for you; one that is a compromise of speed and accuracy. Note every person in the fact pattern and understand who they are, and what each one does in the facts. Now, these are just your basic exam essay notes. You must also outline your <u>arguments</u>—the real key to success—so even if you use half of your allowed time to outline, your writing will go much faster and smoother. Think of this outline as the essay itself but in a coded format, a shorthand format, a map. As you work through practice exams you will develop a personal system of shorthand for yourself.

<u>Structure</u>: Structure your exam essay outline by party, then by claim or by chronological events.

<u>Format</u>: Next, use a format such as ARAC to write the essay. Use the format consistently for each fact pattern and be very formulaic. Make certain to leave enough time to write out your essay! You will not have time to proofread each essay. Trust your essay outline and move on. Proofread only at the end of the exam if there is time. Ignore spelling errors made by the professor. If the fact pattern seems to contain an error, on the other hand,—explain the error—explain what you assume was probably meant—and resolve the issue based on your assumption.

Only cite or use real cases if your professor insists on it. You do not need to memorize case names, just the relevant facts, such as "the case where the car jumped the curb and killed a pedestrian".

<u>Issues that need more information</u>: If a fact suggests a claim or issue, but is missing some information to actually make out the full issue, note it and move on. Never make up facts to fill in for the missing information and never just ignore it. Example: Ann may have a claim for battery because Tony pointed a gun at her. However, we must determine if Ann experienced fear or if she thought that Tony was joking.

<u>"Red Herrings"</u>: Facts that suggest a claim but really do not. Examples are issues that fall outside the scope of the course or the instructions for the question, such as issues that do not involve the client you represent.

<u>Major Inconsistencies in the Law</u>: If your professor has discussed cases that involve major differences in majority and minority opinions, if there were very persuasive dissenting opinions discussed, or if there exists great inconsistency in opinion among different courts—if there was a major split in opinions—that may serve as a counterargument—and a discussion of jurisdictional differences.

In most law schools, comprehensive law exams are held at the end of each semester. Law professors do not want you to recite what you know about the law. They want you to demonstrate analytical skills by finding the issues raised by the facts, by stating applicable rules of law, and by applying the law to the facts to reach a fair and logical conclusion. There is often no single correct answer on law school exams. Your conclusion is not as important as your analytical skill.

The Tradition of Hypothetical Exams

Law professors make up hypothetical essay exams by adapting the facts of case law, real life situations or fictional situations from literature or popular culture. These exams are intended to test your ability to reason (perform legal analysis) by having you read complicated information and use law to resolve issues raised by the facts. Your answer is graded according to individual professors' standards of construction, originality and judgment. You must see the "big picture" without falling prey to incoherence, arbitrariness or subjectivity.

After teaching a law class all semester that focuses on case analysis and issue analysis, law professors base an entire semester's grade on the result of one final exam. Students must demonstrate their understanding of the course material in a way that bears no resemblance to the way in which it was taught all semester. Issues are hidden in facts and severe time limits act together to prevent you from developing and writing detailed answers. Speed is as important as analytical ability. That is why exam practice, in addition to study, is so important.

For professors, essay exams are easy to write but hard to grade. Grading law exams is a chore made easier if the exam is easy to read and supports the professor's subjective point of view—both intangible reactions to an exam. Many law professors simply read an exam answer and decide on a grade based on the impression it left with the reader—a subjective process.

This grading method is based on how the law professor *feels* about the answer without assigning any point values. Some professors value short answers and some value longer answers. Even non-substantive distractions may result in inconsistent grading among students of similar proficiency. Examples include bad penmanship and spelling, ink color, and line spacing.

Another common approach taken by law professors when grading long exam essays is to objectify the answer. Objective exams use multiple choice questions, true-false and short answer formats. Law professors objectify essay exams by using point based answer keys to grade them. Points are awarded for each issue, rule, fact analyzed, counterargument and logical conclusion. This method is an attempt to reduce subjectivity.

Unlike essay exams, objective law exams are easy to grade but hard to write. Law professors do not, as a rule, get any training in how to write valid objective law exams. Not only are essay exams easier to write, but many professors claim that they are a good test of writing skills. Increasingly, however, law schools are hiring legal writing faculty and implementing formal writing courses to develop and test writing skills. As a result, law tests can then be crafted to objectively measure *subject proficiency* apart from writing skills.

Another claim in support of essay exams is that objective exams do not test a student's ability to spot legal issues, organization skills, constructive thought processes, and thought fusion skills (thoughtful insight and creative interpretation).

Tenured law professors tend to prefer essay exams and pre-tenure staff may avoid objective exams to blend in better. Law school professors are attorneys who teach and they have little (if any) training as educators or testing experts. They test based on how they were tested when they were law students—using essay type law exams. They teach how they were taught and they test how they were tested.

Under the traditional testing model a law professor writes an essay question that he never taught his students to answer. Students are taught one way and tested in another. They are only tested on a small amount of the material they were taught during the semester because it is very hard to write an essay exam that tests proficiency in the entire subject matter. Even if a professor *could* write an essay exam that covered everything, it would be impossible for a student to take such an exam in three hours.

If a law school curriculum *could* accurately be tested by a computer graded multiple choice method, then there is no reason that all law courses could not be offered online to thousands of students. Students could have convenient access from home to the finest professors in the country and it would drastically reduce the cost of a law school education. The downside is that many law professors, and even traditional law schools, would become unnecessary.

The reality, however, is that the traditional essay method is used on one part of the bar exam. Thus, reliance on web based law classes and objective law exams may fail to adequately prepare students to pass the bar exam's essay portion.

How do law professors really grade? Watch:

http://legalblogwatch.typepad.com/legal_blog_watch/2010/04/how-do-law-professors-grade-exams.html

ADDITIONAL READING:

Legal Writing

http://en.wikipedia.org/wiki/Legal_writing

Good Legal Writing

http://people.ischool.berkeley.edu/~pam/papers/goodwriting.html

Writing v. Speech: Why Lawyers Write Badly

http://disputedissues.blogspot.com/2008/12/writing-versus-speech-why-lawyers-write.html

Legal Writing: Sense and Nonsense

http://disputedissues.blogspot.com/2008/12/writing-versus-speech-why-lawyers-write.html

LAW EXAM WRITING STYLE

Section E Skill Objectives—Students will be able to:

- Understand the difference between format and style.

- Practice legal writing that is both predictive and persuasive.

Section E Outline:

- Introduction to Legal Writing Style
- Hair Girl
- Sample Grading Criteria

If any man wishes to write in a clear style, let him be first clear in his thoughts.

Goethe

This is the hardest section to write because law exam writing *style* does not follow a set format. I can show you the format to use when briefing a case. I can show the format to use to follow when writing a law exam answer. I can show you a format for a course outline. But writing style on a law exam has nothing to do with formats.

Your own writing style is distinctive and is an element of writing apart from content. Legal writing is highly technical in nature and is used to express legal analysis. But legal writing on a law exam is graded subjectively and different law professors have their own idea of what "good style" is. So you must adopt and practice a new (legal analysis) writing style that will resonate with your law professors. But be prepared: your law professors will give you little (if any) guidance as to what they expect on exams in terms of style or substance.

One aspect of legal writing is <u>legal analysis</u>. Legal analysis is both <u>predictive</u> (based on precedent) and <u>persuasive</u>. For example, an attorney writes memorandums of law to evaluate negative and positive precedent as it relates to a client's unique set of facts and circumstances. This is a form of predictive analysis where the attorney tries to predict the legal outcome of his client's case based on existing law. But legal analysis must also be persuasive. For example, when an attorney writes an appeal or a motion he is attempting to get a judge to decide in his client's favor.

On a law exam, your professor primarily wants you to get to the point. He weighs your conclusions, analysis, and use of relevant facts—relative to the writing of every other student in your class—on a curve. Law professors are busy and do not have the time to wade through long essay answers. Your exam essay must be focused—providing law and facts related to the issues in the exam fact pattern(s). But professors also set aside some points for overall writing *style* aside from content. Those points may make the difference between one grade and a higher grade.

Good writing style on a law exam does <u>not</u> involve opening a vein of thought and letting it gush all over the place. But clarity and brevity are artificial relative to the actual thought process, which tends to ramble all over the place. We become so familiar with the mechanisms of writing undergraduate essays that we do not recognize when we write the same way, automatically, on law exam essays.

A well written exam answer is complete—clear—concise—compelling (convincing).

You will not have time for eloquent writing on law exams. Your writing must be complete (but not flowery). It must prove or disprove every element at issue. It must also cite and discuss every rule, defense, exception and policy argument related to the elements at issue.

Your exam essay must be clear (logical) so follow a format that works for you (example, ARAC). Further, it must be concise and easy to read. Short and simple sentences are most effective. Most importantly, it must be compelling and convincing. NB: Many fact patterns will prove an *exception* to a majority rule that was covered in class.

Do not try to memorize or use case names or other caption information. Just refer to cases by their relevant facts. For example, write "the case where the dog chased the bike and the child fell and broke his neck." This method is just as good as citing a case by name.

I write in simple terms for a reason. My torts professor in law school earned her law degree at Harvard. She was an exceptional professor and a published author. I once asked her what she considered to be the best writing *style* on a law exam and she gave me the following advice:

"Write as if your audience is an extremely intelligent eight grader;

use simple language that is directly to the point and very easy to understand."

In other words, assume that your reader knows <u>nothing</u> about the law and show your entire thought process (show all of your work). You MUST show every step of your analysis. This means that you must lay out a clear <u>step-by-step</u> analysis for your reader to lead him to your conclusions.

During law school, every one of my classes was graded on a traditional curve, except that every class offered only <u>one</u> "A+" grade. There was one student that earned the A+ in almost every class (I call her Hair Girl because she was always playing with her hair during classes). Hair Girl earned the A+ almost every time. I imagined that she was an amazingly gifted writer.

One day I was in the administrative offices of the law school after final exams were over. There was a long table covered with semester exams that had been graded and were ready to be stored. As I looked over the piles of exams one caught my eye—it was a final exam essay booklet written by Hair Girl. I could not resist. When no one was looking I picked up the booklet and read it. At first I was surprised and how short her answers were.

Her entire exam fit into one essay book (I usually used two, maybe three). I was also surprised at how simple her sentences were: short and directly to the point. This made her analysis seem very confident. Her essays were clear and logically presently with no filler.

While law professors do grade subjectively, her writing style earned A+ grades across the board with most professors.

<u>Remember</u>:

An "A" essay follows rules of <u>grammar and usage</u>. Writing style is clear and precise. There is no jargon or conversational tone. Spelling is accurate.

An "A" essay's <u>content</u> is comprehensive, accurate and persuasive. Issue and sub-issue points are stated clearly and are completely argued. The purpose is clear: it is consistent. In a poor essay, issues are identified but not well argued and fail to address important social and policy concepts. Purpose is inconsistent. Relevant facts are ignored as is the reasoning connected to those facts.

As to <u>format and organization</u>, an "A" essay follows some organizational model (ARAC) and it is appropriate in length. The structure (ARAC) of the essay is clear and easy to follow. Good paragraph transitions exist which maintain the flow of thought throughout the essay. Conclusions are logical and flow from the content of the essay. A poor essay lacks a format, omits legal rules, or misstates rules, and it is too short or too long. Structure is not easy to follow, issue introductions are missing and conclusions are either missing or confused (do not flow from the essay's content). Paragraphs seem disjointed and lack an analytical flow of thought. There is no clear progression of ideas.

<u>Style points</u> are awarded for original thought and strong presentation / advocacy. A confident and clear introduction captures my attention and a confidently finished answer is persuasive. Good writing shows a holistic awareness of relevant law, issues, audience and purpose. Finally, writing is thoughtful with insightful links to social and policy issues.

An excellent essay goes beyond repeating or summarizing the law, it offers a *solution* to the issues raised. It explains relevant authority and shows clearly how that authority applies to the facts. It predicts a logical outcome. This analytical process may seem simple in theory but it is very difficult in practice.

You must remember to explain every step of your analysis, even when you know that the reader (your law professor) knows more about the law and facts than you ever will. In light of your professor's knowledge you may be tempted to omit analytical steps that seem too obvious.

It is thus helpful to use a writing outline, map or flowchart before starting to write an essay exam answer. This improves organization and clarity. Never "free write". Good legal writing is a process that will improve with practice. You need to learn to apply new vocabulary and organization methods. Good legal writing style demands precision and economy of language that results from practice.

ADDITIONAL READING:

Law School Exams

http://lib.law.washington.edu/ref/lawexams.html

EXAM ANSWER FORMATS—TO ARAC OR NOT TO ARAC

And COMMON EXAM MISTAKES TO AVOID

Section F Skill Objectives—Students will be able to:

-   Understand and apply the ARAC answer format.

-   Recognize common exam technique mistakes.

-   Practice good law study skills.

Section F Outline:

-   Introduction to ARAC format
-   Sample ARAC application
-   Why Use ARAC?
-   What not to do on a law exam
-   Academic Skills, Good Practices & General Wisdom
-   How To Prepare For A Law Exam

If at first you don't succeed, law exams are not for you.

O. A. Posse

College exams are usually designed to test your knowledge and understanding of a subject. In law school knowledge and understanding are merely threshold aspects of exams designed to test issue spotting and legal analysis skills.

The traditional ARAC format (Answer, Rules, Analysis, and Conclusion) is still preferred by most law professors but distained by some. Even so, I discourage you from using the ARAC (or any other method) in rote fashion. That means that you must <u>not</u> write "The answer is"..." followed by "The rule is"..." followed by "And the analysis is"...". You get the idea.

Writing style is also important. Awkward writing with spelling errors leaves a bad impression.

I used "IRAC" in law school with much success. However, I have <u>modified</u> that approach by replacing the I (Issue) with an A (answer) as follows:

ARAC = **A**nswer (for each issue)

Rule(s)

Analysis (prove or disprove elements)

Counter Arguments ("however") and

Conclusion ("nevertheless")

Sample (simple) ARAC paragraph:

A: Bob has a valid contract as against Mike.

R: A contract requires a valid offer, acceptance and consideration.

A: Here, Bob offered to buy Mike's car for $1,000 and Mike accepted by......

C: However, Mike had enjoyed a beer with Bob prior to accepting the offer and may claim that there was no *meeting of the minds* because he was intoxicated. Nevertheless, a reasonable person may conclude that Mike could not be significantly intoxicated after drinking one beer, and that he understood the nature of the agreement.

Begin by stating the answer to an issue (Answer). Professors love this because they do not have to dig around in your essay to see what your final answer is. By knowing your answer up front, the professor is better able to see if your application of the law fits, and if your logic supports your answer.

Next, state the Black Letter Law / Rule and every element—even if only one element is "at issue" (Rules). Black Letter Law = the elements and exceptions for the tort = rules. Then discuss the facts in light of the rules (Analysis) as shown below.

An element of a tort, for example, is "at issue" if it can be argued different ways in light of the facts given on the hypothetical. Several elements will be clear and uncontested. For those elements, use one sentence to show how the facts prove that element. You will lose valuable points for every element that you do not cite and support with a fact from the fact pattern.

For the elements "at issue" write several sentences showing how the facts can lead to one conclusion or another. Pick one conclusion and *show the reasoning* that leads you to believe that it is the *best* conclusion. Then add any defense arguments or exceptions that apply. Finally, address competing policies and if those different policies can lead to/support different conclusions.

Repeat this process for every tort (or crime, etc.) made out by the fact pattern. Once again, do NOT just recite the law and argue one answer. The facts in the fact pattern are there FOR A REASON. You must use them to prove OR disprove every element (or exception).

While I personally prefer the ARAC method described above, there are many other format alternatives to consider (listed below in additional readings). It is best to test drive all of them and to see which works best for you. You may even create an entirely new format crafted from pieces of those listed here. The bottom line: use what works best for you.

ADDITIONAL READING:

Law IRAC Format

http://en.wikipedia.org/wiki/IRAC

IRAC and CRRACC Format

http://www.law.cuny.edu/academics/WritingCenter/students/strategies-techniques/irac-crracc.html

CIRAC Format

http://www.law.cuny.edu/academics/WritingCenter/students/strategies-techniques/irac-crracc.html

In Defense of IRAC

http://www.threeyearsofhell.com/archive/000802.php

WHAT NOT TO DO ON A LAW EXAM

Common mistakes to avoid on essay type law exams are:

- Avoid fancy / ornate language, superfluous / redundant language and legalese.

- Never waste time recopying the fact pattern.

- Do not recopy full statutes into your exam blue book—just <u>cite</u> the law and apply it to the relevant facts.

- Outline your answer but then craft a well written essay response based on your outline. Never turn in an outline or bullets as your answer. Outline every issue before you start to write your answer and budget a set amount of time to discuss each issue.

- Assume the <u>role</u> that you are asked to assume for the exam. You may be the lawyer for the defense or the prosecution. You may be the judge or his law clerk. You may be a legislator or his legislative clerk. But regardless of your role, you must spot and discuss every issue from all sides of the argument.

- Do not ignore any facts on the fact pattern. They are all there for a reason. Do not invent or add facts.

- Do not make up issues (Negative Issues). Just because you have invested a great deal of study time on issue "X", do not discuss issue "X" if it does not appear on the exam.

- Do not just regurgitate everything you studied during the semester. There has to be organization and structure. If you just spew legal concepts and beat one or two obvious legal issues to death your grade will suffer. On the other hand, "forking" is the process of discussing alternative solutions to the same legal problem and is a good practice.

- Do not pad your answer with general policies or discussions of issues that *might* be involved. Go immediately to the real issues and only mention relevant facts. Do not cite case names or statutes if you do not explain their relevance.

- Do not ever attempt to insert humor or jokes into your answer, even if you have a talent for it. Never.

<u>Never cut classes</u>. In any law class, you will be learning the law from a *particular professor's perspective*. Do not rely on a commercially prepared course outline because they will not show you what <u>your</u> professor emphasized in class—or what he left out. If you cut classes and rely on another student's class notes, they may be incomplete.

ADDITIONAL READING:

Law School Exam Mistakes

http://law-career.blogspot.com/2008/01/law-school-exam-mistakes.html

Writing Law Examinations

http://lawschool.westlaw.com/shared/marketinfodisplay.asp?code=so&id=6&subpage=3

ACADEMIC SKILLS—GOOD PRACTICE GENERAL WISDOM

Common Sense Basics:

- Get a good night's sleep and eat before the exam. Arrive early to set up for the exam and to relax a bit.

- Anticipate time pressure and schedule time for each section of the exam. There will be no time for redrafting, reflection or reconsideration. Pay attention to the <u>weight</u> given to each question when allocating time to answer it. Do not spend 30% of your time on a question that is only worth 10% of the final grade. If the professor <u>suggests</u> time allocations for each question, consider that a hint as to each question's relative credit weight.

- Also allocate time <u>within</u> each question. It is a mistake to presume that a two issue question is a 50/50 situation. Do not presume that each of the two issues should merit 50% of your time and effort. If one issue is more difficult and complicated it will warrant lengthy exploration and explanation. You should always signal your awareness of how open to argument a difficult issue is. If one issue has an easy resolution, just discuss it quickly and move along. Do not beat easy points to death.

- Read the fact pattern carefully (MORE THAN ONCE) and do not add facts. If you need a fact not given to answer an issue, you must state what that fact is and why you need it to reach your conclusion. Never rely on nonspecific statements such as, "Facts are missing that are needed to reach a conclusion." "Assuming the plaintiff…." Missing facts may suggest that you have not understood the issues, or that you are to identify the missing facts and then use them to discuss alternative arguments.

- Underline and take notes while reading the fact pattern so that you do not forget anything that tickles your memory. Highlight relevant facts, parties and harms. Pay attention to dates, odd facts and the relationship between parties as these signal important issues.

- Read the instructions and answer the call of the question. Do not barf up everything you have memorized during the semester regarding the subject matter. You are not being tested on memorized knowledge. You are being tested on your ability to <u>use</u> the knowledge memorized.

  Complete memorization of the subject matter is a basic precondition—a mere starting point. You must use that knowledge to analyze NEW facts and NEW issues never discussed in class. Do not address basic concepts of law when the question asks you to probe advanced topics.

- Use complete sentences. Write legibly. Use a laptop if possible.

- Use proper spelling, grammar and punctuation. Never abbreviate. Do not use texting language.

- Use well organized paragraphs. Limit paragraphs to one thought and use topic sentences and proper transitions that clarify relationships between the paragraphs. In this way, you will make clear your knowledge of every issue and their relationship to each other. Also use headings to organize your answer (according to claims, parties or the specific call of the question).

- Answer any questions that are specifically asked. If a question asks you to consider personal jurisdiction, do not discuss subject matter jurisdiction. If the question asks you to address jurisdiction issues, then it would be correct to discuss both. The scope of your answer must match the scope of the question.

  You will not be asked to write about any issues that pop into your head as you read the fact pattern. You must analyze specific issues from the perspective of specific parties.

- Keep answers very concise and well reasoned. Quality is better than quantity. Excellent answers can be very concise, and long answers can be incomplete and badly written.

- Use a concise approach (IRAC or ARAC) and argue both sides of every issue unless instructed to do otherwise by your professor.

- Practice exams under real conditions. Go sit in the classroom where the exam will take place and restrict your answers to three hour sessions (most exams last three hours).

- Read and outline all of your professor's old exams on reserve—at your law school and at any other law school your professor taught at (when possible).

- Spend enough time practicing how to write a good answer—do not spend too much time just studying class materials.

- Allow some panic. Almost every student panics a bit at the start of an exam. Anticipate this, get it over with, and then get started.

How to Prepare For a Law Exam:

- Commercial materials are an excellent addition and supplement to lecture notes. But base your exam arguments on whatever your instructor stressed during his lectures and not just on the commercial outlines.

- Write your own hypotheticals and trade them with study partners—then analyze your answers.

- Keep your personal life drama free and in order.

- Create a study schedule.

- Practice old exams.

- Memorize the black letter law covered in your courses. Memorize the rules and the elements of each rule. It is also very important to memorize the policies that underlie the rules.

- Compare your outline to web outlines and professionally prepared outlines to check for completeness.

- Study common mistakes made on law exams then avoid them.

- Use study aids such as hornbooks, restatements of law, commercial study guides and outlines.

- Make your own flash cards specific to each your courses.

- Create element checklists and the scope of each (how can a plaintiff satisfy each element)

- Create class <u>outlines</u> and then <u>checklists</u> for each outline for each of your classes. Focus on the law and policies rather than on the cases you have briefed and studied. Include issues that you will be looking for under each major category. Memorize the checklist and test drive it on practice exams.

- <u>Before Class</u>:

  The chances that you will be called on by a law professor are slim in classes that seat over 100 students. But if you ARE called on, and are unprepared, the consequences can be ugly—you may be humiliated in front of the entire class. When I was in law school (first year) one of my professors called on another student (thank God it was not me) and asked him some questions about a case we had for homework. The student was NOT prepared and could not answer even one question. The professor just walked out of the class and did not come back to finish it—he was that disgusted.

  Professors in law school do not merely lecture. They use the Socratic Method. The Socratic Method facilitates learning by employing a series of questions and answers to guide a student through complicated legal material. This is why you cannot afford to go to a law class unprepared. You will not just be required to sit and listen to a lecture. You may be called upon to discuss homework material. Before class: prepare—prepare—prepare.

- <u>During Class</u>:

Never cut class and remain mindful during class. Do not allow yourself to become distracted with web surfing, email, etc.

Edit your topic briefs according to your professor's lectures. What does he emphasize? Write down every hypothetical problem he proposes and his answer (these often signal potential exam topics).

Pay careful attention to the scope of a rule of law and anything that limits that law. Also note any social policy issues as well as how your professor feels about the issues.

Participate in class discussions and, even if the professor calls on another student, think about how you would answer the questions posed.

- <u>After Class</u>:

Never wait to get help if there is anything you do not understand. Discuss confusing issues with study partners. Learn how to use hornbooks to clarify confusing issues. You may also address questions to your professor during office hours.

Review class notes right away while the class is fresh in your memory. Back up all notes on your computer. Take notes from outside readings and assignments posted by your professor. Sometimes, reading hornbooks and nutshells may help you to better understand areas that your professor did not fully explain—or just skimmed over in class.

Hone critical thinking skills by studying with a study group or study partner(s).

Summarize by week or month: For every class topic you should highlight social policy, specific legal tests and related analysis, and how the cases briefed relate to each other. That is, how are they the same—how are they different?

Class Outlines:

First of all, why take time to create your own outlines when you can buy commercial outlines written by experts? Because students who write their own outlines do better on exams. The process of creating an outline takes enormous amounts of class materials and puts them into an organized and understandable format that is easier to memorize. More importantly, making your own outline will train you to think like a lawyer.

The purpose of an outline is to take all of the information covered during the semester and to put it into a readable summary that is used as a memory tool (not a teaching tool). Outlines are not teaching tools because if you read an outline before learning the law you cannot understand it.

The very act of creating an outline will teach you the law and help you to memorize it. As you condense the outline into a mini outline, micro outline and exam outline—single words will trigger large volumes of memories. When well condensed, an outline will help you to consider and argue <u>every</u> issue in complicated fact patterns. If an outline is not condensed enough it will not be easy to memorize or use.

NB: The tort outlines that I have provided for you do not contain case law or policy arguments because these will vary from professor to professor. You should augment my outlines with cases and policy considerations that are stressed in class by your torts professor. Use my outlines as a starting point only. Tailor your version of an outline to suit your particular memory needs. There are also tons of web sites that offer free law class outlines. Again, use them as starting points only. If you use another student's outline, make sure he had the same professor.

The main idea is to condense your outlines down to one that triggers memories of ALL subject matter understanding.

- No one will teach you how to outline in law school.

- Commercial outlines are very helpful. But do not ever be tempted to save time by relying solely on commercial outlines or outlines created by other students. The process of making your own outline will help you to organize class notes, case briefs and textbook readings into one body of information. One logically presented body of law. A good outline will also force you to focus your thinking during an exam. Finally, just writing out rules of law into an outline will help you to memorize them.

- Keep in mind that every law professor teaches differently and emphasizes different material s. If another student's outline is not based on your specific professor's class, do not use it.

- The best outlines I ever used were the BARBRI bar review outlines that I purchased at the <u>end </u>of 3L. Those outlines would have been very valuable to me *during* law school. I would highly recommend that you purchase some used (BARBRI) bar review study materials from someone who no longer needs them. You can then use them throughout law school.

- When creating your own outlines, start early in the semester. While one reason for making outlines is to help you focus during an exam, an equally important reason for outlining is to teach you how to think like a lawyer (the skill of legal reasoning). Some computer word processing programs have an outlining feature. Using your computer's outline mode will save you time in the long term. Organize your outline in a way that makes sense to you (into a template). Whatever outline template you develop, always compare it to your class syllabus and your textbook's table of contents to make certain that you have not left anything important out.

- Once you have a completed, and tested, outline—you will compress the outline into a mini outline (using shorthand) that is no longer than one page. When the exam starts, write the mini outline into the front cover of the exam answer booklet.

Law School Exams Online:

Many law schools keep old law school exam collections available to the public for free. To access a list of law exam links, check *Findlaw: Law School Exams* and *Jurist: Law School Exams*.

- The following law schools also maintain freely available exam collections:

- U. of Arkansas Exam Archive   U. of Missouri-Columbia Exams Online

- U. of Dayton Past Exams   Pepperdine U. Exam Archive

- U. of Kentucky Exam List   St. Thomas U. Sample Exams

ADDITIONAL READING:

Exam Taking Tips—Criminal Law

http://stclguns.homestead.com/ExamTakingTips.html

Preparing for and Taking Law School Exams

http://stclguns.homestead.com/ExamTakingTips.html

Tips & Tricks

STATUTORY RULES OF LAW

Section G Skill Objectives—Students will be able to:

- Apply substantive tort and criminal law principles to hypothetical fact patterns to reach sound legal conclusions based on critical thinking.

- Identify and formulate legal issues and to analyze those issues objectively.

Section G Outline:

- Overview of Substantive Law Tort Law
- Sample Outline of Tort Law
- Writing a Tort Exam Fact Pattern Hypothetical (aka How Law Professors Construct Law Exams)
- Tort Writing Assignment
- Deconstructing A Criminal Law Hypothetical
- Criminal Law Writing Assignments
- Criminal Statutes and Case Law

Overview of Substantive Law Tort Law:

Negligence: To prove negligence you must prove the following:

DUTY—standard of care owed by defendant to the plaintiff

Two Issues: (1) Zone of danger created by defendant.

(2) Standard of Care = What a reasonable person would use.

BREACH—of the above duty—consider the following:

Custom & Negligence *Per Se* (violation of a statute). If a defendant broke a law and harmed another by doing so he is presumed to be liable, but he may rebut that presumption by showing a custom to break that law.

Res Ipsa Loquitur (The Think Speaks for Itself—is plain on its face.) The thing that caused injury was in the exclusive control of the defendant. No one but the defendant could have caused the harm.

CAUSATION—defendant caused the harm / injury

Two Types: Actual causation and proximate cause causation.

1. Actual: <u>But For Test</u> (But for what the defendant did would the injury have occurred?)

 <u>Substantial Factor Test</u> (if many things could have caused the injury, any one that was a substantial factor is held liable.)

2. Proximate Cause: <u>Forseeability Test</u> (If injury is unforeseeable = no proximate cause = no liability.)

<u>DAMAGES / INJURIES</u>—plaintiff was harmed (physical, property damage)

Two Issues: What was the harm and did plaintiff mitigate that harm. The defendant is not liable for injuries if the plaintiff did nothing to limit them, such as by seeing a doctor or taking medicine—which may have made matters worse.

If a defendant caused injury in a willful, malicious or reckless matter the plaintiff may be entitled to punitive damages beyond the actual harm suffered.

<u>Defenses to Negligence</u>:

<u>Contributory Negligence</u>—plaintiff contributed to the careless act.

<u>Last Clear Chance (Common Law)</u>—if both parties are negligent then the one with the last clear chance to prevent injury is liable, otherwise both parties share liability.

<u>Assumption of Risk</u>—plaintiff understood the risk and voluntarily assumed the risk.

<u>Emergency Doctrine</u>—Defendant acted rashly to avoid an even greater harm. This affords a lower standard of care.

<u>Custom</u>—If the harmful behavior was the same as that of everyone else.

SAMPLE TORTS OUTLINE: I have set out (below) an outline of tort law (without the products liability sections). You can make an outline for every law class you take and then (after you memorize it) you can condense it down in any manner you choose.

Part 1 <u>INTENTIONAL TORTS</u>

Intent is defined as follows: either that the defendant desires or is substantially certain that the elements of the tort will occur.

Transferred Intent: Intent can be transferred. For example, if A intends to assault B, and accidentally commits battery against B, A is liable for battery to B.

Mistake Doctrine: Under this doctrine, if a defendant intends a tort it is <u>no defense</u> that the defendant mistakes, even reasonably, the identity of the property or person he acts upon or believes incorrectly there is a privilege. If, for example, A shoots B's cat, reasonably believing it is a rat, A is liable to B.

Insanity and Infancy: Neither insanity nor infancy is a defense for an intentional tort. But intent is subjective and requires that the defendant desires or be substantially certain that the elements of the tort will occur. Thus, if the defendant is extremely mentally impaired or very young, he may not possess the requisite intent.

<u>Battery</u>: Battery is the intentional harmful or offensive contact with another person.

Intent: Battery requires intent, but it does <u>not</u> require intent to harm. It is only necessary that the defendant intend to cause either harmful or offensive contact

Harmful or Offensive Contact: Battery encompasses either harmful or offensive contact. Even trivial offensive contact is a battery. Defendant need not actually touch the victim. Example: A spits on B.

<u>Assault</u>: Assault occurs when the defendant's acts intentionally cause the victim's reasonable apprehension of immediate harmful or offensive contact.

Intent: The defendant must desire or be substantially certain that her action will cause the apprehension of immediate harmful or offensive contact.

Apprehension: The victim must *perceive* that harmful or offensive contact is about to happen to him.

Imminent Harmful or Offensive Contact: The victim's apprehension must be of <u>imminent</u> harmful or offensive contact

Fear v. Apprehension: The apprehension of imminent contact need not produce fear in the victim.

<u>False Imprisonment</u>: When the defendant unlawfully and intentionally causes confinement or restraint of a victim within a bounded area. Accidental confinement does not count.

Bounded Area: The victim must be confined within an area bounded in all directions. The bounded area can be, however, a large area, even an entire city.

Confinement or Restraint: The victim must be confined or restrained. Confinement may be accomplished by (1) physical barriers; (2) force or threat of immediate force against the victim, the victim's family or others in her immediate presence, or the victim's property;

(3) omission where the defendant has a legal duty to act; or (4) improper assertion of legal authority.

Consciousness of Confinement: The victim be conscious of the confinement at the time of imprisonment.

<u>Trespass to Chattel and Conversion</u>: Trespass to chattel and conversion are intentional torts that protect personal property from wrongful interference.

<u>Trespass to Chattel</u>: The intentional interference with the right of possession of personal property. The defendant must intentionally damage the chattel, deprive the possessor of its use for a substantial period of time, or totally dispossess the chattel from the owner. This tort does not require that the defendant act in bad faith or intend to interfere with the rights of others. It is sufficient that the actor intends to damage or possess a chattel which in fact is properly possessed by another.

<u>Conversion</u>: An intentional exercise of dominion and control over a chattel which so seriously interferes with the right of another to control it that the actor may justly be required to pay the other the full value of the chattel. Only very serious harm to the property or other serious interference with the right of control constitutes conversion. Damage / interference which is less serious may still constitute trespass to chattel. Buying stolen property, even in good faith and not aware the seller did not have title, constitutes conversion by both the seller and innocent buyer.

<u>Intentional Infliction of Mental Distress</u>: This tort takes place when the defendant, by extreme and outrageous conduct, intentionally or recklessly causes the victim severe mental distress. The victim does not have to suffer physical manifestations of the mental distress. Extreme and outrageous conduct is behavior which is beyond all possible bounds of decency (atrocious) and utterly intolerable in a civilized community. The victim's vulnerability and relationship to the tortfeasor are important factors.

Intent or Recklessness: The defendant must intend to cause severe emotional distress or act with reckless disregard as to whether the victim will suffer severe distress. Although characterized as an intentional tort, recklessness, in addition to intent, generally proves liability.

Third Party Recovery: Courts award a third-party victim recovery only if, in addition to proving the elements of the tort, she is (1) a close relative of the primary victim; (2) present at the scene of the outrageous conduct against the primary victim; and (3) the defendant knows the close relative is present.

Exception—Common Carriers and Innkeepers: Common carriers and innkeepers are liable for intentional gross insults which cause customers to suffer mental distress. There is no requirement for the defendant to act in an extreme or outrageous manner or that the victim suffer <u>extreme</u> distress.

Part 2 <u>DEFENSES TO INTENTIONAL TORTS</u>

<u>Consent</u>

If the asserted victim gives permission, consent is a defense to intentional tort liability.

Express & Implied Consent: One can convey consent <u>expressly</u> with words or through gestures. Consent is <u>implied</u> when the conduct of the individual reasonably conveys consent.

Consent by Law: Consent can be implied by law. Courts recognize by law consent to emergency medical treatment (by health professionals) when a victim is unconscious and unable to consent.

Invalidating Consent:

Incapacity: Both express and implied consent can be invalid if an individual lacks capacity to consent. Example: Children may consent only to less significant matters. Insanity or retardation may bar consent. Incapacity can also be the result of drug or alcohol use.

Action Beyond The Scope of Consent: Consent is also lacking if the action goes beyond the consent given.

Fraud: Consent is invalid if induced by fraud that misrepresents an essential aspect of the interaction.

Duress: Consent obtained by physical threat is invalid. Economic threat, however, does not negate consent.

Illegality: A person <u>cannot</u> consent to a criminal act.

<u>Self-Defense</u>: Self-defense is a defense which can justify and negate intentional tort liability. Reasonable force can be used where one reasonably believes that such force is needed to avoid immediate harm.

The Threat Must be Immediate: Self-defense must be in response to an immediate threat of harm.

The Response Must be Reasonable: Self-defense is justified if one reasonably believes that force is necessary to avoid an attack. The belief need not be correct. Force intended to cause death or serious injury is only justified if one reasonably believes that they will suffer serious bodily injury or death from an attack.

Retreat From Deadly Force: There is no obligation to retreat from force that does NOT threaten death or serious injury. There is disagreement whether retreat is required when self-defense requires force that may cause death or serious injury. The majority position does not require retreat under such circumstances.

<u>Defense of Others</u>: One may use reasonable force to protect another person from immediate physical harm. The majority view holds there is a privilege to use reasonable force to protect another whenever the actor reasonably believes that the other person is entitled to exercise self-defense.

<u>Defense / Recovery of Property</u>: An individual may use reasonable force to prevent a tort against his property.

Reasonable Force: Only reasonable force can be used to protect one's property. Force intended to inflict death or serious injury is never reasonable to protect property. Even slight force is unreasonable in defense of property if it is excessive. Thus, if a verbal threat would suffice, no force is justified. Also, force in defense of property is only a defense when it is directed at a wrongdoer; even a reasonable mistake that an individual has wrongfully interfered with property is not an excuse.

Mechanical Devices: Intentional <u>mechanical</u> infliction of deadly force is not privileged unless such force is needed to defend oneself (or another) from deadly force. Barbed wire fences and similar deterrents are not perceived as intended to inflict death or serious injury because they are designed to deter entry.

Recovery of Personal Property: One may use reasonable force to recover property when in hot pursuit of the wrongdoer. However, if the force is directed at an innocent party (privileged to possess the property), or against one acting out of a bona fide claim of right, the actor is liable for injuries even if the mistake was reasonable.

<u>Necessity</u>: One may interfere with the property interests of an innocent party in order to avoid a greater injury. Risky behavior is justified if the action minimizes the overall loss. The defense is divided into two categories: public and private necessity. <u>Public necessity</u> exists when one appropriates or injures private property to protect the community. Public necessity is a complete defense. <u>Private necessity</u> exists when one appropriates or injures private property to protect a *private interest* valued greater than the appropriated or injured property. Since private necessity is an incomplete defense, one is privileged to interfere with another's property but will be liable for the damage.

Part 3 <u>NEGLIGENCE AND THE REASONABLE PERSON TEST</u>

Intro: To recover for negligence, a plaintiff must prove all of the following elements by a preponderance of the evidence: (1) duty, (2) breach of duty, (3) proximate cause and (4) damages.

The "Reasonable Person" Test: One must act as would a reasonably prudent person in the same or similar circumstances. If one does, he is protected from negligence liability. Failure to act in such a manner constitutes unreasonable conduct and *breach of duty*. The reasonable person standard is an objective standard that compares one's conduct to that of a reasonable person. In this way, the law imposes on each person an obligation to conform to the objective reasonableness standard.

Characteristics of a Reasonable Person: The reasonable person possesses attributes that represent community norms. The reasonable person is not a real person. The reasonable person's qualities are those expected of others in the community. The reasonable person is *not* perfect, and he possesses the general experience of *his community*.

Emergency: A jury is allowed to *consider* in its determination of the defendant's reasonableness evidence that the defendant was acting under emergency conditions not of the defendant's making. This does not necessarily exculpate the defendant from liability.

Physical Condition: A defendant's own physical qualities may be taken into account by a jury in the breach of duty determination. Sometimes the physical condition of the party requires the use of greater care.

Mental Condition: Most courts treat mental conditions as irrelevant for purposes of negligence liability. The insane are held to a standard of sanity and people with cognitive disabilities are held to a level of normal intelligence.

Superior Abilities, Skill or Knowledge: The standard of care does not change for those with superior skills although a defendant's special or unusual skills may affect a jury's breach of duty determination. The reasonable person standard sets the <u>minimum</u> of community expectations; those able to do more are <u>expected to do so</u>.

Children Standard of Care: Children are held to a standard of care that compares their conduct to other reasonable children of the same age, experience, and intelligence under like circumstances. However, many courts have concluded that children should not be entitled to special treatment if they engage in adult or inherently dangerous activities, such as driving a car or shooting a gun.

Part 4 <u>UNREASONABLENESS: BREACH OF DUTY</u>

Breach of duty is the defendant's failure to act as a reasonable person would have under the same or similar circumstances. Breach of duty is <u>unreasonable conduct</u> by a defendant. A jury decides whether the defendant has breached a duty by considering the following factors:

Probability: The probability factor measures the likelihood of the injury causing event taking place.

Magnitude of Loss: The magnitude of loss factor considers the amount of harm flowing from the injury-causing event. It is what a reasonable person would foresee as *likely* harm.

Burden of Avoidance: An analysis of burden requires consideration of such things as the costs associated with avoiding the harm, alternatives and their feasibility, the inconvenience to those involved and the extent to which society values the relevant activity.

The Role of Custom: Custom refers to a way of performing a certain activity within a community, or within a particular trade or industry. An injured plaintiff may assert that a defendant's deviation from custom is evidence of lack of due care. A defendant may likewise try to avoid liability by showing compliance with norms and customs.

Part 5 <u>BURDEN OF PROOF FOR BREACH OF DUTY</u>

The plaintiff has the burden to prove every element of a negligence case by a preponderance of the evidence. If the plaintiff fails to meet this burden, the case will be decided for the defendant. The plaintiff must provide enough evidence so that a jury can find that <u>*more likely than not*</u> the defendant failed to act reasonably. Just because an accident happens is never enough by itself to allow a jury to decide that a defendant's behavior was unreasonable.

Kinds of Evidence

A plaintiff can use direct and circumstantial evidence to prove breach of duty. Direct evidence is evidence that comes from personal knowledge or observation. Circumstantial evidence is proof that requires the drawing of an inference from other facts. If a jury can draw a reasonable inference (as opposed to speculate) the circumstantial evidence will be admitted. For example: Coming indoors with a wet umbrella is circumstantial evidence that it is raining outside.

Constructive Notice for Slip and Fall Cases

Where a plaintiff slips and falls on the defendant's property, the plaintiff must prove more than the fact that she fell and was injured. The plaintiff must also prove that the condition which caused the fall existed long enough so that the defendant should have discovered it and should have cleaned it up.

Res Ipsa Loquitur

Res ipsa loquitur is a form of circumstantial evidence used to prove a defendant's breach of duty. It means "the thing speaks for itself". Res ipsa loquitur has its greatest impact in cases where the plaintiff is unable to make specific allegations about what the defendant did wrong. The necessary elements needed for the application of res ipsa loquitur are: (1) an accident that normally does not happen without negligence, (2) exclusive control of the instrumentality by the defendant and (3) absence of voluntary action or contribution by the plaintiff.

The Effect of Res Ipsa Loquitur:

Upon proof of res ipsa loquitur by the plaintiff, a jury may elect to infer that the defendant was unreasonable—if it so chooses. With res ipsa loquitur, the case gets to a jury (without specific allegations of what the defendant did wrong) and the jury decides whether the defendant was more likely than not at fault.

Part 6 <u>STATUTORY STANDARDS OF CARE—NEGLIGENCE PER SE</u>

The negligence-per-se doctrine provides that in certain situations a criminal statute may be used to set the standard of care in a negligence case. Criminal statutes make no mention of civil liability but do impose fines or imprisonment as punishment for violators. Such specific legislative standards replace the more general reasonable person standard.

Factors Used for Adopting a Statute as the Standard of Care in A Negligence Case

A judge in a negligence case must determine if a statute provides the sort of specific guidance that justifies its use by a civil court. The judge must examine the statute in order to decide if the statute was designed to protect against the <u>type of harm</u> suffered by the plaintiff and whether the class of persons designed to be protected by the statute includes the plaintiff.

Licensing Statutes: Most courts refuse to use licensing statutes as the standard of care because the lack of a license itself does not establish the lack of due care.

The Role of Excuse

Acceptable excuses for violating a statute include: a sudden emergency not of the actor's making; compliance would involve greater danger than violation; the actor neither knows nor should know of the occasion for diligence; the actor has some incapacity rendering the violation reasonable; or, after reasonable efforts to comply, the party is unable to do so.

Negligence Per Se and Children

Most courts have concluded that the child standard of care should apply even when the child has violated a statute. Rather than using the statute as the standard of care, the standard is that of a reasonable child of the same age, maturity, intelligence and experience.

Compliance with Statute

Compliance with a statute is merely relevant evidence of reasonableness. Compliance does not establish due care.

Part 7 PROFESSIONAL NEGLIGENCE

Because of the specialized training needed to be a doctor, lawyer, etc. courts defer to the expertise of the profession to determine the appropriate standard of care. In the professional negligence cases, custom plays a different role than it does in standard negligence cases. In professional negligence cases the defendant's compliance with professional customs insulates the defendant from negligence liability. Custom establishes the standard of care in professional negligence cases.

Medical Malpractice

The standard of care to which doctors are held is set by the custom of the medical profession. A physician must use the skill common to members of the profession. This standard demands of the physician <u>minimal competence</u>. In medical malpractice cases, liability flows from the physician's failure to conform to the profession's customary practice.

Thus, if a doctor adheres to customary practice, she cannot be found to have committed malpractice. As long as <u>one</u> accepted approach (when several approaches are available) is followed, a doctor is protected from malpractice liability. In a medical malpractice case, plaintiff must prove more than an unwanted result. Plaintiff must also prove that the defendant doctor's deviation from customary practice <u>caused plaintiff's injury</u>.

Informed Consent

Another basis for medical malpractice liability is based upon a physician's failure to provide information to the patient. Liability arises from the defendant's failure to obtain the plaintiff's informed consent. Although most informed consent cases now are based on negligence, when a physician performs a substantially different procedure from that to which the plaintiff-patient agreed or where the doctor significantly exceeds the scope of the plaintiff's consent, a battery action will be the correct cause of action.

Extensions of Informed Consent

Some courts have expanded the informed consent obligation to require disclosure of risks of forgoing a medical procedure or treatment.

Attorney Malpractice

Custom of the legal profession sets the standard of care in a legal malpractice case and breach of duty is shown by the attorney's failure to meet that standard of care. Unless the attorney malpractice is glaringly apparent, a plaintiff can only prevail with expert testimony regarding both the standard of care and breach. The plaintiff must show that, had there been no malpractice, he would probably have prevailed in the underlying action. Thus, the legal malpractice lawsuit requires the resolution of <u>two</u> conflicts: the initial lawsuit and the malpractice action.

Part 8 <u>DUTY IN NEGLIGENCE CASES</u>

The element of duty requires that there exist a legal relationship between the defendant and the plaintiff that obligates the defendant to act (or to refrain from acting) in a certain way toward the plaintiff.

Nonfeasance / Misfeasance / Negligent Omission

<u>Nonfeasance</u> is generally the failure to intervene to confer a benefit upon another. Thus there is usually no duty owed in a nonfeasance case. <u>Misfeasance</u> consists of affirmative acts of doing something that a reasonable person would not do. Misfeasance is also demonstrated by <u>negligent omission</u>—failing to do something that a reasonable person *would* have done. Either misfeasance or negligent omissions generally lead to the finding of a duty. A defendant who is sued based on nonfeasance has not created the risks that ultimately injure the plaintiff. Instead, the defendant failed to prevent harm caused by some other source from occurring. Typically, nonfeasance actions arise where the plaintiff contends that the defendant should have intervened to rescue the plaintiff, or where the claim is that the defendant should have prevented harm to the plaintiff by controlling a third party or by taking measures to protect the plaintiff from injury.

Duty to Rescue

A person does not have a duty to aid another. Courts consistently have refused to require a stranger to render assistance, even where the person could have rendered aid with little risk or effort. However, a well-established exception to the no-duty-to-rescue rule applies when the need for rescue arises because of the defendant's negligence.

Special Relationships

Courts have imposed a duty to rescue when justified by a special relationship between the parties such as a common carrier-passenger, innkeeper-guest and ship captain-seaman.

Undertaking to Act and Reliance

Once a person undertakes to rescue, he must not leave the victim in a worse position. Closely related to the undertaking to act concept is the concept of reliance. Courts have found a duty where the defendant caused the plaintiff to rely on promised aid. Occasionally, a rescue obligation arises from contract. There is debate about the extent to which a defendant's gratuitous promise, without more, gives rise to a duty.

Duty to Control and Protect

A person typically is not legally obligated to control the conduct of another or to take steps to protect another from harm. But exceptions arise where there is a special relationship. The relationships giving rise to a duty to control require some relationship between the defendant and the third party, combined with knowledge (actual or constructive) of the need for control. There can be substantial debate about which relationships give rise to a duty to control.

Suppliers of Liquor

Several jurisdictions now impose liability on commercial suppliers of liquor. A few courts have determined that a social host could be liable to a third party injured by a drunken guest. These decisions are controversial and raise complex policy issues.

Negligent Entrustment

Liability is premised on supplying a potentially dangerous instrumentality (such as a car or gun) to a person the defendant knows or should know is not fit to handle it.

Duty to Protect

As a general principle, there is no obligation to protect another from harm. But if the defendant and plaintiff are in a relationship where the plaintiff has surrendered the ability for self protection, the defendant has a duty to make reasonable efforts to protect the plaintiff.

Business Duty to Protect

The business-patron relationship is rarely enough to itself establish a duty. Courts typically require a high degree of foreseeability to establish a duty.

Police Duty to Protect

Under the "public duty doctrine," a government actor performing improperly is not liable to individuals harmed by the misperformance, because any duty owed is limited to the public at large rather than to any specific individual.

Police Duty

Police departments are typically not liable for failing to protect individual citizens. Most courts fear that if they recognize a duty of protection, they would inevitably be determining how the limited police resources of the community should be allocated. In order for there to be a duty to protect in a police case a plaintiff must establish that the defendant police undertook to act and created reliance, enlisted the aid of the plaintiff, or increased the risk of harm to the plaintiff.

Part 9 <u>LAND OCCUPIER DUTY</u>

Under the common law, the duty owed depended on the *status* of the person entering the land—whether the entrant was a <u>trespasser</u>, a <u>licensee</u>, or an <u>invitee</u>. The status of the person entering the land determined the standard of care owed by the land occupier. Some jurisdictions have rejected the status approach to liability, using a generalized duty of ordinary care instead.

Common Law Approach

The common law approach to landowner liability measured the duty owed by a land occupier to persons entering the property by the status of the entrant. Because of the value attached to private land ownership, the law developed in a way that was highly protective of these interests.

Trespassers: A "trespasser" is one who enters or remains on the property in the possession of another without the permission of the occupier. The duty owed to trespassers was extremely limited. The only obligation imposed on land possessors was to refrain from willfully harming the trespasser. Courts expanded the duty to include requiring warnings about traps.

Frequent or Known Trespassers: Where a land occupier is aware of a trespasser and knows that the trespasser is approaching a non-obvious human made danger, the land occupier is obligated to warn if there is danger of serious harm or death. If the land occupier is on notice of frequent trespassing, an obligation to warn of hidden dangers known to the land possessor and risking serious injury or death may be imposed. No warning need be given of conditions on the land that a trespasser would be expected to discover or which are inherent in the use of the land.

Child Trespassers: Under the <u>attractive nuisance doctrine</u> a child trespasser will be owed a duty of *ordinary care* if a judge balances several factors and finds that they support providing the child trespasser special treatment.

Licensees: A licensee is someone who enters the land with the consent of the land possessor (guests). A land possessor may be liable to a licensee injured by a condition on the property where the land possessor knows of a dangerous condition on the property, fails to make the condition safe or to warn the licensee about the risk involved, and the licensee does not know about the danger nor would be expected to discover the dangerous condition.

Invitees: There are two types of invitees: business invitees and public invitees. Business invitees are on the premises for the potential financial benefit of the land occupier. Public invitees are on land held open to the public at large. As to both, land possessors must use reasonable care in maintaining the premises and in their activities. This often entails taking affirmative steps to discover dangers on the property. The obligation of the land possessor to an invitee then is one of reasonable care.

A Unitary Standard

A minority of states have rejected the common-law status approach discussed above. Under a generalized duty of care approach, a duty of reasonable care is owed any land entrant regardless of status.

Landlord-Tenant

All jurisdictions recognize some or all of the following exceptions: common areas, negligent repairs, undisclosed dangerous conditions known to the lessor, lessor's covenant to repair, premises leased for admission to the public, and dangerous condition to persons outside the leased premises. Most jurisdictions now require a plaintiff to fall within one of these recognized exceptions in order to establish a tort duty owing from the landlord.

Part 10 <u>DUTY LIMITED BY KIND OF HARM</u>

Negligent Infliction of Emotional Distress

In the past, tort law provided compensation for a victim's mental distress only when it followed physical injury. Recovery for such emotional upset is known as "pain and suffering." But in certain limited circumstances, negligently inflicted mental distress that does not follow from physical harm is recognized as a basis for recovery. Traditionally, to recover for mental distress, the defendant's negligence must have caused some form of <u>physical impact</u> on the plaintiff. Today courts only require that the plaintiff have been in risk of physical impact, sometimes referred to as being within the "zone of danger." Most states also require that the victim's mental distress be sufficiently severe to cause physical symptoms of the distress.

A separate development has been the gradual recognition of *bystander* recovery for negligently inflicted emotional distress. A majority of states allow a bystander to recover only if the bystander is also within the zone of physical risk. A few states now allow recovery for bystanders who are not in risk of physical impact if they (1) are physically near the accident; (2) have contemporaneous sensory perception of the accident; and (3) are closely related to the victim. Most of the states following this approach also continue to require that the bystander-plaintiff suffer some physical manifestation of her distress.

Fear of Future Physical Harm

An issue receiving increasing attention is whether emotional distress damages should be recovered for the fear of *future* physical harm. The problem often arises in the toxic tort or defective product context. Most courts are wary of permitting recovery due to the difficulty of measuring damages, potentially crushing liability, and serious proof problems such as the possibility of multiple causes.

Bystander Actions

Recovery for emotional distress suffered from the defendant's negligently inflicted harm *to another* has been particularly controversial.

Zone of Danger

Courts have used the near-impact rule to compensate a bystander for the emotional trauma of witnessing a serious injury to a close relative. Under the zone-of-danger rule, the plaintiff can recover for emotional harm suffered from witnessing negligently inflicted harm causing death or serious injury to a close relative when she is in a position to fear for her own safety.

Wrongful Conception, Wrongful Birth and Wrongful Life

These cases are controversial because the plaintiffs are contending that the birth of a child is a compensable underline. The defendant's negligence has not rendered a healthy child *unhealthy*, but for the defendant's negligence the child would not have been born at all. The case names used in this area varies, but most cases are categorized as follows: the parents' action for the negligently caused birth of a *healthy* child is a wrongful conception case; the parents' claim for damages due to the negligently caused birth of an *unhealthy* child is a wrongful birth case; and the *child's* own legal claim is one for wrongful life.

<u>Wrongful Conception</u>: Plaintiffs are typically permitted to recover damages directly related to the pregnancy and the birth. Some courts also permit the recovery of emotional distress damages. Most courts have refused to permit the parents to recover the cost of raising the child to majority.

<u>Wrongful Birth</u>: The plaintiff must show that "but for" the defendant's negligent failure to diagnose the condition giving rise to the birth defect, the plaintiff would have learned of the potential danger and would have elected to terminate the pregnancy. Most jurisdictions have permitted the wrongful birth plaintiff to recover extraordinary expenses associated with the defect with which the child was born. Some have also permitted recovery of emotional distress damages.

<u>Wrongful Life</u>: A wrongful life action is the action of the infant born in an impaired condition, claiming, in essence, that being born was the injury. The great majority of jurisdictions have refused to recognize such a claim. A central reason for the rejection of a wrongful life claim is the difficulty calculating damages. Courts cannot apply the usual tort damages principles to these cases because the pre-injury condition is non existence.

Loss of Consortium and Wrongful Death

<u>Loss of Consortium</u>: Nearly all jurisdictions permit one spouse to recover against a person who seriously injures the other spouse, usually calling it as an action for loss of consortium. This permits recovery for the economic loss of the of the injured spouse's household services and for loss of companionship, comfort, and sexual services.

<u>Wrongful Death</u>: Every state has passed a statute that permits wrongful death recovery but the scope of recovery varies from state to state. Under a wrongful death statute, plaintiff is suing for loss suffered due to the death of a close relative. A surviving spouse, parents and children are typically permitted to bring an action.

Part 11 CAUSE-IN-FACT

"But For" Test

The traditional test for actual causation is the "but for" test. For the defendant to be held liable, the plaintiff must establish that *but for* the defendant's culpable conduct or activity the plaintiff would not have been injured.

Substantial Factor Test

This test requires that the defendant materially contributed to the plaintiff's injury. The substantial factor test is used by many courts as a <u>supplement</u> to the "but for" test when *redundant multiple* causes would preclude liability under the "but for" analysis.

PROXIMATE OR LEGAL CAUSE

The plaintiff must prove the defendant's culpable conduct is the proximate cause of the plaintiff's injuries. "Proximate" or "legal" cause *adds to the requirement that the defendant's culpable conduct be the actual cause* of the plaintiff's injury and will preclude recovery when the causal relationship between the defendant's conduct and the plaintiff's injury does not justify imposing tort responsibility on the defendant.

Proximate Cause Tests

Foreseeability Test : This test focuses on whether the defendant should have reasonably foreseen the general consequences or type of harm suffered by the plaintiff. The foreseeable harm test requires (1) a reasonably foreseeable result or type of harm, *and* (2) no *superseding* intervening force. The extent and the precise manner in which the harm occurs need not be foreseeable. An intervening force is a new force which joins with the defendant's conduct to cause the plaintiff's injury.

Part 12 <u>DAMAGES</u>

Damages is the money awarded to the person injured by the tort of another. Tort damages include nominal damages, compensatory damages, and punitive damages. Compensatory damages are awarded to a person to indemnify for personal injury, property, and other economic harm sustained by the victim. Compensatory damages are awarded for both pecuniary and non-pecuniary losses. Unlike economic loss, pain and suffering, and other forms of mental distress have no obvious monetary equivalent. This *valuation* issue has generated controversy over the desirability of compensating for pain and suffering at all. Punitive damages are awarded to punish and deter particularly egregious conduct.

Property Damages: Damages for permanent deprivation or destruction of property are measured by the market value of the property at the time of the tort. If real or personal property is damaged but not destroyed, courts compensate for the diminished market value of the property and sometimes award the cost of repairs instead of diminished value.

Personal Injury: Personal injury victims under tort law can be compensated for (1) medical expenses; (2) lost wages or impaired earning capacity; (3) other incidental economic consequences caused by the injury; and (4) pain and suffering.

Punitive Damages: Punitive damages are discretionary and awarded when a tort is committed with malice. The United States Supreme Court has held that punitive damages must bear some relationship to potential harm.

Part 13 <u>DEFENSES</u>

In the past, there were two defenses to negligence: contributory negligence and assumption of risk. Both were complete defenses and completely barred the plaintiff from any recovery. Today in most states contributory negligence has been changed by statute into <u>comparative negligence</u>. Unlike contributory negligence, comparative negligence need not be a complete bar to the plaintiff's recovery, but acts only as partial bar resulting in a percentage deduction from otherwise recoverable damages.

Assumption of Risk

There are thus three basic elements to the assumption of risk. The plaintiff must (1) know a particular risk and (2) voluntarily (3) assume it.

<u>Immunities</u>

Immunity protects a defendant from tort liability. Unlike a defense, it is not dependent on the plaintiff's behavior, but on the defendant's status or relationship to the plaintiff.

Charitable Immunity: Charitable organizations were historically immune from tort liability. Today this immunity has been abrogated.

Spousal Immunity: In the past spouses could not sue each other. Today most states have eliminated spousal immunity.

Parent-Child Immunity: Parent-child immunity precludes tort actions between parents and their non-adult children. Parent-child immunity still exists in some form in many jurisdictions.

Part 14 <u>STRICT LIABILITY</u>

Strict liability is "liability without fault."

Strict Liability for Injuries Caused By Animals

Livestock: The common law rule provided for owner liability without fault for damage done by trespassing livestock. Restatement §504 imposes strict liability for the owner of trespassing livestock *unless* (1) the harm is not a foreseeable one; (2) the trespass by animals being herded along the highway is confined to abutting land; or (3) state common law or statute requires the complaining landowner to have erected a fence.

Domestic Animals: Keepers of domestic animals are liable for injury caused by the animal only where the possessor knew or should have known of the animal's vicious disposition.

Wild Animals: Many jurisdictions have followed the rule of strict liability for owners or keepers of wild animals that cause harm even though the possessor has exercised the utmost care.

Strict Liability for Abnormally Dangerous Activities

Some activities create such serious risks that one may be strictly liable even when he exercises the greatest care. In those cases, a plaintiff must show that with that activity (1) the risk of great harm exists if defendant's safety efforts fail, (2) the impossibility of defendant's complete elimination of the risk of harm, and (3) injury caused.

Activity Was Under Defendant's Control: The activity must have been in the control of the defendant at the time of plaintiff's injury.

Defenses: The plaintiff's assumption of the risk is a defense to a strict liability action based on an abnormally dangerous activity.

Part 15 DEFAMATION

The law of defamation is complicated because it is a blend of common law and First Amendment principles. The tort of defamation permits recovery for harm to one's reputation, which was considered a serious injury in England.

Defamatory Remark

A defamatory remark, is one that harms a reputation by injuring a person's character or causing personal disgrace. A court determines as a matter of law whether the remark *could* be construed as defamatory, while it is for a jury to decide whether the statement in the case before it is *actually* defamatory.

Defamatory to Whom

The plaintiff must show that a substantial and respectable minority would understand the defamatory nature of the remark. This group can be small.

Statements Not Facially Defamatory: Inducement and Innuendo

Some statements are clearly defamatory because nothing needs to be added for one to understand the defamatory nature of the statement. But sometimes the defamatory impact can only be understood by the addition of extra information. In such situations the plaintiff must plead the extra facts needed to make the statement defamatory ("inducement") or to explain the defamatory impact ("innuendo") if not obvious.

Publication / Republication

A plaintiff must prove that the defamatory remark was published, meaning that it reached at least one person other than the defamed plaintiff. The plaintiff must show that either the defendant intended to publish the information or was negligent in doing so. Any repetition of a defamation is considered publication, even if the re-publisher attributes the statement to the initial source.

Damages

General damages provide compensation for the emotional trauma and harm suffered by the plaintiff whose reputation was harmed. There are situations, however, where the plaintiff must plead and prove a specific type of loss, called special damages, in order to win. Special damages are specific economic losses flowing from the defamation. If the plaintiff proves these special damages, he may recover general damages.

Libel / Slander Distinction: Slander is an oral utterance while libel is a written expression.

Defense: Substantial Truth

A defendant may establish truth as a defense. While the defendant has to show the accuracy and truth of the statement in issue, he does not have to show the truth of every aspect—substantial truth is the test.

Public Officials / Public Figures

A public official can only win a defamation case where the public official can prove that the defendant either knew that the statement was false or recklessly disregarded whether the communication was false, a fault standard known as *actual malice*. Public figures generally have access to the media to counteract false communications and they assume the risk of reputational harm by involving themselves in issues of importance.

Private Person

The current law in private plaintiff cases requires that the subject matter of the defamation be analyzed to discern whether it deals with matters of public concern or matters of private concern.

Actual Malice

Actual malice requires plaintiff to prove that either the defendant knew of the falsity or was reckless as to truth or falsity. The plaintiff must prove that the defendant was at least reckless. As to falsity, in cases involving public officials, public figures, or private persons, the plaintiff must prove falsity as part of his case.

Part 16 INVASION OF PRIVACY

There exist four separate torts for invasion of privacy: (1) intrusion upon seclusion, (2) appropriation of plaintiff's name or picture, (3) placing the plaintiff in a false light before the public, and (4) public disclosure of private facts.

Intrusion Upon Seclusion

A person who intentionally intrudes, physically or otherwise, upon the solitude or seclusion of another or his private affairs or concerns, is subject to liability to the other for invasion of his privacy, if the intrusion would be highly offensive to a reasonable person. This interference may also amount to trespass, but there is no requirement that trespass be committed.

Appropriation of Name / Picture and the Right of Publicity

One who appropriates for his own use or benefit the name or likeness of another is subject to liability to that person for invasion of his privacy. The tort applies to an unauthorized endorsement of a product. It does not apply to journalistic articles or books about a person.

False Light: The privacy tort of false light overlaps with defamation. The elements of false light which must be proven by plaintiffs include the defendant's (1) publicizing (2) false facts (3) that a reasonable person would object to.

WRITING A TORT EXAM FACT PATTERN HYPOTHETICAL

In this section I will show you how to write a tort exam hypothetical fact pattern. Remember, a real tort exam may have several small fact patterns or one large one (or a combination thereof). Here, we will write one small fact pattern.

First: Make up the general plot and the parties involved. Here, I will write about a high school cheerleading competition between two competing high schools: high school A and high school B. The parties involved are cheerleaders 1, 2 and 3 for high school A, and cheerleaders X, Y and Z for high school B.

Second: Select a few torts to test on. Here, I select four torts: assault, battery, a negligent tort and defamation.

Third: Decide who will be the plaintiff(s) and who will be the defendant(s). I will make cheerleader 1the evil cheerleader (the defendant) and cheerleader X the injured party (the plaintiff).

Fourth: Specify a role/perspective for the law student. In this case, the law student will be the defense attorney for cheerleader 1.

Fifth: Flesh out the story/fact pattern.

❦

High school A and high school B have been long time adversaries, each with nationally recognized football teams and cheerleading squads. This year, the annual cheerleading competition between the two schools will be held at high school A. A full college scholarship will be awarded to every cheerleader on the winning team. Cheerleader 1 is the head cheerleader for high school A. Cheerleader X is the head cheerleader for high school B.

Cheerleader 1 really needs and wants the scholarship because without it she will not be able to afford to attend college. Cheerleader X comes from an affluent family and will attend college regardless of the outcome of the competition. Further, cheerleader's boyfriend recently dumped her and started to date cheerleader X.

❦

Before we go further, let us review the elements of assault and battery so that we may make out facts to support both torts in the above fact pattern.

Assault: Assault occurs when the defendant's acts intentionally cause the victim's reasonable apprehension of immediate harmful or offensive contact.

Intent: The defendant must desire or be substantially certain that her action will cause the apprehension of immediate harmful or offensive contact.

Apprehension: The victim must *perceive* that harmful or offensive contact is about to happen to him.

Imminent Harmful or Offensive Contact: The victim's apprehension must be of <u>imminent</u> harmful or offensive contact

Fear v. Apprehension: The apprehension of imminent contact need not produce fear in the victim.

Battery: Battery is the intentional harmful or offensive contact with another person.

Intent: Battery requires intent, but it does <u>not</u> require intent to harm. It is only necessary that the defendant intend to cause either harmful or offensive contact

Harmful or Offensive Contact: Battery encompasses either harmful or offensive contact. Even trivial offensive contact is a battery. Defendant need not actually touch the victim. Example: A spits on B.

᠆᠆

When the cheerleaders from high school B arrive at the competition site, cheerleader 1 points her baton (in a menacing manner) at cheerleader X and says, "You are going down!" Cheerleader 1 then throws her baton directly at cheerleader X's head but misses by about two feet. Cheerleader X did not duck or flinch, but laughed and responded, "With that kind of sloppy throwing accuracy your team will surely loose today". Cheerleader X turns to walk away, but cheerleader 1 throws a sneaker at the back of cheerleader X's head and makes contact.

᠆᠆

Here are the tort elements and the corresponding facts which prove the elements:

Assault:

<u>intent</u>   cheerleader 1 intended to create apprehension—done in a *menacing* manner followed by a *verbal threat*

<u>apprehension</u> cheerleader X perceived that harmful contact was about to happen to her since she saw the baton coming at her face

<u>counterargument</u>—there was no apprehension because she did not duck

<u>imminent contact</u> yes

NB: Since cheerleader X did not <u>see</u> the sneaker as it came at her head from behind, there was no assault because the element of apprehension is missing. There was, however, battery, as discussed below.

<u>Battery</u>:

<u>intent</u>   cheerleader 1 intentionally threw her sneaker at cheerleader X's head

<u>contact</u> even though cheerleader 1 did not actually touch cheerleader X, her sneaker did and contact need not be harmful, but here it was clearly offensive

Now, I will add to the story to make out the elements of a negligent tort:

☙

As cheerleader 1 is preparing for the competition she applied hand lotion to her arms and some of it fell on the gym floor where the cheerleaders from high school B were about to perform. Cheerleader 1 saw the mess on the floor but was careless and did nothing about it. As the cheerleaders from high school B excitedly ran into the center of the gym, cheerleader X slipped and fell and broke her ankle. She was disqualified from further competition by the school nurse. Nevertheless, the cheerleaders from high school B won the competition.

☙

The elements of any negligent tort are: (1) duty (2) breach of duty (3) cause (4) injury. Here, cheerleader 1 had a duty to behave reasonably but she was "careless" and thus breached that duty. A reasonable person would have cleaned up the mess as it was forseeable that someone might slip on it since it was on the gym floor where the competition was to take place. Cause, however, is hard to prove since the facts do not say that cheerleader X slipped on the lotion, only that she "slipped and fell". Injury is obviously the broken ankle. It may be argued that cheerleader X caused her own fall by running.

If, however, cheerleader X <u>did</u> slip on the lotion, then cheerleader 1 is liable for her physical injuries. Since cheerleader X's team won the competition, there was no monetary loss to argue. Since the spilled lotion was a careless act (not malicious or intentional) there are no punitive damages to argue.

Finally, I will add to the fact pattern to make out the tort of defamation. Let us first review the three elements of that tort:

<u>Defamatory Remark</u>—A defamatory remark, is one that harms a reputation by injuring a person's character or causing personal disgrace.

<u>Defamatory to Whom</u>—The plaintiff must show that a substantial and respectable minority would understand the defamatory nature of the remark. This group can be small.

Publication—A plaintiff must prove that the defamatory remark was published, meaning that it reached at least one person other than the defamed plaintiff. The plaintiff must show that either the defendant intended to publish the information or was negligent in doing so.

Libel / Slander Distinction: Slander is an oral utterance while libel is a written expression.

Defense: Substantial Truth

Here, then, are some facts to make out the tort of defamation.

Needless to say, cheerleader 1 was very angry because she did not win the college scholarship. That night she went on Face Book and wrote the following about cheerleader X. "Cheerleader X is a whore! She is having sex with my ex boyfriend and is pregnant". The entire student body at high school B read the posted remark and started to call cheerleader X a "slut" to her face. Cheerleader X was extremely embarrassed, especially since she actually *was* pregnant. She was, however, pregnant with the child of one of her teachers having conceived prior to dating cheerleader 1's boyfriend. Cheerleader X slept with several teachers and was not certain which one was the baby's daddy. Most of the faculty was already aware of this behavior, and would have referred to cheerleader X as a whore, except for the fact that she was the principal's daughter and they did not want to be fired.

To get revenge, cheerleader X bought a gun, confronted and then shot cheerleader 1 in the leg.

Here, cheerleader 1 did intentionally publish (by a written comment = slander) defamatory statements which were intended to harm cheerleader X's reputation. However, even though cheerleader X read the posted comment and was humiliated, the statement was substantially true. Also, since her reputation was *already* tarnished at her school even before the Face Book comment was published, her reputation was already destroyed. Cheerleader 1 has a valid defense for this tort.

Here is an outline of the parties and identified torts:

Cheerleader 1   assault, battery, negligent tort and defamation

Cheerleader X   assault, battery and trespass

<u>Here is the complete fact pattern:</u>

⌒⌒

High school A and high school B have been long time adversaries, each with nationally recognized football teams and cheerleading squads. This year, the annual cheerleading competition between the two schools will be held at high school A. A full college scholarship will be awarded to every cheerleader on the winning team. Cheerleader 1 is the head cheerleader for high school A. Cheerleader X is the head cheerleader for high school B. [Introduction to the parties in the fact pattern.]

Cheerleader 1 really needs and wants the scholarship because without it she will not be able to afford to attend college. Cheerleader X comes from an affluent family and will attend college regardless of the outcome of the competition. Further, cheerleader's boyfriend recently dumped her and started to date cheerleader X. [Serves to flesh out the mindset (intent) of cheerleader 1.]

When the cheerleaders from high school B arrive at the competition site, cheerleader 1 points her baton (in a menacing manner) at cheerleader X and says, "You are going down!" Cheerleader 1 then throws her baton directly at cheerleader X's head but misses by about two feet. Cheerleader X does not duck or flinch, but laughs and responds, "With that kind of sloppy throwing accuracy your team will surely loose today". Cheerleader X turns to walk away, but cheerleader 1 throws a sneaker at the back of cheerleader X's head and makes contact. [Assault and Battery.]

As cheerleader 1 is preparing for the competition she applied hand lotion to her arms and some of it fell on the gym floor where the cheerleaders from high school B were about to perform. Cheerleader 1 saw the mess on the floor but was careless and did nothing about it. As the cheerleaders from high school B excitedly ran into the center of the gym, cheerleader X slipped and fell and broke her ankle. She was disqualified from further competition by the school nurse. Nevertheless, the cheerleaders from high school B won the competition. [Negligent Tort]

Needless to say, cheerleader 1 was very angry because she did not win the college scholarship. That night she went on Face Book and wrote the following about cheerleader X. "Cheerleader X is a whore! She is having sex with my ex boyfriend and is pregnant". The entire student body at high school B read the posted remark and started to call cheerleader X a "slut" to her face. Cheerleader X was extremely embarrassed, especially since she actually *was* pregnant. She was, however, pregnant with the child of one of her teachers having conceived prior to dating cheerleader 1's boyfriend. Cheerleader X slept with several teachers and was not certain which one was the baby's daddy. Most of the faculty was already aware of this behavior, and would have referred to cheerleader X as a whore, except for the fact that she was the principal's daughter and they did not want to be fired. [Defamation]

To get revenge, cheerleader X bought a gun, confronted cheerleader 1 at high school A, and then shot cheerleader 1 in the leg. [Assault and Battery, Trespass]

As cheerleader 1's defense attorney you must identify and defend against every tort made out by the facts of this hypothetical story. You do NOT defend cheerleader X's torts since that is not your role. Instead, you must argue why cheerleader 1 has valid tort claims against cheerleader X.

✎✎

ADDITIONAL READING:

Sample Tort Exam

http://www2.law.columbia.edu/faculty_franke/Torts/Sample%20Exam.htm

Tort Exams & Sample Answers

http://guweb2.gonzaga.edu/~dewolf/torts/exams/exam_ind.htm

Torts—Additional Study Materials

http://biotech.law.lsu.edu/courses/old_courses/torts99/torts_study_guides.htm

Tort & Injury Law—Exams, etc.

http://stu.findlaw.com/outlines/injury.html

Deconstructing A Criminal Law Hypothetical

Assignment 1:

Your job is to use the law provided (statutes and case law) to decide which crimes are supported by the facts given in the hypothetical (on the next page). Your <u>role</u> is to play the District Attorney assigned to prosecute John's case. The <u>format</u> that you <u>MUST</u> use to write your paper is ARAC.

Remember, you must prove <u>every element</u> of <u>every crime</u> that you identify <u>by justifying each element</u> with a fact (or multiple facts) from the fact pattern. Your essay must elaborate each crime charged, all of its elements (as stated in the related statute) plus facts that support how each element was proven. Do not add facts to the fact pattern.

Finally, you must incorporate the some of the <u>case law</u> provided into your argument to support your allegations of which crimes were committed by John.

It is also very important for you to recognize any possible defenses that may be argued by John's defense attorney. You <u>must</u> raise any possible counterarguments or defenses <u>and</u> respond to them.

If you can support your answer with the statutes, facts and case law—then it should be correct. You may also use the grading rubric provided on page __ to try to self grade your essay. Remember to use good grammar and to spell check your paper.

Assignment 2:

Write a criminal law fact pattern hypothetical. That is, you must make up a criminal fact pattern that describes <u>any four</u> crimes that were NOT used in the above assignment. To do this you must look up the New York Penal Code online (or at a law library) to select four different crimes to flesh out in a fact pattern. For example, you may use arson because arson was not in assignment 1 above. Your facts must prove every element of every crime you select.

CRIMINAL LAW FACT PATTERN

Here is a criminal law hypothetical that I wrote just like the tort hypothetical earlier referenced. Before we go further, please note that assault and battery are torts and they are also crimes. But the elements are very different. The burden of proof is also different for tort law and criminal law. Keeping that in mind, read the following criminal law fact pattern and then read the penal (criminal) code and case law that follows to determine which crimes were committed.

John, a twenty year old addict, needed money to buy more crack cocaine. It had been several days since his last score and he was desperate. It was winter in Buffalo, New York and his footsteps were muffled by deep snow. His method for obtaining money was to break into homes in the middle of the night, while the occupants slept, and to quietly take whatever valuables he found on the first floor.

On this particular night John used a crowbar to break into a house on Willow Street. He pried open a kitchen window and climbed in. He was dismayed to discover that the house was completely empty. There was no furniture in the house and the electricity had been turned off. John went upstairs and discovered a group of teenagers smoking weed in one of the empty bedrooms. All but one of the teenagers ran away. Mary, an eighteen year old, was too stoned and dazed to run away.

John took advantage of the situation and started to undress Mary. She struggled and scratched John, but she was too frightened and dazed to say anything or to cry out for help. After the sex act, John took out a knife and plunged it into Mary's chest intending to kill her so that she could not accuse him of rape. Mary passed out but did not die. Thinking Mary to be dead, John left the house and went home. He accidentally dropped his knife inside the house before departing.

When Mary regained consciousness she went downstairs to call for help. She was bleeding from a chest wound that had missed her heart. She was screaming for help as she left the house through the front door, but she slipped on some snow, fell backwards and hit her head on the concrete front steps. The blow to the head killed her. An elderly neighbor heard her screams and came to see what was happening. When he saw the dead girl and the blood on the snow he suffered a heart attack and died.

A nearby neighbor saw John go into the house and called the police. The police arrived just in time to witness Mary's fall and the elderly neighbor's heart attack. The police found John's fingerprints in the house and on the knife. They matched John's DNA to a sperm sam-

ple from Mary's body and to John's skin cells found under Mary's nails. John was arrested, convicted of several crimes and sentenced to life in prison.

Parties: John, Mary, Teenagers, Elderly Neighbor.

⮑⮐

Additional Instructions for Analyzing the Criminal Fact Pattern (above):

The criminal code statutes and case law that follow are for you to read and to use when you analyze the above criminal fact pattern. **Not all of them will apply.** You must be selective and use only the ones that relate to the fact pattern. Note: I have modified the statutes to make them easy to read and to understand for the purposes of this assignment. If you need to see what the real statutes look like you can look them up in the New York Penal Code.

For this assignment you must:

- Decide which crimes were committed according to the statutes and cases.

- <u>Prove</u> that each crime you identify <u>was</u> committed by identifying which *facts* from the fact pattern prove out the *elements* of the statutes / cases.

- Apply any defenses that may be useful.

- Raise any counterarguments or potential weakness with regard to crimes.

Applicable Criminal Statutes and Cases

Section 120.10 Assault in the first degree

A person is guilty of assault in the first degree when:

1. With intent to cause serious physical injury to another, he causes injury by means of a deadly weapon or a dangerous instrument; or

2. With intent to disfigure another seriously and permanently, or to destroy, amputate, or disable permanently a member or organ, he causes such injury; or

3. Under circumstances evincing a depraved indifference to life, he recklessly engages in conduct which creates a grave risk of death, and thereby causes serious physical injury; or

4. In the course of and in furtherance of the commission or attempted commission of a felony or of immediate flight there from, he causes serious physical injury.

Section 125.27 Murder in the first degree

A person is guilty of murder in the first degree when:

1. <u>With intent</u> to cause death, he causes the death; and

the victim was killed while the defendant was in the course of committing or attempting to commit and in furtherance of robbery, burglary in the first degree or second degree, kidnapping in the first degree, arson in the first degree or second degree, rape in the first degree, criminal sexual act in the first degree, sexual abuse in the first degree, aggravated sexual abuse in the first degree or escape in the first degree, or in the course of and furtherance of immediate flight after committing or attempting to commit any such crime or in the course of and furtherance of immediate flight after attempting to commit the crime of murder in the second degree; provided however, the victim is not a participant in one of the aforementioned crimes.

2. In any prosecution under subdivision one, it is an <u>affirmative defense</u> that:

(a) The defendant acted under the influence of <u>extreme emotional disturbance</u> for which there was a reasonable explanation or excuse, the reasonableness of which is to be determined from the viewpoint of a person in the defendant's situation under the circumstances as the defendant believed them to be.

Felony Murder

The following cases expand upon the felony murder concept.

Cases:

People v. Davis, 491 N.Y.S.2d 240 (N.Y. Sup. Ct. 1985) (felony murder (§ 125.25(3)))

In re Anthony M., 63 N.Y.2d 270 (1984) (felony murder (§ 125.25(3)))

People v. Hernandez, 82 N.Y.2d 309 (1993) (felony murder (§ 125.25(3)))

People v. Matos, 83 N.Y.2d 509 (1994) (felony murder (§ 125.25(3)))

PEOPLE of the State of New York

v

Jeffrey DAVIS

Supreme Court, Criminal Term,

Kings County, Part VII

128 Misc. 2d 782 (1985)

EDWARD C. ALFANO, Justice.

Defendant has been indicted for felony murder (2 counts) (the underlying felonies are robbery and burglary) and one count of intentional murder. Defendant's confession indicates that at the time of the homicide he was "high" on drugs. In its jury charge this court did not charge intoxication as to felony murder, but did charge intoxication as to intentional Murder. The court wishes to expand on its rationale. 1. Penal Law "§ 125.25 Murder in the Second Degree: A person is guilty of murder in the second degree when:

Acting either alone or with one or more other persons, he commits or attempts to commit robbery, burglary...and, in the course of and in furtherance of such crime or immediate flight there from, he or another participant, if there be any, causes the death of a person other than one of the participants.

2. The court is aware that Criminal Jury Instructions (CJI), N.Y., recommends such a charge (Vol. 2, § 125.25(3), p. 346). Of course, the charges were prepared prior to the decision in People v. Register, 60 N.Y.2d 270, 469 N.Y.S.2d 599, 457 N.E.2d 704.

Other states have discussed the issue of whether voluntary intoxication is a defense to felony murder. Such states as Pennsylvania and New Jersey have at one time held that intoxication is not a defense to felony murder. [n. 3]

3. Although present law in Pennsylvania and New Jersey may now be different the cited cases give some insight into the thinking of other jurisdictions on the issue before this court.

In cases such as Commonwealth v. Wooding, 355 Pa. 555, 50 A.2d 328; Commonwealth v. Hardy, 423 Pa. 208, 223 A.2d 719 and Commonwealth v. Tarver, 446 Pa. 233, 284 A.2d 759, the Supreme Court of Pennsylvania held that neither a specific intent to kill nor premeditation to take life was an element of the crime of felony murder. Thus, the fact that defendant may have been intoxicated during the commission of the crime of felony murder "was of no legal significance (Commonwealth v. Wooding, 355 Pa. 555, 50 A.2d 328, 329, supra; see also, Commonwealth v. Edwards, 380 Pa. 52, 110 A.2d 216, 218-219; Commonwealth v. Simmons, 361 Pa. 391, 65 A.2d 353; Murphy, "Has Pennsylvania Found a Satisfactory Intoxication Defense?", 81 Dickinson L.R. 199; Commonwealth v. Graves, 461 Pa. 118, 334 A.2d 661; Commonwealth v. Haywood, 464 Pa. 226, 346 A.2d 298, 299 n. 3).

Early New Jersey cases also have held that intoxication is not a defense to felony murder. The courts reasoned that except where the defendant has interposed a plea of insanity the state of mind of a defendant accused of felony murder "was not in issue" (State v. Roach, 119 N.J.L. 488, 197 A. 33; State v. Burrell, 120 N.J.L. 277, 199 A. 18). Therefore, a defendant's intoxication was no defense to the crime of felony murder (cf State v. Roman, 168 N.J.Super. 344, 403 A.2d 24, 26-27).

In New York, intoxication, although <u>not a defense to a criminal charge</u>, may be offered by a defendant at trial "whenever it is relevant to negative an element of the crime charged" (P.L. 15.25, emphasis added).

"Elements" of an offense are identified as a "culpable mental state (mens rea) and a voluntary act (actus reus) (Penal Law, § 15.10). Both are required in all but the strict liability offenses." (People v. Register, 60 N.Y.2d 270, 276, 469 N.Y.S.2d 599, 457 N.E.2d 704).

In People v. Register, (supra), the Court of Appeals held that in some crimes there is an "additional requirement" which "refers to neither the mens rea nor the actus reus" (italics in original). This "additional requirement," Register held, "is not an element in the traditional sense but rather a definition of the factual setting in which the risk creating conduct must occur—objective circumstances which are not subject to being negatived by evidence of defendant's intoxication" (id. at 276, 469 N.Y.S.2d 599, 457 N.E.2d 704).

The court must determine whether the underlying felony in the crime of felony murder is an element, or a "definition of the factual setting in which the risk creating conduct must occur..."[p. 784] (i.e., "objective circumstances") (People v. Register, 60 N.Y.2d 270, 276, 469 N.Y.S.2d 599, 457 N.E.2d 704, supra).

It has been held that in "felony murder, the underlying felony is not so much an element of the crime, but instead functions as a replacement for the mens rea or intent necessary for common-law murder..." (People v. Berzups, 49 N.Y.2d 417, 427, 426 N.Y.S.2d 253, 402 N.E.2d 1155; emphasis added). This legal fiction has been substituted for the intent necessary to commit common-law murder because the crime of felony murder does not have as an element an intent to kill or "malice" or "malice aforethought" (People v. Benson, 125 Misc.2d 843, 846, 480 N.Y.S.2d 811; see also P.L. 125.25, subd. 3; People v. Berzups, 49 N.Y.2d 417, 427, 426 N.Y.S.2d 253, 402 N.E.2d 1155, supra; People v. Gladman, 41 N.Y.2d 123, 125, 390 N.Y.S.2d 912, 359 N.E.2d 420; People v. Marwig, 227 N.Y. 382, 387, 125 N.E. 535, People v. Jones, 81 A.D.2d 22, 45, 440 N.Y.S.2d 248; People v. Miller, 108 A.D.2d 1053, 485 N.Y.S.2d 857, 861).

This substituted intent is a general, rather than a specific intent, and cannot be negatived by intoxication (see, People v. Register, 60 N.Y.2d 270, 469 N.Y.S.2d 599, 457 N.E.2d 704, supra; People v. Leary, 64 A.D.2d 825, 407 N.Y.S.2d 313; People v. Roark, 643 P.2d 756, 773-774; People v. DelGuidice, 199 Colo. 41, 606 P.2d 840, 842-844; State v. Shine, 193 Conn. 632, 479 A.2d 218; People v. Harkey, 69 Ill.App.3d 94, 25 Ill.Dec. 487, 489, 386 N.E.2d 1151, 1153).

Thus, the Court of Appeals in People v. Berzups, (49 N.Y.2d 417, 427, 426 N.Y.S.2d 253, 402 N.E.2d 1155, supra), in holding that the underlying felony "is not so much an element of the crime [of felony murder]" has recognized that the underlying felony is not an element of that crime.

As the underlying felony is not an essential element of felony murder it is possible to be found guilty of felony murder notwithstanding that the underlying felony was dismissed for legal insufficiency on that defendant was acquitted of the underlying felony (People v. Davis, 46 N.Y.2d 780, 413 N.Y.S.2d 911, 386 N.E.2d 823; People v. Murray, 40 N.Y.2d 327, 386 N.Y.S.2d 691, 353 N.E.2d 605 [in each case the underlying felony was dismissed for lack of corroboration. The felony murder conviction was upheld as not requiring corroboration]; People v. Lucas, 105 A.D.2d 545, 546-547, 481 N.Y.S.2d 789; People v. Murray, 92 A.D.2d 617, 459 N.Y.S.2d 810 [double jeopardy did not bar a new trial on the felony murder count even if the trial judge at the first trial dismissed the robbery, which was the underlying felony, for insufficiency of the evidence]; People v. Crimmins, 99 A.D.2d 439, 470 N.Y.S.2d 617, affd. 64 N.Y.2d 1072, 489 N.Y.S.2d 879, 479 N.E.2d 224; People v. Scott, 93 A.D.2d 754, 461 N.Y.S.2d 309; People v. Ponder, 77 A.D.2d 223, 433 N.Y.S.2d 288, affd. 54 N.Y.2d 160, 445 N.Y.S.2d 57, 429 N.E.2d 735). Since there can be an acquittal of the underlying felony and a conviction of felony murder also indicates that the underlying felony is not an "element" of felony murder.

It held that voluntary intoxication should have been charged so that if the jury found that defendant's intoxicated condition negatived the intent to rob, the jury having been charged as to the lesser degrees of homicide, would have had the alternative to find defendant guilty of any one of those lesser degrees. Under former law, there existed felony murder and misdemeanor murder. Under present law, this distinction no longer exists. Under present law, as felony murder has no lesser included offenses and a conviction of felony murder will be upheld even though there is an acquittal of the underlying felony, People v. Koerber (supra) is no longer the law.

In accord with Koerber (supra), is People v. Cummings, (274 N.Y. 336, 8 N.E.2d 882), also a felony murder case, where the Court of Appeals reiterated the position taken in Koerber (supra). For the reasons stated above, this case has been overruled by present law.

It is also noted that defenses or legal requirements of the underlying felony are not necessarily defenses or legal requirements of a felony murder based on such underlying felony (People v. Davis, 46 N.Y.2d 780, 413 N.Y.S.2d 911, 386 N.E.2d 823, supra; People v. Murray, 40 N.Y.2d 327, 386 N.Y.S.2d 691, 353 N.E.2d 605, supra). It would appear that although intoxication is a "defense" to the underlying felony, it does not apply to felony murder.

The underlying felony, not being an element of felony murder can best be described as an aggravating circumstance. It describes the "factual setting in which the risk creating conduct must occur—objective circumstances (People v. Register, 60 N.Y.2d 270, 276, 469 N.Y.S.2d 599, 457 N.E.2d 704, supra). Such "objective circumstances" cannot be negatived by intoxication (People v. Register, id. at 276, 469 N.Y.S.2d 599, 457 N.E.2d 704). This court therefore did not charge intoxication as to the counts alleging felony murder.

END OF DOCUMENT

In the Matter of ANTHONY M., a Person Alleged to be a Juvenile Delinquent,

Appellant

The PEOPLE of the State of New York, Appellant

v

Frank CABLE and Denise Godbee, Respondents

Court of Appeals of New York

63 N.Y.2d 270 (1984)

OPINION OF THE COURT

KAYE, Judge.

In the two appeals before us, elderly victims of crime—an attempted purse-snatching, and a robbery and burglary—some days after these incidents, succumbed to heart attacks, having shown no immediate signs of heart trouble. The central issue is whether there was sufficient proof to support the fact-finders' determinations that the stress of the incidents was a cause of the fatalities. Concluding that there was sufficient evidence of causal connection, we affirm the adjudication of Anthony M. for juvenile delinquency based on manslaughter, and we reverse the Appellate Division order and reinstate the conviction and sentence of defendant Frank Cable for felony murder, manslaughter and robbery. While our conclusion as to causal connection applies with equal force to Cable's codefendant, Denise Godbee, she is entitled to a new trial with respect to the homicide charges because in her case the court erroneously refused to charge the affirmative defense to felony murder.

Matter of Anthony M.

Anthony M., a 12 year old, in the early evening of April 17, 1982, was seen loitering near a subway entrance in midtown Manhattan half an hour before the incident and again observed there, for about five minutes, when two elderly women passed, one of them the 83-year-old victim, Lee Gibson. In a matter of seconds, Anthony crouched behind her, grabbed her handbag and, when Mrs. Gibson would not release the bag, he pulled the strap with such force that she was whirled around, thrown to the sidewalk on her left side, and dragged a short distance, whereupon Anthony let go and disappeared into the subway station. Mrs. Gibson was taken to the hospital, where a fractured left hip and other bruises were diagnosed. She was also that day examined by her cardiologist, Dr. Jerome Zacks, who recommended transfer to another hospital for surgery involving the implantation of a pin in order that she might walk again.

In the initial days following the incident, she exhibited no symptoms of heart trouble, despite a medical history that included hypertension, long- standing angina (both believed to be under control), an enlarged heart, arteriosclerosis of the coronary artery and vascular disease. After hip surgery was performed, on April 19, in the second hospital, her condition progressed normally.

On April 25, Mrs. Gibson developed congestive heart failure, and two days later died of a myocardial infarction.

At a fact-finding hearing on charges against Anthony involving <u>manslaughter</u>, <u>attempted robbery</u> and <u>assault</u>, three medical experts testified regarding the cause of Mrs. [p. 277] Gibson's death. The testimony of Dr. Manuel Navarro, Associate Medical Examiner, who had performed the autopsy on April 28, 1982, established that the direct cause of Mrs. Gibson's death was a myocardial infarction, three to five days old.

However, he could not with any medical certainty pinpoint the April 17 incident as a cause of the heart attack, nor could the medical witness called by the defense, Dr. Tina Dobsevage, an expert in internal medicine. Both felt, in substance, that given her general physical condition Mrs. Gibson could well have died at any time even without the stress of the attempted purse-snatching. Dr. Zacks, the cardiologist, while acknowledging that he would not have recommended the hospital transfer and surgery if he perceived an undue risk, and that Mrs. Gibson was doing well postoperatively, expressed the opinion with a reasonable degree of medical certainty that the indirect cause of her death was the "stress of a mugging and subsequent fracture of a hip, surgery for that hip fracture, thereafter, pain and anxiety and fear of never being able to walk again while she was in the hospital prior to her sudden—cardiac arrest * * * [T]he stress precipitated the myocardial infarction with subsequent cardiac arrest and ultimate death."

Finding that Anthony had created a substantial and unjustifiable risk when he selected Mrs. Gibson as his victim, that he was heedless of the peril created by his violence, and that his criminal act set in motion the sequence of events that led inexorably to her death, the trial court found that Anthony had committed acts that if done by an adult would constitute the crimes of attempted robbery in the first degree, assault in the first degree, and manslaughter in the second degree, and placed him with the Division for Youth, Title III, for 18 months. The Appellate Division affirmed, 97 A.D.2d 989, 468 N.Y.S.2d 963, without opinion. Only the finding regarding manslaughter is challenged on appeal.

Cable and Godbee

Arnold Weiner, an 89-year-old retired diamond merchant, and his wife, Anna, on July 23, 1980 were robbed in their Manhattan apartment, threatened with a knife, bound, and left lying face down on their living room floor. [p. 278] Mr. Weiner was also struck in the face. Two days later, he died of a myocardial infarction.

A man identified as defendant Cable was seen entering the Weiners' apartment building early in the morning of July 23. His girlfriend, defendant Godbee, who had recently begun work as a maid for the Weiners, followed moments later. Defendants rode up together in the elevator which stopped at the tenth floor, where the Weiners lived. Godbee was admitted to the Weiners' apartment, but went right out to deliver a newspaper to a neighbor, leaving the apartment door unlocked, as she had done on a prior occasion.

When she returned, she discovered that a male intruder (found by the jury to be Cable) had tied up Weiner, and was in the process of tying up Mrs. Weiner. Godbee, according to her statement to the police, started to call for help, but was threatened by the intruder, who proceeded to take several items of jewelry. Mrs. Weiner later awakened to find herself and her husband, both bound, on the living room floor, her husband bleeding from the mouth. She asked Godbee, who was seated in a chair, to call the superintendent, but Godbee said that she had already called the police. Some 20 minutes after he had entered, Cable was seen leaving the building, attempting to hide his face. Several of the items of jewelry were, later that day and the next, sold by Cable.

Weiner that afternoon was taken to Roosevelt Hospital by a neighbor, treated for the cuts and bruises, and returned home. The next day, July 24, he visited his personal physician, Dr. Walter Liebling, complaining of pains in his left lateral lower chest, just above the waistline; no EKG was taken. On July 25 he again complained of not feeling well and spent the day in bed. Late that day, some 56 or 57 hours after the theft, Weiner suffered heart failure and died.

At the trial of defendants for felony murder, depraved indifference murder, robbery and burglary, Dr. Liebling testified that, despite excess weight and arteriosclerosis, Weiner prior to July 23 was in "good general health." During the four years of their relationship, Dr. Liebling had never detected any sign of heart disease in Weiner, and he had no serious illness.

While the experts agreed that the direct cause of Weiner's death was the myocardial infarction, they differed on when the infarction occurred. For the People, Dr. Elliott Gross, Chief Medical Examiner for New York City, who performed the autopsy, testified as a pathology expert that from the color of the infarct and lack of scar tissue, it most likely occurred 44 to 54 hours before death. In his opinion, it was possible for a 90-year-old man who had been burglarized to suffer a mild cardio-infarction that would not show up for two days, but the infarction also could have occurred without any excitement or trauma.

Testifying in Godbee's behalf, Dr. Steven Factor, a specialist in cardiovascular pathology, dated the infarct at 72 to 96 hours before Mr. Weiner's death—which would have placed it before the theft—basing his opinion on the number of white cells and the presence of fibroblasts, or "scavenger" cells, at the periphery of the infarct. Like Dr. Gross, he testified that it was "possible" that the stress of the robbery led directly to the infarct, but he could not be certain of this, and he further opined that no one could be.

Dr. Millard Hyland, Deputy Chief Medical Examiner for Manhattan and Staten Island, testifying on rebuttal as an expert in forensic pathology, from the white cells and absence of fibroblasts, as well as the red blood cells of the clot and the absence of scar tissue, placed the infarct between 36 and 72 hours before death. Moreover, while acknowledging the possibility of other causes, he expressed the opinion with a reasonable degree of medical certainty, as well as commonsense certainty, that the emotional and physical trauma of the burglary caused Weiner's heart attack.

Defendants were convicted of felony murder, manslaughter in the second degree, robbery in the first and second degrees, and burglary in the second degree. The Appellate Division, 96 A.D.2d 251, 468 N.Y.S.2d 470, two Justices dissenting, reversed the convictions for felony murder, manslaughter and robbery in the first degree, and dismissed the charges underlying them.

In both appeals, defendants urge—as the Appellate Division majority concluded in Cable and Godbee—that the necessary causal connection between offense and myocardial infarction was insufficiently established. Measured by a standard of "whether, after viewing the evidence in the light most favorable to the prosecution, any rational trier of fact could have found the essential elements of the crime beyond a reasonable doubt" (Jackson v. Virginia, 443 U.S. 307, 319, 99 S.Ct. 2781, 2789, 61 L.Ed.2d 560; see, also, People v. Contes, 60 N.Y.2d 620, 621, 467 N.Y.S.2d 349, 454 N.E.2d 932), we believe that there was sufficient evidence to support the finding of causation made at the trial level.

For criminal liability to attach, a defendant's actions must have been an actual contributory cause of death, in the sense that they "forged a link in the chain of causes which actually brought about the death" (People v. Stewart, 40 N.Y.2d 692, 697, 389 N.Y.S.2d 804, 358 N.E.2d 487). "An obscure or a merely probable connection between an assault and death will, as in every case of alleged crime, require acquittal of the charge of any degree of homicide" (People v. Brengard, 265 N.Y. 100, 108, 191 N.E. 850).

A defendant's acts need not be the sole cause of death; where the necessary causative link is established, other causes, such as a victim's preexisting condition, will not relieve the defendant of responsibility for homicide (see People v. Kane, 213 N.Y. 260, 273, 107 N.E. 655). By the same token, death need not follow on the heels of injury. Even an intervening, independent agency will not exonerate defendant unless "the death is solely attributable to the secondary agency, and not at all induced by the primary one" (People v. Kane, 213 N.Y. 260, 270, 107 N.E. 655, supra).

An injury may trigger immediate measurable deterioration and a gradual process of dying for which defendant is responsible (People v. Brengard, 265 N.Y. 100, 104-105, 191 N.E. 850, supra; see, also, People v. Roberts, 73 A.D.2d 954, 424 N.Y.S.2d 13), but that is not to say that a victim who evidences no immediate decline cannot just as surely have been set by defendant's acts on a certain course to death.

Though sometimes perceptible to lay witnesses (see People v. Brengard, 265 N.Y. 100, 105, 191 N.E. 850, supra), the progression from injury to death, often unseen and not readily comprehended, will generally be a subject for expert medical opinion. To establish a causal connection, conclusions which are only "contingent, speculative, or merely possible" (Matter of Burris v. Lewis, 2 N.Y.2d 323, 327, 160 N.Y.S.2d 853, 141 N.E.2d 424) will not suffice, but neither is absolute certainty and the exclusion [p. 281] of every other possibility required. While in both cases other possible causes of the heart attacks suffered by the elderly victims were not eliminated, the medical evidence, viewed from the perspective enunciated in Jackson, supported the fact-finders' determinations that defendants' acts were at least a contributing cause of both fatalities.

In Anthony M., the medical evidence connected the stress of the fall and fractured hip to the consequent stresses and fears of immobility, pain and surgery to correct the condition caused by the fall, leading to cardiac arrest and ultimate death. Similarly, in Cable and Godbee, there was proof in the medical evidence to support the jury determination that the stress arising from defendants' acts was a cause of the infarction that manifested itself two days later. In neither instance was the testimony of the medical expert that there was a causal link so baseless or riddled with contradiction that it was unworthy of belief as a matter of law (see People v. Stewart, 40 N.Y.2d 692, 699, 389 N.Y.S.2d 804, 358 N.E.2d 487, supra; People v. Ledwon, 153 N.Y. 10, 46 N.E. 1046) and, despite contrary medical opinion, the jury was entitled to accept this evidence.

The trial court erred in refusing to charge the affirmative defense to felony murder. We cannot disregard this error. The jury convicted Godbee of reckless manslaughter (as a lesser included offense of depraved indifference murder), thereby demonstrating its acceptance of the People's contention that Godbee caused the victim's death by soliciting, requesting, commanding, importuning or intentionally aiding Cable to engage in such conduct (Penal Law, § 20.00). This verdict would have been unreconcilable with acquittal of felony murder based on the affirmative defense [p. 283] because, to establish the affirmative defense, Godbee had to prove that she did not solicit, request, command, importune, cause or aid the commission of the homicide act (Penal Law, § 125.25, subd. 3,).

Nevertheless, as a practical matter, by erroneously refusing to give the charge the court divested Godbee's counsel of any reason to argue that, while she may have aided in the robbery, Godbee did not participate in the acts causing the victim's death. Success on this issue, absent submission of the affirmative defense to which Godbee was entitled, would have been an empty victory since she would still have been convicted of felony murder.

Consequently, an acquittal on depraved indifference murder or its lesser included offenses could not have benefited Godbee in terms of the sentence imposed. Had counsel been given the opportunity to argue the affirmative defense, as he should have been, we cannot say the jury would have reached the conclusion it did regarding Godbee's complicity in the acts causing the victim's death.

Although this error would on the law entitle Godbee to a new trial on the felony murder count, since the Appellate Division has not yet passed on the facts the order for a new trial must await that court's review of the facts. Furthermore, since the jury's acceptance of the affirmative defense to felony murder would have required an acquittal of reckless manslaughter, the erroneous failure to give the instruction would on the law require a new trial on that charge as well.

COOKE, C.J., and JASEN, JONES, WACHTLER, MEYER and SIMONS, JJ., concur.

MEYER, J., dissents in part and votes to reverse and order a new trial as to both defendants in a separate opinion.

END OF DOCUMENT

The PEOPLE of the State of New York, Respondent

v

David HERNANDEZ, Appellant

The PEOPLE of the State of New York, Respondent

v

Oswaldo SANTANA, Appellant

Court of Appeals of New York

82 N.Y.2d 309 (1993)

OPINION OF THE COURT

SIMONS, Judge.

This appeal raises the question whether a conviction of felony murder under Penal Law § 125.25(3) should be sustained where the homicide victim, a police officer, was shot not by one of the defendants but by a fellow officer during a gun battle following defendants' attempted robbery. Under the circumstances presented, we conclude that it should, and we therefore affirm.

Defendants Santana and Hernandez conspired to ambush and rob a man who was coming to a New York City apartment building to buy drugs. The plan was to have Santana lure him into the building stairwell where Hernandez waited with a gun. In fact, the man was an undercover State Trooper, wearing a transmitter, and backed up by fellow officers.

Once the Trooper was inside the building, Hernandez accosted him and pointed a gun at his head. A fight ensued during which the officer announced that he was a policeman, pulled out his service revolver and began firing. In the confusion, Hernandez, still armed, ran from the building into a courtyard where he encountered members of the police back-up unit. They ordered him to halt. Instead, he aimed his gun at one of the officers and moved toward him. The officers began firing, and one, Trooper Joseph Aversa, was fatally shot in the head. His body was found near the area where Hernandez was apprehended after being wounded. Santana was arrested inside the building.

The evidence at trial did not establish who killed Aversa, but the People concede that it effectively eliminated the possibility that either defendant was the shooter. Separate juries were empaneled for the two cases, and both defendants were convicted of felony murder and other charges.

On appeal, defendants contend that the felony murder charges should have been dismissed because neither one of them fired the fatal shot. The Appellate Division rejected that argument. Even though a fellow officer shot Aversa, the Court concluded that defendants were properly held responsible for felony murder because their conduct "unquestionably 'forged' a critical link in the chain of events that led to Trooper Aversa's death" (186 A.D.2d 471, 473, 588 N.Y.S.2d 567).

Some 30 years ago, this Court affirmed the dismissal of a felony murder charge on the grounds that neither the defendant nor a co-felon had fired the weapon that caused the deaths (People v. Wood, 8 N.Y.2d 48, 201 N.Y.S.2d 328, 167 N.E.2d 736). In Wood, the defendant and his companions were escaping from a fight outside a [p. 313] tavern when the tavern owner, attempting to aid police, fatally shot a bystander and one of defendant's companions. Defendant was charged with assault and felony murder.

At the time, the relevant provision of section 1044 of the former Penal Law defined murder in the first degree as "[t]he killing of a human being without a design to effect death, by a person engaged in the commission of, or in an attempt to commit a felony" (§ 1044[2]). We concluded that by the plain terms of the statute defendant could not be liable for murder, for the killing of the two men was not committed by a person "engaged in the commission of" a felony or a felony attempt.

Relying on the statute's "peculiar wording", we decided the case without addressing whether a similar result would be required as a matter of common law (8 N.Y.2d, at 53, 201 N.Y.S.2d 328, 167 N.E.2d 736; see, Commonwealth v. Redline, 391 Pa. 486, 137 A.2d 472). The Wood case acknowledged that other jurisdictions differed on whether to apply a proximate cause theory under which felons could be held responsible for homicides committed by nonparticipants or an agency theory under which felons would be responsible only if they committed the final, fatal act (People v. Wood, supra, 8 N.Y.2d at 51-53, 201 N.Y.S.2d 328, 167 N.E.2d 736; see, Annotation, Criminal Liability Where Act of Killing is Done by One Resisting Felony or Other Unlawful Act Committed by Defendant, 56 ALR3d 239, 249- 261, §§ 4, 5).

In 1965, the Legislature revised the felony murder statute by removing the language that had been dispositive in Wood and replacing it with a provision holding a person culpable for felony murder when, during the commission of an enumerated felony or attempt, either the defendant or an accomplice "causes the death of a person other than one of the participants"

(Penal Law § 125.25[3]). Thus, this appeal raises the question of whether Wood remains good law despite the recasting of the Penal Law.

The question is one of first impression for this Court, although some Appellate Division panels have continued to adhere to the Wood rule that the shooter must be a participant in the underlying felony (see, e.g., People v. Castro, 141 A.D.2d 658, 529 N.Y.S.2d 554, lv. denied 72 N.Y.2d 1044, 534 N.Y.S.2d 943, 531 N.E.2d 663; People v. Ramos, 116 A.D.2d 462, 496 N.Y.S.2d 443).

The People believe those Appellate Division decisions to be in error. They premise their argument on the established construction of the term "causes the death", which is now the operative language in the Penal Law. That term is used consistently throughout article 125 and has been construed to mean that homicide is properly charged when the defendant's culpable act is "a sufficiently direct cause" of the death so that the fatal result was reasonably foreseeable (People v. Kibbe, 35 N.Y.2d 407, 412, 362 N.Y.S.2d 848, 321 N.E.2d 773; accord, Matter of Anthony M., 63 N.Y.2d 270, 280, 481 N.Y.S.2d 675, 471 N.E.2d 447; People v. Stewart, 40 N.Y.2d 692, 697, 389 N.Y.S.2d 804, 358 N.E.2d 487). In the People's view the evidence here meets that standard.

They contend that it was highly foreseeable that someone would be killed in a shootout when Hernandez refused to put down his gun and instead persisted in threatening the life of one of the back-up officers. Thus, under the People's theory, Hernandez "caused the death" of Aversa. Because his attempt to avoid arrest was in furtherance of a common criminal objective shared with Santana, the People contend that the murder was properly attributed to Santana as well as under principles of accomplice liability (see, People v. Friedman, 205 N.Y. 161, 98 N.E. 471; accord, People v. Wood, supra, 8 N.Y.2d at 52, 201 N.Y.S.2d 328, 167 N.E.2d 736).

In response, defendants assert that People v. Wood, though decided on narrow statutory grounds, states a rule that was followed for centuries at common law and one that has been embraced by a significant number of jurisdictions. The rationale for requiring that one of the co-felons be the shooter (or, more broadly, the person who commits the final, fatal act) has been framed in several ways. Some courts have held that when the victim or a police officer or a bystander shoots and kills, it cannot be said that the killing was in furtherance of a common criminal objective (State v. Severs, 759 S.W.2d 935, 938 [Tenn.Crim.App.]). Others have concluded that under such circumstances the necessary malice or intent is missing (Wooden v. Commonwealth, 222 Va. 758, 284 S.E.2d 811).

Under the traditional felony murder doctrine, the malice necessary to make the killing murder was constructively imputed from the mens rea incidental to perpetration of the underlying felony (Commonwealth v. Redline, 391 Pa. 486, 493-494, 137 A.2d 472; IV Blackstone, Commentaries, at 200-201). Thus, in Wooden, the Virginia Supreme Court concluded that where a nonparticipant in the felony is the shooter, there can be no imputation of the necessary malice to him, and no party in the causal chain has both the requisite mens rea and culpability for the actus reus.

Still other courts have expressed policy concerns about extending felony murder liability. They have asserted that no deterrence value attaches when the felon is not the person immediately responsible for the death, or have contended that an expansive felony murder rule might unreasonably hold the felons responsible for the acts of others—for instance, when an unarmed felon is fleeing the scene and a bystander is hit by the bad aim of the armed victim (see, People v. Washington, 62 Cal.2d 777, 781-782, 44 Cal.Rptr. 442, 446, 402 P.2d 130, 134; State v. Bonner, 330 N.C. 536, 541-542, 411 S.E.2d 598, 601).

Analysis begins with the statute. The causal language used in our felony murder provision and elsewhere in the homicide statutes has consistently been construed by this Court according to the rule in People v. Kibbe (35 N.Y.2d 407, 362 N.Y.S.2d 848, 321 N.E.2d 773, supra), where we held that the accused need not commit the final, fatal act to be culpable for causing death. To accept defendants' analysis would require that we hold that the phrase "causes the death" in subdivision (3), the felony murder paragraph of section 125.25, means something entirely different than it does in subdivisions (1) and (2) of the very same section. That is contrary to the normal rules of statutory construction (see, People v. Bolden, 81 N.Y.2d 146, 151, 597 N.Y.S.2d 270, 613 N.E.2d 145).

That rule of construction must bend, of course, if in fact the Legislature intended the language to have a unique meaning within the context of the felony murder provision, but the legislative history of the 1965 revision reveals nothing about whether the Legislature intended to overturn People v. Wood. Defendants read that silence to mean that no such substantive change in the law was envisioned by the Legislature, and they [p. 316] urge us to reaffirm the common law as it applied to felony murder to limit liability when a nonparticipant is the killer.

Defendants' position is problematic for several reasons. First, it asks us to find in the ambiguous silence of the legislative record grounds for contradicting the unambiguous language of the statute. Second, it assumes that the Legislature intended an unusually narrow construction of the word "causes" even though New York homicide decisions had defined causality more expansively (see, e.g., People v. Kane, 213 N.Y. 260, 270, 107 N.E. 655 [error in medical treatment provided to victim does not relieve attacker of liability]).

It assumes also that in choosing the statutory language the Legislature and the Temporary State Commission on Revision of the Penal Law and Criminal Code, which drafted the amended provision, disregarded the well- defined debate over the difference between "causing" a homicide and "committing" a homicide (see, e.g., Morris, The Felon's Responsibility for the Lethal Acts of Others, 105 UPaLRev 50 [1956]). The Legislature could easily have written into subdivision (3) the limitation endorsed by defendants—as it did with the limitation applying to the death of a cofelon—but it chose not to do so.

Third and more serious, defendants' argument is premised on the assumption that the relevant common law pertaining to felony murder was uniform and unambiguous at the time the Legislature acted in 1965. In fact, the leading American case for limiting felony murder liability, Commonwealth v. Redline, 391 Pa. 486, 137 A.2d 472, supra, which was decided shortly before People v. Wood, overturned prior case law in Pennsylvania.

Variations on the felony murder doctrine were widespread in American jurisprudence, with liability turning on such factors as whether the victim was one of the felons, whether the felons initiated the gun battle and whether the deceased had been used as a shield by defendant (see, People v. Washington, 62 Cal.2d 777, 44 Cal.Rptr. 442, 402 P.2d 130, supra; Commonwealth v. Redline, supra).

Nor can it be contended that the limited view of felony murder liability was clearly the law in New York at the time the Legislature acted. In People v. Wood, we noted that two of our decisions had incidentally endorsed the idea that the felon must be the killer (see, People v. Giro, 197 N.Y. 152, 90 N.E. 432; and People v. Udwin, 254 N.Y. 255, 172 N.E. 489), but we expressly left open questions concerning "the application of the rules of causation and foreseeability" (People v. Wood, supra, 8 N.Y.2d at 53, 201 N.Y.S.2d 328, 167 N.E.2d 736). Earlier, in People [p. 317] v. Keshner, 304 N.Y. 968, 110 N.E.2d 892, we had let stand a felony murder conviction though defendants did not commit the final, fatal act. In Keshner, defendants had plotted to burn down a building and had spread gasoline in the structure but were apprehended by police before they could proceed further. Moments later, an independent force caused the gasoline to ignite, and defendants were held liable for the deaths of those caught in the blaze.

In light of the statutory language and the case law prior to the revision, we conclude that the Legislature intended what appears obvious from the face of the statute: that "causes" in the felony murder provision should be accorded the same meaning it is given in subdivisions (1) and (2) of section 125.25 of the Penal Law.

Unlike defendants and those courts adopting the so-called agency theory, we believe New York's view of causality, based on a proximate cause theory, to be consistent with fundamental principles of criminal law. Advocates of the agency theory suggest that no culpable party has the requisite mens rea when a nonparticipant is the shooter.

We disagree. The basic tenet of felony murder liability is that the mens rea of the underlying felony is imputed to the participant responsible for the killing (People v. Wood, 8 N.Y.2d 48, 51, 201 N.Y.S.2d 328, 167 N.E.2d 736, supra). By operation of that legal fiction, the transferred intent allows the law to characterize a homicide, though unintended and not in the common design of the felons, as an intentional killing (id.).

Thus, the presence or absence of the requisite mens rea is an issue turning on whether the felon is acting in furtherance of the underlying crime at the time of the homicide, not on the proximity or attenuation of the death resulting from the felon's acts. Whether the death is an immediate result or an attenuated one, the necessary mens rea is present if the causal act is part of the felonious conduct.

No more persuasive is the argument that the proximate cause view will extend criminal liability unreasonably. First, New York law is clear that felony murder does not embrace any killing that is coincidental with the felony but instead is limited to those deaths caused by one of the felons in furtherance of their crime (People v. Ryan, 263 N.Y. 298, 189 N.E. 225). More than civil tort liability must be established; criminal liability will adhere only when the felons' acts are a sufficiently direct cause of the death (People v. Kibbe, 35 N.Y.2d 407, 412-413, 362 N.Y.S.2d 848, 321 N.E.2d 773, supra).

When the intervening acts of another party are supervening [p. 318] or unforeseeable, the necessary causal chain is broken, and there is no liability for the felons (People v. Kern, 75 N.Y.2d 638, 658, 555 N.Y.S.2d 647, 554 N.E.2d 1235, cert. denied 498 U.S. 824, 111 S.Ct. 77, 112 L.Ed.2d 50; Matter of Anthony M., 63 N.Y.2d 270, 280, 481 N.Y.S.2d 675, 471 N.E.2d 447, supra; People v. Kane, 213 N.Y. 260, 270, 107 N.E. 655, supra; State v. Baker, 607 S.W.2d 153, 156 [Mo]). Where a victim, a police officer or other third party shoots and kills, the prosecution faces a significant obstacle in proving beyond a reasonable doubt to a jury that the felons should be held responsible for causing the death.

Second, the New York felony murder statute spells out the affirmative defense available to the accomplice who does not cause the death (see, Penal Law § 125.25[3][a]-[d]). Defendants assert that our construction of the statute's causality language will mean that an accomplice whose partner is the shooter will have a defense but one whose unarmed partner causes the death will not. The plain language of the statute does not support that proposition.

The statutory defense is available to the accomplice who (a) does not cause the death, (b) is unarmed, (c) has no reason to believe that the co-felon is armed and (d) has no reason to believe that the co-felon will "engage in conduct likely to result in death or serious physical injury". Thus, by its terms, the defense is not limited to situations where the co-felon kills with a weapon; it applies as well to instances where some other "conduct likely to result in death" is not within the contemplation of the accomplice.

In short, our established common-law rules governing determinations of causality and the availability of the statutory defense provide adequate boundaries to felony murder liability. The language of Penal Law § 125.25(3) evinces the Legislature's desire to extend liability broadly to those who commit serious crimes in ways that endanger the lives of others. That other States choose more narrow approaches is of no moment to our statutory scheme. Our Legislature has chosen not to write those limitations into our law, and we are bound by that legislative determination.

Finally, we conclude that there was no error in the court's instructions on defendant Santana's culpability. The jury was properly charged that more than "but for" causation was required; that it must find the fatal result was the sufficiently direct and foreseeable result of Hernandez's acts (see, People v. Kibbe, 35 N.Y.2d 407, 413, 362 N.Y.S.2d 848, 321 N.E.2d 773, supra).

The evidence established that Hernandez, when confronted by the officers in the courtyard, refused to surrender and continued to move toward one officer with his gun drawn. Immediate flight and attempts to thwart apprehension are patently within the furtherance of the cofelons' criminal objective (People v. Gladman, 41 N.Y.2d 123, 129, 390 N.Y.S.2d 912, 359 N.E.2d 420; People v. Donovan, 53 A.D.2d 27, 385 N.Y.S.2d 385). Moreover, it was highly foreseeable that when Hernandez continued toward the officer with his gun drawn that shots would be fired and someone might be hit.

Foreseeability does not mean that the result must be the most likely event. Undoubtedly, in planning the robbery, defendants did not anticipate that their victim would be a State Trooper or that a back-up unit would be on the scene. Yet, it was foreseeable that police would try to thwart crime (People v. Irby, 47 N.Y.2d 894, 419 N.Y.S.2d 477, 393 N.E.2d 472), and Hernandez was aware that police were on the scene at the point he resisted arrest and remained armed.

As the Appellate Division concluded, it is simply implausible for defendants to claim that defendants could not have foreseen a bullet going astray when Hernandez provoked a gun battle outside a residential building in an urban area.

Accordingly, the order of the Appellate Division should be affirmed.

KAYE, C.J., and TITONE, HANCOCK, BELLACOSA, SMITH and LEVINE, JJ., concur.

END OF DOCUMENT

The PEOPLE of the State of New York, Respondent

v

Eddie MATOS, Appellant

Court of Appeals of New York

83 N.Y.2d 509 (1994)

OPINION OF THE COURT

CIPARICK, Judge.

The issue to be considered in this appeal is under what circumstances a fleeing felon's actions cause another's death for purposes of Penal Law § 125.25(3), the felony murder statute.

There was evidence at trial that, in the early morning hours of October 17, 1989, defendant, Eddie Matos, and two accomplices broke into a McDonald's restaurant on Seventh Avenue and 40th Street in Manhattan by shattering the glass door with a sledgehammer. Once inside, Matos and his accomplices rounded up the employees at gunpoint. A maintenance worker, however, managed to escape and then returned to the restaurant with three police officers.

As they approached the restaurant, they saw Matos run toward the back of the restaurant. The officers ran into the restaurant in time to see Matos climb up a ladder that led to the roof. Police Officer Dwyer hurriedly climbed up the ladder right behind Matos. About 10 seconds later, another officer, Sergeant Flanagan, proceeded up the ladder to the roof and later discovered Dwyer lying on his back about 25 feet down an airshaft. It took emergency services personnel about 45 minutes to rescue Dwyer from the airshaft, but he was later pronounced dead at Bellevue Hospital.

The Appellate Division affirmed the conviction of murder in the second degree, burglary in the second degree and attempted robbery. The Court concluded that the elements of felony murder were established, 191 A.D.2d 383, 595 N.Y.S.2d 207. A Judge of this Court granted leave to appeal and we now affirm.

It is well established that in order for criminal responsibility to attach, a defendant's actions must have been an actual contributory cause of death (People v. Stewart, 40 N.Y.2d 692, 697, 389 N.Y.S.2d 804, 358 N.E.2d 487). It must be shown that the defendant sets in motion the events which ultimately result in the victim's death (People v. Kibbe, 35 N.Y.2d 407, 362 N.Y.S.2d 848, 321 N.E.2d 773). However, the defendant's acts need not be the sole cause of death (Matter of Anthony M., 63 N.Y.2d 270, 280, 481 N.Y.S.2d 675, 471 N.E.2d 447).

Here, defendant's conduct set in motion and legally caused the death of Police Officer Dwyer. Had defendant not first committed an armed violent felony and then attempted to escape by way of the roof, the officer would not have pursued him onto the roof, thereafter plunging to his death in the airshaft.

The trial court stressed to the jury that "but for" causation was only one step in determining cause in the criminal context, an aspect defendant-appellant does not dispute. Additionally, the jury was told that it must also find that defendant's conduct was a sufficiently direct cause of the ensuing death before it could impose criminal responsibility. The defendant's conduct qualifies as a sufficiently direct cause when the ultimate harm should have been reasonably foreseen (People v. Kibbe, 35 N.Y.2d, at 412, 362 N.Y.S.2d 848, 321 N.E.2d 773, supra).

The accused need not commit the final, fatal act to be culpable for causing death. In Kibbe, the fatal act was inflicted by a passing truck driver who struck and killed the victim. The defendants were held to have caused his death, for the event was a directly foreseeable consequence of their own earlier act of abandoning the victim on the shoulder of a [p. 512] highway. In People v. Kern, 75 N.Y.2d 638, 555 N.Y.S.2d 647, 554 N.E.2d 1235, the "Howard Beach" defendants were held to have caused their victim's death even though he was actually killed by the intervening act of a passing motorist.

In People v. Hernandez, 82 N.Y.2d 309, 604 N.Y.S.2d 524, 624 N.E.2d 661, this Court held that the defendants initiated or participated in the chain of events that led to an officer's death by attempting to rob an undercover officer in a failed drug transaction. Since, in initiating a gun battle, they should have foreseen that someone's bullet might go astray, their conduct was a sufficiently direct cause of a backup officer's death even though the shot which killed him was fired by another officer. The Court held (supra, at 319, 604 N.Y.S.2d 524, 624 N.E.2d 661) that "immediate flight and attempts to thwart apprehension are patently within the furtherance of the co-felons' criminal objective," citing People v. Gladman, 41 N.Y.2d 123, 390 N.Y.S.2d 912, 359 N.E.2d 420. The Court further noted that foreseeability does not mean that the result must be the most likely event.

In the instant case, the jury was correctly given the issue as to whether it was foreseeable that upon defendant's attempt to escape by way of the roof, he would be pursued by an officer. In those circumstances it should also be foreseeable that someone might fall while in hot pursuit across urban roofs in the middle of the night.

Accordingly, the order of the Appellate Division should be affirmed.

KAYE, C.J., and SIMONS, BELLACOSA, SMITH and LEVINE, JJ., concur.

TITONE, J., taking no part.

END OF DOCUMENT

RELATED STATUTES:

Section 130.00 Sex Offenses; Definitions

The following definitions are applicable to this article:

1. "Sexual intercourse" has its ordinary meaning and occurs upon any penetration, however slight.

2. (a) "Oral sexual conduct" means conduct between persons consisting of contact between the mouth and the penis, the mouth and the anus, or the mouth and the vulva or vagina.

(b) "Anal sexual conduct" means conduct between persons consisting of contact between the penis and anus.

3. "Sexual contact" means any touching of the sexual or other intimate parts of a person not married to the actor for the purpose of gratifying sexual desire of either party. It includes the touching of the actor by the victim, as well as the touching of the victim by the actor, whether directly or through clothing.

4. For the purposes of this article "married" means the existence of the relationship between the actor and the victim as spouses which is recognized by law at the time the actor commits an offense proscribed by this article against the victim.

5. "Mentally disabled" means that a person suffers from a mental disease or defect which renders him or her incapable of appraising the nature of his or her conduct.

6. "Mentally incapacitated" means that a person is rendered temporarily incapable of appraising or controlling his conduct owing to the influence of a narcotic or intoxicating substance administered to him without his consent, or to any other act committed upon him without his consent.

7. "Physically helpless" means that a person is unconscious or for any other reason is physically unable to communicate unwillingness to an act.

8. "Forcible compulsion" means to compel by either:

a. use of physical force; or

b. a threat, express or implied, which places a person in fear of immediate death or <u>physical injury</u> to himself, herself or another person, or in fear that he, she or another person will immediately be kidnapped.

9. "Foreign object" means any instrument or article which, when inserted in the vagina, urethra, penis or rectum, is capable of causing physical injury.

10. "Sexual conduct" means sexual intercourse, oral sexual conduct, anal sexual conduct, aggravated sexual contact, or sexual contact.

<u>Section 130.05 Sex Offenses; Lack of Consent</u>

1. Whether or not specifically stated, it is an element of every offense defined in this article that the sexual act was committed without consent of the victim.

2. Lack of consent results from:

(a) Forcible compulsion; or

(b) Incapacity to consent; or

(c) Where the offense charged is sexual abuse or forcible touching, any circumstances, in addition to forcible compulsion or incapacity to consent, in which the victim does not expressly or impliedly acquiesce in the actor's conduct.

3. A person is deemed incapable of consent when he or she is:

(a) less than seventeen years old; or

(b) mentally disabled; or

(c) mentally incapacitated; or

(d) physically helpless

<u>Section 130.35 Rape in the First Degree</u>

A person is guilty of rape in the first degree when he or she engages in sexual intercourse with another person:

1. By forcible compulsion; or

2. Who is incapable of consent by reason of being physically helpless; or

3. Who is less than eleven years old; or

4. Who is less than thirteen years old and the actor is eighteen years old or more.

The PEOPLE of the State of New York

v

Martin EVANS, a/k/a Martin Sage, Defendant

Supreme Court, New York County

85 Misc.2d 1088, 379 N.Y.S.2d 912 (1975)

EDWARD J. GREENFIELD, Justice:

The question presented in this case is whether the sexual conquest by a predatory male of a resisting female constitutes rape or seduction.

In making the distinction, we must deal with patterns of behavior which have been exhibited by aggressive males towards gentle or timid or submissive females, the broad outlines of which have been similar for hundreds or maybe thousands of years, but the particulars of which vary markedly in individual cases.

It is a fact, I suppose, that since before the dawn of history men with clubs have grabbed women, willing or unwilling, by the hair, to have their way with them. Techniques have become more varied and more subtle with the years.

As we have become more civilized, we have come to condemn the more overt, aggressive and outrageous behavior of some men towards women and we have labelled it 'rape.' We have attempted to control or deter it by providing for extremely heavy sentences, second to and, in some jurisdictions, equalled by the penalties set by the law for murder.

At the same time we have recognized that there are some patterns of aggression or aggressive male sexual behavior toward females which do not deserve such extreme penalties, in which the male objective may be achieved through charm or guile or protestations of love, promises or deceit.

Where force is not employed to overcome reluctance, and where consent, however reluctant initially, can be spelled out, this we label 'seduction,' which society may condone, even as it disapproves.

There is some conduct which comes close to the line between rape and seduction. This is such a case.

Since a jury has been waived, this Court is called upon to scrutinize the conduct involved and to draw the line between the legally permissible and the impermissible and to determine on which side of the line this conduct falls.

Rape is defined in our Penal Law, Section 130.35, subdivision 1, as follows: 'A male is guilty of rape in the first degree when he engages in sexual intercourse with a female: 1. By forcible compulsion.'

Rape can also be premised upon other conditions which would indicate the incapacity of a female to give consent either in actuality or as a matter of law. We are concerned here with the first subdivision, sexual intercourse by forcible compulsion. That is the essence of the crime.

Forcible compulsion is defined in Section 130.00 subdivision 8, of the Penal Law as 'physical force that overcomes earnest resistance; or a threat, express or implied, that places a person in fear of immediate death or serious physical injury to himself or another person, or in fear that he or another person will immediately be kidnapped.'

Rape, though it sometimes may be abetted by other females, appears to be exclusively a proscribed activity for males.

Seduction, on the other hand, may be freely indulged in by both sexes. It involves allurement, enticement, or persuasion, to overcome initial unwillingness or resistance. Its ends may be achieved by fair means or foul, but seduction eschews the crudities of force and threats. In which category does defendant's conduct fall?

In answering that inquiry, and based upon the testimony in this case, the Court first makes the following findings of fact:

The defendant, a bachelor of approximately thirty-seven years of age, aptly described in the testimony as 'glib', on July 15, 1974 met an incoming plane at LaGuardia Airport, from which disembarked Lucy Elizabeth Peterson, of Charlotte, North Carolina, a twenty-year-old petite, attractive second-year student at Wellesley College, an unworldly girl, evidently unacquainted with New York City and the sophisticated city ways, a girl who proved to be, as indicated by the testimony, incredibly gullible, trusting and naive.

The testimony indicates that the defendant struck up a conversation with her, posing as a psychologist doing a magazine article and using a name that was not his, inducing Miss Peterson to answer questions for an interview.

The evidence further shows that the defendant invited Miss Peterson to accompany him by automobile to Manhattan, her destination being Grand Central Station. They were accompanied in the automobile by other persons, some of whom were introduced by the defendant as colleagues on a professional basis. But it appears that a funny thing happened on the way to the station. There were numerous detours before Beth Peterson ever found her way to Grand Central Station. First, they were taken to an apartment on the east side. Some of the party were left there.

Then the evidence indicates that this defendant and a girl named Bridget took Miss Peterson to an establishment called Maxwell's Plum, which the defendant explained was for the purpose of conducting a sociological experiment in which he would observe her reactions and the reactions of males towards her in the setting of a singles bar. After several hours there, in which Miss Peterson evidently was still under the belief that her stopping for a drink at Maxwell's Plum was part of this psychological and sociological experiment, she was persuaded to accompany the defendant to the west side, upon the defendant's explanation that he was there going to pick up his automobile and drive her to Grand Central Station.

Instead of going to the automobile, she was induced to come up to an apartment on the fourteenth floor, which the defendant explained was used as one of his five offices or apartments throughout the city; and Miss Peterson, still believing that the defendant was in fact what he purported to be, went up and accompanied him there.

That apartment, Apartment 14—D, at 1 Lincoln Plaza, was in truth and in fact the apartment of one Heinz Patzak, who ran the Austrian National Tourist Bureau and who at that time was in Austria. Mr. Patzak has testified that he never had given approval or permission for the defendant to enter, use or occupy that apartment.

Miss Peterson came to the apartment and her questions as to the existence of photographs of children, a crib, stuffed animals and toys, were readily explained away by the defendant as being connected with his treatment of patients as a psychologist, the explanation of the crib and the toys being that there were used for the purposes of primal therapy to enable his patients to associate with their childhood years more readily.

In the apartment the psychological interviewing continued, the defendant having explained to Miss Peterson that he was searching for the missing link between the 'girl-woman' and the 'woman-girl.' Miss Peterson, who was then working in a psychiatric branch of New York Hospital, Cornell Medical School, in White Plains, and who had some training in psychology, believed that all of this legitimately related to a psychological research project which the defendant was conducting.

During the course of the interview in the apartment the defendant probed Miss Peterson's life and she had, during the course of their conversation together, made a revelation of her prior intimacies and her feelings, and her experiences with respect to various people. In the apartment she was asked to participate in an adjective word game, applying five adjectives to certain designated persons, including herself and the defendant.

She had been there for one to two hours when the defendant made his move and pulled her on to the opened sofa-bed in the living room of that apartment and attempted to disrobe her. She resisted that, and she claims that as articles of clothing were attempted to be removed she would pull them back on and ultimately she was able to ward off these advances and to get herself dressed again. At that point, the defendant's tactics, according to her testimony, appeared to have changed.

First, he informed her of his disappointment that she had failed the test, that this was all part of his psychological experiment, that, in fact, this was a way in which he was trying to reach her innermost consciousness, one of the ways in which that could be done. Then, after expressing disappointment in the failure of this psychological experiment, he took steps to cause doubt and fear to arise in the mind of Miss Peterson. He said, 'Look where you are. You are in the apartment of a strange man. How do you know that I am really who I say I am? How do you know that I am really a psychologist?' Then, he went on and said, 'I could kill you. I could rape you. I could hurt you physically.'

Miss Peterson testified that at that point she became extremely frightened, that she realized, indeed, how vulnerable she was. The defendant did not strike her, did not beat her, he exhibited no weapons at the time, but he made the statement, 'I could kill you; I could rape you.'

Then there was yelling and screaming, further to intimidate the defendant, and then an abrupt switch in which the defendant attempted to play on the sympathy of Miss Peterson by telling her a story about his lost love, how Miss Peterson had reminded him of her, and the hurt that he had sustained when she had driven her car off a cliff.

Obviously, Miss Peterson's sympathy was engaged, and at that time acting instinctively, she took a step forward and reached out for him and put her hand on his shoulders, and then he grabbed her and said, 'You're mine, you are mine.' There thereupon followed an act of sexual intercourse, an act of oral-genital contact; a half-hour later a second act of sexual intercourse, and then, before she left, about seven o'clock that morning, an additional act.

The sexual intercourse appears to be corroborated by the findings of the laboratory confirmation of seminal fluid on the underclothing which she had worn at the time.

The testimony indicates that during these various sexual acts Miss Peterson, in fact, offered little resistance. She said that she was pinned down by the defendant's body weight, but in some manner all her clothing was removed, all his clothing was removed, and the acts took place. There was no torn clothing, there were no scratches, there were no bruises. Finally, at approximately seven a.m. Miss Peterson dressed and left the apartment. She says that the defendant acknowledged to her that he was aware that it had been against her will, but he nevertheless gave her three telephone numbers. Miss Peterson then returned to White Plains, where later that day she recited some of the events to a fellow-worker, and then to a roommate.

Ultimately she reported the facts to the New York City Police and to the Westchester County Sheriff's office, resulting in her being taken to New York City by personnel from the Westchester County Sheriff's office where, at the Gulf & Western Building at Columbus Circle they saw the defendant emerging from an elevator. Despite her identification of him at that time the defendant initially denied that his name was Marty, that he knew Miss Peterson, or that he had had any involvement with her in any way.

After he had been placed under arrest in a coffee shop of the Mayflower Hotel, and they had proceeded to the building at No. 1 Lincoln Plaza, the defendant began to make partial admissions as to his identity, his occupation of Apartment 14—D at No. 1 Lincoln Plaza, his knowledge of Miss Peterson and ultimately the fact that he had had sexual intercourse with her, which he claimed was consensual and a matter of mutual enjoyment. He further told the police officers that the whole psychology bit was a 'game that he played with girls' heads.'

The testimony further indicates that after he had been placed under arrest, and while he was in custody, he escaped from the police car in which he had been placed, and that Detective Kelleher chased him in and around the streets and up 15 flights of a building, where he ultimately located Evans on a water tower. The explanation given to Detective Magnusson was that he was looking for a lawyer.

Those being the facts, the Court arrives at the following conclusions:

The Court finds that the testimony of Beth Peterson was essentially credible testimony. The Court finds from the story which she has narrated that the defendant was a person who was crafty, scheming, manipulative, and ever ready with explanations.

From the testimony which has been given there are some factors which tend to point toward guilt and some towards innocence. As factors indicating guilt are the assumption of the false identity by the defendant, his not giving his true name, his denial to the police when first confronted of what his name was, and his denial of any knowledge of Miss Peterson, which denials he ultimately retracted. Then, of course, there is the evidence about flight which is always [p. 1095] evidence that can be considered as evincing some consciousness of guilt. On the other hand, there are some factors pointing to innocence on the part of the defendant, and a lack of criminal culpability on his part.

The fact that Miss Peterson had no bruises or scratches, no torn clothing, that she had been allowed to proceed from the apartment without any further threats or concealment as to location. The fact that she was given phone numbers by the defendant which made it relatively easy to trace his location and whereabouts; the fact that he attempted to call her on several occasions after she had left the apartment; and the fact that he had continued in his prior haunts at the Gulf & Western Building and at No. 1 Lincoln Plaza. From all this, the Court concludes that the defendant inveigled Miss Peterson, deceived her, put her on, and took advantage of her.

The question is whether having had sexual intercourse by the same means described constitutes rape in the first degree. The essential element of rape in the first degree is forcible compulsion. The prevailing view in this country is that there can be no rape which is achieved by fraud, or trick, or stratagem. 75 C.J.S. Rape s 16; Annotation, 91 A.L.R.2d 593.

Provided there is actual consent, the nature of the act being understood, it is not rape, absent a statute, no matter how despicable the fraud, even if a woman has intercourse with a man impersonating her husband (Lewis v. Alabama, 30 Ala. 54); or if a fraudulent ceremony leads her to believe she is legally married to a man (Alabama v. Murphy, 6 Ala. 765), (contra if an explicit statute to that effect exists, e.g., State v. Navarro, 90 Ariz. 185, 367 P.2d 227, 91 A.L.R.2d 586) or even if a doctor persuades her that sexual intercourse is necessary for her treatment and return to good health. Don Moran v. People, 25 Mich. 356; Commonwealth v. Goldenberg, 338 Mass. 377, 155 N.E.2d 187, 70 A.L.R.2d 814, cert. den. 359 U.S. 1001, 79 S.Ct. 1143, 3 L.Ed.2d 1032. 'Fraud cannot be allowed to supply the place of the force which the statute makes mandatory. Mills v. U.S., 164 U.S. 644, 648 (17 S.Ct. 210, 41 L.Ed. 584).' Id., p. 822.

It should be noted that seduction, while not considered to be a criminal act at common law (79 C.J.S. Seduction s 31), has been made a criminal offense by statute in some jurisdictions. In seduction, unlike rape, the consent of the woman, implied or explicit, has been procured, by artifice, deception, flattery, fraud or promise.

The declared public policy of this state looks with disfavor on actions for seduction since the civil action was abolished [p. 1096] more than forty years ago, CPA ss 61—b, 61—d; now Civil Rights Law, s 80—a. The statute did not repeal any Penal Law provisions (CPA ss 61—h, 61—i, now Civil Rights Law s 84), but there are no presently existing penal sanctions against seduction.

The law recognizes that there are some crimes where trickery and deceit do constitute the basis for a criminal charge. Since the common law, we have recognized the existence of larceny by trick. But of course, for a larceny there has to be a taking of property of value. I do not mean to imply that a woman's right to her body is not a thing of value, but it is not property in the sense which is defined by the law.

It is clear from the evidence in this case that Beth Peterson was intimidated; that she was confused; that she had been drowned in a torrent of words and perhaps was terrified. But it is likewise clear from the evidence that the defendant did not resort to actual physical force. There was "no act of violence, no struggle, no outcry, and no attempt to restrain or confine the person...which constitute the usual...and essential evidence' of rape.' Commonwealth v. Goldenberg, supra, citing Commonwealth v. Merrill, 14 Gray (Mass.) 415, 417.

The restraint which was imposed upon Miss Peterson was a restraint imposed by his body weight, which would be the normal situation in which any sexual contact would be achieved. Miss Peterson manifested little or no resistance.

She indicated at some point she kicked. I asked her what she was doing with her arms and hands at the time. The answers indicated that it was not very much. Now, that can be understandable. A woman is not obligated to resist to the uttermost under all circumstances, when her will to resist has been paralyzed by fear and by threats. That is why the law recognizes the existence of a threat as being the equivalent of the use of actual force. As stated in People v. Connor, 126 N.Y. 278, 281, 27 N.E. 252, 253, an ancient but still followed case, in the Court of Appeals:

'The extent of the resistance required of an assaulted female is governed by the circumstances of the case, and the grounds which she has for apprehending the infliction of great bodily harm. 'When an assault is committed by the sudden and unexpected exercise of overpowering force upon a timid and inexperienced girl, under circumstances indicating the power and the will of the aggressor to effect his object, and an intention to use any means necessary to accomplish it, it would seem to present a case for a jury to say whether the fear naturally inspired by such circumstances had not taken away or impaired [p. 1097] the ability of the assaulted party to make effectual resistance to the assault.'

Whether resistance was useless under the prevailing circumstances is a always a question for the trier of facts. People v. Yannucci, 483 N.Y. 546, 550, 29 N.E.2d 185; People v. Dohring, 59 N.Y. 374, 382.

So the question here is not so much the use of force, but whether threats uttered by the defendant had paralyzed her capacity to resist and had, in fact, undermined her will. Now, what was it the defendant said? He said, 'Look where you are. You are in the apartment of a strong man.

How do you know that I really am who I say I am? How do you know that I am really a psychologist? I could kill you. I could rape you. I could hurt you physically.' Those words, as uttered, are susceptible to two possible and diverse interpretations. The first would be in essence that—you had better do what I say, for you are helpless and I have the power to use ultimate force should you resist.

That clearly would be a threat which would induce fear and overcome resistance. The second possible meaning of those words is, in effect, that—you are a foolish girl. You are in the apartment of a strange man. You put yourself in the hands of a stranger, and you are vulnerable and defenseless. The possibility would exist of physical harm to you were you being confronted by someone other than the person who uttered this statement.

Of course, it is entirely possible that Miss Peterson, who heard the statements, construed that as a threat, even though it may not have been intended as such by the person who uttered those words. The question arises as to which is the controlling state of mind—that of a person who hears the words and interprets them as a threat, or the state of mind of the person who utters such words. It appears to the Court that the controlling state of mind must be that of the speaker. She, the hearer, may in fact take the words as a threat and be terrified by them.

Sometimes that may be reasonable under all the circumstances. Sometimes it may be a rather hysterical reaction to words which would not justify the induction of [p. 1098] that terror. But this being a criminal trial, it is basic that the criminal intent of the defendant must be shown beyond a reasonable doubt. It is his intent when he acts, his intent when he speaks, which must therefore be controlling. And so, if he utters words which are taken as a threat by the person who hears them, but are not intended as a threat by the person who utters them, there would be no basis for finding the necessary criminal intent to establish culpability under the law.

So where a statement is ambiguous, where the words and the acts which purport to constitute force or threats are susceptible of diverse interpretations, which may be consistent with either guilt or innocence, the Court, as the trier of the facts, cannot say beyond a reasonable doubt that the guilt of the defendant has been established with respect to the crime of rape.

The words which were uttered both as to what the defendant could do, 'I could kill you. I could rape you.' and subsequent words that he was going to do to the complainant what his lost love had done to him—the Court finds are ambiguous. They were not accompanied by violence. They were not accompanied by a demonstration of the intention to carry out the threats. There was no beating. There was no weapon displayed. There was a statement as to a possibility, a statement of vulnerability.

The Court finds it cannot conclude that there was the utterance of a threat of such a nature as to enable the Court to find the defendant guilty of the crime of rape in the first degree beyond a reasonable doubt. Since the Court, therefore, can find neither forcible compulsion nor threat beyond a reasonable doubt, the defendant is found not guilty on the charges of rape, sodomy and unlawful imprisonment.

Now, acquittal on these charges does not imply that the Court condones the conduct of the defendant. The testimony in the case reveals that the defendant was a predator, and that naive and gullible girls like Beth Peterson were his natural prey. He posed. He lied. He pretended and he deceived. He used confidences which were innocently bestowed as leverage to effect his will.

He used psychological techniques to achieve vulnerability and sympathy, and the erosion of resistance. A young and inexperienced girl like Beth Peterson was then unable to withstand the practiced onslaught of the defendant. The defendant apparently got his kicks through the exercise of these techniques.

He apparently spurned the readily available [p. 1099] women, the acquiescent women, like Bridget, who was living in the same apartment. To him, the game was worth more than the prize. He boasted to the police that this was a game he played with girls' heads. The Court finds his conduct, if not criminal, to be reprehensible. It was conquest by con job. Truly, therefore, this defendant may be called 'The Abominable Snowman.'

So bachelors, and other men on the make, fear not. It is still not illegal to feed a girl a line, to continue the attempt, not to take no for a final answer, at least not the first time. But there comes a point at which one must desist. It is not criminal conduct for a male to make promises that will not be kept, to indulge in exaggeration and hyperbole, or to assure any trusting female that, as in the ancient fairy tale, the ugly frog is really the handsome prince.

Every man is free, under the law, to be a gentleman or a cad. But take heed. Violence, force and threats are totally out of bounds. Their employment will transform a heel into a criminal.

While the Court must conclude that the defendant's conduct towards Miss Peterson cannot be adjudged criminal so as to subject him to the penalty of imprisonment for up to twenty-five years, the Court finds, on the undisputed facts, that defendant did enter Apartment 14—D, at No. 1 Lincoln Plaza, the dwelling of Heinz Patzak and his family, illegally and without permission or authority.

There being no proof that the illegal entry was for the purpose of committing a crime, the defendant is found not guilty of the charge of burglary in the second degree. But he is found guilty of the lesser included offense of criminal trespass in the second degree, pursuant to Section 140.15 of the Penal Law, under Indictment No. 3861 of 1974.

Further, the evidence clearly establishes that the defendant, after having been arrested for a felony, escaped from the custody of the police officers, and he is found guilty of the crime of escape in the second degree, under Section 205.10 of the Penal Law.

It may be ironic that the defendant, having been acquitted of the charges for which he was arrested, is found guilty of attempting to flee from the possibilities of having to face up to the charge. But the facts are clear, and whatever consequences flow from that fact will flow. The defendant fancied himself to be terribly clever, but, as frequently happens with terribly clever men, he made a rather stupid mistake.

END OF DOCUMENT

Section 140.00 Criminal Trespass and Burglary; Definitions

The following definitions are applicable to this article:

1. "Premises" includes the term "building," as defined herein, and any real property.

2. "Building," in addition to its ordinary meaning, includes any structure, vehicle or watercraft used for overnight lodging of persons, or used by persons for carrying on business therein, or used as an elementary or secondary school, or an enclosed motor truck, or an enclosed motor truck trailer. Where a building consists of two or more units separately secured or occupied, each unit shall be deemed both a separate building in itself and a part of the main building.

3. "Dwelling" means a building which is usually occupied by a person lodging therein at night.

4. "Night" means the period between thirty minutes after sunset and thirty minutes before sunrise.

"Enter or remain unlawfully." A person "enters or remains unlawfully" in or upon premises when he is not licensed or privileged to do so. A person who, regardless of his intent, enters or remains in premises which are at the time open to the public does so with license and privilege unless he defies a lawful order not to enter or remain, personally communicated to him by the owner of such premises or other authorized person. A license to enter or remain in a building which is only partly open to the public is not a license to enter or remain in that part of the building which is not open to the public. A person who enters or remains upon unimproved and apparently unused land, which is neither fenced nor otherwise enclosed in a manner designed to exclude intruders, does so with license unless notice against trespass is personally communicated to him by the owner of such land or other authorized person, or unless such notice is given by posting in a conspicuous manner. A person who enters or remains in or about a school building without written permission from someone authorized to issue such permission or without a legitimate reason which includes a relationship involving custody of or responsibility for a pupil or student enrolled in the school or without legitimate business or a purpose relating to the operation of the school does so without license.

Section 140.20 Burglary in the Third Degree

A person is guilty of burglary in the third degree when he knowingly enters or remains unlawfully in a building with intent to commit a crime therein.

Section 140.25 Burglary in the Second Degree

A person is guilty of burglary in the second degree when he knowingly enters or remains unlawfully in a building with intent to commit a crime therein, and when:

1. In effecting entry or while in the building or in immediate flight there from, he or another participant in the crime:

(a) Is armed with explosives or a deadly weapon; or

(b) Causes physical injury to any person who is not a participant in the crime; or

(c) Uses or threatens the immediate use of a dangerous instrument; or

(d) Displays what appears to be a pistol, revolver, rifle, shotgun, machine gun or other firearm; or

2. The building is a dwelling.

Section 140.30 Burglary in the First Degree

A person is guilty of burglary in the first degree when he knowingly enters or remains unlawfully in a dwelling with intent to commit a crime therein and when in effecting entry or while in the dwelling or in immediate flight there from, he or another participant in the crime:

1. Is armed with explosives or a deadly weapon; or

2. Causes physical injury to any person who is not a participant in the crime; or

3. Uses or threatens the immediate use of a dangerous instrument; or

4. Displays what appears to be a firearm; but it is an affirmative defense that the firearm was not loaded.

Section 140.35 Possession of Burglar's Tools

A person is guilty of possession of burglar's tools when he possesses any tool commonly used for committing offenses involving forcible entry into premises, or offenses involving larceny by a physical taking under circumstances evincing intent to use or knowledge that some person intends to use the same in the commission of an offense.

Case Law to Consider:

STATE of New Jersey, Plaintiff-Appellant

v

Thomas STASIO, Defendant-Respondent

Supreme Court of New Jersey

78 N.J. 467, 396 A.2d 1129 (1979)

SCHREIBER, J.

The major issue on this appeal is whether voluntary intoxication constitutes a defense to a crime, one element of which is the defendant's intent. Defendant Stasio was found guilty by a jury of assault with intent to rob, in violation of N.J.S.A. 2A:90-2, and of assault while being armed with a dangerous knife, contrary to N.J.S.A. 2A:151-5.

The trial court sentenced the defendant to three to five years on the assault with intent to rob count and a concurrent term of one to two years on the second count. The prison term was suspended and the defendant was placed on probation for three years. The Appellate Division reversed the convictions and ordered a new trial. We granted the State's petition for certification. 75 N.J. 613, 384 A.2d 843 (1978).

The scene of this incident was the Silver Moon Tavern located at 655 Van Houten Avenue, Clifton. The date was October 7, 1975. The defendant having presented no evidence, what occurred must be discerned from the testimony of three witnesses for the State: Peter Klimek, a part owner of the Silver Moon; Robert Colburn, a patron; and Robert Rowan, a member of the Clifton police force.

Robert Colburn had frequented the Silver Moon Tavern not only for its alcoholic wares but also to engage in pool. On October 7, Colburn arrived at the Tavern about 11:00 a. m. and started to play pool. Sometime before noon the defendant joined him. They stayed together until about 3:00 p. m. when the defendant left the bar. Though the defendant had been drinking during this period, in Colburn's opinion the defendant was not intoxicated upon his departure. Neither [p. 471] the defendant's speech nor his mannerisms indicated drunkenness.

Peter Klimek arrived at the Tavern shortly before 5:00 p. m. and assumed his shift at tending bar. There were about eight customers present when, at approximately 5:40 p. m., the defendant entered and walked in a normal manner to the bathroom. Shortly thereafter he returned to the front door, looked around outside and approached the bar.

He demanded that Klimek give him some money. Upon refusal, he threatened Klimek. The defendant went behind the bar toward Klimek and insisted that Klimek give him $80 from the cash register. When Klimek persisted in his refusal, the defendant pulled out a knife. Klimek grabbed the defendant's right hand and Colburn, who had jumped on top of the bar, seized the defendant's hair and pushed his head toward the bar. The defendant then dropped the knife.

Almost immediately thereafter Police Officer Rowan arrived and placed the defendant in custody. He testified that defendant responded to his questions with no difficulty and walked normally. Klimek also stated that defendant did not appear drunk and that he had not noticed any odor of alcohol on defendant's breath.

At the conclusion of the State's case, the defendant elected not to take the stand. He made this decision because of an earlier conference in chambers [n. 1] at which defense counsel had advised the court that his defense would be that defendant had been so intoxicated that he was incapable of forming the intent to rob. The trial court responded by stating that it would charge that "voluntary intoxication was not a defense to any act by the defendant in this matter."

The defendant on a voir dire made it clear that his decision not to testify was predicated upon the trial court's position. It might be noted that the defendant had no record of prior convictions. Holding that the trial court's declaration in view of the defendant's proffer of proof was erroneous, the Appellate Division reversed the convictions and ordered a new trial.

The Appellate Division reasoned that specific intent is an essential element of the crime of an assault with intent to rob and that voluntary intoxication may be shown to negate that element of the offense.

This Court last considered the culpability of an individual who had committed an illegal act while voluntarily under the influence of a drug or alcohol in State v. Maik, 60 N.J. 203, 287 A.2d 715 (1972). There the defendant Maik had been charged with the first degree murder of his friend, a fellow college student. The defense was insanity at the time of the killing.

Evidence at the trial had suggested that the defendant was schizophrenic and that a psychotic episode may have been triggered by the defendant's voluntary use of LSD or hashish. The trial court had charged the jury that if it found that the underlying psychosis had been activated by the voluntary use of either narcotic, the defense of insanity would not stand.

On appeal Chief Justice Weintraub, writing for a unanimous Court, began by discussing generally the concept of criminal responsibility. After pointing out that although there was a difference in the treatment of sick and bad offenders, he noted that notwithstanding that difference "the aim of the law is to protect the innocent from injury by the sick as well as the bad." 60 N.J. at 213, 287 A.2d at 720. It was in that context that a decision would have to be made whether the voluntary use of alcoholic beverages or drugs should support a viable defense.

He then stated the generally accepted proposition that criminal responsibility was not extinguished when the offender was under the influence of a drug or liquor and the reasons for that rule:

It is generally agreed that a defendant will not be relieved of criminal responsibility because he was under the influence of intoxicants or drugs voluntarily taken. This principle rests upon public policy, demanding that he who seeks the influence of liquor or narcotics should not be insulated from criminal liability because that influence impaired his judgment or his control.

The required element of badness can be found in the intentional use of the stimulant or depressant. Moreover, to say that one who offended while under such influence was sick would suggest that his sickness disappeared when he sobered up and hence he should be released. Such a concept would hardly protect others from the prospect of repeated injury. (60 N.J. at 214, 287 A.2d 720)

The Chief Justice set forth four exceptions to the general rule. First, when drugs being taken for medication produce unexpected or bizarre results, no public interest is served by punishing the defendant since there is no likelihood of repetition. Second, if intoxication so impairs a defendant's mental faculties that he does not possess the willfulness, deliberation and premeditation necessary to prove first degree murder, a homicide cannot be raised to first degree murder. State v. Sinclair, 49 N.J. 525, 544, 231 A.2d 565 (1967); State v. Trantino, 44 N.J. 358, 369, 209 A.2d 117 (1965), Cert. den. 382 U.S. 993, 86 S.Ct. 573, 15 L.Ed.2d 479 (1966).

Under this exception the influence of liquor "no matter how pervasive that influence may be, will not lead to an acquittal. It cannot reduce the crime below murder in the second degree, and this because of the demands of public security." State v. Maik, supra, 60 N.J. at 215, 287 A.2d at 721. Third, a felony homicide will be reduced to second degree murder when intoxication precludes formation of the underlying felonious intent.

Parenthetically, it may be noted that since voluntary intoxication does not eliminate responsibility for the felony, it could be contended that the defendant should remain liable for first degree felony murder. On the other hand, considerations of fairness indicate that such a defendant should be treated the same as one charged with ordinary first degree homicide requiring premeditation. Fourth, the defense of insanity is available when the voluntary use of the intoxicant or drug results in a fixed state of insanity after the influence of the intoxicant or drug has spent itself. Since the defense in Maik may have fallen into the fourth category, the charge as given was erroneous and the cause was remanded for a new trial on the issue of whether the defendant had been insane at the time of the killing and whether that condition continued thereafter.

A difference of opinion has been expressed in the Appellate Division as to the meaning of Chief Justice Weintraub's discussion of intoxication in Maik. In State v. Del Vecchio, 142 N.J.Super. 359, 361 A.2d 579 (App.Div.), certif. den. 71 N.J. 501, 366 A.2d 657 (1976), a conviction for breaking and entering with intent to steal was reversed on the ground that the jury had improperly been charged that voluntary intoxication was not a defense to a crime requiring a specific intent.

The Appellate Division reasoned that, when a specific intent was an element of an offense, voluntary intoxication may negate existence of that intent. Since intoxication may have prevented existence of that specific intent, an acquittal might be in order.

The Appellate Division also held that the only principle to be derived from Maik was the proposition that voluntary intoxication may be relevant in determining whether a murder may be raised to first degree. In contrast, Judge Allcorn's dissent in State v. Atkins, 151 N.J.Super. 555, 573, 377 A.2d 718 (App.Div.1977), rev'd 78 N.J. 454, 396 A.2d 1122 (1979), expresses the opinion that Maik stands for the proposition that voluntary intoxication is not a defense to any criminal offense irrespective of whether a specific or general intent is an element of the offense.

In our opinion the Chief Justice in Maik enunciated a principle applicable generally to all crimes and, unless one of the exceptions to the general rule is applicable, voluntary intoxication will not excuse criminal conduct. The need to protect the public from the prospect of repeated injury and the public policy demanding that one who voluntarily subjects himself to intoxication should not be insulated from criminal responsibility are strongly supportive of this result. We reject the approach adopted by Del Vecchio because, although it has surface appeal, it is based [p. 475] on an unworkable dichotomy, gives rise to inconsistencies, and ignores the policy expressed in Maik.

Del Vecchio would permit the intoxication defense only when a "specific" as distinguished from a "general" intent was an element of the crime. However, that difference is not readily ascertainable. "The distinction thus made between a 'specific intent' and a 'general intent,' " wrote the Chief Justice in Maik, "is quite elusive, and although the proposition (that voluntary intoxication may be a defense if it prevented formation of a specific intent) is echoed in some opinions in our State, see State v. White (27 N.J. 158, 165-167, 142 A.2d 65 (1958)); Cf. State v. Letter, 4 N.J.Misc. 395, 133 A. 46 (Sup.Ct.1926), it is not clear that any of our cases in fact turned upon it." 60 N.J. at 214-215, 287 A.2d at 721.

Professor Hall has deplored the attempted distinction in the following analysis: The current confusion resulting from diverse uses of "general intent" is aggravated by dubious efforts to differentiate that from "specific intent." Each crime has its distinctive Mens rea, e. g. intending to have forced intercourse, intending to break and enter a dwelling-house and to commit a crime there, intending to inflict a battery, and so on. It is evident that there must be as many Mentes reae as there are crimes.

And whatever else may be said about an intention, an essential characteristic of it is that it is directed towards a definite end. To assert therefore that an intention is "specific" is to employ a superfluous term just as if one were to speak of a "voluntary act." (J. Hall, General Principles of Criminal Law 142 (2d ed. 1960))

For a similar analysis see People v. Hood, 1 Cal.3d 444, 456-457, 82 Cal.Rptr. 618, 625-626, 462 P.2d 370, 377-378 (1969). The same point is made in G. Williams, Criminal Law The General Part (2d ed. 1961): The adjective "specific" seems to be somewhat pointless, for the intent is no more specific than any other intent required in criminal law. The most that can be said is that the intent is specifically referred to in the indictment. There is no substantive difference between an intent specifically mentioned and one implied in the name of the crime. (Id. at 49)

The undeniable fact is "that neither common experience nor psychology knows any such actual phenomenon as 'general intent' that is distinguishable from 'specific intent.' " Hall, "Intoxication and Criminal Responsibility," 57 Harv.L.Rev. 1045, 1064 (1944).

Moreover, distinguishing between specific and general intent gives rise to incongruous results by irrationally allowing intoxication to excuse some crimes but not others. In some instances if the defendant is found incapable of formulating the specific intent necessary for the crime charged, such as assault with intent to rob, he may be convicted of a lesser included general intent crime, such as assault with a deadly weapon. N.J.S.A. 2A:90-3. In other cases there may be no related general intent offense so that intoxication would lead to acquittal.

Thus, a defendant acquitted for breaking and entering with intent to steal because of intoxication would not be guilty of any crime breaking and entering being at most under certain circumstances the disorderly persons offense of trespass. N.J.S.A. 2A:170-31. Similarly, if the specific intent to rob were not demonstrated because of intoxication, then the defendant may have no criminal responsibility since assault with intent to rob would also be excused.

Finally, where the more serious offense requires only a general intent, such as rape, see J. Hall, General Principles of Criminal Law 143 (2d ed. 1960), and sources cited, intoxication provides no defense, whereas it would be a defense to an attempt to rape, specific intent being an element of that offense. Yet the same logic and reasoning which impels exculpation due to the failure of specific intent to commit an offense would equally compel the same result when a general intent is an element of the offense

One commentator summed up the situation in the following way: For example, if the defendant is found incapable of formulating the specific intent necessary for the crime with which he is charged, he may be convicted instead of a lesser included general intent offense. Yet in some cases there may be no related general intent offense on which conviction can be based, and complete acquittal will result. See, e. g., People v. Jones, 263 Ill. 564, 105 N.E. 744 (1914) (attempted burglary); Hall, (Intoxication and Criminal Responsibility, 57 Harv.L.Rev. 1045, 1062 (1944)).

Thus, the intoxicated offender may be denied exculpation, receive partial exculpation, or receive total exculpation, depending upon the nature of the crime with which he is charged. As one commentator concludes: "It is thus apparent that the criminal liability of the grossly intoxicated offender depends upon the crime fortuitously committed while incapacitated."

Note, Volitional Fault and the Intoxicated Criminal Offender, 36 U.Cin.L.Rev. 258, 276 (1967). (Comment, 61 Minn.L.Rev. 901, 904 n.14 (1977))

The Del Vecchio approach may free defendants of specific intent offenses even though the harm caused may be greater than in an offense held to require only general intent. This course thus undermines the criminal law's primary function of protecting society from the results of behavior that endangers the public safety. This should be our guide rather than concern with logical consistency in terms of any single theory of culpability, particularly in view of the fact that alcohol is significantly involved in a substantial number of offenses.

The demands of public safety and the harm done are identical irrespective of the offender's reduced ability to restrain himself due to his drinking"(I)f a person casts off the restraints of reason and consciousness by a voluntary act, no wrong is done to him if he is held accountable for any crime which he may commit in that condition. Society is entitled to this protection." McDaniel v. State, 356 So.2d 1151, 1160- 1161 (Miss.1978).

Until a stuporous condition is reached or the entire motor area of the brain is profoundly affected the probability of the existence of intent remains. The initial effect of alcohol is the reduction or removal of inhibitions or restraints. But that does not vitiate intent. The loosening of the tongue has been said to disclose a person's true sentiments "In vino veritas." One commentator has noted:

The great majority of moderately to grossly drunk or drugged persons who commit putatively criminal acts are probably aware of what they are doing and the likely consequences. In the case of those who are drunk, alcohol may have diminished their perceptions, released their inhibitions and clouded their reasoning and judgment, but they still have sufficient capacity for the conscious mental processes required by the ordinary definitions of all or most specific mens rea crimes.

For example, a person can be quite far gone in drink and still capable of the conscious intent to steal, which is an element of common law larceny. (Murphy, "Has Pennsylvania Found a Satisfactory Intoxication Defense?", 81 Dick. L. Rev. 199, 208 (1977).

When a defendant shows that he was comatose and therefore could not have broken and entered into the home or committed some other unlawful activity, such stage of intoxication may be relevant in establishing a general denial. But short of that, voluntary intoxication, other than its employment to disprove premeditation and deliberation in murder, should generally serve as no excuse. In this fashion the opportunities of false claims by defendants may be minimized and misapplication by jurors of the effect of drinking on the defendant's responsibility eliminated.

The significance of the common law approach to voluntary intoxication should not be overlooked. Our criminal law is grounded in large measure in the common law because of its incorporation by our constitutions and statutes. Our first constitution expressly included the common and statutory laws of England. N.J.Const. (1776), par. 22. This incorporation by reference has been retained in subsequent constitutions. N.J.Const. (1844), Art. X, par. 1; N.J.Const. [p. 480] (1947), Art. XI, s I, par. 3. See State v. Young, 77 N.J. 245, 249-250, 390 A.2d 556 (1978).

The Legislature has followed this pattern since 1796 by stating that all offenses of an indictable nature at common law that are not expressly provided for by statute are crimes. An Act for the Punishment of Crimes, par. 68, adopted March 18, 1796 (Laws of New Jersey 244, 262 (1821)); N.J.S.A. 2A:85- 1. See State v. Bynes, 109 N.J.Super. 105, 262 A.2d 420 (App.Div.1969), aff'd o. b. 55 N.J. 408, 262 A.2d 408 (1970).

At common law voluntary intoxication was not a defense. The earliest pronouncement is found in Reniger v. Fogossa, 1 Plow. 1, 19, 75 Eng.Rep. 1, 31 (Exch.Ch.1551), which reads:

"But where a man breaks the words of the law by involuntary ignorance, there he shall not be excused. As if a person that is drunk kills another, this shall be felony, and he shall be hanged for it, and yet he did it through ignorance, for when he was drunk he had no understanding nor memory; but inasmuch as that ignorance was occasioned by his own act and folly, and he might have avoided it, he shall not be privileged thereby. And Aristotle says, that such a man deserves double punishment, because he has doubly offended, viz. in being drunk to the evil example of others, and in committing the crime of homicide. And this act is said to be done ignoranter, for that he is the cause of his own ignorance: and so the diversity appears between a thing done ex ignorantia, and ignoranter".

See Singh, "History of the Defense of Drunkenness in English Criminal Law," 49 L.Q.Rev. 528, 530 (1933). That remained the unwritten law at the time New Jersey attained statehood. For development of the law in England see Director of Public Prosecutions v. Beard (1920) A.C. 479, 12 A.L.R. 846. Our holding today adheres to the central theme of that principle modified only by contemporary circumstances including scientific data on physiological effects of alcohol and our notions of fairness and rightness.

It might be suggested with some justification that we should adhere to the policy expressed in the new Code of Criminal Justice, effective September 1, 1979, N.J.S.A. [p. 481] 2C:98-4. However, the Deputy Attorney General implied at oral argument that the Legislature would be requested to modify the provisions dealing with intoxication and, in view of the possibility that the Legislature might act, in the interim we prefer to adhere to the principle enunciated in Maik. We note that in Arkansas, a law based on the Model Penal Code's provision for a defense of voluntary intoxication was repealed less than two years after it was enacted. Ark. Stat.Ann. s 41-207 (1977).

The repealing legislation was made effective immediately by a finding of emergency which read in part "that the defense of voluntary intoxication is detrimental to the welfare and safety of the citizens of this State in that criminals are at times excused from the consequences of their criminal acts merely because of their voluntary intoxication ." 1977 Ark.Acts, No. 101, s 3. Similarly, Pennsylvania first enacted but then repealed a voluntary intoxication defense which was substantially the same as in the Model Penal Code. 18 Pa.Cons.Stat.Ann. s 308 (Purdon Supp.1978) (prior version at 1972 Pa.Laws, No. 334).

The new Code of Criminal Justice provides that a person is not guilty of an offense unless he acted purposely, knowingly, recklessly or negligently, as the law may require. N.J.S.A. 2C:2-2. It also states that intoxication is not a defense "unless it negatives an element of the offense," N.J.S.A. 2C:2-8(a), and that "(w)hen recklessness establishes an element of the offense, if the actor, due to self-induced intoxication, is unaware of a risk of which he would have been aware had he been sober, such unawareness is immaterial." N.J.S.A. 2C:2-8(b).

These provisions were taken from the Model Penal Code of the American Law Institute, s 2.08 (Prop.Off. Draft 1962). The American Law Institute Committee has explained that in those instances when the defendant's purpose or knowledge is an element of a crime, proof of intoxication may negate the existence of either. Tent. Draft No. 9 at 2-9 (1959). The [p. 482] distinction between specific and general intent has been rejected.

Purpose or knowledge has been made a component of many offenses so that voluntary intoxication will be an available defense in those situations. Thus, voluntary intoxication may be a defense to aggravated assaults consisting of attempts to cause bodily injury to another with a deadly weapon. N.J.S.A. 2C:12-1(b)(2). Intoxication could exonerate those otherwise guilty of burglaries and criminal trespass. N.J.S.A. 2C:18-2; 2C:18-3.

It would be an available defense to arson, N.J.S.A. 2C:17-1, robbery, N.J.S.A. 2C:19-1, and theft, N.J.S.A. 2C:20-3. It could reduce murder to manslaughter, N.J.S.A. 2C:11-3, 2C:11-4, and excuse shoplifting, N.J.S.A. 2C:20-11(b). The Code would also permit the incongruous result of permitting intoxication to be a complete defense to an attempted sexual assault (rape), N.J.S.A. 2C:5-1, but not of a completed sexual assault, N.J.S.A. 2C:14-2. Whether the Legislature will retain any or all these provisions remains to be seen.

Our holding today does not mean that voluntary intoxication is always irrelevant in criminal proceedings. Evidence of intoxication may be introduced to demonstrate that premeditation and deliberation have not been proven so [p. 483] that a second degree murder cannot be raised to first degree murder or to show that the intoxication led to a fixed state of insanity. Intoxication may be shown to prove that a defendant never participated in a crime. Thus it might be proven that a defendant was in such a drunken stupor and unconscious state that he was not a part of a robbery. See State v. Letter, 4 N.J.Misc. 395, 133 A. 46 (Sup.Ct.1926).

His mental faculties may be so prostrated as to preclude the commission of the criminal act. Under some circumstances intoxication may be relevant to demonstrate mistake. However, in the absence of any basis for the defense, a trial court should not in its charge introduce that element. A trial court, of course, may consider intoxication as a mitigating circumstance when sentencing a defendant.

The judgment of the Appellate Division if affirmed.

HANDLER, J., concurring.

If a defendant's state of mind is a material factor in determining whether a particular crime has been committed and if a degree of intoxication so affects the defendant's mental faculties as to eliminate effectively a condition of the mind otherwise essential for the commission of a crime intoxication should be recognized as a defense in fact.

When dealing with the issue of intoxication, the focus at trial should be upon the mental state which is required for the commission of the particular crime charged. This should not ordinarily call for desiccated refinements between general intent and specific intent.

I subscribe to the reasoning expressed in State v. Maik, 60 N.J. 203, 287 A.2d 715 (1972), and endorsed by this Court, which denigrated the attempted differentiation between so-called specific intent and general intent crimes. It is an unhelpful, misleading and often confusing distinction. See People v. Hood, 1 Cal.3d 444, 456-457, 82 Cal.Rptr. 618, 625-626, 462 P.2d 370, 377-378 (1969); J. Hall, General Principles of Criminal Law 142 (2d ed. 1960); G. Williams, Criminal Law The General Part (2d ed. 1961); Hall, "Intoxication and Criminal Responsibility", 57 Harv.L.Rev. 1045, 1064 (1944), authorities cited by the majority opinion. Ante at 1132-1133.

For the most part, the inquiry at a criminal trial should be directed toward the general guilty condition of mind or Mens rea necessary to append responsibility for criminal conduct. See State v. Savoie, 67 N.J. 439, 454-461, 341 A.2d 598 (1975).

Adherence to the distinction between specific and general intent crimes, and the availability of voluntary intoxication as a defense in terms of that distinction, has led to anomalous results. See Annot., "Modern Status of the Rules as to Voluntary Intoxication as Defense to Criminal Charge", 8 A.L.R.3d 1236 (1966); for example, compare State v. Frankland, 51 N.J. 221, 238 A.2d 680 (1968) (intoxication is a defense to a statutory criminal charge of burning with intent to burn) with State v. Kinlaw, 150 N.J.Super. 70, 73, 374 A.2d 1233 (App.Div.1977) (intoxication is not a defense to a statutory charge of wilfully and maliciously burning). Inconsistent applications of the intoxication defense and disparate results can be avoided or reduced by rejecting the dichotomy between specific intent and general intent crimes.

The Model Penal Code of the American Law Institute has eschewed this distinction. It deals with Mens rea primarily in terms of purpose and knowledge and calls for an analysis of the elements of the criminal offense in relation to these components. See Model Penal Code s 2.02, Comments (Tent. Draft No. 4, 1955); Id., s 2.08, Comments (Tent. Draft No. 9, 1959).

The recently enacted New Jersey Code of Criminal Justice, N.J.S.A. 2C:1-1 Et seq., similarly abandons the distinctions between specific and general intent in addressing the area of the mental components of crime. N.J.S.A. 2C:2-2. This approach, in my view, enables a trier of fact to assimilate proof of a defendant's intoxication in a more realistic perspective and to reach a more rational determination of the effect of intoxication upon criminal responsibility, particularly in terms of consciousness and purpose. N.J.S.A. 2C:2-2.

On this point, the majority disapproves of the decision of the Appellate Division in State v. Del Vecchio, 142 N.J.Super. 359, 361 A.2d 579 (App.Div.), certif. den. 71 N.J. 501, 366 A.2d 657 (1976). [p. 487] Ante at 1132-1133. I also disavow that decision to the extent it maintains the distinction between specific intent and general intent crimes and determines the availability of voluntary intoxication as a defense based upon that distinction. I do not think it follows, however, that if the separation between so-called specific and general intent crimes is rejected, voluntary intoxication as a factual defense must also be rejected.

The majority of this Court repudiates the intoxication defense on grounds of general deterrence and a ubiquitous need to protect society from drunken criminals. This approach mirrors a commendable impulse, which I share. But, it fails to consider that enforcement of the criminal law must be fair and just, as well as strict and protective.

The criminal laws need not be impotent or ineffective when dealing with an intoxicated criminal. The question should always be whether under particular circumstances a defendant ought to be considered responsible for his conduct. This involves a factual determination of whether he has acted with volition.

Intoxication, in this context, would constitute a defense if it reached such a level, operating upon the defendant's mind, so as to deprive him of his will to act. Cf. State v. King, 37 N.J. 285, 297-298, 181 A.2d 158 (1962). I would accordingly require, in order to generate a reasonable doubt as to a defendant's responsibility for his acts, that it be shown he was so intoxicated that he could not think, or that his mind did not function with consciousness or volition. Cf. State v. Ghaul, 132 N. J. Super. 438, 440, 334 A.2d 65 (App.Div.1975); State v. Turley, 113 R.I. 104, 318 A.2d 455 (Sup.Ct.1974) (intoxication must be so extreme as to paralyze the will of defendant); State v. Gover, 267 Md. 602, 298 A.2d 378 (Ct.App.1973) (intoxication that suspends defendant's reasoning abilities constitutes a defense); also State v. Bindhammer, 44 N.J. 372, 209 A.2d 124 (1965); State v. Trantino, 44 N.J. 358, 209 A.2d 117 (1965), Cert. den. 382 U.S.

993, 86 S.Ct. 573, 15 L.Ed.2d 479 (1966); State v. King, supra 37 N.J. at 296-297, 181 A.2d 158 (homicide prosecutions).

I disagree therefore with the suggestion by the Court that if voluntary intoxication is recognized as a defense, as it is under the recently enacted New Jersey Code of Criminal Justice, N.J.S.A. 2C:2-8, it will serve to excuse criminal conduct with respect to which purpose or knowledge is a component. Ante at 1136. I do not share the pessimism of the Court that voluntary intoxication as a recognized defense will wreak havoc in criminal law enforcement under the New Jersey Criminal Justice Code.

The fear of condoning criminals, who are also drunks, can be addressed, I respectfully suggest, by imposing a heavy burden of proof upon defendants to show a degree of intoxication capable of prostrating the senses. Drunkenness which does not have this effect does not diminish responsibility and should not serve to excuse criminality. I think it amiss therefore for this Court to forewarn the Legislature, Ante at 1135-1136, on the basis of its own dire prognostications as to the applications of the statutory intoxication defense contemplated under the New Jersey Criminal Justice Code.

In this case, the crime with which defendant was charged is denominated by the statute, N.J.S.A. 2A:90-2, as assault with intent to rob. It serves no useful end to describe the mental state necessary to sustain the charge as a "specific intent" in contradistinction to a "general intent" to do the particular acts revealed by the evidence. I am satisfied that under any formulation of the elements of the crime, defendant on these facts could not be exonerated for reasons of intoxication. The facts, which are fully set forth in the Court's opinion, Ante at 1130, reveal that defendant engaged in volitional, purposeful activity he assaulted his victim with a knife and at the same time unmistakably expressed his purpose by demanding that his victim turn over $80 from the cash register.

He had the requisite Mens rea for affixing criminal responsibility. The evidence of defendant's drinking during the day and before the assault is relevant, of course, to the question of whether he was intoxicated when he committed this crime. But, in light of his unequivocal [p. 489] assault on the bartender with a knife and his loud and clear demand for money from the cash register, the evidence of intoxication was palpably insufficient to negate the volitional character of the defendant's behavior.

Juxtaposed against such overwhelming and clear evidence of purposeful criminal conduct, only intoxication which prostrated the defendant's faculties or deprived him of will would justify his acquittal.

Was defendant nevertheless entitled to have the jury consider the evidence of intoxication as a factor relevant to his commission of the charged crime? Evidence of intoxication, which may under some circumstances be inferred from prolonged, continuous, heavy drinking, should ordinarily entitle a defendant to a charge of intoxication as a factual defense bearing upon his mental state and whether he acted without purpose or volition. E. g., State v. Frankland, supra; State v. Sinclair, 49 N.J. 525, 231 A.2d 565 (1967); State v. Hudson, 38 N.J. 364, 185 A.2d 1 (1962); State v. King, supra.

The charge on intoxication, however, should explain to the jury that unless defendant's intoxication was sufficiently extreme so as to have deprived him of his will to act and ability to reason, and prevented him in fact from having a purpose to rob the bartender, he would not, on this ground, be entitled to an acquittal. The jury, moreover, should be admonished to consider and weigh the evidence of intoxication with great caution. See State v. Tune, 17 N.J. 100, 114-115, 110 A.2d 99 (1954), Cert. den. 349 U.S. 907, 75 S.Ct. 584, 99 L.Ed. 1243 (1955).

Justice CLIFFORD joins in this opinion.

PASHMAN, J., concurring in result only and dissenting.

In this and the companion case of State v. Atkins, 78 N.J. 454, 396 A.2d 1122 (1979), the majority rules that a person may be convicted of the crimes of assault with intent to rob and breaking and entering with intent to steal even though he never, in fact, intended to rob anyone or steal anything.

The majority arrives at this anomalous result by holding that voluntary intoxication can never constitute a defense to any crime other than first- degree murder even though, due to intoxication, the accused may not have possessed the mental state specifically required as an element of the offense. This holding not only defies logic and sound public policy, it also runs counter to dictates of prior caselaw and the policies enunciated by our Legislature in the new criminal code. I therefore dissent from that holding although I agree that the defendant is entitled to a new trial.

II

Today's holding by the majority stands logic on its head. This Court and the Legislature have long adhered to the view that criminal sanctions will not be imposed upon a defendant unless there exists a "concurrence of an evil-meaning mind with an evil-doing hand.' "State v. Williams, 29 N.J. 27, 41, 148 A.2d 22, 29 (1959). The policies underlying this proposition are clear. A person who intentionally commits a bad act is more culpable than one who engages in the same conduct without any evil design.

The intentional wrongdoer is also more likely to repeat his offense, and hence constitutes a greater threat to societal repose. A sufficiently intoxicated defendant is thus subject [p. 494] to less severe sanctions not because the law "excuses" his conduct but because the circumstances surrounding his acts have been deemed by the Legislature to be less deserving of punishment.

It strains reason to hold that a defendant may be found guilty of a crime whose definition includes a requisite mental state when the defendant actually failed to possess that state of mind. Indeed, this is the precise teaching of cases allowing the intoxication defense in first-degree murder prosecutions. To sustain a first-degree murder conviction, the State must prove that the homicide was premeditated, willful, and deliberate. State v. King, 37 N.J. 285, 293-294, 181 A.2d 158 (1962).

If the accused, due to intoxication, did not in fact possess these mental attributes, he can be convicted of at most second- degree murder, See, e. g., State v. Polk, 78 N.J. 539, 397 A.2d 327 (1979); State v. Maik, supra, 60 N.J. at 215, 287 A.2d 715; State v. King, supra, 37 N.J. at 297-298, 181 A.2d 158; State v. DiPaolo, 34 N.J. 279, 295-296, 168 A.2d 401, Cert. den. 368 U.S. 880, 82 S.Ct. 130, 7 L.Ed.2d 80 (1961). That offense, however, can be sustained on a mere showing of recklessness, State v. Gardner, 51 N.J. 444, 242 A.2d 1 (1968), and the necessary recklessness can be found in the act of becoming intoxicated.

Just as the lack of premeditation, willfulness, or deliberation precludes a conviction for first-degree murder, so should the lack of intent to rob or steal be a defense to assault and battery with intent to rob, or breaking and entering with intent to steal. The principle is the same in both situations. If voluntary intoxication negates an element of the offense, the defendant has not engaged in the conduct proscribed by the criminal statute, and hence should not be subject to the sanctions imposed by that statute.

III

The majority ultimately grounds its conclusions on public policy considerations. It professes to be concerned with protecting society from drunken offenders. There are several [p. 495] problems with this approach. First, the majority's opinion is not even internally consistent. Although intoxication is not to be given the status of a defense, the majority states that it can be considered to "buttress the affirmative defense of reasonable mistake." State v. Atkins, supra, 78 N.J. at 460, 396 A.2d at 1125.

It is difficult to comprehend why the public would be less endangered by persons who become intoxicated and, as a result, commit alcohol-induced "mistakes" which would otherwise be criminal offenses, than by persons who get so intoxicated that they commit the same acts without any evil intent. In fact, it appears highly likely that the first group would encompass a larger number of persons and hence constitute a greater menace to society.

Second, the majority's opinion is not likely to deter the commission of alcohol-induced crimes. It is unrealistic to expect that before indulging in intoxicants people will consider the extent of their criminal responsibility for acts they might commit. In this respect, therefore, today's holding will not add to the public's safety.

The most important consideration, however, is that the standards for establishing the defense are extremely difficult to meet. Contrary to the implications contained in the majority opinion, it is not the case that every defendant who has had a few drinks may successfully urge the defense. The mere intake of even large quantities of alcohol will not suffice. Moreover, the defense cannot be established solely by showing that the defendant might not have committed the offense had he been sober. See Final Report of the New Jersey Criminal Law Revision Commission, Vol. II, Commentary (1971) at 68. What is required is a showing of such a great prostration of the faculties that the requisite mental state was totally lacking.

That is, to successfully invoke the defense, an accused must show that he was so intoxicated that he did not have the intent to commit an offense. Such a state of affairs will likely exist in very few cases. I am confident that our judges and juries will be able to distinguish such unusual instances.

IV

The majority and the commentators have criticized as elusive the "specific intent-general intent" dichotomy. See, e. g., LaFave & Scott, Criminal Law (1972) s 45 at 344; Note, "Intoxication as a Criminal Defense," 55 Colum.L.Rev. 1210, 1218 (1955). The majority's difficulty in distinguishing the various mental states should not, however, be sufficient reason to mandate that all intoxicated defendants be incarcerated. The proper approach is to try and outline a more rational rule for applying the defense.

I believe that such a rule is that enunciated in our new Code of Criminal Justice, effective September 1, 1979, which provides that intoxication will be a defense whenever it negates an element of an offense. N.J.S.A. 2C:98-4. The Act defines four mental states purpose, knowledge, recklessness and negligence one of which is necessary to establish guilt depending on the particular offense involved. N.J.S.A. 2C:2-2. Purpose and knowledge may be negated by intoxication, whereas recklessness and negligence may not. Moreover, the elements of recklessness or negligence may, where required by the definition of the crime, be satisfied by the recklessness implicit in becoming voluntarily intoxicated.

Although our current criminal law does not neatly compartmentalize mens rea into four such categories, the same type of analysis can be applied. Whenever a defendant shows that he was so intoxicated that he did not possess the requisite state of mind, he may not be convicted. Intoxication would not be a defense, however, to criminal offenses which may be established by recklessness or negligence as the carelessness in getting intoxicated would of itself supply the necessary mental state.

This analysis would leave intact the long-standing rule that intoxication is not a defense to second-degree murder as that crime may be established by showing recklessness. State v. Gardner, 51 N.J. 444, 458, 242 A.2d 1 (1968).

Although the distinction between specific intent and general intent would be erased by the rule enunciated herein, [p. 497] this does not mean that the different mental states implicit in our criminal law would become irrelevant. Some crimes battery, for example only require that the defendant intend the act that he has committed, while others such as assault and battery with intent to kill require that he also intend to bring about certain consequences.

Certainly it would take a greater showing of intoxication to convince one that defendant had no intent to strike the victim than to show that he did not intend to kill. In the former case, one might well conclude that he must have intended his act unless he was unconscious. Indeed, this is the main reason why the "specific intent/general intent" dichotomy was first formulated.

Inasmuch as defendants in these two cases were charged with crimes requiring intent to rob or intent to steal, their convictions must be reversed and a new trial ordered at which they can attempt to persuade the jury that they lacked those mental states. We must respect the legislative judgment, made explicit in the new Criminal Code, that those persons who, due to intoxication, act without the intent required by law as an element of the crime, are not to be treated as are those who willfully commit the same acts.

Accordingly, I would affirm the judgment of the Appellate Division in this case and the companion case, State v. Atkins, 78 N.J. 454, 396 A.2d 1122, decided this day.

END OF DOCUMENT

The PEOPLE of the State of New York, Respondent

v

Cornelius GAINES, Appellant

Court of Appeals of New York

74 N.Y.2d 358 (1989)

OPINION OF THE COURT

KAYE, Judge.

The felony of third degree burglary occurs when a person "knowingly enters or remains unlawfully in a building with intent to commit a crime therein." (Penal Law § 140.20.) The issue before us is whether, in this case of unlawful entry, the jury should have been instructed that they must find defendant's intent to commit a crime in the building existed at the time of the entry, or whether no such instruction need have been given, because the "remains unlawfully" element of the statute means that such intent may be formed after defendant's unlawful entry. We conclude that Penal Law § 140.20 requires that intent to commit a crime in the building exist at the time of the unlawful entry, and we reverse the Appellate Division order that upheld defendant's burglary conviction.

The People's evidence at trial showed that in the early morning of February 2, 1985, defendant was arrested as he emerged from the window of a building supply company. Over his own clothes defendant was wearing coveralls and a jacket that belonged to a company employee; pens bearing the company name were in the jacket pocket. Inside the building, several desks were in disarray, but other than the garments and the pens, nothing was missing from the premises and no burglar's tools were found.

Taking the stand on his own behalf, defendant testified that on February 2, he left the homeless shelter where he had been staying, because he had inadequate funds to remain there, and he set out for a friend's place, where he planned to spend the night. When defendant found his friend out, he walked further until he reached the building supply company, pushed in a window and entered the building for refuge from the cold and heavy snow that fell that night. Defendant claimed that he did not touch the desks, file cabinets or safe but simply put on the jacket and coveralls to keep warm and stayed near a heating vent until he heard police officers approaching.

In a pre-charge conference, defense counsel requested that the jury be instructed that, where there is an unlawful entry, in order for a burglary to occur the intent to commit a crime within the building must exist at the time of the entry. Counsel also argued that on the facts of this case—where it was undisputed that defendant's entry was unauthorized—any reference to "remains unlawfully" should be omitted from the charge. The court refused both requests and charged, without elaboration, that the jury could find defendant guilty of burglary if, at the time of his knowingly unlawful entry or remaining, defendant intended to commit a crime in the building.

During deliberations, the jury asked the court for further instructions on the difference between burglary and trespass, and specifically asked whether "intent has to occur before or after entering the building." The court reread its earlier [p. 361] instructions. Defense counsel again excepted, arguing that defendant's commission of a crime as an afterthought following unlawful entry would not transform a trespass and petit larceny into a burglary, and that the jury should be so instructed.

In response, the court expressed the view that the Legislature did not intend that a defendant escape prosecution for burglary "in any case where a defendant unlawfully entered a building or premises but not with a specific intent to commit a given crime and thereafter committed a crime in the building". The Appellate Division affirmed defendant's conviction, with two Justices dissenting, 147 A.D.2d 891, 537 N.Y.S.2d 360. Concluding that the trial court erred in denying defendant's requests, we now reverse his burglary conviction and order a new trial.

At common law, burglary was defined "as the breaking and entering of a dwelling of another, at night, with intent to commit a felony therein." (Hechtman, Practice Commentaries, McKinney's Cons. Laws of N.Y., Book 39, Penal Law art. 140, at 5 [1975].) Unless the intent to commit a felony existed at the time of the breaking and entry, there was no burglary. Similarly, under the former Penal Law, a defendant who broke and entered with no intent to commit a crime was not guilty of burglary, though later deciding to commit a crime on the premises (People v. Haupt, 247 N.Y. 369, 371, 160 N.E. 643).

When the Penal Law was revised in 1965, burglary in the third degree was defined as "knowingly enters or remains unlawfully in a building with intent to commit a crime therein." (Penal Law § 140.20; emphasis added.) The People's contention in essence is that the addition of "remains unlawfully"—a concept unknown at common law or in the former Penal Law—abrogates the requirement of intent to commit a crime at the time of unlawful entry. All that is now required, according to the People, is that defendant commit a crime while unlawfully on the premises. On its face, the statute could be read to support this interpretation.

This interpretation is, however, not consistent with the purpose of classifying burglary as a separate and relatively more serious crime. As commentators have pointed out, burglary is in fact a form of attempt crime, since the crime the unlawful intruder intended to commit need not be completed.

The development of burglary as an independent felony resulted from two deficiencies in the early law of attempt: that an attempt could not be penalized until the last act short of completion had occurred, and that the conduct was in any event punishable only as a misdemeanor (see, Denzer and McQuillan, Practice Commentary, McKinney's Cons.Laws of N.Y., Book 39, Penal Law art. 140, at 331-332 [1967]; Model Penal Code and Commentaries, Official Draft and Revised Comments § 221.1, at 62-63).

These gaps in the laws of attempt have now been remedied. An attempt need not encompass the final act toward the completion of the offense (People v. Bracey, 41 N.Y.2d 296, 300, 392 N.Y.S.2d 412, 360 N.E.2d 1094), and is punishable as an offense of the same grade or a single lesser grade of severity as the completed crime (Penal Law § 110.05).

Nonetheless, the Legislature has continued to penalize burglary as a serious felony—rather than simply punish the trespass and the attempted or consummated crime within a building—because of the heightened danger posed when an unlawful intrusion into a building is effected by someone bent on a criminal end. A defendant who simply trespasses with no intent to commit a crime inside a building does not possess the more culpable mental state that justifies punishment as a burglar.

This is not to suggest, however, that the People are required to prove that defendant intended to commit any particular crime within a building. Moreover, defendant's intent to commit a crime may be inferred from the circumstances of the entry, under a proper instruction (see, People v. Barnes, 50 N.Y.2d 375, 381, 429 N.Y.S.2d 178, 406 N.E.2d 1071).

We conclude, therefore, that the Legislature had no such purpose. The statute contains no clear and explicit direction to change the long-standing rule (see, People v. King, 61 N.Y.2d 550, 554, 475 N.Y.S.2d 260, 463 N.E.2d 601). To the contrary, the Legislature was plainly addressing a different factual situation—not one of unlawful entry but of unauthorized remaining in a building after lawful entry (as a shoplifter who remains on store premises after closing). As we observed in People v. Licata, 28 N.Y.2d 113, 320 N.Y.S.2d 53, 268 N.E.2d 787, " '[t]he word "remain" in the phrase "enter or remain" is designed to be applicable to cases in which a person enters with "license or privilege" but remains on the premises after termination of such license or privilege.'" (Id., at 117, 320 N.Y.S.2d 53, 268 N.E.2d 787, quoting Denzer and McQuillan, Practice Commentary, op. cit., at 341-342; 2 CJI [N.Y.] PL 140.20; 2 LaFave & Scott, Substantive Criminal Law § 8.13[b], at 468.) By the words "remains unlawfully" the Legislature sought to broaden the definition of criminal trespass, not to eliminate the requirement that the act constituting criminal trespass be accompanied by contemporaneous intent to commit a crime.

In order to be guilty of burglary for unlawful remaining, a defendant must have entered legally, but remain for the purpose of committing a crime after authorization to be on the premises terminates. And in order to be guilty of burglary for unlawful entry, a defendant must have had the intent to commit a crime at the time of entry. In either event, contemporaneous intent is required.

New York's pattern criminal jury instructions place the word "remains" in brackets, indicating that the defendant has either entered or remained unlawfully, but not both (see, CJI[N.Y.] PL 140.20).

The trial court committed error in denying defendant's charge requests. The court should not have referred to unlawful remaining in its burglary charge, since the situation to which that language applies was not present in the case. Most importantly, defendant was entitled to a charge clearly stating that the jury must find that he intended to commit a crime at the time he entered the premises unlawfully.

Failure to give such an instruction compels reversal in this case. The jury could have concluded from defendant's testimony that he intended no crime when he broke into the building. Notably, by their specific questions, the jurors indicated that they had focused upon the time defendant's criminal intent was formed, in the correct belief that it should be determinative of whether defendant had committed a trespass or a burglary. However, the charge given by the court could have misled the jurors into thinking that any illegal entry constituted a burglary when coupled with a subsequent crime, and it was therefore reversible error (see, People v. Blacknall, 63 N.Y.2d 912, 914, 483 N.Y.S.2d 206, 472 N.E.2d 1034).

In that a new trial is necessary, we do not reach defendant's additional contention that he was improperly sentenced as a predicate felon because the Mississippi burglary statutes (under which he was previously convicted) lacked an essential element of the analogous New York crime.

Accordingly, the Appellate Division order should be reversed and a new trial ordered.

WACHTLER, C.J., and SIMONS, ALEXANDER, TITONE, HANCOCK and BELLACOSA, JJ., concur.

Order reversed, etc.

END OF DOCUMENT

The PEOPLE of the State of New York, Respondent

v

Herbert E. MACKEY, Appellant

Court of Appeals of New York

49 N.Y.2d 274 (1980)

OPINION OF THE COURT

MEYER, Judge.

Defendant was indicted and charged with rape in the first degree and burglary in the second degree. The burglary count accused defendant of "knowingly entering and unlawfully remaining in the dwelling of (complainant) with intent to commit a crime therein", but did not specify the crime he was accused of intending to commit.

The fact setting in which these issues arise is sufficiently indicated by the following summary of the relevant testimony: Complainant was awakened at about 1:30 a. m. in her bedroom by a man who, she testified, was a stranger to her and who had no authority from her to enter her house. After the man left she found a window open in one of the other rooms.

A textbook, pamphlet, registration and receipt card with defendant's name on it and a schedule of classes for City College, which defendant attended, were found 10 to 12 feet from complainant's house. Defendant identified the books, card and schedule as his. A storm window screen had been removed [p. 278] from a window of the house and was propped against the side of the house about three feet from the window.

The window faced an alleyway between complainant's house and the adjacent building, was in a poorly lighted area and was surrounded by shrubbery. When apprehended a short distance from the house defendant first stated "I live here" but then stated "Well, I don't live here. I used to live here. I'm visiting friends." The house was a two-family house in which the complainant's sister had previously resided in the apartment which at the time of the incident was occupied by complainant and in which house two other sisters resided as tenants in the basement apartment.

The tenant sisters and a man friend of theirs all testified that complainant had been present with defendant on a number of occasions, that the house was like "open house" to the two men who were friendly with both sets of sisters. Complainant's sister testified that she had moved out of the house about three months prior to the incident and admitted that she had socialized with the tenant sisters and the men, but swore that though defendant had been present in the house while complainant lived there, defendant and complainant were never in each other's presence.

I

Defendant's motion for particulars as to the burglary count requested "that The People be required to inform (the defense) as to the specific crime which it will allege that the defendant intended to commit inside of the complainant's premises". He relies upon our holdings in People v. Iannone (45 N.Y.2d 589, 412 N.Y.S.2d 110, 384 N.E.2d 656) and People v. Fitzgerald (45 N.Y.2d 574, 412 N.Y.S.2d 102, 384 N.E.2d 649) as supporting his contention that denial of the requested particulars was an abuse of discretion to such a degree as to amount to reversible error. That reliance is misplaced.

Iannone and Fitzgerald held that indictments which stated no more than the bare elements of the crimes charged and in effect parroted the statute were sufficient, while noting that the defendants could discover the particulars of the crimes by requesting a bill of particulars. But the particulars to which a defendant indicted by such a document is entitled are the particulars of the crime charged, here burglary in the second degree, which requires only a knowing entry "with intent to commit a crime therein" (Penal Law, s 140.25; emphasis supplied).

The predecessor sections of the Penal Law of 1909 were phrased in terms of "some crime" (ss 402, 403), "a crime" [p. 279] (s 404) and "any crime" (s 406) and we are told by Professor Arnold Hechtman's Practice Commentary (McKinney's Cons. Laws of N.Y., Book 39, Penal Law, s 140.20, p. 37) that "Similarly the Revised Penal Law's definition of burglary is satisfied if the intruder's intent, existing at the time of the unlawful entry or remaining, is to commit any crime."

Thus, to secure a conviction for burglary the State "need not establish what particular crime the intruder intended to commit" (Hechtman, loc. cit.), nor is it necessary that the intended crime in fact be committed (id.). Nor is there any unfairness to a defendant in so holding, for as we pointed out in Iannone 45 N.Y.2d, at p. 598, 412 N.Y.S.2d, at p. 116, 384 N.E.2d, at p. 662): "The need to utilize the indictment as the means of resolving any double jeopardy inquiry has been considerably alleviated by the modern practice of maintaining full records of criminal proceedings which may be considered by subsequent courts. Similarly, the function of the indictment as the vehicle for assuring that the crime for which the defendant is tried is the one for which he was indicted by the Grand Jury is of less significance due to the practicability of using sources extraneous to the indictment should a challenge be made on those grounds (see CPL 210.30)."

The reason for the rule is pragmatic: intent is subjective, and must be established by proof of defendant's conduct and other facts and circumstances (see McCourt v. People, 64 N.Y. 583, 586; People v. Oliver, 4 A.D.2d 28, 31, 163 N.Y.S.2d 235, 238, affd. 3 N.Y.2d 684, 171 N.Y.S.2d 811, 148 N.E.2d 874). If the State must prove an intent to commit a particular crime as distinct from the general intent to commit crime, the trial of a burglary indictment becomes an exercise in hairsplitting similar to that which, prior to 1942, engulfed the Penal Law's larceny article in a sea of technicalities (see, e. g., People v. Noblett, 244 N.Y. 355, 155 N.E. 670; and Hechtman, Practice Commentaries, McKinney's Cons. Laws of N.Y., Book 39, Penal Law, s 155.05, p. 113).

Had the Legislature intended the result for which defendant argues it could easily in revising the Penal Law have inserted the word "specified" or the word "particular" between "a" and "crime". It did not do so and the dissent points to nothing in the legislative history of the present provisions or in our prior holdings that requires such a result, relying instead on decision of Federal and State courts construing the statutes of other States. We have not in the past and do not now find those decisions persuasive.

Thus, in People v. Gilligan, 42 N.Y.2d 969, 398 N.Y.S.2d 269, 367 N.E.2d 867 we made clear that the People need prove only that defendant intended to commit a crime during his illegal presence in the building, for we there held that defendant's intent to commit a crime on entering the building "could be inferred beyond a reasonable doubt from the circumstances of the breaking". Similarly, People v. Henderson, 41 N.Y.2d 233, 391 N.Y.S.2d 563, 359 N.E.2d 1357, citing People v. Terry, 43 A.D.2d 875, 351 N.Y.S.2d 184, recognized that the intent necessary for burglary can be inferred from the circumstances of the entry itself.

The out-of-State cases on which the dissent relies proceed from the premise that the burglary statute "is a proscription on entry of a dwelling with any one or more of a certain category of specific intents and not merely a proscription against entry with a generally evil or criminal intent" (United States v. Thomas, 144 U.S.App.D.C. 44, 47, 444 F.2d 919, 921). If that premise be accepted, it follows that intent to commit a specific crime being an element of the offense, a due process problem might exist if the specific crime is not particularized. But unless there is read into the words "a crime" more than the Legislature has stated, intent to commit a specific crime is not an element, and the necessity for particulars, and with it the due process question, disappears.

The fallacy involved in the contrary view is pointed up by the suggestion of the dissent that "in the absence of indicia of a different criminal intent", larceny may be specified as the intended crime (p. 284). The cases cited in support of that proposition do clearly so hold, but they also make clear that the jury may infer from the circumstances of the entry if not explained to their satisfaction that larceny was intended (United States v. Thomas, 144 U.S.App.D.C., at p. 49, 444 F.2d, at p. 924, supra ; State v. Woodruff, 208 Iowa 236, 243, 225 N.W. 254; Commonwealth v. Ronchetti, 333 Mass. 78, 81, 128 N.E.2d 334) and that the rationale behind the rule is that the usual object of burglary is theft and that unless a presumption of larceny is indulged "the burglar caught without booty might escape the penalties of the law" (State v. Woodruff, 208 Iowa, at pp. 239-240, 225 N.W., at p. 255, supra ; United States v. Thomas, 144 U.S.App.D.C., at p. 49, 444 F.2d, at p. 924, supra). To hold that a specific not a general intent is required, but allow the specific intent to be proved by inferring it from the same evidence that would prove the general intent, is simply to indulge in circular reasoning.

Had defendant's motion for particulars demanded the basis upon which the People would contend that he intended to commit a crime its denial may have been error (CPL 200.90).[p. 281] But the demand as framed asked only for information that was not a necessary element of burglary the specific crime that defendant intended to commit and its denial, therefore, was not an abuse of discretion. Moreover, there not only was clear evidence from which the jury could infer general intent to commit a crime,[n. 2] but it also is clear that defendant's trial strategy was in no way affected.

Defendant took no exception to the failure to charge intent to commit a specific crime; he did, however, consistent with his strategy of showing prior association, permission to enter and inferentially consent to intercourse, make a number of requests for a charge that the People had to prove beyond reasonable doubt that he had no license or privilege to enter complainant's dwelling. There is, therefore, no basis for reversal.

Accordingly, the order of the Appellate Division should be affirmed.

FUCHSBERG, Judge (dissenting in part).

COOKE, C. J., and GABRIELLI, JONES and WACHTLER, JJ., concur with MEYER, J.

FUCHSBERG, J., dissents in part and votes to modify in a separate opinion in which JASEN, J., concurs.

END OF DOCUMENT

STATUTES TO CONSIDER

Section 120.00 Assault in the Third Degree

A person is guilty of assault in the third degree when:

1. With intent to cause physical injury , he causes such injury; or

2. He recklessly causes physical injury to another person; or

3. With criminal negligence, he causes physical injury to another person by means of a deadly weapon or a dangerous instrument.

Section 120.05 Assault in the Second Degree

A person is guilty of assault in the second degree when:

1. With intent to cause serious physical injury to another person, he causes such injury to such person or to a third person; or

2. With intent to cause physical injury to another person, he causes such injury to such person or to a third person by means of a deadly weapon or a dangerous instrument; or

3. With intent to prevent a peace officer, police officer, a fireman, or an emergency medical service paramedic or related personnel in a hospital emergency department, from performing a lawful duty, by means including releasing or failing to control an animal under circumstances evincing the actors intent that the animal obstruct the lawful activity of such peace office, police officer, fireman, paramedic or technician, he causes physical injury to such peace officer, police officer, fireman, paramedic technician or medical or related personnel in a hospital emergency department; or

4. He recklessly causes serious physical injury to another person by means of a deadly weapon or a dangerous instrument; or

5. For a purpose other than lawful medical or therapeutic treatment, he intentionally causes stupor, unconsciousness or other physical impairment or injury to another person by administering to him, without his consent, a drug, substance or preparation capable of producing the same; or

6. In the course of and in furtherance of the commission or attempted commission of a felony, other than a felony defined in article one hundred thirty which requires corroboration for conviction, or of immediate flight there from, he, or another participant if there be any, causes physical injury to a person other than one of the participants; or

Section 120.10 Assault in the First Degree

A person is guilty of assault in the first degree when:

1. With intent to cause serious physical injury to another person, he causes such injury to such person or to a third person by means of a deadly weapon or a dangerous instrument; or

2. With intent to disfigure another person seriously and permanently, or to destroy, amputate or disable permanently a member or organ of his body, he causes such injury to such person or to a third person; or

3. Under circumstances evincing a depraved indifference to human life, he recklessly engages in conduct which creates a grave risk of death to another person, and thereby causes serious physical injury to another person; or

4. In the course of and in furtherance of the commission or attempted commission of a felony or of immediate flight there from, he, or another participant if there be any, causes serious physical injury to a person other than one of the participants.

Section 120.45 Stalking in the Fourth Degree

A person is guilty of stalking in the fourth degree when he intentionally engages in a course of conduct directed at a specific person, and knows or reasonably should know that such conduct:

1. is likely to cause reasonable fear of material harm to the physical health, safety or property of such person, a member of such person's immediate family or a third party with whom such person is acquainted; or

2. causes harm to the mental or emotional health of such person, where such conduct consists of following, telephoning or initiating communication or contact with such person, a member of such person's immediate family or a third party with whom such person is acquainted, and the actor was previously clearly informed to cease that conduct.

Section 120.50 Stalking in the Third Degree

A person is guilty of stalking in the third degree when he:

1. Commits the crime of stalking in the fourth degree against three or more persons, in three or more separate transactions, for which the actor has not been previously convicted; or

2. Commits the crime of stalking in the fourth degree against any person, and has previously been convicted, within the preceding ten years of a specified predicate crime, and the victim of such specified predicate crime is the victim, or an immediate family member of the victim, of the present offense; or

3. With intent to harass, annoy or alarm a person, intentionally engages in a course of conduct directed at such person which is likely to cause such person to reasonably fear physical injury or serious physical injury, the commission of a sex offense against, or the kidnapping, unlawful imprisonment or death of such person or a member of such person's immediate family.

Section 120.55 Stalking in the Second Degree

A person is guilty of stalking in the second degree when he:

1. Commits the crime of stalking in the third degree and in the course of the commission of such offense: (i) displays, or possesses and threatens the use of, a firearm, pistol, revolver, rifle, shotgun, machine gun, electronic dart gun, electronic stun gun, cane sword, billy, blackjack, bludgeon, metal knuckles, chuka stick, sand bag, sandclub, slingshot, slung shot, shirker, "Kung Fu Star", dagger, dangerous knife, dirk, razor, stiletto, imitation pistol, dangerous instrument, deadly instrument or deadly weapon; or (ii) displays what appears to be a pistol, revolver, rifle, shotgun, machine gun or other firearm; or

2. Commits the crime of stalking in the third against any person, and has previously been convicted, within the preceding five years, of a specified predicate crime, and the victim of such specified predicate crime is the victim, or an immediate family member of the victim, of the present offense; or

3. Commits the crime of stalking in the fourth degree and has previously been convicted of stalking in the third degree; or

4. Being 21 years of age or older, repeatedly follows a person under the age of 14 or engages in a course of conduct or repeatedly commits acts over a period of time intentionally placing or attempting to place such person who is under the age of fourteen in reasonable fear of physical injury, serious physical injury or death; or

Section 120.60 Stalking in the First Degree

A person is guilty of stalking in the first degree when he commits the crime of stalking in the third or second degree and, in the course thereof he:

1. intentionally or recklessly causes physical injury to the victim of such crime; or

2. commits a class A misdemeanor.

Section 125.15 Manslaughter in the Second Degree

A person is guilty of manslaughter in the second degree when:

1. He recklessly causes the death of another person; or

2. He commits upon a female an abortion act which causes her death; or

3. He intentionally causes or aids another person to commit suicide.

Section 125.20 Manslaughter in the First Degree

A person is guilty of manslaughter in the first degree when:

1. With intent to cause serious physical injury to another, he causes the death of such person or a third person; or

2. With intent to cause the death of another person, he causes the death of such person or of a third person under circumstances which do not constitute murder because he acts under the influence of extreme emotional disturbance; or

3. He commits upon a female pregnant for more than 24 weeks an abortion act which causes her death; or

4. Being 18 years old or more and with intent to cause physical injury to a person less than 11 years old, the defendant recklessly engages in conduct which creates a grave risk of serious physical injury to such person and thereby causes the death of such person.

Section 125.25 Murder in the Second Degree

A person is guilty of murder in the second degree when:

1. With intent to cause the death of another, he causes the death of such person or of a third person; but it is an affirmative defense that:

(a) The defendant acted under the influence of extreme emotional disturbance for which there was a reasonable explanation or excuse, the reasonableness of which is to be determined from the viewpoint of a person in the defendant's situation under the circumstances as the defendant believed them to be; or

(b) The defendant's conduct consisted of causing or aiding, without the use of duress or deception, another person to commit suicide. Nothing contained in this paragraph shall constitute a defense to a prosecution for, or preclude a conviction of, manslaughter in the second degree or any other crime; or

2. Under circumstances evincing a depraved indifference to human life, he recklessly engages in conduct which creates a grave risk of death to another person, and thereby causes the death of another person; or

3. Acting either alone or with one or more other persons, he commits or attempts to commit robbery, burglary, kidnapping, arson, rape in the first degree, criminal sexual act in the first degree,

sexual abuse in the first degree, aggravated sexual abuse, escape in the first degree, or escape in the second degree, and, in the course of and in furtherance of such crime or of immediate flight there from, he, or another participant, if there be any, causes the death of a person other than one of the participants; but it is an affirmative defense that the defendant:

(a) Did not commit the homicidal act or in any way solicit, request, command, importune, cause or aid the commission thereof; and

(b) Was not armed with a deadly weapon, or any instrument, article or substance readily capable of causing death or serious physical injury and of a sort not ordinarily carried in public places by law-abiding persons; and

(c) Had no reasonable ground to believe that any other participant was armed with such a weapon, instrument, article or substance; and

(d) Had no reasonable ground to believe that any other participant intended to engage in conduct likely to result in death or serious physical injury; or

4. Under circumstances evincing a depraved indifference to human life, and being 18 years old or more the defendant recklessly engages in conduct which creates a grave risk of serious physical injury or death to another person less than 11 years old and thereby causes the death of such person.

Section 125.27 Murder in the First Degree

A person is guilty of murder in the first degree when:

1. With intent to cause the death of another person, he causes the death of such person or of a third person; and

(a) Either:

(i) the victim was a police officer who was at the time of the killing engaged in the course of performing his duties, and the defendant knew or should have known that the victim was a police officer; or

(ii) the victim was a peace officer who was at the time of the killing engaged in the course of performing his duties, and the defendant knew or should have known that the victim was such a uniformed court officer, parole officer, probation officer, or employee of the division for youth; or

(iii) the victim was an employee of a state correctional institution or was an employee of a local correctional facility who was at the time of the killing engaged in the course of performing his duties, and the defendant knew or should have known that the victim was an employee of a state correctional institution or a local correctional facility.

......

(vii) the victim was killed while the defendant was in the course of committing or attempting to commit and in furtherance of robbery, burglary in the first degree or second degree, kidnapping in the first degree, arson in the first degree or second degree, rape in the first degree, criminal sexual act in the first degree, sexual abuse in the first degree, aggravated sexual abuse in the first degree or escape in the first degree, or in the course of and furtherance of immediate flight after committing or attempting to commit any such crime or in the course of and furtherance of immediate flight after attempting to commit the crime of murder in the second degree; provided however, the victim is not a participant in one of the aforementioned crimes; or

(viii) as part of the same criminal transaction, the defendant, with intent to cause serious physical injury to or the death of an additional person or persons, causes the death of an additional person or persons; provided, however, the victim is not a participant in the criminal transaction; or

(ix) prior to committing the killing, the defendant had been convicted of murder, or had been convicted in another jurisdiction of an offense which, if committed in this state, would constitute a violation of either of such sections; or

(x) the defendant acted in an especially cruel and wanton manner pursuant to a course of conduct intended to inflict and inflicting torture upon the victim prior to the victim's death. As used in this subparagraph, "torture" means the intentional and depraved infliction of extreme physical pain; "depraved" means the defendant relished the infliction of extreme physical pain upon the victim evidencing debasement or perversion or that the defendant evidenced a sense of pleasure in the infliction of extreme physical pain; or

(xi) the defendant intentionally caused the death of two or more additional persons within the state in separate criminal transactions within a period of twenty-four months when committed in a similar fashion or pursuant to a common scheme or plan; or

2. It is an affirmative defense that:

(a) The defendant acted under the influence of extreme emotional disturbance for which there was a reasonable explanation or excuse, the reasonableness of which is to be determined from the viewpoint of a person in the defendant's situation under the circumstances as the defendant believed them to be. Nothing contained in this paragraph shall constitute a defense to a prosecution for, or preclude a conviction of, manslaughter in the first degree or any other crime except murder in the second degree; or

(b) The defendant's conduct consisted of causing or aiding, without the use of duress or deception, another person to commit suicide. Nothing contained in this paragraph shall constitute a defense to a prosecution for, or preclude a conviction of, manslaughter in the second degree or any other crime except murder in the second degree.

Section 130.25 Rape in the Third Degree

A person is guilty of rape in the third degree when:

1. He engages in sexual intercourse with another person who is incapable of consent by reason of some factor other than being less than seventeen years old;

2. Being 21 years old or more, he engages in sexual intercourse with another person less than 17 years old; or

3. He engages in sexual intercourse with another person without such person's consent where such lack of consent is by reason of some factor other than incapacity to consent.

Section 130.30 Rape in the Second Degree

A person is guilty of rape in the second degree when:

1. being eighteen years old or more, he or she engages in sexual intercourse with another person less than fifteen years old; or

2. he or she engages in sexual intercourse with another person who is incapable of consent by reason of being mentally disabled or mentally incapacitated.

It is an affirmative defense to the crime of rape in the second degree that the defendant was less than four years older than the victim at the time of the act.

Section 130.35 Rape in the First Degree

A person is guilty of rape in the first degree when he or she engages in sexual intercourse with another person:

1. By forcible compulsion; or

2. Who is incapable of consent by reason of being physically helpless; or

3. Who is less than 11 years old; or

4. Who is less than 13 years old and the actor is 18 years old or more.

Section 135.05 Unlawful Imprisonment in the Second Degree

A person is guilty of unlawful imprisonment in the second degree when he restrains another person.

Section 140.00 Criminal Trespass and Burglary; Definitions

The following definitions are applicable to this article:

1. "Premises" includes the term "building," as defined herein, and any real property.

2. "Building," in addition to its ordinary meaning, includes any structure, vehicle or watercraft used for overnight lodging of persons, or used by persons for carrying on business therein, or used as an elementary or secondary school, or an enclosed motor truck, or an enclosed motor truck trailer. Where a building consists of two or more units separately secured or occupied, each unit shall be deemed both a separate building in itself and a part of the main building.

3. "Dwelling" means a building which is usually occupied by a person lodging therein at night.

4. "Night" means the period between thirty minutes after sunset and thirty minutes before sunrise.

5. "Enter or remain unlawfully." A person "enters or remains unlawfully" in or upon premises when he is not licensed or privileged to do so. A person who, regardless of his intent, enters or remains in or upon premises which are at the time open to the public does so with license and privilege unless he defies a lawful order not to enter or remain, personally communicated to him by the owner of such premises or other authorized person.

A license or privilege to enter or remain in a building which is only partly open to the public is not a license or privilege to enter or remain in that part of the building which is not open to the public. A person who enters or remains upon unimproved and apparently unused land, which is neither fenced nor otherwise enclosed in a manner designed to exclude intruders, does so with license and privilege unless notice against trespass is personally communicated to him by the owner of such land or other authorized person, or unless such notice is given by posting in a conspicuous manner.

A person who enters or remains in or about a school building without written permission from someone authorized to issue such permission or without a legitimate reason which includes a relationship involving custody of or responsibility for a pupil or student enrolled in the school or without legitimate business or a purpose relating to the operation of the school does so without license and privilege.

Section 140.05 Trespass

A person is guilty of trespass when he knowingly enters or remains unlawfully in or upon premises.

Section 140.20 Burglary in the Third Degree

A person is guilty of burglary in the third degree when he knowingly enters or remains unlawfully in a building with intent to commit a crime therein.

Section 140.25 Burglary in the Second Degree

A person is guilty of burglary in the second degree when he knowingly enters or remains unlawfully in a building with intent to commit a crime therein, and when:

1. In effecting entry or while in the building or in immediate flight there from, he or another participant in the crime:

(a) Is armed with explosives or a deadly weapon; or

(b) Causes physical injury to any person who is not a participant in the crime; or

(c) Uses or threatens the immediate use of a dangerous instrument; or

(d) Displays what appears to be a pistol, revolver, rifle, shotgun, machine gun or other firearm; or

2. The building is a dwelling.

Section 140.30 Burglary in the First Degree

A person is guilty of burglary in the first degree when he knowingly enters or remains unlawfully in a dwelling with intent to commit a crime therein, and when, in effecting entry or while in the dwelling or in immediate flight there from, he or another participant in the crime:

1. Is armed with explosives or a deadly weapon; or

2. Causes physical injury to any person who is not a participant in the crime; or

3. Uses or threatens the immediate use of a dangerous instrument; or

4. Displays what appears to be a pistol, revolver, rifle, shotgun, machine gun or other firearm; except that in any prosecution under this subdivision, it is an affirmative defense that such pistol, revolver, rifle, shotgun, machine gun or other firearm was not a loaded weapon from which a shot, readily capable of producing death or other serious physical injury, could be discharged. Nothing contained in this subdivision shall constitute a defense to a prosecution for, or preclude a conviction of, burglary in the second degree, burglary in the third degree or any other crime.

Section 155.05 Larceny; Defined

1. A person steals property and commits larceny when, with intent to deprive another of property or to appropriate the same to himself or to a third person, he wrongfully takes, obtains or withholds such property from an owner thereof.

2. Larceny includes a wrongful taking, obtaining or withholding of another's property, with the intent prescribed in subdivision one of this section, committed in any of the following ways:

(a) By conduct heretofore defined or known as common law larceny by trespassory taking, common law larceny by trick, embezzlement, or obtaining property by false pretenses;

(b) By acquiring lost property.

A person acquires lost property when he exercises control over property of another which he knows to have been lost or mislaid, or to have been delivered under a mistake as to the identity of the recipient or the nature or amount of the property, without taking reasonable measures to return such property to the owner;

(c) By committing the crime of issuing a bad check, as defined in section 190.05;

(d) By false promise.

A person obtains property by false promise when, pursuant to a scheme to defraud, he obtains property of another by means of a representation, express or implied, that he or a third person will in the future engage in particular conduct, and when he does not intend to engage in such conduct or, as the case may be, does not believe that the third person intends to engage in such conduct.

In any prosecution for larceny based upon a false promise, the defendant's <u>intention</u> or belief that the promise would not be performed may not be established by or inferred from the fact alone that such promise was not performed. Such a finding may be based only upon evidence establishing that the facts and circumstances of the case are wholly consistent with guilty intent or belief and wholly inconsistent with innocent intent or belief, and excluding to a moral certainty every hypothesis except that of the defendant's intention or belief that the promise would not be performed;

<u>Section 155.10 Larceny; No Defense</u>

The crimes of (a) larceny committed by means of extortion and an attempt to commit the same, and (b) bribe receiving by a labor official, and bribe receiving, are not mutually exclusive, and it is no defense to a prosecution for larceny committed by means of extortion of for an attempt to commit the same that, by reason of the same conduct, the defendant also committed one of such specified crimes of bribe receiving.

<u>Section 155.15 Larceny; Defenses</u>

1. In any prosecution for larceny committed by trespass taking or embezzlement, it is an affirmative defense that the property was appropriated under a claim of right made in good faith.

2. In any prosecution for larceny by extortion committed by instilling in the victim a fear that he or another person would be charged with a crime, it is an affirmative defense that the defendant reasonably believed the threatened charge to be true and that his sole purpose was to compel or induce the victim to take reasonable action to make good the wrong which was the subject of such threatened charge.

<u>Section 160.05 Robbery in the Third Degree</u>

A person in guilty of robbery in the third degree when he forcibly steals property.

<u>Section 160.10 Robbery in the Second Degree</u>

A person is guilty of robbery in the second degree when he forcibly steals property and when:

1. He is aided by another person actually present; or

2. In the course of the commission of the crime or of immediate flight there from, he or another participant in the crime:

(a) Causes physical injury to any person who is not a participant in the crime; or

(b) Displays what appears to be a pistol, revolver, rifle, shotgun, machine gun or other firearm; or

3. The property consists of a motor vehicle

Section 160.15 Robbery in the First Degree

A person is guilty of robbery in the first degree when he forcibly steals property and when, in the course of the commission of the crime or of immediate flight there from, he or another participant in the crime:

1. Causes serious physical injury to any person who is not a participant in the crime; or

2. Is armed with a deadly weapon; or

3. Uses or threatens the immediate use of a dangerous instrument; or

4. Displays what appears to be a firearm; except that it is an affirmative defense that such firearm was not a loaded weapon.

Section 240.25 Harassment in the First Degree

A person is guilty of harassment in the first degree when he or she intentionally and repeatedly harasses another person by following such person in or about a public place or places or by engaging in a course of conduct or by repeatedly committing acts which places such person in reasonable fear of physical injury. This section shall not apply to activities regulated by the national labor relations act, as amended, the railway labor act, as amended, or the federal employment labor management act, as amended.

Section 240.26 Harassment in the Second Degree

A person is guilty of harassment in the second degree when, with intent to harass, annoy or alarm another person:

1. He or she strikes, shoves, kicks or otherwise subjects such other person to physical contact, or attempts or threatens to do the same; or

2. He or she follows a person in or about a public place or places; or

3. He or she engages in a course of conduct or repeatedly commits acts which alarm or seriously annoy such other person and which serve no legitimate purpose.

Subdivisions two and three of this section shall not apply to activities regulated by the national labor relations act, as amended, the railway labor act, as amended, or the federal employment labor management act, as amended.

<u>END</u>